EXPLORERS AND COLONIES

Frontispiece: Sir Francis Drake (National Portrait Gallery)

EXPLORERS AND COLONIES:
AMERICA, 1500-1625

DAVID B. QUINN

THE HAMBLEDON PRESS
LONDON   AND   RONCEVERTE

Published by The Hambledon Press 1990

102 Gloucester Avenue, London NW1 8HX (U.K.)

309 Greenbrier Avenue, Ronceverte WV 24970 (U.S.A.)

ISBN 1 85285 024 8

British Library Cataloguing in Publication Data

Quinn, David B. (David Beers)
   Explorers and colonies: America, 1500-1625
   1. North America. Exploration to 1599
   I. Title
   970.01

Library of Congress Cataloging-in-Publication Data

Quinn, David B.
   Explorers and colonies: America, 1500-1625
   /David B. Quinn
   Includes bibliographical references
   1. America – Discovery and exploration
   2. North America – Description and travel
   3. America – History – To 1810
   I. Title   E121.Q48   1990
   970.01 – dc20   89-48056   CIP

Printed on acid-free paper and bound by
W.B.C. Ltd., Maesteg, Wales

CONTENTS

PREFACE

The problems and consequences of the early expansion of Europe have presented to historians many and complex issues. Before analytical work can be done on many areas of this process it is first of all necessary to find out what happened. A few of these essays, the majority of them focused on North America, do not avoid general discussion but they are mainly concerned with the discovery and elucidation of particular episodes which help to lay the groundwork for more wide-ranging studies. Many of them are interesting in themselves, which the author hopes will engage the reader for their intrinsic interest, while at the same time adding some small facet to our knowledge and eventual understanding of how and why Europeans left home. They do not, in general, deal with the usually catastrophic effects of European intrusion on the indigenous peoples of the Americas, which have been ably handled by other hands and which should never be overlooked. The essays vary in character a good deal: some are academic in that they are loaded with evidence in the form of footnotes; others are more straightforward accounts of particular episodes, or the exposure of hitherto unknown documentary sources. There is inevitably some repetition, but it is hoped not too much. Cumulatively, the author's hope is that they will indicate how many and various are the facets of early enterprise in distant areas and how many ways of looking at them there are.

The essays are the product of many years of study and follow on an earlier collection, *England and the Discovery of America* (1974), though they traverse different ground. They, or many of them, are the product of close collaboration with Alison Quinn, who helped at every stage in their production (she even made the index to this volume). Among my many friends who have encouraged and helped me I may single out Professor P.E.H. Hair, who went over my miscellaneous publications with me and helped me to sort them into possibly republishable groups. I owe much to A.N. Ryan, and to K.R. Andrews who have steered me clear of many mistakes and otherwise assisted me. Finally, I would like to thank Martin Sheppard of the Hambledon Press for his kindly and effective editorial guidance.

David B. Quinn

March 1990

ACKNOWLEDGEMENTS

The articles reprinted here first appeared in the following places and are reprinted by kind permission of the original publishers.

1   *Rapports*, I, Comité International des Sciences Historiques, XIIe Congrès International des Sciences Historiques (Vienna, 1965), pp. 45-60.

2   *The Hakluyt Handbook*, edited by D.B. Quinn, I, Hakluyt Society, 2nd series, nos. 144 and 145 (London, 1945), pp. 133-152.

3   *The Hakluyt Handbook*, I, pp. 244-253.

4   *The Mariner's Mirror*, LXXII (1986), pp. 244-273.

5   *First Images of America: The Impact of the New World on the Old*, edited by Fredi Chiapelli (Berkeley, University of California Press, 1976), II, pp. 635-658.

6   *Transactions of the Royal Historical Society*, 5th series, XXVI (1976), pp. 73-93.

7   *Terrae Incognitae*, VIII (1976), pp. 91-97.

8   *The History of North American Discovery and Exploration*, edited by Stanley H. Palmer and Dennis Reinhartz (Walter Prescott Webb Lectures, 1987 (College Station, Texas, Texas A. & M. University Press, 1988), pp. 10-33.

9   *Early Maryland in a Wider World*, edited by D.B. Quinn Detroit, Wayne State University Press, 1982), pp. 119-148.

10   *Sir Francis Drake and the Famous Voyage, 1577-1580: Essays Commemorating the Quadricentennial of Drake's Circumnavigation of the Earth*, edited by Norman J.W. Thrower (Berkeley, University of California Press, 1984), pp. 33-48.

11   *Terrae Incognitae*, XIV (1982), pp. 97-104.

12   *KM 80: A Birthday Album for Kenneth Muir, Tuesday, 5th May, 1987* (Liverpool, Department of English Language and Literature, Liverpool University, 1987), pp. 120-121.

13   Newfoundland Historical Society Pamphlat, 7 (1983).

14   This piece appears here for the first time.

15   *Thomas Harriot, Renaissance Scientist*, edited by John W. Shirley (Oxford, Oxford University Press, 1974), pp. 36-53.

16   *The Works of Jacques le Moyne des Morgues*, edited by Paul Hulton (London, British Museum, 1977), I, pp. 18-44.

17   *Canadian Historical Review*, XLIV (1962), pp. 328-343.

18   *Early European Settlement and Exploitation in Atlantic Canada*, edited by G.M. Story (St. John's, Memorial University of Newfoundland, 1982), pp. 9-30.

19   *Journal of Imperial and Commonwealth History*, II (1974), pp. 235-252.

20   *Bulletin de l'Institut Historique Belge de Rome [Miscellanea Charles Verlinden]*, XLIV (1974), pp. 513-534.

21   *The American Neptune*, XXXI (1971), pp. 85-103.

22   *Virginia Magazine for History and Biography*, LXXVII (1969), pp. 347-360.

23   *Welsh Society and Nationhood: Essays Presented to Glanmor Williams*, edited by R.R. Davies, R.A. Griffiths, I.G. Jones and K.O. Morgan (Cardiff, University of Wales Press, 1984), pp. 90-107.

24   *William and Mary Quarterly*, 3rd series, XVI (1959), pp. 551-555.

25   *William and Mary Quarterly*, 3rd series, XXIII (1966), pp. 136-145.

LIST OF ILLUSTRATIONS

1

EXPLORATION AND THE EXPANSION OF EUROPE

If 'acculturation' is a term of art in social anthropology and is consequently unfamiliar to many historians it is none the less a category which historians need. The interpenetration of cultures is clearly a field for the historian as he expands his interests in the world of the past as he must do in the world of the present, since one outstanding feature of the twentieth century is the coming to fruition of a process of culture-mingling which has been in progress at an accelerating rate for the past five centuries. At the same time, although remembering that 'acculturation' is the more widely embracing term, many historians will be content in formulating their approach to intercultural history to use the simpler and less comprehensive term 'exploration'. If 'acculturation' requires a complex approach and a highly technical analysis, 'exploration' is easier to define, as, in its initial stages, merely the visual interpenetration of one culture by another, the explorer being the active cultural factor, the society being explored the passive, yet with little passing immediately from one to the other except the superficial impression of what was seen, recorded by the explorer most likely, and also in some cases by the explored. In this connection I remember with pleasure a diorama which used to be seen in the Smithsonian Institution in Washington showing the Arawak Indians of the Bahamas 'discovering' Columbus and sending signals of his arrival to their fellows, and so reversing the conventional European centred picture of the world-exploring process. It is also an advantage that 'exploration', provided we see it as a reciprocal process, is a neutral term. In the expansion of European men, ships, arms, trade, commerce, government and concepts into Africa, Asia and the Americas in the centuries after 1400 A. D., and the reciprocal influence of non-European lands and peoples on the Europeans, we are very much in need of neutral terms, since in our present century those like nationalism, imperialism and exploitation necessarily carry an emotional charge from which we may need categories such as 'acculturation' and 'exploration' as a shield. To some writers even acculturation has not seemed a neutral term but a process the infliction of which is only one stage less drastic than death. Dr. John C. Huden prefaces his *Indian place names*

of *New England* (1962) with the statement that the Amerindians of
northeastern North America had been, since the arrival of Europeans,
"mauled, expelled, exhorted, acculturated or killed". Better, perhaps, in
his view to be acculturated than killed but not very much more so.

Exploration is essentially the act of leaving one's own cultural environment in order to inspect a new physical and cultural terrain, and
it is necessarily accompanied or followed, if it is to have effects percep-
tible by historians, by the recording of the resulting experience (though
it may, of course, deposit residual artifacts in the explored culture as
well). The record may be in the form of maps or drawings of the coastlines and things seen on the journey, or in a journal which sets down the
day-to-day impact of new sights and experiences in words, but which
may find its ultimate expression in a reflected form into which the
experience of exploration has been distilled through writing, drawing,
printing or engraving. Since human motives are rarely unmixed, there is
not, in our modern history at least, much pure exploration in the sense
that the urge to find and to survey visually new land and peoples far
from home is entirely the effect of curiosity, unalloyed by desire for gain
or power, or proselytising. The nearest we come to disinterestedness is
where exploration is set on foot to find proof or disproof of an intellectual speculation, a cosmographical guess. At the same time, the explorer
as such is set apart from the traveller, who is primarily a merchant, a
soldier, or a missionary, by his capacity to excite a vicarious curiosity in
those who hear him or read his accounts of travel. A sense of wonder
may not take an observer very far into the understanding of the complexities of human cultures but it may very well excite those to whom an
explorer possessed of it expresses his discoveries. The explorer, of course,
may be a liar and so may lose his power to interest and influence men in
the end. The tall tales and myths of Sir John Mandeville had a long run,
but in the end they were less effectively influential than the truths of
Marco Polo. The explorer can clearly have an enduring influence when
his words convince those who hear him that it is worth while repeating
and extending his experience. In the conviction which he carries he can
also convince later generations that what he recorded is valid evidence
for the cultural history of the regions he explored, as well as indicative
of the cultural background and preoccupations from which he, himself,
derived.

No culture, even our own science-based, international one, allows its
products to see another precisely as it is; something is carried over. The
Portuguese we see in seventeenth century Japanese and Chinese drawings
are admirably shown, the details of their appearance being often meticu-
lously rendered, and yet they are turned in some degree into Orientals,
they have a Chinese or a Japanese attitude, a few Mongoloid facial
touches, a way of standing or walking, a manner of wearing their clothes
which is not European. The fine bronze figures of Portuguese soldiers

made in Benin, or the ivories which followed them, are yet subtly African. The American Indians put on record by European drawings of the sixteenth century are not quite Amerindian but partly Europeanized, just as the Spaniards seen by Aztec artists are both European and non-European. But when we say this we do not say enough, because in all good delineation in words or by line there is, where the writer or artist willed it and has had the skill, an objective carry-over from the seen to the seeing culture. Christopher Weiditz's Aztecs, seen in Spain in 1529, are living, vigorous expressions of a non-European culture: so are the Carolina Algonkians seen in North America by John White between 1584 and 1587. And drawings such as these are equally valuable as documents in the pre-European history of Mexico and the Carolina Tidewater as they are in the story of expansion from its European end. But side by side with the good is the second- and third-rate record, or the valueless invention. What is true of visual representations is equally so of written description. An educated and sophisticated writer, a Pigafetta or a Verrazzano, for example, can produce a many sided account of an exploring voyage, but his education, his knowledge of classical lore about the barbarians known to the old Mediterranean cultures, often stands in his way and distorts his account when he is putting down what he sees or thinks he sees. The educated man can with an effort, make a leap towards the understanding of a strange, even an apparently repulsive culture, as De Léry did in his study of the Tupinambá, but it often is the simple seaman or soldier, a Bernal Diaz, a Hans Staden, a Miles Philips, who can bring the new scene and the newly envisaged cultural landscape most sharply and objectively to light. Soldiers and sailors are often cruel and narrow minded; they are not often moralists and they often have a considerable capacity for identifying with the enemy. In the documentation of early exploration many of the most useful narratives are by such men, limited though they may be in scope. On the other hand, the cleric, and more especially the missionary, is more likely than any other to distort by condemnation and exaggeration the non-compatible culture. Africans, Asians, Amerindians have been misreported and maligned far more by pious European clergy than by any other observers. These men looked at the new cultures primarily with the aim of transforming their ideology, and this kept the great majority of them from seeing clearly what it was that they proposed to alter. Yet there are exceptions to this in the sixteenth century also. Las Casas tried hard, if not too clearly, to see the conquest from the Amerindian point of view: Oviedo expressed his disgust at Amerindian practices yet gave some of the best descriptions of the way the native peoples got things done; Hakluyt swayed between his strong Protestant reaction against paganism and his objective curiosity about the non-European world and its inhabitants. The Jesuits who applied a more detached and critical intelligence to the problems of conversion swept aside the more elementary missionary misconceptions of non-European and non-Christian society. To Jesuits in China, in India, in Canada the first necessity came to be the observation, the description, the understanding of the new societies, not as an end in itself but as a sophisticated means towards getting them to accept the religion of Catholic Europeans. In the Jesuit letters the external descriptions provided by lay travellers were paralleled by attempts to reveal the inner character of the extra-European societies. They are the first consciously to attempt the psychological interpenetration of one culture by another, though they too, even at their best, carry over inevitably and confusingly something of their educational background in Europe.

One question on the literature of early European expansion which may help us to look at it in relation to later developments is to what extent it is nationalistic? Do the historians of a particular imperial country report and emphasize the achievements of their own nationals only? The expansion literature of both Spain and Portugal tends to be so narrow that each is concerned almost solely with the overseas achievements of its own monarchy. Peter Martyr, being Italian by birth, is the least constricted of the writers on Spain: Oviedo and Gómara occasionally refer to non-Spanish activities: Herrera very rarely. The achievements of the Spaniards in the Americas and in the farthest Orient are the whole, or almost the whole, of the story. The Portuguese writers are narrower still — from Resende through Barros to Galvão and beyond the theme is Portugal in Africa, in Asia, in Brazil. Italians, a few Portuguese, in the Spanish service and, somewhat later, Germans also, meant that writers of Spanish expansion history could not entirely ignore other Europeans though they could cut down references to them to a minimum. Portuguese writers scarcely mention foreigners, even Spaniards, except when, briefly, they get in the way of Portuguese conquerors, though there are exceptions here in, for example, the publication of the first narrative of De Soto's North American travels in Portugal not Spain. But these exceptions are not very considerable. It may be argued, however, that Spanish and Portuguese writers are not being excessively nationalistic in reporting in this exclusive way the early stages of overseas penetration. Portugal held the lead on the road to Asia and retained it at least until the union with Spain in 1580. Why should her historians bother to record the very minor penetrations, none of them lasting, by the more northern European states, France and England? Similarly, apart from the eminent Italians, Columbus, Vespucci and Sebastian Cabot, and the Portuguese, Magellan and Gomes, in their service, why should the Spaniards take much account of any except their own achievements in the Americas? Though it may be said that there is a certain mutual blindness in the references to Brazil in Spanish works and to Spanish South America in those of the Portuguese.

We might very well imagine that, outside the Iberian peninsula, the newsgatherers and printers would be only too pleased to be able to publish anything and everything about the new discoveries by Portugal and Spain they could find, whether in print or in manuscript. (We must remember that a certain secrecy, maintained by the Portuguese in particular, would remain to be overcome.) This is, in practice, found to be only very partially true. The interest which would justify publication was slow and uneven in its rise in a number of European countries. It was evident first of all, where we should expect it, in Italy. The share of individual Italians in the discoveries created a wide human interest in what was being done. The relatively large size of the Italian intellectual audience and the many centres of printing in Italy made the diffusion of materials on the discoveries peculiarly rapid and extensive. Moreover, since so many of the tracts published in Spain and Portugal were in the vernaculars, it was important for the further diffusion of such materials that so much Italian printing was done in the international language of educated Europeans, Latin. Yet the extent to which information on the expansion of Europe penetrated the German lands and was published there was exceptional and its appearance relatively rapid. It has not yet been fully explained or explored. The links between pioneer German printers in Spain and Portugal and their home environments, the central position of the greater German cities for disseminating books, the rivalry between the printers, the publication of much in Latin as well as in German — these and other factors are evidently part, if not the whole, of the story. At the same time, the contribution of German publishers to the European understanding of the achievements of Columbus and Vespucci was much greater than we might expect where so few Germans were themselves involved in the earliest discoveries and where a great political stake was not held by them. Antwerp, as a half-open door to the new lands, was one channel through which information on the discoveries reached Germany. The political link of Spain with the empire in the person of Charles V between 1519 and 1556 also provided Germany with a small stake in the New World and in Asia. A few Germans were directly concerned in exploration and wrote of what they saw. To the early report of Springer it was possible to add later the accounts of Staden and Schmidel, and also of the German merchant houses in Venezuela. The imperial connection, however exclusive Spain might remain in prohibiting non-Spaniards from direct intercourse with her possessions, undoubtedly increased the contribution of Germans to the publicizing of the extra-European lands. For the most part contributions to non-European travel and conquest had still to be drawn from outside Germany, from Spain, Portugal and from the Italian middlemen. In the later sixteenth century the German publishers were able to extend their range and assemble much material for translation and republication from England, France and the Netherlands as well.

Both in Italy and Germany the fusing of individual travel narratives into syntheses of discovery stories had begun very early, commencing indeed with the Vespucci material, which was associated in several publications with accounts of Portuguese voyages, and so helped to unify in men's minds the eastern and western phases of extra-European activity. Francanzano de Montalboddo's collection, *Paesi novamente retrovati* (Venice, 1507), went through fifteen editions in four languages, Italian, Latin, German, French, and was, in the words of Lawrence C. Wroth, the distinguished American scholar, 'More instrumental than any other work in disseminating knowledge of the worlds of America, Africa, and the Far East'. But it was Ramusio in Venice between about 1530 and his death in 1557, who first assembled a varied team of narrators who could bring European expansion to life, and present it as an interesting and truly significant international process. The contribution he made both to the literature of discovery and to the diffusion of knowledge about the extra-European lands is enormous. In the first place he was not cramped by nationalistic prejudice: his aim was to produce a mosaic of information drawn from the most diverse sources he could tap; in the second he refused to put into his *Viaggi* only syntheses by himself of what he could assemble from scattered sources. He insisted, so far as possible, on obtaining *actualités,* first hand impressions by men who had been on the voyages, whose impressions were fresh, vivid, uncensored. Unable to achieve this in every case, and being forced to leave gaps for a number of the areas into which spectacular European penetrations had already been made, he was nevertheless able to bring a panorama of overseas activities before European readers of whatever nationality (provided they could read Italian, which increasing numbers could), and also provide a series of documents on which subsequent students of the expansion movement could continue to depend. The completion of the work after Ramusio's death and its continued improvement for another generation brought a new understanding of the expansion movement throughout Europe. At the same time the achievements of the synthesizers, who assimilated much of the overseas material into general surveys of all human history, were not outstandingly successful. Sebastian Münster (1550), a pioneer, and perhaps significantly a product of the German school of publicizers, Belleforest (1570) and Thevet (1575) were prepared to put into their cosmographies a good deal of dubious (Mandevillian-type) material as well as offering summaries, often rather jejune, of original realistic narratives. There are no great historical syntheses of the early overseas process: the documentary collections were much more revealing.

France occupies a curious position in the assimilation of expansion material. Publication on the Spanish and Portuguese discoveries in the early sixteenth century is appreciable in quantity, but much of it is derived from Italian sources. Apart from publishing Vespucci material, France's contacts with Spain and Portugal are not evident before 1520. This was possibly the result of political divisions, but it also reflects the dominance of Italian ideas and publications. Moreover, though we now recognise the substantial contribution the voyages of Verrazzano, of Cartier and of Parmentier made before 1550 to the knowledge of overseas lands, nothing was published on any of them in France before 1545. Thevet's publications on Brazil were the first contributions of any considerable range and they were not of outstanding quality. Material such as De Léry's on Brazil in the 1550ties had to wait nearly a generation to find publishers. Indeed, until the Englishman, Richard Hakluyt the younger, inspired Frenchmen to publish these overseas materials in the 1580ties France showed a considerable measure of indifference to the achievement of her own nationals and even to the historical productions of Spain and Portugal which gave such important glimpses of the overseas world. The story of English reactions to the discoveries is stranger still. No publication of any significance on the overseas discoveries made by Spain and Portugal appeared until after 1550. Nor has this found any really convincing explanation. From 1553 onwards there is a trickle, but only after 1575 is the quantity substantial.

The range of the illustrative material available to the European student on the non-European world, expanded rapidly in the last quarter of the sixteenth century. American plants were beginning to be described and illustrated in the herbals. Costume books from De Bruyn (1577) onwards provided a certain number of tolerable illustrations of non-European peoples — though no costume book before 1590 can be said to be of substantial value for the New World. The cartographers of the Netherlands were making an impressive contribution to the visual knowledge of the non-European lands in such achievements as the Mercator world map of 1569 and in the great series of Atlases issued by Ortelius, Mercator and others from 1570 onwards. Illustrations of ethnological value were to be found in Oviedo, Thevet, Staden and a few other writers, but it was not until Theodor de Bry commenced the publication of his *America* in 1590 that the resources of the engraver were systematically directed towards giving such a comprehensive view of the people and cities and plants and animals in their own setting as could bring the new lands to life. De Bry was fortunate in building on the illustrative work of John White and Jacques Le Moyne for his first two volumes. The copperplate engravings from their drawings set a wholly new standard of intelligibility. In his later volumes De Bry often had to invent where he had no, or no adequate, first-hand views, but even so he did a remarkable job, though he was followed by many lesser imitators. The Dutch, as they began publishing independent accounts, built on De Bry's foundations in Van Linschoten's *Itinerario* (1596), where visual material — maps, plans, views — and narrative are knit into a fine unity, and which was the precursor of a number of similar works to appear in the Netherlands.

Catholic-Protestant divisions, combined with national antagonisms, contributed to the circulation of partial views of the overseas achievement. Spaniards and Portuguese became less and less willing to publicize achievements in the overseas field by French Huguenots, English Protestants and Dutch rebels at a time, in the later sixteenth century, when these were becoming significant, except when major defeats and repulses could be reported. The Protestant north, in its turn, began to take a sceptical view of the Iberian conquests. Were the missionary achievements of the Catholic powers a sham and were American and Asian peoples being converted only to a nominal or a debased form of Christianity? Were the Spaniards not, in their conquests, brutally cruel to the simpler societies which they invaded and destroyed? Las Casas was published in six languages throughout the Protestant North between 1578 and 1599 as evidence for Spanish iniquities. This certainly created a 'black legend', since the earlier attacks on Spanish actions had arisen in Spain itself through the emergence of a Spanish conscience about them. This propaganda against Spanish imperialism raised also, often for the first time, the moral issue of conquest and expropriation for those peoples like the English who were only beginning to consider expansion seriously. Hakluyt used Las Casas not only to belabour the Spaniards but to exhort the English, whom he was urging into overseas ventures, to behave themselves in a quite different and morally superior way. That his advice was by no means invariably followed does not minimize his importance as a moralist

The best example of the nature of nationalist influence and of the limits of internationalism in the circulation of information on the overseas world is given by Richard Hakluyt. By the two editions of his *Principal navigations* he literally put the English on the overseas map, collecting from a great variety of sources, mainly unpublished, all the material he could which showed to what an extent they had participated in the discoveries. Because his collection was so complete it gave the English more than their due share in the expansion achievement. But he also set new objectives for the collector of exploration narratives. He was not content merely with getting some account of every voyage he could: he sought for the fullest and most objective one he could find and ruthlessly scrapped in his second edition unsubstantiated and mythical tales or less adequate first-hand accounts. He did not alter what his narrators had seen, but he was capable of editing out things he did not think significant and of suppressing things to which he did not wish to give publicity. Hakluyt's build-up of the comparatively limited English overseas effort was designed to pave the way for more effective voyages and colonizing attempts. It was also intended to bring out the full range of interest which the overseas lands might have for Englishmen, which is why Hakluyt added to his second edition narratives of regions not yet touched by the English from Spanish, Portuguese or other non-English sources. Completeness in the world coverage of his work was his objective in 1598/1600: his attempt to make it still more complete on too large a scale is probably the reason why he never finished the vast third edition which he had in preparation up to within a year or two of his death in 1616. Thus his geographical-ethnographical interest was always tending to become dominant over his more narrowly nationalistic one. An international aspect was already evident in his earliest work, *Divers voyages* (1582), where he tried to assemble all he could from European publications on the eastern seaboard of North America and to add to it what he could find in English sources. The object was primarily geographical, but it was applied geography for national ends, as the book was intended to provide briefing for English voyagers. When he went to France in 1583 Hakluyt began to extend his range of interests still further. He induced the French to put in print the best account of their Florida ventures, that of Laudonnière (and after published it in English). He put out an unedited text of Espejo's New Mexico expedition in both Spanish and French within a year after its appearance in Madrid. He published an effective Latin edition of Peter Martyr in 1587, the first complete one for nearly sixty years. These were all activities which, if he hoped they would encourage English and French enterprises, were primarily governed by a respect for texts and an interest in the lands they described. He kept up this process, though in the narrower sphere of translations into English, in his editions of Galvão, Peter Martyr and the Fidalgo de Elvas in the later years of his life. Hakluyt's individual contribution to the nationalistic material on the expansion was, in the case of England, enormous: in publicizing the literature of European expansion in general, especially that of France, his achievement was very substantial, and compares with that of Ramusio earlier in the sixteenth century.

The period of the consolidation of the early sources ends about 1630 with the appearance of the chief works of Purchas, Gottfried and Bergeron. This marks the end of the initiation of the Dutch, the English and the French into the extra-European field as occupiers and not simply as tentative explorers. Thereafter, these nations are less interested in re-exploring older materials on the earlier phase of expansion than in providing new descriptive and propagandist works on their latest achievements and projects. So long as they were making progress in their imperial race they seldom looked back at the origins of European expansion, though occasionally they returned to the past to refurbish old ideological weapons. (The revival of 'black legend' literature in the 1650ties during the English struggle with Spain is an example.) When decline in imperial effort sets in, it seems that interest in and research on origins revives. Thus Pieter Van der Aa publishes much in the Netherlands on every phase of the early expansion at the opening of the eighteenth century, while many important texts appeared for the first time or were re-edited in Spain and Portugal in the same century, at a time when each of these nations was loosening its grip on the extra-European world.

A characteristic eighteenth century activity is the attempted publication of complete (or allegedly complete) collections of voyages. From Churchill to Pinkerton this follows a steady course in England. During this period, however, narratives included in these collections on the early expansion period were mostly re-issues of earlier versions, sometimes in inferior forms, while little new material was produced and none of it was competently edited. In France, too, such collections as the Abbé Prevost's *Histoire universelle de voyages* were very similar in aim. The eighteenth century made more progress through such men as Raynal and Voltaire, who gave the early narratives some critical reconsideration in the light of expanding knowledge of human perception and concepts.

The systematic exploration and re-exploration of the world in the nineteenth century, characterized, for example, by the formation of important geographical societies in Paris, London and Berlin between 1821 and 1831, brought with it a great revival of interest in the study of the early voyages and of their sources. The geographical societies helped to create a public which had a new interest in exploration history and its documentation. The novelty of this lay partly in its reliance on archival sources. M. F. de Navarrete's *Colección de viajes* (1825/37) began the modern documentation of the Spanish discoveries while his transcripts from the immensely rich Spanish archives laid the foundations for the *Collección de documentos inéditos para la historia de España* from 1842 onwards and influenced the later *Colección de documentos inéditos de Indias*. Henri Ternaux-Compans followed a similar though not identical path in France, his *Voyages* combining both printed and manuscript materials on the discovery of America, and being in effect the most comprehensive assembly of such materials since De Bry.

The foundation of the Hakluyt Society in 1846 came more directly through the influence of the geographical societies, in particular of the Royal Geographical Society. Formed to present documents of the early period of European expansion in English, it took on from the beginning a new academic responsibility, not merely reprinting old published texts in translation, but adding a scholarly commentary to them (giving them the kind of status which only documents from classical history had hitherto enjoyed) and combining published narrative sources with archival material under topics or regions. Set on the course which had\produced some 260 volumes in under 120 years, the Society concentrated on the fifteenth and sixteenth centuries. But it did not ignore the seventeenth and eighteenth. At the same time, its continued connection with the Ramusio-Hakluyt-De Bry-Purchas tradition has kept for it an enduring place in the historiography of European expansion in the formative period. The Hakluyt Society was a typical reflection of Free Trade optimism, the English belief that their right to penetrate the farthest corners of the earth to sell their goods had a strong historical foundation which would be strengthened by the publication of well-edited materials on how exploration and European expansion came about.

The end of the eighteenth and the beginning of the nineteenth century saw too the appearance of a completely new approach to the beginnings of European expansion. This was that of the people of the

United States and of the independent Latin American countries. They were colonists who were developing, under the stress of revolution, strongly nationalist views on their past history; as such they looked freshly at the discoveries, since in them were to be found the origins of their own history. The documents of the first period of the discoveries were of particular interest and value to them because they found there the earliest expression of the exploring and colonizing movement on the part of the European powers. As their perspective was different from that of European editors and writers their interest shifted from materials concerned with expansionist motivation to the results of discovery and settlement, that is from the central to the local level, for example, to Argentina or Brazil rather than to Spain or Portugal. What had hitherto been of peripheral interest now became central. Most Latin-American historians concerned themselves closely with shaping a history for their own country and giving it a strongly nationalist flavour, often anachronistically. A few, José Toribio Medina in Chile is a good example, rose beyond local preoccupations and brought fresh and learned minds to the problems and bibliography of the discovery of the Americas as a whole.

In the United States the concern of historical students was at first largely with the English sources for the earliest attempts to discover North America and to establish colonies. Thus Ebenezer Hazard's *Historical collections* (1792-4) were almost wholly filled with English documents, and so were the earliest source publications of the Massachusetts Historical Society of a similar period. It was not until well into the nineteenth century that the sources on the early activity of other European powers in North America began to arouse effective interest. Buckingham Smith was one of the pioneers in the investigation and publication of Spanish materials, as were E. B. O'Callaghan and Henry C. Murphy of Dutch. Prescott in the 1840ties gave a classic exposition of Spanish exploration and conquest outside the area of the United States, while Parkman followed from the early 1850ties with a comparable survey of France's relations with North America. The preoccupation of New England and Virginia with the older English sources was thus invaded and it is significant of this expansion of interest that Justin Winsor's *Narrative and critical history of America*, with its emphasis on sources, and a range as wide as could then be conceived, was planned and edited in New England in the 1880ties. Bancroft from the 1870ties was laying a groundwork of Spanish material for the study of western United States history, while the inspiration of Parkman on Reuben Gold Thwaites, a little later, made Madison, Wisconsin, the Middle West base for editions of the *Jesuit Relations* and so much other material on early French exploration and expansion, paralleling and developing the work of French-Canadian historians impelled by the surviving French cultural nationalism in Quebec.

Twentieth century Latin America had another facet to add in the study of the history of American exploration in the classical period of the expansion of Europe. The new look at the history of expansion which came from both North and South America in the nineteenth century was that of colonists turned into members of new national states. It had not reflected vitally the experiences and the history of the pre-European populations and their descendants. The Mexican revolution of the twentieth century saw the re-emergence of the American Indian as a factor in contemporary history and this, in turn, brought about a parallel revolution in the study of the early sources of European expansion, their examination for what they could tell both about the preconquest history of the indigenous population and also the largely submerged history of these populations during the colonial and early national periods. The Mexican historical school associated with the names of Silvio Zavala, the Colegio de México and the *Programa de la Historia de América* has already altered many of the perspectives of the colonial period, and its influence is still extending both north and south through the Americas.

Thus, in that area of the globe covered by European expansion to the west, three phases, Europe-centred, new-nation-centred, indigenous peoples-centred, have followed, each of them still viable but all necessary for the full realization of the others in research and synthesis. But it is the last, with its insights on the history of the oppressed and submerged, which has perhaps the greatest relevance to the problems of historical study in the field of early European expansion in other areas at the present time.

In Asia the progress of studies of early European expansion has been very different. The advanced societies of India, China and Japan, amongst others, had something significant of their own to bring to the history of European expansion, namely a sophisticated reaction which could find expression in chronicle, song and story. The Jesuits realized something of this in the late sixteenth and early seventeenth century and tried to tap both Chinese and Indian scholars to get a rounded impression of the effect which European penetration was having on their societies. Their perception of eastern reactions was valuable but it was also limited and it was not sustained in its earlier integrity throughout the seventeenth century. The Enlightenment helped to keep the spirit of inquiry into the East alive amongst Europeans, though with very imperfect tools, since there was still so little reciprocity of aim and of scholarship. Chinese and Japanese alike looked back at this time on the earliest European explorations and intrusions with indifference or contempt.

The great change here came in the nineteenth century, when French, English and Dutch scholars made more effective contact with the older civilizations through their literature and scholarship. As the English became established throughout India they could afford the luxury of scholarship. But the Asiatic Societies of the late eighteenth and early nineteenth centuries in both India and Great Britain were not in effect mere luxuries but genuine bridges between West and East, allowing some of eastern and western culture slowly to interpenetrate. It was under these circumstances that the editing and understanding of the documents relating to early European expansion took a great step forward, for Sir Henry Yule and others like him could call on the authority of the East to support the researches of the West. The curiosity of learned Europeans and their influence on the traditional scholarship of the East had a part in the revival of modern Asian nationalism, and also, and to some extent consequently, the emergence of an Asian view of European expansion, at once radically critical and intellectually constructive. From Japanese critical editions of early European sources on the Far East to syntheses like K. M. Panikkar's *Asia and western dominance,* the Asian review of the sources, of the motives, of the harms and benefits, the repressions and stimuli of European expansion has played and is playing an immensely important part in the re-interpretation and re-evaluation of that movement.

Within very recent years former French and English colonies have begun, in some cases have just begun, to look back at the sources for the history of what was to become their country. In many cases they find their first literate historical materials in the records of early European expansion. Just as in the Americas earlier the focus shifted from London, Madrid and Lisbon to New York, Rio de Janeiro and Buenos Aires, so now the focus on this type of documentation shifts to the new capitals in Africa where state historical societies and universities to feed them are still in many cases only beginning. European settler communities in Africa have not made many outstanding contributions to the understanding of African backgrounds, being mainly concerned with the history of settlement in a period later than that of the earliest European contacts. Consequently, every scrap of early exploration material on almost every part of Africa takes on a new significance and has to bear a new weight of historical interpretation. This situation promises to bring about a most lively and interesting use of such sources. One danger is that the artificial boundaries of the modern states, relics of colonial divisions rather than of indigenous social entities, will lead to these sources being used in insufficiently meaningful fragments. Another is that they will become too rapidly imbedded in the national legends, which are, in new nations, the almost inevitable prelude to national histories, and from which it may prove difficult to extract them.

It may prove useful here to recapitulate what has been said so far. The earliest accounts of the overseas world by Europeans were, if often naive, the least biased. Later descriptions and narratives were strongly influenced by the particular national bias of their country of origin, though they had a certain basic similarity in their approach and character and content derived from the degree of homogeneity which Western European culture had attained by the sixteenth century. It depended to some extent on the uses to which the early narratives could be put by the competing European colonial powers, whether they were preserved or destroyed, published or concealed, recalled from time to time or forgotten until modern research workers uncovered them. From the phase of empire-breaking which began in the late eighteenth century the liberated nations of ex-Europeans in the Americas came to contribute a new nationalist element of their own to the use of these materials. In the late nineteenth century a parallel Asian development to this began to appear: it was not the same but it had similarities. In the twentieth century the indigenous cultures have been taking over the exploration materials as tools for a still newer set of national histories, those of the former conquered societies which did not in the main belong to either Asian or European literate communities.

Marx initiated a new way of looking at and thinking about European expansionism but his characterizations of what he called the early phases of merchant capitalism were not very precise: Lenin was primarily interested in the analysis of a later phase of imperialism. Since Marx a Marxist element in the interpretation of the earlier stages of European expansion has been evident both in Asia and in the Americas. At the same time there do not seem to have been major works written from a purely Marxist angle on this particular aspect of European expansion. Instead, Marxism has remained an ingredient, sometimes an important one (as in Indian historiography), sometimes a relatively minor one (as in Mexican) in the reinterpretation of the early sources from the point of view of the peoples subjected to European domination. In the hands of African historians it will be interesting to see what balance will be struck. It may be that an at least semi-Marxist approach may prove to be a tool to rationalize the emotional excesses of a purely nationalist history.

The novel and varied value of the records of early exploration and expansion by Europeans in the current situation makes it peculiarly important that historians who are trying to see through the varying approaches towards a historical synthesis should think out a coherent policy towards the documentation of these early centuries. Clearly almost every source ought to be looked at again with the greatest care and with a many-faceted approach. Already we appreciate better than we did the significance of data on natural history contained in the early exploration documents. Professional anthropologists have long known the vital importance of early documents for their cultural studies, though only a minority have understood enough about the critical study of sources to make full use of what is to be found in them. It is now clear that it will be necessary for Africans and Asians to take into their own hands the greater part of the interpretation of the early documents in so far as they refer to their own societies. Indeed they are bound to do so. But it is also highly desirable for European historians to have access to their work and to contribute to the explanation of the character of the documents which emanate from European cultures. Neither type of contribution ought, of course, to exclude the other. Should we not now envisage what we should need for a critical edition of an early exploration text? This will require the collaboration, ideally, of European and non-European historians each working from his own cultural standpoint towards a full interpretation, and aided by scientific specialists so far as is necessary. This kind of collaboration is desirable as much for European as for non-European historians. The final use that is made of such documentary editions once they are made available, is bound, for a long time, to have nationalist or imperialist or Marxist overtones, but in the preparation of texts and commentaries international association can bring historians around the world towards some common approaches. This may in the end, perhaps, bring them towards a synthesis of views on the nature and character of early European exploration of the non-European world and the subsequent expansion of Europe outside its own territorial limits.

2

HAKLUYT'S REPUTATION

The story of Hakluyt's reputation is still incomplete,[1] but it is now possible to see some of the elements, at times rather puzzling ones, which accounted for its survival and growth. In his own lifetime Hakluyt's achievement won him no spectacular rewards or exceptional literary prominence. An Oxford college fellow-ship, two country livings, two cathedral prebends, a Savoy chap-laincy, a modest fortune were his rewards as a scholar, business consultant and clergyman as well as a compiler and editor. He owed much of his rise in the little circle of voyage-promoters and voyage-recorders to his elder cousin, and it was largely through him that, in the first place, he made the essential contacts with merchants, maritime speculators, sailors and ministers of state. His role as consultant on certain overseas matters, more particularly on American prospects, to Walsingham, Burghley and Robert Cecil, between 1578 and 1612, was far from being a continuous one. From 1581 to 1588 he had some appreciable influence on Walsingham: though his contacts with Burghley went back to 1578, his close association with the elderly statesman on the St Lawrence voyages covered only a few years in the 1590s: from 1596 to about 1609 he had a rather limited range of connections with Robert Cecil and perhaps some influence with him during the crucial years 1605–7 when the Virginia Company was being created. He had very close connections with most of the North American adventures and adventurers between 1580 and 1607: besides the Virginia Company he had some share in determining the form and objectives of the East India Company in 1600 and

[1] A particularly useful estimate of the limits of what has already been done is that by Federico Marenco in his introduction to *I viaggi inglesi . . . di Richard Hakluyt*, I (Milan, 1966), 27–33.

the North-west Passage Company in 1612. Yet it is difficult to trace a continuous association between Hakluyt and very many of the individuals whose careers overlapped, as did Hakluyt's, the Elizabethan and Jacobean periods. Michael Lok he knew from at least 1581 and was still in fairly close touch with him in 1612. Ralegh he was close to between 1583 and 1589 but he was only loosely in contact with him from 1590 to 1603, and only occasionally, it is thought, after his disgrace in 1603. It seems probable that one of his most stable contacts in London from 1582 until his death was Thomas Smith, though we have few indications of precisely how close or continuous their co-operation was over either the East India Company or the Virginia Company.

Hakluyt had, it is true, other circles of influence. The little band of senior members of Christ Church which William Gager celebrated in Latin verse in 1583 included Hakluyt.[1] And in 1598 or a little later Gabriel Harvey noted, 'I looke for much, as well in verse, as in prose, from my two Oxford frends, Doctor Gager, & Master Hackluit: both rarely furnished for the purpose.'[2] Gabriel Harvey (d. 1630) and his brother Richard (d. 1623) both outlived Hakluyt and appear to have retained an interest in him for the rest of his life. At the same time, there is no indication that Archbishop Toby Mathew (d. 1628), or the mathematician, Nathaniel Torporley (d. 1632), both of whom were also included in Gager's gallery, kept up any contact whatever with Hakluyt. Such men could provide, however, some extension of his reputation into the decade or two after his death. He was active also in the intellectual circle which included William Camden (d. 1623) and Sir Henry Savile (d. 1622), but our evidence of close contact with them is largely from the 1580s, and evidence of developing links with younger scholars in the years before his death is slight. His links with geographers in the Low Countries are not known to have survived the deaths of Mercator (1594) and Ortelius (1598), with the exception of some contact with Emanuel van Meteren (d. 1612). He did not leave, therefore, so far as we know,

[1] B.M., Additional MS 22583, the Hakluyt verse being on f. 62.
[2] Gabriel Harvey, *Marginalia*, ed. G. C. Moore-Smith (1913), p. 233.

a continental reputation, based on correspondence in his late years, behind him. Of the long list of men whom he had aroused to help him or to translate texts which he considered worth English editions, beginning with John Florio and including Martin Basanier, Philip Jones, Robert Parke, Abraham Hart\ well, William Phillip, William Walker, Pierre Erondelle, John Pory and Michael Lok, none became his disciple and continued his professional interests, though Pory (d. 1635) may at times have aspired to do so. Captain John Smith continued to exploit Hakluyt's works with an occasional acknowledgement between 1612 and 1624,[1] as did William Strachey in his then unpublished 'Historie of Travell into Virginia Britania' (1610–12).[2]

It was left largely to Samuel Purchas to carry on Hakluyt's work, and on the whole, to enhance his reputation. The details of the transition in materials from Hakluyt to Purchas are given above[3] and are very important in the record of the transmission of Hakluyt's collections. The sequence of tributes too, between 1613 and 1625, which Purchas paid to Hakluyt were important as placing on record his most significant follower's appreciation of Hakluyt's work and in helping to consolidate his fame. Whatever problems Purchas encountered in acquiring part of Hakluyt's collections – and they still remain somewhat obscure – he did not shirk paying a due tribute to his master, most forcefully con\ veyed in the engraved title to his last major work, *Hakluytus posthumus or Purchas his pilgrimes*, 1 (1625), even though the printed title\pages stress rather his own contribution and read *Purchas his pilgrimes* alone. After his immense labours, Purchas both in his titling and in his grumbles about the difficulties of obtaining some of Hakluyt's papers, which he expressed in his preface, was in two minds about precisely what tributes should

[1] John Smith, *Works*, ed. Edward Arber (1884), pp. 148, 267, 305, 465, 772. How far Smith had personal contacts with Hakluyt is not clear, but he claimed some.

[2] William Strachey, *The historie of travell into Virginia Britania*, ed. L. B. Wright and V. Freund (1953), p. xxvii; S. G. Culliford, *William Strachey, 1572–1621* (1965), pp. 48–50. Strachey could have encountered Hakluyt but we have no definite record that he did so.

[3] *Hakluyt Handbook*, I, 74-96.

be paid to Hakluyt's example and memory, but it is clear that by attempting to distinguish materials culled from Hakluyt and those collected by himself, he was honestly concerned to establish and enlarge the reputation of his master, while not forgetting to claim originality for his own methods, 'the whole Artifice (such as it is) being mine owne'.

It would seem that shortly after 1600, the word 'Hakluyt' became a portmanteau expression for the *Principal navigations* or *Voyages* (as they were more generally known). Soon after their publication, Purchas' *Hakluytus posthumus or Purchas his pilgrimes* joined the *Principal navigations* under the general bracket of 'Hakluyt', and both collections came to be treated as a general store which could be employed and pilfered with little or no acknowledgement by geographical writers and littérateurs. Robert Burton, for example, used materials from Hakluyt freely in *The anatomie of melancholy* (1621 and subsequently), but he made only one reference to his collections in a long list of geographical writers.[1] Nathanael Carpenter, *Geographie delineated* (1625 and subsequently),[2] used Hakluyt freely without any acknowledgement whatsoever. Though Hakluyt had long been known to the Harvey circle, his death in November 1616 passed Richard Harvey by without any precise impact, but when he heard of it he thought it worth writing 'R[d] Hakluyt dead, 1616–17' in his copy of Hakluyt's edition of Peter Martyr's *Decades* (1587):[3] the circumstance was important even if the particulars were vague and imprecise. This may well indicate the reputation which remained to Hakluyt after his death, his name was well enough known but the particulars of his achievements soon became somewhat unclear in men's minds.

Perhaps, George Hakewill's reference, in his influential book, *An apologie of the power and providence of God in the government of the world* (1631 and subsequently), marked the beginning of something of a revival in his reputation. Hakewill wished,[4] that *The*

---

[1] *Anatomy of melancholy*, ed. A. R. Shilleto, II (1903), 103 (though he bequeathed his *Principall navigations* (1589) to Christ Church where it still is).

[2] *Geography delineated* (Oxford, 1625 and 1635).   [3] B.M., pressmark 45.b.10.

[4] *An apologie* (1631), p. 253 (3rd edn., 1635), pp. 310–11.

principal navigations in their original form (he almost certainly means that of 1598–1600) and as 'lately enlarged and perfected' (i.e. by Purchas in 1625) could be translated into Latin: 'it were to be wished as well for the honour of the English name, as the benefite that might thereby redound to other Nations, that his collections and relations had been written in Latin, or that some learned pen would be pleased to turn them into that Language.' What Hakewill is saying, it is clear, is that the collecting and editing work of Richard Hakluyt was of such high quality and intrinsic interest that it should be made fully available not merely to those who read English but to the learned world of continental scholarship. The texts with which Hakluyt had supplied De Bry in 1588 had been used and reused on the continent and other borrowings were made before and after his death for voyage-collections published then, but the complete translation of *The principal navigations*, not to mention the *Pilgrimes*, was too much for even the most energetic Frankfurt or Amsterdam entrepreneur. The myth of a French translation of *The principal navigations* in 1629 is a hardy one,[1] but there is clearly nothing in it. It seems to have stemmed from careless references to the works of Pierre Bergeron. His *Traicté de la nauigation et des voyages de descouuerte et conqueste moderne* (Paris, 1629), and *Relation des voyages en Tartarie* (Paris, 1634), utilized extensively, and with due acknowledge-ment, first Hakluyt's more modern contributions and then, in more depth, his medieval contributions. He referred to him in the first work as 'le docte et laborieux Richard Hakluit' and in the second as 'le docte Geographe', thus placing his name before a French readership not too long after his death.[2]

The publication in 1658 of Sir Ferdinando Gorges' tract on his New England enterprises and of a rewritten version of it by his grandson, another Ferdinando Gorges, in 1659,[3] provided an occasion both for acknowledging Hakluyt's work on providing materials on North America and reviving the link between his promotional activities and those of an entirely new generation.

---

[1] Reappearing, for example, in M. van Durme, ed., *Correspondance Mercatorienne* (Antwerp, 1959), p. 161.

[2] *Traicté*, pp. 51–2; *Relations*, sig. a3r.   [3] *America painted to the life* (1659).

Hakluyt had a certain following in Restoration England. Thomas Fuller's posthumous *Worthies of England* (1662)[1] had a useful and amusing though rather inaccurate notice of Hakluyt (though Aubrey wholly ignored him), which helped to revive his reputation, notably his reference to the 'useful Tracts of *Sea Adventures*, which before were scattered as several Ships, Mr. Hackluit hath embodied into a *Fleet*, divided into *three Squadron*, so many volumes, a work of great honour to England', which usefully characterized and commended *The principal navigations*. Thomas Dinely, noting in 1680 several Hakluyt tombs in Leo-minster Church,[2] remarked, 'of this family of Hacluit is Richard who wrote learnedly, as a traveller concerning Geography & History'. (It may be noted that Dinely seems to have thought that some of Hakluyt's 'Voyages' were his own.) Anthony à Wood in his *Athenae Oxonienses*,[3] again writing not wholly accu-rately on the man, speaks of *The principal navigations* as being 'per-formed with great care and industry' which 'cannot but be an honour to the Realm of England', in the last words echoing Fuller.

The French connection also continued into the later seventeenth century. Melchisedech Thévenot had used Hakluyt and Purchas when preparing his voyage-collection and included their names in his title-page, *Relations de divers voyages curieux, que n'ont point esté publiés ou ont esté traduit d'Hacluyt, de Purchas et d'autres voyageurs*[4] but in fact he took only one Anthony Jenkinson narrative from Hakluyt and nine others (some of which had come from Hakluyt in the first place) from Purchas. Nonetheless, Thévenot remained genuinely interested in Hakluyt. He had picked up from Purchas the information that not all the voyage-narratives collected by Hakluyt had been included in his own collection. When a friend of his, one N. Toinard (or Thoynard), was writing to John Locke on 24 August 1680 (N.S.), Thévenot added a note of his own to inquire whether there was any hope of finding these

[1] Ed. John Nichols (1811), p. 453.
[2] *History from marble*, ed. J. G. Nichols (1867), p. clvii.
[3] *Athenae Oxonienses*, I (1691), 350; ed. P. Bliss, II (1815), cols. 186–8.
[4] Paris, 1663–72, 4 parts in 5 volumes.

unpublished pieces which he might possibly then translate and publish.[1]

Locke was himself a connoisseur of voyage literature and owned a copy of *The principal navigations*,[2] but he was unable to locate (as indeed his modern successors have been) the Hakluyt papers, used and unused, which Purchas had had.[3] Thévenot's attitude to sources would have pleased Hakluyt himself: his inquiry too may have been the first time a question on the fate of Hakluyt's papers was asked (we still do not know the answer).

There are some indications towards the end of the century that, however much his publications may have been cherished by their owners, and his memory kept alive by biographers, compilers and collectors, Hakluyt was thought to be fading out of the historian's ken as his works became less accessible through want of a new edition. Edmund Bohun, in his *Character of Queen Elizabeth* (1693),[4] was rather pessimistic in tone: 'Mr. *Richard Hacluit*, who

[1] 'Japris par la lecture de Purchas, que de son temps cest adire vers lannee 1625 il y avoit encores des ecris d'Hackluit qui n'avoient point este Imprimés, Purchas en parle commes de pieces qui meritent d'estre données au public, Il fauderoit s'informer en quelles mains peuvent estre tombes ces ecrits, et Sauver ces ouvrages en faveur du Public et dun homme dont on se souviendera tousjours pour lobligation que nous luy avons de nous avoir sauvé beaucoup de bonnes choses

il a sauvé des pieces et des ouvrages de quelques uns de nos conquerans Francois, Je vouderois bien estre assez heureux pour luy rendre la pareille et sauver de loubly par ce soin que J'en prens quelques uns de ses ouvrages

ce seront une diligence a faire encore pour les ouvrages de Purchas il est difficle quil ne soit reste quelques pieces quil avoit ammassées pour en enrichir son receuil.' Bodleian Library, MS Locke C. 21, ff. 55–6. I owe this reference to Dr Esmond de Beer.

[2] In the collection of Mr Paul Mellon, see Peter Laslett and John Harrison, *The library of John Locke* (Oxford Bibliographical Society, n.s., XII, 1965), p. 28.

[3] Locke to Toinard, 30 August [1680]: Et si quid post se reliquit Hacluit quod nondum editum est id totum interijsse credo.' B.M. Additional MS 28728, ff. 9–10. This reference also I owe to Dr de Beer. Locke transcribed a section on Russia from Hakluyt (headed 'excerpts from Principall Navigations') in Bodleian Library, MS Locke C. 30, ff. 56–7 (reference from Mr Colin Steele).

[4] P. 264. A selection of seventeenth and eighteenth century views of Hakluyt may be found in C. W. Moulton, ed., *Library of English and American literary criticism*, I (New York, 1910), 445–6. An unpublished sketch by William Fulman (1632–88) is in Corpus Christi College, Oxford MS 308, f. 43v.: the sketch by

lived in these times, took a particular care to collect and publish
the journals of all these Voyages, by which he deserved very well
of the Nation; and it is a great pity that his works are becoming
so scarce and so little known, and that no man has since pursued
the same method; these Discourses being of great use for all
Mariners, and serving very much for the enlarging and clearing
the Geography of the World.' Though there was still a long way
to go before a new edition of Hakluyt was to be possible, 'the
same method', or at least a comparable method, if not so scholarly
or comprehensive as Hakluyt's, was to produce a long series of
general voyage-collections, from the beginning of the eighteenth
century onwards until the early nineteenth. These were frequently
to invoke the name of Hakluyt on their title-pages, though sometimes with less justification even than Thévenot, and were to be,
in a sense, substitutes for the real thing, Hakluyt reissued and
restored. G. R. Crone and R. A. Skelton point out[1] that most of
these collections were not produced for purely geographical or
scientific reasons, or even for political ones, but almost solely to
provide desultory reading for educated country gentlemen, and
were consequently distinguished rather by 'eclecticism and
amateurism' than by scholarship or practical value. The effect
was to keep the name of Hakluyt alive indeed, but also to annoy,
even infuriate, the few who were devoted to his text. William
Oldys may have been an unusually articulate representative of
this view, but it is possible to sympathize with him when he
complained in 1757 that 'Hakluyt went on, to be pillaged,
abridged, and reduced, as he had been; to be transposed and
transformed; so he has been published and republished, little or
much of him, from one end to the other, in a confused, or indis-
tinct conjunction with other collections; and no true genuine
Hakluyt, or grateful acknowledgement to Hakluyt, after more
than one hundred and fifty years, revived yet'.[2]

White Kennett (1660–1728) in B.M. Lansdowne MS 983, f. 273, also remains
unpublished.
[1] 'English voyage collections, 1625–1846', in E. Lynam, ed., *Richard Hakluyt and
his successors* (1946), pp. 66, 78–9.
[2] *Biographia Britannica*, IV (1757), 2472.

However, the first of the major eighteenth-century collections, *A collection of voyages and travels* (4 vols. 1704), best known as *Churchill* from its publishers, contained in its first volume a long discourse[1] entitled 'The catalogue and Character of most Books of Travels'. This was first advertised as being by Edmond Halley, though afterwards was 'supposed to be written by the celebrated Mr. Locke'. The attribution to Locke is false; that to Halley very doubtful, and the author was most probably some Churchillian hack. Not without interest as reflecting eighteenth-century taste and knowledge, the critical remarks on Hakluyt help to indicate why it was not in this period easy to contemplate a new edition of the original text. Hakluyt was starred as 'the first Englishman that compil'd any Collection of Travels now extant', but the *Principal navigations* was characterized as both too bulky and too uncritical. Hakluyt is said to have been responsible for 'stuffing his Work with too many Stories taken upon trust, so many trading Voyages that have nothing new in them, so many Warlike Exploits not all pertinent to his Undertaking, and such a multitude of Articles, Charters, Letters, Relations, and other things little to the purpose of Travels and Discoveries', and to have failed to concentrate on what 'was really authentick and useful'. Viewed as a historical source-book, this is a bad misjudgement of *Principal navigations*, but in the context of eighteenth-century taste and of the amateur readership of the time it was not unreasonable. Nor is it unfair to say that Hakluyt's reputation with the broader reading public in the later nineteenth and twentieth centuries has been based on rigorous selection in anthologies of his more dramatic and colourful pieces. Hakluyt was valuable to the Churchills, as was frankly admitted, 'for the good there is to be pick't out', though the selection made in 1704

---

[1] [Awnsham and John Churchill], *A collection of voyages and travels . . . with a general preface giving an account of the progress of navigation from its original to this time*, I (1704), xcii–xciii. Curiously enough, the writer found Ramusio's *Navigationi et viaggi* 'judiciously compiled and free from the great mass of useless matter, which swells our English Hakluyt and Purchas'. John Harris, *Navigantium atque itinerantium bibliotheca*, II (1705), i–ii, speaks well of Hakluyt. Other editors tend to ignore him, as did John Knox, *A new collection of voyages*, I (1767), iv, when he commended in turn Purchas, Churchill and Harris.

was not unconscientious. Purchas too was regarded very similarly, following Hakluyt, 'whom he has imitated too much'. How much and how little the travel collections in fact exploited Hakluyt can be gleaned from Crone and Skelton and need not be laboured in detail. When the Abbé Prévost began his extensive work, *Histoire générale des voyages*, he prefaced his first volume in 1746 with a tribute to Hakluyt.[1] He had used both the 1589 and the 1598–1600 editions and regarded them as sheet-anchors in a general collection such as he aimed at, remarking that with Hakluyt and Purchas the English had an advantage over any other country in putting the voyages of their countrymen on record. He paid a special tribute to the detail in which earlier English enterprises were known.

A collection of voyages and travels . . . Compiled from the . . . library of the late earl of Oxford published by Thomas Osborne,[2] had rather a different character from those which took items or snippets or abstracts from *Principal navigations*, as it consisted largely of reprints of earlier volumes of travels, including Hakluyt's translation of Galvão and three other books translated at his prompting, all of which helped to increase the Hakluyt material in circulation and enable a more comprehensive view to be taken of his achievement. William Oldys, however, proved that a new edition of *Principal navigations* was not yet a practical proposition. His 1736 prospectus was for a 300-sheet edition in weekly parts to be

[1] Antoine Francois Prévost, *Histoire générale des voyages* (20 vols. Paris, 1746–79), I, i–ii: 'Mais il n'y a point de plus de Nation qui en ait publie plus que les Anglois, de qui nous en avons déja trois générales, . . .; celle de Hakluyt, en trois Tomes in folio celle de Purchass, en quatre Tomes, . . . & celle de Harris, en deux. He criticized Harris for leaving out many of the best narratives in Hakluyt, and said that while the intention of the collectors was to put together the best authors from the beginnings of commerce and discovery down to their own times, their fear of multiplying volumes (which was not to deter Prévost) led them to suppress many excellent pieces. 'C'est par cette raison que Hakluyt est borné aux Auteurs Anglois, & que n'écrivant pas plus de cinquante ans après les premieres navigations de ses Compatriotes, il n'a pas laissé d'en omettre plusieurs, qui n'ont pas même trouvé place dans son Supplement.' (He had already noted that 'Hakluyt se crut obligé en 1599, c'est a-dire, dix ans après sa première Addition, d'en donner une Seconde avec un supplément considerable.')

[2] 2 vols., 1745.

assembled in a single folio volume. Not only was the whole of the 1598–1600 edition to appear, but also biographical material, some notes and corrections and an appendix of Hakluyt's 'remains' from Purchas were to be added.[1] This would surely have made up one of the bulkiest and most indigestible volumes it is possible to imagine, and it is perhaps, for all Oldys' enthusiasm and scholarship, a good thing for Hakluyt's reputation that he did not reappear in this form. There was insufficient response, and Oldys had to content himself with a full analysis of the contents of *Principal navigations* and a further plea for its republication in his *British Librarian*.[2] It is now clear that Oldys' biographical knowledge of Hakluyt and his enthusiasm for his works made his contribution of his Hakluyt article to *Biographia Britannica* in 1757,[3] though unsigned, a real turning-point in the history of Hakluyt's reputation. Oldys understood, as earlier critics had not done, both the precise nature and extent of Hakluyt's labours in compiling and editing his collections, paying tribute to 'his vigorous endeavours' and to 'this undiscourageable spirit' with which he went about his task. His assessment is entirely contrary to that in the Churchill collection: 'For this edition is built up on a very comprehensive plan, and may, at all times, be no less serviceable many ways, than reputable to the nation; as it is a magazine, so nobly stored with some of the most adventrous atchievements of our ancestors, that were of the most national concern, attested by eye-witnesses, as well as other most credible and authentic vouchers.' Oldys' biographical information cleared up many problems and was authoritative for another century, while his bibliographical data were comprehensive and accurate. If his eulogy sounds at times a little excessive, it should be remembered that the article was deliberately aimed to rescue a major historical authority, for so Oldys considered him, from undeserved misunderstanding and neglect. Subsequent biographical studies in the eighteenth century, for example, that in Joseph Towers, *British biography*,[4] largely followed Oldys.

One factor in arousing and maintaining an interest in Hakluyt

[1] *Biographia Britannica*, IV, 2472.   [2] No 3, March 1737, pp. 136–58.
[3] *Biographia Britannica*, IV, 2461–74.   [4] III (1767), 299–302.

in the eighteenth century was the rise of naval history. But the earlier naval historians, as Oldys was to point out about Joseph Burchet's *Most remarkable transactions at sea* (1720), paid very little attention either to the Elizabethan period or to Hakluyt. Yet Hakluyt's significance as a source-book in this field had previously been pointed out, Fuller having remarked that 'his Genie urging him to the study of History, especially to the Marine part thereof'. Thomas Lediard in *The naval history of England*[1] both used and acknowledged Hakluyt, stating, 'I have given my Readers an Abridgement of the most curious Accounts contained in Hackluyt and Purchas.' To Oldys he was, as so much else, 'our most eminent and worthy Naval Historian in the reign of Queen Elizabeth'; but there was a chauvinistic purpose too to be served by reviving Hakluyt. The argument here was that Hakluyt had both recorded and stimulated overseas exploration and aggression: now in an era of world-wide war with France might he not be used again for a similar purpose? Oldys winds up with a rhetorical call to Englishmen to 'animate their posterity to dispise all hazard,...bloodshed and death itself, for a knowledge of the uncultivated world, and the honour that may be reaped in it, to their own advantage, and the aggrandizement of their country'. The revival of Hakluyt in a scholarly manner was thus to be involved once,[2] and, similarly, again, in the later nineteenth century, with the glorification of British imperialism.

The growth of bibliographical studies in the hands of men like Oldys, Joseph Ames and William Herbert, and the appearance of reasonably reliable catalogues of the major libraries, made it possible for interested students or scholars to find out what pub-lished works, besides *Principal navigations*, Hakluyt had been responsible for, so that both *Principall navigations* (1589) and *Divers voyages* (1582) came to light again in that way.[3] The eighteenth century too saw the first beginnings of an interest in the biblio-

[1] 1 (1735), sig. A2r.
[2] The eighteenth-century boast is echoed in his own manner by William Robert-son, *The history of America* (1777), bk. ix, on Hakluyt 'to whom England is more indebted for its American possessions than any man of that age'.
[3] See Quinn, *Richard Hakluyt, editor*, pp. 40–2.

graphy of the history of North America for its own sake. White Kennett's *Bibliothecae Americanae primordia* (1713) was the pioneer work in English in this field and it contained, some twenty-four years before *The British Librarian*, a full catalogue of the contents of *The principal navigations*. An occasional American colonist had already begun to collect books on the North American past in England:[1] and to add to the stocks brought over by earlier settlers. The *Bibliotheca Americana* (1789), apparently compiled by Leman Thomas Rede, continued to feature Hakluyt's writings. The way was thus opening for men like John Carter Brown, Obadiah Rich, and James Lenox, not to mention Henry Stevens, who put Hakluyt's publications into the front ranks of growingly expensive Americana.

Thomas Zouch in 1808 could write[2] that 'Every reader conversant in the annals of our Naval transactions will cheerfully acknowledge the merit of Richard Hakluyt'. They might indeed do so, but largely on the basis of second-hand recommendations, for copies of the original editions were by now genuinely scarce. However, buoyed up by the boom in publishing and bookselling of those years, Robert Harding Evans was well on the way to publishing the first edition of Hakluyt for over two hundred years. A successful bookseller and auctioneer, Evans was also an old boy of Hakluyt's school, Westminster, so that piety may have worked with him as well as profit. His introduction was a puff for his publication ('This elaborate and excellent collection') as well as a boost for Hakluyt. It was so useful to authors in cosmography, navigation and history, and 'a LEADING STAR TO THE NAVAL HISTORIES since compiled'.[3] However, the edition lived up to its advertisement. The text of *Principal navigations* was well produced in four stout volumes, as well as a few additional items from *Principall navigations* (1589), and volume five (1812) added *A selection of voyages . . . chiefly published by Hakluyt, or at his*

---

[1] Either William Byrd I or William Byrd II had acquired a copy of *The principal navigations* during a visit to England, which was in the family library when it was dispersed in 1777–8 (C. L. Cannon, *American book collectors* (1941), pp. 16–18).

[2] *Life of Sir Philip Sidney* (York, 1808), p. 317. John Stanier Clarke, *The progress of maritime discovery* (1803), pp. xii–xiii, has a favourable sketch of Hakluyt.

[3] I (1809), xxvi–xxvii.

suggestion, but not included in his celebrated compilations, comprising Hakluyt's own translations and most of those published under his inspiration. Therefore, although the Evans edition was a limited one of only 325 copies and was expensive, it made up at last a coherent body of Hakluyt material in an unabridged form, from which the greater part of his output could be read, studied and judged.

From 1812 onwards we are in rather a different world so far as Hakluyt scholarship is concerned. Study of the early expansion of Europe overseas, for which Hakluyt was essential, and the continued preoccupation of Englishmen and others with the exploration of the less accessible parts of the earth's surface, meant that Hakluyt formed part of the basic reading of geographers, explorers, and even civil servants engaged in some way with distant colonies. After 1815 curiosity tended to replace xeno-phobia for a time in the international sphere and in relation to the lesser-known regions: the atmosphere for this became more favourable as concepts of free trade and *laissez-faire* became more general. Sir William Foster has explained the circumstances under which the Hakluyt Society came into existence in 1846 as the result largely of the efforts of the geographer, William Desborough Colley.[1] It was a time when the names of eminent Elizabethans such as Matthew Parker and William Camden were being used to cover the activities of publishing societies. As the Camden Society published historical texts and the Parker Society ecclesi-astical texts, so the Hakluyt Society was 'formed for the purpose of printing, for distribution among the members, the most rare and valuable voyages, travels, and geographical records, from an early period of exploratory enterprise to the circumnavigation of Dampier'. Thus launched, the Society might have proceeded, as indeed the Camden Society proceeded, with little regard for its guiding light, but there were enthusiastic Hakluytians amongst its members from the first, and John Winter Jones' fine edition of

[1] 'The Hakluyt Society, a retrospect', in Lynam, ed., *Hakluyt* (1946), pp. 143-5. J. Payne Collier, 'On Richard Hakluyt and American discoveries', *Archaeologia*, XXXIII (1849), 282-92, however questionable some of its statements, also reflected the revival of interest in Hakluyt.

Divers voyages in 1850, with its copious additions to the Oldys biography of Hakluyt in its introduction, ensured that Hakluyt's reputation and its furtherance remained a primary purpose of the Society. This was reflected by the gradual appearance of editions of his and his pupils' translations and the slow sorting out and editing of sections of the voyage collections along with new and hitherto unpublished material. By 1898, the year following Queen Victoria's diamond jubilee, the Society had put out one hundred volumes and thought it time to begin a second series.

The Hakluyt Society had, however, missed an opportunity to publish the most important Hakluyt work which still remained in manuscript, 'A particuler discourse concerninge the greate necessitie and manifolde comodyties that are like to growe to this Realme of Englande by the Westerne discoueries lately attempted written in the yere 1584, by Richard Hakluyt of Oxforde.' Leonard Woods, searching for materials on the history of Maine, located the only surviving contemporary copy at Middle Hill (as Phillipps MS 14097) in 1868, and had it recopied for publication with the blessing of Sir Thomas Phillipps. Charles Deane completed the editing of Wood's edition, to which was given the short title, *Discourse on western planting* (which has, with a few minor variations, held the field since 1877 when it appeared as *Documentary history of the state of Maine*, II (Cambridge, Mass., 1877), and also separately). Even though it was not sufficiently appreciated then, and has not always been since, that this was a confidential paper, prepared for the use of Queen Elizabeth and her advisers without any idea of publication, the contents of this work as the first major prospectus for the English occupation and exploitation of North America on a grand scale, won for its author an additional and significant place in the history of the beginnings of English enterprise in America as a major contributor to the foundation of the colonies from which the United States emerged.

I have written elsewhere[1] that 'the Hakluyt Society was a typical expression of Free Trade optimism, the English belief that

---

[1] Comité International des Sciences Historiques, XIIe Congrès International des Sciences Historiques, *Rapports*, I (Vienna, 1965), 54. See above, p. 10.

their right to penetrate the farthest corners of the earth to sell their goods had a strong historical foundation which would be strengthened by the publication of well-edited materials on how exploration and European expansion came about'. But this too was to alter rapidly; Hakluyt was to change in the period of the new imperialism of the late nineteenth century from the great Free Trader to the protagonist of nationalistic empire. It is not without significance that it was J. A. Froude, as the prophet of imperial revival, who should have characterized the Evans edition, as early as 1852,[1] as 'the Prose Epic of the modern English nation'. The Elizabethan period was to him an epoch of heroic endeavour, an inspiration for future generations: 'They [the Voyages] contain the heroic tales of the exploits of the great men in whom the new era was inaugurated; not mythic, like the Iliads and the Eddas, but plain broad narratives of substantial facts, which rival legend in interest and grandeur.' He pays a scholarly tribute too by saying that 'very little which was really noteworthy escapes the industry of Hakluyt himself', but he saw the voyages, in inflated rhetorical terms, 'which with their picturesqueness and moral beauty shone among the fairest jewels in the diamond mine of Hakluyt'. The Hakluyt Society was reproved for its scholarship: it should, instead, have been publishing Hakluyt in penny numbers, since 'What the old epics were to the royally or nobly born, this modern epic is to the common people'. Hakluyt's approach was, of course, that of a strongly biased English nationalist, and so statements from his writings could be used in support of the later British Empire and its makers. At the same time these fluctuations in the ideological context in which he was seen, with consequent changes in his reputation, did not affect the continuing study of his work and the growth in the appreciation of its historical value.

It will be evident that to a considerable degree Hakluyt's reputation with scholars has depended on knowledge of and accessibility of his works. Edmund Goldsmid's edition of the *Principal navigations*, published elaborately in sixteen volumes in Edinburgh

---

[1] 'England's forgotten worthies', *Westminster Review*, July 1852, reprinted in *Short studies in great subjects*, II (1867), 102–59.

between 1884 and 1890, added to the number of texts of the work available to students and collectors, but the editorial apparatus was, unfortunately, almost valueless. It was only in 1899 that the Hakluyt Society at last seriously considered publishing a critical edition.[1] By 1903, when one volume was nearly ready, it was found that the firm of James MacLehose of Glasgow were about to publish an edition of their own. A portion of this edition was eventually adopted by the Society for its extra series, and has remained a mainstay of all students of Hakluyt since its completion in 1905. It contained, in volume twelve, a vivid and penetrating study of the book and, incidentally, of its compiler by Professor Walter Raleigh which became and has remained a classic of its kind. There was a full index of names and places, many illustrations, and an almost entirely reliable text. There was loss, however, as well as gain in the abandonment by the Society of its own project. C. Raymond Beazley's version of *The texts and versions of John de Plano Carpini and William de Rubruquis*, added by the Society to the extra series in 1903, contains collations of Hakluyt's texts, notes and explanations, intended to appear in the first volume of the Society's projected edition, which, if maintained in quality, would have gone far beyond the handsome MacLehose edition in scholarly value. Indeed, the formidable task of producing a critical edition of Hakluyt still remains a challenge which the Hakluyt Society has never, so far, managed to meet. This does not mean that it has abandoned the attempt to build on what Hakluyt laid down. Many of its volumes have continued the earlier policy of the Society by incorporating sections from Hakluyt's texts in wider annotated collections of material, so that scattered throughout its publications critical annotation of much of what Hakluyt published is to be found. In 1928 the Society obtained a stimulus from an outside source. The American Geographical Society published *Richard Hakluyt and the English voyages* by a young professor of English literature, George Bruner Parks. This was the first full study of Hakluyt inside the context of his own time. It revealed also the significance of the profession (or occupation) of geographical consultant in Tudor England,

[1] Lynam, ed., *Hakluyt* (1946), p. 162.

and so made possible a much more accurate assessment of Hakluyt's role in Elizabethan overseas enterprise. Its scholarly appendices also contained comprehensive lists of the material on Hakluyt and his elder cousin which still survived. This stirred the Hakluyt Society to publish in 1935, under the devoted editorship of E. G. R. Taylor, two volumes of *The original writings and correspondence of the two Richard Hakluyts*, with a characteristic introduction placing the Hakluyts still more firmly in their geographical setting.[1] It now became possible for the first time, through George Parks' book and the Taylor texts, to estimate the respective contributions of the elder and younger Hakluyt in their roles as collectors and advisers (with some redress of the balance in favour of the older man). The younger Hakluyt's efforts to rake in material from every possible source and his own willingness to supplement those sources by his own writings if he was at the last resort unable to get a first-hand account of an enterprise which he felt should be recorded, stood out more clearly. Moreover, the weight and scholarship of 'A particuler discourse' ('Discourse of western planting', was the form chosen for a short title) became more evident in the edition of it contained in Professor Taylor's second volume: Hakluyt emerged as a peculiarly learned and formidable advocate of western expansion by the Elizabethan state.

In the 1950s the advance of photolithography enabled the Hakluyt Society to contemplate the republication of Hakluyt's *The principall navigations* (1589), still largely unknown in its original form to many scholars. Full annotation did not seem practicable, as the main objective was to make a usable text available fairly rapidly. Accordingly, the editors, D. B. Quinn and R. A. Skelton, and the indexer, Alison Quinn, concentrated on providing a mainly bibliographical introduction and a fully analytical index. Though a black-letter text offers some discouragement to casual readers, it has some corresponding advantages for scholars who can see from it precisely what the author and

---

[1] Her *Late Tudor and early Stuart geography* (1934), pp. 1–38, had already presented a succinct and searching review of Hakluyt's geographical achievement and reputation.

his printers put into their text, but it is a far from complete substitute for a fully annotated version. A similar technique was subsequently adopted for the publication by a private firm of *Divers voyages* (1582) and *A shorte and briefe narration of the two navigations to newe Fraunce* (1580).[1] It will be unfortunate if some further attempt is not made to grapple with the problems of a fully explanatory edition of the work by which Hakluyt is rightly and most universally known, *Principal navigations* (1598–1600).

We might even, with perhaps undue optimism, envisage a programme which began with a facsimile edition of the second edition on similar lines to those employed for the first edition. It might proceed with a facsimile edition of the manuscript of 'A particuler discourse' (1584) with a transcript and notes. It could then go to a multi-volume edition, with full elucidations, of all Hakluyt's works and those he influenced. Some of these suggestions may well be accomplished in due course if humane scholarship survives. But it would be a mistake to regard the publication and editing of Hakluyt's works as an end in itself: they are not, after all, the sacred texts of an inspired writer. Yet they are to an increasing degree basic sources for a widening range of inquiry. Hakluyt assembled invaluable materials on the reciprocal relations between the European and the non-European world at a formative stage in their many and varied aspects. They are not limited in interest to 'the English nation' but contain vital elements of the early history of many more recent nation states. The catholicity of Hakluyt's interests and the integrity of his documentation – however this was limited by the conventions and circumstances of his own time – ensure to his collections both an enduring and expanding place in the fields of historical, geographical and anthropological scholarship on a world scale.

Hakluyt's reputation is not something static, but one reflecting the scholarly values of each generation of students of his work and of the society in which he lived. Continued scholarly concern with his works is the means by which successive groups of scholars can review and revise Hakluyt's status and significance

[1] Edited by D. B. Quinn, under the general title, *Richard Hakluyt, editor*, 2 vols. (Amsterdam, Theatrum Orbis Terrarum, 1967).

within Elizabethan and Jacobean England, reconsider and refine opinions on his editorial capacities and limitations, and may, above all, exploit the materials he collected for new and varied ends. By these means Hakluyt's reputation can, continuously, be re-assessed, his changing relevance estimated. Hakluyt's reputation is not, however, only a matter for scholars. His popular reputation not only survives but grows through repeated selections and anthology pieces from his collections. These circulate more widely, it might seem, in each decade. For those who continue to read books, the narratives he collected, told, or got others to tell have a continuing and lively appeal. His name and something of his fame adheres.

3

HAKLUYT'S USE OF MATERIAL: NORTH AMERICA

Richard Hakluyt was the outstanding advocate of English exploration of and settlement in North America between 1580 and 1600, and he continued to take an influential part in North American occasions in the later years of his life. He had excep, tional opportunities for collecting material on the colonizing voyages and in the two editions of his voyage-collection, *The principall navigations* (1589) and the third volume of *The principal navigations* (1600), he put together much the greater part of what is now known of the colonizing enterprises.

For the early English voyages to America he was able to draw on the materials on John and Sebastian Cabot (including the manuscript Cabot patent of 1496) which he had collected and printed in *Divers voyages* (1582)[1] and was able to add appreciably to them, mainly from published sources, but with the addition of a document on Cabot's second licence,[2] though he failed to discover the later Bristol grants of 1501 and 1502 in the Rolls Office. This was almost all that could be put together on these ventures before the nineteenth century, even if it left many pro, blems unsolved and, in particular, left the respective roles of John and Sebastian Cabot unclarified. For the reign of Henry VIII Hakluyt had Robert Thorne's very general treatise of 1527 which he had already published in 1582.[3] He obtained some additional material on the 1527 voyage but assimilated it to some vague hints of a voyage in 1516, while his attempt to combine two defective accounts on the 1536 voyage was only partly successful.[4] It is

---

[1] *DV*, sigs. A1–4; Quinn, *Richard Hakluyt editor*, I, 10; II, 13–19.

[2] *PN* (1589), pp. 509–14; Quinn and Skelton, edd., *PN* (1589), I (1965), xxviii; II, 507–14.

[3] *DV*, sigs. B1–D4; Quinn, *Richard Hakluyt editor*, I, 10–11; II, 21–43; *PN* (1589), pp. 250–8.

[4] *PN* (1589), pp. 515–19.

hard, however, to see what more he could have done, though he missed John Rastell's *A new interlude and a mery of the nature of the iiii elements* [1519], which would have given him some insights on English knowledge of North America before 1520.

Having eschewed in his first edition all accounts of non-English voyages, Hakluyt had very little indeed to use between 1536 and 1578. He gives one short extract from Laudonnière's *History* (which he had published separately in translation in 1587),[1] and a vivid impression of Florida, with an account of John Hawkins' brief call in 1565, from John Sparke.[2] He also had a letter on Drake's visit to California in 1579.[3] It is with the grant of a colonizing patent to Sir Humphrey Gilbert on 11 June 1578[4] that he gets into his stride. He was able to reprint from *Divers voyages* (which he had compiled as propaganda for Gilbert's venture) his cousin's notes on colonization in North America in 1578.[5] He adds also a valuable letter on Newfoundland to his cousin by Anthony Parkhurst,[6] but he gives us nothing on the first abortive voyage of Gilbert in 1578-9, which he could well have obtained and which would have resolved some problems of interpretation.[7] For the second colonizing project of 1580-3, however, he obtained a very good narrative by Edward Hayes,[8] and a short addendum to it by Richard Clarke,[9] and printed them together with a Latin letter from Stephen Parmenius to himself[10] and a note from Thomas Aldworth to Walsingham.[11] He also reprinted three tracts with whose original publication he had had something to do, those by David Ingram, Christopher Carleill and Sir George Peckham.[12] There was very little else he could hope to obtain on the 1583 voyage itself, though he does

---

[1] *Ibid.*, pp. 543–5.   [2] *Ibid.*, pp. 538–43.

[3] *Ibid.*, Drake leaves; Quinn and Skelton, edd., *PN* (1589), II (1965), 643G–643I.

[4] *PN* (1589), pp. 671–9.

[5] *DV*, sigs. K1–3v; Quinn, *Richard Hakluyt editor*, I, 12–13, 113–18; *PN* (1589), pp. 636–8.

[6] *PN* (1589), pp. 674–7.   [7] Cf. Quinn, *Gilbert*, I, 37–46.

[8] *PN* (1589), pp. 679–97.   [9] *Ibid.*, pp. 700–1.

[10] *Ibid.*, pp. 697–9.   [11] *Ibid.*, p. 718.

[12] *Ibid.*, 557–62, 718–25, 701–18; Quinn and Skelton, edd., *PN* (1589), I (1965), xxxii; II, 557–62, 718–25, 701–18.

not waste much space on the extensive preparations for it during the years 1580–3 of which his own propaganda compilation, the *Divers voyages*, comprised only a very small part.

In the years from 1584 onwards Hakluyt was deeply involved in the Roanoke voyages as adviser to Sir Walter Ralegh (even though he spent the greater part of the time in France) and, in return, he was able to get from Ralegh, Thomas Harriot and John White materials with which he could put together a very full documentation on the voyages from 1584 to 1588.[1] Ralegh's patent[2] was followed by Arthur Barlowe's discourse of the 1584 voyage.[3] Somewhat censored and prettied up, this version is more likely to have been Ralegh's than Hakluyt's. For 1585 he had the *Tiger* journal,[4] somewhat cut it seems, and a list of colonists.[5] He gives one letter from Lane to his cousin, the elder Richard Hakluyt,[6] but Sir Francis Walsingham had others,[7] which he evidently did not pass on to Hakluyt. For the Roanoke colony of 1585–6 he relied mainly on Lane's discourse[8] whose coverage was incomplete, since it concentrated on a few episodes only, and on a reprint of Thomas Harriot's *A briefe and true report* (1588). He did not obtain Harriot's narrative of the voyages and his detailed observations, 1584–7, which have disappeared,[9] though it is possible that some of the documents he prints may have come from the documentary collection on which Thomas Harriot based his own chronicle, and which would have been in Ralegh's possession. He was not able, either, to reprint Walter Bigges [*et al.*], *A summarie and true discourse* (1589), which had something on Drake's removal of the Roanoke colonists in 1586. Hakluyt was very conscious that these sources still left the picture of the colony incomplete. Consequently, he was working to enlarge its scope by getting Harriot to write notes for John White's Indian

---

[1] Quinn, *Roanoke voyages*, I, 3–76, is largely a critique of these materials and of Hakluyt's handling of them; Quinn and Skelton, edd., *PN* (1589), I (1965), xlii–xliii.

[2] *PN* (1589), pp. 725–8.   [3] *Ibid.*, pp. 728–33.

[4] *Ibid.*, pp. 733–6.   [5] *Ibid.*, pp. 736–7.

[6] *Ibid.*, p. 793.

[7] See Quinn, *Roanoke voyages*, I, nos. 25–7, 29, 30 (a map), 34.

[8] *PN* (1589), pp. 737–47.   [9] See Quinn, *Roanoke voyages*, I, p. 387.

drawings which, with a further reprint of the Harriot tract, Theodor de Bry brought out as *America*, part i, at Frankfurt in 1590. Nevertheless, information collected on Chesapeake Bay during the winter of 1585-6 was held back, evidently for security reasons. For the 1586 voyage, Hakluyt failed to pick up from its participants any coherent narrative at all and was forced to compile one himself from obviously imperfect materials:[1] if he had tried harder he might have had better success. In the case of John White's colony of 1587, he obtained the very full narrative written by White himself,[2] quite adequate for Hakluyt's purpose, but a little one-sided in its judgements for ours. White's abortive attempt to bring aid to the colonists in the Armada year was also narrated by him for the benefit of Hakluyt's readers.[3] To keep them involved with the ventures he was even able to slip in later in the volume a document assigning rights in 'Virginia', dated as late as 7 March 1589.[4]

In the decade between the appearance of *The principall navigations* (1589) and the publication of volume III of *The principal navigations* in 1600, Hakluyt was less closely concerned in North American voyaging, if only because there were very few expeditions in which to be involved. His original contributions to the material on North America in 1600 were therefore much fewer than in 1589 – his coverage, in any event, having been very full for the ventures of 1578-88. He was, however, able at this time to expand somewhat his earlier programme through the decision to include foreign sources where no English voyage narrative adequately covered the ground. He was thus able to give something like a complete coverage to eastern North America and to bring in something about the west.

Hakluyt obtained nothing new to add to his scattered information on the English voyages of the reigns of Henry VII and Henry VIII though he managed to clarify somewhat his account of the 1527 voyage,[5] but he was able to fill out the picture of the early discovery of the eastern seaboard and the river valleys by

[1] *PN* (1589), pp. 747-8.   [2] *Ibid.*, pp. 764-70.
[3] *Ibid.*, pp. 771-3.   [4] *Ibid.*, pp. 815-17.
[5] *PN*, III (1600), 1-10, 129-31.

resuscitating Verrazzano from *Divers voyages*, and also the accounts of the Cartier voyages already published in 1580.[1] To them he was able to add incomplete accounts of the Cartier voyage of 1541–2 and the Roberval expedition of 1542–3, together with some material from the *Cosmographie* of Jean Alfonse de Saintonge.[2] The main novelty for the first half of the century came with the addition of a reasonable selection of the Spanish materials for the exploration of western America. He was able to proceed from Fray Marcos de Niza to Coronado and thence to Ulloa and Alarcón, the texts taken from Ramusio and from Gómara, the latter having been published in English in 1596.[3] He continued into the second half of the century with a new English translation of the Espejo material which he had published in Spanish and French in 1586.[4] There is a mention in May 1590 of a further new expedition to Cíbola being planned[5] under Rodrigo del Río.

Hakluyt was, similarly, able to fill out the picture of the eastern coastline. He brought in the whole of Laudonnière's *Notable history*, which he had already published, to give a full picture of French Florida, 1562–8, along with two depositions taken in 1586,[6] though he had nothing to balance it with on the Spanish side. Indeed, the whole scale and nature of Spanish enterprise in eastern North America remained under-represented. This may have been partly due at least to the need to play down the role of Spain for propaganda purposes, so that eastern North America should appear to be much more an exclusive preserve of the

---

[1] Taylor, *Hakluyts*, II, 226.   [2] *PN*, III (1600), 301–42.

[3] *Ibid.*, pp. 362–82, 397–439; Francisco López de Gómera, *The pleasant historie of the conquest of Weast India, now called New Spaine* (1596).

[4] See pp. 468–9, 534–5, below.

[5] *PN*, III (1600), 397. Rodrigo del Río de Loza was an important official in the northern frontier district of Mexico, and governor of Nueva Viscaya. It does not seem that he himself planned an expedition into New Mexico in 1590 but he was concerned about this time in trying to stop the slave-hunting raid by Gaspar Castañade Sosa directed into this area (cf. P. W. Powell, *Soldiers, Indians and silver* (1952), pp. 186–9, 197, 217–18, 280–2, and G. P. Hammond and A. Rey, *The rediscovery of New Mexico, 1580–94* (1966), p. 302).

[6] *PN*, III (1600), 361–2.

French and English than it was in practice: it may also have been partly due to lack of suitable sources, though Hakluyt had at least a copy of the detailed narrative published by the Gentleman of Elvas[1] of Hernando de Soto's expedition, which he was to publish in translation in 1609 as *Virginia richly valued*. He does not seem to have had at hand anything on the Spanish Florida colony from 1565 onwards or on the attempt to establish a Spanish mission on Chesapeake Bay 1570-2, though Drake's destruction of the fort at San Agustín in 1586 appears briefly.[2]

Hakluyt's investigation of surviving Cartier–Roberval materials during his stay in France had thrown up a few items on subsequent French activities in the early 1580s, but he made no reference to the fact that he had obtained Jacques Noël's map of the St Lawrence valley which for the first time showed Lake Ontario, though he had this information incorporated in the general map included in volume II.[3] He did not publish 'The relation of Mr Stephen Bellanger', a copy of which he had sent to Dr Julius Caesar, judge of the High Court of Admiralty, in 1584,[4] nor the other scraps of information on French activities in Canada which he had used, along with a summary of Bellenger, in his 'A particuler discourse' in the same year.[5]

The largest body of materials on North America surviving from the 1589 edition related to the English ventures of 1578-88. Consequently, for this period, Hakluyt had no striking novelties to offer. He contented himself with going over the existing materials carefully and in detail so as to present his material in a form which satisfied him more adequately, the 1589 edition having been rushed through the press with consequent blemishes in the text. He also both culled and added a few items to make the coverage more effectively complete. From the documents on the

---

[1] Fidalgo de Elvas, *Relaçam* (Evors, 1557); see John Brereton, *A briefe and true relation of the discouerie of the north part of Virginia* (1602), p. 46, for information from this book, probably by Hakluyt.

[2] *PN*, III (1600), 235-6.

[3] See above, p. 68.

[4] First printed in D. B. Quinn, 'The voyage of Étienne Bellenger to the Maritimes in 1583; a new document', below, pp. 285-300.

[5] Taylor, *Hakluyts*, II, 233, 278-9.

Gilbert ventures he cut out David Ingram's narrative as being unreliable, and added the Latin poem by Stephen Parmenius, *De nauigatione Humfredi Gilberti . . . carmen*, as revised by the Hungarian poet shortly before he sailed to his death on Gilbert's 1583 expedition.[1] Hakluyt had been largely responsible for the first appearance of the poem in print in 1582 as propaganda for Gilbert's voyage, and it was included now more as a memorial to Parmenius than as a document of evidential value.[2] Two small items on Bristol's involvement in Christopher Carleill's share of the venture were also inserted for the first time.[3] Similarly, in regard to the Roanoke voyages, Hakluyt eliminated the account of the abortive 1588 voyage as being no longer of interest, and also the 1589 assignment of rights in Virginia which had ceased to operate. This time he put in the Bigges account of Drake's expedition of 1585–6 which contained something on San Agustín and the aiding of the Roanoke settlement.[4] He was also able to round off the series with John White's account of his last attempt to find the Lost Colonists in 1590, adding also the letter of 1593 (or 1594) which enclosed the narrative.[5] There was more to the voyage than was contained in the narrative, but Hakluyt did not elucidate its context. We hear nothing of further voyages to the Roanoke–Chesapeake Bay area, though there is a possibility that a visit was contemplated in 1591,[6] and we are told later that Samuel Mace's expedition of 1602 marked the fifth attempt to find them, which, since we know only of those of 1588 and 1590, leaves three voyages, some of them possibly carried out before 1600, unaccounted for.

Hakluyt did include one group of new English documents concerning relatively recent voyages to the Maritimes, the Magdalen Islands, Anticosti, and parts of western and southern Newfoundland, with which he had, himself, some association,

---

[1] *PN*, III (1600), 138–46.

[2] Edited by D. B. Quinn and N. M. Cheshire in *The new found land of Stephen Parmenius* (Toronto, 1972).

[3] *PN*, III (1600), 181–2.   [4] *Ibid.*, pp. 546–8.

[5] *Ibid.*, pp. 288–95, 287–8.

[6] K. R. Andrews, *Elizabethan privateering* (1964), pp. 165–6; *English privateering voyages, 1588–95* (1959), pp. 102, 110.

and which covered areas not hitherto represented by English narratives. The St Lawrence voyages of 1591–7[1] are reasonably well represented in the chosen narratives but Hakluyt did not reveal the name of the Basque pilot employed by the English or admit that the 1597 voyage was planned to create a settlement of radical nonconformists in the Gulf of St Lawrence.[2] Hakluyt did not include anything at all on the English fishery in south-eastern Newfoundland between 1583 and 1600 during which time it had proliferated at the expense of the Portuguese and Basques. This was scarcely because he could not obtain adequate information, but either because he did not consider the area sufficiently dramatic for inclusion or else because he preferred to keep activities there, which included a good deal of fighting and pillaging, to some extent under a security blanket. Hakluyt's frankness about the recent St Lawrence voyages is, when we recollect there was a war on, somewhat surprising. It may be that by 1600 it had already been decided to concede that area wholly to the French, so that English activities there, as recently as 1597, were only of geographical and historical interest.

In general, with the exceptions mentioned, Hakluyt presented in 1600 a very adequate coverage of the voyages which had revealed North America to Europeans. There is not to our know-ledge very much on English expeditions that he could easily have obtained. Nor, judging by what Purchas later printed from his collections, was he able during the last stage of his collecting activity between 1600 and about 1613 to add more than a small number of documents on English ventures prior to 1600. He had a good deal more on Spanish activities in North America than he published, but not enough, except in the case of the Soto and Cabeza de Vaca material, to make much difference to the general picture he presented. We are therefore indebted to him for what

[1] _PN_, III (1600), 189–200.

[2] See D. B. Quinn, 'England and the St Lawrence, 1577–1602', in J. Parker, ed., _Merchants and scholars_ (1965), pp. 117–44; 'The first Pilgrims', _William and Mary Quarterly_, 3rd ser., XXIII (1966), 59–90; and J. Rousseau, 'Les toponymes Amérindiens du Canada chez les anciens voyageurs anglais, 1591–1602', _Cahiers de Géographie de Québec_, X (1966), 263–77.

can only be regarded as an exceptionally detailed and comprehensive coverage of an area in which he had a unique personal
interest.

During the years between 1580 and 1590 Hakluyt's main
official sponsor and mentor was Sir Francis Walsingham and it
was largely while he was under his influence or in his service that
Hakluyt found and assembled the North American material
included in his 1589 collection. In the 1590s his patrons were the
Cecils, first Lord Burghley and later Sir Robert Cecil. It was
with Burghley's encouragement that Hakluyt interested himself
in the St Lawrence ventures. Sir Robert Cecil had called him in
to advise on the further conduct of the Guiana question in 1596
and it was to him that Hakluyt dedicated volumes II and III of
the enlarged edition. He made no secret, in his dedicatory epistles,
of his desire to involve Cecil in support for further North American ventures, and he also drew attention to his own part in
making North America and its prospects known in England
through the publication of narratives about it. In 1600 he claimed,[1]
and was largely justified in doing so:

> Of this New world and euery speciall part thereof in this my third volume
> I haue brought to light the best & most perfect relations of such as were
> chiefe actours in the particular discoueries and serches of the same, giuing
> vnto euery man his right, and leauing euery one to mainteine his owne
> credit.

He concluded with his famous statement to Cecil: 'Thus Sir
I haue portrayed out in rude lineaments my Westerne Atlantis or
America.'

He had indeed done his best to find effective narrators and to
give them their heads in telling their own story. He did not object
to tampering in detail with the texts they put before him.[2] He
suppressed from time to time material it might be impolitic to
print, but was, nonetheless, willing to allow his narrators at

[1] *PN*, III (1600), sigs. A2v, A3v.
[2] See Quinn and Skelton, edd., *PN* (*1589*), I (1965), li–lii; Quinn, *Roanoke
voyages*, I, 82–8; *Richard Hakluyt editor*, I, 38–40. Other detailed analyses require
to be done before a definitive picture emerges.

times to be surprisingly frank about recent events and controversial issues. (It should be remembered, too, that his text was
censored before publication, in 1589 by Dr John James and in
1598–1600 by Sir Robert Cecil himself.) It is notable, too, that
he preferred, when he could get them, straightforward accounts
of what had happened by participants in the North American
voyages to propaganda tracts on what might be found there by
future searchers. He re-used an appreciable amount of the promotion material for the Gilbert ventures, but none, except Harriot
(and that had independent merit), for the Roanoke voyages.
Because he was himself involved in most of the ventures between
1580 and 1597 he took special trouble to obtain narratives on
them, and, precisely because he knew the people concerned, he
was, in the great majority of cases, able to obtain them. His
success can be judged in the end by the very high proportion of
the materials on North America for the period 1578–97 which
have survived only because he evoked and conserved them.

4

ARTISTS AND ILLUSTRATORS IN
THE EARLY MAPPING OF NORTH AMERICA

THE tradition of painting and decorating maps goes back into the
Middle Ages. The figurative world maps of the thirteenth century,
such as the Hereford Map and the Ebstorf Map, were given much of
their character as monumental pieces by their colour. The portolan charts,
compiled from the sailing directions or rutters of the Mediterranean were, as
practical tools of seamanship, mainly undecorated, though they might be
drawn with a brush as well as a pen. But after 1300 marine charts began to
take on colours of a decorative character and to be used in the headquarters
of maritime states like the Italian trading cities or by merchants and by
nobles and sovereigns who wished to have them for reference or merely
because they liked them. The marriage of the world map with the portolan
chart may be said to date from the Catalan (or Majorcan) atlas of Abraham
Cresques made in or about 1375[1] which combined a highly decorated view
of the world in eight panels, covered with pictures as well as coastlines, and
having specific charts of the Mediterranean added to it as well. It appears to
have been given by Pedro III of Aragon either to Charles V of France in his
last years or perhaps as a present to the young Charles VI when he ended his
minority. It may be taken as a starting point for one of the themes of this
lecture, the use of elaborately coloured maps, charts and atlases as presents
between monarchs or other men of high rank, illustrating their high esteem
as works of art.

In the fifteenth century the portolan chart increased its range from the
Mediterranean to Western Europe, out into the Atlantic and down the coast
of Africa. The majority of those which survive have a decorative quality,
though in some of them this did not prevent them being useful to voyagers
who were probing the Atlantic Ocean and following the African coast
southwards. But besides the marine charts which held closely to the coasts,
there were new and elaborate world charts, one at least of them commissioned by a monarch in an attempt to formulate a world picture on a newly

1 George Grosjean, ed., *Mappamundi: the Catalan atlas of the year 1375* (Zurich, 1978); L. Bagrow
and R. A. Skelton, *History of cartography* (London, 1964), 66, pl. XXXVII–XL.

elaborate scale. This was the map made in Venice for Afonso V of Portugal by Fra Mauro and his assistants in 1458 or 1459, which assembled much material hitherto unknown to the Portuguese and speculated on areas well outside their vision hitherto. The map sent to Portugal is lost but Fra Mauro and his assistants made the surviving replica of it which still adorns the Marciana Library in Venice.[2] It was decorated with scenes comparable with those of the Catalan atlas, mostly imaginary, but suggestive of the kinds of persons and products to be met with over the whole landmass, and offering new hints on westward as well as southward and eastward voyaging.

The world maps of the later fifteenth century were more scientific, in that some of them married the new (or revived) Ptolemaic system of presenting the earth's surface inside a frame of latitudes and longitudes and included elements of what were believed to be classical geography in the world picture, which towards the end of the century revealed that there was a large area of the earth's surface from east to west as well as from north to south which had not been explored. These maps were mostly austere in their appearance, as Ptolemy's (or those believed to have been Ptolemy's) had been, but alongside them marine charts, showing something of the new discoveries, tended to become more ornate again, as clients on land sought information on the expanding shores of maritime discovery. Thus, after the discovery of the outlying islands of the Americas by Columbus in 1492, a new series of ornate world maps began to depict something, however tentative, of the new western lands, and increasingly cautiously differed as to whether they showed unfinished coastlines or linked the new lands boldly with eastern Asia. They also, cautiously at first, and less cautiously later, began to decorate their New World, when it slowly began to be recognized as such, with figures of men, of birds, of animals, of trees, of human habitations. The more practical of these charts and world maps were either used up or were assimilated into government offices concerned, in the Iberian peninsula, with further exploration and exploitation, so that comparatively few originals survived. If we had them alone we should have only a small unrepresentative sample of what was put down on vellum or paper during the crucial years of discovery between the 1480s and the 1530s.

What I have said so far is known to every student of historical cartography and there is nothing novel about it. However, in the remainder of this lecture I intend to stress two points, first that the tradition of painted decorative charts and maps does not adhere to professional chart-makers only but was one of the branches or aspects of European art in the sixteenth century, and which enshrined traditions of miniature painting in particular. And, secondly, I would suggest that it was the artistic and decorative value of a number of these charts and maps which led to their survival and that this survival was significant for the historian of cartography. Moreover, they survived largely because they were exchanged as gifts by princes and nobles, and, without these art objects, which are also maps, we should know substantially less than we do about the exploration of North America and certain adjacent areas. This is, I believe true to the extent that the contribution of cartography to the study of American discovery, and that of other parts of the globe as well, would be gravely diminished if these very special examples of the art had not survived and been cherished even when they escaped from the custody of the princely or noble houses of which they were long the treasures.

While the traditional Mediterranean portolan continued to be made for two centuries at least after the discovery of America, and many of the surviving examples are decorated, some of them lavishly, they represent only one aspect of a European phenomenon. If, to begin with, they were the product of Italians working in Italy or in the Iberian lands, the Portuguese soon came to dominate the chart- and map-making art, but were followed rapidly by Spaniards, Frenchmen and inhabitants of the Low Countries. While there is something of an international style, even amongst the most highly artistic productions of the period, there are significant developments of regional differences in techniques and ornamentation, and there are strong traditional features also, derived from the evolution of miniature painting in particular areas.[3] These, again, have been examined in detail by students of the subject. Here the emphasis will be on those crucial cartographic links which exist between the presentation maps of various schools and the conservation of knowledge which, but for the artistic value of the maps, might have been lost entirely.

Portugal and Spain were in the lead in producing both practical and decorative charts because their discoveries created a demand by seamen for them, and officials, merchants, nobles and kings wished to have a record of new discoveries in an attractive painted form. Italians were the pioneers in importing portolan-making and -decorating techniques to Portugal. But soon Portuguese were trained in these techniques and themselves began to rival the Italians. This process was helped by the development of the establishment of an official training school for pilots at the *Casa da India* in Lisbon where training in portolan-making was given as well as in navigation. This was imitated in Spain, which had an indigenous school of Catalan cartographers, after the establishment of the *Casa de la Contratación* in 1503. From the first the Spanish service was manned largely by Italians (Amerigo Vespucci was the first pilot-major to be put in charge of these activities in 1508, though Portuguese-trained men were soon employed under him.) But there were independent craftsmen as well, even though the official policy was to keep the discoveries secret. Pilots had, in both countries, to give up the

3 The subject is touched on by Janet Backhouse in Wallis, *Rotz* (see f.n. 15), and Paul Hulton, *The work of Jacques le Moyne de Morgues*, I (1977), and incidentally by Wilma George, *Animals and maps* (1969). See also Anthiaume, *Cartes marines* (Paris, 1916), I, 177.

charts they had made at sea. Both countries kept a standard chart on which new discoveries were entered, and written sailing directions maintained in parallel with them. But unofficial work was also done in these offices and outside them. Decorative charts were made for admirers, or for persons whom kings wished to honour or impress; secrets of the *padrón real* – the standard official chart – were leaked to foreigners. Pedro Nunes, who attempted to teach pilots and chart-makers a more scientific approach to their tasks, added to his *Tradado da sphera* (1537) an appendix a 'Tratado em defensam da carta de marear' in which he urged chart- and globe-makers to be more careful about how they laid out their works and urged them not to over-decorate them with too much gold, and cover them with banners, elephants and camels (*muyto ouro: & muytas bandeyras Illifantes & Camelos & outras couses iluminadas*).[4] His warning may have had some effect, but not much, since Portuguese makers of decorated painted charts were to make and sell their wares all over Europe in the sixteenth century, irrespective of prohibitions or attempts to enforce secrecy or scientific rigour. It was inevitable that the discoveries of Columbus should lead to an outburst of chart-making and to their circulation to powerful and interested persons outside the Iberian kingdoms.

If misuse of decoration was to be deprecated, the continued use of decoration was nonetheless enjoined in one of the most popular of all navigation books of the early centuries of the modern period, Martín Cortés *Breve compendia de la spera y de la arte de navegar* (Seville, 1551). Richard Eden's version in 1561 was the first of eight editions in English during the next sixty-four years.[5] The book, after providing for the laying out of the plane chart correctly in outline, went on

> This one, then with a small pen shall you describe in the card [= chart], all the places and names of the coast in that part where they are and as they are seen in the pattern [*padrón* in Spanish]. And first you must describe in red, the ports, principal capes, famous cities, with other notable things, and all the residue in black. Then shall you draw or paint [the Spanish has *debuxan*, paint, only] cities, ships, banners and beasts, and also mark the regions and other notable things [*ciudades/naos/vanderas/y animales/senalan regiones y otras notable cosas*]. Then with colours and gold shall you garnish and beautify the cities, compasses, ships, and other parts of the card [*y despues con colores y oro hermosean las ciudades/agujas/naos/y otras partes de la costa*]. Then shall you set forth the coasts with green, by the shore or banks of the land, and make them fair to sight with a little saffron, or otherwise, as shall seem best.

This was how, with regional variations, sea charts were to be made in many parts of Europe over the next century or more. How far these decorative versions were of use and were used at sea is another matter.

For the Americas, as they were disclosed, it is not possible to pin down precisely when the first of these decorative world charts was made and for whom. The world map of Juan de la Cosa, even if its known history goes back

4 *Tradado da sphera* (Lisbon, 1537), 2nd register,, sig. B4r.
5 (1551), f. 64r; (1561), f. 58r.

1 Map of the West Indies, Florida and Virginia by John White, from a survey of Virginia of 1585-1586 *(British Museum, Prints and Drawings, 1906-5-9-1(2))*

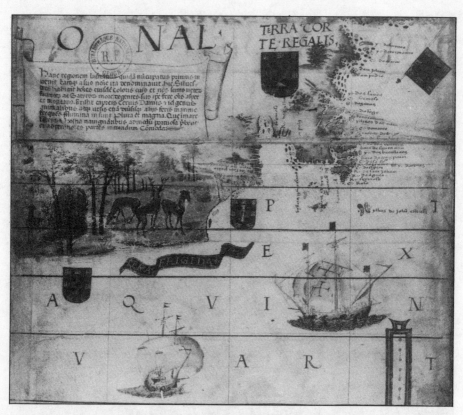

2 North-eastern North America from the Miller Atlas by Pedro (or Jorge) Reinel, 1519
(-30?) *(Bibliothèque Nationale, Rés. Ge AA. 640)*

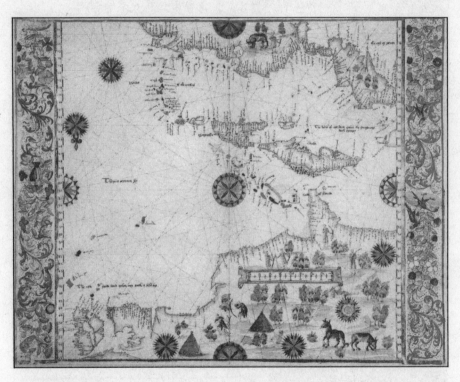

3 Chart of North America in Jean Rotz, 'Boke of Idrography' *(British Library, Royal MS 20.E.IX, ff. 23v. -24r.)*

4 Chart of North America in the Atlas of Diogo Homem made for Queen Mary, 1558
(British Library, Add. MS 5415A, ff. 19v -20r.)

little more than a century, is the first elaborate, gift-type map we have show-ing the discoveries in the west.[6] The Old World portion is traditional in style, offering some decoration of a not very distinguished sort. It is the western portion which is notable. For the first time it gives a continuous coastline to what was to be eventually defined as North America and also a stylised interior, a green-painted area in which worm-like rivers wriggle. The figure of St. Christopher skilfully hides the possible breach or continuity bet-ween the central and northern parts of the new lands, while the termination of the western land surfaces, without any clear indication of whether or not they tie in with Asia or are separate, suggests a considerable degree of sophistication. Juan de la Cosa was an experienced seaman but his map is a work of art, as well as one of the more important documents on the western discoveries. It was begun in 1500 but whether it was finished then is still open to discussion. It appears to me the kind of map which could only have been done for a patron, skilfully combining information and ambiguity, but of little or no use for navigational purposes.

The La Cosa map is most remarkable to historians of North America for its first representation of English discoveries along the eastern coast. There have been endless discussions on whether the lines on the map represent latitudes traversed on the first and second voyages of Cabot in 1497 and 1498, or whether they are derived from an unscaled and stretched out sketch of Newfoundland from the 1497 expedition. The balance of opinion is now towards the latter explanation, but in any event the La Cosa map lies at the beginning of the cartographical implications of the Bristol voyages. One of its objectives may have been to warn King Ferdinand and Queen Isabella of threatened English intervention beyond the zone fixed for Spanish expansion in 1493 and 1494. They were certainly aware at this time of a potential threat from this direction.

There is no such ambiguity about the world map sent by Alberto Cantino from Lisbon to his master, Ercole d'Este, duke of Ferrara, late in 1502.[7] This

6 The La Cosa map, Museo Naval, Madrid, is discussed by R. A. Skelton in J. A. Williamson, ed., *John Cabot and the Bristol voyages* (1962), 298–307, and in D. B. Quinn, *England and the discovery of America* (1974), 98–100. The map is believed to have been taken to France during the Napoleonic wars and was acquired by the Dutch collector-diplomat Baron Walckenaer in a Paris sale-room. On the sale of his collection on 12 April 1853 it was bought by the Hydrographic Department, Madrid, for 4,321 francs (the under-bidder being Henry Stevens) and has since been in the Museo Naval (A. Vassano, *Ensayo Biográfico del . . . cosmografo, Juan de la Cosa y de su carts* (Madrid, 1892), 97–109). It consists of two pieces of cowhide measuring approximately 1830 mm. long by 960 mm., and is in two parts, the one being a map of the Old World, onto which is grafted an overlapping chart of the New. The inscription that it was made in October 1500 by Juan de la Cosa is now thought to refer to the beginning rather than the completion of the map.

7 The Cantino map, Biblioteca Estense, Modena, is discussed at length in A. Cortesão and A. Teixeira da Mota, *Portugaliae monumenta cartographica* [hence *PMC*], I, 7–13, pl. 4; R. A. Skelton, in W. P. Cumming, R. A. Skelton and D. B. Quinn, *The discovery of North America* (1971), 36 [hence Cumming, Skelton and Quinn, *Discovery*]. The map was looted from the Palace in the mid-nineteenth century and was recovered hanging in a butcher's shop.

is a highly professsional view of the world's surface created by a cartographer who was also an artist. He was probably an Italian who had worked for a considerable time in Portugal. It represented in the west the Spanish discoveries so far as they were known, but it stressed the Portuguese view of the west based on the discoveries of Gaspar Corte Real in 1500 and 1501 and showed the Portuguese concept of the line drawn between the areas of Spanish and Portuguese enterprise in the treaty of Tordesillas in 1494. The newest discoveries are placed east of the line (Labrador and Newfoundland were actually well to the west but this was not yet known). They are detached from the Spanish discoveries of a mainland (part of Asia?), the Caribbean islands, and the new Portuguese discovery of mainland Brazil. The lands discovered by Corte Real are distinguished by a decorative miniature forest of enormous mast-trees and Brazil by brilliant parrots (sent back by Cabral after its discovery in 1500), along with a vague vegetational background. It is sufficiently well illustrated to be regarded as a work of art but it was primarily intended to convey information. It is possible that more distinguished rulers than the duke of Ferrara attempted to obtain comparable data from behind Portuguese and Spanish censorship but we cannot pin down others of the earliest American maps to specific recipients. However, the information the Cantino map provides about the western enterprises of the Portuguese made it an essentially important link in our chain of knowledge about the Americas, as well as being very informative about Portuguese knowledge of Africa and India at that time.

R. A. Skelton believed that the atlas of sea charts, known as the Egerton atlas, of *circa* 1508,[8] which revealed Spanish discoveries in the west, including what they knew about North America (though without credit to the English), was an escape from the official Spanish records and represented an early attempt to establish a standard chart (*padrón real*) at about the time Amerigo Vespucci took over as first pilot-major at the *Casa de la Contratación* in 1508 and was entrusted with the task of making such a chart. Since its provenance cannot be traced back to a contemporary source, it is pure speculation that it was the product of contemporary espionage by another European power, but it may well have been. It is a possible 'gift', but it is not artistically outstanding, the coasts and names being clearly but modestly painted, and by a professional hand. It gives us a useful summary of Spanish knowledge of North America and the more important western discoveries at this time.

In 1507 the bold assumption was made that two new continents stood on the way to Asia, and, after much hesitation, this had been accepted by about 1520.

One of the finest illuminated records of the discoveries is the atlas of 1519 (or thereabouts), often known, from the name of a former owner, as the

---

8 British Library, [hence B.L.], Egerton MS 2803. Cumming, Skelton and Quinn, *Discovery*, 59.

Miller atlas, which is now in Paris (Pl. 2).[9] This was the work of a master painter-cartographer. The six sheets in the atlas and a separate world map which probably originally belonged to it, give us the brightest picture of the enlarged world so far composed. There is a sharp division of opinion about its probable makers, Pedro (and possibly Jorge) Reinel or Lopo Homem or all three. All were distinguished Portuguese chartmakers but none of their other surviving productions reach this level of sophistication. The maps are evidence, however, that in Portugal by this time a high artistic standard was being set for makers of such maps. Whether they were produced as a result of training in official chartmaking or were the commercial products of the demand for artistic renderings of newly discovered lands is not clear.

The traditional habit of painting scenes over the territory of an interior still almost wholly unexplored was here carried to considerable lengths. The parrots of Brazil could have been seen in Portugal but the Tupinamba-Guaraní Indians, shown with some realism assisting in the collection of brazilwood, could well have been the result of sketches made on the spot by explorers who had engaged in the brazilwood trade. Were the painters who made these sketches the cartographers themselves or were already journals returning from the New World embellished with sketches from painter-cartographers who could draw? This we cannot answer. A considerable part of northeastern North America, as revealed by the Corte Real and subsequent voyages, is shown, with only a nominal attempt to link it with the Spanish discoveries farther south, but the decoration in the interior has an attempt at realism in the configuration of deer and trees even if there is no indication that they derive from sketches made in this area.

That the atlas was made as a magnificent gift for a monarch seems to be agreed, but provenance is again lacking. It may be suggested that it could have been a gift from Manoel of Portugal to the young Francis I to emphasize Portuguese power overseas at a time when the relations of the Valois line with the newly elected Hapsburg emperor, who was also king of Spain, had not yet been defined. That it is an art object of distinction is undoubted. That it contains valuable information on the Portuguese empire and, as here stressed, on the Americas is also certain.

It is to Charles V that we owe the most valuable information on North

9 Bibliothèque Nationale, Paris [hence B.N.] Rés. Ge, DD 683. There has been considerable controversy about this atlas and about the world map loosely associated with it. Myriem Foncin, Maurice Destombes and Monique de la Roncière, *Catalogue des cartes nautiques sur vélin conservées au Département des Cartes et Plans* [hence Foncin, *Catalogue*] (1963), 36–42, consider both atlas and map to be the work of Lopo Homen, saying (p 33) 'Leur décoration [est] d'une somtuousité remarquable. Il est l'oeuvre d'un grand artiste'. Cortesão, *PMC*, I, 55–61, pl. XVI–XXIV, suggests that it was commissioned by King Manoel as a present for Francis I of France in 1518 and that Lopo Homen was employed to work on it, but was joined by Pedro and Jorge Reinel to complete it, apart from 'the beautiful illumination [which] is undoubtedly the work of an artist specially engaged for the purpose'. He probably underrates the artistic skill of the artist-cartographers of Portugal at this time and there is no evidence of an outside hand in the decoration. There is also a suggestion that the map of South America may be somewhat later in date than 1519 (Wallis, *Rotz*, 70).

America and other areas of the overseas world. He was on the one hand King Charles I of Spain, whose administration was committed to the maintenance of secrecy about the details of the growing American empire so as to limit or exclude intervention by outsiders, and he was also a European figure as Holy Roman Emperor who had contacts with rulers and nobles all over Europe whom he appears often to wish to impress, for political or personal reasons, with information about the overseas empire which he controlled. The result of this not entirely altruistic generosity is that we have a handful of surviving maps and charts which are mostly of high artistic quality without which our knowledge of North America would be considerably constricted. These too may represent only a small sample of such gifts, since so many maps of his long reign have not survived.

The first such gift by Charles V that we know of for certain was made to the permanent papal nuncio, Baldassare Castiglioni, possibly for presentation to Pope Clement VII in 1525, and contained an accurate account of Esterão Gomes' discoveries in North America.[10] It was a world map by the official cosmographer, Diogo Ribeiro, a very finely painted though not decorated work. It was clearly based on the *padrón real*, and is thought to have been completed, except for the eastern North American coastline, when Gomes arrived at La Coruña in September 1525. Ribeiro is believed to have been there and to have sketched in lightly part of the coast already known to the Spaniards and that, farther north, derived from the Portuguese: Gomes' charts were then used to fill in the coast traversed by himself. These included the shores of the later New England, and included for the first time Cape Cod and the Penobscot River. The latitudes given on the map were too low and although they became regular features of the official Spanish profile of eastern North America, they were lowered still further on later redactions and finally assimilated with what appears to have been the entry to Chesapeake Bay, thus creating a very misleading impression of the coast. The map has remained throughout in the family archives, and the precise date of its presentation to the envoy is unknown. While the circumstances of the map's completion depend on circumstantial evidence, they are widely accepted. A papal nuncio was considered a safe person to whom confidential materials could be entrusted and on the assumption that, in some manner, they would be conveyed to the Pope.

A comparable world map was given by Charles to Cardinal Giovanni Salviati, special papal nuncio in Spain, apparently in 1526.[11] In the interim, not only had there been harsh and unresolved diplomatic conflict between

---

10 Archivo Marchesi Castiglioni, Mantua. *PMC*, I, 95–8, Pl. XXXVII: L. A. Vigneras, 'El viaje de Estebán Gomes a Norte America', *Revista de Indias*, 68 (1957), 13–17 (a corrected version was later issued separately): 'The primary cartographical records of the years, 1524–1529', in Lawrence C. Wroth, *The voyages of Giovanni da Verrassano* (1970), 165–77 (the almost definitive study of this and following maps). See also Cumming, Skelton and Quinn, *Discovery*, 74.

11 Bibliotheca Medicae-Laurenziana, Florence. Cumming, Skelton and Quinn, *Discovery*, 72.

Spain and Portugal over where the eastern line of demarcation lay, but also substantial exploration of the eastern North American coast in two separate phases – one connected with the attempts of Lucas Vásquez de Ayllón to establish a Spanish colony in the southeast of North America (which had brought the Spaniards some knowledge of the coast as far as 35°30′ or even 37° north). Estevão Gomes' intensive exploration of the coast between just north of 40° to approximately 45° N had, we have seen, linked the two up. Though much had still to be learned about these shorelines, at least they now had, for Spain, a continuity which marked a way ahead if conquest and colonization of this territory seemed feasible. The 'Salviati' world map showed a bright and gleaming Portuguese Africa and Orient, with Spanish claims on the line of demarcation, putting the Moluccas on their side, but it also included an extended view of eastern North America, incorporating some of the information brought back by Gomes, but in rather a generalized and imprecise form (much more so than in the Castiglioni map). The picture, however, was an attractive one, with decorative trees scattered loosely over the landscape and animals, not too clearly specified, revealed among them. The bright colours and the pleasing aspect of the map as decoration made it a noteworthy gift, even if its information on eastern North America was not of outstanding value except in the general terms that Spain now knew something in detail of the coast from Florida to Newfoundland. Such gifts as these were to form a pattern for others where the emphasis was to be more directly on terms of political advantage.

The rapid deterioration of Francis I's relations with Charles V after 1520 led on to a struggle between Hapsburg and Valois which was to last for almost forty years (ending only in 1559). Francis I and his successor, the later Henry II, both intermittently, in the middle of their absorbing European affairs, concerned themselves with the overseas world, Brazil, a passage to China by the west, the possibility of competing with Portugal on the African coast and in Southeast Asia. The desire to find out more about North America, whether it could be traversed or rounded to give a passage to China, or to reveal its own secrets, became a significant object of French mercantile interests, spurred on and subsidized by the crown. The return of the *Victoria* led to Giovanni da Verrazzano's voyage of 1523–24, sponsored by Francis I, in which he was to search for a passage to China indeed, but, more immediately, to put on the map the eastern shores of North America. Verrazzano in 1524 effectively charted the east coast from north of Florida (for which he had a Spanish chart) and returned rapidly to France, reporting his discoveries to the king. His charts were soon reduced to generality by his brother Girolamo,[12] a sound cartographer, who may or may not have been on the voyage. These showed a coastline, broken only by some river entrances, from approximately 32° to 46° N. If there was no passage to China, however,

12 Formerly in the Royal Library, Milan, but destroyed in World War II. (Wroth, 170–1.)

there seemed to be an isthmus at about 35° across which access to the Pacific would be easy. Hence the westward extent of North America at any point could not be too great. Giovanni's letter to Francis I, followed by Girolamo's map, did not however produce any response, since Francis was, and was to be for some years, too preoccupied in Italy. The lost map by Girolamo is, perhaps, represented by Maggiolo's version. Girolomo made another world map for Henry VIII of England and either delivered it himself or had Giovanni do so. It excited some interest and was displayed in the royal palace (from which, as late as 1582, Michael Lok derived his published map). It interested Henry seriously in North America for the first time, though he preferred to wait until 1527 to send out his own expedition rather than to entrust Verrazzano with one in 1525. Giovanni eventually got funds for a new expedition but it came to a disastrous end in the Caribbean in 1528. Shortly after that, Girolamo, most probably at the instigation of Francis I, prepared another world map, for Pope Clement VII.[13] This was plainly but precisely drawn. It showed the New France which Francis I was claiming in virtue of Verrazzano's voyage and the new shape of North America. It has survived in the Vatican and may have helped to lead Clement VII to inform Francis I in 1533 that the papal bulls sanctifying the Iberian division of the non-European world did not cover lands not then discovered (even if he never formalized that concession in a bull).

In the same year that Girolamo's map was presented to the Pope he received from Charles V one of the finest world maps of the period, one which, alongside Verrazzano's, still adorns the Vatican Library. This was Diogo Ribeiro's finest work.[14] It was finely detailed and painted in restrained colouring. It gave a complete picture, so far as the Spaniards knew it, of the discoveries made so far, and is believed to be an accurate copy of the *padrón real* of 1527, but made after Spain and Portugal had at last in 1529 resolved their differences on the location of the far eastern dividing line. The North American section is notable for the inscriptions on the map which assign Labrador to the English and Newfoundland to the Portuguese, while the Spanish 'Tiera de Estevāo Gomez' and 'Tiera de Ayllon' are clearly described. Formalized trees and mountains are shown but (in distinction from South America) no men or animals. It is possible, though direct evidence is lacking, that the Ribeiro map was intended to counter the Girolamo Verrazzano map, since no account is taken of the French discoveries. Stress is laid in the inscription at the base of the map that the

---

13 Vatican Library, Borgiana I. R. Almagià, *Monumenta cartographica Vaticana* [hence *MVC*], I (1944), 53–55, pl. XXIV–XXVI. The Verrazzano chart in the BN is earlier (7 February 1525). It is not the original made for Francis I which has disappeared, but has an imperfect inscription to one 'L [ ] de [ ]' who remains unknown (Foncin, *Catalogue*, p. 4). A map of a similar type, probably by Girolamo da Verrazzano, is in The National Maritime Museum. This is reproduced in Derek Howse and Michael Sanderson, *The Sea Chart* (Newton Abbot, 1973), Chart V.

14 Vatican Library, Borgiana III, Almagià, *MCV*, I, 50–2, pl. XXI–XXIII.

representation is that agreed by the Treaty of Tordesillas, which, though an international treaty, had been later confirmed by a papal bull. If these two maps are indeed evidence of the Hapsburg-Valois rivalry, then the political importance of the formal, usually decorated, map as a historical document is enhanced.

From 1500 or 1502 at latest to 1529 most of the important developments in the uncovering of the eastern North American coastline can be traced by modern scholars on the painted and usually decorated maps which have been discussed. Without them we should be left without invaluable detailed information on a series of discoveries in the west. In at least some cases, too, it was the highly decorated character of the map, chart or atlas which led to its survival. As works of art, even if in some cases they escaped from the custody of their first recipients or their heirs, they were preserved because of this characteristic. Then, again, the Norman School, makers of finely painted maps and charts, and centring around Dieppe, owed much to this tradition which had been well established before they originated and developed it.

Dr Helen Wallis has made and directed valuable research into the Dieppe School in the course of the work done on *The Boke of Idrography*, published by Viscount Eccles for the Roxburghe Club (1981).[15] The view of the origins of this school which now emerges is that it took its beginning in the worldwide trading enterprises of the firm of Jean Ango and Son of Dieppe and the collection of maps and other representations made by and for the company which both inspired and were the result of its activities. This data inspired mapmakers to graft the production of decorative charts on to the indigenous miniature-painting tradition of the region, with striking artistic results. The return of the survivors of the Parmentier expedition to Sumatra in 1530 appears to have given it a start. That expedition had on it 'Jean Sasi le Grand Peintre' (so far unidentified) and also Pierre Crignon who made charts as well as verses, and whose exotic data opened an eastern and southern world to French eyes, which had also turned early, as we have seen, to the west. One of the earliest individuals to have been influenced by this material was the artist-cartographer Jean Rotz, whose work has at last seen the light in the finest of reproductions. But he was only one of a number of men, working in a small area of Normandy, who produced for rich and powerful patrons a series of maps which, judging from their surviving representatives, reached a new level of both artistic and cartographic development. The archive on which they were ultimately based, if it survived the Civil Wars of the sixteenth century, may well have perished in the English bombardment of Dieppe in 1694.

In the successive phases of the development of the Dieppe School, which are not yet wholly clear, there was undoubtedly a Portuguese influence. Jean

15 *The maps and text of the BOKE OF IDROGRAPHY presented by Jean Rotz to Henry VIII now in the British Library*. Edited by Helen Wallis with a foreword by Viscount Eccles. (Oxford 1981). [Hence Wallis, *Rotz*.]

Alphonse (or Fonteneau) of Saintonge, was otherwise a Portuguese (João Afonso) who had come to France by way of Spain, bearing no doubt Spanish charts with him. He was to influence Rotz and other chartmakers, while there was another Portuguese, so far unidentified, involved also. Rotz (who if his Scottish father had returned to Scotland might have been known as Ian Ross) was a man of action, a sea captain and merchant,[16] who may have been with Parmentier and certainly had been in Brazil in 1539. His major interests were in the study of navigational theory and instrumentation and, above all, in making decorative charts. It was probably with a portfolio of these that he made his way to the French Court in 1540 (we surmise) hoping for employment from the king or from the great patron of the Dieppe artists, the dauphin Henry. When he failed to establish himself he came to England and eventually in 1542 presented to Henry the fine atlas, which made up a very large world map, and to which he added a more up-to-date pair of hemispheres to complete his view of the globe. Of those charts which concern North America in the atlas itself there is some complexity in distinguishing his sources (see Pl. 3). Clearly he had information on Jacques Cartier's first voyage in 1534 and was the earliest to record it on his chart, though without placenames.[17] He had also some novel information on Cape Breton Island (which he shows as such) and on the coast immediately south towards the Penobscot. However for the rest of the east coast he follows the Spanish *padrón real* of 1536, which was evidently available in Dieppe. For New-foundland and Labrador his nomenclature is Portuguese and he stresses the latter as a great peninsula, extending northeastwards almost to Iceland,[18] a distortion caused apparently by failure to note compass variation. He also showed an open route round the north of America. Another novel feature lay in the marking of the fishing banks by a boundary line extending from northern Labrador to the vicinity of Cape Breton (in which he was to be followed by the Harleian map). In the western of the two hemispheres he added in 1542[19] he was able to show the general outline of Cartier's penetra-tion into the St Lawrence valley, again for the first time, but also without placenames. His Labrador here too is also restrained. Cumulatively, his con-tributions are very significant ones and they put Henry in his debt (well acknowledged by rewards and salary given over the next five years). However well Henry was now equipped with knowledge of the New World (and Rotz had valuable information on other parts than North America), he failed to exploit it in his last years.

The Portuguese influence on the Dieppe School was stronger in two other surviving collections. The first is the anonymous 'Hague' atlas, which shows

16 Wallis, *Rotz*, pp. 1–22 includes the main biographical materials; a short account is given by her in 'The Rotz atlas, a royal presentation', *The Map Collector*, **20** (September 1982), 40–42.
17 Wallis, *Rotz*, 39–40, 48–9, 51, ff. 23*v*–24*r*.
18 Ibid., 49–51, ff. 21*v*–22*r*.
19 Ibid., 48, 55–6, f. 29*r*.

much of the stylistic character of maps in the series but is solidly based on Spanish knowledge filtered through Portuguese sources. It was made for the dauphin Henry, later Henry II, and his mistress Diane de Poitiers, it is now thought between 1540 and 1545 (though earlier Avelino Teixeira da Mota and Armando Cortesão put up a strong case for a date of about 1538 for it).[20] An atlas in the same tradition, and fully embodying French discoveries, though still with a strong Portuguese influence, is that made by an unnamed artist for Nicolas   Vallard   of   Dieppe   in 1547 .[21] This indeed is famous for showing not only the St Lawrence Valley in detail but also for depictions of Roberval and his colonists of 1542 – 3.

The man who has hitherto been regarded as the doyen of the School (though clearly Rotz must now take precedence of him) was Pierre Desceliers. Most of the other members of the School were themselves involved in maritime affairs, but he was not. He lived quietly as parish priest of Arques, near Dieppe, made maps of the highest quality and taught others how to make them. His earliest dated chart is that now in the John Rylands Library in Manchester.[22] It belongs to 1546, was well informed on French discoveries in the west, showing Cartier's discoveries up the St. Lawrence in detail, and constituting an important view of the world. It is the first chart to show Basque whalers in action off the Labrador coast, which is significant in view of recent discoveries of their whaling stations there. It is believed to have been made, like the 'Hague' atlas, for the Dauphin Henry, though certain proof is lacking. He went on to make a number of fine charts of a comparable character over the next fifteen years or so. Nicolas Desliens is thought to have been his pupil. But his lost map and surviving materials belong to the 1560s,[23] after the main work of the School was completed. The most brilliant world chart from Desceliers' atelier, though the artist is anonymous, is the Harleian map in   the   British   Library.   [24] Its quality is unusual (it certainly was a gift to or a commission from the Dauphin) and it depicted Cartier and his men, triumphant on the St Lawrence in 1535. It is one which

20 Koninklijke Bibliotheek, The Hague. *PMC*, V, 132–6, pl. 614–700. The arms of France and of the Dauphin are on ff. 5*v*–6*r*., along with the badge of Diane de Poitiers. Cp. Wallis, *Rotz*, 39, 41.

21 Huntington Library MS HN 1547, inscribed 'Nicolas Vallard de Dieppe dans l'année 1547'. *PMC*, V, 136–9, pl. 621–4. The inscription is generally held to be that of the recipient. There is a problem in that the style is distinct from other atlases of the Dieppe School. Cp. Wallis, *Rotz*, 38, 45, 59 (Fig. 8).

22 John Rylands Library, University of Manchester – Charles H. Coote, *Autotype facsimiles of three mappemondes* (Bibliotheca Lindesiana, Aberdeen, 1898); Anthiaume, *Cartes marines*, I, 85, who is confident that it was intended for the Dauphin, as is C. A. Burland, 'A note on the Desceliers Map-pemonde of 1546 in the John Rylands Library', John Rylands Library, *Bulletin*, XXXII (1950–1), 237–41; Wilma George, *Animals on maps* (1969), 66–7, lists eleven species of animals on the South American portion, though the North American area is not so rich in fauna. Wallis, *Rotz*, 39, notes also his B.L., Additional MS 24065 (Fig. 7, p. 49 gives an extract) and Pierpont Morgan Library MS 506, see also 36, 74–5.

23 1561, 1566, 1567. See Wallis, *Rotz*, 39, 40, 48.

24 B.L., Additional MS, 5413, Wallis, *Rotz*, 25–6, 39, 42, 48, 50, 53–4, 74–5.

carried on the tradition that North America was narrow and that the Verraz-zanian isthmus existed, giving easy access for France to the Pacific.

Guillaume Le Testu is the last outstanding figure here.[25] He stands somewhat apart, even if he seems to have worked from the basic stock of charts available to the other map- and chartmakers. A Huguenot, and a man of action, he was based at Le Havre, whereas the Dieppe artists were, apparently, in the Catholic camp. He made for his patron, the admiral of France, Gaspard de Coligny, in 1555 [1556] a fine world atlas. This and a world map of 1566 for the same patron demonstrated an individual style, embodying most of the recent discoveries in America, but embellishing them with a touch of fantasy. R. A. Skelton said of his work that it provided a basis for Coligny's attempts to involve France, in the Huguenot interest, in Brazil, the Caribbean and Florida, all ventures which had failed by the time of Coligny's murder in 1572 and Le Testu's own death less than a year after on the Isthmus of Panama while engaged in a raid on the Spanish treasure train in company with Francis Drake. Ironically, the French survivors complained that their Protestant English allies monopolised the loot.

The Norman artist-cartographers, through their fine productions, not only informed the world of the French discoveries (and some of them were incorporated on the Sebastian Cabot printed world map of 1544[26] so that not all were kept in the privacy of collections), but involved leading men of their time like Henry VIII, Henry II of France and Coligny in the revelation of the extra-European world, with or without political results. Outstanding, however, was the character and quality of the decoration liberally dispersed over sea and land. Rotz, especially, derived naturalistic figures from the Parmentier voyage, gained information on North American Indian tepees and drew for himself a Tupinamba village in South America and showed credible South American Indian figures associated with the brazilwood trade. Comparable naturalistic scenes, real or imagined but credible, illuminated many other examples of the work of the School.[27] They conveyed to the royal or noble patrons who received them not only a sense of the topography of the new discoveries but also a glimpse of the reality which did, or might, lie

25 Ministère de L'Armée, Paris, D.I.Z.4. Cumming, Skelton and Quinn, *Discovery*, 94–5, 129, 135, 152; Anthiaume, *Cartes marines*, I, 96–12; C. de la Roncière, *Histoire de la marine Française*, IV, 120–1: the 1566 world map is in B.N., Paris, Rés. Ge. AA.525 (having the arms both of Coligny and of his vice admiral, Foncin, *Catalogue*, pp. xiv, 77–9).

26 The unique copy of the 1544 map is in the Bibliothèque Nationale, Département des Cartes et Plans. The English edition of 1549 is known only from references to copies being in Whitehall Palace, 1566, Oxford, 1569, Chenies, 1577, Whitehall and London, 1584 and 1589; Whitehall, 1625; post-1660 (R. A. Skelton, 'The royal map collections in England', *Imago Mundi*, XIII (1956), 181–3); last heard of in 1688 as no. 39 in a list of royal maps (Rawlinson MS A 171, ff. 17; *see* Helen Wallis, ('Some new light on early maps of North America, 1490–1560', C. Koeman, ed., *Land- und Seekarten im Mittelalter und in der frühen Neuzeit Wolfenbütteler Forschungen* (München and Wolfenbüttel, 1980), 102–4). It (or 'they' since the reference is sometimes to Sebastian Cabot's *maps*) may have been lost in the fire at Whitehall in 1698.

27 Wallis, *Rotz*, 67–72, f. 28r.

behind the shorelines. Old stereotypes in decoration were not abandoned but a new naturalistic element appears in them. As a group the Norman maps best illustrate my basic theme that new discoveries called into existence patrons of map- and chartmakers who were inspired (and trained) to supply outstandingly beautiful as well as accurate charts, maps or atlases for them. In turn, the very quality of these artefacts led to their preservation and so enable us to reconstruct the cartographic history of North America at a crucial stage; while also enlarging our knowledge of many other parts of the world at that time.

In the case of the Norman painter-cartographers there was a mix of professions, the artist who was also a pilot or commander and the civilian who painted maps without a sea-going background or a training in maritime techniques. In the case of the workshop which Battista Agnese maintained at Venice for a generation, between approximately 1534 and 1564,[28] there is no suggestion of any maritime experience whatsoever. The Agnese atlases were purely art objects made for rich clients as show pieces, though capable of being informative as well on the geography and shorelines of the world. The respect they received and the pleasure they gave accounts for the survival of more than seventy of them down to our time. Varying in the number of maps, the Mediterranean items were scarcely changed from those of the fifteenth century. But the decorative oval world maps with which they opened, with putti in the sides blowing from the directions of the principal winds, were the workshop's trademark, though the series of charts making up a map of the world which often followed were more serious guides to the coasts of the globe. His representations of North America varied with his clients. Normally it is true that the western extent of the continent is indicated by the faintest of shadings, but its extent might be wide or narrow according to whom the client was. Many of the oval world maps keep alive the Verrazzanian profile and some show the isthmus, a few, even, a line of dashes marked as 'the French way' through the isthmus to the Pacific, clearly made for French clients. Then, too, from 1542 onward, he shows the peninsula of California charted by Francisco de Ulloa in 1539, and from 1544, frequently also, the discoveries of João Rodrigues Cabrilho farther north in 1542. This sensitivity to western coastal discoveries is the most novel feature of his contribution to North American cartography. Usually stereotype precludes novelty. All the work produced was wholly professional, not all was of the highest artistic quality. Agnese was the Fabergé of the cartographical world of the sixteenth century. The grandest example of his work is the atlas in the John Carter Brown Library, which Charles V presented to his son Philip on

28 The standard treatment of the Agnese atlases is R. H. Wagner, 'The manuscript atlases of Battista Agnese', Bibliographical Society of America, *Papers*, XXV (1931), 1–110 (also issued for private circulation) listing 71 items; four more atlases are added in his 'Additions to the manuscript atlases of Battista Agnese, *Imago Mundi*, IV, 28–30. For Mlle Myriem Foncin, Agnese is a 'vulgarisateur'.

his sixteenth birthday in 1543.[29] The decorated title leaf contains a medallion of the emperor, a panel showing the handing down of the gift from father to son, with mythological figures in the baroque style of the Venetian painters of the time. The oval map, needless to say, did not show 'the French way' through North America. There is some irony connected with one of his atlases which is believed to have been made in 1542 and subsequently presented to Henry VIII, conceivably in the same year that Rotz completed his atlas for the king. This, unlike the Rotz volume, escaped from the royal collection. It was brought to Europe in the next century by a Scottish Catholic cleric and eventually ended in the Vatican Library where the inscription to the King as 'defender of the faith' seems more than a little incongruous.[30] Agnese provided blank shields on the atlases (a number of which were bound in his workshop) so that his clients' arms and crest could be added. Only a few had this done and some of these have and some have not been identified. They do not include any persons of European fame, but, all the same, judging by the number which survive, most of the courts and castles of Europe must have had at least one. But this mass production of painted atlases has no direct parallel. Agnese was mostly prepared to repeat what he had done before; his sensitivity to new discoveries on the west coast of North America alone remains to be explained.

We know little enough about England's knowledge of or concern with North America before the reign of Queen Elizabeth I. Dr Wallis found that Henry VIII hung maps on the walls of the Palace of Westminster. But Cabot's London-printed map of 1549 had at least placed something of its eastern outline, and the St Lawrence valley on record. After 1550, too, Englishmen were involved overseas, with the Mediterranean, West Africa and, especially, with Muscovy. Cabot lived on until 1558. It was apparently in that year that Diogo Homen, the younger of two very accomplished Portuguese chartmakers of that surname, visited England. He was employed by Queen Mary to make an atlas, possibly for presentation to her absent husband Philip II (see Pl. 4). At least the European map contains an escutcheon impaling the arms of both, while the world chart has the arms of England only. From this it has been deduced that the atlas was unfinished at Mary's death on 17 November 1558 and was taken over and completed for the young Elizabeth I, especially as Philip's arms have been partly erased from the map on which they appeared. It is a painted atlas of high quality, but one which would have given the young queen strange concepts of North

29 John Carter Brown Library, see Samuel J. Hough, *The Italians and the creation of America* (1980), no. 104.

30 Almagià, *MCV*, I, 68–9; Wagner, 'Manuscript atlases', pp. 77–8 (no. 38). Almagià firmly places it as 1542 as against Wagner's *c.* 1545. We do not know anything of it from English sources, including the date of presentation or how it escaped from the royal collection.

America.[31] The Penobscot, for example, becomes a great gulf penetrating the land, and the St Lawrence has its north shore broken into islands beyond which is open sea. This could very easily have produced the idea that a passage round the north of America was easy and have set Englishmen thinking in these terms. This may have led the young queen to interest herself in America, since by 1566 Humphrey Gilbert saw Sebastian Cabot's map (and we later have the plural used as if there were a number) hanging 'in the Queens majesties privy gallery in White hall'. Clearly the hanging of maps on walls as interesting and beautiful objects was developing rapidly. John Dee wrote in 1570[32] of the new fashion (as he thought it) of displaying them, hanging them 'some to beautify their halls, parlours, chambers, galleries or libraries with'. There is a little evidence to corroborate this, but the sudden interest in the Northwest Passage which arose after 1575 had something to do with this interest, and may have helped to lead to the abortive voyages of Martin Frobisher (1576 – 8) in search of a North-West Passage, which the Queen supported.

Dee, who cast the Queen's horoscope for her, was asked by the Queen to write down her title to distant lands. He found reason to allege that Madoc in the twelfth century and John Cabot in the late fifteenth century had acquired title to translatlantic lands for England. His report in 1578 was written 'in twelve vellum skins of parchment' and in 1580 he drew a large map of the western hemisphere which gave an extensive picture, though not a very novel one of the coasts of North America, and also a largely imaginary one of the interior which he interlaced with rivers. On the back he wrote down in summary form the evidence he had gathered on the Queen's title. Ironically, the elaborate manuscript of 1578 has disappeared, and the map has survived. But the map was discarded by her or her immediate successor at a later date and was collected by Sir Robert Bruce Cotton and still survives.[33] It is not as decorative as those of Rotz but it fitted well into circumstances which led to English attempts at colonization in North America in the years immediately following its compilation and was indeed used as a standard map on the basis of which Sir Humphrey Gilbert made grants of land in 1582 – 3. Once again, a presentation (or commissioned) map had some influence on history.

The case of Jacques le Moyne de Morgues, who was in the ill-fated French colony in Florida in 1564 – 5, and John White, who was in the first Virginia

---

31 B.L., Additional MS 5415A; *PMC*, II, 13 – 15, pl. C – CVII. Cortesão's reconstruction would be strengthened if we knew for certain that Diogo Homen was still in England in 1558; he was certainly there in 1547 (Skelton, *Explorers' maps*, 158; Helen Wallis 'Some new light on early maps of North America, 1490 – 1560', *Wolfenbütteler Forschungen* 7 (1980), 101.

32 Euclid, *The elements of geometrie*, tr. H. Billingsley (John Daye, 1570), S.T.C. 10560; preface by John Dee; see E. G. R. Taylor, *Tudor geography*, 283; Alan Debus, ed. John Dee's *Mathematicall preface* (1980).

33 B.L., Cotton MS. Augustus I.i.l. The title is 'Atlantides, vulgariter Indiae Occidentalis nominatae, emendiator descriptio, quam huc est divulgata'; Taylor, *Tudor geography*, 22.

of 1584 – 7, is different from any we have encountered hitherto. Le Moyne was an artist at the Court of Charles IX in France and had had no connection with cartography or the sea until he was commissioned to go to Florida to record the Indians, plans and topography of the area round the colony on the St John's River.[34] He had perforce to become a cartographer and found himself making sketches of river entries and eventually compiling a general map of the areas the French reached.[35] In these latter pursuits he doubtless received the help of experienced pilots and chartmakers. For a man trained to paint flowers and fruit in the manner of traditional miniaturists this was a strange commitment, but one he attempted to fulfill as well as he could. He evidently soon sent home some results of his labours as he can have escaped with very little when he ran from Fort Caroline during the fatal night attack on it by a Spanish force. We suspect he used memory as well as surviving sketches to redo his American drawings, only one of which survives. When, as a Huguenot, he first left France for England he was patronised by Sir Walter Ralegh to make as full a pictorial record as he could of his American experiences, but he died before, we think, he had completed and presented his collection to Ralegh, though it is just possible that Ralegh did receive a portfolio of maps and drawings from him. Certainly, it is only through the engraving of a set of drawings obtained from his widow and published in 1591 that we know of his coastal sketches and a general map of southeastern North America which was both novel and misleading. His pictures of Indian life are another matter, unique for their period. They certainly gave Englishmen and Frenchmen a better idea of that area than they had had before. But, characteristically, much of le Moyne's later life was spent in painting exquisite studies of plants and insects, many of which have fortunately survived.

Something very similar can be said of John White, though almost nothing is known of his early life. He appears to have learnt his trade as a journeyman painter in London (where he was a member of the Painter Stainers' Company) before he accompanied Martin Frobisher to Baffin Island in 1577, where his task was to paint Eskimos and not, so far as we known, to draw maps. His assignment by Sir Walter Ralegh in 1585 was very similar to that of Le Moyne's in 1564 though considerably elaborated.[36] But he was not to

34 Paul H. Hulton, *The work of Jacques le Moyne de Morgues*, 2 vols. (1977), is definitive on the American and European material; the American engravings appeared in T. de Bry, *America*, pt. ii (1591). Richard Hakluyt, dedicating in 1587 to Ralegh his translation of René de Laudonnière's *Histoire notable de la Floride*, speaks of the drawings as 'liuely drawen in coulours at your no smale charges by the skilfull painter Iames Morgues', (*A notable historie*, sig. 2v; E. G. R. Taylor, ed., *The original writings and correspondence of the two Richard Hakluyts*, II (1935), 373).

35 See the discussions of the map in Hulton, *Le Moyne*, I, 37 – 54, 201 – 3.

36 Paul H. Hulton and D. B. Quinn, *The American drawings of John White*, 2 vols (1964), contains full versions of White's drawings, and can be used with the annotated edition of Thomas Harriot, *A briefe and true report of the new found land of Virginia* (1588) in D. B. Quinn, *The Roanoke voyages,* I (1955). P. H. Hulton, *America in 1585* (1984), includes all the American drawings.

be sent alone to map the new coastline and interior found in 1584 on and behind the Carolina Outer Banks, the new Virginia, but was to be partnered by a man who knew about maps and their making, though perhaps more from theory than practice, Thomas Harriot. Together they would map inlets and harbours, land and water. But White was to do much more. He was to draw almost everything he could see, fish, birds, animals, Indians, especially Indians and their ways of life. These were to be linked with verbal descriptions so that the evolving map, the notes and the drawings would make up a complete picture of the area, a thorough survey.

Several years before a prescription had been written for this sort of exercise.[37] The cartographer and his associate were to record everything they saw in their 'writing tables' or notebooks, to enter subsequently in their journals. They were to build up their map by surveyed sheets, using a plane table and a 'topographical instrument', marking them so that they could be united into a large map from which a final map or 'plot' could be reduced and drawn. Map symbols were to be used to show certain physical features, sample trees were to be shown where they occurred in quantity; the settlements, the people, the fauna and flora were all to be incorporated in the map, a council of perfection if ever there was one, but consonant with the precedents of the traditional painted and decorated map – in this case these accurately drawn examples were to 'garnish your plot' as the instructions put it. But, independently, the collection of drawings of objects, persons, activities, fauna and flora was to go on as an end in itself so that an art gallery was to be built up alongside the map.

Some such procedures were observed by White and Harriot. We have no surviving sketches of coastal features worked up into perfection, but we have a rough sketch, and an engraving, with the intervening drawing missing, of the 'entry of the Englishmen'[38] which gives some indication of their character, the shore outlines, the characteristic trees, the Indian settlement, in miniature, the shoals which the pinnace shown passing from Outer Banks to Roanoke Island was avoiding. Nor have we any of the sheets from which the final map was made. That map,[39] in the painted replica by White which survives (see Fig. 3), is simple, undecorated except for Ralegh's arms, with locations and names of villages, but bearing evidence of systematic and accurate survey, the first such survey to be made in North America. Thus White was turned from pure painter into a cartographer. When he launched out on his own, without Harriot's aid to connect a map of Le Moyne's Florida to his own, ignorance of the intervening shorelines led him to make major

37 B.L., Additional MS 38823, ff. 1–8; printed in full in D. B. Quinn, A. M. Quinn and S. Hillier, *New American world*, 5 vols., III (1979), 239–45, pl. 111a.

38 Public Record Office, *MPG* 584 T. de Bry, *America* part i, pl. I.

39 The map, in colour, is in Hulton and Quinn, *White*, II, pl. LIX; it is discussed in I, 52–7, 136–7.

mistakes.[40] Here, he confined his graphic decoration to the painting of Ralegh's crest on the land and filling the sea with fishes, amphibians and ships, thus carrying on, in a more realistic manner, the old traditions. But White's independent drawings of fish and plants and, above all his pictures of Indians, are painted with exceptional skill and penetration of character. They are much more than ornaments to 'garnish his plot' – the artist has been let loose to make pictures in his own medium. The volume, now in the British Museum, which contained White's original drawings and maps was clearly one which fits into the category of such presentation sets as the atlases we have considered before, but dominated by the coloured drawings rather than the maps (see Pl. 1).   The pictures are replicas painted from the originals for presentation to the Queen or to some great man, probably not Ralegh himself, perhaps Sir Francis Walsingham. Their provenance between the sixteenth and eighteenth centuries is lacking, but in a sense they are a culmination of the process which I have been describing, the gradual accumulation of detail about North America in individual maps, charts and paintings which would not have survived unless they had been designed as presentation gifts, and thus by their loss would leave us poorer, very much poorer, in our knowledge and understanding of how exploration was recorded by the painter cartographers.

This is far from the whole story of course. Other maps survive, despite the loss of official collections in the Iberian lands, which were not known to have been made for presentation and were, many of them, used for navigation or as fuel for the growing map-printing trade. Indeed, we have seen how the decorated manuscript maps of the Dieppe School, designed for a patron, were partly superseded by the Cabot maps of 1544 and 1549. Similarly the White-Harriot map was engraved in 1590 and that of Le Moyne in 1591 and both were widely used. But in none of these cases was the engraved and printed version as full or as accurate as the painted manuscript. It would do up to a point, but would not give us the insights, the knowledge, or the beauty of the manuscript survivals.

This is probably the significant part of my story, but it has several appendices. Maps were, in sixteenth century Italy at least, mural decorations, as well as pictures on vellum to be retained in rolls, shelved in book form, hung on walls or framed for display on walls or in cases. It is significant however that the remarkable series of murals of maps which decorated the Terza Loggia in the Vatican was based on printed maps, first painted in the pontificate of Pius IV (1559–65) and redone by Ignazio Danti in that of Gregory XIII. The two hemispheres on the landing of the Loggia, were painted by Antonio Vanosino in 1583, the year of Gregory's death, and do not rest so firmly on obvious sources.[41] It is possible that he used manuscript maps

---

40 In colour, Hulton and Quinn, *White*, II, pl. LVIII, discussed in I, 135–6.
41 Almagià, *MVC*, IV (1955), 28–9 (with a colour plate between the two pages).

which have not survived or added and subtracted details of his own invention. In his western hemisphere it is interesting, for example, that the 'Mare Congelatum' lying to the north of America comes down to meet the land at certain places and so makes it likely that the long-sought Northwest Passage was impassible on account of ice. The western termination of America, too, along with the shores of the Old World which stretch out almost to meet it are not at all like current representations of the 'Strait of Anian' which was supposed to divide America from Asia. We may have here an echo of other presentation maps in the papal collection which have not survived, though this is far from certain.

Then, too, chartmakers as professional painters of new and old maritime subjects on the traditional vellum, continued to work throughout the seventeenth century and into the eighteenth, supplying mariners with sea charts, traditional and novel to be taken to sea. The Thames School, in which masters trained apprentices in a single tradition, extending from the late sixteenth century to the early eighteenth, has left many examples of its production.[42] These were all plane charts, unreliable for direction and east-west distance, but still, in the hands of skilled pilots aware of their treacherous nature, a useful substitute for the absence of printed Mercator charts of marine features in usable sizes and prices.[43] This defect began to be remedied only in the late seventeenth and early eighteenth centuries – the first set of detailed coastal charts for North America appearing in 1689. The techniques of painting are those of the efficient craftsman as contrasted with the artist, if we set them against the fine charts of the earlier presentation types. Their bold painted lines and the broad coloured borders to the land change little over the period the School survived. They were certainly used. Seventeen were captured by the French from one East Indiaman in 1701.[44] A number of them were collected for the use of the Lords of Trade in the 1680s as official reference guides to new and old coastlines and seaways – one of Albemarle Sound, shown by White nearly a century earlier, makes the contrast.[45] The most spectacular achievement of the School which survives

42 Definition and discussion of the Thames School has been vigorously pursued in recent years. The best introduction is Jeanette Black, ed., *The Blathwayt atlas*, I (1970), *Commentary on the Blathwayt atlas*, II (1975), 15–22; the fullest list in Thomas R. Smith, 'Manuscript and printed sea charts in seventeenth century London; the case of the Thames School', in Norman J. Thrower, ed. *The compleat plattmaker* (1978), 45–99, and see Tony Campbell, 'The Drapers' Company chartmakers', in H. Wallis and S. Tyacke, eds., *My head is a map* (1973), 81–106. A chart very similar in style, the so-called 'Virginia chart', is in the I. N. P. Stokes collection, New York Public Library. It was probably made after 1610 and contains valuable information on New England and the discovery of the Hudson River (Quinn, *New American world*, V, pl. 139).

43 On the survival of the plane chart, 'that beautiful and treacherous medieval survival', see J. H. Parry, *The discovery of the sea* (1974) 162–9.

44 Foncin, *Catalogue*, 307, for J. Thornton's contributions to this group.

45 They are included in the Blathwayt atlas of *c.* 1685 in the John Carter Brown Library. The plate of Albemarle Sound is by James Lancaster, 1679, and illustrates the strength (the bold outlines) and the weaknesses (raw colouring and careless detail) of the School. In Jeanette Black's edition of the facsimile of the atlas (1970) it is pl. XXI.

revives the presentation character of the sixteenth century models. William Hack, a leading member of the Thames School, took on the task of copying the large atlas, actually an illustrated set of sailing directions, for the seas and harbours of the Pacific coast of America, which the Spaniards had kept secret until it was captured at sea in 1681. Having made and presented a copy to Charles II in 1682, Hack went on to make others. No less than fourteen still survive, representing a vast amount of patient labour.[46] They are clear, detailed and accurate and are much prized. But they are still the achievement of an artizan rather than an artist. They do not compare in any way with the art of Ribeiro, Rotz, Desceliers, Le Testu or even Agnese. But they were novel and useful. The second duke of Albemarle took one to the West Indies when he went out as a governor. The South Sea Company acquired one when it was founded in 1711 to penetrate the area which was described and illustrated in detail.

The Dutch were the dominant suppliers of printed maps to Europe in the seventeenth century, but even they continued to use the painted vellum chart for recording new discoveries and for keeping certain of their routes to their overseas possessions secret. When Adraien Block returned from his exploration of southern New England and the Hudson Valley in 1614 his so-called 'figurative map' was presented to the States General in 1616 in support of the movement to establish a New Netherlands in North America. It was the first original contribution by the Dutch to the cartography of North America,[47] though Hudson had brought a partial record back in 1609 (which is likely to have been confiscated in England). But the Dutch East India Company (V.O.C.), throughout the seventeenth century and into the eighteenth, employed plane charts on vellum for the use of its directors, its pilots and its officials in Asia as well as many specially printed charts. They too were scattered at the end of the eighteenth century but very many have survived.[48]

The tradition of the painted chart was thus a very long one. It could be used as a confidential tool on seagoing voyages. For that purpose it was usual-

46 A fine example of this 'Wagoner of the Great South Sea', is in the John Carter Brown Library and another in the William L. Clements Library. Its range is from Patagonia to Lower California. The atlas (or highly illustrated rutter) is discussed and listed in Thomas R. Adams, Jr., John Carter Brown Library, *Report for 1966*, 21–4, 45–52. Copies presented to Charles II, 1682, 1683 and 1684, and James II, 1686, are included in Adams, *A Buccaneers' atlas;* Basil Ringrose's *South Sea Waggoner,* ed. Derek Howse and Norman J. W. Thrower, Univ. California Press, places it fully in its context.

47 Algemeen Rijksarchief, The Hague. 'The figurative map', painted by Adraien Block after his return from the exploration of the New England coasts and the Hudson River, was attached to a petition to the States General in 1616 which ultimately helped to involve the Dutch in New Netherland. See I. N. P. Stokes, *Iconography of Manhattan Island*, II, 63–75, pl. XXIII; Cumming, Skelton and Quinn, *Discovery*, 264–5 (partial colour plate). A facsimile (c. 1890) is in John Carter Brown Library, Maps Cabinet Cc 614.

48 See Marcel Destombes, *Cartes Hollandaises. La cartographie de la Compagnie des Indies Orientales* (Saigon, 1941) (part of his then proposed 'Catalogue des cartes nautiqes manuscrits sur parchemin 1330–1700').

ly undecorated or minimally adorned. But from the time that it began to be used for lands outside the Mediterranean and especially for the Americas and other lands of the European maritime empires, it could take highly decorated forms, becoming more an art object than a working map or chart. If we knew more about the provenance of the many beautiful surviving portolans and atlases we could construct a more satisfying picture of how far they were used both as gifts and as articles of commerce. By concentrating on those known to have been gifts, or believed to have been so, and in specializing, too, on what knowledge they supplied on a specific area, North America, one aspect of their significance has been tentatively explored and summarized.

5

NEW GEOGRAPHICAL HORIZONS: LITERATURE

In relation to the New World, new geographical ideas were largely old ideas shifted westwards; genuine novelty emerged only very slowly. What I am concerned with is the image, the icon, in words and in visualization, of the New World. The changing map gives us its face; the concept gives us the framework in which it was set; the rest is a combination of visual and verbal images (I do not think the two can rightly be separated since they are two sides of the same perspective) which gradually altered to fit the facts of the new geographical milieu. Yet the earliest writings on the New World made up the essential materials for the descriptive geography which slowly emerged as the New World came to be accepted in its own right.[1]

The first point, which must be both emphasized and illustrated, is that to a substantial degree and for a considerable time, the New World was seen and described in terms of the Old. The first viewers of America perceived it in terms of the literature of the myth and with the capacity for observation—the two often inextricably intermingled—which they had at their disposal. They saw the islands and mainland of the western ocean, therefore, largely through transference, through the exchange of verbal and visual images from an Old World context to a New. We should remember that the New World was strange before it was entirely new. Until the second decade of the sixteenth century, and residually after that, it was regarded as an extension of the Old World, as Asia or some land in close touch with Asia. Not till after the return of the *Vitoria* in 1522 did America sail off into the seas of complete novelty. We find still in Verrazano in 1524 the wonder that America is so vast, so

---

1. The terms cosmography, geography, topography, and chorography shade into one another in this period. Geography cannot be considered as an integrated, space-oriented study in the fifteenth and early sixteenth centuries. François de Dainville, *La géographie des humanistes* (Paris 1940) 47-54, 67-68, indicates how the two geographies, the study of the earth in relation to the heavens and that concerned with describing in detail the layout and characteristics of lands, waters, regions, and peoples, began to fuse only towards the end of the sixteenth century. Ptolemy's *Geography*, however limited in its descriptive aspect, may be regarded as containing the elements of both.

separate, so New. The passage in his letter of 8 July 1524 shows how slowly the image of a New World impressed itself on the mind of an exceptionally intelligent and well-educated Italian of the time. He says:

> My intention on this voyage was to reach Cathay and the extreme eastern coast of Asia, but I did not expect to find such an obstacle of new land as I have found; and if for some reason I did expect to find it, I estimated there would be some strait to get through to the Eastern Ocean. This was the opinion of all the ancients, who certainly believed that our Western Ocean was joined to the Eastern Ocean of India without any land in between. Aristotle supports this theory by arguments of various analogies, but this opinion is quite contrary to that of the moderns, and has been proved false by experience. Nevertheless, land had been found by modern man which was unknown to the ancients, another world with respect to the one they knew, which appears to be larger than our Europe, than Africa, and almost larger than Asia, if we estimate its size correctly.[2]

The images of the Old World were still being only adapted: men saw in the New the Old, altered but not fundamentally changed. Just as the maps of the late fourteenth and fifteenth centuries often carried visual images of camels and caravans crossing a still largely unexplored Africa, or Tartar tents and horsemen on the Central Asian wastes, so too the words of Sir John Mandeville and of Marco Polo (which were often rein-forced by poorly-remembered scraps of information from classical writers), both in manuscript and in the newer print, rode the atlas of the mind. The strange, the fantastic, and the unreal were familiar and to that extent real. New World sights should, it was felt, and therefore to some extent did, confirm the lore of the Old. And so they did in the earliest writings, illustrations, and maps. Where they did not, where novelty was total, it was conceived as an extension of the old rather than as novelty itself. Only gradually did consciousness and language extend to take in the objects and the names of objects in the New World. As they took on names so they took on reality and were convincingly new. The *canoe*, the *petun*, or *tobacco*, the *maize*, the *manioc*, the *cacao*, the *cacique*, the *wiroans* populated the literature of the New World with tangibles, with boats, with plants, with holders of office and the like that were new, and which could not by tricks of etymology (which were duly tried with many of them) be drawn into the network of the known vocabu-laries and their associated Old World contexts.

A basic fact about the geographical literature of the New World is that until his death in 1506, the Discoverer, Christopher Columbus, remained firmly anchored in the Old World. Almost everything he said

---

2. Lawrence C. Wroth, *The Voyages of Giovanni da Verrazzano, 1524-1528* (New Haven 1970) 142.

or wrote has this character, and it is especially evident in the small but significant contributions he made to the published literature of the subject, so much so that he was the major influence in preventing Europeans from regarding the new western discoveries as anything more than an extension of the Old World. On his cosmographical views I need do no more than mention that he believed in a small world, in which Asia could be found by a relatively brief voyage from Europe, and that he maintained this view for the rest of his life. In his day-to-day journals he could and did describe effectively the voyages which he made, so that he clearly had the capacity to add novelty to the geographical literature of Europe, though in what was published in his own lifetime he did not do himself justice. Yet he was constantly referring the New World to the Old—not to establish that what he saw was different from the Old World but to emphasize that it was, for all intents and purposes, the same.

In 1492 Columbus was equipped with a selection of written materials which appeared to him prophetic of the discoveries he expected to make, though we have only the books of prophecies he compiled later in his life. He may have carried with him printed and manuscript copies of Marco Polo and possibly of Mandeville and Prester John's letter, as well as manuscript illustrations or prints which he showed to Amerindians to help gain information.[3] If he gathered that in the new islands there were dog-faced men, he must have shown pictures to his Arawak informants, and the same would be true of the one-eyed men he was also convinced were there. The isle "entirely inhabited by women without men" he could have got from Polo, but what kind of illustration would he have shown them, except perhaps a drawing done on the spot by himself or by one of his men?[4] Las Casas, as Morison points out, simply thought Columbus had misunderstood his Arawak informants. Yet the "Matinino" of his journal became the "Matrimonio" of his published *Letter*, and survives as the name for Martinique down to the present day. By the

3. See *Journals and Other Documents on the Life and Voyages of Christopher Columbus*, ed. S. E. Morison (New York 1963) 84-89, 103. Columbus used Marco Polo (in the edition printed by Gerard de Leeu at Antwerp between 1485 and 1490) and annotated the text extensively: see *Raccolta di documenti e studi pubblicati dalla Reale Commissione Colombiana pel quarto centenario dalla scoperta dell'America*, Part 1, ed. Cesare de Lollis (3 vols. Rome 1892-94) 2. 471-472. There is no clear evidence that he had either Sir John Mandeville's *Itinerarius* or the Prester John letter (in the form *De ritu et moribus Indorum* or another). So far as I have been able to determine, the editions of these three works published before 1492 are not illustrated.

4. Dog-faced men in *Mandeville's Travels: Texts and Translations*, ed. Malcolm Letts, Hakluyt Society, Ser. 2, 101-102 (2 vols. London 1953) 1. 138 and in *The Book of Ser Marco Polo, the Venetian, Concerning the Kingdoms and Marvels of the East*, ed. and trans. Sir Henry Yule, ed. 3 rev. by Henri Cordier (2 vols. London 1903; v. 3, 1920) 2. 309-311. Cyclopean men were in Mandeville (p. 142) but not in Polo. Both, of course, were in Pliny, but Columbus did not make any notes on these references: see *Raccolta* (n. 3 above) *ibid*.

time the *Letter* was written the women had turned into classical
Amazons, using the arts and arms of war.[5] Indeed Fernando Colón
makes this analogy when referring to Columbus' contact with the island
in 1496.[6]

The spices—cinnamon and other—which he claimed to have seen,
as well as the rhubarb and aloe wood, were derived from the names and
concepts of the earlier literature and not from the actual plant species of
the New World: they were the product of wishful thinking.[7] But the
Letter's claim is elaborated in the secondary literature derived from additional accounts of his voyage, notably in the second New World tract,
Nicolò Scyllacio's *Ad sapientissimum Ludovicum Sforzam* (1494 or 1495)[8]:
"I should be justified in calling this island Hispaniola fertile whether it
be an Arabian or an Indian isle." He then attributes to the island all the
products known to come from Asia (many of them enumerated by
Polo)—"large quantities of cinnamon, which men of ancient times were
not permitted to harvest except with a god's permission. Ginger grows
there as well as Indian spice. . . . It abounds in silk. . . . The place
abounds in rhubarb, a useful remedy in all maladies," and so forth.

In 1498 Columbus was still as infatuated as ever with his Old World
authorities. He had just discovered the mainland of South America, "An
Other World" (*otro mundo*, as he described it), but it was still the same
Old World. His long list of products, of which he brought samples for
Ferdinand and Isabella, included pepper, cinnamon, sandal-wood,
aloes, ginger, myrobolans, and "reddish pearls, which Marco Polo says
are worth more than the white." Morison wryly comments, "Sad to
relate, in all this list only the brasil (dye-wood), the pearls and the cotton
were the genuine articles."[9] Was it merely that Columbus was no bot-
anist? Surely there were men on board who were more critical than this?
Does the self-deception indicate that for some of the discoverers,
including the Discoverer himself, the New World could *only* be seen
through the literature of the Old?

On the flesh-eating men he had heard about from the Arawaks on the

5. *Journals* (n. 3 above) 42, 146, 151-153, 155, 185, 249; Mandeville (n. 4 above) 1. 111;
Polo (n. 4 above) 2. 404-406. Columbus, to judge by his glosses on "Ymago mundi" and,
especially, Aeneas Sylvius, *Historia rerum* in *Raccolta* (n. 3 above) *ibid.*, 360, 311-331,
was somewhat obsessed by Amazons.

6. *The Life of the Admiral Christopher Columbus by his Son Ferdinand*, ed. Benjamin Keen
(New Brunswick, N. J. 1959) 171.

7. *Journals* (n. 3 above) 42, 88, 90, 141, 144, 186.

8. *Raccolta* (n. 3 above) Part 3, ed. Guglielmo Berchet (2 vols. Rome 1892-93) 2. 83-94;
translated in *Journals* (n. 3 above) 229-245. See Hirsch, *First Images*, Appendix I, no. 14
(2.553). Further references to this work are given with *Hirsch* and the number referred to in
his list.

9. *Journals* (n. 3 above) 281-283.

rist voyage, Columbus had read much in both Polo and Mandeville, while anthropophagi infested classical literature also. He took what he had read for granted, before he had made any contact whatever with people who ate men. He also, of course, took over the Arawak name, so that *Caribes* and *Caníbales* came into Europe through him and were interchangeable at the outset. They were *Caníbales* in the *Journal* as early as 23 November 1492,[10] but the word did not appear in the printed *Letter* in 1493, even though we hear of an island "inhabited by a people who are regarded in all the islands as very ferocious and who eat human flesh."[11] Scyllacio picked up the word *Camballi* for *Carib* from sources close to Columbus a year or so later,[12] and so *Cannibal* henceforth came to Europe as proof that indeed the mythical man-eaters had at last been discovered. This constitutes the simplest and clearest case in which classical and medieval tales reinforced what was seen or heard of in the New World. The idea was old, only the name was new: the new name became the thing. Even more striking, of course, was that the old name for the new thing stuck in the case of *the Indies* and the *Indians*.

It was perhaps a blessing for Columbus' reputation even a little after his own time that his letter to the Catholic kings recounting his third voyage discoveries did not reach print. His theory about the western hemisphere ascending into incredibly high altitudes and his view of the Earthly Paradise as a nipple on a pear-shaped continent which somehow lay off the shores of eastern Asia were too ludicrous to be permitted to emerge.[13] His only other contemporary publication came out after the first appearance of both Vespucci's *Mundus novus* and his *Lettera*. This was the so-called *Lettera rarissima (Copia de la lettera per Columbo mandata a li serenissimi re e regina di Spagna: de le insule et luoghi per lui trovate)*, which appeared at Venice in 1505 and incorporated his letter of 7 July 1503 about his fourth voyage. Its passages of narrative and of weather-description have some geographical value, but he was still mainly concerned to reveal how closely his observations confirmed older views of the world: "The world is small. The dry land covers six-sevenths of it, and only one-seventh is covered with water." In Central America he located Veragua only ten days' journey from "the Ganges River": in 1503 Cuba was still Marco Polo's Mangi "which

10. *Ibid.*, 100.
11. *Ibid.*, 185.
12. *Ibid.*, 237-238.
13. *Select Documents Illustrating the Four Voyages of Columbus*, ed. Cecil Jane (2 vols. London 1930-33) 2. 1-47 esp. 30-42; excerpted in *Journals* (n. 3 above) 285-288.

borders on the province of Cathay."[14]

So far as Europe's knowledge of the new islands is concerned we must remember that the *Letter* of 1493 remained for several years the only source, even though the 17 or 18 editions in four years, and its appearance in the principal languages of Europe—Latin, Spanish, Italian—and at places as widely dispersed as Barcelona, Valladolid, Rome, Florence, Antwerp, Basel, Paris, and Strasbourg, point to the geographical interest it created.[15] Until 1503 it remained virtually unchallenged and unsupplemented for most readers. As the *Letter* was permeated with Old World thinking, there is little doubt that the novelty of what Columbus had found was thoroughly obscured. The New World thus remained merely an extension of the image of the Old, the Indians of the papal bulls of 1493 were merely another group of Orientals. So far as the literature of discovery is concerned, Columbus did not discover the New World, even if he made vital geographical contributions to its discovery.

On the other hand, the contributions of Amerigo Vespucci to the geographical literature of the New World were of first-rate importance. His *Mundus novus* (1503), it must be realised, however diluted from Vespucci's own text, was the first printed and published account of an authentic expedition (1501-02) to a continental landmass across the Atlantic. It was, moreover, concerned with a major landmass in latitudes which had, in the Ptolemaic world picture, no equivalent. Thus, though Vespucci appears to have had little doubt that his discoveries should be related to Asia and were not in a continent which could be sharply distinguished from the main block of Old World territory, his designation of it as a New World was appropriate from the first. It was not mere islands, like those which Columbus believed lay off the shores of Asia, but a great new mainland, extending along thousands of miles from far north of the equator to far south, right through the same latitudes as those the Portuguese had penetrated in the 1480's with the voyages of Cão and Dias along the African shore.

This is what brought the *Mundus novus* to all the main publishing

14. *Raccolta* (n. 3 above) Part 1, 2. 175-205; translated in *Journals* (n. 3 above) 372-385. Though Columbus' own published contributions to the geographical literature of the discoveries was so limited, it should not be forgotten that Peter Martyr and Angelo Trevisan between them gave his first three voyages a good showing, in straightforward narrative, in *Libretto di tutta la nauigatione de Re de Spagna de le isole et terreni nouamente trouati* (Venice 1504), facs. ed. with intro. by Lawrence C. Wroth (Paris 1929). The account of the first voyage was Martyr's and that of the second and third voyages Trevisan's, while the voyages of Alonso Niño and Vicente Pinzón were also included (Columbus getting 23 pages out of 27).

15. Carlos Sanz López published 17 editions in facsimile in his *La Carta de Colón, anunciando la llegaua a las Indias y a la provincia de Catayo (China)* (Madrid 1958). *Hirsch*, 1-13, 15-18, with 9A doubtful.

centres of Europe (London almost alone excepted) in the years between 1503 and 1508: Florence, Venice, Paris, Basel, Antwerp, Augsburg, Leipzig, Cologne, Nuremberg, Magdeburg, Rostock, Strasbourg, and Pilsen in Latin, German, Dutch and Czech. The preponderance of Latin editions in the early years show that it was regarded as a learned work,[16] unlike the Columbus letter which was brought out more frequently in the vernaculars, and the total of 37 editions was spectacular. The claim to have followed the landmass beyond the fiftieth parallel to the south was striking, and though the geographical data were meagre, the ethnography was strikingly vivid and effective.[17] If Vespucci was a better publicist than Columbus, which he was, he also had more to offer the reader's interest, once given the idea of western lands.

Vespucci's second published work, *Lettera delle isole novamente trovate* (Florence 1505 or 1506), best known as the *Letter to Soderini*,[18] was more significant for the growth of his geographical reputation and the New World's. Its most prominent feature, the claim to have made a voyage in 1497-98 along continental shores around the Caribbean, and to have found mainland territories wherever he went, was invented by Vespucci to forestall the legitimate Columbus claim to have discovered a mainland on his 1498 voyage. So Vespucci installed himself as the first discoverer not of islands but of the *Mundus novus*. His claim was tricked out with detail acquired on the genuine voyage (as his second) and a further version of the 1501-1502 voyage (as his third): there was a brief account of a fourth voyage to the south in 1503-1504. Thus described, the four voyages built up Vespucci into a formidable figure and his discoveries into an epoch-making series of events. His skill in presenting himself as the principal in all his voyages (he was so in none of them), his paucity of detail on the actual routes, and the vividness and detail of his descriptions of the land and of the lives of the peoples he encountered, made his writings acceptable, even though the *Lettera* for a time fell flat and did not find an immediate market outside Italy.

16. *Mostra vespucciana, Catalogo* (Florence 1954-55), nos. 56-70, describes the principal editions: the latest checklist is *Hirsch* 19-30, 32-34, 38-50, 57, 60-65. Later publications in German outran the Latin.

17. Text and translations into Spanish and English in Roberto Levillier, *Amerigo Vespucci. El Nuevo Mundo* (Buenos Aires 1951). The statement about latitude is on pp. 144 (Ital.) and 289 (Engl.).

18. Besides that in Levillier (n. 17 above) 307-337 (Engl.), there is a useful facsimile and translation, *The First Four Voyages of Amerigo Vespucci,* in Narratives of the Discoverers of America 3 (London 1893); *Lettera di Amerigo Vespucci delle isole novamente trovate in quattro suoi viaggi,* and the translation by G. T. Northup, *Letter to Piero Soderini . . . 1504,* are in Vespucci Reprints, Texts and Studies 2-4 (Princeton, N.J. 1916). A not very satisfactory translation also appears in *The Letters of Amerigo Vespucci . . .,* ed. Sir Clements R. Markham, Hakluyt Society 90 (London 1894) 1-56. Northup's translation has been used in citations.

Can we say that in his published writing Vespucci remained Old World-centered? To a limited degree. He takes over Columbus' cannibals as "Camballi" for the Carib man-eaters, but when he proceeds to describe the Guaraní of Brazil he gives us their man-eating habits in the context of their own society and not as horror-features drawn from travel-tales.[19] Even in the diluted *Mundus novus* he describes a society in which eating human flesh is an ordinary matter of diet, though he indicates that he and his men tried to reason the Guaraní out of adherence to the custom. There is much more of the observer than the moralist about him and he does not propose, as Columbus did, that man-eaters be punished by death or slavery. In the Bartolozzi letter, unpublished at the time,[20] he tells us:

> The meat which they eat commonly is human flesh. . . . When they can have other flesh of animals and birds they eat that too but they do not hunt for it much because they have no dogs and their land is very full of woods which are filled with fierce wild beasts, so they do not ordinarily enter the woods unless with a crowd of people.

He went on to give details of the context in which they take prisoners and sacrifice them to feed both their appetites and, he thinks, their beliefs.

It is true, too, that Vespucci brings back a story of giants.[21] He tells how on Curaçao during his voyage with Ojeda in 1499 they saw at first "only five women, two old ones and three girls, so lofty in stature that we gazed at them in astonishment . . . they were in stature taller than a tall man, . . . inasmuch as we were all of a mind to take away the three girls by force; and to carry them to Castile as a prodigy." However, 36 men then appeared, "much bigger than the women: men so well built that it was a famous sight to see them: who put us in such uneasiness that we would much rather have been in our ships than in the company of such people." The Europeans retreated and were stalked back to the boats by the islanders: "They went entirely naked like the others. I call that island the Isle of Giants, because of their great size." Curaçao duly appeared as *Gigantes* on the maps for some time thereafter.

19. *Lettera* (n. 18 above) sig. B4r, C1v, *The First Four Voyages* (n. 18 above) 26, 36. In the letter of 18 July 1500 (Vaglienti Letter) Vespucci wrote: "Your Excellency may rest assured of this fact. They do not eat one another . . . they bring their prey from the neighbouring islands. . . . They never eat any women, unless they consider them outcasts. . . . Still they are a people of gentle disposition and beautiful stature. . ." (n. 17 above) 276.

20. The letter of September or October 1502, partly retranslated by S. E. Morison in *The European Discovery of America: The Southern Voyages, A.D. 1492-1616* (New York 1974) 285.

21. *Lettera* (n. 18 above) sig. B5v; *The First Four Voyages* (n. 18 above) 30-31.

His Old World preconceptions, too, took hold when he saw the native people cooking the iguana and saw many specimens kept alive in the village for food. The creature resembled the dragon or serpent of European lore[22]:

a serpent save that it had no wings and was in its appearance so foul that we marvelled at its loathsomeness . . . their feet are long and thick, and armed with big claws; they have a hard skin, and are of various colours; they have the muzzle and aspect of a serpent; and from their snouts there rises a crest like a saw which extends along the middle of the back as far as the tip of the tail: in fine we deemed them to be serpents and venomous, and [yet] they were used as food.

Here we combine good observation of a new lizard species, plus the domination of European preconceptions, and the admission that reality was not the same as myth: the dragon could be eaten and was neither dangerous nor poisonous.

On the whole, in viewing the letters which were not published at the time as well as those which were, we must regard Vespucci as a good geographical observer. He displayed a serious, even academic interest in rivers and landforms and in ocean currents, latitude, and longitude. These, together with his skills as an ethnographer, made his contributions to the geography of the emerging New World, even from his published writings alone, of great significance.[23] Unlike the materials on or by Columbus which were published during his lifetime, he brought the New World to life, and provided much of the data to render it at the same time acceptable and novel to educated European readers. This may be held to balance his defects in other respects, his exaltation of himself as leader of expeditions in which he was only a subordinate and, above all, the invention of the 1497-98 voyage, primarily an affair of intellectual pride, the determination of the educated Florentine to score over the self-taught Genoese.

The wide publicity which Vespucci received led his publishers and readers to think in more visual terms of the people of the new lands than Columbus did. Vespucci's giants, for example, were such as had stalked the literature of the past, but they soon began to show what puny mortals were attempting to invade the new lands. The print which depicts his ships entering a river estuary, now in the James Ford Bell Collection, has them overtopped by gigantic men.[24] Then too the word-

---

22. *Lettera* (n. 18 above) sig. A6ʳ; *The First Four Voyages* (n. 18 above) 15-16.

23. On this see especially Carl Sauer, "Terra firma: Orbis novus," in *Festschrift Hermann von Wissmann*, ed. A. Leidmair (Tübingen 1962) 268-270.

24. Attributed to G. Stuchs at Nuremberg. It seems rash of Carlos Sanz López to refer to it as a depiction of Vespucci's entry into the Río de la Plata: Carlos Sanz López, *Bibliotheca americana vetustissima: Ultimas adiciones* (2 vols. Madrid 1960) 2. 430-431, and *Comentario crítico e índice general* . . . (Madrid 1960) 28-29. The date ascribed to it is 1505 or 1506: *Hirsch* 44C.

5

Wild man and his wife,
Epistola Albericii, De novo
mundo *(Rostock ca. 1505).*

pictures drawn by Vespucci fitted in with the Renaissance "Wild Man"
carrying a club, a brutal yet misty figure who haunted the woods.[25]
It was this image which inspired, I am convinced, the woodcut of the
Rostock edition of the *Mundus novus* (Pl. 5),[26] though the savage man
there, bearded and long-haired, is waving arrows, not a club, at his
naked, long-haired wife. Similar figures, the man, however, presenting
his bow to the woman, appear in the Dutch edition, published at
Antwerp about 1508 and now in the John Carter Brown Library (Pl. 6).[27]
But these were all purely imaginary figures.

Possibly somewhat nearer to reality were Vespucci's man-eaters,
who appear to have had considerable popular appeal. The young man
who was eaten by the Guaraní in 1501 achieved a degree of personal
immortality (Pl. 7) by appearing on the manuscript map of 1502
known as Kunstmann II, [28] though this was not published at the time and
the drawing probably bore no resemblance to the victim. More important
and more famous is the so-called Munich woodcut of 1505 or 1506

25. Richard Bernheimer, *Wild Men in the Middle Ages: A Study in Art, Sentiment, and
Demonology* (Cambridge, Mass. 1952) 19-20. A major study is *The Wild Man Within: An
Image in Western Thought from the Renaissance to Romanticism,* ed. Edward Dudley and
Maximillian E. Novak (Pittsburgh 1972).
26. *Mostra vespucciana* (n. 16 above) no. 66 (pp. 43-44). *Hirsch* 28.
27. *Mostra vespucciana* (n. 16 above) no. 70, Plate 14 (a); *Hirsch* 64. The Wild Man was
more usually shown without a female companion.
28. Formerly in Bavarian State Library, Munich. There is a coloured reproduction in
*A Collection of Maps and Documents Shown . . . in Florence on the Quincentenary of the Birth of
Amerigo Vespucci,* ed. Alberto Giraldi (Florence 1954-55), Plate 11.

6

Wild man and his wife, Van der niewer wereld (*Antwerp ca. 1508*).

7 *Cannibal preparing one of Vespucci's men for a meal,
Kunstmann II map, 1502.*

(Pl. 8). Though artistically not very advanced, it has a crude realism which might suggest that it was derived at several removes from a sketch made on a voyage. It shows a group of 11 people—men, women and children—engaged in domestic pursuits or carrying weapons, while human limbs are being eaten, or are drying in the smoke or hanging in the store. The people are using a crude poled shelter on the sea shore, with ships shown out to sea. The versions in Munich and in New York are different impressions, but each had a passage printed underneath derived from Vespucci[29]: "They also eat one another, even those who are slain, and singe their flesh in the smoke." The cannibals thus take shape visually. Derivatives of parts of this picture came into the hands of Jan van Doesborch at Antwerp (Pl. 9), who used them in at least two publications, one a broadsheet in Latin, *De nouo mondo* (of which there is a copy in the Henry E. Huntington Library),[30] and also in the first book in English with a reference to America (as "Armenica"), *Of the Newe Landes*.[31] In each case he has combined them with versions of the famous Burgkmair woodcuts of African and Indian subjects from the Balthasar Springer text of his East Indian travels, published at Augsburg in 1508 and reprinted at Nuremberg in 1509 and 1511. Different sources place these publications between about 1511 and sometime after 1520, though it is clear that the blocks were used much later still.[32] But the Brazilian Indians appear in a far more sophisticated form in Burgkmair's "Triumph of Maximilian" (first published in 1526) and in company with the Springer figures, which might suggest that Burgkmair made earlier and more elegant engravings of the Brazilian Indians himself and that all the other crude cuts derive from them.[33] This concern with visual representations is not without significance in tracing the influence of geographical literature on the slowly-emerging image of the New World. Though they were by-products of the narrative and an accompaniment to it, these illustrations undoubtedly contributed to building up a picture of the New World and its inhabitants as these appeared to the explorers.

Vespucci's cannibals did not fade quickly from the maps, at least from those of northern Europe. Sebastian Münster's edition of Ptolemy in 1540 has on its South American map an engraving of their activities

29. Both reproduced in Rudolf Schuller, "The Oldest Known Illustration of South American Indians," *Museum of the American Indian, Heye Foundation, Indian Notes* 7 (1930) 484-497. I owe my copy of the Munich version to Dr. William C. Sturtevant, Smithsonian Institution. *Hirsch* 18B, places it not later than 1504.

30. The Rostock copy was reproduced and discussed in *De novo mundo* (Antwerp about 1520), ed. Maria E. Kronenberg (The Hague 1927).

31. S.T.C. 7677, British Library copy. Dates between 1511 and 1523 have been suggested for it: I favour earlier rather than later dates but cannot be dogmatic. *Hirsch* 93.

32. See Walter F. Oakeshott, *Some Woodcuts by Hans Burgkmair* (Oxford 1960).

33. *The Triumph of Maximilian*, ed. Stanley Appelbaum (New York 1964) nos. 129-132.

Die figur anzaigt vns das volck vnd insel die gefunden ist durch den cristenlichen künig zü Portigal oder von seinen vnderthonen. Die leüt sind also nackent hübsch, braun wolgestalt von leib. at l... t...
... isch.am. füß. frawen vnd man ain wenig mit federn bedeckt. Auch haben die mann iren angesicht vnd brust vil edel gestain. Es hat auch nyemant nichts sunder sind alle ding zü... ...
Vnd die mann habend weyber welche in gefallen. es sey mütter. schwester. oder freundt. darinn haben sy nit vnderschayd. Sy streyten auch mit ainander. Sy essen auch ainander selbs die er...
w...dan vnd ha... en das selbig fleisch in den rauch. Sy werden alt hundert vnd fünffzig iar. Vnd hat ... kain regiment.

8 *Brazilians at home, "Munich" woodcut, 1505 or 1506.*

9

Derivative Brazilians, J. Van Doesborch, De nouo mondo (Antwerp ca. 1520).

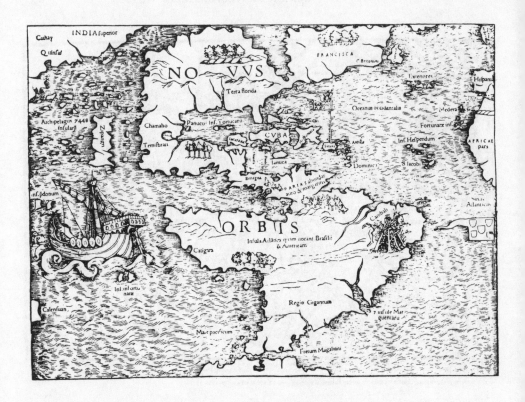

10 *Map with* CANIBALI, *in Ptolemy*, Geographia, *ed. S. Münster (Basel 1540).*

(with CANIBALI boldly captioned)   (See Plate 10), and they appear too in the map in the *Cosmographia* of Peter Apian in 1545, though with a somewhat less explicit engraving.[34] Yet these survivals from older legend and new story began to fade out, as the cannibals themselves became domesticated. Members of the Tupinamba-Guaraní tribes were brought to Europe from 1504 onwards by the French and in the 1530's by the English also, and did not attempt, it would appear, to eat their hosts. Some "cannibals" were fully incorporated into a European art-form in 1550 when Henry II saw a whole village reconstructed in Rouen as part of a pageant.[35] The tribal group brought there behaved well enough, though the conflict staged between the Tupinamba and their "enemies"

34. They are conveniently reproduced in R. A. Skelton, *Decorative Printed Maps . . .* (London 1952) Plates 7-8.

35. Margaret M. McGowan, "Form and Themes in Henry II's Entry at Rouen," *Renaissance Drama*, n.s. 1 (1968) 218-220, fig. 16, plate facing p. 248. As well as the series of plates of the fête there is a large separate engraving of the village. The materials are reproduced in Jean Ferdinand Denis, *Une fête brésilienne célébrée à Rouen en 1550* (Paris 1850): see in this collection figure 78.

("Tabagerres")[36] was fought so vigorously as to create alarm in the onlookers. They were then shipped home but not before Montaigne had seen them, and Vespucci's contribution could not be better demonstrated than in Montaigne.

The long-term effects of Vespucci's writings on the world map were even more striking. In 1506 or early in 1507 Martin Waldseemüller and his friends obtained a manuscript version of the *Lettera*.[37] The four voyages described in it excited their particular interest and led to the making of the map and globes which contained the two great assumptions: first, that the new discoveries made up a new pair of continents, and second, that it was appropriate to give the name of Amerigo Vespucci, in the form AMERICA, to the southern one. Moreover, to the elementary treatise on cosmography that was to explain the map and globe was added a Latin edition of the *Lettera*. So, we have no less than nine printings of the Vespucci material all of which are linked in one way or another with the New World map (though the name "America" was not rigidly maintained on subsequent versions of the map).[38] The constant reprinting of Vespucci's account of the four voyages kept him and his writings and his name in full view between 1507 and about 1519.

We can say therefore that for most readers of the literature on the New World between 1503 and about 1520, Vespucci's two small books constituted the most important geographical literature on the western discoveries, and that the early geographical image of America emerged principally from them.

By 1520 they had lost this hegemony. Peter Martyr had been writing letters about the discoveries of Columbus from May 1493 onwards (though the letters did not appear in print until 1530).[39] From 1494 onwards also he had been compiling coherent narratives of successive expeditions, especially of those made by Columbus himself. The *Libretto* of 1504 tended to keep Columbus' fame alive through the period in which Vespucci dominated the literary scene, while it also presented coherently the early Caribbean voyages, as distinct from those to the southern mainland. In turn it led to the *Paesi nouamente retrouati* pub-

36. On "Tabagerres," Tobagara, see Alfred Métraux, *La civilisation matérielle des tribus Tupi-Guarani* (Paris 1928) 15-16.

37. The basic authority on the Waldseemüller map and text remains Joseph Fischer and Franz von Wieser, *The Oldest Map with the Name America of the Year 1507* (Innsbruck 1903; rpt. Amsterdam 1968).

38. *Mostra vespucciana* (n. 16 above) nos. 81-89 (*Hirsch* 51-55, 66-70), the first eight issues and editions retaining the title *Cosmographiae introductio*.

39. *Opera. Legatio babylonica. Occeani decas. Poemata. Epigrammata* (Seville 1511) printed the first decade only; *De orbe novo decades* (Alcalá 1516), the first three decades; *De orbe novo decades octo* (Alcalá 1530); *Opus epistolarium* (Alcalá 1530). As Petrus Martyr de Angleria, *Opera*, the complete series was published in facsimile (Graz 1966).

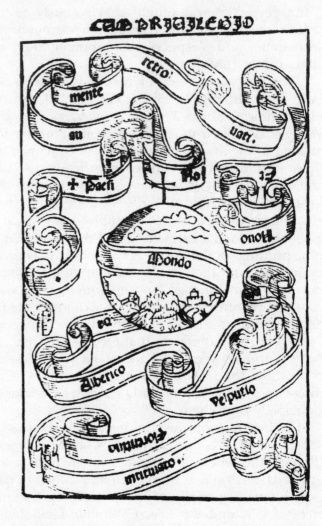

11

Castles in the New World,
Paesi nouamente retro-
uati *(Venice 1507).*

lished in Venice in 1507 (Pl. 11)[40] and followed by ten further editions between that date and 1519.[41] This significant travel collection was devoted to narratives of Portuguese voyages, including that of Cabral and those to the west. The *Libretto* material reappeared, reinforced both by an account of the Ojeda expedition of 1499-1500 (which did not appear to be the same as that which Vespucci claimed as his second voyage) and also by a version of the 1501-02 voyage of Vespucci from his *Mundus novus.* Thus provided with coherent accounts of the main

40. The 1508 edition, with the same title and texts, reprinted in facsimile in Vespucci Reprints, Texts and Studies 6 (Princeton, N.J. 1916).
41. *Mostra vespucciana* (n. 16 above) nos. 71-79; *Hirsch* 55-56, 58-59, 72, 77-80, 82-83.

12

Castles in the Indies,
Epistola Christofori Colombi
(Basel 1493).

overseas enterprises, the reader of geographical narratives could put together a general picture of the Discoveries and establish at least the main lines of development during the period from before 1460 to 1502 (Plates 12 and 13).

When Peter Martyr's first account ("Decade One") of the Columbus voyages appeared in his *Opera* (Seville 1511), a new period of fuller and more reliable narratives was beginning. The New World was being accepted as a fact of life. Through the first "Decade" and the successive publications which made up *De orbe novo decades* between 1511 and 1530, Columbus was rehabilitated. The revised and extended image of the New World, created by narrative and map alike, had room for Columbus. In this respect, Peter Martyr occupies a special place in the dis-

13

Castles in Hispaniola, 1493,
C. Columbus, De insulis in
mari Indico repertis
(Basel 1494).

semination of information on the New World. He helped to form a
climate of opinion in which acceptance of the distinctness of America
became possible. Lacking first-hand experience, however, in his *Decades*
he was better at telling a story than in building up a physical or topographical picture, even though the map included in the 1511 edition was
a valuable adjunct to his text.

During the decade from 1510 onwards the New World was increasingly regarded as wholly separate from Asia. Its outlines, its peoples, its
products emerged as unique, comparable with those of the Old World,
but distinctive. Humanistic and traditional knowledge was still employed to explain America: not to link it into the older scheme of knowledge but rather to throw up contrasts. America slowly acquired a unique
geographical personality.

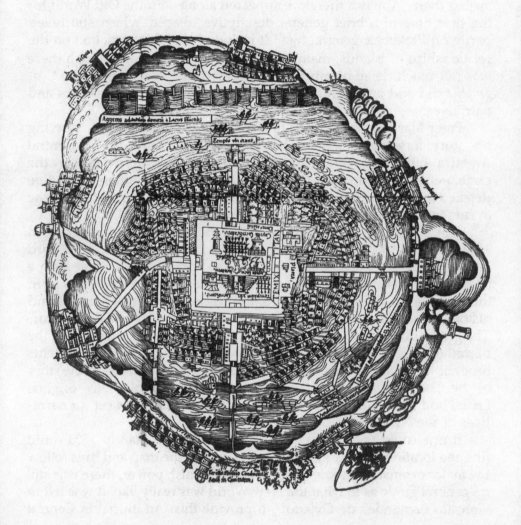

14 *Tenochtitlan with castles, in Cortés, Praeclara (Nuremberg 1524).*

Though maps made considerable progress in the period from 1507 to 1519, a verbal outline of the geographical relationship of the parts of the New World was still lacking. Martín Fernández de Enciso in his *Suma de geographia* (Seville 1519) finally provided it. Enciso had himself been in America and collected sailing directions for places he had not visited there. America therefore appeared along with the Old World for the first time in a brief general descriptive treatise, which still relied partly on Ptolemaic geography.[42] It included useful information on the relationships of islands, mainland, rivers, and so on, and though there was not much detail or much imagination in its presentation, the *Geographia* did add an essential topographical dimension to the maps and narratives.

Peter Martyr's second and third *Decades* came out in 1516, carrying his story forward to the establishment of the Spaniards in Central America. But shortly after 1520 all this early material was overlaid by the excitement of the conquest of Mexico. The rapid publication of the fine detailed letters which Cortés sent from Mexico makes it evident that the events to the west were important news in Europe.

The second and third letters of Cortés, published respectively in 1522 and 1523, and the fourth in 1525 with a Latin translation of the third letter and a map of Tenochtitlan (Pl. 15), produced in serial form a nearly contemporary series of accounts of the conquest of Mexico from the Conqueror himself. These took the reader into a geographical and historical context almost as closely as if he had been an actual spectator. The geographical detail was sufficient, though not a major feature of the narratives, but their immediacy and the exciting nature of their contents brought home to Europeans the most striking single episode in the story of the Conquest in a way that nothing, not even Columbus' original *Letter*, had done hitherto. A high standard had thus been set for narratives of the New World.

If one could take for granted that an educated man in 1525 could find the location of places in the New World on the map and thus follow the major extensions of knowledge and of Spanish power, there was still no general guide as to what the New World was really like. It was left to Gonzalo Fernández de Oviedo[43] to provide this. An official in Central

---

42. Enciso was reasonably generous in apportioning space to America, allocating to it 18½ pages (sig. G6^V.–H7^V.) though the part (sig. H7^r.–H7^V.) devoted to North America was very limited both in length and in content.

43. There is a valuable series of studies on Oviedo containing details of his life and of his ethnology, natural history and attitudes to the Indians in "Homenaje a Fernández de Oviedo," *Revista de Indias* 17 (1957) 391-705. See also the introduction by Juan Pérez de Tudela Bueso to Gonzalo Fernández de Oviedo, *Historia general y natural de las Indias*, Biblioteca de Autores Españoles 117-121 (5 vols. Madrid 1959), which is basically a reprint of the edition by José Amador de los Ríos (4 vols. Madrid 1851-55).

America since 1514, he played an active part under Pedrarias in not always reputable proceedings, but he was more a scholar than an administrator and he was horrified at the behaviour of some of his compatriots towards the peoples of the Americas. He began not only to compile a chronicle of what had occurred within his own knowledge (and before) in the Spanish-occupied lands but also to collect everything he could about the people, their way of life, the plants and animals of his new environment. Out of his expanding diaries and narratives Oviedo compiled a relatively brief report for Charles V in 1525. Printed in 1526 under the title *De la natural hystoria de las Indias*[44] but better known as the *Sumario*, it covered the islands and mainland as far as the borders of Mexico. It was marked by its knowledge, a great deal of which is still invaluable, its objectivity, its comprehensiveness, and above all by its author's determination to take America on its own merits, as a series of lands to be described in a manner which would make its people as well as its fauna and flora intelligible to Europeans. It stands as a landmark in the geographical literature of America.

Oviedo was a great admirer of the Elder Pliny and used his *Natural History* extensively, even imitating its form in certain respects. But he was no slavish follower. He did not try to make Pliny conform to the New World or the New World conform to Pliny. The new independent attitude is well shown in his treatment of the *jaguar*, which he called for convenience a tiger[45]:

> In my opinion these animals are not tigers, nor are they panthers or any of the numerous known animals that have spotted skins, nor some new animal that has a spotted skin and has not been described. The many animals that exist in the Indies that I describe here, or at least most of them, could not have been learned about from the ancients, since they exist in a land which had not been discovered until our own time. There is no mention made of these lands in *Ptolemy's Cosmography*, nor in any other work, nor were they known until Christopher Columbus showed them to us.

This is the spirit and language of the new geographical literature which takes the novelty of the New World for granted. And it is also a sign of the emergence of a New World geographical literature in its own right. The tentative gropings of Columbus, Vespucci, and Peter Martyr were being replaced by the bold narratives of the Cortés letters on the one hand, and by analytical discourses on American peoples and

44. Toledo 1526. Published in facsimile, University of North Carolina Studies in the Romance Languages and Literatures 85 (Chapel Hill 1969); English translation by Sterling A. Stoudemire, *Natural History of the West Indies*, University of North Carolina Studies in the Romance Languages and Literatures 32 (Chapel Hill 1959).
45. *Natural History* (n. 44 above) 47.

products such as that of Oviedo on the other. The *Sumario* was only a foretaste of the *Historia general y natural*[46] which began to appear in 1535; it progressed somewhat further in 1547 and 1557, but only the first 20 books (of 50) were published during the sixteenth century.[47] Yet whatever criticisms one can make of his digressions and his *politique* reticences, the combined narrative and analytical surveys were sufficient to make Oviedo's fame.

Not content with giving a story of events and a parallel treatment of the ethnographic, botanical, and zoological features of the New World, Oviedo had realised that the visual image was significant also to complete the geographical picture of what he had to describe. As a young man Oviedo had lived in Italy and had been at the centre of the High Renaissance culture of the time. Realising that words alone were inadequate to paint America, he regretted that Leonardo da Vinci and Andrea Mantegna—painters whom he had known in Italy—and Pedro Berruguete were not available in America to add colour and form to the words which he himself commanded.[48]

Oviedo himself drew pictures to illustrate his Amerindians, his plants and animals. But he was not an able artist; he could only draw poorly, and his drawings were more nearly diagrams than pictures. A surviving manuscript of seven books of his *Historia general y natural*[49] contains 24 illustrations, all apparently in his own hand. The printed *Sumario* of 1526 had a few outline engravings, the succeeding volumes in 1535 and 1557 a few more, but they did not convey very much though they had some value. He himself could thus only partially convey his visual impression of the New World.

Still, with Oviedo, Europeans had gained a broad and essentially

46. The *Sumario* drew its material from Books 5 to 15 of Part I of the *Historia general y natural*.

47. *La historia general de las Indias* (19 bks. Seville,1535) took the story down to the eve of the conquest of Mexico and drew its natural history and ethnographical materials from the islands and mainland where Oviedo had resided 1514-25. *La hystoria general de las Indias agora nueuamente impressa corrigida y emendada* (Salamanca 1547) contained Oviedo's dedicatory epistle to Cardinal Loaysa, but did not carry the history further, though to some copies was added Francisco de Xerez, *Verdadera relación de la conquista del Peru* (ca. 1534, ed. 3 Salamanca 1547). *Libro XX de la segunda parte de la general historia de las Indias* (Valladolid 1557) added Oviedo's account of Magellan's and certain other Pacific voyages only. The history as a whole was not published until the middle of the nineteenth century.

48. "porque es mas para ver le pintado de mano de Berruguete o otro excelente pintor como el o aquel leonardo de vince o Andrea mantheña famosos pintores que yo conocieren en Ytalia: que no para darle a entender con palabras. E muy mejor que todo esto es para visto que escripto ni pintado": *Hystoria general* (1547) 91ᵛ. "The Role of the Artist in the Voyage of Discovery," in Paul Hulton and David B. Quinn, *The American Drawings of John White, 1577-1590* (2 vols. London and Chapel Hill 1964) 1. 29-36, considers Oviedo in this setting.

49. Henry E. Huntington Library, MS HM 177, two volumes containing Books 4, 6, 7, 9, 11, 32, 37, of Part I.

complete geographical idea of the New World. Together with the maps and the cosmographic concepts behind them, the literature of the New World had all the elements, though it still lacked many of the details, needed to understand the New World's outstanding physical, natural, and human characteristics.

Looking back over the emergence of a geographical literature on the New World, we must reemphasize a number of points. In the first place there was very little available before 1507 to enable the reading public (supposing it could gain access to all that had appeared—a small handful of pamphlets) to make any balanced estimate of the nature or implications of the Discoveries. People learnt there were new islands and then new mainlands, gold and cannibals. But the literature and the maps which emerged in manuscript and were beginning to appear in print (for example, that of Contarini-Rosselli [1506][50] to which Norman Thrower refers) were Old World-centered; their essential feature was that the new discoveries were physically, humanly, and naturally an extension of the Old World, not something basically novel.

Only in 1507 with the appearance of *Paesi novamente retrovati* and the linking of Vespucci's *Lettera* and *Mundus novus* to a revolutionary concept of two distinct continents, linked by name with Americus Vespuccius in the *Cosmographiae introductio*, did the discoveries in the west and east stand out in contrast: the Vespucci tracts offered the concept of a distinctive New World. Subsequent developments—the Peter Martyr narratives, the Enciso sailing directions, and the Oviedo *Natural History*—enabled scholars and educated men generally, if they read the appropriate languages (and a number of the essential pieces were in Spanish or Italian still, rather than in the learned *lingua franca* of Latin), to gain something of a balanced geographical concept of the Americas by 1530. In the next generation, with Oviedo continuing his history, with Gómara providing a further general survey, and with tracts becoming more numerous and detailed, the picture emerged, still slowly, in more refined detail. America became part of human experience; it was assimilated, even if imperfectly, into European concepts. Embellishments on the maps became less specific, more generalized, in line with decoration on maps generally. America can be seen to come of age in 1562[51] when Gutiérrez showed a rococo Neptune and his Car

50. The Contarini-Rosselli world map of 1506, engraved in Florence by Francesco Rosselli (British Library) was the first to show the new discoveries in print. North America was still regarded as an extension of Asia, the land to the west of the Caribbean islands as probably insular, while South America, as *Terra Sancte Crucis siue mundus nouus,* was a great independent continent. It is conveniently reproduced in James Alexander Williamson, *The Cabot Voyages* . . . (Cambridge 1962) 304.

51. The northern portion of the important printed map of Diego Gutiérrez (British Library) is reproduced in R. A. Skelton, W. P. Cumming, and D. B. Quinn, *The Discovery of North America* (New York and London 1971) 142-143 (fig. 156).

riding across the seas westward from the old to the new Spanish empire:
it symbolized America's incorporation in a revised and enlarged classical
geographical tradition.

APPENDIX

Some Old World Survivals in New World Geography

Nomenclature, descriptions, and representations of the New World
continued to be coloured by the Old. Cabral called the land he had
touched in the west the Land of the Holy Cross (Terra de Sancta Cruz),
but it was known first for the parrots, which he sent home in 1500 as
evidence of the new riches, as Terra de Papagaios. They duly appeared
in all their red and gold glory on the Cantino map of 1502.[52] They symbolized that these lands were indeed the Indies. They are Aristotle's
elephants in another guise: "those who imagine that the region around
the Pillars of Hercules joins on to the regions of India . . . produce also in
support of their contention the fact that elephants are a species found at
the extremities of both lands."[53] Aristotle was both history and proph-
ecy to educated Europeans in 1500: if there were no elephants in the
New Indies, parrots would have to symbolize the links between the new
discoveries and Africa and Asia. Columbus, indeed, gave the name
"Cabo de Elefante" to Haut Piton, Hispaniola, in 1492.[54]

Writing in 1493-94, Peter Martyr confirms this approach (I quote
from the English version of 1555)[55]:

> albeit the opinion of Christophorus Colonus (who afirmeth these lands to be
> parte of India) dothe not in all poyntes agree with the iudgement of auncient
> wryters as touchynge the bignesse of the Sphere and compasse of the Globe
> as concernynge the nauigable portion of the same beynge vnder vs, yet the
> Popingiaies and many other thynges brought from thence, doo declare that
> these llandes fauoure somwhat of India, eyther beynge nere vnto it, or elles
> of the same nature: forasmuche as Aristotle also . . . and likewise *Seneca*,
> with diuerse other authours not ignorant in Cosmography, do affirme that
> *India* is no longe tracte by sea, distante from Spayne by the weste Ocean.

52. In colour in Armando Cortesão and Avelino Teixeira da Mota, *Portugaliae monumenta cartographica* (6 vols. Lisbon 1960-62) 1. Plate 9.
53. *On the Heavens* [*De Caelo*], trans. W. K. C. Guthrie (London and Cambridge, Mass.
1939) 253.
54. Samuel Eliot Morison, *Admiral of the Ocean Sea: A Life of Christopher Columbus* (2 vols.
Boston 1942) 1. 367.
55. *The First Three English Books on America*, ed. Edward Arber (Birmingham 1885) 67.
This is from Decade One.

It is curious how early and how often the castle appears as a European construct in a New World setting. Two editions of the Columbus *Letter* illustrate this clearly. *De insulis inuentis*, the so-called "pictorial" edition,[56] has a scene in Hispaniola which includes European-type castellated buildings. In the *De insulis nouo repertis*[57] the islands first seen in 1492 and 1493 are named and tiny ships make their way through them, while prominent in view are large European castles. Similarly, the first edition of *Paesi nouamente retrouati* (Venice 1507)[58] has on its title-page a globe with castellated buildings stretched across the newly-discovered lands, while the same motif was taken up in a German edition of Vespucci, *Newe unbekanthe landte* (Nuremberg 1508).[59]

It was more than a quarter of a century after the first discovery that Europeans saw stone structures which could be regarded as castellated. Cortés indeed saw such in 1519. When in 1524 he sent home his plan of Tenochtitlan,[60] which he had by then totally destroyed, great castles appeared in it, some perhaps modified in the engraver's hands to appear more European. Bernal Díaz saw them also and described them in a famous passage, as being "like the enchantments they tell of in the story of Amadis, on account of the great towers and cues and buildings rising from the water, and all built of masonry."[61]

56. Sanz López (n. 15 above) no. 7. Facsimile also in *The Letter of Columbus and the Discovery of America*, ed. Wilberforce Eames (New York 1892).

57. Sanz López (n. 15 above) no. 8.

58. *Mostra vespucciana* (n. 16 above) no. 71, Plate 14 (b).

59. Copy in Bodleian Library, call number Mason Z 157.

60. In his *Preclara narratione* . . . (Venice 1524).

61. Bernal Díaz del Castillo, *The True History of the Conquest of New Spain*, trans. A. P. Maudslay, Hakluyt Society, Ser. 2, 23-25, 30, 40 (5 vols. London 1908-16) 2. 37.

6

RENAISSANCE INFLUENCES
IN ENGLISH COLONIZATION

Every Country left to it selfe, and not much molested with famine, or devoured
by warres, will at length grow too populous, unable to sustaine its owne weight,
and relieve its owne Inhabitants. Whence it hath bin a policy practised by most
Kings & States in such cases, to make forraine expeditions, and send forth
Colonies into other Countryes lesse peopled, to disburden their owne of such
encombrances; as we see the Kings of Spaine to have sent many into the West
Indies; and we at this day discharge many Idlers into Virginia and the
Barmudas.

(Nathanael Carpenter, *Geographie delineated*, London, 1625, bk. ii, p. 137)

THE New World of the sixteenth century grew directly out of the
Old not merely in a physical but in an intellectual sense. The men
of the late fifteenth and early sixteenth centuries, who found the
new lands overseas, were educated in a humanistic tradition which
made the classical past, especially the Roman past, alive and relevant to them. Consequently, there is an element of continuity in the
thinking about the discoveries and the problems they presented on
the basis of older intellectual concepts, which continues to influence
much of the thought of the sixteenth century about cosmography,
natural history and about the planting of colonies in lands unknown
to the ancients. It is astonishing how Ptolemy remained the stan-
dard-bearer of the new discoveries: maps of the New World and
other novel areas, added to his *Geography* for the first time in 1513,
continued to proliferate in edition after edition until by the later
sixteenth century the original maps and text had been so overlaid
with new matter that they bore even less relationship to the original
than the first issue of Gray's *Anatomy* has to the current edition. It was
much the same with Pliny: the *Natural History* remained the starting
point for New World and Asiatic botany and zoology throughout
the sixteenth century. Oviedo in 1526 paid his respects to the
master before suggesting that genuine novelties could now be added

to his text: well before the end of the century Pliny too had been swamped in new material, though his text was also retained intact.

So far as colonies were concerned many commentators proved to be willing to compare what was being done in the Americas with what had been done long before by the Romans and to seek inspiration from the narratives of Livy, Sallust, Caesar and the rest. Moreover, classical writings, when they suited the particular axes they had to grind, were being used by political commentators in Italy as guides to action. The most notable of these was, of course, Machiavelli, whose advocacy of colonization on Roman models pervaded his writings. To men brought up on Livy the narratives of the historian and the commentaries of the *Discorsi* became almost indistinguishable; both were guides to action not merely subjects for reflection.

There was an English reaction to the first generation of novel, oceanic voyages which took place between 1487 and 1522, but it was, so far as we can tell at present, a muted one. John Cabot certainly represented an Italian Renaissance view of the earth, originating, it is thought, in Florence and with Toscanelli, that the ocean between Europe and Asia might be crossed by westward voyaging. There is no evidence so far that Cabot had any direct impact on English humanists, unless we class Henry VII as one, or had any positive influence on concepts of colonization, even though in 1498 he proposed to bring convicts with him to lay foundations for a halfway house on the route to Asia. The voyages he initiated petered out in the prosaic fishery off Newfoundland.[1] At the same time it may not be wholly without significance that the first Latin translation from the Greek of one classical text on cosmography was made by an Englishman, Thomas Linacre, Proclus's *De sphaera*, appearing at Vienna in 1499 and being thereafter frequently reprinted.[2] This was one of the very few early works which proclaimed that the whole surface of the globe was habitable. Linacre had apparently been in contact with Thomas More at Oxford and became his friend in London. He may perhaps, have been influential in introducing him to the new as well as the old cosmography.[3]

[1] See especially J. A. Williamson, *The Cabot Voyages and Bristol Exploration*, Cambridge (1962), and the not uncontroversial account in D. B. Quinn, *England and the Discovery of America* (London, 1974).

[2] Proclus, Diadochus, *De sphaera* (Vienna, 1499, Leipzig [1500], Vienna, 1511, London c. 1522, Paris 1534); translated into English as *The description of the sphere or frame of the worlde*, by William Salysburye (London, 1550).

[3] More commented favourably on 21 October 1515 on Linacre's work in translating part of Aristotle's *Meteorologica* and a commentary on it, though neither of these works were published (Elizabeth F. Rogers, *St Thomas More: Selected Letters*,

Certainly More seems to have soaked himself in the reports of the new discoveries overseas, though there is little evidence that he did so before he visited the Netherlands in 1515. Antwerp, above all, was a centre for the dissemination of knowledge of the new lands in northern Europe (at least five printings of American tracts had taken place there between 1493 and the time of More's visit), and it was there he picked up much of his information. While the setting of *Utopia* (published at Louvain in 1516) was in the New World, he never uses the name America which was only slowly taking hold from 1507 onwards. He may also have learnt there something of the great debate which was already taking place in Spain on the treatment of the Amerindians and on the legitimacy of both colonization and enslavement. What is striking in *Utopia* for our purpose, is his emphasis on the legitimacy of colonization. He poses the question[4] whether it is right for the Utopians to send their people out to form colonies in other lands which are insufficiently occupied even though the inhabitants may resist. He concludes that 'wherever the natives have much unoccupied and uncultivated land, they found a colony under their own laws (*coloniam suis ipsorum legibus propagant*). . . . The inhabitants who refuse to live according to their laws, they drive from the territory which they carve out for themselves. If they resist they wage war against them. They consider it a most just cause for war when a people does not use its soil but keeps it idle and waste nevertheless forbids the use and possession of it to others who by the rule of nature ought to be maintained by it.'[5] More appeared to identify himself with this somewhat rigid view of natural rights, but it nonetheless represents a considered view and, since More appears to be the first Englishman to use the word *colonia* in a Roman meaning, he provides an essential starting point for this study. His hint is clear; to colonize can be legitimate, even good.[6]

It is highly probable that it was under More's influence that his brother-in-law John Rastell took up the study of the new lands and especially of colonizing prospects there.[7] He aimed to be the first

---

New Haven, 1961, pp. 52–53). More made further reference to the discovery of new lands in his 'Confutacion' (1532), in *The workes* (London, 1557), p. 428.

[4] *Utopia*, edited by E. L. Surtz and J. H. Hexter (Yale edition of the Works of St Thomas More, iv, New Haven, 1965), p. 136.

[5] *Ibid.*, p. 137, and see pp. 415–46.

[6] New English settlements in Ireland had already been suggested about 1515, but we have no evidence that More had Ireland in mind (see *State Papers, Henry VIII*, ii (1834), p. 25; 'to send one man oute of every paryshe of England, Cornwale, and Wales, into this lande, to inhabit').

[7] John Clement (in 1515) and Thomas Lupset (1518) were drawn to More's work on *Utopia*, and so involved, if only peripherally, in New World literature (Rogers, *Selected Letters*, pp. 73, 110).

English colonizer of the new continent which lay between England
and Asia. He had read Waldseemüller's *Cosmographiae introductio*,
in its 1507[8] or a later edition, which had named America (after
Americus Vespuccius) as the southernmost of two novel continents.
Indeed, he is amongst the first to carry the name to North America
as well as South. He planned a colony there and set out to establish
it in 1517, though his men refused to sail off into the ocean beyond
Ireland to the west and he lost his substantial investment. His
Interlude of the four elements,[9] which appeared several years later,
showed he had not lost his belief in the value of colonial experiments
across the Atlantic. His words are well known, but significant:

> O what a thing had been then
> if that they that be Englishmen
> might have been the first of all
> that there should have taken possession
> and made first building and habitation
> a memory perpetual.

Rastell was, however, a lone voice crying in the wilderness; he was
not heard or at least not regarded, even if he seems to have encouraged his son William to go on a prospecting voyage to the Strait
of Belle Isle in 1536, though this voyage too was failure.

The appearance in the works of Machiavelli of fairly frequent
references to the need to imitate the Romans and send out colonies
to increase the power of the state or the ruler[10] was directed mainly,
of course, to Italian city states which might thereby extend the
range of their power into the territories surrounding them. This
might be applied by easy extension to the Irish lordship of the king
of England as well as, by a further extension, to the new lands
across the Atlantic. It is still not clear that, before the reign of
Queen Elizabeth, Machiavelli was indeed being cited in support of
such enterprises, but the use of Roman precedents can be found,
and where they were in question Machiavelli's hand, in the *Discorsi*
at least, may not have been far behind.

If colonization is not heard of again in England in connexion
with America for a generation, it crops up from time to time from
1521 onwards in relation to Ireland, though when an English administration was installed in Dublin in 1534 the proposals to resettle

[8] Published at St Dié, Lorraine, see J. Fischer and F. von Weiser, *Die älteste Karte
mit dem Namen Amerika aus dem Jahre 1507* (Innsbruck, 1903).

[9] *A new interlude and a mery of the nature of the iiij. elementes* [London, c. 1525] sig.
Clv.

[10] *Principe*, chap. 3; *Discorsi*, bk. i, chap. 1, bk. ii, chap. 6, bk. iii, chap. 19;
Istorie, bk. ii, chap. 1. See J. H. Whitfield, 'Machiavelli's Use of Livy', in *Livy*, edited
by T. A. Dorey (London, 1971), pp. 73–96.

Ireland with more Englishmen were submerged for some years by a tide of conciliation. They were to re-emerge at the opening of the reign of Edward VI in a context of military necessity. Two great forts, Governor and Protector (later Philipstown and Maryborough), were established on the western border of the settled English area, the Pale, to defend it against Irish incursions, and these forts grew into towns which gradually spread their influence and their settlers over the surrounding country, very much as a Roman colony would have done. Sir Thomas Smith, one of the most academic of English statesmen of the period, later looked back to the achievements of Sir Edward Bellingham, the rather obscure lord-deputy of the years 1547–48, as beginning a new era of colonization in Ireland, and may already have been struck by the Roman analogy. As secretary of state, 1548–49, he was partly responsible for the policies which brought women to join soldiers in the forts and encouraged cultivation outside them, while the lord deputy, Sir James Croft, moved on in 1551 to plan settlements over a considerable area. In 1552 Edward Walshe, an educated Waterford man, gave us the first clear indication that Roman precedents were being invoked when he put forward the example of 'the politic Romans' as an argument for keeping holdings small and making settlement intensive.[11] Clearly colonization was developing in Ireland though the terms used were 'inhabiting' and 'planting' rather than 'settling colonies'. The plantation of Leix and Offaly went on with repeated set-backs until it finally took hold in the 1560s. What we still cannot determine is at precisely what point settlement in Ireland and colonization in America came to be considered in parallel and equivalent terms.

It was in the 1550s that colonization in America came to be discussed openly in England, even though the word 'colony' had been slow to appear; indeed Ralph Robinson avoided using it when translating *Utopia* into English in 1551.[12] When Richard Eden published *A treatise of the newe India* in 1553 he drew attention to the riches which Englishmen, like Spaniards, might draw from empire-building overseas, but refrained from using the word 'colony' and

---

11 See D. B. Quinn, 'Edward Walshe's "Conjectures" Concerning the State of Ireland [1552]', *Irish Historical Studies*, v (1947), pp. 302–22. Walshe (who saw service at Boulogne in 1544) showed in his pamphlet, *The office and duety in fightyng for our countrey* (London, 1545), dedicated to Sir Anthony Saintleger, that he was well acquainted with Livy and other classical histories. (I am indebted to Dr Dean White for suggesting that this pamphlet would be worth examination.)

12 'Then they chewse out of euery citie certeyn cytezins and buylde vp a towne vnder their own lawes in the next land. . . .' *A fruteful and pleasaunt worke of the beste state of a publyque weale and of the newe yle called Vtopia* (London, 1551), fo 15v., and in 2nd edn (London, 1556), fo 15v.

from direct advocacy of overseas colonization by the English. By 1555, when his *The Decades of the newe World* appeared, he was less reticent. He translated a dialogue between two Italians who considered that modern peoples ought to emulate Alexander and Caesar 'by assigning colonies to inhabit divers places of that continent (America).' He told also how, in his opinion, the Spaniards in their settlements improved the conditions, and religion, of the Indians, while enriching themselves in the process. He was the first to describe in English the North American expeditions by Cartier and Coronado and to ask 'Oh what did Christian princes mean that in such lands discovered they do not assign certain colonies to inhabit the same?'[13] This was the first clear call since Rastell for English colonization in North America, though it may have been caution which suggested that settlements be made well to the north of the empire of King Philip. Here classical precedents simply provide an excuse for raising the question of colonization in an English context. At the same time the question was very slow to emerge as a topic for debate. Even when, in 1563, a half-hearted attempt was being made to prepare a colonizing expedition to occupy a deserted French fort in Florida, the publisher of a translation of a French tract advocating the advantages of the southeast coast of North America for settlement could do no more than point to the pleasure and profit of overseas voyaging, 'as well for the enlarging of the Christian faith as the enriching of kingdoms'.[14] It was not, indeed, until the late 1570s that Englishmen began talking in earnest about American colonization, though when at last they had begun to do so, they surpassed all other European nations of the time in the amount of discussion of objectives, ways and means, and so on, which took place. Indeed, between 1578 and 1630 talking and writing about colonies was rather more frequent in England than attempts to establish them and may even have paved the way for success in the longer run in the difficult process of planting really viable colonies in temperate latitudes in North America.

By the time such discussion began, however, many Englishmen were familiar with at least some of the problems of colonization because they heard enough about the subject in an Irish context and had become aware of experiments made there. In this process Sir Henry Sidney, during his lord-deputyship of Ireland, 1565–1571, and Sir Thomas Smith in England, between 1565 and 1577, played outstanding parts, while the young captain, Humphrey

---

[13] In *The First Three English Books on America*, ed. E. Arber (Birmingham, 1885) pp. 49–60, 285–8.

[14] Jean Ribault, *The whole and true discouerye of Terra Florida* (London, 1563), sig. *2v.

Gilbert, from 1566 onwards, focused his mind on techniques of exploiting Irish lands through English settlers which he was afterwards, in the late 1570s, to translate into an American context.[15] There was, in this period, both discussion and experiment Roman precedent, with possibly the indirect influence of Machiavelli's writings, came to play some part in shaping both ideology and concrete plans for settlements.

Smith, it would appear, was already under the influence of the Roman historians as well as Machiavelli when he revived with William Cecil the possibilities of large scale colonies in Ireland in 1565,[16] for the following year showed that his library at Hill Hall[17] contained not only an array of Greek and Roman historians but Richard Eden's *Decades* (Smith had been his tutor at Cambridge) and Machiavelli's *History of Florence*, his *Discorsi* and *The Prince*, all three works, of course, expressing the view that a ruler who wished to extend and enforce his rule should not merely conquer but colonize. In the *Discorsi*, in particular, he had stressed that the Romans had sent out compact bodies of men not only to hold down conquered territories, but to bring Roman law and custom to the occupied areas, and provide a loyal nucleus of inhabitants, an argument which fitted in very well with Smith's views on Ireland and indeed with the whole situation which was emerging there.

We can see Sidney steadily advocating colonization here and there in the island, largely under private auspices though with government supervision,[18] and using classical terminology such as 'that there might be induced there some colony',[19] and also being answered in a royal letter by a reference to 'deducing some colonels of people out of our realm to inhabit the same.'[20] This was in 1568–69, though we cannot link Sidney directly with Machiavelli's injunctions. Smith, however, after his admission to the privy council in March 1571 and especially when he became secretary of

[15] See D. B. Quinn, *The Voyages and Colonising Enterprises of Sir Humphrey Gilbert* 2 vols., (London, 1940), I, 9–12, II, 490–97.

[16] Smith to Cecil, 6 June and 7 November 1565, P.R.O., State Papers, Foreign SP 70/78, 1007 and 1302; Smith to Sidney, May 1565, State Papers, Ireland, SP63/13, 51, see Mary Dewar, *Sir Thomas Smith* (London, 1964), pp. 156–57.

[17] John Strype, *The Life of the Learned Sir Thomas Smith* (Oxford, 1820), pp. 276–77. *See* Christopher Morris, 'Machiavelli's Reputation in Tudor England' *Il Pensiero Politico*, II (1969), no. 3, p. 90. (I am indebted for this reference to Dr Cecil Clough.)

[18] Nicholas Canny, *The Elizabethan Conquest of Ireland. A Pattern Established 1565–1576* (Hassocks, 1976).

[19] Sidney to the Queen, 12 November 1568. P.R.O. State Papers Ireland, SP63/26, 18.

[20] Queen to Sidney, 6 June 1569. T. ÓLaidhin, *Sidney Papers, 1565–70* (Dublin, 1962), p. 108.

state in 1572 and so took on, under the Queen, responsibility for directing Irish policy, became obsessed with Roman-style colonization as the model for Ireland. Moreover, he proposed to engage himself in the creation of a model 'Roman' colony, equipping his illegitimate son, Thomas, with a patent and some corporate backing to found the city of 'Elizabetha' in the Ards in Ulster, and issuing a printed pamphlet, a prospectus and a map to draw in men and money. Curiously, he avoided in this printed publicity any mention of Rome and even of the word 'colony' and spoke only of 'inhabiting' the Ards, but in his correspondence he reiterated time after time for some four years the classical jargon about colonies which had become for him a living directive to action.[21] His didactic letters spoke of his son as 'a leader forth of men, who in ancient time were *deductores coloniarum* and the action was called *deducere coloniam*'.[22] 'The truth is', he said several years later, 'that I and my deputies be indeed *Coloniae deductores*, the distributors of land to English men in a foreign country.'[23] Smith was talking nonsense of course, since Ireland was a kingdom under the English crown and the very land involved in his grant had been part of the earldom of Ulster which Edward IV had inherited in 1461. A young scholar[24] put it to me recently that Smith seemed throughout to be thinking in terms of an independent entity where English laws (or Smith's laws perhaps) would run, not those of the royal administration in Dublin, so that the inhabitants would be carrying English law, like Roman colonists, into a new environment. It does indeed appear that he thought in some such terms with emphasis on the city. This was to be a strong town, as a magazine of victuals, a retreat in time of danger, and a safe place for the merchants. 'Mark Rome', he said, 'Carthage, Venice, and all other where any notable beginning hath been.'[25] After his son had been killed, he sent a further expedition to erect the city which he described in detail, together with an elaborate plan for its govern-

[21] See D. B. Quinn, 'Sir Thomas Smith (1513–1577) and the Beginnings of English Colonial Theory', *Proceedings of the American Philosophical Society*, lxxxix (1945), 343–60; Dewar, *Sir Thomas Smith*, pp. 156–70; N. Canny 'The Ideology of English Colonization: Ireland to America', *William and Mary Quarterly*, 3rd ser. xxx (1973), 575–98.

[22] Smith to Sir William Fitzwilliam, 17 July 1572. Bodleian Library, Carte MS 57, fo 38.

[23] Smith to Fitzwilliam, 31 July 1574, Carte MS 56, fo 218. In the same letter he designated *de facto* leaders of the colony 'Colonel, and *coloniae ductor* and *agrorum divisor*.'

[24] Mr Barry Langston.

[25] Smith to his son Thomas, May 1572, *Calendar of State Papers, Foreign 1583, and Addenda*, pp. 491, and see 467–68, 492. John R. Hale, 'To Fortify or not to Fortify', *Essays in Honor of John Humphreys Whitfield*, ed. H. C. Davis, D. G. Rees, J. M. Hartwell and G. W. Slowey (London, 1975), p. 110, shows that Machiavelli

ment,[26] which was that of a virtually independent principality. But his fantasy was finally revealed for what it was when this expedition too collapsed. He must have become something of a laughing stock before he died in 1577, but his words about Roman colonies and the means by which they might be brought to life again went widely round official circles in England. After Smith, few officials can have had any doubts about the supposed nature or at least the terminology of Roman colonization, though they may have had many doubts about its relevance to Irish conditions.

It was between 1576 and 1578 that the notion of planting American colonies took hold in England. The debate on their nature and function was really opened in 1577 by the elder Richard Hakluyt and was later taken up by his younger and better known cousin of the same name. Sir Humphrey Gilbert, Edward Hayes, a Liverpool man, Christopher Carleill, Sir George Peckham and Thomas Harriot were the other main protagonists during the following decade. [27] This discussion was almost wholly empirical and pragmatic, based on what America was like or was thought to be like, and not to any appreciable extent on long-term historical precedent or the Machiavellian precept. The discussion turned on the possibility of creating in North America such amenities as mining camps, military garrisons, trading posts, great aristocratic estates, communities of village size which would operate small holdings, and large-scale company plantations. There was strong English nationalist sentiment behind it as hostility to Spain developed from piracy to open war. There was a missionary impulse, too, but it was tentative and perhaps, hypocritical. The discussion was based also, to some extent, on practical experiments, Frobisher's unsuccessful mining camp on Baffin Island,[28] Gilbert's aborted territorial colony in 1583 in the later New England,[29] the moderately successful garrison-colony on Roanoke Island in 1585–86, and the village community which John White planted in 1587 and which was never

---

stressed both the importance of fortifying conquered territories and of colonizing them, but he did not put the two themes together. Smith, rather than Justus Lipsius, *Politicorum Libri sex* (1589), in *Omnia opera*, iv, (Wesel, 1675), 73–74, who is cited by Hale, appears to be the earliest, or at least one of the earliest, to do so.

[26] See Dewar, *Sir Thomas Smith*, pp. 164–68 and review by D. B. Quinn *Irish Historical Studies*, viv (1964–65), 285–87. The emphasis is again on the city: 'The chief strength to fortify a colony is to have a city or town of strength well walled and defended.'

[27] Listed in *Appendix*, pp. 116-17 below.

[28] See V. Stefansson, *The Three Voyages of Martin Frobisher*, 2 vols. (London 1938).

[29] See Quinn, *Gilbert*. 2 vols. (London, 1940), and *England and the Discovery of America* (London, 1974).

seen again,[30] experiments which were in the shorter run failures but which provided in turn the material for further discussions.

The younger Richard Hakluyt impressed on Queen Elizabeth in 1584 the need for her to assert her personal authority across the Atlantic to enhance her majesty no less than her territory,[31] but he did so without reference either to Roman precedent or to Machiavelli, though he found scripture useful, as a clergyman could, to reinforce his arguments. Laudonnière, the French historian of French Florida ventures in the 1560s, used Roman precedents to justify French actions, but Hakluyt translated and published his words without comment.[32] Sir George Peckham used scriptural precedents too, but the only references to the Romans in his tract were in prefatory poems by John Ashley and John Hawkins. The naval hero lollops along in good style, reducing the Roman analogy to its lowest common denominator:

The Romans when the number of their people grew so great
As neither wars could waste nor Rome suffice them for a state
They led them forth by swarming troops to foreign lands amain
And founded divers colonies unto the Roman reign.

We must, however, analyse the underlying assumptions and conclusions in social and economic terms and not in those of Roman influence. In summary we can say that they revolved round three main considerations and a number of minor ones, the complementary economy, the supplementary economy and the emigration thesis.

The first of these, the idea that the colonies must exist mainly to supplement English production, was of primary importance. Settlers established along the North American coast from about latitude 30° to 60° N. could produce almost all the products which England would normally obtain from European trade and a certain number of sub-tropical exotics as well. The English economy would thus become virtually independent of imports from all but tropical lands. This programme could well have been deduced from Spanish and Portuguese precedents in dealing with their overseas empires, but in the English discussions it was developed coherently and in detail, in a way which became stereotyped only in the following century.[33]

[30] See D. B. Quinn, *The Roanoke Voyages, 1584–90,* 2 vols. (Cambridge, 1955).

[31] 'A particuler discourse', the so-called 'Discourse of Western Planting', in E. G. R. Taylor, *The Original Writings and Correspondence of the Two Richard Hakluyts,* 2 vols. (London, 1935), ii, 211–326.

[32] R. Laudonnière, *A notable historie containing foure voyages made by certayne French captaynes vnto Florida* (London, 1587), sig. A1–A1v.

[33] G. L. Beer, *The Origins of the English Colonial System, 1578–1660* (New York, 1908), is still the fullest account, though his interpretations have been modified

The second of these, the idea of a supplementary economy, arose from the realization that North America could produce many of the products which England herself produced but in greater quantities. The English share in European and Newfoundland fisheries, if boosted into domination of all North American fisheries, could create a profitable monopoly in the international fishery which at that time was booming. Timber was clearly another complementary product. Not only could Baltic timber be done without, but English timber would be supplemented and conserved by bringing in masts and yards, barrel staves and clapboards, building ships on the spot, and above all substituting American timber for English in expensive timber-using heavy industry—iron-smelting, glass-making, potash manufacture—as well as by providing tar and resin. The vision of an infinite resource in timber, especially oak, was attractive. Then, too the cultivation of English grains and other food plants would enable the colonists to adjust their diet to that to which they were accustomed and obviate the need for food exports to them. This was an original idea. It did not take into account the possibility (which developed with New England in the next century) that certain colonies might produce *only* products of a complementary nature and could only produce an unmarketable surplus or else become direct competitors with England, nor did it stress the great mercantilist plank of the next century that the colonies would offer a major closed market for English manufactures.

The last major consideration was the presumed need for the export of English men and women. The tendency for population to increase after the mid-century, together with endemic unemployment associated with the decline of certain branches of the cloth trade, impressed—over-impressed—almost all those who thought about it with the idea that there was a surplus population which ought to be exported. Those who read Machiavelli seem to have turned their thoughts especially to Ireland as a home for surplus English people, and they had some influence, but 'the Americans', as we may call the group of projectors with whom we are here concerned, thought America was more suitable. Here there would be a free hand to experiment. And in the social blueprints for colonies there was wide agreement that attempts should be made to re-create something very like ideal English communities, whether they were the great feudal lordships of Gilbert's dream or the compact and democratic village communities envisaged by the Lost Colonists of 1587 and created at last in 1620 by the Pilgrims.

and developed in books such as Ralph Davis, *The Rise of the Atlantic Economies* (London, 1973) and K. G. Davies, *The North Atlantic World in the Seventeenth Century* (Minneapolis, 1974).

Linked with the desire to plan newer Englands in North America, was the incentive of upward social mobility. It is constantly stressed that persons going to America could expect to move at least one or two steps, if not more, up the steeply graded ladder of Elizabethan social hierarchy. Moreover, groups who sat uneasily at home, penally-taxed Catholic gentry, or Puritans of one denomination or another, might there be able to carry with them ideological idiosyncrasies which might not be so easily tolerated at home.

There were other incentives less original. There was the hope of selling to Amerindians vast quantities of woollen cloth or receiving rich furs and other products in exchange for worthless trinkets. Gold, silver and jewels were powerful incentives but they were muted in propaganda appeals after Frobisher's fiasco in finding worthless and not golden metals on Baffin Island. There was, too, the possibility of converting the heathen. Very often this appeared as a competitive necessity, since the Spaniards were attempting it, rather than as a moral imperative, or else it was thought of as a precondition for setting the Amerindians to work for the settlers, though too much optimism was not expressed after early reports had reached England on the attitudes of native peoples to European servitude.

Over the whole picture the idea of creating in North America another England or Englands, on a larger scale, with more generous opportunities (in theory at least) for all settlers though retaining essentially English social gradations, was dominant in this thinking. How far it went back to *Utopia* or Utopianism, how far it was influenced by a humanistic education, how far simply by self-interest is difficult to say. We may suggest that the total picture represents the practical approach of the Northern Renaissance, moulding its dreams and projections into specific, possibly attainable, social and economic objectives. New and improved Englands in North America, and an England improved by its American colonies, took shape on paper at this time.

It was in Ireland that the first large English colonial settlement was achieved. The plantation of Munster was developed between 1585 and 1594, wrecked in an Irish rising in 1598 and slowly reconstituted after 1603.[34] It was there, after the initial pangs of settlement, that the holders of some great Irish seignories began to think in terms of Roman models and Machiavellian warnings. Sir William Herbert, Richard Beacon and Edmund Spenser were all prepared to quote classical precedents and the works of the more recent

[34] R. Dunlop, 'The Plantation of Munster', *E.H.R.*, iii (1888), 250–69; D. B. Quinn, 'The Munster Plantation: Problems and Opportunities', *Journal of the Cork Historical and Archaeological Society*, lxxxi (1966), 19–40.

political master, Machiavelli, to justify what had been done in Munster and to commend its extension over the rest of Ireland. Sir Walter Ralegh, largest planter of all, may well have been in their company but has left no written record.[35] The reason may have been only personal idiosyncrasy or an intellectual game worked out in their Irish semi-exile. Yet Machiavelli's talk about colonies being instruments of strong government and a means of reforming and consolidating an existing regime had in some degree a special application to Irish conditions. Herbert, a scion of the Montgomeryshire family, was the most articulate. In 1588–89 he wrote a Latin treatise, entitled *Croftus, sive De Hibernia liber*, in honour of the lord-deputy of the 1550s, which was probably intended for publication as a learned excursus on English policy in Ireland, though it did not find its way into print until the late nineteenth century.[36] Herbert was concerned to explain why the conquest begun by Henry II had failed and how the reconquest of Ireland could be made fully effective. He was full of classical analogies and terminology and made several bows in the direction of 'that perceptive Italian', Machiavelli.[37] Briefly, the earlier conquest failed because, as he said, 'the transplanting of the colonies was without towns, castles or sufficiently satisfactory regulations': such colonies degenerate 'when colonists imitate and accept the morals, customs and laws of the native peoples.' Machiavelli had stressed the need for giving wide powers to regional officials (men no doubt like himself who held wide seignories) and he was said also to endorse the wiping out of the native inhabitants if they remained, in the last resort, irreconcilable. The objectives of the regime Herbert favoured in Munster and wished to extend to the rest of Ireland were 'the building of cities, the planting of colonies, the defending of the powerless against the harshness and oppressions of the rulers, the periodic calling up and levying of soldiers from among the more vigorous inhabitants, and finally the educating of the flower of the youth in English academies.'[38] It is interesting to compare the emphasis here, a contrast with what was being discussed regarding America.

Richard Beacon's treatise, *Solon his follie, a politique discourse, touching the reformation of commonweales*, was published at Oxford in 1594. Ostensibly it was about the relations of two hypothetical

---

[35] P. Lefranc, *Sir Walter Ralegh écrivain* (Paris, 1968), pp. 237–40, 633–35.

[36] Edited by W. E. Buckley (Roxburghe Club, 1887). For Sir William Herbert of St Julians, Monmouthshire, see biography by A. H. Dodd in *Dictionary of Welsh Biography* (London 1959), p. 355, and *Herbert Correspondence*, edited by W. J. Smith (Cardiff and Dublin, 1963), pp. 4, 8, 61–64.

[37] Pp. 35, 41.

[38] P. 54, see also pp. 26, 35–8. I am indebted to Dr Cecil Clough for translations.

states, 'Athens' and 'Salamina', but in fact about Anglo-Irish relations. Beacon generalized from his experiences in Munster.[39] In
Ireland England should do as the Romans had done. He said:
'the Romans in all countries by them conquered did labour nothing
more than to protect and defend the feeble and weak, and to deliver
the people from oppression'. Earlier colonies had failed since,
'instead of planting of colonies, we placed garrisons.' Saturation
settlement was desirable, therefore 'let us lose no opportunity of
deducting colonies': such 'a reformation of a declined common-
weal is an happy restitution unto his perfection'.[40] The whole tract
is informed by reading amongst Italian and French writers, though
acknowledgments are seldom specific. Beacon is very eloquent if at
times obscure, but an able exponent of this theme. Spenser in his
View of the state of Ireland, published only in 1633, found justification
for plantation in the defects of the Irish as well as in the achievements of the Romans. He cited Machiavelli, 'where he commendeth
the manner of the Romans' government, in giving absolute power
to all their consuls and governors, which, if they abused, they
should afterwards clearly answer.'[41]

A third writer of this period, who comes chronologically between
Herbert and Beacon, was Matthew Sutcliffe, who afterwards, as
Dean of Exeter, was prominently associated with the Plymouth
Company, the northern branch of the Virginia Company. His substantial work, *The practice, proceedings, and lawes of armes* (1593),
criticized Machiavelli as an amateur soldier who wrote about wars
he did not understand, but was content to use the *Discorsi* to help
out his plentiful citations from the Roman historians. He cited with
approval Vegetius' maxim 'The Romans did subdue the world by
the exercise of arms.' Moreover, he saw Roman colonization, by its
soldiers after conquest in the field, as an example to be followed in
subjecting conquered territories in his own time. Such colonies were
also economical: 'To maintaine a force therefore without great
charge, the meane is to send Colonies of the English nations into
the country conquered.' Such a programme had, he felt, a special
relevance to Ireland, saying 'And if Colonies had now of late bene

[39] For Richard Beacon, fellow of St John's College, Cambridge, Queen's
Attorney in Munster, 1586–91, grantee of 6,000 acres in Munster, 1591, see
Joseph Foster, *Alumni Oxonienses*, i (London, 1891), 94, and, for the grant of 1591,
Calendar of Patent and Close Rolls of Ireland, 18–45 Elizabeth, edited by James Morrin
(Dublin, 1862), p. 266.

[40] Pp. 81, 108, 114. I am indebted for information on *Solon* to Dr Sydney Anglo
who is making a study of the text.

[41] *A View of the State of Ireland*, ed. W. L. Renwick (Oxford, 1970), pp. 98–100,
125, 169; *Prose Works* (Variorum Spenser, ix), edited by R. Gottfried (Baltimore,
1949), pp. 229, 279, 286, 304, 397, 429.

sent into Ireland, not as now scattering and disunited, and few in number, but in good strength and united by lawes, and dwelling in townes as the Romans did, I doubt not, but the countrey would bee better assured, and the charge farre lesser then now it is.' Nor should there be any compunction about dispossessing the native inhabitants in such a case: 'If any man say, that it is hard to dispossesse the ancient inhabitants of the countrey out of their dwellings: he considereth not that rebels, and enemies are so to be used; and that if they be placed other where, it is of mercie rather then desert.' Sutcliffe, indeed, sums up very neatly the application of Roman and Machiavellian military-colonial precedent to contemporary Irish affairs.[41a]

Both Beacon and Spenser had a narrow, almost purely Irish perspective, but Sir Thomas Smith's Roman city could well have been envisaged in an American setting. Sutcliffe's also was narrow, set inside a purely military perspective, and applicable primarily to Ireland though capable of more general extension once external conquest was embarked on. Herbert's viewpoint lay somewhere in between: he was concerned with ancient history and the analogies it could supply both to point to political and military reforms and also to advocate a new beginning in dealing with the whole problem of intruded colonial settlement, which might in certain respects have been appropriate to America as well as to Ireland. These Irish instances, especially those applied to Munster, bring out clearly that Machiavelli was concerned with colonies as instruments of government in territories adjacent to or degenerated from the rule of the parent power. In Ireland colonization was primarily one means of solving the problem of government; colonies are associated with power rather than with the expansion of peoples into new areas. In America the problems seemed initially almost wholly concerned with establishing a secure social and economic base, while those presented by the native inhabitants and by the government of the colonies appeared to be of secondary significance.

Once expeditions with colonizing objectives had begun to be despatched to America a main element in published promotion material was narrative—accounts of what had actually occurred on particular expeditions—which could be analysed and compared with the experience of the French, Spanish and Portuguese at an earlier stage in other parts of the Americas. When colonies had actually been set up in America, from 1607 onwards, the achievements of the colonists, in however discreetly censored a form, in turn became the main ingredient in colonial promotional literature.

[41a] Sig. B4r., pp. 205–06.

The Virginia Company, throughout its career from 1606 to 1624, tried its best, and with some considerable success, to control the material which was published on its American colony. Consequently, much published colonization material is promotion matter in a narrower sense than that of the earlier phase. There was not, consequently, much need to look back into the Roman, or indeed any other past, and the main influences were more likely to be men with colonial experience rather than theorists like Machiavelli. None-the-less, especially when things were going wrong in the colony, some appeal to the past was still part of a continuing tradition.

The habit of reference to the Roman past continued in Ireland during the growing pains of the great Ulster plantation, which was to surpass Munster and Virginia alike as a new colony in the period before 1630. Thomas Blenerhasset in 1610 thought James I should preen himself like a Roman emperor on the strength of his colonizing achievements in Ulster,[42] while Sir John Davies,[43] making still another review of the mistakes of the initial Norman conquest, before going on to praise the Ulster plantation, could not refrain from pointing out how the Romans would have done much better than Henry II and the rest. In the Virginia Company literature, Roman example comes up also from time to time. Robert Gray, in *A good speed for Virginia* (1609), maintained that for the Romans colonization was the chosen means for dealing with a population surplus and should be for England also.[44] Robert Johnson in 1609 and 1612 also glanced at Roman precedents.[45] It was really only when there were serious problems arising in Virginia, and a closer look at the longer perspective was needed, that serious consideration was given to historical precedent. The learned writer of *A true declaration of the estate of the colonie in Virginia* (1610), was one who thought in this way. The Virginia Company's settlement of 1607 in Virginia, though reinforced twice in 1608, had singularly failed to root itself firmly at Jamestown. The first large reinforcement in 1609 had been no more successful; so many died and food had run so short that a further relief expedition in 1610 had barely arrived in time to prevent the colonists leaving Virginia. Much of this was blamed on the incapacity of the colonists to rule themselves. *A true declaration*, therefore, was intended to explain failures and to recommend

[42] Dedication to *A direction for the plantation in Ulster* (London, 1610).

[43] *A discouerie of the true causes why Ireland was neuer entirely subdued, nor brought vnder obedience of the crowne of England, vntill the beginning of his maiesties happpie reigne* (London, 1612), pp. 77, 124–25, 156, 164.

[44] Sig. B4.

[45] *Nova Britannia* (London, 1609), sig. C2, E2v., and *The new life of Virginia* (London, 1612), sig. F1, G4.

reforms which would create a successful colony. The author had a long excursus on the prevalence of colonization throughout the ages, ending with the Romans, who 'deduced 53 colonies out of the city of Rome into the womb of Italy'. The chief lesson to be learnt was the need for order and discipline in the colonizing process: 'how easily might ambitious discord tear in pieces an infant colony,' he said, 'where no eminent and respected magistrates had authority to punish presumptuous dissentience.' He worked up into a fine rhetorical passage: 'Tacitus hath observed that when Nero sent his old trained soldiers to Tarantum and Autium, but without their captains and centurions, that they rather made a number than a colony. Every soldier secretly glided into some neighbouring province, and forsook their appointed places, which hatched this consequent mischief. When therefore license, sedition and fury are the fruits of a heady daring and unruly multitude, it is no wonder, that so many in our colony perished. . . . A colony is heretofore denominated because they should be *coloni*, the tillers of the soil and stewards of fertility. Our mutinous loiterers would not sow with providence, and therefore they reaped the fruits of too dear-bought repentance.'[46]

In this case the Roman analogy was not merely academic but the headline of a new policy, namely a plan to place the colony under a firm administration in a legal strait-waistcoat, in which the settlers would be compelled to obey orders, to work, to build, to grow crops and to behave as they were told to do. The legal code developed in 1610–11 and imposed on the colony was as draconic as any which could have been derived from classical authorities. William Strachey, who wrote the introduction to *For the colony in Virginea Britannia. Lawes divine, morall and martiall*, published in 1612, presented the code as 'a transcript of the Toparchia or state of those duties by which their colony stands regulated and commanded, that such may receive due check who maliciously and desperately heretofore have censured of it.'[47] In his own work, 'The history of travell to Virginia Britania', which he wrote about the same time, but did not publish, Strachey maintained that had the Romans not conquered and civilized the Britons, England would be savage yet. Perhaps this may be the last case where Roman law and precedent regarding colonies was called in to justify a particular line of policy.[48] And indeed, whether the Roman influence was effective or not, the

---

[46] In Peter Force, *Tracts . . . Relating Principally to the Origin . . . of The Colonies in North America*, III (Gloucester, Mass. 1963), no. 1, pp. 4, 15.

[47] Sig. A2v.

[48] *The Historie of Travell into Virginia Britania (1612)*, ed. L. B. Wright and V. Freund (London, 1953), p. 24.

colony did survive and begin to grow under its hard taskmaster, the code of 1611, until it could be gradually relaxed after 1616.

There were a few traditional echoes still to come. The clergy in particular liked to show off their learning by citing Roman as well as biblical precedents for colonization. The Reverend William Symonds in his *Sermon* (1609) asked rhetorically, when insufficient colonists were coming forward for Virginia—'Is only now the ancient planting of colonies, so highly praised among the Romans and all other nations, so vile and odious among us that what is and hath been a virtue is all others must be sin in us?'[49] But he did not provide an answer to his own question. The Reverend Richard Eburne compiled, in *A plaine path-way to plantations* (1624), the fullest compendium of all on why England should establish colonies in America, especially in Newfoundland. Among his many reasons was that plantations were 'both usual and ancient . . . above all to the Roman state, which from their very first years, *ab urbe condita*, after that Rome itself was builded, fell apace to that practice and had ever on hand one or other colony.'[50] We need not conclude, however, that he placed Roman precedent high on his list of incentives. We may take the Reverend John White of Dorchester a little more seriously. *The planters plea. Or the grounds of plantations examined, and usuall objections answered* (1630), was the last of the early classical treatises, by an eminent pioneer who sent many settlers to New England. The argument throughout is a mixture of religious and economic incentives and imperatives. There are side glances at Roman colonizing precedents. The bringing in of religion was the main thing to be hoped for, religion for colonists and the Indians alike, but, obliquely, the Romans are brought into it too. 'I make no question,' he said, 'but God used the same way to other barbarous nations, which he held with us, whom he first civilized by the Roman conquests and mixture of their colonies with us, that he might bring in religion afterwards, seeing no man can imagine how religion should prevail upon those who are not subdued to the rule of nature and religion:'[51]—a statement which contained the germ of a programme for settlers and Amerindians alike in the new Commonwealth of Massachusetts Bay, which was then just forming.

We can see that in most respects Roman analogies and precedents and the reading in Machiavelli which may well have lain behind many of them, had only marginal and occasional practical importance in the later development of colonial planning in early seven-

[49] Sig. C4.
[50] *A plaine path-way to plantations* (London, 1624), p. 17, and *A Plain Pathway to Plantations*, ed. Louis B. Wright (Ithaca, N.Y., 1962), p. 41.
[51] P. 11, other references to Roman colonies are on pp. 37, 43–44.

teenth century England. The broad considerations of economic and social policy, sketched before 1600, were in the main followed during the period when theorizing was turned into effective, if risky, experiments in colonization. They were inevitably modified in their application as practical lessons were learnt. The real America proved in many ways different from the America which appeared in the early debates and projects. It had its own distinctive climate and its own faunal and floral characteristics which made some of the early plans for economic exploitation fruitless. Its natives were not the simple, obedient savages whom some theorists hoped for, but they were not wholly intractable barbarians either: a sophisticated native policy was called for. Ideas on the organization of particular types of settlement had to be worked out by trial and error. A chartered company, for example, proved excellent for raising capital if it had high-level government sponsorship, as had the Virginia Company for most of its existence: it proved unsatisfactory for developing a colonial community. It led, on the other hand, by a process of trial and error, to the production of a viable cash crop, tobacco, which made Virginia self-supporting in the end. Similar organizations failed in Newfoundland partly because of undue optimism about the climate, but principally because its main harvest, that of the sea, could best be handled by unco-ordinated seasonal fishing voyages from Europe. In New England hard experience revealed that a small village-type community could indeed make a living for itself within a span of about four years, but it needed outside help if it was to do more than survive its early growing pains and prosper. In 1629–30 the Massachusetts Bay Company was to begin to demonstrate that capital, if put up by the settlers themselves and used to feed the colony through its early years, together with a process of adapting company organization to the task of internal self-government,[52] could work wonders in enabling a New England in the end to be created.

Did any of these later developments owe anything substantial to earlier discussions which involved looking back to Rome or to Machiavelli or other Renaissance theorists? It is hard to give any precise answer. Renaissance learning certainly contributed to the spread of Europe overseas in all sorts of ways, many of them indirect, rather than direct, but it was gradually subsumed as an immediately

[52] General guides to the early development of colonies in North America are J. E. Pomfret, and F. M. Shumway, *Founding the American Colonies* (New York, 1970), W. F. Craven, *The Southern Colonies in the Seventeenth Century* (Baton Rouge, 1949); C. M. Andrews, *The Colonial Period of American History* (New Haven, 1934), i, and D. B. Quinn, *North America from First Discovery to Early Settlements. The Norse Voyages to 1612* New York, 1977).

effective force. In the case of England, it was clearly only one among a wide spectrum of influences. We may consider that Roman precedent, however imperfectly understood, directed Englishmen's attention to certain incentives to colonization, perhaps the issue of presumed pressures of population and that of intensive forward planning for the government of both settlers and natives. Other means and other channels would have probably brought them to very similar positions, though perhaps by longer routes. While in a few cases some concrete effects can be deduced from theoretical reliance on Rome or Machiavelli for guidance, it is hard to regard either as decisive over a very wide area of discourse or experiment. Perhaps the main significance of their appearance at all is that they indicate that the new colonial situation created by the overseas discoveries was being envisaged very much inside a historical context.

Appendix

English Discussions of Colonization in North America, 1576–1602.

In the following list individual colonizing projects are dated as closely a possible, but they are placed in sequence under date of publication if they appeared before the end of Queen Elizabeth's reign. Later publication is referred to in a few instances.

(i) Sir Humphrey Gilbert, *A discourse of a discouerie for a new passage to Cataia* (London, 1576);

(ii) Richard Hakluyt, the elder, 'Notes framed by a Gentleman', [1578]; in Richard Hakluyt, the younger, *Diuers voyages touching the discouerie of America* (London, 1582);

(iii) Christopher Carleill, *A breef and sommarie discourse vpon the entended voyage to the hethermoste partes of America* (London, 1583, 2 edns);

(iv) Sir George Peckham, *A true reporte, of the late discoueries, and possession taken in the right of Englande, of the New-found Landes* (London, 1583), 2 issues;

(v) Richard Hakluyt, the younger, 'A particuler discourse' (Discourse of Western Planting, 1584), in E. G. R. Taylor, *The Original Writings and Correspondence of the Two Richard Hakluyts*, vol. ii (London, 1935), pp. 211–326;

(vi) Richard Hakluyt, the elder, 'Inducements to the lykinge of the voyadge intended to that parte of America which lyethe betwene 34. and 36. degree of Septentrionall Latytude', [1584–85], in *Ibid.*, ii, 339–43;

(vii) Edward Hayes, 'Discourse of the Newfounde lande,' 1586, Brit. Lib., Lansdowne MS 100, fols 83–94;

(viii) Thomas Harriot, *A briefe and true report of the new found land of Virginia* (London, 1588);

(ix) Edward Hayes, 'A report of the voyage and success thereof, attempted in the yeere of our Lord 1583, by Sir Humphrey Gilbert knight', in Richard Hakluyt, *Principall nauigations* (London, 1589), pp. 679–97;

(x) Edward Hayes, 'A discourse conserning a voyage intended for the planting of chrystyan religion and people in the Northwest regions of America' [1592], C.U.L. MS Dd. 3. 85, No. 4;

(xi) Anon., 'Plantacion in America' [c. 1595–1600], P.R.O., State Papers, Colonial, C.O. 1/1, 9;

(xii) Charles Leigh, 'A brieffe platforme For a voyadge with three ships vnto the Iland of Ramea in Canada', 1597, Brit. Lib., Additional MS 12505– fols. 77r–77v;

(xiii) Edward Hayes, 'A treatise' [c. 1592–3], in John Brereton, *A briefe and true relation of the discouerie of the north part of Virginia* (London, 1602), both edns, sig. B4–C4;

(xiv) Richard Hakluyt, the elder, 'Inducements to the liking of the voyage, intended towards Virginia,' 1585, in *Ibid.*, 2nd edn, sig. D1–E2V.

NOTE: Items 1-xi, xiii-xiv have been published in full in D.B. Quinn, A.M. Quinn and S. Hillier, *New American World*, 5 vols. (New York, 1979), I, 1-180, and xii in IV, 79-80.

7

THE ENGLISH CONTRIBUTION TO EARLY OVERSEAS DISCOVERY

With this subject, and with the impression that S. E. Morison has conveyed (not wholly seriously) in *The Northern Voyages* that it is possible for an Irishman to be an English nationalist,[1] you may expect a eulogy of English achievement in this field. To do this might be to stretch the truth somewhat, since, though Englishmen made some very interesting contributions to early discovery, they did not, in most cases, follow them up, but left it for others to exploit them or, alternatively, in other cases stepped into some other nation's shoes and exploited what had first been pioneered by others. Activity in the overseas discovery area is not in itself a measure ot the contribution made by any one individual or any single country; the quality of what was contributed must be taken into account also.

If I was trying to find a theme where I think the evidence points to a clear case of English priority in discovery and exploitation in North American waters it is that of the cod. The cod (*Gadus* sp.) does not differ in character in the western Atlantic from what it is in the east, except in the crucial factors of size and quantity. The cod offshore is bigger and fatter (has larger livers which produce the "train" oil) and is found - or used to be found - in unsurpassed numbers on the many Banks from the Gulf of Maine to the Labrador coast where natural conditions are most propitious for its breeding. To emphasise this creature so near the shores of Lake Michigan*might appear inappropriate if I did not consider that the major initial discovery by the English was of the numbers and characteristics of the North American codfish and that they were, so far as we know, the first to exploit it as a source of food for protein-deficient western Europe, and so paved the way for the establishment of the first major European industry based on North American resources.

Having recently put a case in my book *England and the Discovery of America*[2] for an English discovery of the Isle of Brasil in 1481 by the ships *George* and *Trinity* sailing from Bristol, I am in danger of repeating myself in unnecessary detail. These vessels certainly sailed westwards into the Atlantic in this year, carrying a certain amount of salt, apparently looking for new fishing grounds. When they returned they were said to have been "to serch and fynde" the Isle of Brasil.[3] Whether this meant they had gone to search for and had found the island or whether the phrase is injunctory only and their instructions were couched in the terms "search" and "find" is a semantic matter which cannot be firmly resolved without further evidence. All I have been able to do is try to put this event in a

* This chapter was given as a paper in Minneapolis.

[1] *European Discovery of America. The Northern Voyages* (New York, 1971), p. 208.
[2] New York and London, 1974.
[3] *Ibid.*, p. 8.

fuller context of Bristol's concerns with the Atlantic in the later fifteenth century
in the hope that we can reach a little nearer to a decision one way or the other.

The next alternative is that either there was a further discovery between either
1490 and 1491 and 1496 or that Englishmen were attempting to exploit a fishery
established on the basis of an earlier voyage, as the Spanish envoy, Ayala, stated
in 1498 that the Bristol men had been sending out for seven years two to four
ships a year to search, he considered, for the Isle of Brasil and the Island of Seven
Cites.[4] There is good ground for maintaining that all these ships could not have
been sent out simply for exploration purposes and must have produced an economic return. The reference, ambiguous though it is, adds another strand to an
argument that the English were exploiting North American fisheries before John
Cabot took a hand in Bristol voyaging.

Finally, we have John Day writing to Columbus at the end of 1497, it appears, to indicate that Cabot's recent voyage had produced information on what
he thought was the Isle of Brasil and the Island of the Seven Cities, and stating
that Columbus already knew that the discovery of the Isle of Brasil had been made
by the English in times past *(en otros tiempos)*[5] which certainly does not suggest
that it was made very near the time of writing, or even as recently as 1492. Taken
together these data amount, I believe, to good if not decisive circumstantial evidence that a discovery of some sort was made ahead of any other European power
in the west. My own preference is for dating that discovery in 1481, but it can be
preference only, without conclusive proof. Admiral Morison takes the view that
John Day, however reliable his evidence on the Cabot voyage of 1497, that he was
merely repeating Bristol gossip about an earlier discovery to Columbus, and that
in any event Henry VII would have behaved very differently toward Cabot had a
Bristol discovery of any western land been made.[6] We cannot be certain that
Edward IV, Richard III or Henry VII would be aware of a Bristol discovery in, say,
1481 or even later, but had they known of it I am sure that it would not have the
connotation which Morison gives it.

There were large numbers of islands on the maps which we know were available in England by about 1480[7] and the discovery of one of them might or might
not have excited any comment, indeed it is probable that various false sightings
of islands had been made from time to time. Islands in the Atlantic, indeed, were
not of any great account as discoveries at the time of their first sighting. We have
almost nothing in the way of records of first discoveries of the very large number
of islands of the Canary, Madeira, Azores and Cape Verde groups from the later
fourteenth century onwards which the Portuguese and Castilians had made.
Islands became important to monarchs, notably to the Portuguese monarchs,
when it was found that they had some territorial value, good soil, some strategic
value, or even, possibly, use as bases for fisheries. The discovery of an island which
was merely regarded as a useful landmark for a fishery as would be the discovery

---

[4] *Ibid.*, pp. 9-10.
[5] *Ibid.*, pp. 6-7.
[6] *The European Discovery of America. The Northern Voyages* (1971), pp. 208-209, *The Southern
Voyages* (New York, 1974), p. xi (where he suggests the supposed discovery to be in 1480 which
is not proposed).
[7] *England and the Discovery of America*, pp. 57-60.

of the Isle of Brasil (supposing it to be some fragment of island or mainland in the Newfoundland area) would not be more significant, or worthy of more publicity, than the use of certain islands off the west coast of Iceland would have been earlier in the fifteenth century for the fishing vessels sent out regularly from England. The situation would be completely altered by a discovery like that of Columbus where the islands found were alleged to lie off the coast of Asia, to be gold- and spice-bearing, and which led to immediate major diplomatic moves by the Papacy, Castile and Portugal. Once this had occurred, Henry VII was bound to consider seriously any approach made to him by such as Cabot who could hold out the hope of reaching Asiatic lands by a short and direct passage westwards from England. In fact, the question of the discovery of some outlying scrap of North American land by the English before 1493 has the same kind of relevance to the eventual exploitation of the Americas subsequent to Columbus' voyage as the discovery of the Azores earlier in the fifteenth century had to the same matter.

The question of priorities has an appreciable but limited interest. For the general historian it may be tedious and uninteresting, but for the Society for the History of Discoveries, for example, it is the kind of puzzle which is worth chewing over from time to time as new ideas, and above all, new evidence, emerge. An English "first" in the rediscovery stakes is not so important as anything Columbus or John Cabot achieved, though if it was made and exploited before 1492 it adds a new facet of interest to our knowledge both of England and the Atlantic in the fifteenth century.

My all-important American codfish does not stand or fall by an English discovery of a cod fishery before 1497, since John Cabot was the first to publicise the discovery of seas swarming with fish after his return in 1497, thus giving the Bristol seamen a clear priority in any event. But we have still to inquire who started the fishery on an economic basis. All the hints of an earlier discovery are silent about this matter except the claim that Robert Thorne and Hugh Elyot were the first to make an effective discovery of the new found lands.[8] Whether they did so or not they were clearly the first to exploit the fishery after John Cabot's death. Dr. Alwyn A. Ruddock has very recently published new information[9] from the customs records which show that these men sent their ship *Gabriel* in 1502, apparently to fish, and followed with the *Gabriel* and *Jesus* in 1504, the latter bringing back salt fish and fish livers worth £ 207 10s. This is the first recorded catch of the soon-to-be-ubiquitous Newfoundland cod. It seems to have marked too the first independent voyage of Sebastian Cabot whom Dr. Ruddock finds was given his pension on April 3, 1505 for services done in connection with the finding of "the new founde landes." The English priority seems clear but it did not stand for long. It was probably no more than a year before the first French ships went to Newfoundland to fish and the Portuguese are known to have been bringing cod by 1506.[10] Thus if there was, on present evidence, a clear priority

[8] *Ibid.*, p. 11.
[9] Alwyn A. Ruddock, "The Reputation of Sebastian Cabot," Bulletin of the Institute of Historical Research, XLIII (1974), pp. 96-99.
[10] See H. A. Innis, *The Cod Fisheries (1940), pp. 14-15;* C. A. Julien, *Les voyages de découverte et premiers établissements* (Paris, 1948), p. 25; C. de la Morandière, *Histoire de la pêche de la morue dans l'Amérique septentrionale* (2 vols, Paris, 1962), I, 219, 224; Morison, *Northern Voya-*

both in discovering and exploiting the Newfoundland fishery for the English, no exclusive rights in it were either claimed or exercised, and indeed English vessels were soon in a small minority as the great international fishery took off. The cod of Newfoundland and the search for it made every summer by hundreds of European vessels constituted, until well after 1600, the only positive and valuable result of the discovery of North America,[11] in which the fish brought to Europe played a considerable part in enlarging the protein resources available to the common people as well as providing ships' stores for countless other exploring and trading voyages to many parts of the earth's surface.

Voyages from Bristol by Azorean Portuguese in association with Bristol seamen between 1501 and 1505, in the later of which Hugh Elyot had a share, were directed to other parts of the North American coasts besides Newfoundland,[12] so that it is worth while considering whether those who made them still considered themselves, as John Cabot did, to be reconnoitering the shores of Asia. If they did not, and so anticipated Waldseemüller's 1507 hypothesis that North America was a continent intermediate between Europe and Asia, then Sebastian Cabot's voyage in 1508-9 in search of a Northwest Passage round America may rank as an English "invention."

It may, however, be argued that the 1507 map could already have been known in England before Cabot set out.[13] No definitive answer can be given. Cartographic evidence suggests that well before the end of the first decade of the century the Portuguese too, were familiar with the trend of the Labrador coast and may themselves have been making deductions similar to those of Cabot.

We may see that England may have had a technical priority in the rediscovery of America before Columbus, but, because she did not exploit it at a political level, it could have little practical effect, except, perhaps, in providing some measure of experience which made the voyages of the period 1497-1509 more effective than they might otherwise have been. The priority gained in exploring a long stretch of coast in 1497 was soon, by 1501, paralleled by the Portuguese, so the priority there had likewise a limited effect. And though Sebastian Cabot appears to have invented the concept of a Northwest Passage, he did not get the backing to exploit it after 1509 and was passed by Henry VIII, along with his knowledge of the new lands, to Ferdinand of Aragon in 1512. The fishery, if begun by the English, rapidly came to be dominated by French, Portuguese and Spanish Basques, though the English retained their share. In general then, English pioneering did not produce, apart from the fishery, any tangible results.

So far as the subsequent discovery period down to 1550 is concerned the English have little claim to originality in discovery. They followed the French to eastern North America after Verrazzano and to the Gulf of St. Lawrence after Cartier's first voyage.[14] It may also seem that the English followed the French to

ges, p. 254.
[11] This is not to deny that the fur trade and the Gulf of St. Lawrence whale fishery did have some economic importance before 1600.
[12] *England and the Discovery of America*, pp. 111-130.
[13] *Ibid.*, p. 138: since we know thanks to Dr. Ruddock's paper ("The Reputation of Sebastian Cabot," pp. 96-99) that Sebastian had been on at least one voyage to America before 1505 our inferences on the possible extent of his knowledge before 1508 can be more extensive.
[14] *Ibid.*, pp. 171-189

Brasil from 1530 onwards as well. The record of a single English ship in the Caribbean, in 1527, shows that England played no part in any of the major American discoveries of the period and did not even successfully batten on them as the French managed to do. By 1550 her earlier priorities, though Sebastian Cabot was back in England trying to capitalize on them, were faded memories. Nor, after 1550 were there many major original ventures. The most surprising was the decision to send the 1553 expedition to Asia by way of the North east Passage rather than the Northwest, and this has never been fully explained. Nonetheless, the failure of this attempt was accompanied by the development of the   north-eastern   route to Muscovy and this proved to be of some novelty and economic value, in the exchange of cloth and metals for furs, wax and naval stores.

Though the probing of the approaches to the Passage continued and produced limited results, the more valuable effect of the development of the Russia trade was some overland contacts with the Trans-Caspian region and Persia, since they gave some hope of being able to approach the nearer parts of Asia behind the back of the Portuguese. These developments did not, however, lead very far, even though their achievement had some degree of originality.

We probably have to wait for the Drake voyage of 1577-1580 before we get a major novelty. The conception of a voyage to the Pacific was in itself a striking one, even if K. R. Andrews is correct,[15] and he probably is, that Drake's task was to prey on the southern fringes on the viceroyalty of Peru, since at least wider issues, the questions of Terra Australis and of the Strait of Anian, had been ventilated in England before he sailed. What else Drake did in the Pacific was apparently governed by the circumstances that he had upset the Spaniards too much to have any chance of getting back through the Strait of Magellan. He did, therefore, search halfheartedly for the opening of the Strait of Anian, and, apparently, as a casual gesture, went through the formalities of annexing New Albion to the crown of England, and even carried out important pioneer contacts with the Moluccas. His main importance was twofold. He showed that the Pacific, a Spanish lake since its discovery, could be invaded by hostile forces, while he also demonstrated that the voyage of the *Victoria* was not a freak achievement but a practicable venture – a fact which Cavendish was to demonstrate again with his following voyage in 1586-1588. Spain had to extend her military and naval cover widely as a result, even though the English did not again successfully raid the Pacific shores of the southern viceroyalty. Drake's voyage was, however, the greatest psychological achievement of the English overseas; thereafter the Spaniards had much greater respect for their potential maritime achievements than they had reason to have hitherto.

The Roanoke voyages were an original achievement too. Having written so much about them[16] I might be expected to stress them. Perhaps the most significant achievement of the years 1584-1590 in North America was the amount and nature of the information brought back in a digestible form. Hariot's tract, White's drawings and their multilingual dispersion in print throughout Europe

[15] K. R. Andrews, "The Aims of Drake's Expedition of 1577-1580," *American Historical Review*, LXXIII (1968), 724-741.
[16] Especially in *The Roanoke Voyages* (2 vols., Cambridge, England, 1955), and in P. H. Hulton and D. B. Quinn, *The American Drawings of John White* (2 vols., London and Chapel Hill, 1964).

made them a major revelation of the character of the country and people of the east coast of North America. The Spaniards, not unnaturally in view of their vast experience elsewhere in the Americas, took North America for granted, and did not write much about it. They also tried out there a variety of the expedients – military, colonizing and missionary – which had grown familiar to them elsewhere and discarded those which did not succeed. The English proceeded more tentatively. The settlement of 1585-1586 had the important effect of showing that Englishmen could remain healthily for a year in an North American environment, even if it did not tempt them to remain there for longer. The English, it appeared, too, were prepared to learn from their mistakes. An exploring base in 1585-1586 was replaced in 1587 by a varied colony with family units: if this disappeared by 1590 it was thought to be both alive in the wilds and a pattern fit to follow for a long time after.[17] Indeed the Virginia experience after 1607 was also a series of somewhate painful experiments, in which experience was gained by failure, until in the end tenacity was repaid, and viable settlements established.

Something like the same process occurred in New England. The early inspection of 1602-1605 provided a varied range of experiences and insights but they did not suffice to maintain the Segadahoc colony in 1607-1608. John Smith had to start the process off again after 1614. Once again the English showed something of a genius for publicity since the invention of the name New England helped to ensure that Englishmen would try to make it so. And so, indeed, they did.

The claim for originality rests rather on a certain persistence and determination to achieve adaptation rather than in some rapid illumination which made settlement at once possible and effective. The other leading characteristics of the English settlements, the breadth of the social cross-section which their settlers represented, and the great extent to which many of them were let alone to work out their own adaptation without government and corporate interference, sprang partly, it might seem, for the earlier process of trial and error, and the attitudes which it engendered.

There is, of course, much of interest in other aspects of English overseas activity in its early stages, their privateering in the Caribbean, distinguished in the end for its scale and persistence; the experiments in exploring and raising tobacco in Guiana, which led them to nibble at the fringes of the Spanish tropical empire; their West Africa trade; their appearance in the wake of the Dutch in the East Indies, and their homing on India, under Dutch pressure, which was to have such great significance later. In none of these activities is there much that is wholly novel.

Perhaps the Northwest Passage voyages from 1576 to 1631, even if they were in the end barren of result, or appeared to be so, were of the greatest originality in revealing, expensively, the wide expanses of Davis and Baffin straits and of Hudson Bay, with the lands around them, which permanently enlarged the geographical perspective of North America, and made ground for fur-trading and further probing at much later stages. This, perhaps, is as much as can be said briefly.

Is there still research and analysis to be done, it may well be asked? Ac-

[17] *England and the Discovery of America*, pp. 432-481.

cidental discovery may still throw up striking documents which can alter our perspectives radically, especially so far as the early explorations in the Atlantic are concerned. But, apart from some further clarifications of the nature of English enterprise in Guiana, the Amazon and Brazil, which we may probably expect, I do not consider that major discoveries of materials in the later sixteenth and early seventeenth centuries are likely, though reassesment may well change the emphasis which would be now given to various aspects of early activity. Advances in this field must surely come rather from the comparative assessment of English achievement in relation to those of other powers, especially as regards North America, rather than by documentary novelties.

We ought really to begin comparing, inch by inch as it were, the various activities of the western European powers in the earliest stages of overseas expansion. We still do not know if there was an English way of doing this, a French way of doing that, a Spanish way of doing the other. This is where analytical techniques of all sorts, not only quantitative but qualitative as well, will need to be brought into play. To take only one obvious example, we still know virtually nothing about French privateering in the sixteenth century, and nothing at all about the differences between French and English privateering and how they developed. We could investigate too, in this way too details of French, Spanish, and English ways of attempting colonization in North America and comparing these activities with happenings in similar circumstances in other parts of the Spanish and Portuguese empires in the Americas. And there are other similar lines of approach deserving consideration.

The greatest field for both quantitative and comparative studies in the very early period is in connection with the cod and the cod fishery with which I began. There are masses of notarial materials in western European countries other than England which have lain almost unused. There is much less contractual material in England but more narrative. The mass of French notarial records has only been scratched in a few locations.[18] The great treasurehouse in northern Spain is only now being investigated on behalf of the Canadian Archives department, and the first reports are promising.[19] Nothing has been done, to my knowledge, to locate and search similar records in Portugal. In the end these materials will provide much material for our quantitatively-minded historians to find out precisely how this major European industry worked in different parts of Europe. Contractual documents can be supplemented in many cases by court records. The latter will, at least prevent the human element from being ignored. Gillian T. Cell has already given us a concise monograph on one section of the English experience, and has pointed the way to others.[20] I am convinced that there are materials for the understanding of a unique international business enterprise, which can, incidentally, throw much light on English overseas enterprise at successive stages in its development.

---

[18] E.g. by C. de la Morandière, *Histoire de la pêche de la morue.*
[19] Mrs Selma Barkham has subsequently revealed the great extent of the Basque whale fishery.
[20] G. T. Cell, *English Activity in Newfoundland, 1577-1660* (Toronto, 1970).

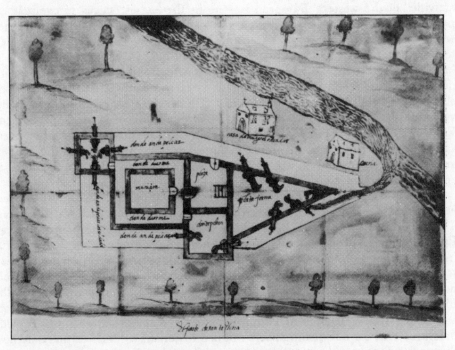

15 Spanish Fort at Santa Elena (now Parris Island, S.C.) *(Archivo General de Indias, Seville)*

8

COLONIES IN THE BEGINNING:
EXAMPLES FROM NORTH AMERICA

IT IS ONLY appropriate, since these lectures are in memory of Walter Prescott Webb, that I should start with a quotation from *The Great Frontier*. "Many explorers," Webb said, "made mistakes in the American wilderness, but nevertheless came back with or sent back valuable information."[1] My subject is in the first place about European governments that made many early attempts to penetrate North America. They made many mistakes. They sometimes learned enough from these mistakes to sponsor viable settlements in the end, but even if the attempts brought back or sent back useful information, for a long time they obtusely failed to learn enough to do so. I can illustrate this part of my topic only empirically from the experiences of England, France, and Spain, though not in that order, and will end my discussion of government policy and the more or less state-sponsored colonizing efforts just at the point in the seventeenth century, in the 1620s, when enduring colonies were finally being inserted into the casually appropriated lands of the inhabitants of the continent, when a "frontier," in Webb's terms, was at last being created, even if I am not going to be concerned with frontier theory as such.

It is a truism, but one we must not lose sight of, that the European colonies in the Americas sprang out of the distinct historical experiences and traditions of each of these states, but it is one that, for my purposes, must be briefly developed. It is, for example, traditional to say that the Spanish empire was born out of the experiences of the *reconquista,* the long process of conquest, town-building, ecclesiastical fervor, and institutionalism that removed Muslim rule from Spain in the very year Columbus sailed, leaving Spain open to venture into the West. While this is basically true, its strict relevance for Spanish activity in North America between 1512 and 1620 is not so clear. By the time North America came within the range of the *conquistadores* the ideals and methods of the *reconquista* had been profoundly modified by earlier enterprises in the New World, first in the Caribbean

1. Walter Prescott Webb, *The Great Frontier* (Austin: University of Texas Press, 1963; London: Secker and Warburg, 1963).

and then, much more drastically, in Mexico and still more in the conquest of Péru. Consequently, Spanish policy in North America was, in my view, influenced more by these experiences after Columbus's time and by the governmental devices and institutions that evolved to cope with unprecedented problems of government from a distance rather than by anything that had gone before.

Similarly, though in a very different perspective, the activities of both France and England in North America must be seen against the background at home, though here the influences tended to be negative rather than positive. Both nations were held back by more urgent domestic commitments and by lack of institutions which could cope with colonies lying several thousand miles away, and also by lack of capital, which Spain did not lack from the 1520s onward. France, for example, had expelled the English only in the middle of the fifteenth century and had regained a measure of unity only by the beginning of the sixteenth century. In that century France looked to the east and southeast for opportunities for expansion, not to the west, though her seaboard towns did involve themselves deeply in the Newfoundland fishery and were the eventual sources for much of French activity in the western Atlantic. In the case of England the Tudors found themselves fully occupied in reestablishing royal control over their more distant lands in England and in assimilating Wales and attempting, unsuccessfully, to do the same for Scotland, while they were faced with continuing problems in creating some degree of stability in Ireland, which continued until Queen Elizabeth I died in 1603. In the succeeding reign of James I, there were more positive pressures on the part of both merchants and gentry to assert an expansionist policy. Both countries were hampered by religious problems. Henry VIII took over much of the property of the medieval church and Elizabeth had to find means of reconciling most of her subjects to a form of Protestant worship. In France religious wars broke out repeatedly and prevented effective unity in the latter part of the century, until the victory of Henry IV and the Edict of Nantes in 1598 gave France an opportunity to look westward with more effect than hitherto.

I cannot do more here than indicate some of the ways in which these influences, above all governmental influences, affected European attempts to open up North America by exploration for settlement. I may, perhaps, stress too much the mechanisms that governments tried to use to bring about colonial expansion and say too little on the nature of the brief colonial communities that were created and then failed to take root in so many instances. There is often a good deal of documentation on what governments hoped to achieve and too little on what was actually done. Yet as Webb suggested in the quotation with which I began, something in the way of information, and sometimes a great deal, emerged from even the most unsuccessful ventures.

Then too, there is a process of learning to be observed, not by any means a continuous improvement in the methods adopted or in the use of the knowledge acquired by earlier attempts, but it is possible to see that something survived from even the worst failures and in the end had enough influence to lead to a measure of success, although even here the amount and nature of the capital investment in colonization had a good deal to do with the narrowing of the margin between success and failure.

There is, obviously, one vital difference, already noticed in general terms, between the position of Spain and that of the other two states. At the time when Spain seriously became interested in North America she already had bases and an organization behind her ventures, first to the Caribbean, where the *audiencia* of Santo Domingo was a continuing if declining source of strength, but more especially in New Spain from the mid-1520s. In Mexico the viceroys had immense resources at their disposal and a substantial degree of autonomy, while at all times the central supervisory machinery created in Spain, the *Consejo de Indias* and the *Casa de la Contratación*, held the initiative and the ultimate responsibility for expansion and determined the form in which successive *entradas* into North America should be made.[2] The major problem is why with such resources Spain did not achieve more and do so more quickly than she did. Her success in so many areas was so spectacular that North America clearly presented unique problems. Basically, they perhaps centered around the slowly appreciated fact that North America did not appear to contain resources that could be exploited both quickly and profitably in areas accessible to Mexico or the Caribbean, however much these areas were to prove such a rich resource to Europeans in later times. More specifically, there were great problems in keeping in touch with expeditions that had apparently disappeared into the unknown, together with the obstructions of a bureaucratic system that often hampered rather than helped operations in which action was the key to success. We must take into account the fact that although interesting information, often embodied in spirited narratives such as that of Cabeza de Vaca,[3] came out of North America, much of the information sent back to Mexico or to Europe was about distances and physical resources and the nature and habits of the indigenous population, and was highly colored and

2. The basic textbook on the administration of the Spanish empire remains Clarence H. Haring, *The Empire in America* (New York: Oxford University Press, 1947).

3. Alvar Núñez Cabeza de Vaca, the English version of whose "Relation" is in David B. Quinn, Alison M. Quinn, and Susan Hillier, *New American World. A Documentary History of North America to 1612*, 5 vols. (New York: Arno Press and Hector Bye, 1979), II, 15–59, translated from *La relactión qui dio Núñez Cabeza de Vaca* (Zamora: Augustín de Paz and Juan Picardo for Pedro Musetti, 1542). Additional report in Quinn, *New American World*, II, 59–89.

unreliable.

Compared with Spain, both France and England were handicapped to some extent by the absence of institutions that were concerned with overseas developments. The way that Irish affairs, for example, were handled by both Crown and Privy Council must appear amateurish in the extreme when contrasted with the professionalism of the *Consejo de Indias*, however paper-ridden it tended to become. Much depended on the individual monarch. It is now clear that Henry VII was much more continuously interested in the western voyages than was once believed;[4] Henry VIII had only intermittent curiosity about the new lands when he saw what Spain was getting from her discoveries but did not apply himself to compete. It was not until Queen Elizabeth I had been on the throne for some years that gradually a focus of interest outside and inside her court was created and what we may call an "American" party emerged. It was small but occasionally influential and then only in the last third of her long reign and when she was becoming ever more closely involved in antagonism toward Spain. Thus, English concern with North America in the sixteenth century may be described as peripheral, and such efforts as were made to intervene there were empirical and lacked effective official support. A very different approach and a more varied, if not immediately more successful, response came with the accession of James I in 1603 and culminated during the next generation.

In France much of the initiative in some significant if intermittent achievements came from individual port towns and their merchants rather than from the state. This phenomenon was to influence the later forms that French intervention took in America. True, Francis I was personally interested in what lay across the western ocean, but his preoccupation with his European wars and with North America as a possible stepping stone to the Pacific governed most of the initiatives he took. The decade 1533–43, indeed, saw some significant initiatives that gave France some presumptive rights over the Saint Lawrence Valley. After 1547 the initiative passed from the Crown to the Huguenot Admiral of France, Gaspard de Coligny, whose attempted colonizing expeditions to Brazil in the 1550s and to modern South Carolina and Florida in the early 1560s were of considerable value in bringing information, despite their having only the tolerance if not the full support of the reigning monarchs. There were for many years only a few tentative efforts to maintain French claims, but under Henry IV it was different. As he slowly fought his way to unchallenged power between 1589 and 1598, Henry IV, backed by pressure from towns like Rouen, St. Malo, and La Rochelle, developed a strong sense that a French presence in North America was necessary. But be-

4. See ibid., I, 91–123.

fore his murder in 1610 only a little had been done, although what was done was important enough to make France a factor in North American affairs. His successors were to build only slowly on what Henry had begun.

It is well to remember that Spain continued into the seventeenth century to claim prior rights over the whole of North America, though she was prepared to admit some Portuguese rights to Newfoundland and its surrounding mainland areas. The long procession of enterprises that she sponsored in North America gave substance, it might appear, to that claim even if she had so few successes to record. Even if alarm at the increasing ramifications of her commitment led in the 1540s to limitations on new enterprises, her Florida and New Mexico ventures showed that she was not complacent or wholly inactive. Her Florida venture in the 1560s, in particular, gave her a permanent stake in southeastern North America, even if it was a much smaller one than had been intended. Spain continued to base her claim to the widest authority on the papal division of the non-European world in 1493, but as late as 1607, Philip III's minister, the duke of Lerma, could assert that the Americas were "to them *Regum Novum* . . . The division and possession was theirs and therefore lawful both by reasons of nature and nation to appropriate it to themselves and exclude others."[5]

Spain's expectations in North America were not only of gold and silver and jewels; she also expected to create great estates such as had been built up in Mexico, Péru, and elsewhere, based partly on a pastoral economy brought from Spain but primarily dependent on an experienced and servile population of native farmers who would supply, as the people of Mexico and Péru did, the labor force needed to operate estates and mines and also to provide a surplus of food for the urban complexes that were at the core of Spanish society in both the Old and the New World. North America did not do this. Except to some degree in the Pueblo country, Indians were not tied to the soil, even if in many places they grew crops; they were not content to serve as laborers and they resented rather than tolerated alien European intervention and harassed its representatives in most places whenever they could.

The one incentive that remained alive in the Spanish attempt to advance into North America was the missionary impulse. The expansion of Spain in the Indies was considered to be a function of her mission to convert the heathen. This had peculiar connotations in Spanish thinking; it was an important part of Spain's imperial mission and had little relation to the Counter-Reformation. Just as the Jesuits under

5. David B. Quinn, "James I and the Beginnings of Empire in America," *Journal of Imperial and Commonwealth History* 2 (1974): 146; below, p. 334.

their Spanish founder had been "soldiers of Christ" in many parts of the Portuguese and Spanish empire, so in North America the Franciscans took their place (the Jesuits indeed retreated in 1572 from all attempts to convert North American Indians). It was the Franciscans who dragged the Spanish forward, hiding their fierce aggressiveness under a cloak of meekness. It was they who eventually made Florida an extended mission field when secular Spaniards had failed to colonize it or to maintain more than a military outpost there, and it was they, as we will see, who involved Spain irrevocably in New Mexico. Part of the ardor of missionary Spain arose from the blood of the martyrs. The Spanish had an impressive roll of them before the end of the sixteenth century — a Dominican on the Gulf Coast, Jesuits on the Chesapeake, Franciscans in the Sea Islands, and another string of Franciscans in New Mexico from 1542 onward. This characteristic masochistic reaction of Christianity to the challenge of heathendom continued to provide incentives to expansion, though it was dulled for a time after the first third of the seventeenth century.

The incentives of both French and English were more prosaic. Both hoped to get through, or in the case of the English, to get around, North America to the Pacific. This was an element in much of the exploration and attempted colonization by both countries. Both set increasing store on the Newfoundland fishery. Although the English were the first to aspire, unavailingly, to take it over in the 1580s, it remained significant in the minds of Frenchmen as well. But from this point the English and French diverged. The English set their minds on the sale to the Indians of English cloth and metal objects but were unsure of what they expected in return. The English convinced themselves that North America in latitudes comparable with those of Spain and Portugal would produce Mediterranean-type agricultural products. They also hoped for metals, precious or otherwise, and so did the French. But the French concentrated on commodities, and to their merchants the fur trade gradually became all-important. Colonization, when it came, had to be fitted into fur trading, while Frenchmen, after countless wars at home, did not for a long time wish to leave France for North America. English men and women proved more willing to leave home; they set their eyes on land, land where they would cultivate exotic crops and richly endow their country and themselves with their produce. Only later in New England did the settlers reconcile themselves to growing English crops and Indian cultivars. English people wished to move as families to new land in North America, in harmony with Indians if they would surrender land to the newcomers, in hostility if they did not. Spain was only interested in the domination of great areas with large estates (if there were no mines), whereas Englishmen were content to exploit small or moderate-sized holdings (larger, however, than they might ever acquire at home). For the French, North

America was an area of commercial opportunity, where an adventurous man could make a good living and return with his surplus to France. These are a few of the broad contrasts in the approaches of the three European peoples with whom we are concerned.

What is clear is that Europeans of whatever nation, at most times and places, believed that they had a right to enter and occupy lands in any part of North America they fancied, without any regard for the rights and the safety, even the survival, of those whose possession had been ensured for millennia without interference from the outside. Spanish arrogance in this regard was without comparison. Buoyed by her sense of mission, Spain considered it her duty and her right to occupy non-Christian lands and subordinate non-Christian peoples, even if she did slowly evolve rules that gave them, at least on paper, some legal protection. The English, for the most part, if with some exceptions, followed the same path more slowly, perhaps with less arrogance and less of a sense of mission. The French were the least concerned with disrupting and taking over native territory until missionary activities were added to the fur trade, when she too became involved in the long genocidal process that was to mark European intervention in North America as it had done already in so many parts of the Spanish dominions.

There is a certain degree of irony, even of humor, in the fact that both Spain and England endorsed the first major explorers who were to make an impression in the lands of the western Atlantic with such grandiose paper powers and authority. Columbus, it will be remembered, in the Capitulations and *titulo* of April, 1492,[6] was to be admiral and viceroy of all lands found by him, and to enjoy these offices and pass them on to his heirs, while he was also to have a tenth of all the bullion and jewels he might find. These terms were ludicrously inappropriate to such a minuscule expedition as this when its objective was the Asiatic mainland, where it was known that great empires existed and would present an impenetrable barrier to such a handful of men as Columbus commanded. These articles were to cause endless trouble when his discoveries proved to be only those of primitive and unremunerative Caribbean islands. As for John Cabot, his sons, and successors, the patent granted to them in March, 1496, by Henry VII, accorded them the rights to occupy as governors under the Crown all lands "in whatever part of the world which before this time were unknown to all Christians."[7] These provisions were as unrealistic as those granted to Columbus, even if never realized in any manner whatsoever.

6. In English, Samuel Eliot Morison, *Journals and Other Documents on the Life and Voyages of Christopher Columbus* (New York: Heritage Press, 1963), pp. 27–30.

7. In Latin and English, H. P. Biggar, *The Precursors of Jacques Cartier* (Ottawa: Public Archives of Canada, 1911), pp. 7–10.

By the time Ponce de León began planning conquests to the north of the Caribbean Spain had begun to plan expansion by grants on paper which both licensed and limited the activities of her *conquistadores* in their *entradas* into new territories. To follow these Capitulations in detail is to see how Spain's concern with North America developed, even if the results hoped for were not achieved and the grantees in practice had little intention of abiding by their contracts, although a few might in the end be punished for glaring failures to do so.

The first Spanish grant to Ponce de León on February 23, 1512, was simple and nontechnical; bureaucracy had not yet come into its own.[8] If he could discover Bimini he could occupy it and make settlements, though fortresses, if needed, would be provided by the Crown. After his first voyage, the Capitulations of September, 1514, were much more formal. By that time, following complaints about the treatment of native peoples in the Islands, a cynical device had been invented to provide a nominal shield for future *conquistadores*. This was the *requerimiento*, a proclamation to be read in Spanish to any concentrations of native people the invaders encountered, which in Spanish (which they could not understand) commanded them to become subjects of Spain and accept Christianity.[9] If they did not acquiesce (and how could they?), then they could be treated as enemies and enslaved or distributed in *repartimiento* (almost the same thing) among the Spaniards. Ponce de León was to use this contract as the first step toward seizing and dividing the land that he had found. Other than some limits to the numbers of Indians that could be assigned to a single Spaniard, the grantee was to have unlimited powers. This grant became, with variations, the pattern for most later Capitulations. But those signed with Ayllon on June 12, 1523, were much more bland.[10] The *licenciado* was to explore lands discovered between thirty-five and thirty-seven degrees north latitude (between thirty-three and thirty-five degrees would be more accurate I believe). There was no mention of the *requerimiento*, although the Christian religion was to be spread by the priests Ayllon was to take with him. Indians were to be taken

8. Capitulations with Pedro Ponce de León, in English, Quinn, *New American World*, I, 231–33; in Spanish, *Colección de documentos inéditos de Indias*, 1st series (42 vols. Madrid, 1864–84), XIII, 26–32. There is a brief overall view of these arrangements for North America in Eugene Lyon, "Spain's Sixteenth Century North American Settlement Attempts," *Florida Historical Quarterly* 59 (1980–81): 275–91, the main focus being Florida.

9. In English, John H. Parry and Robert G. Keith, *New Iberian World. A Documentary History of the Discovery and Settlement of Latin America to the Early 17th Century*, 5 vols. (New York: Times Books and Hector and Rose, 1984), I, 285–90.

10. Capitulations with Lucas Vásques de Ayllon, in English, Quinn, *New American World*, I, 249–53; in Spanish, Fernández de Navarrete, *Obras*, 4 vols. (Madrid: Biblioteca de Autores Españoles, 1964), II, 102–107.

into service only for wages and were to be treated well; this followed the disgraceful exploitation of captives as slaves in Hispaniola when taken by Ayllon's men in an earlier raid. There was much detail on what sort of colony was to be created. The governor was to have a great estate for himself, but the settlers were to be placed in towns under their own magistrates. He was to pay for this, although subsidies might be given later if he began well. Ayllon did indeed establish the town of San Miguel de Gualdape somewhere on the South Carolina coast, conceivably on the Waccamaw River, but we know more about the quarrels that took place when Ayllon died than we do about the settlement itself. Indeed, it came voluntarily to an end, though many colonists were lost on their way back to the Caribbean. Ponce de León had failed utterly and died of wounds in 1521. Ayllon was only a shade more effective in 1526, even if for a short time a Spanish colony subsisted on North American land.

There was no respite after these failures. Narváez on December 11, 1526, was commissioned to conquer and settle the Gulf coast at his own cost, except for three forts which the Crown would maintain.[11] According to the Capitulations he was not only to be governor-for-life but *adelantado*, a hereditary governor-conquerer (the title had not been granted to his precursors), passing his powers on to his heirs, but accompanied by treasury officials (*oficiales reales*) to see that he paid dues to the Crown. Settlers were to be given grants according to social status, and *caballeros* were to get double quantities of land. His own estate was to be a large one. What was new was the incorporation of a letter dated November 14, 1526, one sent throughout the empire, enjoining governors to protect the rights of the natives and to limit their exploitation of them, although the establishment of missions was to have a high priority.[12] This was a consequence of the growing fear in Spain that labor would be wiped out in the course of conquest, while souls would not be saved from heathendom if cruelty and murder were to be permitted without limitations. Narváez, as is only too well known, failed utterly; his expedition was lost and only the apparently miraculous appearance of Cabeza de Vaca in western Mexico in 1536 brought news of the disaster as well as amazing tales of the interior. This is a case where Webb's dictum, cited at the beginning, holds true.

There was then a breathing space until one of the conquerors of Péru came forward with stolen gold to finance a great *entrada* into North America. The Capitulations made with Hernando de Soto on

11. Capitulations with Panfilo de Narváez, in English, Quinn, *New American World*, II, 4–10; in Spanish, *Colección de documentos inéditos de Indias*, 1st series, XXII, 224–45.

12. In English, Quinn, *New American World*, II, 6–10; in Spanish, Archivo de Indias, Seville, Justicia 750A, ff. 236–87.

April 28, 1537, were the most elaborate to date.[13] He was to take on the conquest of all the lands previously granted to Ayllon and Narváez, was to be governor and *adelantado*, and was to establish colonies wherever he could, with assignments to settlers according to rank, outside his own great estate. But he was not to escape some royal supervision: his chief justice was to be appointed by the Crown, as were the treasury officials, while the letter of 1526 was to govern his relations with the native peoples, and he was bound to do his utmost to bring them to Christianity. His great expedition did not get under way until 1539, but its wanderings over much of the southern part of what is now the United States have led historians a dance, as he chopped and changed his plans, moved from one winter quarter to another chasing moonshine gold, making no settlements, and finally dying in the wilderness, leaving Moscoso, daringly, to bring a substantial remnant of his men home in 1543. The contract system had brought no rewards, only disaster.

Two Spanish initiatives differed fundamentally from those covered by Capitulations. The first was Coronado's in 1540.[14] Directed to the supposed Seven Cities of Cíbola, it was primarily an official advance into hitherto unconquered territory. Coronado carried it through effectively (if not without bloodshed), putting the Pueblo country, parts of the Great Plains, and the lower stretch of the Colorado River on the map, but returning with a disciplined force when remaining seemed pointless, without promise of a civilized society in the interior. He did little to support the friars who accompanied him, although a few remained behind to attain martyrdom, but his expedition was efficient and in its way successful in dispelling myths and providing new geographical insights into America. On his return, he was not accorded the honor he deserved.

The second venture of this sort was even more ambitious. Luna was equipped by the viceroy of New Spain in 1559 with a large expedition that was to land on the Gulf coast of Florida and make its way to the coast of South Carolina to take possession of land around the Punta de Santa Elena, where French privateers had been active.[15] Had

13. In English, Quinn, *New American World*, II, 93–96; in Spanish, Buckingham Smith, *Colección de Varios Documentos para la Historia de la Florida y Tierras Adyacentes* (London: Trübner, 1857), I, 140–46.

14. Fully documented in George P. Hammond and Agapito Rey, *Narratives of the Coronado Expedition, 1500–1542* (Albuquerque: University of New Mexico Press, 1940). The appointment of Francisco Vásques de Coronado is extracted in English, pp. 83–86; in Spanish, in *Hispanic American Historical Review* 20 (1940): 83–87.

15. The expedition of Tristán de Luna is fully covered in Herbert I. Priestly, *The Luna Papers, 1559–1561*, 2 vols. (Deland: Florida State Historical Society, 1928), instructions in Spanish and English, I, 18–43; in English also in Quinn, *New American World*, II, 207–11.

he done so, the whole of the Florida peninsula would have been secured for Spain. Spaniards and the Indians of Mexico were to become colonists on the land. He was not only to have treasury officials to keep watch on him but he was to consult a junta of his leading men when it was necessary to change plans. Almost everything went wrong, largely because the geographical information brought back by Soto's men was wholly inadequate. We know almost nothing of the temporary settlement at Nanipacana (though a town plan was included in his instructions). We do know that ignorance, misuse of supplies, and inertia prevented any effective move toward the Atlantic coast. Finally, Villafañe took over in 1561 and was ordered to take a colony by sea to settle Santa Elena if he could find it. He could not and had to return. Spain had not yet learned how to colonize in North America. In 1561 orders came from Spain that no more attempts were to be made in Florida.

The French Huguenots changed all that. First they settled a small group on Port Royal Sound—the Spanish Santa Elena—in 1562. Although they deserted it in 1563, a larger force under Laudonnière settled on the Saint John s River in Florida in 1564, the possible precursor of many others, as Spanish reports had it. This time a combined operation was planned. Pedro Menéndez de Avilés, an able and rich naval commander, was to be *adelantado* of Florida with wide powers and was to use his own resources as well as the extensive official help to be given.[16] His Capitulations echoed those of his predecessors in other respects. His destruction of the French settlement and the settlers alike left him free to plant soldiers and clergy round the peninsula, establish a base at San Agustín (which had to be moved later), occupy San Mateo, where the French had been, and finally select Santa Elena as a site for a garrison and a city, the latter to be inhabited by tough Asturian farmers. But Menéndez was distracted by other calls for his services; supplies failed several times; the outposts were withdrawn under Indian pressure; and his own great slave-run estate was never laid out. San Agustín lost inhabitants rather than grew (it was laid out, we think, rather on the lines of the plan with which Luna had been entrusted in 1559); the settlers at Santa Elena were harassed by Indians and by the soldiers of the garrison alike. Gradually Florida declined until it was only a chain of small garrisons, despite a further injection of settlers in Santa Elena. After Menéndez's death in 1574, Florida was soon threatened with total desertion as most of the gar-

16. Capitulations with Pedro Menéndez de Avilés, in English, Quinn, *New American World*, II, pp. 384–89; in Spanish, *Colección de documentos inéditos de Indias*, 1st series, XXIII, 242–58. See especially Eugene Lyon, *The Enterprise of Florida, 1565–1568* (Gainesville: University Presses of Florida, 1976); he prints a supplementary contract of March 15, 1565 (Lyon, *Enterprise of Florida*, pp. 213–19).

rison and then all of the Santa Elena settlers departed.[17] But Pedro
Menéndez Marqués, the old man's nephew, restored a limited Spanish presence; San Agustín began to grow again. Yet in 1586 Drake cut
down San Agustín to the ground and it had to be rebuilt from scratch,
while Santa Elena was abandoned. Slowly, San Agustín settled down
as a frontier garrison town, kept alive only by new threats of English
intervention, and populated mainly by the soldiers' wives, a few merchants and craftsmen, and by Indian-occupied suburbs that provided
a market. The town scarcely changed for several generations. But
Florida, for all its problems, did become the one solid achievement
of Spanish colonization in the sixteenth and early seventeenth century. San Agustín, its plaza, its church and monastery, its tiled houses,
and its large wooden fort constituted a genuine accomplishment even
if a small one.

Apart from the Luna and Menéndez expeditions, undertaken primarily for strategic reasons, the failure of both Soto and Coronado
to found effective colonies or to discover workable mineral resources
marked the end of Spanish initiatives in North America for a long time.
The New Laws of the Indies in 1542 brought a stronger humanitarian
impulse into official policy toward the Indians, even if it did not put
a *terminus ad quem* to the holding of Indians in *encomienda,* that
is, in tutelage to great landholders. The laws were followed by the setting of a limit to further expansion. In the future there was only to
be infilling in areas already under Spanish control, with one elastic
proviso: if missionaries penetrated beyond the known limits, then soldiers might be sent in to protect them and their converts. The mission
field was not to prove too profitable in North America in the following
years. Fray Cancer was killed in western Florida in 1549 when he attempted an unprotected mission; a Jesuit group was wiped out on
Chesapeake Bay in 1571 while attempting a comparable venture. Even
under protection, Jesuits so completely failed to make converts in Florida that they left the area in 1572. Though the Franciscans penetrated
tentatively into Florida in the years following 1573, they made little
progress, and their missions were marred in 1576 and 1597 by revolts
in which missionary lives were lost. But the urge to persist, to find
ways in which they could become effective, survived. In the meantime, the *Recopilación* of the New Laws of the Indies in 1573 offered
some fresh cautions and some fresh loopholes for expansion. One notable paragraph stated: "The term 'conquest' is not to be used to describe exploring expeditions. These expeditions are to be made in the
spirit of peace and love, and we do not wish them to be described by

17. Documents in Quinn, *New American World,* II, 277–471; see also David B.
Quinn, *North America from Earliest Discovery to First Settlements* (New York: Harper
and Row, 1977), pp. 240–61.

a word that might be thought to authorize the use of force against the Indians."[18] However, there were provisions for new settlements inside or outside existing borders. The key passages are: "In planning settlements, whether in territory already explored, pacified, and brought to obedience to Us, or in areas to be explored and pacified in future . . . the land should be inhabited by natives who can be evangelized, that being the chief object of settlements authorised by Us."[19] It is then set down that "once the general area has been selected by competent explorers, the sites for principal towns and satellite villages should be chosen. To avoid injury to the natives, they should be unoccupied or freely offered by their inhabitants." At the same time "Indians may be recruited for the new settlements as laborers and craftsmen, provided that they go voluntarily." This was all very humane, if scarcely practical. Indeed, the decree went on to provide that *adelantados* might still be appointed with the rights to hand on their governorship to an heir; they might, if they acquitted themselves well when subjected to the *residencia*, the periodic review of their performance, be entrusted with perpetual ownership of the land and ennobled. Moreover, the *adelantado* might still place Indians in *encomienda* (under legal restrictions on what tribute might be exacted from them) for three generations. The old system was in fact given a humanitarian gloss, genuine on the part of the bureaucrats who drew up the decree, but impossible to enforce at a distance from centers of effective authority. Under these provisions, however, the Franciscan Order, increasingly powerful in Mexico, could continue to exert pressure to expand outward, and to demand civilian protection, even if this meant extending the range of existing authorities in Florida or forcing the civilian authorities to take on new colonizing responsibilities in New Mexico.

Compared with the Spanish initiatives between 1512 and 1543, those of the French look puny. Spain was impelled by the success of her earlier conquests, by the expectation of land and Indians to exploit, of treasure to be found, and not least by missionary aspirations. France, in contrast, had mainly commercial objectives, inspired by Breton and Norman towns and by the desire to find a western way to Asia. Verrazzano did indeed bring the coastline of much of eastern North America to French attention in 1524, but he had found no passage to the South Sea nor indeed did he raise any commercial expectations.[20] But in the late 1520s reports from fishermen suggested that there were water passages into the interior north of Newfoundland. These inspired Francis I to inquire from Pope Clement VII in 1533 if France was excluded

18. Parry and Keith, *New Iberian World*, I, 368.

19. Ibid., I, 370-71.

20. Lawrence C. Wroth, *Voyages of Giovanni da Verrazzano* (New Haven, Conn.: Yale University Press, 1970), is the authoritative narrative.

from the Americas. The reply, not couched in formal terms, was that as North America had not been found in 1493 France was not excluded from it.[21] When Cartier sailed in 1534 it was to explore these tentative openings, and his exploration of the Gulf of Saint Lawrence might not have had further results had he not brought home Indians from far upstream who inspired further ventures. Cartier did penetrate a thousand miles from the Atlantic in 1535 and survived a Canadian winter at Québec, but he brought only faint hope of passages to the Pacific, though rather more hope of founding a fur trade. Cartier's commission in 1535 merely empowered him to search beyond the New Lands (*oultre les Terres Neufves*), not to appropriate lands or settle.[22] But since Spain was still sending her great expeditions into the interior, even if their failure was not yet known, Francis decided to imitate her at least to the extent of commissioning Roberval as lieutenant general of the lands that Cartier had discovered and authorizing him to settle them and govern them.[23] Cartier went ahead in 1541 to prepare the way for settlers, and although he did build a base on the Saint Lawrence, his men insisted on returning after a single winter. Roberval, bringing gentlemen and their wives, craftsmen, and convicts to labor for him, also managed only a single winter, returning in disgrace from his strongly fortified settlement, *Francy Roy*, in 1543. With his return and disgrace, France's attempt to imitate Spain's efforts in North America ended for more than a generation. If the Huguenot colonies, only semiofficial ones, had succeeded, the tale might have been different.

As for England, there was virtually no enthusiasm for a long time, although it began to be talked about in the 1550s and a reinforcement of the Huguenot colony in South Carolina was planned but not carried out in 1563. It was not until the 1570s that a small group of enthusiasts for North American colonization appeared. The first English plans and the revival of French ambitions to appropriate parts of North America appeared almost at the same time. In March, 1577, Henry III commissioned the Marquis de la Roche to appropriate such lands there as he could master,[24] and this was followed in January, 1578, by a formal commission to him as viceroy of New France, a territory which was not defined. His attempts to set expeditions on foot in the next six years came to nothing. But on the English side, the coincidence

---

21. Charles-André Julien, *Les voyages de découverte et les premiers Etablissements* (Paris: Presses universitaires de France, 1948), pp. 115–16.

22. H. P. Biggar, *Collection of Documents Relating to Jacques Cartier and the Sieur de Roberval* (Ottawa: Public Archives of Canada, 1930), pp. 44–45 (in French).

23. Ibid., pp. 178–85.

24. Alfred Ramé, *Documents inédits sur le Canada* (Paris: Librairie Tross, 1867), 2nd series, pp. 6–10 (in French).

in time is striking.

In 1577 a patent to a commercial syndicate to exploit the supposed gold mines on Baffin Island, revealed in an unsuccessful attempt to discover a Northwest Passage a year before, led to a spacious grant to Sir Humphrey Gilbert in June, 1578.[25] This empowered the Englishman to occupy and colonize, with himself as governor with wide powers, lands hitherto unknown to or occupied by any Christians. This area was too vague for Spanish agents to penetrate for some time, but it involved in fact a preemptive strike at the North American shores between thirty-four and forty-five degrees north, a bid to forestall Spanish Florida from further expansion. Although authorized by Queen Elizabeth I, the venture was to be a privately financed one. Gilbert had to find financial assistance where he could. Between 1578 and 1583 he did his best to do so, selling much unexplored land to subscribers to his ventures, the first expedition never reaching America and the second in 1583 leading to the formal annexation of Newfoundland, though no more, followed by his death at sea on his way home. The transfer of his patent to his half-brother Walter Ralegh in February, 1584, showed that the "American" party at court and among the gentry, with a little support from London merchants, was a serious one.[26]

After an initial reconnaissance, the establishment at the "New Fort" on Roanoke Island of a little more than one hundred men, who survived there in 1585–86 with small loss for ten months, was a significant beginning. This was essentially a colony of soldiers and specialists. The site did not prove suitable for a privateering base against Spain at a time when its mounting hostility to her was leading England into open war. The colony did not discover, any more than comparable Spanish ventures, any important mineral resources. It did find that Indians resented English occupation of their lands, but intensive geographical and other surveys led to discovery of a deepwater harbor, Chesapeake Bay, and land to the south of it not fully occupied by native settlements. Although lack of supplies led the colonists to return prematurely with Sir Francis Drake, the way was paved for a genuine colony of settlement, which was planted in 1587 after many mishaps in the lands that constitute the most southerly part of modern Virginia. These colonists were only occasionally remembered during the long sea war with Spain. They had not been found again before fresh English ventures began in earnest in 1607, having been wiped out shortly before by the jealous Indian overlord of the Virginia Tidewater,

25. David B. Quinn, *The Voyages and Colonising Enterprises of Sir Humphrey Gilbert* (London: The Hakluyt Society, 2nd series, nos. 83–84, 1940), I, 188–97.

26. David B. Quinn, *The Roanoke Voyages, 1584–1590* (Cambridge: The Hakluyt Society, 2nd series, nos. 104–105), I, 82–89.

Powhatan.[27] The Roanoke voyages did much to create a tradition of attempted colonization, but the objectives of the English differed from those of France and Spain. Hopes of trade with the Indians were indeed raised, but the main emphasis was on settling people, in the belief that England was overpopulated. The colonists were to cultivate Mediterranean and subtropical products, which, it was believed, could flourish between thirty-five and thirty-seven degrees north latitude in North America — olives, vines, sugar, pineapples, and the like — though the Lost Colonists of 1587 hoped that Indian cultivars — corn, beans, and squashes — could provide basic sustenance for the English people who grew them. English hopes of reviving settlement lingered on through the war period and were kept alive by the publication of narratives of the voyagers and colonists.

France was held back from major colonizing activity in America by the wars of religion, especially by the war of succession, 1589–98, but Henry IV, once firmly on the throne, rapidly revived them. He recommissioned La Roche as lieutenant general of Canada, Newfoundland, Labrador, and Norumbega — the whole stretch between about forty and sixty degrees north latitude.[28] This was in direct defiance of Spain and also in competition with English claims. It made sense, for French commercial interests had been expanding. France's share of the fisheries off Newfoundland and the Maritimes had been growing, and her merchants were fur trading in the Maritimes, the Gulf of Saint Lawrence, and the Saint Lawrence River (the summer fur-trading mart at Tadoussac had been active for some years so that to empower some individual with royal authority over these activities was not unreasonable). La Roche, however, concentrated his activities on the commercial exploitation of Sable Island from 1598 onward, but the venture ended in disaster in 1603. Meantime, merchants were given a license to occupy a post at Tadoussac, but it failed in 1600–1601 to establish itself. La Roche was set aside in 1603, since his oversight on behalf of the Crown had had no effect. Pierre du Gua, Sieur de Monts, commissioned for ten years to exploit the territory south of Cape Breton, was to be financed by levies on the Saint Lawrence fur traders.[29] His first colonial site on Sainte Croix Island, near the Bay of Fundy, was laid out in 1604 on civilian lines, but severe weather forced him to

27. David B. Quinn, *Set Fair for Roanoke* (Chapel Hill: University of North Carolina Press, 1985), pp. 341–78.

28. Marc Lescarbot, *History of New France*, ed. W. L. Grant and H. P. Biggar, 3 vols. (Toronto: Champlain Society, 1907–14), II, 196–201.

29. Ibid., II, 211–26. The narrative by Samuel de Champlain forms the basic source. Champlain, *Works*, 7 vols. (Toronto: Champlain Society, 1922–36), I, 233–469. See David B. Quinn, "The Preliminaries to New France. Site Selection for the Fur Trade by the French," *Wirtschaftskräfte und Wirtschaftsweg* (Nuremburg: In Kommission bei Klett-Cotta, 1978), IV, 9–25.

move across the bay to found Port Royal. There de Monts developed the characteristic type of French trading settlement, the *habitation* — living quarters and storehouses within a single defensible structure. From there explorers worked their way around the Maritimes and to southern New England. But his patent was withdrawn in 1607 when it became clear that furs in sufficient quantity were not to be obtained in this area. Champlain, employed by de Monts, had shown himself to be a shrewd and effective observer of the geography and resources of the area. In 1608 it was he who was entrusted by the merchants, under royal authority, to found the first permanent settlement on the Saint Lawrence. Québec was established in 1608 with its own *habitation*, copied and developed from that at Port Royal, as the base from which fur trading up and down the river and the lands nearby could be carried on. France was set in her own peculiar mission in North America, which we may characterize as to use as few men as possible to maximize profits. From 1612 there was a nonresident royal governor, but with Champlain as his lieutenant. Before 1627 this was all, except for a few tentative missionary attempts, which came to little. Trudel has called the period down to 1627 "Le Comptoir"—the period when the exchange of goods for furs constituted almost the whole of France's activity.[30] There were plans to do more, but nothing happened until after 1633, when colonization and missionary work began in earnest. France in the sixteenth and early seventeenth centuries showed little consistent desire to stake out territorial claims and to reinforce them by colonies. So long as trade could be safeguarded and developed, that was enough. This differed greatly from the designs of Spain and even of England in this period.

It was Spain that, after its long respite from new adventures in North America, took up again the colonization of New Mexico as her last early venture into the continent. As northern Mexico began to lose its attractions, though its mineral wealth was far from worked out, parties of adventurers made their way from Santa Bárbara northward to the Pueblo region on the upper Rio Grande. These expeditions aimed to explore for minerals and to carry a few friars in search of new Indian communities to convert, even to colonize, between 1580 and 1591.[31] The authorities in Mexico were at first skeptical, then hostile, and finally, largely under Franciscan pressure (the Order being now a powerful force there), inclined toward official intervention. It took some time

30. Marcel Trudel, *Histoire de la Nouvelle France*, II. *Le Comptoir, 1604–27.* (Ottawa: Fides, 1906); Champlain, *Works*, II, 1–226, contains the crucial account of the establishment of the French on the Saint Lawrence, 1608–12.

31. These are fully documented in George P. Hammond and Agapito Rey, *The Rediscovery of New Mexico, 1580–1594* (Albuquerque: University of New Mexico Press, 1966).

to find an entrepreneur who would invest his own money in an enterprise that also had official backing and financial support. Oñate finally emerged as such a figure. It took some additional time for him to reach an agreement with the viceroy, Velasco, the contract to which he agreed in September, 1595, being very different in form from earlier Capitulations but reminiscent of them in the new circumstances of the definitions under which new discoveries could be made.[32] The primary document consists of a number of requests from Oñate with answers by Velasco. Most of the requests the latter was able to say that he could accept, provided they were kept within the limits of the printed Ordinances of 1573. These Oñate referred to by number, and it is clear that the viceroy was being very careful to keep within the limitations set down there, which, as it has been shown, were indeed wide enough. But Oñate wanted more than he could be given. Some of his requests were absurdly ambitious; he wished his ultimate authority to extend from the Pacific to the Atlantic and to have his province detached from New Spain and come directly under the *Consejo de Indias* so as to have its own *audiencia* or court of appeal. About these demands Velasco temporized as he had no power to grant them. In any event, he was just winding up his affairs before handing over to the new viceroy, Monterrey, who vigorously repudiated such pretensions and made it clear in his final contract that Oñate was going as a governor subject to recall. In 1598 Oñate finally reached New Mexico and formally annexed it to Spain. His train of soldiers, civilians, and friars (eight of them) had a very mixed experience in the Pueblo country, sending out some useful and some useless reconnaissance missions and installing the friars in many of the pueblos (they took the one they named Santo Domingo for their own headquarters), while Oñate quartered himself first in one and then in another pueblo. These were not entirely unsuited to Spaniards (reinforced in 1599). Coronado had likened them to the Granada of his day, but we have little information on how daily life was conducted, except that soldiers and civilians for the most part, and some of the friars also, found it intolerable: While Oñate was absent on an expedition in 1601, the greater part of them deserted the colony and retreated to Mexico. Velasco, who returned to Mexico as viceroy soon after, refused Oñate's demands for reinforcements and for punishment of the deserters and eventually relieved him of his office in 1607 but required him to remain at the pueblo of

32. The agreements between Juan de Oñate and the viceroy, Luis de Velasco, are in George P. Hammond and Agapito Rey, *Oñate: Colonizer of New Mexico*, 2 vols. (Albuquerque: University of New Mexico Press, 1952), I, 42–64. The volumes contain all that is known about New Mexico between 1584 and 1609.

San Gabriel until a final decision could be reached.[33] The Franciscans in Mexico and in Spain pleaded that they had converted so many thousands of Pueblo Indians already (a vast exaggeration if not a downright lie) that Philip III was persuaded to reestablish the colony. Peralta was sent north in 1609 to do so. It was made clear that he was to be simply a salaried governor, subject to orders from Mexico, and his contingent of fifty soldiers, a handful of civilian colonists, and a dozen friars showed that little opposition was expected. The greatly divided Pueblo groups were not inclined to resist. Peralta's main task, as set out in the ordinances, was to establish a city as a nucleus of Spanish power, and so the *Villa* of San Francisco de la Santa Fé was duly established in 1610. We know very little of its character. An adobe church, which soon fell down, official quarters for the governor, officials, and soldiers, and a monastery at least took form around the central plaza. But forced labor had to be used. In the meantime the friars, distributed among the pueblos, were asserting their moral authority over the individual villages, using Pueblo labor to construct churches and serve them in other ways. The Franciscan commissary, Ordoñez, who had followed Peralta, proved to be a man of paranoic ambitions; he declared himself at one point to have all the authority that any pope ever had and soon was treating Peralta as his servant. A grim struggle ensued, the friars dividing soldiers and citizens into two parties. Peralta had lost much of his authority by the time he was relieved in 1614.[34] Although the struggle of church (embodied in the friars) and state (personified by the governor) continued, a *modus vivendi* was slowly established. By means of a strong public relations campaign the friars won official support in Mexico and eventually an assurance of generous supplies for themselves and less generous ones for the officials and soldiers. The colony survived but remained small, except for the attached Christianized Pueblo peoples. They, in fact, became as Catholic as seemed necessary on the surface, while continuing in secret their native religious observances. New Mexico remained an anomaly, hundreds of miles from the Mexican border, never powerful or populous, but a showpiece for supposed Franciscan missionary triumphs. It was to be the last Spanish intrusion into North America for almost a century, and it did little to demonstrate that Spain was prepared to con-

33. Ibid., I, 32–35. A Spanish study of Oñate's venture, Luis Navarro García, *La conquista de Nuevo Mexico* (Madrid: Cultura Hispanica del Centro Ibero-américano de Cooperación, 1978) heads its last chapter "Tierra de Desencanto."

34. Pedro de Peralta's instructions of March 30, 1609, were printed by Lancing B. Bloom, "Ynstrucción a Peralta por Vi-Rey," *New Mexico Historical Review* 4 (1929): 178–87, although the translation is not too reliable. The best-documented study of Peralta's experiences at the hands of Fray Isidro Ordoñez is France V. Scholes, *Church and State in New Mexico, 1610–1650* (Albuquerque: Historical Society of New Mexico, Publications in History, No. 7, 1937), pp. 19–67.

quer or rule any substantial part of the continent.

The English contribution to North American colonization of course begins with the Roanoke voyages and all the pro-colonization arguments that accompanied them. But it was not until another dynasty took over in England that continuous attention was paid to transatlantic settlement. James I, if inclined to be timid when threatened by Spain, was by instinct imperially minded. He had reason to be: he was the first unchallenged ruler of Ireland for many centuries; he joined the kingdoms of England and Scotland in his person and tried to join them constitutionally as Great Britain. It was almost inevitable that he would assist attempts to penetrate North America. Moreover, there was now merchant capital available in London, permitting the long process of colonization (longer and more painful than had been expected) to begin. The Virginia Company charter of April, 1606, took up where the Elizabethans had left off, but with a difference.[35] Whereas all sixteenth-century grants of monopoly for exclusive trading rights or settlement projects had been solely private enterprises financed by individuals, as were so many of those of Spain, with royal authority remaining in the background, the Virginia charter attempted to join English and Spanish traditions. The companies that would exploit the long coastline between the old limits (thirty-four to forty-five degrees) were to be merchant companies, that of Plymouth to concern itself with Norumbega (the later New England) and that of London with the Chesapeake. Yet, they were to be governed by rules laid down by a royal council, imitating in a sense the *Consejo de Indias*, but composed of relatively minor officials and nonofficial merchants and gentlemen. Settlement was to be financed by the companies, which had much freedom of action, subject to·directives from the royal council. The Plymouth Company's settlement on the Kennebec did not survive more than one winter;[36] it concentrated too much on providing against a French maritime threat, which did not in fact exist, and too little on exploiting the fur trade with expertise that could have been learned from the French or even the local Indians.

The Chesapeake settlement was different. It was to be located well inland and was to concentrate on exploiting indigenous products and reviving the mythical suitability of Virginia for exotic cultivars, while not forgetting to search for minerals. Decimated by disease in the first few months, the colony of little more than a hundred men could do little. Reinforcements in 1608 provoked Indian hostility, which intensified when new settlements were begun by a larger influx of colonists

---

35. April 10, 1606. Quinn, *New American World*, IV, 197–98.

36. David B. Quinn and Alison M. Quinn, *The English New England Voyages, 1602–1608* (London: The Hakluyt Society, 2nd series, no. 161, 1983), pp. 376–468.

in 1609. The instructions of the royal council did not help.[37] In any event, the existence of the council tended to irritate Spain further, even though she had protested since 1606, and so the second charter in 1609[38] (1) left the London Company to take on some royal powers of direction and, (2) with a further revision in 1612 and the financial assistance of a public lottery in 1613, set it free to experiment. All it could do for some years was to hold on, tightly governing a small community, almost wholly masculine. Until 1616 the colonists were servants of the company and until that year had not sent many useful cargoes to England, but at that point Trinidad tobacco began to provide a staple saleable crop. With the distribution of land to settlers in 1618 and reforms in internal administration, the colony grew, indeed grew too fast to absorb its new settlers. The tobacco boom soon burst. Indians killed many settlers, the company crashed, and the English monarch had to take over Virginia and learn to govern from a distance from 1625 onward.[39]

Virginia is not the whole story, of course. A company colony had done well in Newfoundland in 1610, though less well after a few years, and in 1620 the Pilgrims had, without any effective authority, established their intentionally self-supporting settlement in New Plymouth. Indeed, it cannot be said that really effective English colonies were operating before 1630, but the emphasis on population movements had been established. To move people from England, to make them produce commodities for export, or else to become self-sufficient — these were the established premises of English colonization and the secrets, most probably, of its later success.

In comparing the experiences of Spain, France, and England in North America we are not effectively comparing like with like. The sixteenth century was Spain's imperial century. If she did not develop new capital resources and industry in Spain itself, she obtained them vicariously in the form of precious metals from the success of her imperial ventures in Mexico and Péru. She did not stand at the beginning of a revolution in industry, although it can argued that she, with Portugal, accomplished a revolution in commerce. Yet even here, failures to make an effective impact on North America are puzzling. Had she applied the administrative talents that held her empire together to the

---

37. December 10, 1606. Quinn, *New American World*, V, 197–98 (May, 1609), mistakenly placed under the second not the first charter; Quinn, *New American World*, V, 212–18. The fullest documentation is in Philip L. Barbour, *The Jamestown Voyages, 1606–1609*, 2 vols. (Cambridge: The Hakluyt Society, 2nd series, nos. 136–37, 1969).

38. Second charter, May 23, 1609; third charter, March 12, 1612. Quinn, *New American World*, V, 204–12, 226–32.

39. The history of the Virginia Company is pungently described in Edmund S. Morgan, *American Freedom: American Slavery* (New York: Norton, 1975), pp. 44–130.

systematic exploitation of that area, she could have done much more than she did. Either her bureaucracy was too hidebound to do more than point out guidelines for *conquistadores* that were more of a hindrance than a help, or her agents were not of the stuff that made Cortés and Pizarro the most lucky and successful villains and heroes of early modern history. Essentially, the lack of an amenable labor force in North America was probably the clinching factor in her failures. Without such a force it seems doubtful whether the conquerors of Mexico and Péru could have been more than temporary raiders. They were not the founders of great imperial provinces which had a substantial Spanish and black population to stiffen and support the initial invaders, who in turn were bolstered by the strong network of bureaucratic controls that were placed on them. This sequence did not take place in North America. The networks of missions in both Florida and New Mexico were flimsy substitutes for the tight administrative controls and infrastructure of so much of the rest of the empire. But, however we look at it, the expenditures of so many lives for so little gain and for so much damage to an indigenous society, shows that Habsburg Spain proved ineffective in this particular environment, whether on the east coast or in the interior. We must leave it at that with something of a query in the end; it may be that chance had a good deal to do with it or that there are other factors which have not been taken into account.

Comparing Spain, France (though her population was greater), and England (though her maritime resources were or became substantial), the capacity of any of them effectively to penetrate and control any substantial parts of North America was almost insignificant. Yet, the accumulation of capital in the French port towns and cities (in Spain matched only by a small area in the north of the country) enabled them to reach out to the natural resources of the more northerly parts of North America and to glean wealth from both fish and furs, and, for long, to do so without disrupting, even though influencing, aboriginal society. In the end missionaries were to alter this and eventually the state was to take a hand, but that was beyond the period with which we are dealing. The French state, as such, did not assert itself as an imperial power during this early period.

England was, again, somewhat different. She was concerned with financing privileged corporations from the midcentury onward, but they were not directed to the western Atlantic but to Muscovy, the Levant, and eventually to India and the Far East. The East India Company brought home its first rich cargo three years before the first charter was granted to the Virginia Company. The eyes of a substantial number of Englishmen were indeed directed toward the west in the last quarter of the sixteenth century, but their actual efforts were puny and ineffective, except in so far as they provided precedents for more effective action early in the following century. The state was too short of money and resources to aid merchants' private western ventures. Yet, after the war was over in 1604 it became possible to mobilize merchant and gentry capital to make a major drive into the Chesapeake. If it emerged in the end that the privileged commercial corporation was not the correct instrument for doing this, the lesson had to be learned and was learned by experience, often bitter experience. But behind the slow and significant growing mercantile power of England, the desire of a sufficient number of her people for new land and for new opportunities did give her expansion an advantage over the efforts of France and even of Spain to insert her presence significantly into eastern North America. There were factors, not touched on here, that contributed to her success there, notably religious ones, which came into operation effectively only from 1630 onward. But by that time her teething troubles were already almost over, and she had become the first effective North American colonizing power.

I think that the comparison tells something about government. Spain, having virtually invented (in modern times at least) government from a distance, was obsessed with paper. Her officials really did think that rules set out on paper could and would control the men and their followers engaged in penetration of untraversed areas in North America, and that when they were ready to settle there, that they could be influenced by being told what to do. The somewhat dreary episodes we have pursued do, I think, show that this did not work. The French, on the other hand, were skeptical about the effects of bureaucratic intervention. For a moment in 1541–42 they may have felt that Roberval could establish a living colony in Canada. After that, even if they set up viceroys and their lieutenants to do things in America, they never cared much whether they did anything or not. They were not concerned with the workings of bureaucracy; they were affected by what pressures important merchant groups could bring on them, and this is how French Canada got started in its own peculiar way. How it changed in the 1630s is not part of my story here.

As for the English, their rulers were prepared to go through the motions of handing out charters but not to supervise their operation, but to let nature, in the shape of men like Gilbert or Ralegh, take its course. If they failed, so much the worse for them. In the one attempt between 1606 and 1609 that was made to insert a bureaucratic element into the colonizing process, it took only from April, 1606, to May, 1609, to demonstrate that this was more a hindrance than a help. The merchants and their supporters had to go ahead without government intervention. That too was to begin changing in 1625 and thereafter. But for the period with which we are concerned, I think the comparison will stand.

This topic, I am sure, should form the opening chapter in any attempt to survey the European penetration of North America. Its tentative character contrasts sharply with the following period of rapid development and change, so that it may be tempting to begin a course on the Colonial Period in 1607 or 1620, but this, I strongly believe, is misleading. The scale of European enterprise in North America before these dates is such that it must form the correct introduction to what follows; the subsequent history of North America cannot be fully understood unless this is done. I hope I am preaching to the already converted, but if not, I hope that they will take what I have said to heart and that students and lecturers alike will understand how vital the pre- and protosettlement periods are to the understanding of what came after.

9

WHY THEY CAME

There is no easy way in which the question of why individuals and groups came to settle in North America as the earliest European invaders can be answered. For the sixteenth and most of the seventeenth century, it is a matter of looking at individual and collective incentives and propelling forces. Settlement may be understood best in a developmental context: the initial arousing of expectations in Europe (or in the case of Spain, perhaps in Mexico and the Caribbean) led, through various stages of planning, to summer visits for mainly trading purposes, to small-scale experiments in colonization, and finally, through many interim stages, to the creation of new European social and economic groupings across the Atlantic by the exploitation of natural resources in different regions, mainly in eastern North America.

The Americas were already well populated in 1492, and the population of North America is now known to have been appreciably higher than was believed until very recently. It can be said at the beginning that the existence of an aboriginal population and its prior rights to North American land played a surprisingly limited role in the planning of permanent settlement by Europeans. Spanish monarchs, like English and French rulers and many of their subjects, cut and carved North America on paper many times, without more than a passing glance at the existence of an established population. Colonies such as Maryland were to come into existence as the result of private schemes aimed at aggrandizing individuals or small groups. They induced the ruler to sanction their plans on the assumption that land could be appropriated freely in indefinitely large quantities from those who had lived there for millennia.

It is true that, in certain circumstances, the existence of native peoples played a considerable part from the first. While the offshore and onshore fisheries were carried on for the most part with little contact with the Indians, fur-trading involved direct contact, and it grew to be the main channel by which European products entered North America. In the end the fur trade greatly influenced Indian society, creating an almost symbiotic relationship between natives and intruders.[1] In their settlement plans, Spaniards always assumed that natives, if they would not work for the settlers, could be pushed out or killed off unless they could be gradually pacified by missionaries, settled in villages, and made liable for taxation in kind or in limited labor services. This was the pattern of established Spanish colonies in Florida and New Mexico. But Hernando de Soto had been concerned with Indians only as beasts of burden and suppliers of foodstuffs, without any regard to their rights, and he was typical of the conquistadores who entered North America. France assumed that exploration by Verrazzano gave her rights to settle anywhere along the eastern North American coast, irrespective of the wishes of the Indians. The English felt the same, very often without even invoking "rights" of discovery by John or Sebastian Cabot. Nonetheless, in early English plans there was usually the expectation that the occupants would cooperate with the intruders by engaging in trade with them, forming a market for European goods and producing the still largely unknown products of their soil in exchange. Richard Hakluyt was the most optimistic of the planners as far as trade was concerned. There were often injunctions in English plans that the natives should be treated kindly and sometimes that they should be Christianized and Europeanized, but it was always assumed that they would not object to great portions of their land being taken from them or that they would be placated by nominal payments for the right to settle in particular tribal areas. These assumptions often rested on theories about the superiority of Europeans over supposedly savage people[2] and on the belief

1. Our understanding of this relationship has been greatly assisted by a recent work revealing the symbiotic relationship between the Indians and animal life, a relationship gradually weakened and broken down in the period after white contact. See Calvin Martin, *Keepers of the Game: Indian-Animal Relationships and the Fur Trade* (Berkeley, 1980), esp. chaps. 1, 2.
2. In one   recent work on this topic, Bernard W. Sheehan, *Savagism and Civility* (Cambridge, 1980), however, appears to go much too far in asserting that this attitude, though it was prevalent, was solely responsible for Englishmen's actions toward Indians in Virginia from 1607 to 1622.

that much of North America was either uninhabited or so sparsely occupied that European settlements would scarcely impinge on existing inhabitants.

The reality, of course, was different. Indians would be swept off the land only by the fortuitous passage to them of epidemic European diseases or by long and savage military campaigns. In practice, early settlers depended on them for instruction on how to grow native food crops and on surpluses of corn and other foodstuffs to help out deficiencies in their own supplies. The Indians in turn came to depend on Europeans for metal goods (which rapidly transformed their cultural status) and for many articles of clothing and equipment. In many areas settlement involved a process of mingling between the two cultures, the extent of which has only recently come to be fully realized. But, except in the fur trade and to a very limited extent in other superficial contacts, this mutual learning process could not be forecast or provided for unless settlement had actually begun, and even then it was imperfectly understood by both native and invader.

This is, of course, only one aspect of a complex development. The main reasons why Europeans thought of settling in North America and did so arose out of problems in their own European societies. In the case of Spain, of course, North America was just another of the vast areas in the west which Spain could invade and settle as and when she chose: the incentives which led Spaniards to North America were marginal to those which led them to the Islands, to Mexico and Peru. For other Europeans, English, French, and Dutch, it was largely social and economic uncertainties in their particular polities which turned their attention to American lands and preoccupied them as they planned to go or even went there. If Indian lands and rights impinged on them in the end, it was secondarily only, and at a comparatively later stage in the process of deciding why they went.

We may remember that when we think of early America, we are dealing with two very different periods. From the discovery (or rediscovery) of America by Columbus down to the early seventeenth century, a substantial number of Europeans thought of going to live in North America, but only a few actually went, and most of these either returned home or died where they had tried to settle. Only a handful of Spaniards remained to live in North America before 1607. Thus the sixteenth century was a period of discussion and experiment only, one in which North America slowly came within

the consciousness of English, French, Spanish, and Portu-
gese and which led to exploration, to experiments in settlement and to failures to establish, except in Florida, permanent European colonies. Yet it is an interesting and exciting
period, when North America emerged physically, was talked
about as a possible outlet for non-Iberian people, and when
individuals and groups gradually began to think of going to
settle and attempted to do so. The early seventeenth century
is different: people came and stayed. We take the existence
of North America for granted, but the people who lived in the
sixteenth century could not do so; they had to learn gradually
(the relatively small number who even heard of it) what it
might be like and what possible reasons there might be for
moving from the England or France they knew to pioneer a
new life for themselves overseas.

One incentive we must face up to at the very beginning:
imitation of what was happening elsewhere in the Americas.
Europeans became interested in North America because they
thought it was or might be like places where Spaniards and
Portuguese were settling and becoming rich. Throughout the
sixteenth century, thousands were going each year from
Spain—officially only from the part of Spain known as Castile, but unofficially from other parts and from Portugal.
Small handfuls also went from almost every country in western Europe; we can trace Italians, French, English, Irish,
Greeks, and many others who had evaded the Spanish restrictions in some way or another and had joined what was in
effect a gold and silver rush to Mexico and Peru. Altogether
about 200,000 Europeans, predominantly Castilians, are
thought to have settled in Spanish America in the sixteenth
century;[3] how many other Spaniards and Portuguese there
were is not known, and there were only a few indeed of all
the rest. Portuguese, too, went to settle in some numbers in
their own colony in Brazil. The whole process contrasts quite
sharply with the position in North America.

From the time of Columbus's first letter in 1493, stories
and rumors about America had been seeping into Europe.
Once Cortés discovered and conquered Mexico, these stories
took on many romantic colorings, and the gold and silver

3. A figure of 200,000 persons who came to, survived in, and remained in the Spanish empire in the sixteenth century is given
by Woodrow Borah, "The Mixing of Populations," in Fredi
Chiapelli, ed., *First Images of America*, 2 vols. (Berkeley,
1976), 2:709.

which followed in a growing stream as Peru was also found and conquered built up a simple-minded picture among Europeans of a New World full of easily obtained riches, an Eldorado which the Spaniards reserved for their own people, and which they would not allow other Europeans (especially Protestants) to share.[4] This picture was indelibly imprinted as Spanish gold (in reality mainly Spanish silver)[5] became a controversial issue in Europe, as the rivalries of France and Spain and of England and Spain developed into wars on land and at sea. The incentive to non-Spaniards to go to America sprang from this simplified view of the Spanish empire, though it was overlaid by more sophisticated concepts which produced added incentives to go, not just to the Americas, but specifically to North America.

It was only very slowly that any firsthand information about North America became readily available in Europe. Giovanni da Verrazzano, exploring the North American coast for France in 1524, and Jacques Cartier, exploring the St. Lawrence also for France between 1534 and 1536, were the first to give some clear and enthusiastic pictures of both the coastlands and a small part of the interior. Verrazzano was charmed by the trees and flowers and by the apparent fertility of the land as he worked his way from the Carolinas to Maine. Cartier thought the woods and animals of the St. Lawrence area would make it possible for Europeans to prosper there, though he had his doubts after he and a small exploring party stayed at Quebec through the cold Canadian winter in 1535–36. Their accounts only became widely accessible to Europeans when they were published in Italian in Venice by Ramusio in the 1550s.[6] It is surprising how

4. The many-sided impact of the Americas on the rest of the world in the century after 1492 can best be traced in Chiapelli, ed., *First Images.*
5. There are impressive figures in Pierre Chaunu, *Conquête et exploitation des nouveaux mondes* (Paris, 1969).
6. Diffused from materials in G. B. Ramusio, *Navigationi et viaggi*, 3 vols. (Venice, 1550–59), the North American materials being first published in vol. 3 in 1556. For Verrazzano, see D. B. Quinn, ed., *New American World: A Documentary History of North America to 1612*, 5 vols. (New York, 1979), 1:281; for Cartier and Roberval, see H. P. Biggar, ed., *The Voyages of Jacques Cartier* (Ottawa, 1924). Richard Hakluyt was the main diffusing agent in England, for whose works see D. B. Quinn, ed., *The Hakluyt Handbook*, 2 vols. (London, 1974).

often these accounts were used over the rest of the sixteenth
century to describe what North America was like. It was only
after another generation (in 1588) that the first directly observed description of part of North America, Thomas Harriot's little book on an area of modern North Carolina and
Virginia, appeared to provide something like a true picture of
the resources of part of the continent by an Englishman who
lived there.[7]

As soon as there was any concrete information, a few
men in France and England began to build on it, to turn their
eyes toward the part of the America where there were no
Spaniards and where they, too, might make their fortunes
overseas. The men who advised them at home had to turn to
Spanish America for analogies to fill out the very limited
materials at their disposal by applying things that were
known about the West Indies and Mexico to North America.[8]
They were bound, for example, to ask why, if gold and silver
were to be found in quantity in Mexico and Peru, they
should not also be found in North America? If sugar could be
profitably transplanted from southern Europe and the Atlantic islands to the Caribbean and to Brazil, why not to North
America also? If Spanish cattle, pigs, and sheep, not to mention horses, could multiply in Hispaniola and Mexico, why
not on the mainland to the north?[9] These were only the simplest questions which could and did arise. They were certainly present in the minds of the French who between 1562
and 1565 tried to settle in what are now South Carolina and
Florida. The discovery of a certain amount of both gold and
silver in native Indian hands seemed to suggest these suppo-
sitions were correct. Only the more sophisticated of the colonists discerned that the bullion came from the wrecks of

7. *A brief and true report of Virginia* (London, 1588).
8. There are lists of commodities known or supposed to exist in
Richard Hakluyt, *Divers voyages touching the discoverie of
America* (London, 1582); George Peckham, *A true reporte* (London, 1583), in Quinn, ed., *New American World*, 3:51–52; and
in John Brereton, *The discoverie of the north part of Virginia*
(London, 1602).
9. See Quinn, ed., *New American World*, 3:143, 285, and the drawings of West Indian fruits and other items made by John White
on the Virginia voyage of 1585, in Paul Hulton and D. B. Quinn,
The American Drawings of John White, 2 vols. (London and
Chapel Hill, N.C., 1964).

Spanish ships on those hurricane-infested coasts.[10]

The first real gold rush in North American history took place on the unlikely shores of Baffin Island in 1577 and 1578, when an attempt to find a route around North America to Asia under Martin Frobisher led to the belief, fostered by inefficient or corrupt mineral experts, that stone brought from Baffin Island was auriferous. A fleet in 1577 and another in 1578 brought some thousands of tons of ore to England to be smelted before it was found that no metal could be extracted from it.[11] After that there was some caution exercised in claiming that North America must inevitably be rich in gold and silver. Yet mineral wealth remained one great incentive of exploring and colonizing expeditions, even though copper, lead, and iron came in as humbler alternatives to gold. Ralph Lane, after a year on Roanoke Island in 1585–86, said that unless a good mine or a passage to the South Sea were found, he could see little hope of an English colony succeeding.[12] John Smith thought he would find gold in the Potomac valley (and indeed there was a little alluvial gold, though he did not discover it).[13] The Calverts hoped there would be mineral riches in Maryland; so did the settlers in New England. The first settlers in Newfoundland in the early seventeenth century found excellent iron ore, but they did not exploit it to any extent;[14] no one successfully worked iron on a commercial scale before the Massachusetts men in the 1640s.

The incentive most often talked about in the sixteenth century, however, was timber, the most widely used natural product in European society, especially among the seagoing peoples of western Europe. They were using up their best oak and other hardwoods and did not have much good coniferous timber at their disposal. For planking and masts they depended very largely on the Baltic countries, which could

10. See the evidence for this in Paul Hulton, ed., *The Work of Jacques Le Moyne*, 2 vols. (London, 1977).
11. Vilhjalmur Stefansson and Eloise McCaskill, eds., *The Three Voyages of Martin Frobisher*, 2 vols. (London, 1938).
12. Quinn, ed., *New American World*, 3:300.
13. This was at Great Falls, on the Maryland side of the river. It was worked out in the late nineteenth century (personal information from Dr. P. L. Barbour).
14. See Quinn, ed., *New American World*, 4:34–35; Gillian T. Cell, *English Enterprise in Newfoundland* (Toronto, 1969), pp. 59, 63, 72 (for Bell Island).

also supply such products as pitch, tar, resin, hemp, and flax.[15] All observers noted that North America had unlimited timber. Communities that could build houses of wood and make ships and boats were, it was thought, off to a good start; other timber products might profitably be exported. In fact, the first and only product of the short-lived English settlement of 1607–8 on the Kennebec River (Fort St. George) was a stout pinnace of thirty tons burden, the *Virginia*, which was later employed between England and Chesapeake Bay.[16] New England was to get some of its early and much of its later prosperity from building vessels of all sorts. But what had to be learned by hard, backbreaking experience was how much of a problem trees created. Most land suitable for settlement (if it was not on Indian-cleared sites) had to be cut over. Eventually the roots had to come out as well. Slash-and-burn techniques with crops grown between the stumps was a temporary expedient. The labor and cost of transporting timber across the ocean to England proved prohibitive in most cases; Baltic timber remained cheaper. Exceptions were masts (sent from the Kennebec in 1608, from Virginia in 1611) and fine woods like cedar (brought from Roanoke Island in 1585, from New England in 1602, and from Virginia continuously from 1607). Other woods, such as cypress and walnut, followed cedar. Timber, processed for barrel staves or clapboard, could also be marginally profitable; timber in bulk could not.[17]

The idea of using American lumber to stoke furnaces for making iron arose early. This was tried in Virginia from 1608 on, but the bog iron available there was hardly suitable for mass production, while the large-scale ironworks planned in 1620 was aborted by the Indian rising of 1622; samples only appear to have found their way back to England.[18] The same was true of glass, though some glass was made in 1608–9 and

15. Replacement of Baltic commodities by North American ones was constantly advocated between 1583 and 1612 (Quinn, ed., *New American World*, 3:28, 64, 75, 76, 174; 4:34; 5:242, 351).
16. Ibid., 3:425–26; 5:286, 293, 296.
17. Ibid., 3:442–54, passim; 5:357.
18. Ibid., 5:358; Edmund S. Morgan, *American Slavery—American Freedom* (New York, 1975), pp. 45, 85, 87, 95, 100, 109; Susan M. Kingsbury, ed., *Records of the Virginia Company of London,* 4 vols. (Washington, D.C., 1906–35), 3:612–13; 4:11–12, 23.

in the 1620s.[19] Potash was made successfully, though it never became a major export in the early days; neither did resin nor tar. In the end the greatest value of timber was as a building material, essential for the development of any settlement, and so primarily an internal resource rather than an export crop.

A much wider appeal was made by that most basic of commodities, land. To Europeans in early modern times, land was not only what they lived on but what they lived off, since agriculture was the only major industry. But land was also the only major object of investment. Renting or purchasing land was the equivalent of investing in a business enterprise today, even though colonial trading and settlement companies were also among the first to issue shares publicly for cash. But many of them, notably the Virginia Company between 1606 and 1624, offered as dividends on the shares not money but land, and it was as dividends on cash invested or other consideration given that many of the Virginia settlers after 1617 and until the company expired in 1624 got their land.[20]

Land seemed almost like an abstraction to some of the people who were interested in North America. Sir Humphrey Gilbert began dealing in real estate (or maybe "unreal estate" would be more accurate) in quantity in 1582, when he handed out estates of 30,000 acres or larger to any of his supporters who put up more than one hundred pounds in cash. He got rid of 20 million acres in what we know as New England in this way. He never saw the land himself, and none of the men to whom he sold ever saw any of it either. Gilbert was only the first of many land speculators in North America who have raised money from insufficiently suspicious buyers down to our own day.[21] Landed estates were the dream of the gentry when they did not have land or enough land in England. We know that it was large estates that attracted the shrewder London businessmen to Virginia once land became freely available, and that the shrewdest and hardiest of them laid the foundations of the great plantations

19. Jean C. Harrington, *A Tryal of Glasse* (Richmond, Va., 1972).
20. See Morgan, *American Freedom—American Slavery*, pp. 93–97.
21. See D. B. Quinn, ed., *The Voyages and Colonising Enterprises of Sir Humphrey Gilbert*, 2 vols. (London, 1940). vol. 2; D. B. Quinn and Neil M. Cheshire, eds., *The New Found Land of Stephen Parmenius* (Toronto, 1972); and documents (still unclassified) of June 1582, acquired in 1978 by the ⏐National Archives of Canada, Ottawa.

there. Maryland, above all, was a land speculation by a section of the English aristocracy and gentry, as the manors that
were envisaged and to some extent created there under the
paramountcy of the Calverts testify. Even in Massachusetts,
where land holdings were to be so much smaller in general
than in the south, it is clear that the families who came from
England with capital, the means to exploit land, or were able
and ambitious, took up sizable holdings for themselves, and
that substantial estates in Massachusetts increased as the colony took hold.[22] In the 1630s, when Maryland was being
divided, the first attempts to do the same thing were begun
on the St. Lawrence. Extensive seigneuries were offered to
French settlers who would bring men and women with them
to work their holdings (though there the progress of the seigneurial system was to be very slow indeed until after 1663).[23]

Land in North America attracted only a few people who
were already great landowners in England (or later, in
France), though estates across the Atlantic which could be
managed for them in absentia could be added to their European holdings. But the ocean was still too wide for such
investment in land to be important in the early seventeenth
century. Many of the richest subscribers to the Virginia Company did not take up their landed dividends. Nevertheless,
the younger sons of lords and lesser landowners were especially attracted by North American land. Under the legal system by which the eldest son inherited all the landlord's land,
the younger sons had to make their way in a profession, in
commerce, at court, or by marriage if they were to acquire
estates of their own. Many coveted and some obtained land
in North America; certainly the attraction of North America
for younger sons was widely advertised from the 1580s to the

22. Most grants were made to proprietors of towns, who were ex-
    pected to dispose of at least fifty acres to each household in the
    township. But there were major grants, if not so great as in
    Virginia and Maryland, to the principal investors. Sylvia D.
    Fries, *The Urban Idea in Colonial America* (Philadelphia,
    1977), p. 47, says that "the basis was laid for a landed gentry in
    New England" between 1630 and 1640. Of grants to individuals
    in this decade, she traced sixty ranging from fifty to fifteen
    hundred acres.
23. See Richard C. Harris, *The Seigneurial System in Early Canada*
    (Madison, Wis., and Quebec, 1968).

1620s and even later.[24]

There were many other reasons, too, why persons sprung from the owning and ruling groups in Europe would be enticed to America by hopes of building up holdings there: pressures on them for religious reasons, because they were in debt, or because they had committed some offense for which it was desirable that they should leave their own country. Always such people expected that they would get land, but land where other people would do the work for them or pay them rents and services. They would move from the ruling upper class in the Old World to assume the same status in the New. The Spanish Indies, especially Mexico and Peru, had provided Spanish aristocrats or would-be aristocrats with just this translation. Even where the original inhabitants had been killed off, black slaves could be brought in to produce plantation crops on the new estates. This generally was not the case in North America. North American Indians were not willing to turn themselves into a laboring or even a tenant class for intruding white landlords, though they did so occasionally under coercion.[25] The problem was not obvious so long as the aspiring landlord looked at his potential estate from Europe. It could become critical when he came to America; thousands of acres were of little value if they remained both virgin and unprofitable.

There were ways of getting round the problem. A few settlers brought their family servants and estate tenants with them to Virginia and Maryland. More usually, indentured laborers were hired, normally through agents who made a business of it; individuals bound themselves into a steady occupation with some hope of land and an independent existence at the end of the period.[26] Later, criminals too might be sent to serve the remainder of their sentence as servile laborers on American land. Finally, blacks could be brought in expensively, first as indentured servants and later as slaves

24. See, for example, Quinn, ed., *New American World*, 3:31, 104 ("the planting of younger brethren").
25. D. B. Quinn, *North America from Earliest Discovery to First Settlements* (New York, 1977), pp. 104, 123, 162, 167, 211, 222, 293, 306; Elizabeth A. H. John, *Storms Brewed in Other Men's Worlds* (College Station, Tex., 1975), pp. 58–97, passim.
26. Abbot E. Smith, *Colonists in Bondage* (Chapel Hill, N.C., 1947) remains the standard authority.

from Africa.[27] By such means, sometimes even including the extreme of the landowner and his family doing some work themselves (which they would never condescend to do in Europe), some great plantation estates were built up in the south, but there were still very few of them by the midseventeenth century. Many of the farms in Virginia and Maryland were small. There were no great plantations farther north; the big farms of Massachusetts were working farms, not estates for gentlemen. Sir Ferdinando Gorges and his friends in Devonshire spent a whole generation trying to evolve some form of manorial estate for themselves and their followers in Maine, but they never succeeded on any substantial scale.[28] In Canada the early seigneurs found it difficult to hold their tenants once they had got them to Canada; there were too many opportunities for a freer and potentially profitable life on the frontier.

Apart from bullion and jewels, Spaniards might make fortunes from Old World crops like sugar or New World products like cochineal; they might learn to produce and export large quantities of hides (leather was, after wood, the most important raw material for the equipment of early modern societies), but English colonies made heavy and unsuccessful weather of trying to find a novel American staple. Oranges and lemons, like sugar, were not suitable crops for Virginia or Maryland. Silkworms, tried repeatedly, did not flourish; they died from insufficient care, or they did not like the mulberry as found in America, or ultimately their culture failed because a pioneer society was not really suited for the specialized task of assembling and spinning the delicate filaments into usable thread.[29]

Tobacco—Trinidad tobacco, *Nicotiana tabacum*—was the savior.[30] When John Rolfe successfully raised a crop at

27. Wesley F. Craven, *White, Red, and Black* (New York, 1977), pp. 77–85, examines the exiguous evidence.
28. James P. Baxter, *Sir Ferdinando Gorges and His Province of Maine,* 3 vols. (Boston, 1890) and Robert E. Moody, ed., *Letters of Thomas Gorges, 1640–1643* (Portland, Maine, 1978) contain all the documentary materials.
29. Charles E. Hatch, "Mulberry Trees and Silkworms in Virginia," *Virginia Magazine of History and Biography* 65 (1967) :1–61.
30. There is, of course, a large literature on tobacco. The essentials are made clear in Morgan, *American Freedom—American Slavery,* but see Richard S. Dunn, "Masters, Servants, and Slaves in the Colonial Chesapeake and the Caribbean" in *Early Maryland.*

Jamestown in 1612, the Virginia colony had a reason for keeping going. Tobacco was far from being Virginia's only export for some years, but it became the only really profitable one, and the infant colony, after the Virginia Company expired, drew itself by its aid to some degree of prosperity between 1624 and 1640. Maryland might have been founded even without tobacco; it was not intended that it should be grown and certainly not that it should become dominant as it did. But the colony would have found much more difficulty in taking root without it. Monoculture in an export crop always had its dangers—the tobacco market was always vulnerable to merchant pressures, as well as to the vagaries of the seasons and of markets (and in England to governmental interference)—but it made the southern colonies viable exporting communities. For many years one of the main objectives Englishmen had for crossing the ocean was to grow tobacco, even though for a substantial number their actual occupations in America were different. If they had any useful skills or trades at their command, they often carried on with them in their new environment, while learning and developing other skills as planters. This trend arose largely from the dispersed patterns of settlement associated with tobacco cultivation and commerce, which did not encourage the development of towns and certainly not of cities. Farther north, urban life began much earlier; because of the carrying to the New World, most specifically to New England, of patterns of nucleated settlement analogous to those in Europe. Northern craftsmen often did better by continuing their trades in a town rather than becoming farmers, especially if they were specialized ones, like those of jewelers, printers, and booksellers. This fact was early true of Boston, for example, but in smaller townships the basic craftsmen, such as smiths, carpenters, and shoemakers, usually held and worked land as well.

One basic obstacle to all early attempts to plan settlements in North America was the obstinate convictions of Europeans that climate in North America could be equated precisely with climate in western Europe. Since eastern North America has a continental climate dominated by the great land mass that lies behind it, extremes of heat and cold as compared with western maritime Europe were unexpectedly great. The Gulf Stream so moderates the climate of western Europe that the British Isles, for example, have a much more equable climate than eastern North America, equivalent to that of latitudes five or more degrees to the south. It is also now realized there was a little Ice Age in the sixteenth and seventeenth centuries, and that cold winters, bad harvests, and floods in western Europe provided an incentive to leave home, but the first settlers found comparable conditions in North America, whose natural differences were exaggerated by this phenomenon. The decade 1600–1610 saw especially cold winters, as Champlain and the settlers at Jamestown and on the Kennebec were to find to their cost. The double defect in knowledge, difference in climatic zones, and the carry-over of specially severe weather from Europe to America meant that most planning of settlements, when only summer voyages had previously been made to American shores, was very faulty, and that consequently incentives offered to potential colonists were grossly misleading. It was only gradually in the early seventeenth century that this came to be fully understood and fully appreciated, so that the necessary social and economic adjustments made empirically to meet it could be incorporated in the social pattern of a particular area.[31]

So far we have ranged widely and slightly over the more obvious attractions North America had or might have had for Europeans. The incentives, and we might say the impulsion, that affected particular groups ranged over a wide spectrum of possibilities. The Roanoke settlers of 1585 were employees of a syndicate headed by Sir Walter Ralegh; they had little choice about what lay ahead of them. This fact did not prevent many of them from complaining at the indignities of pioneer life, at no soft beds or servants and no gold to spice their future if they stayed. The little group who came in 1587 and were lost were different again. We think that in the main they were craftsmen who wanted to turn themselves into independent farmers and may well have succeeded in doing so, but we do not really know. A handful of radical English Puritans took a look at the Magdalen Islands in the Gulf of St. Lawrence in 1597 with the idea of escaping religious persecution and establishing their little "gathered church" on the

---

31. There is little realistic material on climate, though there is some in John Smith's works. Edward Hayes attempted to account for the weather in Newfoundland (Quinn, ed., *New American World*, 4:32–33), while weather diaries were kept in Newfoundland 1611–13 (that for 1612–13 is printed ibid., pp. 157–78). See also Geoffrey Parker, *Europe in Crisis, 1598–1648* (London, 1979), pp. 17–22.

basis of a walrus and cod fishery, but they decided in the end that Amsterdam was better.[32] A band of French convicts, placed on Sable Island in 1598 to catch seal and walrus, were supplied annually for several years; when supplies did not come they turned on and killed their jailers and then one another.[33] Only a few desperate men survived and were eventually pardoned. A small party of Frenchmen at Tadoussac on the St. Lawrence lost most of their men from scurvy in 1600–1601, and did not persevere. Cartier's pioneers in 1535–36 were merely on a reconnaissance, but his colonists of 1541–42 wanted to stay, though one winter was too much for them. Roberval's settlers of 1542–43 hoped for farms and furs and a richer life than they had had in Europe, but they, too, were driven off after one Canadian winter. Laudonnière's men in Florida in 1564–65 were mainly an anti-Spanish garrison but hoped to lay foundations for a settlement based on agriculture and gold. Jean Ribault had women and children with him when be brought reinforcements in 1565; they were overrun by the Spaniards and had no opportunity to experiment. Champlain's men in 1604–5 on St. Croix Island also were almost driven out by the extreme cold, but found at Port Royal a place where they could winter fairly safely and carry on a useful but not too profitable fur trade with the Micmac Indians from 1605 to 1607.[34]

It is hard to find a common denominator for these settlers of the pre-1607 period. Some were men who were prepared to go anywhere for pay; a few were sent by force; a few thought of coming to obtain religious freedom. (The Florida colony could have become a refuge for the French Huguenots if it had been allowed to survive.) Many must have thought that land was the one really desirable item and that it could be had easily. Spanish civilian settlers in Florida in the 1560s and 1570s had hopes of becoming free farmers, but all

32. See D. B. Quinn, *England and the Discovery of America* (New York, 1974), pp. 316–33.
33. Gustave Lanctot, *Réalisations françaises de Cartier à Montcalm* (Montreal, 1951), pp. 29–50.
34. D. B. Quinn, "The Preliminaries to New France. Site Selection for the Fur Trade by the French, 1604–1608," *Wirtschaftskräfte und Wirtschaftswege. Festschrift für Hermann Kellenbenz*, 4 vols. (Nuremberg, 1979), 4:1–25; see also Samuel Eliot Morison, *Samuel de Champlain* (Boston, 1974) and Douglas R. McManis, *A Historical Geography of New England* (New York, 1975).

lost their land and stock. The *adelantado,* Pedro Menéndez de Avilés, never realized his plans for a great slave-worked plantation. Soldiers assigned for duty there, their wives and families, a few officials, and a few craftsmen to serve their needs, together with a scattering of missionary friars, made up the population of Spanish Florida after 1576.

Many sixteenth-century immigrants who returned to Europe as failed colonists were henceforth hostile to colonization.[35] Because North America, for one reason or another, did not give them a living, they considered it unhabitable by Europeans. Hundreds of Spaniards, French, and English formed that opinion. The drive to colonize came rather from a few enthusiasts, some of whom had good reasons for their optimism; others had very little except a desire to take part in marginal speculations. These attitudes did not change in the earlier years of the seventeenth century. There were a number of groups of failed colonists who came back to speak against Virginia or Maine or the Maritimes or Canada. But by then the pressure of propaganda and the existence of more mobile capital which rich men were willing to invest in America (after the peace treaties made with Spain, by France in 1598 and England in 1604) made a difference. Rising costs of living and declining resources at home made movement more attractive. The state was taking a greater part in stimulating commerce and so gave more encouragement, if little cash, to overseas developers. North America, like the West Indies and the Spice Islands, became a better field for speculative investment in a variety of new export crops and, later, in tobacco, and so propaganda for colonization became both greater and more effective.

The one area little affected by this change was Florida, a frontier garrison of the Spanish empire. By limiting their aims to maintaining two or three small garrisons, Spain had succeeded in establishing the first permanent roots for Europeans in North America.[36] This early assertion of a military presence was not to be without influence in later colonial experiments.

---

35. See Thomas Harriot on failed English colonists in Quinn, ed., *New American World,* 3:140–41; for Spanish ones, ibid., 2:590–92; 5:15–17.
36. For San Agustín ca. 1612, see Antonio Vásquez de Espinosa, *The Compendium and Description of the West Indies* (Washington, D.C., 1947), pp. 106–9.

It was from 1607 on that incentives began to pile up for Englishmen, but it was a long time before North America provided either a good living or cozy subsistence. The colonial theorists kept harping on three advantages.[37] First, North America could supply products to vary and expand English imports; the products that formerly had come from the Iberiàn peninsula and from Mediterranean Europe (olive oil, wine, and dried fruit, for example) could be produced abundantly in North America, and such exports would profit colonizing companies, replacing the need for European imports and giving settlers a good living. As we saw, all these experiments were failures except, in the end, tobacco, and in the much longer run, rice and cotton.

Second, the North American colonies could supplement commodities which England produced herself but in quantities insufficient for her own needs, or which she could in turn export herself. Fish and timber were the chief of these. Both timber production and fishing did indeed occupy the lives of many of the early settlers—the fishing settlement at Richmond Island, Maine, and the Newfoundland settlements are examples. Although few settlers made fortunes, some did find in them a way not only to provide for their own needs, but also to trade with some profit.[38] Furs and skins lay rather between the first and second categories; they were of some importance to English settlers in Virginia and Maryland, and especially in certain parts of New England (where they provided incentives to expand settlement in, for example, the Connecticut valley), but furs were scarcely enough in themselves to lead people to leave England for America. They occupied a very different role in the seventeenth century for the French and the Dutch.

The third and final major economic advantage to be gained from colonies, it was urged, was freedom from population pressure. This, people were told, was why there was unemployment in England (sturdy beggars, accused of being idlers, were often mainly able-bodied men and women out of

37. This theme is developed in D. B. Quinn, "Renaissance Influences in English Colonization," *Transactions of the Royal Historical Society*, ser. 5, 25 (1976) :73–93 ; see above, 97-117.
38. See Harold A. Innis, *The Fur Trade in Canada*, 2d ed. (Toronto, 1956); Quinn, *North America from Earliest Discovery*, pp. 533–36; Van Cleaf Bachman, *Peltries or Plantations* (Baltimore, 1970); Martin, *Keepers of the Game*.

work and going from place to place looking for it).[39] The state was urged to encourage emigration to colonies because its burden would thereby be lightened; propaganda was therefore directed to potential settlers to suggest that overpopulation was causing them to become poorer and that they would inevitably be better off in places like North America, where there would be plenty of space for them. Continuing (though less severe) inflation made the population argument more plausible, especially when it was combined with downward pressure on real wages.

Modern economic historians tell us that unless agricultural production per head of those employed in it rose appreciably, there could be no substantial population rise in general, or growth in the urban population in particular, without some hardship. Towns, though they were congested, dirty, smelly, and disease-ridden by the lowest of modern standards, were nevertheless expanding. London doubled in size in the sixteenth century and had almost doubled again by the middle of the seventeenth century, though it is true that her growth was exceptionally large. London's growth did encourage more intensive use of agricultural land in southeast England, but not sufficiently to meet the rise in population. There were also many interesting attempts from 1540 to 1640 to diversify and expand industrial production in the country.[40] Many failed, some succeeded, but cloth export indus-

39. Edward Hayes and Richard Hakluyt thought England's population was too great to avoid unemployment, but Hakluyt considered that developing colonies would encourage home employment (Quinn, ed., *New American World*, 3:82, 84, 127).
40. Joan Thirsk, *Economic Policy and Projects: The Development of a Consumer Society in Early Modern England* (Oxford, 1978) shows how population growth from about 2.25 million in the 1520s to 3.5 million in 1603, and a rise continuing to 1640 (p. 159), was partly met by the development of consumer industries in England, but even so there were incentives to go elsewhere to look for economic prosperity or to avoid abject poverty (cf. Andrew B. Appleby, *Famine in Tudor and Stuart England* [Stanford, Calif., 1978], for the subsistence crises of the period). There was a push-pull relationship among emigration, external commerce, and internal development (see Carole Shammas, "English Commercial Development and American Colonization, 1560–1620," in K. R. Andrews, H. P. Canny, and P. E. H. Hair, eds., *The Westward Enterprise* [Detroit, 1979], pp. 151–74).

tries, even if the content altered from unfinished to finished goods, remained both dominant and inelastic, often being on the edge of depression. The amount of additional employment provided by new ventures was not nearly enough to take up the population increase of several million within the century.

There was, then, some basis for the argument that England was overpopulated, and certainly the idea that to get out was to get on because there would be less pressure from one's neighbors was to some extent effective. It combined with the more strictly commercial arguments into a fairly attractive set of incentives: land, easily grown or gathered products, easy subsistence when in America, and good profits from an assured market in England. We can see now that North America had the potential for meeting these criteria, but as it existed in the period before white exploitation and as it was to exist in the early stages of white settlement, it could not and did not universally offer these rewards. Good health, good fortune, and hard work might bring them to a few, though only a few, of the early settlers. Most of the rest might well find that the likelihood of death or disease, the sheer hard physical labor of creating a homestead, the power that a handful of men with large holdings of land could exercise over them (so that their working conditions could be as bad as in England) and, finally, the economic hold of English merchants on the prices they got for their produce made many of the alleged incentives look like lies told to the unwary. Optimistic colonists hoped to exploit the land; instead they were frequently exploited themselves.

There were other influential incentives which arose from people's attitudes in matters of politics and religion. Many Englishmen felt unhappy at the rule of the foreign Scottish dynasty after 1603 (as others were to feel unhappy at the rule of a German dynasty after 1714), and neither James I nor Charles I did very much to placate English nationalistic—almost xenophobic—feelings, but it is not clear that this in itself provided any great incentive to emigrate, though some people did go to the Netherlands for this kind of reason. The Stuarts were soon to quarrel with their parliaments, which in the end produced a political crisis and then a revolution. But there is little evidence in the first part of the century that ordinary people cared very much (Parliament was something that concerned the rich, not the common people), though it became so gradually after 1629, when Parliament was in abeyance.[41]

Religion was more important. A considerable number of people in England felt either insecure or unhappy about the religious situation as it affected them and became pessimistic about the possibility of it improving in the way they wished it to improve; these individuals were inclined to leave England for North America so as to have greater opportunities to develop their views on church organization and religious life. On the other hand, it must be remembered that sixteenth-century England was one of the least intolerant countries in Europe. The state demanded a somewhat nominal show of conformity from all its citizens; in peacetime a few appearances at the parish church and the taking of communion once a year would be sufficient. In a worldly society these requirements were much less onerous than the interrogations, threats of death, and frequent executions which hung over Protestants in most Catholic countries and which in a comparable form characterized the few highly integrated Calvinist centers like Geneva. In England nonattendance at church involved fines, though those who went to church irregularly were scarcely troubled. Persistent refusal to attend could lead in the end to confiscatory fines for Catholics (though in the early Stuart period they were enforced only where local judges were vindictive or when there was a real or imagined threat of treason), or even when the right to levy them in a particular area had been leased to a courtier. Catholics were, officially, not allowed to have the services of their priests (who could be executed if identified); unofficially, so long as the priests were kept discreetly disguised as servants or craftsmen, neither they nor their sponsors were systematically persecuted. (After all, the two queens of the period 1603–40 were both Catholics, had private chapels, and could admit to their services the Catholic aristocrats who were in favor at court.) Protestants who refused wholly to conform were more systematically punished, though this depended very much on the local authorities of the established church, but they were harassed rather than threatened with extreme penalties. Unless there was a treason scare (and there were treasonable plots by Catholics), or unless some Protestant extremist gave public utterance to outrageous sentiments (for

41. The range of public and private grievances is best developed in
    Carl Bridenbaugh, *Vexed and Troubled Englishmen, 1590–
    1640*, rev. ed. (New York, 1976).

example, attacked the existence of the Trinity or preached
the expropriation of all wealth on religious grounds), no one,
except for priests in periods of tension, had the threat of
death hanging over him as he might well have done in most
parts of the Continent.[42]

But we must recall too that it was a religious age. Very
many people considered their religious allegiance and practices their strongest emotional and intellectual tie to their
country. It seemed to an increasing number of Protestants
that England had never had a Protestant Reformation. The
state church was reputably Christian, but it was neutral or
negative about things which many people felt vitally needed
reform. The Church of England was the nearest of the Protestant churches to the Lutherans in its organization and relationship to the civil powers, but it lacked the evangelical
touch which Luther had given to his church, the emphasis on
personal contact with God and with the Scriptures. The
Church of England was inclined to leave enthusiasm out; the
Book of Common Prayer and the two sacraments were
enough; preaching was a matter of putting forward state policies or academic theology, but not of inspiring people to
heights of religious emotion. The label "Puritan," when it is
extended to all those people who wished to introduce a Protestant reformation into the Church of England, is somewhat
misleading. Nor were there, until Arminianism attracted the
Stuarts and their bishops, mainly after 1620, any deep theological divisions. Most of the bishops and clergy accepted the
basic Calvinist tenets on predestination, even if they did not
apply them to society quite as Jean Calvin or John Knox had
done. Reducing the status and power of the bishops and reducing or eliminating the remaining traditional Catholic symbols and liturgical practices were topics constantly being
brought up in Parliament between 1604 and 1629 (as they
had been under Elizabeth) and rejected by the crown. But
the biggest desire was for an emotional drive, based on sermons and on Bible readings and interpretations; many of the
local clergy shared this desire, but not the hierarchy or the
crown. It was despair at attaining reformation and the intense
desire to carry it out themselves which played an important—
some would say vital—part in leading to the first mass emigration of Englishmen to North America, that to New England. Between 1630 and 1640 some 20,000 people left En-

42. Ibid., pp. 374–410, gives a good conspectus.

gland to settle there.[43]

The opening of the Bible to individual interpretation had produced, quite early in the Reformation period, radical groups who hung closely together, perhaps because of some common tenet (adult baptism was one such), or because they felt that they could live a holy, God-fearing life only inside the bounds of a single, untrammeled congregation, "a gathered church" separated from all others. Such Protestants were self-regarding; they were rarely evangelical once they had built up their little congregation; they disliked state churches of any sort; they wanted to be left alone; they insisted on being so. Of all recalcitrants, it was they whom Queen Elizabeth disliked most. The Brownists were persecuted from 1593 onwards, while James I's clergy stepped up the persecution after 1604. The little group who pathetically turned to ideas of a colony on the Magdalen Islands in 1597 (whom I have called "the first Pilgrims") formed a congregation which had been imprisoned wholesale between 1593 and 1597. When walrus and cod in the Gulf of St. Lawrence were found to be monopolized by hostile Catholic fishermen, they turned instead to tolerant Dutch Amsterdam, where as "the Ancient Church" they were an inspiration to the congregation that migrated to Leiden from Scrooby in Lincolnshire in 1607.[44] They were moved in turn in 1618 to consider emigrating to America, and some eventually did so in 1620 to form the Pilgrim colony of New Plymouth. A village community, centered on the religious services and experiences which were its core and raison d'être, with fishing and fur-trading as incidental economic necessities, produced the first surviving, self-sustaining settlement in New England. The prime incentive was the desire for religious community in a

43. There is still no agreed figure for pre-1640 emigration to New England. Russell Menard, "Immigrants and Their Increase," in Aubrey C. Land, Lois Green Carr, and Edward C. Papenfuse, eds., *Land, Society, and Politics in Early Maryland* (Baltimore, 1977), p. 109, accepts the traditional figure of 21,200 in Edward Johnson, *Wonder-Working Providence,* ed. J. Franklin Jameson (New York, 1910), p. 58, while McManis, *Colonial New England,* pp. 41–81, in the course of an extended demographic analysis, is prepared to accept the United States Census Bureau, *Historical Statistics of the United States* (Washington, D.C., 1960), p. 2, which has 13,700, a figure almost certainly too low. Twenty thousand has been taken as a reasonable approximation.

44. Quinn, *England and the Discovery of America,* pp. 316–33.

free environment. They never quite achieved it, but on the whole their incentive proved powerful enough for them to succeed in doing most of what they wanted.

A good deal of what was put forward in the sixteenth century in the way of incentives to go to North America was based on guesswork or promotional exaggeration arising from brief summertime visits. Only a few people caught on relatively fast to the realities of the situation in the seventeenth century. The hopes of most of the people who went to Virginia in the first ten years were not realized. Very often they died, or went home, or continued barely to exist. Yet a few tough old hands, we now know, did survive from the beginning and probably made a better living than they would have done in England, but they were very few indeed.[45] They paved the way for the cleverer people who followed. By the time individuals could acquire land in quantity in Virginia, the way to use it profitably by exploiting white indentured labor (or, appreciably later, black labor) to cultivate tobacco had been learned. E. S. Morgan has shown how, within half-a-dozen years from the time land was thrown open to speculation by the Virginia Company, many large holdings had been grabbed by a handful of resourceful operators who proved able to grow crops for their own use, to sell them inside the colony, and to get most of the profitable new export crop, tobacco, into their own hands. However, they never blocked the opportunities for small landholders to establish themselves, even if they had to reach out into frontier territory to do so. The later arrivals, if they were also resourceful, efficient, and, maybe, unscrupulous could make a living and perhaps a success out of moving to Virginia. Of course this possibility attracted others to imitate the great land accumulators, but only a very small proportion succeeded in doing so. The prospects for mixed agriculture and animal husbandry were enough, for example, to lead to the foundation of Maryland. The Calverts and their friends and dependents hoped to be more comfortable in their religion by settling in Maryland, but they also expected to make their

45. Compare Irene W. D. Hecht, "The Virginia Muster of 1624/5 as a Source for Demographic History," *William and Mary Quarterly* 30 (1973):65–92, and Morgan, *American Slavery—American Freedom*, pp. 115, 395–97. Though information is incomplete, it is clear that a minority survived from the period of crisis, 1607–12, until 1625.

fortunes as successful planters, just as a handful of Virginians were doing; they were quite prepared to exploit other settlers in order to do so, whether they were Catholic or Protestant, white or, eventually, black. They had sincere doubts about the fluctuating and speculative nature of the tobacco market, though they soon overcame them in practice.

The incentives to success in New England were somewhat different. In the early seventeenth century, the idea slowly caught on that this was a place where there was less chance of encountering strange diseases, and where crops could be grown and animals kept on lines almost identical with those of England itself, but supplemented by indigenous cultivars such as maize. Realistic views of climate, of soils, and of the possible means of settling the land began to develop after John Smith's productive tour of 1614 (when he contributed the considerable incentive of renaming the old Norumbega "New England"). The Pilgrim colony's attractions for nonseparatist Englishmen were not great, but the publications that emerged from it made clear a way of life not substantially differing from that of England was perfectly feasible there.[46] Several other small fishing settlements farther north on Massachusetts Bay in the 1620s provided adequate evidence that this was so.

One major asset was that, though there were plenty of trees, there were also considerable tracts of open land. Partly this was a matter of geology, but also of historical accident, since so much Indian-cleared land lay vacant. Conservatively minded Englishmen who did not wish to risk the novelties of Virginia (or of the West Indian islands, which were just being opened for settlement) could regard New England as a sensible place in which to invest their capital and to which to emigrate. The reforming Protestants of East Anglia and other places in the south and southeast of England, despairing of church reform and of the curbing of the monarchy, could therefore regard New England as providing sufficient incentives to move. These considerations produced the great migration to Massachusetts Bay in 1630 and after.

Many of the emigrants had property in England and intended to exchange it for property in America; they could afford to bring their whole families and to pay passages for servants who would remain with them for some years. The

46. George D. Langdon, Jr., *Pilgrim Colony* (New Haven, Conn., 1966) gives the basic information.

Winthrops and their friends did not think in terms of great plantation estates, but of substantial English farms or modest estates. This was what most of the leaders soon acquired, though some were to add to them very considerably a little later on.[47] Moreover, coming over in large groups and from a fairly wide social spectrum, they were able to envisage an urban element in the colony almost from the beginning.[48] John Winthrop's "City upon a Hill" was not the vision which created Boston, but it was one element in its emergence. The settlers were not going to spread themselves widely, but rather create village nuclei and move outward slowly from such of them as offered the best opportunities. They were people who brought a good deal of capital equipment with them, including tools, furniture and books; some of them were able to leave part of their resources in money, land, or credit behind them in England and send for necessities and luxuries to help them adjust more comfortably to the new setting.

However, almost everybody seems to have worked hard enough in the early days (the Protestant work ethic, much derided as a concept by professional historians today, had something in it). They were not distracted by frivolities, even if their puritanism was not as narrow as it used to be depicted. On the whole, the greatest incentive New England provided lay in the fact that the anticipations of the earliest settlers— apart from those of the Pilgrims—had been found to be realistic. People could live traditional English-style lives, however reformed in religion and social habits, in New England, and increasing numbers of people wished to try to do so. Indeed, the New England township tended to become more a traditional community than more rapidly changing England itself. The stream of emigrants slowed after 1635 only because of restraints imposed in England, but a sympathetic Parliament, on the eve of the Civil War, was willing to send out children to

47. See n. 22, above.
48. Rutman, *Winthrop's Boston* (1965) and Fries, *Urban Idea* give convincing evidence of the urban impulse, but Rutman tends to stress that most settlers came from nucleated villages in England and not from developed urban communities. Hugh Kearney, "The Problem of Perspective in the History of Colonial Society," in Andrews, Canny, and Hair, eds., *Westward Enterprise,* pp. 290–302, suggests that these township communities tended to become fossilized into rigid traditional patterns.

be cared for and to swell Puritan households.

Virginia's attractions, mostly the wealth or at least the competence to be derived from tobacco, also acted as incentives to bring out more people once the initial trials of the Virginia Company period has passed. But Virginia's high death rates and the fear of Indian attacks such as that of 1622 were partial disincentives. Virginia's population in the years 1624–40 rose more slowly than New England's, though it did grow substantially—from little more than one thousand to eight or perhaps ten thousand, though remaining chronically short of women.[49] Maryland too did not have any spectacular population growth to record, even though a minority of complete families with their dependents did go there. New England attracted something like twenty thousand people in its first six years; Maryland, as the latest research has shown, had not many more than four hundred survivors at the end of the same period.[50]

It will, I think, be clear that, as North America emerged from myth to reality, so the incentives for leaving Europe to attempt a new kind of life there became more specific and realistic. As they did so, they attracted more people to follow the pioneers. Success, or the news of success, in settling in North America was the best incentive of all. Of course, there were many who were unlucky or who were more optimistic about their prospects than they might have been if they had not believed too much of the propaganda which circulated in England. Most of those who came were sensible, clear-sighted, and prepared to work hard to improve their positions above those they had had in England, either in respect to religious and political freedom or to economic circumstance. But they could not wholly escape from England; social and class differences crossed the Atlantic, and the majority of set-

49. Craven, *White, Red, and Black*, p. 33, is inclined to be skeptical about population figures, preferring the reported 2,500 of 1630 to the estimated 3,000 of 1628, but he reports the 15,000 estimate of 1649 as acceptable, though with some caution. Menard, "Immigrants and Their Increase," pp. 88–110, prefers a figure of ca. 11,000 for 1640 which seems somewhat high.

50. Estimates of Maryland's population growth from 1634 to 1650 have tended to be considerably reduced as the result of recent research. Lois G. Carr and Lorena S. Walsh, "The Planter's Wife," *William and Mary Quarterly* 34 (1977) :543 and Menard, "Immigrants and Their Increase" give the latest views on the subject.

tlers became subject in some measure to those who started with initial advantages of birth, wealth, or education. Yet it became clear also that there were opportunities in America for men and women with the initiative to seize them. In Virginia most of the aristocrats gave place to more efficient entrepreneurs. Most of all, it gradually became apparent that North America, if not the Eldorado or Utopia of some of the early pamphleteers, was a good place for Europeans to live. They could push aside the original inhabitants, the Indians, and turn their lands into extensions of England and France; many of them could, by about 1640, already consider that North America was not after all so different from their homeland. It was an extension of Europe rather than a wholly new world.

10

EARLY ACCOUNTS OF DRAKE'S FAMOUS VOYAGE

"The famous voyage of Sir Francis Drake into the South Sea, and there hence about the whole globe of the Earth, begun in the yeere of our Lord, 1577," as published in 1589 by Richard Hakluyt, is the earliest account of the circumnavigation. As such, it has received much critical attention and has inspired much speculation. What Hakluyt says about his plans for a narrative in his address to the reader prefacing *The principall navigations*[1] may or may not be precisely true. He writes that he is able to print an account of Thomas Cavendish's recently concluded circumnavigation, which gives fuller details on the Far East and St. Helena than are extant for Drake's voyages—which proves that he possessed a narrative of that voyage. But Cavendish alone may not satisfy his reader, Hakluyt says, so he makes a somewhat lame excuse for not printing an account of Drake's voyage:

I must confesse to haue taken more then ordinairie paines, meaning to haue inserted it in this worke: but being of late (contrary to my expectation) seriously delt withall, not to anticipate or preuent another mans paines and charge in drawing all the seruices of that worthie Knight into one volume, I haue yeelded vnto those my freindes which pressed me in the matter, referring the further knowledge of his proceedinges, to those intended discourses.

In spite of all this, Hakluyt did manage to insert the narrative we know as "The Famous Voyage" into his volume. He did so after everything had been printed but before the book was in public circulation. A six-leaf gathering, the first three leaves signed Mmm 4-6, the remainder unsigned, and without page numbers, was inserted between pages 643 and 644, and the correct catchword was added at the foot of the last page.[2] It has been argued that the insertion was made later, perhaps in 1594 or 1595,[3] but this is not so. The vast majority of

---

1. *The principall navigations* (London, 1589), sig. *4v.
2. These are reprinted in the facsimile edition, ed. D. B. Quinn and R. A. Skelton, of Richard Hakluyt, *The principall navigations* (1589), 2 vols. (Cambridge, Eng., 1965). In the modern index by Alison Quinn, the notation 643A to 643L has been used for material from them (II, 836).
3. H. R. Wagner, *Sir Francis Drake's Voyage Around the World* (San Francisco, 1926), p. 238.

the surviving copies of *The principall navigations*[4] have the Drake leaves, and a certain limited number of them have been established as strictly contemporary; so the insertion was made at the end of 1589 or the beginning of 1590 (it is not known precisely when the book appeared).[5] It is clear too, from internal evidence, that Hakluyt received a substantially longer narrative and pared it down, possibly with the help of one or more of his assistants, to a size which would be possible to insert. This editing was done masterfully, for the account of the voyage is very complete, and it retains throughout a relaxed and personal tone. Hakluyt reprinted it in 1600 with hardly any changes.[6] It has remained since 1589 the basic authority for the voyage, however much *The World Encompassed* (1628) and materials from manuscripts in England and Spain have supplemented it.

This section, which is written in the third person and refers throughout to Drake as "our Generall," has the character of a continuous narrative by a single hand. We know that this was not the case, as will be indicated below. It could not, therefore, unless our analysis is hopelessly at fault, have been by a man who accompanied Drake on his voyage. Hakluyt had taught himself to transform written material from crude data to coherent and personal narrative. The Reverend Philip Jones, who assisted him in putting together *The principall navigations* (and who may have had a larger share in the task than the evidence shows)[7] had demonstrated that he could translate a Latin text in an easy, flowing style: he had by then completed Albertus Meierus' *Methodus describendi regiones* (1587) as *Certaine briefe, and speciall instructions for gentlemen, merchants, students, souldiers, mariners, &c. employed in services abroad* (1589).[8] He had, indeed, dedicated the translation to Drake and in it had commended Hakluyt to him, but this was in January 1589, before Drake had gone to Portugal (Jones used the calendar dating, not the legal dating, on the dedication: 24 January 1589). Jones could have done the conflation and contraction of documentary material in a hurry if Hakluyt had been too fully engaged in other matters connected with his large book. But I like to think that the compression and its carefully balanced selection of events was in some ways indicative of Hakluyt's special skills, which he demonstrated more fully in the

---

4. See the discussion in D. B. Quinn, ed., *The Hakluyt Handbook*, 2 vols. (London, 1974), II, 477–489. A total of 121 copies is listed, but there are some duplicates. All but 10 have the Drake leaves, which were never reprinted for later insertion. This proves that the copies which went out in 1590 had the Drake leaves already inserted (except, possibly, a small number), but there is no clear correlation with the Bowes leaves; many of the unsophisticated copies have these in the second state, as we should expect (9 of 13 copies in Oxford and Cambridge, pp. 481–482), but the equally unsophisticated Weld-Blundell copy (p. 488) has the Drake leaves with Bowes in the first state.

5. *The principall navigations*, 1589, I (1965), xxii–xxiii.

6. *The principal navigations*, III (1600), 730–742; he had also printed the California portion earlier (III, 440–442) to stress the English claim on the west coast of North America.

7. *The principall navigations*, 1589 (1965), xviii–xx.

8. First published at Helmstadt in 1587. The English translation is Short Title Catalogue (S.T.C.) 12003.

second edition and in some of the narratives he handed on to Samuel Purchas. Indeed, clergymen, when they were not intent on theological argument among themselves, were accustomed to putting across complex theological or moral precepts to their congregations in their sermons and were particularly suited for this kind of high-grade journalism. "The Famous Voyage" indeed shows what they (or he, if it was Hakluyt alone) could do in this regard, at great speed and with an absolute limit on length.

There is no clear evidence about the original text that was delivered to Hakluyt, which he kept and did not print, except that he was asked, he said, not to print it so as not to forestall the efforts of another would-be author working on a book on Drake. Neither is there direct evidence about the origin of the text which Hakluyt actually printed as "The Famous Voyage," though there are indications that sources extant in other versions were employed in some way in it. In the absence of evidence, all we can do is either say we do not know the answers or make some hypotheses about both texts which can form a basis for discussion.

One overriding fact must be kept in mind. Hakluyt compiled *The principall navigations* when he was in the employ of Sir Francis Walsingham, Queen Elizabeth's principal secretary of state.[9] Clearly, he owed a number of documentary items to this association. He was, moreover, under Walsingham's orders regarding what he could and could not print. The corrector or censor, Dr. John James, was appointed by Walsingham; the book was dedicated to Walsingham; and, very exceptionally, Walsingham himself certified it to the Company of Stationers for publication. When Walsingham found that the account of Sir Jerome Bowes, which had been passed by him or by the censor, was considered by the Muscovy Company as likely to prejudice their future trading relations in Russia, it was removed from the earliest printed copies and a somewhat milder version was substituted. Walsingham was also in a position to tell Hakluyt what to print and what not to print about Sir Francis Drake.

It seems likely that Walsingham, not some competing author, was the source of the omission of the original narrative which Hakluyt possessed about the circumnavigation.[10] It is clear that Walsingham had a dossier on Drake's activities during the circumnavigation as a necessary part of his official duty to investigate Drake's actions on the voyage and afterward. However, with the dispersal of the Walsingham archive and the loss of much of its content (the residue among the State Papers in the Public Record Office is far from complete), we cannot particularize it in any great detail.[11] Walsingham was there-

9. *The principall navigations* (1589), I (1965), xx–xxi.

10. If this is so, some modification should be made of the statement in ibid., p. xxi, that the substitution of the Bowes leaves is our only indication of censorship.

11. Walsingham's involvement in the Drake affair is well brought out in documents in Wagner, *Sir Francis Drake's Voyage*, pp. 442–443 (from Public Record Office, London, SP94/1, fol. 57), and in Zelia Nuttall, *New Light on Drake* (London, 1914), pp. 420–428 (from P.R.O., SP12/143, 30, and SP12/1/444, 17), as well as (in my opinion) in the notes in British Library Harley MS 280, fol. 81 (printed in W. S. W. Vaux, ed., *The World Encompassed* [London, 1854], pp. 175–177), of which Hakluyt made use in 1600.

fore in a position to provide Hakluyt with at least some of his materials when it had finally been decided, with the book already printed, to add "The Famous Voyage" to it—though it is too much to say that it can be *proved* that he supplied such material. What is clear is that in November 1589 *The principall navigations* was planned to appear without any account of the most famous English expedition made to date. It was also to appear without any narrative (or with only an incidental reference to one small part of it) of the almost equally flamboyant West Indian voyage of 1585–86; perhaps the publishers of *Sir Francis Drakes West Indian voyage* were unwilling to release it for reprinting.

Any discussion of the publication of materials on Drake's voyages in *The principall navigations* must take into consideration Drake's position at the time of the work's compilation and publication. In June 1589 Drake returned from his voyage to Portugal in disgrace. An investigation established to the satisfaction of the Queen and her ministers that his inaction at crucial stages had prejudiced the success of the expedition—the greatest single force sent against Spain during the whole course of the war.[12] Whether or not Drake was a principal cause of the failure, from the summer of 1589 until 1593 he lived as a private gentleman in the West Country and was excluded from state affairs—as Raleigh was, but for very different reasons, during part of the same period. To publish anything about Drake, especially anything laudatory, was likely to have political implications because his public popularity was as great as his official disgrace was unqualified. The less said about him the better. The suppression of the original narrative given to Hakluyt about the circumnavigation was therefore most likely to have been an official measure of Walsingham's. The omission of an account of the 1585–86 voyage can be explained along similar lines, though this cannot be demonstrated because Hakluyt made no claim to have possessed a narrative of this voyage which he had withdrawn.

One of Drake's possible lines of defense, and a line of publicity which might have helped toward his rehabilitation, would have been to prepare narratives of the positive services he had done for the state before the Portugal voyage. There is evidence that he did this, but it is not yet clear when he began—perhaps soon after his return to the West Country. A possible hypothesis is that Drake, or someone he employed for this purpose, was the author of the suppressed version of the circumnavigation which Hakluyt withdrew (under pressure from Walsingham). At some time between 1589 and 1595 Drake employed the Reverend Philip Nichols to compile narratives of some of his voyages. We know of Nichols from the small book on the Isthmus voyage of 1572–73, *Sir Francis Drake revived*, which did not appear until 1626.[13] This book is said to have

12. For the disastrous Portugal voyage see K. R. Andrews, *Drake's Voyages* (London, 1967), pp. 135–146, and for Drake's long period of disgrace Sir Julian Corbett, *Drake and the Tudor Navy*, 2 vols. (London, 1898), II, 334–374.

13. S.T.C. 18544, under Philip Nichols as author; no. 18545 is another edition of 1628. The title is a translation of the Latin title of a Dutch tract, *Franciscus Dracus redivivus* (Amsterdam, 1596), upholding Drake and Cavendish as champions of Protestantism in the struggle of the United Provinces and England against Spain. It is reprinted in I. A. Wright, ed., *Documents Concerning English Voyages to the Spanish Main, 1569–1580* (London, 1932), pp. 245–396.

been based on the reminiscences of a number of seamen and to have been revised and supplemented by Drake himself. It was therefore completed well before Drake left on his last voyage in 1595, and it could have been in progress some years earlier.

The other volume which is likely to have been put together by Nichols with Drake's aid, though we have no direct evidence on this point, is the longer narrative of the circumnavigation, *The World Encompassed,* issued in 1628 and, like *Sir Francis Drake revived,* published by Sir Francis Drake, Bart., Drake's nephew.[14] This volume claimed as its base the journal of the Reverend Francis Fletcher (chaplain on the circumnavigation), supplemented by narratives of other participants. It is a reasonable assumption, though one which does not seem to have been made until now, that *The World Encompassed* was also put together under Drake's auspices before 1595. This work may have been the basis for the discarded account of 1589, and it may even have been used in the account of the later part of the voyage in "The Famous Voyage" narrative. These claims cannot, except for the last, be made with any certainty, but they can be used to explain much that is otherwise inexplicable.

There is no doubt whatever that Drake intended to publish under his own name a narrative of all his voyages up to and including the Portugal one as a means of convincing the Queen of the extent of his services to England. He wrote a preface to this effect addressed to her and dated 1 January 1592.[15] The English legal year began on 25 March, so this would be 1593 by our reckoning. But it could have been 1592. Hakluyt, for example, often and confusingly used calendar dating instead of what was known as English style, just as we have seen Philip Jones do. In this preface, Drake complained that writing came hard to him. Indeed, we do not have any example of his narrative style, or even of his relaxed epistolary style; his surviving letters are brief, on immediate matters of business. It is almost certain that he did not complete any such narrative. If the date was 1593 he would not have had time to do so, for he was soon after that gradually taken back into the confidence of the higher officials and eventually the Queen.

How then, in light of the draft preface, can the thesis expounded above be explained regarding the material in *Sir Francis Drake revived* and *The World Encompassed*? The explanation would be that Drake's early plan was to obtain the services of others better qualified at writing than he to write up successive narratives of his voyages from his own material, together with whatever his assistants could glean from survivors of the voyages and his own recollections and documents, so that a full, clear, and exculpatory narrative could be put together. The Reverend Philip Nichols would be perfectly capable of doing this in the manner stated on the 1626 title page: "out of the report of Master Christopher Ceely, Ellis Hixom and others who were in the same voyage with him . . . and much holpen and enlarged by divers notes, with his own hand

14. S.T.C. 7161, under Sir Francis Drake the younger; no. 7612 is another edition published in 1635.
15. Prefixed to *Francis Drake revived,* sig. A3.

[Drake's] here and there inserted." This is excellent evidence that the narrative was composed and completed under Drake's own eyes. There is much less specific evidence about *The World Encompassed,* which was said to have been "carefully collected out of the notes of Master Francis Fletcher Preacher in this employment, and divers others his followers in the same." There is no doubt that Fletcher's narrative was used extensively in this book; the only copy of the journal itself, the first part (extending to 25 November 1578), dated 1677, establishes this clearly.[16]

We are left then with two alternatives: first, that in 1589 Drake was having Philip Nichols and possibly someone else write up the materials so far as he could assemble them or, second, that narratives of the circumnavigation (and possibly also the account of the 1572–73 voyage) were already in existence before the end of 1589. The publication of the circumnavigation was stopped; or it could have been, as Hakluyt stated, "withdrawn." Drake's collection of voyages would therefore, at this time, have been a series of narratives published as having been compiled by another man (Philip Nichols?) but backed secretly by Drake's authority. The publication of "The Famous Voyage" did at least give Drake public recognition, and this may have satisfied him for a time, but it can be argued that by the end of 1592, at the latest, he was taking on a different task. He would revise and rewrite, in his own hand and in his own style, the narratives already compiled for him and present them to Elizabeth. This, and perhaps this alone, can explain the mysterious preface of 1 January 1593. "Madam," he said,

> Seeing divers have diversely reported and written of these voyages and actions which I have attempted and made, every one endeavouring to bring to light whatsoever inklings of conjectures they have had; whereby many untruths have been published, and the certain truth concealed, as I have thought it necessary myself, as in a card to prick the principal points of the counsel taken, attempts made and success had, during the whole course of my employment in these services against the Spaniard.

He denied that he was apologizing for anything he had done, but said rather that he was merely trying to put the record straight in order that he should not be excluded from service in future, "not as setting sail for maintaining my reputation in mens judgement, but only as sitting at helm, if occasion shall be, for conducting the like action hereafter." He wrote for later ages, he claimed, so "that posterity be not deprived of such help as may happily be gained hereby,

16. This can be seen in N. M. Penzer, ed., *The World Encompassed* (London, 1926), where the 1677 copy is printed in full except for some of the crudely copied sketches, all of which are in Wagner, *Sir Francis Drake's Voyage.* This account indicates Fletcher's basic hostility to Drake, which came to a head later in his voyage and explains the lack of any further contact between them. The Fletcher text was considerably modified to Drake's advantage for the first part of the 1628 edition of *The World Encompassed,* and presumably comparable modifications were made to the lost portion of the original.

and our present age, at least, may be satisfied in the rightfulness of these actions, which hitherto have been silenced." He hoped his labor would not be lost because it had not been easy—"also in writing the report thereof, a work to him no less troublesome."[17]

This document has every indication of authenticity, and it very much contains the flavor of a seaman's bold writing. But why should Drake write such a preface if he had not completed anything substantial himself? The answer could be that he had already had both the 1572-73 and 1577-80 voyages written up for him by a professional hand or hands, and that he was engaged not in writing them from the beginning but in revising them with touches of his own in order to make it appear that he had written the whole series himself. This argument implies that Philip Nichols, and possibly others, had originally been employed to write on their own account voyage narratives that they could publish under their own names, but that well before 1 January 1593 Drake had decided to use them instead as his ghost writers and to base his own final narrative on the work they had done for him. This scheme was not followed, it is suggested, because in 1593 Drake saw signs that he would eventually be rehabilitated, and he therefore consigned to limbo among his papers the two narratives already discussed, together with the preface and whatever original notes and papers he had retained. These arguments are not conclusive and cannot be so in default of new evidence, but they are worth putting forward as part of the context within which "The Famous Voyage" was conceived and executed.

There are a few further significant facts. First, there is no evidence that Drake was able to retain the log of the circumnavigation. He surrendered his illustrated journal, written by himself and his relative John Drake, to the Queen, who subsequently suppressed it. It is now lost. The Queen probably demanded and impounded his log: if he had to depend on Fletcher's journal and other narratives for *The World Encompassed* (if in fact it was written before 1595), he cannot have had the log in his possession. On the other hand, it is highly probable, indeed almost certain, that he impounded Fletcher's journal on or before his return in 1580 together with as many of the unofficial journals of his men as he could get hold of, since none have survived in their original state. Nothing was heard of the Fletcher journal except in *The World Encompassed*— when it was presumably still in the Drake archive—until one John Conyers, now identified as a well-known London pharmacist, copied the first part of it in 1677, nearly a century after its compilation, without naming its location. But no body of papers deriving from Drake survive in the Drake family archives, so it must be concluded that most or all were dispersed during the civil struggles of the mid-seventeenth century.

The World Encompassed, apart from the initial paragraphs perhaps added by Drake's nephew, is a clear, straightforward narrative of the whole voyage. It differs from *Sir Francis Drake revived* in that the latter is written in the third

17. *The World Encompassed,* sig. 4v.

person, whereas *The World Encompassed* is written in the first person, though it does not purport to be Drake's own narration. His nephew writes in his dedication to the Earl of Warwick as if it were: "I rather choose to say nothing, rather than too little, in praise of the deceased author." Henry R. Wagner thought the 1628 volume was the work of the compiler of the 1626 volume, but he considered both roughly contemporary with their dates of publication, and he insisted that *The World Encompassed* contained much padding, which he thought of as seventeenth-century additions. On the contrary, the narrative is fluid and coherent, with only the occasional moralizing and comment on fauna and flora that the 1677 copy of the first part of Fletcher's narrative contains. Wagner does make some good points, notably that the compiler used Edward Cliffe's narrative of John Winter's portion of the voyage (Hakluyt printed it in 1600), and this seems highly probable. There is no reason why it should not have been available to Drake after his return; Drake would doubtless have demanded full details of Winter's voyage before and after he left him. Otherwise most of *The World Encompassed* is Fletcher, but Fletcher purified of any adverse comments on Drake (at least in the part where we have the full journal and can compare the two).

There is no doubt that the second part of the voyage also largely depended on the part of the Fletcher journal of which the full version is missing. No doubt this part, too, was purged of comments on Drake which were not to his credit. Even for the first part of the voyage, the compiler had available other sources than Fletcher. With some version of this narrative already existing in 1589, there seems no reason why it too should not have been put in its present form by Philip Nichols. No doubt it benefited from "the notes of . . . divers others his followers in the same" from Fletcher's journal, and certainly from Drake's memory and any miscellaneous notes he had managed to salvage.

We are now in a position to say something about the manuscript Hakluyt received, as has been proposed, either from Drake or from his assistant (Philip Nichols appears the obvious candidate). The manuscript was almost certainly favorable to Drake and had some of the modifications in Fletcher's journal noted above. This alone could have made it unacceptable to Walsingham or his censor. But Hakluyt evidently retained his copy even when he was not allowed to print it. He says of the Cavendish narrative, "in relation of the Philippinaes, Iapon, China, and the Isle of S. Helena it is more particular, and exact; and therfore the want of the first made by Sir Frauncis Drake will be the lesse." It is not certain whether he is speaking of the voyage made by Drake or the narrative made by him.

Wagner has traced, as far as possible, the surviving sources from which it can be deduced that "The Famous Voyage" (as printed) was derived. Wagner establishes that much of the earlier parts of "The Famous Voyage" derived from John Cooke's narrative (B. L. Harley 540, ff. 93–100ʳ)[18] and that what can be

18. This is a copy made by John Stow some time before he completed the 1592 edition of *The annales of England from the first inhabitation vntill 1592* (1592: S.T.C. 23334). The heading of the document is "For Francis Drake. Anno Domini 1577" and is ambiguous. It could, indeed,

termed its middle course derived from the "Anonymous Narrative" (B. L. Harley 280, ff. 83–90).[19] Internal evidence suggests that both these documents in their existing form were written after Drake's return, probably some time after, and that they were based on journals kept during the voyage and are not those journals themselves. Both are critical of and sometimes biased against Drake, but both contain significant information on the voyage which is not obtainable from Fletcher's journal for the first part of the voyage or from *The World Encompassed* for the later stages. We cannot be certain where Hakluyt obtained them, but it is reasonable to assume that if Walsingham (or his censor) was responsible for suppressing the first version supplied to Hakluyt, then Walsingham was the source of these and probably other items from which "The Famous Voyage" was finally put together.

Wagner stresses that for the first part of the Hakluyt narrative there is no definite trace of the use of Fletcher or any derivative of Fletcher, though he gives one or two instances where such a use might have been possible. The "Anonymous Narrative" is only some three thousand words in length, and it concentrates mostly on that part of the voyage between the Island of Mocha, off Chile, and Guatulco, Mexico. Wagner is obliged to concede that, thereafter, Hakluyt appears to depend on Fletcher. By this he means the version attributed to Fletcher and others in *The World Encompassed*, for we have no text of Fletcher's journal for this part and there are few discrepancies in Hakluyt (though there is much compression) from what was printed in 1628. This would indicate that Hakluyt had recourse to a version of this text written before the end of 1589.

It is unlikely that Hakluyt had Fletcher's journal; if he had, he would almost certainly have either used it in 1600 or else bequeathed it to Purchas, who would at least have referred to it in his *Pilgrimes* of 1625, where he relies on "The Famous Voyage." The probable explanation is that for the first two stages of the voyage, up to the departure from the Spanish settlements at Guatulco, Cooke and the "Anonymous Narrative" were sufficient to give a balanced picture, even in the small scale to which they were being reduced; but for the later stages (the California one and the trans-Pacific and homeward ones), Hakluyt was driven back on the original narrative which had been suppressed. Because it is not likely to have contained such controversial matter about Drake as Fletcher's original account of the Doughty affair had included, using the original would not lead him into trouble with Walsingham and the censor, who

mean that it was presented at some point to Drake, but in the context it must merely be Stow's indication that he intended to use it for his chronicle of the year 1577, which he did. It is difficult to accept its citations of speeches as containing the exact words spoken at the time; and it was probably written in its present form to support the case of John Doughty in his charges against Drake, though much has a ring of authenticity.

19. This is in a contemporary hand but bears no indication of its origin or author. It is certainly a redaction of an earlier journal because it records, e.g., news of the sending back to Spain of Nuno da Silva, Drake's former pilot (put ashore by him at Guatulco), which took place in 1582, thus making the narrative later than this year.

are likely to have objected to a pro-Drake version of the Doughty episode and other controversial incidents on the outward voyage. That Hakluyt had kept this version is sufficiently indicated in his remarks already quoted.

The argument, then, is that the first narrative was suppressed as giving too much credit to Drake for certain episodes, and that it was replaced almost certainly from official (Walsingham) sources when it was finally realized that to omit the circumnavigation entirely would distort the picture of English overseas enterprise. Hakluyt and his associates were then able to use parts of the original version, which was basically Fletcher as modified in *The World Encompassed,* to round off and balance the latter part of his narrative. This again brings us back to the point that what emerged as *Sir Francis Drake revived* and *The World Encompassed,* in 1626 and 1628, respectively, were compiled for and partly by Drake with the assistance of the Reverend Philip Nichols between the summer of 1589 and the end of 1592 (or perhaps 1591). Further, *The World Encompassed* was in existence in some form before November 1589—it was excluded from *The principall navigations* at that point, yet partly resuscitated by Hakluyt when he had to hastily put together "The Famous Voyage" a month or two afterward. There is a great deal of conjecture in all this, and it is not possible to support firmly many of the points made here, but it seems desirable to attempt an hypothesis or series of hypotheses which would put "The Famous Voyage," and with it the principal English sources for Drake's circumnavigation, into a reasonable perspective. As for the Reverend Francis Fletcher, there is nothing to say. He disappears in September 1580, leaving nothing but his journal—in Drake's hands, to use or misuse, as he thought fit.

"The Famous Voyage" is, in its contracted state, only about fourteen thousand words long, yet it contains a clear, coherent, and basically complete account of the voyage. As such it is a considerable achievement in compression and elucidation. A good many of the criticisms which have been levied against it, notably by Wagner, have been somewhat misconceived. It does contain mistakes, and it does not cover all the episodes of the voyage fully. But it must be remembered that the only other complete account of the voyage, *The World Encompassed,* is almost precisely three times as long and therefore has space for much more incident than Hakluyt could afford. The 1677 Fletcher journal of roughly one-fifth of the voyage is some twenty-four thousand words in length; the complete Fletcher journal would have run to some seventy or eighty thousand words at least if it had been continued on the same scale. (Of course, parts of the later sections of the journal are used in *The World Encompassed,* but almost certainly not the whole of it.) Even John Cooke's narrative (which again covers only the first part of the voyage), with its "Anonymous Narrative" of the final two-thirds, is over twelve thousand words in length. Edmund Cliffe's account of this stage of the voyage out and of Winter's return is also on a modest scale, under seven thousand words.[20]

20. *The principal navigations,* III (1600), 748–753.

The question of length must be taken into account in any evaluation of "The Famous Voyage." Compression—and hasty compression at that—was bound to leave gaps and almost certain to produce mistakes and ambiguities in detail. It is remarkable that no more weaknesses of this sort show. The most outstanding feature of the narrative is that it reads freshly, like the account of a participant in the voyage; and indeed, it does contain some statements in the first person. It is therefore a major achievement on the part of Hakluyt and his assistant or assistants to have turned a composite account into this simple, direct, first-person narrative. If this reading is correct, Hakluyt's skills as an editor, long before he tried himself at greater length and scope in the second edition of *The principall navigations,* were well developed.

At the same time, there are signs here and there that the compression was done in haste. It can be argued that too much space is given to some comparatively minor episodes and too little to some major ones. Altogether very little light is thrown on the methods and personality of Francis Drake himself, except perhaps in his dealings with the ship *Cacafuego* and with the California Indians. The early stage of the voyage is treated, perhaps, in too leisurely a fashion in view of the compression needed later. Most readers are inclined to complain that far too little is said about the Doughty affair; but not only was it still very much a controversial matter in 1589, it was in fact a minor episode in the geographic picture which Drake's voyage drew for Englishmen for the first time.

Drake's primary objective—the exploration of Patagonia and of the Chilean coast—is, after all, well covered, as is his voyage through the Strait of Magellan. Insufficiently described are his violent struggles with the westerlies after he had emerged into the Pacific, as well as his discovery that Tierra del Fuego was an archipelago, not a solid land mass extending to the South Pole. The main facts of the robberies of the Spanish ships are given as effectively, if in less detail, as in Cooke's narrative and *The World Encompassed.* The stay in New Albion is given disproportionate emphasis because of Hakluyt's view that North America was the proper field for English imperial enterprises and colonization. If the crossing of the Pacific is skimped like the crossing from Africa to Brazil, this accorded with Hakluyt's later practice of cutting down open sea passages as boringly repetitive for his readers. His detail on the Moluccas is firm and precise: again, English contacts with the Spice Islands were part of his, and even more his elder cousin's, program for English commerce. The final voyage home is also skimped, and the abortive call at the African coast north of the Cape of Good Hope is denied.[21]

21. The "Anonymous Narrative" says they entered a great bay to the west of the Cape of Good Hope, but finding no water had to go to sea again, where they obtained enough water from a rainstorm to carry them forward. But "The Famous Voyage" insists that "the Cape of Good Hope, which was the first land we fel withall: neither did we touch with it, or any other land, vntill we came to Sierra Leana." Either the text Hakluyt was using differed from the Cooke text we now have, or in compression of his sources Hakluyt slipped on this point.

The overall impression is of a narrative that picks up a great deal of what was novel about the voyage and, especially, what was likely to be important for future English voyagers. Clearly, Hakluyt saw in the Drake material which he could print in 1589 a close complement to what he could reveal on the much more recent circumnavigation of Thomas Cavendish. All in all, "The Famous Voyage" deserves its fame as the best short account of the circumnavigation. Indeed, in many respects it is an outstanding account. But to say this is not to deny its shortcomings and errors, which are mostly venial, the results of its hasty preparation and compression.

In his second edition, where he was not under the same pressure as when he added "The Famous Voyage" to the first edition, Hakluyt remained satisfied with the narrative—perhaps too satisfied. His customary improvement of the forms of place names and addition of side notes was characteristic of his dealing with other texts of 1589. He removed a nonsensical sentence, the intended meaning of which he could, indeed, have supplied by revision.[22] He also added a brief paragraph on the voyage along the South American coast which is paralleled in a series of notes evidently made shortly after 1582, now in B. L. Harley MS 280, fol. 81.[23] The mistakes on the depth of water in the Plate estuary point conclusively to a direct relation between John Cooke's narrative and Hakluyt's 1589 version.[24] His alteration from 55°20 to 57°20 of the southernmost latitude that was reached on the voyage can be ascribed to his use of material from Nuno da Silva, though he may also have had other evidence,[25] and his alteration of the latitude at which the California coast was reached from 42° to 43° may have been similarly based.[26] His removal of the mention of snow on the coasts of western North America,[27] which reappears in *The World Encompassed,* is likely to have come from conversations with persons who had been with Drake—or perhaps because he thought the incident improbable. The fact that Hakluyt supplemented "The Famous Voyage" only with a narrative

22. Sig. 3M6r. "Wee had by proofe in this place, as also at the furthermost Islands, that the sunne being at the least 8. degrees from the Tropike of Capricorne, the night was but two howers long, and scant that, so that we perceiued that when the sunne should be in the Tropike, there would be no night at all." (See Wagner, *Drake's Voyage,* p. 263.)

23. See n. 11 above, associating the document with Walsingham. It is a series of supplementary answers by one of Drake's men to an interrogation, the major parts of which do not appear to be extant.

24. Hakluyt turned the Cooke narrative's "54 and 3 $\frac{1}{2}$ fathoms" into "54 and 53 $\frac{1}{2}$ fathoms" of fresh water. (This is brought out by *The principal navigations,* III (1600), p. 744.)

25. *The principal navigations,* III (1600), p. 744, where Nuno da Silva says "seven and fiftie degrees."

26. Ibid., p. 737. Compare *The principall navigations,* sig. 3M7r. "in 42. degrees."

27. "Lowe plaine land, & clad and couered ouer with snow."

from Nuno da Silva[28] and Edward Cliffe's[29] account of Winter's phase of the voyage (taken from Linschoten, as published in English in 1598) perhaps signifies his satisfaction with the account as it stood. He also added a list of the kings of Java and a brief vocabulary of Javanese words, obviously obtained from someone who had been on the voyage.[30] It would seem that direct contact between him and Fletcher can be ruled out.

The conclusion must be that, even though Hakluyt felt that "The Famous Voyage" could be supplemented in certain particulars, as above, it was still as authoritative as he could make it. The fact that it was retained in the second edition shows that he was not in contact with the Drake family and its archive. Walsingham had died in 1590 and his papers were not available. Hakluyt's failure to include further critical material on Drake would, perhaps, follow naturally from the reticence he showed with regard to dead heroes and his desire not to revive old controversies; his deletion from the 1589 version of some personal remarks in Luke Ward's narrative of the Fenton voyage of 1582 is a case in point.[31] If the volumes published in 1626 and 1628 still cause difficulties (perhaps resolved above), they nevertheless greatly increased the available material on Drake. The revelation of the British Library version of Cooke, the edition of "Anonymous Narrative" by Vaux in 1854 (even if inaccurately transcribed), and the meticulous work of Zelia Nuttall and H. R. Wagner in English and Spanish repositories have revealed materials which can be used both to enlarge greatly "The Famous Voyage" and to call into question some

28. In Jan Huygen van Linschoten, *Jan Huygen van Linschoten his discours of voyages into the Easte and Weste Indies* [trans. W. Phillip] (London, 1598; S.T.C. 15691), printed in *The principal navigations*, III (1600), 742–748. In order to be able to include some English material in his section on western North America, Hakluyt printed separately the portion of "The Famous Voyage" relating to Drake's California visit (III, 440–442), with a long heading stressing his taking possession of New Albion. (This is the only instance of Hakluyt's duplication of part of a narrative.) Here he made the change, noted above, to 43° as in the main narrative; but he also took the opportunity (which he did not do in "The Famous Voyage") of setting the sequence right in placing the cleaning and caulking of the ship at the island of Caño before instead of after the raid on Guatulco. He was always uncertain whether to stress potential mineral resources where there was no clear evidence for them. He did draw attention to the "great shewe of rich minerall matter" to be found in New Albion, though he could not make up his mind how to express this in the text. In 1589 (sig. 3M8r.) it appeared as "There is no part of earth here to be taken vp, wherein there is not a reasonable quantitie of gold or silver". In the main narrative in 1600 this becomes "There is no part of earth here to bee taken vp, wherein there is not some speciall likelihood of gold, and silver" (III, 442), whereas in the subsidiary version (III, 738) it is "There is no part of earth heere to bee taken vp, wherein there is not some probable shew of gold or siluer." We have no indication from what source he obtained this information because it does not appear in other extant document sources. Perhaps Drake himself was the source, noting the possibility of bullion (rather than its proved existence) to attract future English expeditions to the place.

29. *The principal navigations*, III (1600), 748–755.

30. Ibid., p. 742.

31. *The principall navigations* (1589), I (1965), i.

of its details.[32] But the narrative remains basic, and it contains celebrated and vivid passages without which our knowledge of the circumnavigation would be much the poorer. What Hakluyt can be especially criticized for is having failed to use the material on the maps, manuscript and printed, which he had seen'.[33]

Hakluyt was cautious, as he had to be, in regard to the more controversial aspects of the circumnavigation. He ignores many of John Cooke's critical remarks, and he makes his account of the Doughty controversy as neutral as possible, but he neither glorifies nor denigrates Drake. Throughout, he concentrates on the voyage rather than the man. This is characteristic of his treatment in both editions of his great collection. Biography, not Hakluyt's primary concern, emerges from voyage narrative only as incidental to action; he sticks firmly to the "nauigations, voiages and discoueries" of his title page. Samuel Purchas, his successor, shows much more interest in the personality of his characters.

Given the tightrope Hakluyt was obliged to walk, his "Famous Voyage" is both comprehensive and fair, and it reflects great credit on his capacity to present a complex pattern of sea voyaging concisely, on the whole accurately, and in a style which conveys something of its excitement and novelty. Along with the narrative of "N. H." on the Cavendish circumnavigation,[34] as well as some other materials about that voyage, the 1589 edition of *The principall navigations* gave Englishmen, for the first time, direct evidence from English sources of expeditions which multiplied substantially the areas covered by earlier attempts and which strongly reinforced Hakluyt's propagandist purpose: to stress that by this time Englishmen had the resources and knowledge to penetrate any part of the oceanic world, if only they had the will and the capital resources necessary. "The Famous Voyage" narrative played an important part in making the coverage of English maritime activities truly worldwide.

32. Zelia Nuttall, ed., *New Light on Drake* (1914), provided the greatest addition we have on the circumnavigation through her researches in Spain and Mexico; H. R. Wagner, *Drake's Voyage* (1926) added translations of a few additional Spanish documents and much commentary on earlier materials. E. G. R. Taylor, "More Light on Drake," *The Mariner's Mirror*, 16 (1920), 134-151, added the draft plan of 1577, the fragmentary character of which has caused much difficulty in interpretation (see also John Hampden, *Francis Drake Privateer* [London, 1972], pp. 111-113), and John Winter's brief outlines of his voyage (British Library Lansdowne MS, 100, no. 2), written on 2 June 1579 (a modern version is in Hampden, pp. 239-243). There is some tendency in Wagner to expect Hakluyt to have put much more into "The Famous Voyage" than was physically possible; this arises from failure to take into account the limitation of the narrative to a bare twelve pages.

33. See British Library, *Sir Francis Drake: An Exhibition to Commemorate Francis Drake's Voyage around the World, 1577-1580*, ed. Helen Wallis (London, 1977).

34. *The principall navigations* (1589), pp. 809-815: Hakluyt replaced this with a fuller account in the second edition.

APPENDIX

The biographies of Philip Nichols and Francis Fletcher are crucial to the arguments put forward in the preceding pages, though it cannot be claimed that all the suggestions made here can be fully established from what is known at present. As both men attended Cambridge University, the main secondary authority, which does not cite sources, is John Venn and J. A. Venn, *Alumni Cantabrigiensis*, pt. 1, vol. I (Cambridge, Eng., 1922), henceforth cited as Venn.

There are no great lacunae in what we know of the life of Philip Nichols "of Lincoln," who matriculated in 1569 and was a member of Corpus Christi College, proceeding to the B.A. degree in 1573-74, the M.A. in 1577, and a fellowship at his college from 1576 to 1583. He was ordained deacon and priest in the diocese of Lincoln on 31 May 1576, and in 1579 he was incorporated as a member of Oxford University. He disappears from sight for some years after 1583, having possibly married and or become a chaplain at sea or in a noble household. Nichols would seem to have been available to enter Drake's service on the latter's return from Lisbon in June 1589, and to have been available to prepare the first (rejected) draft of "The Famous Voyage" for Hakluyt in 1589; and he is likely then or shortly thereafter to have written up for Drake the account of the 1572-73 voyage which we know as *Sir Francis Drake revived*. In the fair copy of this work which Sir Francis Drake, Bart., the younger, prepared for publication in 1626 (and which is now in the British Library, Sloane MS 301) the title is simply: "A Relation of the rare occurrances in a third voyage made by Sir Francis Drake into the West Indies in the years 72: and 73, when Nombre de Dios by him and 52 others only in his company surprised. Faithfully taken out of ye Reports of Mr Christopher Ceelie, Ellis Hixom and others who were in the same voyages with him by Phillip Nicholls Preacher. Reviewed also by ye same Sir Francis Drake, and much holpen and enlarged by divers notes with his own hand here and there inserted." The published title contained this information but was preceded by the more flamboyant title *Sir Francis Drake revived: calling upon this dull or effeminate age to follow in his noble steps of gold and silver.* In the absence of other evidence, the title can tentatively be attributed to the publisher, Nicholas Bourne. Bourne went on to print the other work, which Nichols may have had a major part in compiling, based largely on Fletcher's journal: *The world encompassed by Sir Francis Drake, being his next voyage to that to Nombre de Dios formerly imprinted; carefully collected out of the notes of Master Francis Fletcher preacher in this imployment, and diuers others his followers in the same: offered now at last to publique view, both for the honour of the actor, but especially for the stirring vp of heroick spirits, to benefit their countrie, and eternize their names by like noble attempt.* It is worth noting that both these books were published during a renewed war with Spain and that they took the nationalistic slogans on their title pages from the war fever of the time; so they themselves became war propaganda against Spain by reviving the achievements of Francis Drake more than half a century before.

Whether through Drake's influence or not, Nichols spent the rest of his ecclesiastical career in the West Country. He was briefly vicar of Stoke Climsland, near Falmouth, in 1591 and rector of Mylor, within easy reach of Plymouth by water, from 28 November 1591 to May 1592; so he could have remained closely in touch with Drake during the years when Drake was (we think) contemplating turning the narrative which Nichols had written for him into direct speech as his own accounts of his ventures. Nichols moved, later in 1592, to be rector of Wembworthy, in central Devonshire, the living of which he held until 1606 (he was made a prebendary of Exeter Cathedral in 1599 and held his canonry until 1606). He then moved to the rich rectory of Honiton, in the east of the county, where he remained until his death in 1614. Venn is incorrect in saying that he died in 1606; W. H. Wilkins, "The Rectors of Honiton, 1505–1907," *Transactions of the Devonshire Association*, 66 (1937) 406, gives a valuable summary; his will, and the administration, were destroyed in the Exeter Probate Registry in 1942, but they are noted in E. D. Fry, ed., *Wills and Administrations Relating to . . . Devon and Cornwall* (London, 1903), p. 131; there was a contest over his property outside the diocese of Exeter in the Prerogative Court of Canterbury, and letters of administration were given first to his sister, Dorothy Gredicot (née Nicholls), and then revoked and reissued to his widow, Joan Nicholls (née Beaumont), Public Record Office, London, PROB 6/8, fol. 140.

Venn admits that the ground for Francis Fletcher is much less sure. Fletcher can probably be identified with a man of that name who entered Pembroke College in 1564 but did not take a degree. Though record of his ordination has not been found, he must surely be the rector of St. Mary Magdalene, Milk Lane, London, who, after holding the preferment for a short time, resigned in July 1576 to join Drake in his preparations (see George Hennessy, *Novam repertorium ecclesiasticum Londonense* [London, 1898], p. 268). Venn believes that Fletcher was next the rector of Bradenham, Buckinghamshire, between 1579 and 1592 (the first date covers the period when Drake's Francis Fletcher was still at sea). But in fact, the rector of Bradenham from 1575 until at least 1581, when he became one of the Queen's chaplains, was Richard Fletcher, on his way to high episcopal office. If Francis Fletcher served at Bradenham (and he may indeed have been placed there at some point as the result of some relationship) it was as curate or vicar. From Venn it then appears that in 1593 Francis Fletcher became vicar of Tickhill, Yorkshire, but he does not appear in the Public Record Office, Certificates of Institutions to Benefices (E331) or in the Composition Books (E334). But he was certainly vicar of that parish when, in 1605, he married Margaret Gallard, a widow of the parish (*Yorkshire Archaeological Journal*, 101 (1891) 215), and his benefice was filled by another in 1619. His will has not been found. For reasons indicated above, it does not appear that he retained his valuable journal of the circumnavigation, but surrendered it to Drake in 1580; nor has any further contact between them been discovered. The surviving transcript of the first part of the journal was made by John Conyers, "Pharmacopolist," in 1677 (British Library, Sloane MS 61) and is more likely to have come from a Drake source than from Fletcher's papers. There seems little doubt that his journal was used by Drake, probably through the agency of Philip Nichols, at various times between 1589 and 1594, and that it appeared in a form which had Drake's approval as *The World Encompassed* in 1628.

11

TURKS, MOORS, BLACKS, AND OTHERS
IN DRAKE'S WEST INDIAN VOYAGE

Drake's raid, in 1585–86, on northwest Spain, the Cape Verdes, Santo Domingo, Cartagena, and San Agustín, with calls at Cape San Antonio in Cuba, at Oristan (St. Helena Sound, South Carolina), and at Hatarask on the North Carolina banks, ended when he brought Ralph Lane and his hundred colonists from Roanoke Island to England in July 1586. The course of the expedition presents some curious features. Drake did not try to penetrate up the Chagres and repeat his exploit of 1573, even though he was carrying a number of knocked down pinnaces for this purpose. He did not attack Havana, which was the key point in the Spanish Caribbean system—a "Discourse" of 1591 declared that Havana was "the key of the Indies insomuch that he who is Lord of that obtaineth the rest"—or even Vera Cruz, or rather its port of San Juan de Ulúa, to avenge his and Hawkins's defeat there in 1568.[1]

The publication of Mary Frear Keeler's *Sir Francis Drake's West Indian Voyage* answers some of the outstanding questions about the voyage and puts the events more fully in view than ever before.[2] But Keeler does not take us very much further with one of the oddest features of the expedition, namely its collection of an assorted bag of liberated prisoners and galley slaves, Europeans, Moors, and "Turks"; of black predial slaves; and of Indians from the Cartagena area. These individuals were still with Drake (though some, like many of his sailors, may have died of fever) when he left San Agustín in ruins in May 1586, but only a small number of them are known to have come all the way to England with him. Why did he make this collection of people? What did he intend to do with them? The minority we hear about later seem to have been mainly "Moors" and "Turks"—how many of them got back safely to their homelands? These questions are still unanswered and perhaps unanswerable, yet it may be worthwhile putting together what little is known at present about this puzzling aspect of Drake's voyage.

[1] London, Public Record Office, CO 1/32, "A Discourse of the Indies," dated 23 December 1591, printed in *Calendar of State Papers, Colonial, 1675–1676, also Addenda, 1574–1674* (London: H.M.S.O., 1894), p. 50.

[2] Mary Frear Keeler, ed., *Sir Francis Drake's West Indian Voyage, 1585–1586* (London: Hakluyt Society, 1981).

The sequence of events so far as we can reconstruct it from surviving documents is this. According to a Spanish source, Drake "carried off the Moors from the galleys at Cartagena and at Santo Domingo, about 200, whom he promised to send to their own country . . . [and] he carried off 150 negroes and negresses from Santo Domingo and Cape Verde—more from Santo Domingo."[3] The collection thus began when he was halfway across the Atlantic, at the Cape Verde Islands, and grew thereafter, in the Caribbean. A report which reached England in May 1586 states that from Santo Domingo he took away 1200 Englishmen, Frenchmen, Flemings, and "Provincials out of prison, besides 800 of the countrey people."[4] However much exaggeration this involved, it must have aroused interest and perhaps some surprise in England, where it was probably interpreted as meaning that Drake was collecting reinforcements for an attack across the Isthmus of Panama, over which he hoped to carry his pinnaces.[5] Later in the voyage, according to a Spanish document, some soldiers at Cartagena, "especially Moors, deserted to the Englishman, as did the black slaves of the city, whom they find very useful."[6] Another Spanish report gives rather more detail: "Most of the slaves and many of the convicts from the galleys went off with the English as did some of the negroes belonging to private owners."[7] An English narrative confirms the Spanish reports by stating that at Cartagena general orders were given "for the well usage of Strangers, namely Frenchmen, Turks and Negroes."[8] Finally a Spanish prisoner, released by the English in Cuba, stated that Drake "took 300 Indians from Cartegena, mostly women, [as well as] 200 negroes, Turks and Moors, who do menial service, and he carries them along, though they are not useful to his country."[9] We have no confirma-

---

[3] Summary of a deposition made at Havana, 26 June 1586, by Pedro Sanchez, in Irene A. Wright, ed., *Further English Voyages to Spanish America, 1583–1592* (London: Hakluyt Society, 1951), p. 212.

[4] Public Record Office, SP 12/189, 42, letter of Nicholas Clever to Nicholas Turner, merchant, 26 May 1586.

[5] The figures are cut down drastically in an English narrative which states that "wee had from thence 80 slaves, Turkes, Frenchmen, Greekes & Nigros"—unless *80* is a mistake for *800:* a repetitive passage says "we had manie Turkes, Frenchmen, Nigros, Moores, Greekes & Spaniards went with us from this Towne" (Keeler, pp. 197, 202, from British Library, Royal MS 7. C. XVI, fols. 170v, 171v). A French account suggests that the overall number can hardly have been as low as eighty: "Il y avoit au port une galère qui fut bruslée, et les esclaves qui estoient dedans, desquelz y avoit dix-huit ou dix-neuf François, mis en liberté" (Louis La Cour de la Pijardière, ed., *Mémoire du voiage en Russie fait en 1586 par Jehan Sauvage, suivi de l'expédition de Fr. Drake en Amérique à la même époque* [Paris: Aubry, 1855], p. 23). Ten of the Frenchmen were brought back to Morlaix in a Norman vessel which accompanied Drake in the Caribbean (Julian Strafford Corbett, ed., *Papers Relating to the Navy During the Spanish War, 1585–1586* [London: Navy Records Society, 1898], p. 95).

[6] Pedro Fernández de Busto to the Audiencia at Panama, 12 March 1586, in Wright, p. 54. It seems very unlikely that the Spaniards had soldiers who were Moors: the Moors we hear about later were sailors, the crew of galleys.

[7] Don Luis de Gúzman and Alonso de Topia to the Crown, Cartagena, 1 June 1586, in Wright, p. 159.

[8] Journal of the "Leicester," 23 February 1586, in Keeler, p. 169.

[9] Alonso Suarez de Toledo to the Crown, Havana, 27 June 1586, in Wright, p. 173. One Spaniard argued that the capture of Cartagena by the English was divine retribution for local immorality, including the "unrighteous intercourse between the Moors of these galleys and slave women and Christian Indian women, and even other women of every sort, moved to desire which overmasters every other consideration" (Wright, p. 197).

tion of this one report about the removal of Indians from Cartegena, but otherwise have ample evidence that, when he left the Caribbean, Drake took with him a very mixed bag of rescued persons.[10]

At San Agustín, when Drake drove the population and garrison into the woods and then significantly stripped the houses of all movable objects, doors, locks, and so forth, which he took with him, two Frenchmen and a number of blacks joined him. But at least three other blacks who might have gone with him and thus escaped from their Spanish masters, preferred to stay and give their versions of Drake's actions to the governor, Pedro Menéndez Marquéz, when he emerged from hiding. According to a dispatch from Havana in September 1586, they gave the following reason for Drake's taking blacks with him: "He meant to leave all the negroes he had in a fort and settlement established at Jacan [Roanoke Island] by the English who went there a year ago. He intended to leave the 250 blacks and all his small craft there, and cross to England with only the larger vessels."[11] A similar statement is given in a later dispatch from the governor: "All the negroes, male and female, the enemy had with him, and certain other equipment which he had taken in Santo Domingo and at Cartagena, were to be left in the fort and settlement which they say exists on that coast."[12] Presumably the doors, locks, and so forth pilfered at San Augstín were also for Roanoke.

Drake's intentions with regard to the Virginia settlement when he left England in September 1585 are unknown. What can be said is that, as he journeyed towards Roanoke, he must have expected it to contain far more than the mere hundred Englishmen Richard Grenville had actually left there in August 1585, since it had been originally thought at least 300 men were needed to establish the settlement. Grenville had assembled 600 men in England, though Drake knew that several hundred of these, instead of being a reinforcement for Roanoke as planned, had in June 1585 been instead diverted to a Newfoundland venture. Perhaps, then, we may assume that, from an early stage in his raiding, and certainly once the Chagres venture had been given up, Drake intended that the rescued individuals (apart from the Turkish and Moorish galley slaves who had been promised freedom and repatriation) should reinforce the Roanoke colony, providing it, for instance, with free black settlers. If the party did include the Indians from the Cartegena region, perhaps they, too, were to be unloaded at Roanoke: having previously suffered under the Spanish yoke, they might be expected to provide a screen for the colony against the Spaniards or against the local Indians. Drake's interest in Roanoke is undoubted: as soon as he returned to England he told a foreign visitor at court that his main purpose in destroying San Agustín and calling in at the Carolina banks was to safeguard Roanoke and warn the settlers that a

---

[10] The removal of the Indians may have been only rumor, though the statement sounds as if it were better founded. If Drake did take Indians, one possibility is that he merely put them ashore again further up the coast.

[11] Diego Fernández de Quiñones to the Crown, Havana, September 1586, in Wright, p. 204.

[12] Idem, Havana, 22 March 1587, in Wright, p. 230.

Spanish force was being prepared, which would attempt to wipe it out.[13] This was indeed the Spanish plan, though Drake's raid hampered its execution, and though the Spaniards' next attempt, in 1587, to find the colonists, who were assumed to be on Chesapeake Bay, failed to locate them or to enter the bay.

Unfortunately, the English sources on Lane's colony tell us nothing of Drake's plans to reinforce it. Lane's men were short of food and on bad terms with the local Indians, while Lane himself wanted only to explore Chesapeake Bay and then bring his Englishmen home. What Drake's response to this situation was we cannot say, but it is bound to have affected his plans for the blacks—and perhaps Indians—he intended to leave behind. Did he give them the choice—either to disembark and settle in North America, where they could take their chance with the local Indians, or else to go back with him to England and face whatever future that might hold for them? In the event, we are told that the colonists were already boarding a vessel Drake had supplied for their exploration of Chesapeake Bay when a storm struck and destroyed a number of Drake's ships, including all his smaller ones. In the sunken vessels may well have perished many of his black and Indian passengers. Though some may have survived, this may explain why we hear nothing further about blacks and Indians. Lane was offered a larger ship, unsuitable for exploration of inland waterways, and he and all his men instead went home to England.[14] Who else returned with Drake? We hear only of "Turks." Perhaps we can assume that a handful of blacks also crossed the Atlantic and were given their freedom in England. However, if several hundred blacks and Caribbean Indians, male and female, had been landed at Portsmouth and had had to be cared for and assimilated, we should surely have had some record of it. Somehow the facts about what actually happened at Roanoke went unrecorded, and hence the exact fate of the many people Drake "rescued" in the course of his voyage from Spain to San Agustín may now never be known.

The galley slaves ascertained to be "Turks"—that is, subjects of the sultan—were another story. As early as August 4, 1586, the Privy Council wrote to the Levant Company to ask them to consider how "the 100 Turkes brought by Sir Francis Drake out of the West Indyes (where they served as slaves in the Spanishe Galleyes) may uppon the arrivall of the shippes to Wolwich and Blackwall (whether they are appointed to brought and there to be discharged) be receyved by order of their Companie and enlarged untill they shall sende some of their shippes into those partes, in which they maye be conveyed home and presented by the Ambassador [William Harborne] unto the Grand Seignour." The Privy Council was anxious to do this, as it was hoped that the repatriation would benefit the company and enable its agents to "drawe on greater favor and liberties unto themselves then they yet enjoye," and also lead

---

[13] David Beers Quinn, ed., *New American World: A Documentary History of North America to 1612,* 5 vols. (New York and London: Macmillan, 1979), 3:307–10, an unpublished anonymous letter of 1 August 1586 from Archivo General de Simancas, Estado Francia, K.1564 (B57, nos. 100–168).
[14] What is known about this episode is given in Quinn, *The Roanoke Voyages, 1584–1590,* 2 vols. (Cambridge: Hakluyt Society, 1955), 1:249–55, 288–308; and in Keeler, pp. 209–10, 270–74.

to the release of some English captives still in Turkish hands. It was considered that the rewards received from the sultan would more than repay the cost of transport of the Turks to Contantinople.[15] Probably about one hundred Turkish subjects who survived the Atlantic voyage were eventually repatriated. This was done not in a single operation, but by putting parties of Turks aboard vessels which were undertaking routine voyages to the eastern Mediterranean.

The return of one party of Turks was not without incident. Laurence Aldersey left Bristol in the *Hercules* of London on 21 February 1587 and was given twenty Turks to transport. According to Aldersey, when he reached Patras, which was then in Turkish hands, the local magistrate showed great interest in the repatriation:

> They brought us to the house of the Cady, who was made then to understand of the 20. Turks that we had aboord, which were to go to Constantinople, being redeemed out of captivitie, by sir Francis Drake, in the west Indias, and brought with him into England, & by order of the Queens Maiestie, sent now into their Countrey. Whereupon the Cady commaunded them to be brought before him, that he might see them: and when he had talked with them, and understoode howe strangely they were delivered, he marvailed much, and admired the Queenes Maiestie of England, who being but a woman, is notwithstanding of such power and renowme amongst all the princes of Christendome, with many other honorable words of commending her Maiestie. So he tooke the names of those 20. Turkes, and recorded them in their great bookes, to remain in perpetuall memorie.[16]

In this case the propaganda value of returning the galley slaves was considerable. But Aldersey's repatriates did not have such a good reception from the Greeks at Chios, which had been captured by the Turks fairly recently, in 1566:

> As we remained at Sio, there grew a great controversie betweene the marriners of the Hercules, and the Greekes of the towne of Sio, about the bringing home of the Turkes, which the Greekes tooke in ill part, and the [Greek] boies cried out, Vive el Re Philippi: whereupon our men beate the boies, and they threw stones, and so a broile began, and some of our men were hurt: but the Greekes were fetcht out of their houses, and manacled together with yrons, and threatned to the gallies: about fortie of them were sent to the prison, and what became of them, when wee were gone, we know not.[17]

[15] *Acts of the Privy Council of England*, n.s. 14 (1587–87) (London: H.M.S.O., 1897), pp. 205–6. In the account of expenditure after Drake's expedition reached England there is an item for laying out ten pounds on clothing for the Turks and other charges (British Library, Lansdowne MS 52, no. 36). Compare Corbett, p. 95, and Keeler, p. 62n.

[16] Richard Hakluyt, *Principall Navigations* (London: George Bishop and Ralph Newberie, 1589), p. 224.

[17] Ibid., p. 225. In saluting Philip of Spain, the Greeks no doubt had in mind his contribution to the recent naval defeat of the Turks, at Lepanto in 1571; and it is conceivable that some of the Turks now being repatriated by the English had become prisoners of Spain on that occasion. But if so, some of them, being sailors, may not have been ethnic Turks but renegade Greeks, and this would explain the extreme hostility of their compatriots. One account included Greeks among those liberated by Drake (see note 5), and since the Greeks were not mentioned subsequently, they may have been later counted as Turks.

Laurence Aldersey left the *Hercules* at Tripolis (present-day Tarabulus esh Sham, Lebanon), from which port she presumably sailed on to Constantinople, before returning to England on 26 March 1588.

It is not altogether clear whether our sources systematically distinguish between "Turks" and "Moors." Although Iberians were inclined to class all Moslems as Moors, we have seen one Spaniard distinguishing between Turks and Moors when describing those liberated by the English on Santo Domingo. In Elizabethan England, the term "Moors" was applied rather indiscriminately to genuine Moors (i.e., North Africans), to "Turks," and to Middle-East Arabs; nevertheless, in the 1580s, as commercial relations with the Porte became closer, Turks were often more precisely distinguished. Furthermore, because England was at this time also in close commercial contact with Morocco, Drake and the English government should have been capable of identifying Moors, at least those who were subjects of the king of Morocco, and distinguishing them from Turks.[18] It is, therefore, a little strange that we do not hear of any repatriation of liberated Moors to Morocco. However, since there were ships making fairly freqent voyages to and from that kingdom, the passage of small numbers of Moors from England may have occured without being thought worthy of record. We can therefore be reasonably certain that the "Turks" whose repatriation was of concern to the Privy Council and the Levant Company were individuals who genuinely derived from the sultan's dominions.

But not all of the Turks returned home. One, at least, formally became a Christian, and the occasion of his baptism was made the subject of a published sermon by Dr. Meredith Hanmer, *The baptizing of a Turke*.[19] This sermon was preached at Saint Catherine's-by-the-Tower on 2 October 1586, when Chinano, a Turk born at Euboea or Negroponte, was baptized. In his dedication to Ralph Rokeby, Hanmer says:

> I suppose it needfull to certefie your worship what moved this Turk to becom a Christian: not holie words but workes, not the name of faith, but the viewe of fruites, not the learning of Clarks but the lives of certain good Christians, whose love & kindnes did so ravish him . . . that he confessed the God of the christians to be the onely true God. And among others he named Sir F. Drake that worshipful knight & W. Hawkins that worthy Captaine. The tree is knowne by the fruits, Gods children are known by their holines, the true professors are knowne by their love.[20]

The Turk did not speak English, so a Spanish interpreter was employed. Through this interpreter, the man is reported to have said that

> the experience of the wicked world, at Nigropontus his native country, his misery and captivitie under the Spaniards, his travaile hither, and the

---

[18] Anglo-Moroccan relations are treated in detail in T[homas] S[tuart] Willan, *Studies in Elizabethan Foreign Trade* (Manchester: Manchester University Press, 1959), pp. 92–312.

[19] Meredith Hanmer, *The baptizing of a Turke* (London: Robert Waldegrave, [1586]), S.T.C. 12744, the copies in the British Library and the Folger Shakespeare Library having been examined.

[20] Ibid., sig. A3v–A4r.

view of this lande, had beaten into him . . . the knowledge of the true God. And further he saide, that if there were not a God in England then was none no where. Two things (he did confesse) moved him to the Christian faith. The one before his comming to England, the other after his arrivall. Before his comming, the vertue, the modestie, the godlines, the good usage, & discrete government of the English Christians, & among othere (as he chiefly noted) he was most beholden unto the Right worshipfull knight, S. Frauncis Drake, and the worthy captaine, W. Haukins, terming them most worthy Christians. After the arrival, he saw curtesie, gentlenes, frendly salutations of the people, succour for him & his cuntrimen, pitie & compassion of the English men, & withall he learned that the poor, the aged, the impotent, the sicke & diseased Christians were provided for, whereas in his cuntry, & wher he had bene in captivitie, the poore, & sicke, & diseased were scorned, despised, & accounted of as dogs.[21]

When he was asked whether the Spaniards had not, during his twenty-five years of captivity, tried to convert him, "his aunswere was: that he had beene by a Friar solicited thereto, & that he heard no more of him but the name of Christ, without instruction or opening to his comfort any poynt of the faith. . . . Again that there were two things which he utterly misliked in the Spaniard, his cruelty in shedding of bloud, and his Idolatry in worshipping of Images."[22] Hanmer could not here forbear to refer to *The Spanish Colonie,* the English translation of Bartolomé de las Casas's *Brevissima relacion,* which had appeared in London in 1583, for further evidence "of the crueltie of the Spaniard."

In this sermon Hanmer is adding his weight to the anti-Catholic and anti-Spanish propaganda of the time. This is the only occasion in this period (as far as I know) when a Moslem made a public confession of adherence to the Church of England. Yet the episode was an answer of a sort to those Catholic propagandists who had, ever since the early 1560s, been inquiring why, if the Church of England was, as it claimed, a universal church, it had never converted anyone outside the British Isles. The episode also shows, however, that Drake was indeed an evangelizing Protestant, who took every opportunity to spread the faith (he had earlier in his voyage attempted the conversion of Catholics). But the conversion of Chinano may have contained an element of unrealized irony: coming as he did from a Greek island in Turkish hands, he may well have been a Greek by origin, and so conceivably not a Moslem from birth.

Hanmer's general attitude towards non-whites was ambivalent. He has a long disquisition of the falsity of Islam, and the credulity of Islam's peoples, and hence eventually reaches the Moors: "The Moores calld Mauri inhabit Mauritania in Affrike, they are (sayth Isodor) of the progenie of Cham, whose posterity Noe accursed, and no marvail accursed people receive the cursed doctine of Mahomet. . . . These people inhabiting Mauritania in Affricke, are because of their hewe and colour of the Latins called Nigritae, in our vulgar Speach Nigros." It will be noted that Hanmer did not specify whether Chinano was black, brown, or indeed a Moor at all: he simply assumed that *Moor* was a

[21] Ibid., sig. C3v–C4r.
[22] Ibid., sig. C4r–C4v.

generic name for all Muslim. However, even if "Nigros" were followers of "Mahomet," they were not irredeemable. Hanmer cites Cà Da Mosto: "The Nigros in the kingdome of Senega ... are not malicious nether stubbornely bent against the Christians. ... The king of Senega was in maner thoroughly persuaded to renounce the laws of Mahomet but he feared his Nobility, and the losse of his Crowne."[23] "Nigros" were thus worthy of conversion and, by implication at least, their color did not prevent them from becoming good members of the Church of England.

To set against Drake's Turk, it appears that one of Drake's blacks deserted to the continent and gave out counterpropaganda. Edward Stafford, the English ambassador in Paris, wrote to Francis Walsingham on 20 August 1586, only shortly after the Turk was baptized in London:

> There is in this town a Negro with a cutt one his face that sayethe he camme with Sir Frances Drak and stole away from him when he was landed in England, he giveth out that what Sir Frances Drak hathe brought home is lyttle or nothinge, and thatt he hathe confessed that the takinge of Cartagena Nombre de dios, and the rest by him is false, but he is never awaye from the Spanish Imbassador [Bernardino de Mendoza]. And I thinke him a man supposed by him to give out these thinges. I wold be gladde to here whether anie such hathe skaped awaye from Sir Frances Drake or no, and doo [send] yf itt maye plese yow as mutche as maye be knowen of the particular successes of Sir Frances Drakes voyadge. I wold make them blowen abroade to his honor and to the discontentment of the Spanish faction.[24]

Nothing more has been found in English or Spanish documents about this episode, and it remains unclear whether the black was an agent of the Spanish embassy, set up to ridicule Drake, or a genuine refugee, who could not bear to remain in England and was returning to Spanish protection and custody. No influx of Spanish-speaking blacks into either Plymouth or London is recorded at this time. The fate of those blacks (and they may only have been a handful) who were brought to England by Drake and who remained there is as yet undiscovered.

---

[23] Ibid., sig. C5r–C5v: in margin "Aloys Cadamus Navigat cap 6." The passage referring to the king's possible conversion is not, however, in *Paesi novamenti retrovati*, 2d ed. (Milan: Giovanni Giacomo and fratelli Da Legnano, 1508), sig. Div., in chapter 6 but in chapter 23; it also appears in [Giovanni Battista Ramusio], *Navigationi et viaggi*, 3 vols. (Venice: Stamperia di Giunti, 1550–59), 1: fol. 111v, but here chapters are not indicated. In fact, Hanmer (or his source) paraphrases Cà Da Mosto and improves on what he said. The passage actually reads (in translation), "He was much pleased with the actions of the Christians, and I am certain it would have been easy to have converted him to the Christian faith, if he had not feared to lose his power, for his nephew, in whose home I lodged, often told me so," *The Voyages of Cadamosto*, ed. G[erald] R[oe] Crone (London: Hakluyt Society, 1937), p. 41.
[24] Public Record Office, SP 78/16, fol. 9.

12

VISIONS, 1567

The credulity of hard-headed Elizabethans is well-attested. 'H. G.' recorded 'Visions' experienced by him and John Davis his 'skrier' (i.e., scryer, seer, one with second sight) between 24 February and 6 April 1567 (British Library, Add. MS 36674, ff.59 recto-62 verso). Humphrey Gilbert, as it almost certainly was, managed to see apparitions of many persons of historical or mythical importance who had messages for him. Some of these messages were worldly enough, such as this (ff. 59v-60r): 'then sayd Adam to hym doe this seyde he / Goe cleane in apparell; and be good to the poore; and leave swaring ... then nothing thou shalt lacke'. Several messages indicated that he should obey John Davis, some of whose crystal-gazing took place in 'the house of Solomon', wherever and whatever that was. In one session in particular Davis conjured up angels who told him that 'he should feare nothing. And y^t he had a good seruante of Solomon, whose counsell he should followe; ... for he would advise him for the best and doe nothing to his hindrance / And that they would appeare to him in the element which he would; And they would teach him all the arte*s*, and how to make bookes.' (Gilbert had recently written the first draft of his work on the North-West Passage.)

The most incredible of the episodes recorded is the raising of St Luke the Evangelist; the last item states that 'my boy went to Solomons house in the morning, & came home to me againe about 9. of the clock in the forenoon, And brought me fro*m* them a book written by St Luke the Euangelist'. There is no further information about this book.

It seems quite clear that the boy John Davis, whether or not he was the later navigator who succeeded Gilbert as the great proponent of the North-West Passage, was trying to establish an ascendancy over Gilbert by means of these apparitions (however they were produced). Here is one example of Gilbert's credulity. On 15 March he notes, 'And as I came homeward ther I sawe a greate brended dog commyng toward me. And then I turned my horse and my skryer turned his horse also / And galoped towardes hym, And whe*n* I mett he would need*es* have pressed vpp*o*n me, And my skryer / And then I said vnto him, O thou wicked & rebellious spirit I charge thee to stand ... ' (f.61*v*). The dog, he makes clear, was the devil, and Davis evidently encouraged him in the belief. Presumably it was a real dog, who ran towards them and then when they chased it ran away.

Davis was not necessarily a rogue; he may have believed some of what he told Gilbert. And it must be added that Gilbert is known to have been addicted to boys. Sir Thomas Smith, with whom he was to have dealings about alchemy in the seventies, told someone having difficulty with him that he should send him a boy, as that was the only thing to put him out of his 'stormes'. The command given by 'Adam' that Gilbert should cease swearing suggests rather strongly that Davis had seen Gilbert in some of his rages.

There is another facet to the 'Visions'. They came into the hands of Gabriel Harvey, perhaps through the means of Sir Thomas Smith, and as was his habit Harvey annotated them fully. On a preliminary leaf he wrote in his well-known hand: 'Certaine straung Visions, & apparitions of memorable note. Anno 1567. Lately imparted vnto mee for secretes of mutch importance.' To the document itself he added to the title 'Visions' his own 'or apparitions', and, below the title, '(A notable Iournal of an experimental Magician)'. Mostly the notes are directly related to the text, signalling features which impressed him, but at the foot of the first leaf (f.59) he has 'the vision of *Sir* Th. S. himself: as is credibly supposed. Though *Master* Ion Wood imagines one G.H.' Is the 'G.H.' Harvey himself? It certainly seems that parallel seances were being held by other people, including Sir Thomas Smith, at that time Provost of Eton, not long before his recall to the Privy Council and eventually to the office of Principal Secretary of State. On the verso of the last page Harvey lists 'his principal Autors' as 'Salomon, Iob, *S. Luke*, Bacon, Agrippa', and cites in Latin two texts from Luke and one from John, adding 'These two Gospells, with ye vij psalmes, ye Litany, & De profundis; commonly read of the Salomonical Artisth ˜ [*sic*] in their greatest Experimentes'.

The episode indicates how firmly the Yates thesis of the permeation of necromancy among the Elizabethan elite can be substantiated.

13

SIR HUMPHREY GILBERT AND NEWFOUNDLAND

The name of Sir Humphrey Gilbert[1] will always be indelibly associated with Newfoundland, arising from the fact that he annexed the island, and much else, on 5 August 1583 by the Julian calendar (or 26 July by the Gregorian calendar which we now use) to the crown of England, and that by the chances of colonization and war, Newfoundland became one of the dominions of the British crown, and held a direct relationship with it until 1949, when this was exchanged for the indirect relationship it has as part of Canada. The four hundredth anniversary of Gilbert's arrival at St. John's Harbour on 3 August, is therefore to be marked as 24 July in the year 1983.

Why Newfoundland? This is a long story and it is as much a matter of accident, almost, as design that Gilbert made his first North American landfall on 23 July (13 July) well to the north along the east coast, and did not, instead, make directly for southern New England, then known as Norumbega, as he had at first intended. It was there he had planned a colony for himself and for his Catholic associates, who wished to leave England, as Lord Baltimore's family was to do later, in order to worship more freely than they could in England. Baltimore tried Newfoundland first and then turned to Chesapeake Bay. Gilbert concerned himself first with the mainland well to the south and then, on his final voyage only, made for Newfoundland instead, and became, as his companion Edward Hayes was to say, "a Northern man altogether."

The island of Newfoundland was, without doubt, the core of the richest part of North America at this time (especially if we add to it the southern shore of Labrador and Cape Breton Island) not from its attractions as land to

1. A useful short biography is in *Dictionary of Canadian Biography*, vol. I (1965); a longer one, together with almost all the documents we have on his American ventures, is in D. B. Quinn, *The voyages and colonising enterprises of Sir Humphrey Gilbert* (2 vols., London: Hakluyt Society, 1940). Some additional material is to be found in D. B. Quinn and N. M. Cheshire, *The New Found Land of Stephen Parmenius*, (Toronto University Press, 1972). A number of documents are reprinted in volumes III and IV of D. B. Quinn, A. M. Quinn and S. Hillier, eds., *New American world* (5 vols., New York: Arno Press, 1979). Peter Bower (and others), *What strange new radiance* (Public Archives Canada, 1979), introduced documents now held in Ottawa, and exhibited there in 1979 and at St. John's in 1980.

be lived in, but from the fish which thronged the seas along its coast and on the offshore Banks, and also the whales which ran through the Strait of Belle Isle in late spring and returned to the ocean towards the end of the year.[2] John Cabot in 1497 was the first to make public the great stores of cod in its waters, though there may well have been English and Portuguese fishermen before him who had at least sighted its coasts. After that the "New Found Isle" can be traced through a number of English voyages between 1497 and 1505, two of which first brought fish to Bristol from its shores in the years 1502 and 1503. Since the English were the first to exploit the cod and the oil to be obtained from cod liver (train oil) they already had a real priority in the discovery. But much of its earliest association with England was forgotten later.

Fish were important in England but fishing was a lowly trade and for long not thought to be worth political attention. It was only in 1582 that the Reverend Richard Hakluyt of Christ Church, Oxford, unearthed the royal grant of 3 March 1496 by which Henry VII of England authorized the Cabots, John and his sons, to search for and occupy lands in the west, and it was in the following year, 1497, that John Cabot made a landfall at some part of the coast (we do not know which part though several places have asserted their priority to it), formally claimed the land for King Henry the Seventh, but also raised the flag of Venice (his first adopted country) and possibly that of Pope Alexander VI as well, on Newfoundland's shores.

It was not long after the English discovery that Portugal followed Cabot in the imperfectly-known voyages of the Corte Reals. Certainly Gaspar Corte Real reached it in 1501 and Miguel in 1502. Certainly, too, from 1504 onwards European ships, other than English ones, began to arrive off its shores to fish. The Normans in 1508 were perhaps preceded by the Bretons; the Spaniards planned to go there in 1511 with the aid of a Breton pilot but we do not yet know if they succeeded. Yet from the beginning there were two distinct areas where the cod might be caught — on the foggy Banks where ships might anchor in the mist and their boats go about to take cod by line to store, wet but salted, in the holds, and might never need to touch land at all, but carry their catch direct to Europe. The Banks fishery in the sixteenth century is the least known of all the aspects of European near-contact with Newfoundland. The inshore fishery was very different. The arrival of the spawning caplin on the island's beaches brought cod inshore in vast numbers, and gradually attracted more and more fishermen to her harbours. The southeast of Newfoundland, especially, was plentifully supplied with harbours which allowed the small fishing vessels which had

2. An account of the cod fishery will be found in D. B. Quinn, *North America from earliest discovery to first settlements* (New York: Harper and Row, 1977), pp. 347-368, and of the whale fishery in Selma Barkham, "The documentary evidence for Basque whaling ships," in G. M. Story (ed), *Early European Settlement and exploitation in Atlantic Canada* (St. John's: Memorial University, 1982) pp. 53-96.

worked their way across the Atlantic to anchor safely. Their boats could then fish freely along the shores and quickly accumulate a cargo. Here the fishermen had a choice on what to do about their fish. They might carry it "green" (salted but wet, as was done from the Banks), or they might prepare it dry. "Dry" fish kept longer and made a better price. The technique had been worked out in Iceland, and probably in Portugal too, long before. The fish was split, gutted, had the head removed and was then opened, treated with a little salt and spread out to dry, maybe on rocks, but maybe, very soon, with plentiful timber near the shore, on "flakes", platforms of poles and rods, covered with green coniferous boughs. The fish had to be regularly turned to keep it exposed to the sun as much as possible. When it was dry it was stacked in heaps and eventually bedded down in the hold. This process meant that fishermen had to work on shore in Newfoundland during the inshore season from late May to September. The ships carried men whose job it was to work on land as well as those who were to fish from boats along the coast. They built stages running out into the water at which boats could unload their catch. On these was normally placed the cutting-table, where the fish were prepared for drying, the livers being segregated from the rest of the offal (we know too that roes were often put aside for salting, but we do not know when tongues were first retained as a delicacy). Cod livers could be rotted down to produce oil in time, but it was more effective to extract it by boiling it on land, so cookhouses for this purpose were constructed for this to be done. Moreover, the men needed shelters, and so they had to build rude huts for themselves as well. They might also create facilities for the repair of boats when the fishing was on a large enough scale. Ships grew in numbers from a few dozen to several hundred in a short time.

The Portuguese Crown considered that by discovery and by the papal division of extra-European lands between Spain and Portugal in 1493 (modified by the treaty of 1494) Newfoundland fell to Portugal's share. Spain frequently recognized Portuguese sovereignty over the island (then thought to be an archipelago) and the surrounding lands. Then, after the voyages of Verrazzano in 1524 and of Cartier in 1534 and later, Newfoundland was included in the "New France", which France had claimed as of right of discovery and use. The Spanish Basques began fishing in the 1520s mainly on the south coast and, in the 1540s, developed the whale fishery on the Strait of Belle Isle, and thereafter regarded the island and Labrador as the "Provincia de Terra Nova". We do not hear of any general English claims for a long time, though their ships went on fishing from the western ports, but on a smaller scale than those of the other western European nations, which were building up the fishery into one of Europe's most important overseas activities. But there is one curious thing with regard to the English fishery. Fish caught in the open sea or in home waters were not charged with subsidy (the five per cent duty which imports paid): Newfoundland fish were not charged and so we have almost no records of their entry after 1503. But if they were dried cod, as we suspect an increasing number must have been, they were prepared on shore and so might be, like Iceland dried fish, foreign goods. Can it have been that Newfoundland was reckoned to be part of the crown's dominions? This is only a guess but it could just possibly be one which was based on a continuous tradition.

It is Anthony Parkhurst who first throws some significant light for us on England's participation in the fishery not very long before Gilbert's time. The owner of Bristol fishing vessels sailing to the fishery from 1575 onwards, Parkhurst accompanied them and is the first-known explorer of the island. With his mastiff and eel-spear he probed the harbours and sampled the interior. He also picked up much gossip from non-English seamen. By this time St. John's Harbour had become a rendezvous for the international community. French, Portuguese and Spanish ships came in there as well as English, to get and exchange supplies — the Portuguese brought the English salt in return, we think, for cloth. They also reckoned after a season's fishing to relax and visit each other's ships in a social round, the captains, masters and cape merchants (representatives of the owners), exchanging food and drink in each other's ships. The harbour too was ringed by flakes and stages, cook houses and huts owned by fishermen of several nations. Parkhurst tells us that the English share in the fishery was expanding rapidly in the 1570s and that up to 50 ships were engaged in it in the year 1579. Two years later another Englishman claimed, exaggeratedly, that no less than 500 French vessels were employed in the fishery as a whole. But the English seem already to have enjoyed a special position at St. John's: the port admiral, accepted as the person to settle disputes as chairman of a committee of the ship's captains in harbour for that time, was (Parkhurst said) always an Englishman, though we have no clear confirmation when and how this came about. What was important is that Parkhurst wrote letters in 1577 and 1578 urging Englishmen to colonize Newfoundland, since it offered many attractions and, if settled, would put control of the fishery largely in English hands. One of these letters went to Richard Hakluyt of the Middle Temple, the elder, lawyer cousin of the younger Reverend Richard Hakluyt who produced the Cabot patent for Gilbert in 1582.

Gilbert comes on the Newfoundland scene when, in 1577, in the first of his numerous anti-Spanish projects to survive, he proposed that the English should seize all the Iberian ships at the fishery, convert them to her own use, and so cripple the mercantile marine of both Spain (a semi-hostile power) and Portugal (at that time a friendly one). Whether he got this idea from Parkhurst or not we cannot say, but it is clear he was well aware by 1578 of the strategic importance of the fishery, to which Englishmen had hitherto seemingly given no thought. When, in June 1578, Queen Elizabeth gave him a patent to explore and occupy for the crown lands not held by other Christian powers, he took it to mean, and was correct in doing so, that this included the whole of eastern North America, north of Spanish Florida (Florida, Georgia and South Carolina at the most) up to the most northerly lands known as the coast of Labrador. Whether he took seriously Parkhurst's proposal to the elder Hakluyt that Newfoundland could and should be colonized by the English, we cannot tell, for he set out on his first American expedition in November 1578 and he certainly was not directing his ships to Newfoundland at that time of year. He intended to sail to the Caribbean and then up the east coast of North America searching for suitable places at which to plant colonies. He was clearly thinking in the first place of sites not too far north of the light Spanish footholds in the South-east, but he may well have had it in mind to carry on up the coast and touch at Newfoundland on his way back to England to see what value the reports of it, recently received from Parkhurst, might have. But he got nowhere. One part of his squadron left him and plundered vessels off the western European coast. The rest ran into a storm which drove Gilbert and some of his ships back to Ireland and made it impossible for him to proceed further. He had, ignominiously, to come home. His young half-brother, Walter Ralegh, did a little better in getting to the Canaries and possibly to the Cape Verde islands, but his ship was too poorly found to attempt the Atlantic crossing and she too returned to England. By the early summer of 1579 Gilbert's American plans and preparations, on which he spent much of his own, his wife's and other people's money, had got precisely nowhere.

ii

Having put Gilbert into what we may call the Atlantic picture, it is time to turn back and look at something of his early career. In Tudor England one of the most venturesome groups in society, a small but not unimportant one, was made up of the younger sons of the gentry and nobility. The governing class in England remained small throughout the period of Tudor rule. It was not a closed caste. Men of humble birth might with luck, ability, and often the patronage of a person already a member of that class by birth, rise to be a gentleman or even a noble. But among those who were of gentle family by birth, those whose fathers held land in some quantity or occupied royal or local office were accepted as gentry even if they had newly risen by their own exertions. Outstanding in status, if not always in wealth, was the tiny group of noble families, not more than a hundred in all, while there were more than a thousand gentry families spread over the land, where land was tightly held in primogeniture, so that the eldest born inherited all, or almost all, the hereditary possessions of his father. This left the younger children often without means of support except by their own exertions. Their parents could give them an education, perhaps at a university, sometimes at the Inns of Court, where they mixed with lawyers and perhaps learned some law as well as the polite behaviour which was current in high society. Some might be apprenticed to merchants and become merchants themselves. Rather more of them might be introduced at Court where the ruling monarch kept round him or her other young men who might some day be suitable for office, or for service in war or who might merely have a decorative and attractive presence. But for others there was nothing to be found unless they became lawyers or clergymen (monasteries ceased to exist after the 1530s) or went to seek their fortunes in foreign armies. Even for many of those who obtained an entry to the Court there were frustrations. They could adorn the Court, indeed, and get fed, but they needed active employment and sources of income which could sustain the position in society they felt themselves accustomed to by birth and breeding. To them adventure at sea, legal as privateers in time of war or as pirates in peacetime (though this had its serious risks), had growing attractions in the reign of Queen Elizabeth. They were often restless men, hard to settle into any one occupation, yet often intelligent, innovative, prepared to take risks. If there had been enough of them they could have been a danger to a settled society such as Tudor rulers aimed to maintain. Queen Elizabeth and her ministers found it necessary to find things for them to do, to command soldiers in the unending struggles in Ireland, where English power was only slowly and unevenly being established; or to allow them to serve the Queen's friends on the continent, the Huguenots in France, the Dutch rebels in the Low Countries (even if those who opposed Spain in arms there were not continuously favoured by the Queen). Best of all they might be encouraged to plan adventures overseas, at sea in the search for northerly passages, for plundering raids on the Spanish West Indies, or for ventures such as Humphrey Gilbert was to involve himself in, and his half-brother, Walter Ralegh after him, of planning colonies in the western continent which was gradually becoming known across the Ocean in latitudes near to those of England itself.

Unless we take circumstances like these into account it is impossible to understand a man like Sir Humphrey Gilbert. His father, Otho (we would say Otto) Gilbert was a wealthy gentleman in south Devon with two major residences not very far apart, one at Compton, near modern Torquay, the other at Greenway, overlooking the port of Dartmouth. Humphrey was his second son, born about 1537, as near as we can establish. His elder son, who became Sir John Gilbert, was to inherit their father's wealth. Humphrey seems to have been sent to Eton and, briefly, to Oxford University. While there is no certainty about this, he was certainly living at New Inn for a time, which was one of the minor Inns of Chancery, where some preliminary legal training was usually given before the young man moved to one of the Inns of Court which had greater prestige and where legal knowledge could be gained. There is some evidence that Gilbert had a legalistic mind and did absorb something from his stay at New Inn even if he went no further. Before Elizabeth I succeeded to the English throne on 17 November 1558 young Gilbert had been introduced to her household by a female relative, and he was welcomed at Court after her accession. He gained some experience as a soldier in an abortive English attempt to seize and hold, in the Huguenot interest, the port of Le Havre in 1562-1563. References in later writings might suggest he met there some Frenchmen (André Thevet, possible if unlikely; Jean Ribault more probably) and one or two Englishmen (Richard Eden not improbably) who were already interested in the New World, but certainly it was being discussed in Court and in City of London mercantile circles in the 1560s.

Gilbert, for all his scrappy education, had an academic turn of mind and gave some attention to the possibilities of a passage to Asia through northern latitudes. The body by then known as the Muscovy or Russia Company had arisen out of an attempt to find an eastern passage to the Orient. If it had turned into a business trading with Russia, it had not given up hope of reviving the project. Anthony Jenkinson, its most intrepid explorer — he had been to Bokhara and into Persia — somehow got to know Gilbert and they commenced an argument about the supposed Passage. Gilbert's reading and geographical interpretation led him to advocate a western venture, Jenkinson's an eastern. Some of their letters survive and Gilbert drafted an academic statement of his case in 1566. But the chance of military service in Ireland, and his activities there as a captain of a company, and latterly as temporary military governor of part of Munster (in which he showed a gift for command along with some especially cruel traits), for which he was knighted in 1570, diverted him from speculations about northerly passages and turned him instead to the possibility of finding a permanent future prosperity for younger sons like himself by seizing and colonizing lands taken from their occupants in Ireland. He interested many young gentlemen from the south-western counties in such projects, but the Queen, wisely, decided not to risk entrusting him and his friends with such a task (in any case experiments of a similar sort in northeastern Ireland were under way and were to prove failures). But the idea of acquiring land (and much land), for landless gentlemen stuck in his mind and influenced his later actions. Again, however, he was diverted since on his return to England he had a chance to join a party of English volunteers who went to aid the Dutch rebels against Spanish authority. He was there, very unofficially, for a few months in 1572 and gained military experience to add to what he had already acquired in France and in Ireland: by the time of his return he was very much the professional soldier even if he had no where else, for the time being, to fight.

By this time, too, he had acquired a wife and a seat in parliament. We do not know how he succeeded in marrying an heiress, Ann Aucher, member of a Kentish gentry family, who was to bring him wealth (which he was to spend lavishly on his overseas ventures) and who bore him six children. His connections with the leading men of the southwest over his Irish plans had brought him to some prominence and to acquaintance with the hardened veteran of transatlantic voyaging, John Hawkins, with whom he shared the parliamentary representation of Plymouth in the parliament of 1571, where he distinguished himself as an advocate of unlimited royal power to the embarrassment of the politicians who wished to avoid issues of principle in the House of Commons. He became interested, along with the learned and eccentric Sir Thomas Smith, in an alchemical venture organized by a charlatan, but when it did not succeed in turning lead into antimony got furious at the ineffectiveness of the alchemist. Sir Thomas is the source of our information that he was liable to go into furious rages. He suggested that a boy be sent to calm him — indicating an addiction to currently fashionable pederasty. He could not settle to the life of a country gentleman of means on his wife's lands in the Isle of Sheppey in Kent. He was indeed active in the study, revising his ideas on a Northwest Passage venture, arranging (on paper) things as he would like them in Ireland, and proposing a reform of higher education which would equip young gentlemen better with the arts, sciences, literature and languages of their own day instead of the crusted antiquities of the universities and law schools.

None of his schemes took effect until some London promoters got going with the Northwest Passage scheme and money was raised to send Martin Frobisher to search the seas between Labrador and Greenland for a route. Gilbert's friend George Gascoigne sent a copy of Gilbert's argument and scheme to the printers and so his first publication, *A discourse of a discoverie for a new passage to Cataia,* appeared in 1576. It showed him to be capable of intellectual argument on the geographical ideas of his time and of suggesting English colonies along a route he thought might lie across northern North America at no very high latitude until the Pacific was reached. These settlements would service the trade between England and China. This was an original idea, not hitherto set out in print in the current reign. But he took little part, even as an investor, in the Company of Cathay which brought ore from Baffin Island in 1577 and 1578 in the hope that it contained gold (which it proved not to do), but turned his attention to other plans for exploiting opportunities in western waters. He was now accepted as an authority on America by the secretary of state, Sir Francis Walsingham, and by other would-be experts on the Northwest Passage like Dr. John Dee. Dee was busy in 1578 trying to convince Queen Elizabeth that she had valid title to North America in the light of very early discoveries, and she seems to have been so far convinced as to issue as we have seen, in June 1578, the vague and elaborate patent by which Gilbert acquired rights, sole rights for six years, to exploit the parts of the continent not occupied by Spain (and clearly including Newfoundland) in the interests of England, though his earlier plan for the seizure of foreign vessels at Newfoundland and another design to occupy an island in the centre of the Spanish Caribbean had been rejected. So in 1578 Sir Humphrey Gilbert returned to the planning of what was to preoccupy him for the last five years of his life, the colonization and exploitation of eastern North America.

iii

The failure of his first American expedition has already been noted. Gilbert was obliged to find other employment, as commander of a small naval force made up largely or wholly of his own ships, off the south coast of Ireland in 1579, and in parliament in 1581 as a member for the borough of Queenborough, Kent. But he had not given up his American plans. He worked with John Dee on the cartography of North America. Dee drew a map for the Queen which indicated that there were passages through as well as round North America and persuaded Gilbert that the best place to settle colonies was "Refugio" (Narragansett Bay), the site most praised by the French expedition of 1524 led by Giovanni da Verrazzano, at 41°20' N. latitude. Later Dee drew another map for Gilbert indicating even more open channels through or round the continent. In return Gilbert gave Dee rights to all lands north of 50°, namely the northern tip of Newfoundland, the Strait of Belle Isle, Labrador and all that lay along the northern shores until the Pacific was reached. Dee did some thinking, planning, and consulting spirits (he was a spiritualist) about this during the years 1580-1583, but was diverted to an alchemical venture in Poland in 1583, remaining on the continent for some years and failing to contribute further to American imaginings or journeys.

Gilbert, on the other hand, gave all his energies to thinking out and planning a vast colonizing project. He may have been influenced by Sir Thomas Smith, an authority on Roman law, who planned a highly structured, self-contained and hierarchical colony in Ireland in 1571, which neither fitted the circumstances nor was something a private individual could maintain. But Gilbert went further, almost into fantasy we might think, and on feudal precedents formed ideas of a great new state in America, a territory which he would head as Lord Paramount, which worked downward from him through a hierarchy of great and lesser landholders to mere tenants of small holdings at the bottom. There were to be armies, a navy and a monopolistic trading system, in which some particular towns in England were to be the agents (he settled finally on Southampton). Law was to be imposed by the Lord Paramount, though it seems that he promised his chief landholders representation in some kind of advisory council or parliamentary assembly. With this in mind, he began approaching all the possible groups he could think of — the southwestern gentry, in the interest largely of their younger sons, who would emerge as great landed proprietors under him; courtiers who might get high profits from investment in lands let to tenants in America; townsmen who were offered economic opportunities in a new capital city; small freeholders and tenants who might for a small investment acquire holdings or tenancies of land much greater than was conceivable in England. A specialized effort was made from 1581 onwards to enlist a great measure of support from the Catholic gentry.[3] Uneasy in co-operating in any way with the Anglican establishment, they were being

---

3. A discussion of the Catholic problem, so far as it relates to America at this time, will be found in D. B. Quinn, *England and the discovery of America* (New York: Knopf, 1974) pp. 364-82.

urged by the Pope and by the Spanish king to resist Queen Elizabeth, and some few were involved in plots which brought radical penalties on their heads. Parliament in 1581 hoped to coerce them, or bankrupt them, by very high penalties for not attending their parish churches. Sir Francis Walsingham appreciated the loyalty which the great majority of them felt for their country, but saw that the new law could easily drive many of them into subversion. He co-operated with Gilbert in persuading a number of their leaders to plan to go to America where they would get much more land and infinitely more freedom, even if a nominal Anglican establishment was to be maintained. Sir Thomas Gerard, representing the powerful Lancashire Catholics, and Sir George Peckham, those of the south midlands and southeast, were the leading figures in this project. Gilbert began, in June 1582, disposing of millions of acres on paper to them and to a few other supporters, like Sir Philip Sidney, who seems to have hoped to create some sort of Arcadia in the west, though not a Catholic one. Peckham and Gerard in June laid off four million acres of their hypothetical land grant (based on Dee's 1580 map) to a group of Midlands gentlemen, mainly Catholic but including Sir Edmund Brudenell, who was Protestant, and arranged that a "General" should lead a reconnaissance force (with Sir William Stanley, Richard Bingham and Martin Frobisher as commanders of vessels) to search on the mainland for a place suitable for settlement, along with a requisite number of islands, for subsequent distribution to investors. The elaborate details of these arrangements are set out in a document now in the Public Archives of Canada.[4]

This task was to be completed by March 1583 and yet was never attempted. We suspect lack of money as the initial obstacle. Additional ones were soon provided: the Spanish ambassador in London and the leading English Jesuit in exile, Robert Parsons, each let it be known that Catholics going to America were deserters from the Faith and that the Spaniards would cut their throats if they attempted to settle there. As the Spaniards had indeed cut the throats of hundreds of Frenchmen in Florida in 1565, this was no idle threat. Gerard resigned from the enterprise and so did others, so that Peckham was left virtually alone of the Catholic adventurers by the summer of 1583.

iv

Gilbert had, in the meantime, been building up another reconnaissance squadron at Southampton. This would verify the sites to be assigned to his grantees and also those for himself and his family who were to have enormous portions. He planned to found a base for some 220 men in which he would remain for a year and proceed from there to investigate the

4. See Bower (and others), *What strange new radiance*, pp. 12-13.

adjoining coasts and interior. In relation to what else we know, this is likely to have been intended to be in some part of what we now know as Massachusetts, to the east of Narragansett Bay. But the expedition did not get away in the summer of 1582, through various mischances. It lingered throughout the autumn and into winter until it finally had to be temporarily abandoned, having eaten up stores and money all the time. This was due partly to exceptional weather, partly to poor organization. But as late as December he hoped to sail, this time obviously by the long route through the Caribbean and up the North American coast, but finally had to desist. Yet in the spring of 1583 a great effort was made and finally the squadron got to sea in June, first calling at Dartmouth and then at Plymouth, finally out to the Atlantic on the track of the Newfoundland fishermen, running down the latitude of 50° N. and then proposing to carry his exploration southward from there. A fine new ship had been bought from the Southampton shipowner Henry Oughtred by Walter Ralegh, Gilbert's younger half-brother, who was now well on the way to high favour at Court, and was named the *Bark Ralegh* of 200 tons burden. She was intended to be the flagship of the expedition but was replaced as such by the *Delight*, 120 tons, on which Gilbert sailed as commander or "General" of the expedition. Other ships of the squadron were the *Golden Hind*, 40 tons, owned and captained by the Liverpool-born seaman and adventurer, Edward Hayes, whose journal provides us with most of what we know of the voyage; the *Swallow*, 40 tons under a young man, Maurice Browne, from whose letters written in 1582-83, we know a good deal about the preparation of the voyage, and finally, Sir Humphrey's own little frigate, the *Squirrel* of a mere 10 tons (she had made a brief and successful preliminary reconnaissance across the Ocean to what may have been Narragansett Bay in 1580). Two days out, on 11 June, the *Bark Ralegh* deserted (there was sickness on board and not enough food, it was alleged). This impoverished the expedition and made it vulnerable. On the way, also, the *Swallow* stopped a French fishing vessel and, on the excuse of buying some fish, stripped her in a piratical fashion, Captain Maurice Browne being unable to stop the crew, many of them recruited from pirate ships.

At the end of July the ships were off Newfoundland and three of them made a rendezvous in Conception Bay (at 48° N.), picking up the fourth, the little *Squirrel*, as they moved down the coast. The short-term objective was St. John's Harbour. The primary reason for going there was to acquire stores of food and other necessities from the fishing vessels who came in to barter as well as to fish. Whether Gilbert had any long-planned intention of making a claim to the island on behalf of the Crown and of himself we do not know. It is probable that he had, since Parkhurst had pointed out possible advantages for England if this was done. Hayes may have been the man who suggested that, if English control could be established at St. John's Harbour, then some authority might be exercised over the inshore fishing vessels there and in nearby harbours, and some levies made from fishermen to finance a military settlement at St. John's with armed vessels at the disposal of the settlers to enforce English authority on English and foreign fishing vessels.

Fishermen were never easy to govern, as was to be found by long experience in the future, but they had a professional solidarity which over-rode national identity. In 1582 two armed English ships had attacked and robbed Portuguese fishermen in several harbours south of St. John's. English fishermen tried to prevent them and protested in vain when they did so: some even appeared as witnesses for the Portuguese in the English courts when they tried to gain redress for their losses in 1583. Gilbert and his ships were first of all thought to be another set of marauders. All fishing vessels were armed at this time and the preparations they could make to resist interference, in an enclosed harbour like St. John's, would make it extremely dangerous for Gilbert to force an entrance. However, he did make contact with some of the English fishermen, probably through the inshore fishing boats which plied in and out of the harbour, and convinced them, by showing the Queen's commission, that he had some official status and had not come as an enemy. These fishermen in turn convinced other doubters and they agreed to permit the entry of the ships of the expedition. There was then an anticlimax to Gilbert's dignified entry when the *Delight* went aground on a rock which formed a bar at that time in the harbour mouth and was to remain a peril to incautious pilots for many years to come. At this stage the fishermen showed their capacity for co-operation. A flotilla of boats was got together and pulled the vessel off and she and her three consorts anchored safely inside the harbour. The port admiral was captain of an English fishing vessel and this helped to cool the still tense atmosphere. Gilbert's first step was to call together the captains and leading men of the English ships in the harbour, among whom was the young Richard Whit-bourne, who was to set down his memory of this episode thirty-seven years later. In the harbour were sixteen English ships, while there were twenty from other nations, mostly French and Portuguese, with perhaps one or two Spanish Basques. Once friendly relations had been established the captains of the non-English vessels came with gifts and compliments to Gilbert on the *Delight*, consisting of wine, sweet oil (mostly olive oil one would imagine), marmalade (a conserve, usually but not then invariably made from oranges), and other delicacies. They were, to be sure, also asked for fish, fresh and cured, for the seamen, since the officers and gentlemen alone would hoard the finer gifts. They may even have paid for the fish. From their ships Gilbert's men could see along the western parts of the harbour long and untidy lines of stages, cookhouses, flakes and huts, with boats and the smaller ships docked and the larger ones riding at anchor. When Gilbert, Hayes, the young Hungarian poet Stephen Parmenius and some others went ashore on Sunday, 4 August, after service on board the ships, they were shown the "Garden" when they could walk. It seems to have been behind the shore installations towards the southern end of the harbor and probably represented ground more or less cleared of trees by earlier fisher-men. But as Hayes said, "nothing appeared more there than Nature itself without art, who confusedly hath brought forth roses abundantly, wild but odiferous, and to sense very comfortable. Also the like plenty of 'raspis berries' which doe grow in every place." It was for most of them a pleasant change from shipboard life. Yet Parmenius did not find the scenery attrac-tive: it was not strange enough for him:[5] "The whole terrain is hilly and forested: the trees are for the most part pine. Some of these are growing old and others are just coming to maturity, but the majority have fallen with age, thus obstructing a good view of the land and the passage of travellers, so that no advance can be made anywhere. Nature seems even to want to struggle towards producing corn; for I found some blades and ears that resembled rye and they seem capable of being adapted to cultivation and sowing in the service of man. There are blackberries in the woods, or rather sweet straw-berries growing on bushes." The prospects for a settled life in Newfound-land seemed to these men only fair. They were mostly men from towns and cities, or from the prosperous and fruitful English countryside. They knew little of the seasonal rise and fall of the complex fishing industry. Nor had they any knowledge of weather conditions between October and May.

Gilbert, however, now knew what his next steps should be. He sent men ashore with a large and, no doubt, ornate tent or pavilion. This he had erected in a level space, above the northwest part of the harbour. He then called (by trumpet calls or messengers in boats?) the fishermen who were ashore and in the harbour to come to hear him. Though he spoke in English, he probably had interpreters in French and Portuguese or at least had his men explain his speech. Taking his place as Lord Paramount, he formally annexed the land, being handed a rod and a turf as tokens of English sovereignty. He announced that as it was now part of the Queen of Eng-land's dominions and he was her representative, laws promulgated by him for the future conduct of affairs in the Harbour (and by implication in the whole island) would have the force of law. The laws were firstly, that there was to be no public observance of religion except according to the rites of the Church of England (the Catholic majority would have to worship in private on their ships). Secondly, any challenges to the Queen's authority would be adjudged treasonable and punished as such by English law, the dreadful penalties for which he no doubt spelt out. Thirdly, words spoken against the Queen would lead to the man uttering them losing his ears and, most important, his ship by way of punishment. The "general voice" which Hayes says accepted these precepts were those of the English seamen, and of foreigners who did not dare to do otherwise, as no doubt armed guards surrounded the assembly. After the assembly had dispersed he had a permanent token of English sovereignty erected in the shape of a pillar to

5. A new translation by Neil Cheshire of his Latin letter from St. John's, in Quinn and Cheshire, *New Found Land of Stephen Parmenius*, p. 171, is cited here.

which was affixed the arms of England engraved on lead. Then his men
went to survey the "grounds", the holdings claimed by each ship's captain
for his fishing and drying gear. These Gilbert now appropriated, and leased
in perpetuity to their holders in return for a promise of rent. He did the same
for "grounds" yet unseen of which he was told in other harbours, though
precisely in which we cannot say. This upset long-standing tradition by
which those who came first could pick their "grounds". He next issued
passports to the foreign captains authorizing them to continue to fish under
the terms he imposed. One of these licences or passports to a Portuguese
fisherman survives in a Spanish translation in the Spanish archives.[6]
After that it only remained to impose a levy of fish from every ship
together with other supplies. There was no resistance, so military force must
have been evident throughout.

While Gilbert's men were making these arrangements — which were
futile unless he left a strong garrison and officials to enforce them — and no
one is known to have wintered in Newfoundland before this time and a
garrison would have to be on a year-round basis — his "mineral man"
Daniel was looking for minerals, and finding traces of some. Others were
surveying the harbour and ascertaining its precise latitude. How far afield the
survey parties went we cannot say. All records of these activities (which we
would find invaluable) were later to be lost. We would know much more
about St. John's Harbour and about Newfoundland at this time if they had
survived. Edward Hayes, and no doubt Parmenius too, were inquiring
about the climate of the land, and gathered that it was tolerable from spring
to autumn but was thought to be cold in winter though no one was found
who had tried it. News of white bears, of lynx and other creatures, birds and
so on were collected. No Beothuk Indians were seen and they were said to
have deserted the south of the island, greatly to the disappointment of
Parmenius. When Hayes came to reckon up the assets of the island, besides
fish and oil, he put resin, pitch, tar, potash, boards (sawn timber), hides, furs,
flax, hemp, corn, cables, cordage, line, metals — in that order — as possible
products — a list we can see to have been largely unrealistic. Gilbert was
excited about some ore discovered by the mineral man, which he said
contained silver, but was not to be spoken of until they had left harbour. The
view the English obtained was of part of the Avalon Peninsula alone,
scarcely representative of the island as a whole. At some point, perhaps in
his own annexation speech, he proposed that his own principality in the area
should extend 100 leagues in all directions: 300 miles north, south and
westward from St. John's represented an enormous area.

Edward Hayes, our reporter of the voyage, was an honest man. While
Gilbert was asserting the very tenuous authority he carried from the Queen
and assessing the potential value of the new acquisition of the Crown to

6. First printed, in translation, in Quinn and Cheshire, *New Found Land of Stephen
    Parmenius*, pp. 209-10.

himself and his country, Hayes did not conceal that the expedition was in a state of chaos. Many of the men were recruited from Channel pirates and some took the chance of making off to another harbour and stealing the fish belonging to a vessel there. Others hid in the woods, determined to go no further with their commander, who clearly did not command their effective loyalty. They hoped to get carried home by English fishing vessels. Others still were sick, though we are not told with what disease. In this state of disorder Gilbert cut his losses, assigning the *Swallow* to return with the recalcitrants and the sick, and transferring Browne to be captain of the *Delight*, while he himself went aboard the little frigate *Swallow* so that he could investigate harbours and other features on the way south. Hayes thought they were well enough equipped for further exploration when they set out on 20 August. The ships sailed rapidly south and, as they reached Cape Race, off which they were becalmed for a time, the same night as they left St. John's, little if any investigation of the coast of the Avalon Peninsula south of St. John's Harbour can have been done.

v

The vessels went on, heading for Cape Breton, but came too close to Sable Island with its treacherous shoals. There the *Delight* went aground and rapidly broke up, losing at one stroke most of the stores and all the specimens, maps and charts assembled at St. John's. Most of the men were lost. Maurice Browne and Stephen Parmenius, with the mineral man, Daniel, were among them. Richard Clarke, the master, and a handful of men got on board the shallop, which was being towed and, after much hardship, reached the southeastern shore of Newfoundland, where eventually they were carried back to Europe by Basque fishermen and repatriated. Gilbert was now left, effectively, with one 40 ton ship, the *Golden Hind*, and the tiny frigate. There was nothing left for him but to make for home and give up the voyage. After all his hopes and plans, Gilbert had been forced to admit defeat. But he spoke to Hayes of his having become "a Northern man altogether" and of having moved his own personal objectives to Newfoundland and its adjoining territories. He stressed to Hayes that he had already at St. John's claimed for his own patrimony the vast area of 100 leagues square, as we have seen. But he regretted not having been able to go on to search for and lay out the lands on the mainland granted to his other associates. He had not given up all hopes of Newfoundland, but most of what he had invested in the expedition, as well as his most effective associates, were gone forever.

As the remaining vessels sailed eastward, he alternated between hope, disappointment and rage (cruelly beating his boy from pure exasperation). He was still keeping command of the frigate, though visiting the *Golden Hind* to have a cut on his foot dressed. Hayes tried to convince him then to

move to the larger and safer ship, but he would not do so. Though they had
initially fine weather, autumnal storms soon drove them onward as they
sailed southeastward towards the Azores, the *Squirrel* being nearly
swamped on one occasion but recovering gallantly. Hayes's last picture of
Gilbert, as seen from the *Golden Hind* is a well-known and memorable one:
"the General sitting abaft with a book in his hand, cried out to us in the *Hind*
(so oft as we did approach within hearing,) 'We are as near to heaven by sea
as by land'." The book was almost certainly Sir Thomas More's *Utopia*,
where the phrase, or one very near it, occurs; it was most appropriate for a
man in his position and with his record. Hayes took it as a sign of confidence
that God would care for him as he goes on "Reiterating the same speech,
well beseeming a soldier, resolute in Jesus Christ, as I can testify he was."
There is no need to doubt that Gilbert was a sound member of the Church of
England but not a single testimony except this suggests that Christian
influences on his life were significant. But in the night, Monday, 9 September
(our 31 August) the frigate was overwhelmed by the waves and Gilbert was
never seen again. There were no survivors. The *Golden Hind* reached port
at Falmouth on 22 September with news of his failure and death.

vi

How then are we to assess Sir Humphrey Gilbert's significance for later
Newfoundland? At the time, in 1583, there were hopes, in spite of his death
at sea, of following up his ambitious — over-ambitious, we would say —
plans. Sir George Peckham published a pamphlet late in 1583 in an attempt
to revive his own project and paid tribute there to Gilbert's achievement, as
he saw it through the eyes of Edward Hayes, who remained a stout upholder
of English claims to Newfoundland and an advocate of its exploitation. But
few responded to his propaganda. Sir Humphrey's elder brother, Sir John,
seems to have discovered rapidly in 1584 that the assumption of authority
by his late brother meant nothing. His representatives are not known to have
collected any tribute from the fishermen, nor did they try again in 1585 or
later. Edward Hayes, however, was for a time indefatigable in pressing
Newfoundland's claims on the Lord Treasurer, Lord Burghley.[7] In 1585-6
he addressed to him elaborate memoranda on the resources of Newfoundland and projected various ways in which it could be exploited for English
ends — including a naval flotilla which would patrol the coasts and mulct the
non-English fishing vessels. But even Hayes desisted when he got no
response from Burghley, though the number and importance of English
vessels engaged in the fishery increased steadily for some thirty years after
1583 (though the French still kept somewhat ahead of them).

The most lasting memorial to Gilbert was the narrative of his last expedi-

7. Printed for the first time in Quinn (and others), *New American World, III*, pp. 124-138.

tion by Edward Hayes, published by Richard Hakluyt in his great voyage-collection, the *Principall navigations* of 1589[8] and again in the third volume of his second edition, *Principal navigations*, volume III, in 1600. These editions were widely read and may well have played an important part in the revival of colonizing plans from 1610 onwards. We know at least that Richard Whitbourne, too, in his *Discourse*, published in 1620 and 1622,[10] recalled his own presence on a fishing vessel in St. John's Harbour when Gilbert entered in 1583 and dated his, and his country's, concern with the island from that time forward. The failure of so many colonial attempts in the seventeenth century and the long and successful struggle of the fishermen against the settlers meant that Gilbert passed into forgotten history, except for occasional students of English expansion overseas. But in the late nineteenth and early twentieth century the early history of Newfoundland began to arouse some interest in Newfoundland itself (largely through Judge Prowse),[11] in the United States and in England, so that Gilbert's association with the island, and the annexation of 1583,[*] which is now being celebrated, appeared (whatever its failure to have immediate practical results) to mark a significant stage in the beginnings of the first British empire. It did indeed do so though more as a symbol than a reality. But Newfoundlanders can sincerely regard his annexation of 1583 as a beginning, a promise at least, that there would be in the end a Newfoundland settled by people from the British Isles, as indeed it has been.

*This essay was written to mark the 400th anniversary of the annexation.

8. Pp. 679-97. It appears in the facsimile edition, with an introduction by D. B. Quinn and R. A. Skelton (2 vols., Cambridge: Hakluyt Society,1965).
9. III (1600), pp. 143-62, and reprinted in the 12-volume edition, (Glasgow: MacLehose, 1903-5), VIII, pp. 34-77.
10. See Gillian T. Cell, *Newfoundland discovered* (London: Hakluyt Society, 1982), p. 122.
11. D. W. Prowse, *A History of Newfoundland* (London: 1st edition 1895, 2nd edition 1896) has remained the classic history of the island, though much of it has now been superseded. A full life of Gilbert was first published by W. G. Gosling, *Sir Humphrey Gilbert* (London: 1911) which is still readable, though somewhat overtaken by later discoveries. The first attempt to collect and discuss the documents on Gilbert's American ventures was made by Carlos Slafter (ed). *Sir Humfrey Gylberte* (Boston: Prince Society, 1903), and is still of some use for the basic texts.

QVID NON:

VIRGINIA

Sᵣ Humphry Gilbert knight

Heere may yee see the pourtrait of his face
Who for his countries honour oft did trace
Along the deepe, and made a noble way
Vnto our growing fame Virginia
The picture of his minde if yee do craue it
Looke vpon vertues picture and yee haue it

16 Sir Humphrey Gilbert. Engraving by Robert Boissard, in Henry Holland *Basilωilogia* 1618) *(Ashmolean Museum, Oxford)*

14

STEPHANUS PARMENIUS BUDAEUS:
A HUNGARIAN PIONEER IN NORTH AMERICA

Stephan Parmenius Budaeus, as he called himself, was a young Hungarian scholar who, by way of England, made a voyage to North America on which he perished, though not without leaving us some record of his intentions and his early reactions to new transatlantic lands.[1]

The unlikely appearance of a Hungarian in a North American exploring enterprise in the 1580s stems from the convergence of two streams of activity. On the one side Englishmen were becoming interested in exploring and exploiting North America; on the other side there was the arrival into the English circle, interested in such activity, of a young scholar who was concluding his course of scholarly travel by a visit to the University of Oxford, one of the places of learning in England to which many European scholars came on such a pilgrimage.

Sir Humphrey Gilbert, an English gentleman-adventurer, had determined to attempt to carve out landed estates for Englishmen in hitherto unexploited North America. Gilbert had set out in 1578 to go to North America by way of the West Indies to investigate the coast of what is now Virginia but his ships were scattered in the Atlantic and, apart from a little fighting with Spanish and Portuguese vessels, achieved nothing: he had to return. He settled down after 1579 to plan a more systematic programme of American exploitation.[2] He did not set out in the end until 1583 but by that time he had drawn a varied group of people

---

[1] An earlier version of this essay was published as 'Budai Parmenius István: as elsö magyar utazó Észak-Amerikában,' *Irodalomtörtèneti Közlemènyek* (1974), pp.203-10. The preliminaries have been completely revised. The book on which it is founded is D.B. Quinn and Neil M. Cheshire, *The New Found Land of Stephen Parmenius* (Toronto: University of Toronto Press, 1972).

[2] D.B. Quinn, ed., *The Voyages and Colonising Enterprises of Sir Humphrey Gilbert* (London: The Hakluyt Society, 2nd series, LXXXXIII-IV, 1940). There is a short survey in D.B. Quinn, *Sir Humphrey Gilbert* (St. John's: Newfoundland Historical Society, Pamphlet Series no.7, 1983), pp.1-31, and another in *Dictionary of Canadian Biography*, I (Toronto University Press, 1965), 331-6. Some new information on him appears in Quinn and Cheshire, *Parmenius*.

into his North American enterprise including Stephan Parmenius of Buda.

The search for details of this rather strange association began with Richard Hakluyt, the younger, and the well-known compiler of English travel narratives and, himself, a considerable scholar. It was carried further through collaboration with Neil Cheshire, whose knowledge of Renaissance Latin and its context, and his exceptional ability as a translator, made it possible to reveal in detail such writings of Parmenius as survive, and to piece together something about the arrival and stay of this young Hungarian humanist in England, so that we could publish in 1972 a book, *The New Found Land of Stephen Parmenius*, containing his Latin poems and translations in their context, as then known previous attempts in Hungary to make something of the scattered English references to this man and to fill in his background before 1581 proved to be trivial, mistaken or merely imaginative. Subsequently, however, after both authors had the opportunity to visit Budapest and discuss Parmenius with scholars there, Tibor Klaniczay, director of the Centre for Renaissance Studies in the Hungarian Academy of Sciences, undertook research on the person we know as Parmenius, and has provided something of a setting for his earlier experiences.[3]

It may first of all be said that there is no Hungarian name that can be linked with 'Parmenius', and Klaniczay has been forced to come to the conclusion that this name was adopted by István Budai during his travels, perhaps only when he came to England, as an affectation of a kind much favoured by humanist scholars who liked to provide themselves with a classical-sounding epithet to give them a touch of distinction and to enable them to have an individual handle by which they could be known. In this case, however, it is not easy to determine what was the origin of the word: Klaniczay suggests that it may well derive from one of several Greek words, in a Latinized form, meaning 'steadfast', or something of that sort, indicating Stephan's devotion perhaps to scholarship, to his homeland or even to England. But Parmenius he called himself in the setting in which we know him and so he will remain, unless a better explanation can be found. However, even if the detailed Turkish records do not record any István Budai in Buda itself, those of the town of Ráckové do; István Budai appears as a new arrival in 1559 and as a resident in 1562. This man could well have been our Stephan's father and, if Stephen was over twenty-one years old or thereabouts when we believe he came to England, he could well have been born in Buda as he claimed to have been. There is thus a probable

---

[3] Tibor Klaniczay, 'A Contribution to the Stephen Parmenius Research', *Acta Litteraria Academiae Scientiarum Hungaricae*, XVIII (1976), 191-200. Personal correspondence with Dr. Klaniczay has indicated that no additional information has appeared down to late 1988.

but not a certain indication of his background. There seems little doubt that at Rakové he could have received the elements of a good classical education as a boy and adolescent. To follow him further has involved even less certain conjecture, but much of it possible if not certain.

He himself does not help us much. In his dedication of his principal poem he merely says (in Neil Cheshire's translation): [4]

> Although I was born in the servitude and barbarism of the Turkish empire, my parents were, by the grace of God, Christians, and I was even educated for some part of the time. After I had made some academic progress, thanks to the efforts of my erudite teachers, such as have always been the pride of my native Hungary (and are particularly so now, among her still surviving relics), I was sent away to visit the universities of the Christian world.
>
> On these travels I saw not only many centres of culture but also a number of wisely constituted states and the impeccable administration of many branches of the Church, spending almost three years in the process, I had conceived the object of this expedition to be not merely to have a look at the cities and way of life of different peoples, but to make friends, or at least acquaintances, with some of their eminent men.

Tibor Klaniczay has indicated from this that the most likely place for István Budei, the younger, to have gone from Rákové was the Unitarian College at Kolozavar in Transylvania where Prince Báthory maintained a tolerant and humanistic regime. This college evidently did not turn the Calvinist István into a Unitarian, as he remained a Trinitarian, but it would most probably have given him the training in secular humanism which he was to display in England, an interest in religion it is true, but also a concern, as he himself said, in politics and society and in the intellectual life of the humanist élite in the countries he was to visit. From Kolozavar István is most likely to have made his way to Wittenberg where he apparently matriculated on 29 September 1579 (not at the time of his entry but presumably just before he left). This was a leading Lutheran university but famous for its humanistic leanings. He is likely to have arrived there with some knowledge of the cult of Queen Elizabeth as a peculiarly tolerant and attractive Protestant monarch which was current in Transylvania. This cult can be traced from 1564 through the 1570s, and may well have turned his attention first of all to England. Klaniczay suggests he may even have encountered Paleologus's *Cathechesis Christiana* (1570), where American Indians were set out as simple, uncontaminated people who could be compared favourably with the 'irrationalism of Catholicism'. It is thus not impossible that István carried with him some slight early interest in the Americans which was to be fully developed in England. One probable contact which may have turned his footsteps to Wittenberg was the

[4] Quinn and Cheshire, *Parmenius*, pp.76-7.

eminent Hungarian humanist Andreas Dudith, then living at Breslau (Wróclaw), whose English connections were considerable.[5] He had been visited in 1574 by the young Philip Sidney (whose association with Richard Hakluyt, István's associate in England, was close) and he was also visited by the English scholar Henry Savile (in company with Robert Sidney and Henry Neville) in 1581, establishing a friendship which his son Thomas, who was to be István's close friend in England, was to continue until Dudith's death in 1589. The indications of a contact between Dudith and István are circumstantial but probable. An introduction from him would have been invaluable in his later travels.

A foreign tour was the usual way in which young men of scholarly bent continued their education by way of introductions from one university to another, without remaining long at any one place. The two or more years between 1579 and 1581 were spent, as he indicates, at such centres of learning but it is exasperating that before he came to England we have no firm indication of where he went. He might for example have been to Protestant universities such as Heidelberg or Strasburg, perhaps to the Geneva Academy, under the redoubtable Theodore de Béze (incidentally a close contact of Dudith), whose links with English theologians were considerable. He would, through his interest in and knowledge of the Latin classics, have been in Italy. Protestants could and did travel to cities such as Florence or Bologna, Venice or Milan, and even to Rome so long as they had influential sponsors and maintained a low profile in matters of religion. A number of Englishmen already tended to complete their education by Italian tours. In only one case is there some circumstantial evidence that István found a means by which his plan ultimately to come to England, which he asserts in his writings, had been assisted, that is by meeting one or more members of the Unton family at an Italian university. This was almost certainly at Padua where a number of Hungarian students are known to have gone and where Protestants would not be molested. Henry Unton and his friend Charles Merbury were in Italy, and for a time at Padua during the appropriate period (so was another brother, Edward). But the first two were back in England before the end of 1581, a possible time for István to have accompanied them. We know that when he was at Oxford he was closely in touch with this family, especially with Henry, and stayed at their house, Wadley, at Faringdon not too far from the university. Charles Merbury had had Laurence Humfrey of Magdalen College as his tutor, a man known for befriending many visiting scholars, most of them refugees from Catholic persecution. He, in turn, could well have been the means by which István came to be linked with Richard Hakluyt, if it

---

[5] Pierre Costil, *André Dudith, humaniste hongrois, 1533-1589* (Paris, 1935), especially pp.147, 202-3, 207-8.

was not through one of the Savilles – Thomas had just entered Merton College at this time.

Armed with a sheaf of introductions gathered on his travels, the wandering scholar István, who now emerges as Parmenius, Stephen Parmenius of Buda, can be traced in some detail between late in 1581, when he must have become 'my bedfelowe in Oxforde' as Hakluyt describes him. Hakluyt was a 'Student', a teaching member of Christ Church,[6] the grandest of the Oxford colleges. Through Richard Hakluyt, the elder, a cousin who was a lawyer in the Inner Temple, the younger Richard had been drawn into the study even the teaching of geography at Oxford, and involved in the mainly London-based group which was interested and involved in discussions about the overseas world, in particular about the possibility of England's exploring and colonising North America and had been for some time collecting materials on the New World. Into this circle Parmenius was eventually drawn. But this would be to anticipate, as his primary aim would be to make friends with men of scholarly interests and through them to explore not only the classics but also the political institutions and polity of England, as well as the precise nature of its ecclesiastical institutions as part of the educative process on which he had embarked since leaving Wittenberg, and in which his sojourn in England he regarded as its climax before returning to his native land.

Hakluyt, the Saviles, Jean Hotman, a French humanist then residing in Oxford, and Scipio and Alberico Gentili, the latter an Italian professor of civil law at Oxford, were members of a group of scholars who corresponded with each other and with persons outside Oxford, notably in London where the rising historian, William Camden, was closely in contact with the Oxford circle as was Richard Garth, clerk of the petty bag, one of their associates. It had other members too though so far we know little about the ramifications of the circle.[7] It was into this group that Parmenius was drawn and where he must have found satisfaction for some of his intellectual curiosity though unfortunately no examples of his own correspondence in this period have survived.

Parmenius was not confined to Oxford. He saw something of the countryside of Oxfordshire and Berkshire when he had an open invitation from Henry Unton to stay at Wadley, a large country house at

---

[6] Most of what we know about Hakluyt is contained in D.B. Quinn, ed., *The Hakluyt Handbook* (London: The Hakluyt Society, 2nd series, CXLIV-V, 1974). Documents concerning him are in E.G.R. Taylor, ed., *The Writings and Correspondence of the Two Richard Hakluyts* (London: The Hakluyt Society, 2nd series, LXXVI-VII, 1935). George Bruner Parks, *Richard Hakluyt and the English Voyages* (New York, 1928), is still valuable.

[7] Letters of the English *Literati* are to be found in Thomas Smith, ed., *V. cl. Gulielmi Camdeni et illustrius virorum . . . epistolae* (London, 1691); B.L., Cotton MS Julius C. and Add. 22583; Jean and François Hotman, *Epistolae* (Amsterdam, 1700).

Faringdon, over the border in Berkshire. He saw the way of life of the English gentry, and of which we can see a little in a remarkable picture now in the National Portrait Gallery, depicting in a memorial portrait the life of Henry's father.[8]

From Oxford too Hakluyt took him to London, an experience which made a deep impression on him. It was almost certainly Hakluyt who wrote to William Camden, the historian, then second master at Westminster School, who wrote back in a letter which is not addressed (it is a draft only) saying, in Neil Cheshire's translation of the Latin, 'I will look after Master Parmenius of Buda since you have commended him to me'.[9] Camden could have told him much about the English past and about contemporary scholarship and politics in the capital. There too he may have seen something of the royal court and of the Palace of Westminster. Hakluyt may well have had already the *entreé* to Sir Francis Walsingham, the principal secretary of state, who was to be so significant an influence on Hakluyt's own career from 1583 onwards. He might also have been received by the ageing Lord Burghley, the lord treasurer, to whom Hakluyt was known. At a lower level he is not unlikely to have been brought into touch with Thomas Vautrollier, the Huguenot printer and publisher, who was eventually to publish Parmenius's second poem. Vautrollier was well known to the Sidney family, for example – and Parmenius may also have met Philip Sidney in one or more visits to London. Vautrollier was admired for his expertise in printing in Latin and Greek. The most important introduction of all which Hakluyt effected was that to Sir Humphrey Gilbert, whose personality and projects immediately attracted Parmenius and created in him an intensive desire to see more of the world than he had hitherto envisaged and to involve himself in Gilbert's American venture.

If for the first year in which he was in England, that is from some time in the latter part of 1581, we think, until the summer of 1582 the activities of Parmenius were mainly literary and scholarly, he was gradually drawn to the brink of more practical activity, namely participation in an American exploration venture. It would appear that in the last months of 1581 and the first of 1582 Parmenius was busily studying alongside Richard Hakluyt. We should have to guess at many of the subjects they discussed together: amongst them was, almost certainly, Ptolemy's *Geographia* and the ways in which the classical geography had been vindicated, modified and enlarged by the new discoveries overseas. We are on somewhat firmer ground when we say that they were reading through together the great voyage collections in as many European languages as were at their disposal, to see what was known about the

[8] Quinn and Cheshire, *Parmenius*, pl.3.
[9] Idem, p.215.

American continents which had been newly brought to view in the sixteenth century, with particular reference to what was known about North America, since that had an immediate practical bearing on the preparations which Sir Humphrey Gilbert was making. The primary source for this was the third volume of the great collection, prepared by Giovanni Battista Ramusio at Venice and published there between 1550 and 1559. Hakluyt owned this work, or at least as copy of volume three, and was now engaged in putting together anything he could on what was known of eastern North America for Gilbert's main venture. From Ramusio he took a number of documents which he translated. It is highly probable that Parmenius helped Hakluyt with this selecting task, and that they read together many volumes which did not contribute useful information on this field. Hakluyt was able to add some material from unpublished sources as well. He clearly also enabled Parmenius to read much on the exploits of earlier English explorers in other areas which he had available in manuscript or print. Parmenius seems to have been particularly interested in the English expeditions which opened the northern route to Russia from 1553 onwards, led by men like Willoughby and Chancellor, Stephen and William Borough, and by the land traveller, Anthony Jenkinson, who had brought back much material on Russia and the Muslim lands to the northeast of Persia. He also learnt of notable English adventurers like John Hawkins. Francis Drake and Martin Frobisher, with perhaps a particular interest in Drake's Pacific exploration.

Hakluyt's collection, *Divers voyages touching the discoverie of America*,[10] was intended both to inform the reading public about North America, and also to act as somewhat sophisticated propaganda for Gilbert's western ventures: it appeared late in May 1582. It must therefore have been completed by early March in this year. It was probably in these months that Parmenius was brought into fairly close touch with Sir Humphrey Gilbert and had been inspired by the thought that he himself might have something to contribute towards the venture, not at this stage by taking part in it in person, but by celebrating in print its inspirer and his objectives in a congratulatory poem in the classical idiom. The Latin poem which he composed during the spring of 1582 – his 'stately poem' as Hakluyt was to call it – was probably ready by May of that year, which was intended to continue, at a more elevated intellectual level, the propaganda for Gilbert's American venture. The poem, *De navigatione . . . Humfredi Gilberti . . . carmen*, which appeared in June 1582, was a eulogy of England and of Sir Humphrey Gilbert. It combined classical references in the humanist tradition, using a largely classical vocabulary,

---

[10] There is a detailed study of this collection by D.B. Quinn, *Richard Hakluyt, Editor*, which accompanies a facsimile of *Divers Voyages* (Amsterdam: Theatrum Orbis Terrarum, 1967).

to glorify England and its Queen and the intrepid voyagers who were about to usher in a new Golden Age. More particularly he saw the English expanding over North America, from the north-west of which Sir Francis Drake had so recently returned, so he envisaged, at least in poetic terms, an English empire extending from east to west, from Norumbega to New Albion, while forgetting what effect this might have, if it was ever accomplished, on the inhabitants of that continent, living simply in *their* Golden Age. There is agreement between my collaborator Neil Cheshire and Tibor Klaniczay, who are competent to judge Latin verse, that it was a very reputable performance. To Cheshire it was 'a highly accomplished humanistic exercise'[11] though showing some signs of immaturity. To Klaniczay[12] it was something more: he says 'when we read [it] . . . we do not have the feeling that it is filled with swiftly adopted commonplaces and fashionable phrases in vogue in contemporary England. It is rather a well-deliberated mature poetico-poetical series of concepts'. He sees Parmenius setting up the New World as a passport to a Golden Age, free of Pope or Turk, and governed as England itself is (to him) governed 'by the virgin Astraea' who is similar to a goddess. The roots of this myth lie deep in what Frances Yates, in her *Astraea*,[13] called 'the labyrinth of Elizabethan symbolism'. She traces how the One ruler (the Emperor) of the Catholic imperialist writers became the One Virgin who was to bring down the papacy and usher in 'a golden age of pure religion, peace and plenty'. She goes on to point out that 'the religious side of the imperial legend was easily turned', as it was by John Dee, 'in a nationalist direction as England's power and greatness expanded under Elizabeth's rule'. Parmenius's poem stands directly in this line of succession.

When the little book appeared Parmenius was staying at the country house of his friend, Henry Unton, at Wadley. The head of the family, Sir Edward Unton, was lying ill, and the apothecary who came to visit him and to prescribe medicine became friendly with Parmenius. This was the French Huguenot, Geoffrey le Brumen, who was in the service of Sir Francis Walsingham, and was a militant Calvinist. To him Parmenius inscribed a copy of the printed poem with a flattering reference to his friendship. This copy has by good fortune survived and retains for us one of two surviving examples of Parmenius's handwriting. It is in the Henry E. Huntington Library, San Marino, California.

It was perhaps very shortly after this time that Parmenius began his second surviving poem, his *Paean* on the 104th Psalm, a thanksgiving hymn for his safe journeying from Hungary all the way to his present haven in England. It is a humanist exercise, elegant in style and perhaps

[11] Quinn and Cheshire, *Parmenius*, p.17.
[12] 'Contribution', p.127.
[13] Frances A. Yates, *Astraea* (London, 1975), pp.29–87, especially pp.49–50.

reflecting his contacts with the refinements of the Oxford Latinists of Christ Church and other Oxford colleges. But, as Neil Cheshire says, 'it contains more classical myth and humanist expertise than either Christian doctrine or autobiographical information'. It was dedicated to Henry Unton and was sent to the Huguenot printer, Thomas Vautrollier to print. Though dated 1582 it may not have appeared until the early months of 1583, the English year extending to March 25, though we find the calendar year also frequently used in scholarly circles. It was early in February 1583 that we know it to have been in print since it was then that he inscribed, affectionately, a copy to his young friend Thomas Savile, at that time in his third year as an undergraduate at Merton. The copy was duly presented to Eton College by Henry Savile, subsequently Provost, after Thomas's premature death in 1592, remaining in the college library where Neil Cheshire found it.

In the later spring of 1583 Parmenius took out his earlier poem again and attempted to refurbish it, since Gilbert had not, for reasons that will be explained, got to sea in 1582. He altered some of his references to Gilbert and modified a few of his statements on earlier English explorers, while he also polished the expression and language in places. He put in a side note calling attention to Drake's 'New Albion' being implied in the text. He retained Parmenius's fanciful picture of Gilbert sailing down the Thames and waving farewell to the Queen at her riverside palace at Greenwich; but this was as unreal for 1582 as it was for 1583. He dated his renewed dedication to Gilbert on 31 March 1583. It seems not unlikely that this was done as part of a revived programme of publication in support of Gilbert's delayed enterprise, as there were other pamphlets in the press about this time, but it may never have appeared in a second printed edition since no copy is known to survive. Hakluyt had a copy, however, and published it in the second edition of his great voyage-collection, *The principal navigations . . . of the English nation* in 1600.[14]

Sir Humphrey Gilbert had intended, sensibly, to set out for North America in May or June 1582. He brought some of his shipping safely to Southampton, but the winds turned unfavourable; other vessels could not make their way from London to join him. Frustrations mounted, month after month. Parmenius, at Wadley and Oxford, and possibly with visits to London and even Southampton in between, must have been sadly aware of these setbacks, as must Hakluyt. We have a vivid account of the frustrations they set up in gossippy letters of Maurice Browne.[15] He was a member of Walsingham's household, a young man with a little military and maritime experience and with aspirations himself to write, who was to be brought into close association with

---

[14] *Principal Navigations*, III (1600), 138–43; VIII (1904), 23–33.
[15] Thynne Papers V, MSS of the Marquess of Bath, Longleat; relevant extracts in Quinn and Cheshire, *Parmenius*, pp. 189–210.

Parmenius for some months in 1583. But in December the venture was called off until a new sailing season opened. By this time Parmenius had made his great decision. He would go to America too.

Gilbert accepted him as the scholar poet of the expedition; Maurice Browne was to be its more prosaic chronicler, and it was probably when their respective roles were being worked out that these young men became acquainted. It is to Maurice Browne that we owe the vivid accounts in his letters to his friend John Thynne of the trials of 1582; he tells a little of how the plans were taken up again the following spring, though, unfortunately, he does not mention Parmenius and we cannot tell precisely when he was drawn into the preparations. He would have had to be in Southampton in the second half of May and he probably received there, as Browne did, farewell letters from his friends, together with gifts of small luxuries as tokens of friendship. But by the beginning of June the ships were ready, the winds were right, the course of the expedition was determined, Parmenius having joined the *Swallow*.

The expedition left Southampton at the beginning of June 1583, the ships which composed it making for Dartmouth and then, at Plymouth on June 11, saying farewell, for many of them a last farewell, to English shores.[16] The *Swallow*'s stores were found to be inadequate and the men, rough sailors, with experience of piracy as well as peaceful sailing, were inclined to mutiny: in spite of their captain they robbed a French fishing vessel. The weather was bad for the time of year and winds contrary so that progress was slow and difficult. Once the northern coast of Newfoundland was reached after fifty days, the arrangement for a rendezvous of the ships which had been separated on the journey, worked out very well. As each ship sighted land to the west she made her way south. The squadron gradually assembled and was complete before it reached St. John's Harbour. There Gilbert proposed (unrealistically) to take formal control of the international fishery centred at St. John's before going south to reconnoitre what is now New England where he hoped later to settle colonists.

When the four vessels which now formed Gilbert's squadron attempted to pass the narrow and rock-ridden channel which led to the fine harbour of St. John's, the captains of the fishing vessels anchored inside first thought he was a simple pirate come to rob them and prepared to resist his entry. He was eventually admitted, with some relief, when it was found he came with a commission from the English queen and declared his purpose was not to attack but to protect the fishery. The twenty French and Portuguese vessels did not resist him; the English captains, of whom there may have been about as many again, received him with some enthusiasm. Gilbert gradually announced his plans; he would issue them with permits to continue fishing and he would lease

---

[16] Hakluyt, *Principall Navigations* (1589), pp.679–701, the narrative of Edward Hayes.

them the drying grounds they occupied on shore. For the time being he asked not a money rent, but supplies for his vessels, mainly dried fish which they could easily supply, but also gifts of luxuries such as wine which they might spare him. Presents were brought to the vessels, and Gilbert prepared to make a formal gesture on behalf of his personal and national claims.

Parmenius would have finally set foot on American soil on Sunday, 4 August, when Gilbert made his first shore excursion. Some of the merchants who came with the English fishing ships accompanied them to what was known as 'the Garden', a walk through bushes where raspberries and wild roses made something of a rural retreat, and which was no doubt a welcome change after fifty days at sea. But the land bore out few of Parmenius's expectations. He was expecting a pastoral beauty, strange beasts, strange men, which Newfoundland, this part of Newfoundland at least, could not offer. The bare rocks of the hills and headlands from which snow had not long retreated; the grass, long and untidy, just like grass anywhere else; the bushes rough and not exceptionally attractive; behind there was only the unbroken sweep of the virgin forest. There were no non-Europeans to be seen. The Beothuks, the original redskins, had long been driven away from the vicinity of St. John's. He could not feel that this busy fishing scene, a centre of economic activity such as he might have seen in many parts of western Europe, was really new, exciting or any fit theme for heroic verse.

On 5 August Gilbert formally annexed the island and proclaimed laws for the governance of the fishermen. Then came a brief and limited attempt at exploration. Gilbert, Parmenius and other leading men in the expedition worked their way inland to the forest edge, but found it impenetrable, the old timber having died and clogged up newer growth. Gilbert turned to the bare hills and worked over them with his mineral man (a Saxon miner named Daniel) collecting stones and earth which seemed to have mineral traces. Parmenius does not seem to have been greatly interested in the mineral side but paid some attention to the plants he saw growing, and commented with interest on one or two young Polar bears which had been rescued from icebergs on which they had, involuntarily, floated south.

By this time some rearrangement of personnel had been carried through. The captain of the *Delight* did not wish to continue, and he was assigned to take the *Swallow* back to England. Maurice Browne took over the command of the *Delight* and Parmenius transferred to her also. Thus when, on 6 August, Parmenius took out his writing materials it was almost certainly in the cabin of this ship. Maurice Browne was, in all probability, like Parmenius, settling down to put on record what he had recently seen; Parmenius too may have been jotting down impressions of his feelings, scraps of verse and so on. But he took his quill to write also to his friends. It was only the fact that there were English fishing vessels in the harbour which made transatlantic correspondence of this sort possible. First on his list of correspondents he put Laurence Humfrey, an indication perhaps of the closeness of the friendship which had grown up between them at Oxford, of which we have found no further evidence. When he had finished his letter (which has not survived) he started a letter in fluent Latin in almost identical terms to Richard Hakluyt which we, most fortunately, have.[17] He said he did not yet feel ready to write to Henry Unton but wished Hakluyt to convey his good wishes to him. The contents of this letter to Hakluyt vividly expressed his sense of disappointment that America, so far, was not so different or exciting as his imagination had painted it in advance. In English translation part of his letter read: 'Now I ought to tell you about the customs, territories and inhabitants, and yet what I am so say, my dear Hakluyt, when I see nothing but desolation? There are inexhaustable supplies of fish . . . The whole terrain is hilly and forested: the trees are for the most part pine. Some of these are growing old and others are just coming to maturity, but the majority have fallen with age, thus obstructing a good view of the land. All the grass is tall but scarcely different from ours. I have found some blades and ears that resembly rye and they seem capable of being adapted easily to cultivation and sowing in the service of man. There are blackberries in the woods, or rather very sweet strawberries growing on bushes [actually raspberries]. Bears sometimes appear round the shelters and are killed, but they are white . . . and smaller than ours. I am not clear whether there are any inhabitants in this area (and who could be there, I ask you, since it is impossible to travel any distance?) nor have I met anyone who is in a position to say. Nor do we know any better whether there is any metal in the mountains; and for the same reason, even though their appearance may indicate underlying minerals.' He looked forward mainly to what he would see in more attractive lands farther south: 'the more that is reported about the region we are making for,' he said, 'the greater will our expectations be from day to day.' The Golden Age and new land with its simple, uncorrupted people had faded in contact with harsh reality.

When the three remaining ships set out from St. John's on 20 August, Gilbert was in the tiny frigate, the *Squirrel*, so that he could the better reconnoitre the bays and inlets; Maurice Browne and Parmenius, with the mineral expert, Daniel, were in the *Delight* which could not be brought into the smaller barred harbours; the *Golden Hind*, a ship of intermediate size, was under the command of Edward Hayes. They sailed southwards. Instead of making at once for Cape Breton, from

[17] Idem, pp.697-9: Hakluyt's translation, together with a modern translation and the text, with notes, are in Quinn and Cheshire, *Parmenius*, pp.167-85; facsimile of Latin text p.65.

which he intended to follow the mainland coast to Norumbega, the modern New England, Gilbert decided to turn a little off his course and put in at Sable Island, where, years before, Portuguese had put animals ashore to breed and where some fresh meat might be obtained. On the morning of August 29 they were very near the island, nearer than they realised. There was a sea mist, very poor visibility and a strong wind. The *Golden Hind* began sounding and, realising the water was very shallow indeed, sent out signals to the *Delight* to change her course. The *Golden Hind* and the *Squirrel* managed to sheer off at the last possible moment, but the *Delight* was unable to do so, struck a shoal, foundered and broke up very rapidly. The other ships knew that disaster had struck her but were unable to turn to her assistance. It seems that she was aground on the western spit of Sable Island and was breaking up from the bows when a number of the seamen raced to the stern where the long-boat was still afloat, at the end of the rope tied to the sternpost. A few of them got into her, cut off and began picking up survivors. But amongst the men they rescued were neither Parmenius nor Maurice Browne. They had gone down with the ship. The boat's crew after many adventures and much hardship, got back to England and told something of the last moments of the *Delight*.[18]

Gilbert, having cast about in vain for survivors, was forced to the conclusion that the *Golden Hind* and the *Squirrel* were now too weak and depleted in resources to go on and so, very reluctantly, they put back across the Atlantic. Insisting on sailing in the tiny *Squirrel*, he was half way across when, in heavy seas, the *Squirrel* was swamped and lost with all hands. Hayes brought the *Golden Hind* home alone. Parmenius was lost; Browne was lost; Sir Humphrey Gilbert was lost. All were eulogised by Edward Hayes when he came to write the story of the tragic loss the expedition had suffered. Amongst those whose loss bore heaviest on him was that of 'a learned man, an Hungarian, borne in the Citie of Buda, called thereof Budaeus, who of great pietie and zeale to good attempts, adventured in this action, minding to record in the Latine tongue, the gests and things worthy of remembrance, happening in this discoverie, to the honour of our nation, the same being adorned with the eloquent stile of this Orator, and rare Poet of our time.'[19]

The failure and the losses incurred were almost total. But there was something left. Gilbert's notion of settling depressed groups of gentlemen on North American shores was to inspire others later. The busy propaganda carried on before Gilbert sailed, and the attempts made by his followers, after his failure was known, to carry on with his ventures, showed that the 'Americans', those who wished to intervene in this way in North America had grown greatly in numbers as a result,

---

[18] *Principall Navigations* (1589), pp.700-1.
[19] Hayes in Idem, p.692; Quinn and Cheshire, *Parmenius*, pp.52-60.

partly, of the pamphlets and other literature, amongst them Parmenius's poems, which had been called out by Gilbert's venture.

Parmenius was a minor figure in the process of discovery and colonization, but he was an interesting and significant one for all that. It was novel for a young scholar, especially one from a country so far from the western ocean as Hungary, to be inspired by the vision of a New World, to be willing to learn about it, and to embody his learning and his new enthusiasm in a traditional literary form. It was still more novel – though Camões had done it on the East India voyage from Portugal – for a poet and scholar to be an adventurer himself, to try to play his own part in opening up America to European eyes, to prepare to enshrine his experiences in what he hoped to be enduring verse. That all his interest and his striving came to nothing was sad, but what he has left us, his story as far as it has been possible to tell it, and his small sheaf of works, are there as evidence of his abiding interest as a literary and historical figure.

15

THOMAS HARRIOT AND THE NEW WORLD

THOMAS HARRIOT lived from 1560 to 1621: during at least half that period the New World, the Americas, north and south, the tropical river valleys of Amazon and Orinoco, the sounds and islands and rivers of the first Virginia (which comprised those parts of North Carolina and Virginia which lay between the Neuse River and the James River), fur- and fish-rich Canada, the northern passages to the west of Greenland, the routes across the Atlantic to America north and south, were in his mind. His active concerns with the Americas can be traced from 1584 to 1613 and his interest almost certainly extended some way on either side of these dates. Between 1584 and 1590 he was himself involved in American activities, including temporary residence in North America, not merely as an adviser but as a participant. Otherwise he stayed in the background, giving technical advice and assistance in the solution of problems which lay ahead of the actual participants, or making some response to the discoveries, or problems connected with the discoveries, of others. Some of his activities we can follow in detail; others can only be glimpsed; in still other cases we are forced to speculate on what precise part he played and trust that time, study, and possibly the discovery of new materials may allow such speculations to be confirmed or fruitfully altered so that gradually a full and balanced picture of his place in New World exploration and its popularization can be more fully and accurately assessed.

When Harriot graduated at Oxford in 1580 he was equipped with a rather stereotyped scientific knowledge in mathematics and astronomy. How far he had begun to specialize in mathematics and its applications we are wholly unable to say, except to indicate that his basic intellectual equipment was mathematical though he had a scholar's interest and capacity in a wide range of other areas of knowledge. From St Mary's Hall he presumably took himself to London; it is not unlikely that he entered the household of some gentleman or merchant who had need of a tutor for his children. One might speculate on the possibility that wherever he settled it was in the company of men who were interested not in theory but in practice, in the problems of applying mathematics to such questions as navigation at sea, in the expansion of trade, and in the extension of knowledge about the world outside Europe. Such matters were being discussed in London in the years 1580 to 1583 and at the end of them Harriot emerges as a man who is vitally concerned with them.

Drake's return in 1580 had revealed to many that the world could be encompassed by Englishmen and not by Portuguese and Spaniards alone. Interest in instrumental navigation among merchants, gentlemen, and scholars was beginning to produce English books on the subject.

In 1582 the younger Richard Hakluyt was urging the establishment of a lectureship in London where those interested could be trained: Drake at one point offered to endow it. Later it was financed by the elder Thomas Smith, customer of London, and his son Thomas, who was to head so many companies concerned with the overseas world. English sailing-masters were efficient in the use of older rule-of-thumb methods of navigation, but these were not enough for exploration of new and extensive oceans and coastlines. Nor was it sufficient any longer for a gentleman to be a competent commander of men at sea: he needed himself to know enough of the theory of navigation to understand what the specialist seamen were doing, to conduct effective discussions with them when he wished his view of what should be done to be effective; to be able to plan ahead flexibly where ships could safely, or possibly with safety, go. Drake had shown how vitally important such training and capacity was to a wide ranging expedition. A young man-about-town, a close friend of the younger Thomas Smith, Maurice Browne, who had spent a few months at sea at the Azores, came back to London to study maps and navigation. 'I will apply my tyme', he wrote on 6 July 1582,[1] 'to the studdy of Cosmography, and the art of Navigatione'. He was planning to do so with his friend John Thynne: 'we will device to have somme convenient tyme . . . to have an excellent fellowe who dwelleth here at London to read Cosmography and to instruct us and to make us learned in the art of Navigation, that with the more easines we may come to the full knowlege thereof by experience'. We have no evidence that the 'excellent fellowe' mentioned by Browne was Thomas Harriot but it could well have been.

Maurice Browne was to seek his experience at sea in command of one of the ships of Sir Humphrey Gilbert's American expedition of 1583 and, ironically, was to die of the results of defective seamanship when the *Delight* went down at Sable Island later that year. But he was not the only one of his kind who felt the need to learn what should be done at sea.

Walter Ralegh had taken part as captain of the *Falcon* in Gilbert's earlier voyage in 1578–9 and had drifted rather aimlessly in the Atlantic to the Canaries and farther south, instead of sailing on to America. It may have been then that he learned to regret that he did not know enough to direct his Portuguese pilot, Simon Fernandes, to set an effective trans-Atlantic course. Ralegh too was involved in 1583 in Gilbert's final venture. About the beginning of May 1583 Maurice Browne reported that Ralegh had bought a new ship from Henry Oughtred at Southampton and had equipped it for sixty men,

1. D. B. Quinn and N. M. Cheshire, *The new found land of Stephen Parmenius,* Toronto, 1972. pp. 39, 191.

and that it was to be the flagship of the expedition.[2] When Ralegh bought and renamed his ship the *Bark Ralegh* he may have thought of going in her himself; he may even have begun to think of equipping himself with sufficient navigational knowledge to command her effectively. But he had now climbed into the inner circle of courtiers; it would be risking his future if he asked to leave too soon on a dangerous voyage, and in any case the Queen would not allow him to go. *Bark Ralegh* sailed with the fleet on 13 June without him, but two days later her captain turned back and she returned to Plymouth, the men forcing her captain, Michael Butler, an old companion in arms of Ralegh, to do so because they were afraid to take the risk of crossing the ocean in a ship in whose equipment they did not have confidence. By the end of September one ship alone had come back from American waters to report the loss of the *Delight* and probably of the *Squirrel* with Gilbert on board as well.[3] But Ralegh had his ship; if he was to use her, he must, he felt, learn how to do so.

This is where Harriot came in; he was certainly the 'excellent fellowe' Ralegh employed to teach him cosmography and navigation as he had perhaps taught Maurice Browne before. Whether Ralegh was installed by the Queen in spacious apartments in Durham House in the Strand before the end of the year is not clear. But it was then that the idea took hold of Ralegh that he should take on Gilbert's task of exploring and exploiting, if he could, eastern North America; though he convinced himself he must train not only himself but also his probable associates and such sailing masters as were still flexible enough in mind to learn the new language of the sea. Over the winter of 1583–4, probably latterly at Durham House, Harriot held his classes for Ralegh and for his friends and dependents, to instruct them how to follow a course by the use of instruments and charts, and also how to make charts themselves at sea. His textbook, the *Arcticon*, we know by name but it has not survived.[4] Authority for the transfer of Gilbert's rights of exploration and settlement to Ralegh was given on 16 March, but already his preparations for a reconnaissance were well advanced and his two ships, under the command of Philip Amadas and Arthur Barlowe, put to sea on 27 April. Besides the captains, we are given in Barlowe's account of the voyage the names of eight other members, but John White the artist, when he claimed that his 1590 voyage was his fifth to Virginia,[5] was clearly informing us that he too had been on the 1584 voyage. We might well ask, since White and Harriot were to be close partners in the newly named Virginia in the next year, whether they did not serve an apprenticeship together on the 1584 voyage; in other words

2. *Ibid.*, pp. 203–4.

3. D. B. Quinn, *The voyages and colonising enterprises of Sir Humphrey Gilbert*, 2 vols., Hakluyt Society, 1940, II: 420, 446.

4. British Library, Additional MSS 6788, f. 487. See E. G. R. Taylor. 'Hariot's instructions for Ralegh's voyage to Guiana, 1595,' *Journal of the Institute of Navigation*, V (1952): 345; 'The doctrine of nauticall triangles compendious', *Ibid.*, VI (1953): 131.

5. P. H. Hulton and D. B. Quinn, *The American drawings of John White*. 2 vols., London and Chapel Hill, 1964. I: 13–14.

whether Harriot's practical experience of America did not begin in 1584 rather than in 1585.

This is not a matter on which we have any direct evidence, but there are some indications in the surviving materials which make it not improbable, though it must be stressed that his presence on the first Virginia voyage of 1584 is a conjecture rather than an established fact. It is at least probable that Arthur Barlowe and Philip Amadas (or one of them) had been Harriot's pupils before he set sail; Amadas was to sail again in 1585 as 'admiral of Virginia' and was something of an authority on maritime affairs. Hitherto it has been supposed that Harriot became involved with North America directly only after the return of the ships to England in September; that it was then he learnt to understand something of what the two Indians brought home had to say and was able to teach them some English. The narrative of Arthur Barlowe, as we have it in the form in which it was first published in 1589,[6] was almost certainly prepared for circulation as promotional material for the 1585 venture as early as November or the beginning of December 1584. It contains geographical information which would seem to have required some linguistic bridge to be established before it could become intelligible. Since the Indians brought back were reported on 18 October to be still unable to make themselves understood in English, but were referred to in mid-December as sources of information on the new land discovered by Amadas and Barlowe, it is clear that remarkable advances in contact with them were made during a very short period, so short as to raise serious doubts on whether it was possible in the time available. Nonetheless it was Harriot who was credited with making the bridge; it was he who by July 1585 had a working knowledge of Carolina Algonquian; and who was sent out then to take special note of everything concerning the Indians which was relevant to the English plans for settlement. It might seem much more possible for Harriot to have done what he did if he had indeed been able to go on the 1584 reconnaissance. This would have given him some practical knowledge of the problems of navigation on which he had been theorizing for some time; it would have given him six weeks of fairly intensive contact with the Indians in which to get some inkling of their language and of the topography of their tribal arrangements; he would, too, have had some weeks on the ship going back to England to begin the communication of English to the two Indians, Manteo and Wanchese, who were being taken with the ship; there would then be a good possibility that, with his rapid capacity for learning new techniques, he had himself established some command over the language by the time of their return in the middle of September 1584. Even if the Indians were not able to make themselves understood by the middle of October, their English was probably sufficient, and Harriot's Algonquian adequate, for a good deal of information to be incorporated rapidly in the version of Barlowe's narrative which, it is suggested, was circulated, and for the statement in the bill put before the

6. D. B. Quinn, *The Roanoke voyages*, 2 vols., Hakluyt Society, 1955. I: 15–17; 91–115.
7. *Ibid.*, I: 127.
8. *Ibid.*, I: 375.
9. *Ibid.*, I: 389.

House of Commons on 14 December to confirm Ralegh's American rights to be justified on the basis that by 'some of the people borne in those parties brought home into this our Realme of England . . . singuler great comodities of that Lande are revealed & made knowen vnto vs'.[7] Thus, though there is no direct evidence that Harriot was in Virginia in 1584, if we accept him as the main (or sole) linguistic link between the Algonquian-speaking Indians brought to England and the English public, his employment on the 1584 voyage would appear to be a necessary concomitant.

The role which Harriot was designed to play, alongside John White, in the 1585 colonizing voyage also becomes more intelligible if we concede that their partnership was not new, and that each had had an opportunity in 1584 to make sufficient contact with the land, the products, and the people of the Carolina Outer Banks in 1584 to have some influence on the shaping of the tasks that were set them in 1585 so as to make them manageable in scope. We need not assume that White was and remained wholly ignorant of Algonquian (his naming of many of his drawings with the appropriate Indian words show he was not), but it is clear that Harriot was the main instrument in bridging the linguistic gap between the Amerindian language and English. Harriot was well enough informed as to be able to discuss the indigenous religion with the priests, to note the occurrence of dialectal differences from place to place and to admit that he and his associates lacked 'perfect vtterance in their language' (which did not exclude on his part fluency and academic understanding).[8] He developed a system of orthography for the recording of the sound values which could not be expressed by letters of the English alphabet,[9] and he knew some phrases of the language in 1602 (and possibly taught something of it to even later voyagers).[10]

On the 1585 voyage Harriot, especially if he had already been out in 1584, would be able to test the problems of relating celestial observations at sea to the rather crude dead reckoning which was all that was normally available for recording the route and longitudinal distance run, and of estimating the effects of winds and currents on the course. Whether in fact he developed any instrumental novelties in the course of his voyages we cannot tell, though he was very much interested in practical applications and made some later on.[11] No doubt he tried to reckon longitude with the aid of the eclipse of the sun on 19 April 1585 on the outward voyage though it is doubtful whether he saw very much of it and its partial nature in any event would have rendered it of little value for this purpose.[12] Once the ships arrived at the site of the colony Harriot and White had to begin their survey. They had the seemingly impossible task of mapping as much as they could of the land they explored. One

10. D. B. Quinn, 'Thomas Hariot and the Virginia voyages of 1602,' *William and Mary Quarterly*, XXVIII, no. 2 (April 1970); 273–4.

11. See especially E. G. R. Taylor in *Journal of the Institute of Navigation*, VI: 134–7; also D. B. Quinn and J. W. Shirley, 'A contemporary list of Hariot references,' *Renaissance Quarterly*, XXII (1969): 13–17; 26.

12. Quinn, *Roanoke voyages*, I: 53; 380–1.

small surviving sketch shows how rough the first attempts were,[13] even though such sketches were much better than nothing. But a good deal of work was done with the plane table and other surveying instruments so that accurate directions were established and maintained. This work was probably begun on 11 July, when the two men formed part of the boat expedition across Pamlico Sound from Wococon to the Pamlico River and other swamp-enclosed inlets which marked the mainland shores.

Since we have no examples of their journals or notebooks we cannot tell precisely how they carried out their tasks from day to day. It would seem from the map which emerged at the end of the year-long survey that they worked up and down the Carolina Outer Banks by boat, and checked the whole of the coastline from Wococon (approximately the modern island of Ocracoke) north to Cape Henry and westwards up the Roanoke and Chowan Rivers, into the numerous bays and river channels of the north shore of Albemarle Sound, and, farther north in Virginia proper, examined the southern shore of Chesapeake Bay as far as the site of modern Portsmouth and perhaps made an excursion across the James to Kecoughtan.[14] We would conclude therefore, that Harriot accompanied Lane up the Chowan and Roanoke Rivers and that he and White made a number of smaller and more localized excursions to the sites of the numerous villages included on their map. It would also follow that both were members of the party which spent some time during the winter of 1585–6 in the vicinity of modern Norfolk and at no great distance from Chesapeake Bay.[15] Harriot would thus make contact with Chesapeake and possibly Powhatan Indians in the north, and with Chawanoac, Moratuc, Weapemeoc, Roanoke, Croatoan, Secotan, Neuse, and possibly other Algonquian-speaking peoples further south. It is thus possible to see that he would have had ample evidence of such variations as dialectal differences and also of culture traits of other sorts.

It is evident that the surviving drawings of Indians by John White belong largely to the Secotan, Pomeioc, and Roanoke village complexes.[16] It is probable, indeed almost certain, that he made drawings of much more distant groups. Indeed it is not at all unlikely that the original notebooks which White and Harriot made between them consisted of detailed descriptions of each Indian village which was examined, with notes of unusual customs and details of ceremonial objects and of cultivation variations, amongst other things, and that the notes were united each day with the sketches which White drew.[17] If this was so it is clear that the failure of these records to survive has robbed us of a unique ethnographic record which, had it been fully published, would have set an entirely new standard in the description of a non-European

13. *Ibid.*, I: 215–17.
14. Hulton and Quinn, *American drawings of John White*, I: 136–7; II: pl. 59.
15. *Ibid.*, I: 15, Quinn, *Roanoke voyages*, I: 244–6.
16. See the catalogue in Hulton and Quinn, I: 84–113.
17. Quinn, *Roanoke voyages*, i: 47–55.

people.

As it is we have a summary only of Harriot's general report, one prepared for popular consumption, a selection of the drawings which White worked up for preservation and later copying on his return to England, and a series of rather limited notes by Harriot on the small selection of the John White Indian drawings chosen for engraving.[18] We have something from Harriot on plants, those of medicinal value and those cultivated by the Indians, but very little either from him or from White on the wild flora.[19] We have rather more from both Harriot and White on the animals, fish, and birds found on their travels (not all on the mainland but some from the Caribbean and from the sea voyage as well);[20] we have some rather generalized matter on climate, vegetation, soil, mineral resources, and such like from Harriot.[21] Here, in addition to notes and drawings, specimens were no doubt collected, though whether these were confined to mineral specimens or included dried plants and skins as well cannot be specifically established. Some botanical specimens and seeds were, we know, brought home, and it is probable that Harriot was responsible for many of them.[22] It might seem also that by continued activity Harriot and White had carried through the greater part of their task (so far as it could be done by sampling a territory of some 5000 square miles) by the time Drake arrived off the Carolina Outer Banks in June 1586. When it was finally decided to take them off, much of their work was ruined. According to Lane,[23] in their haste to get the settlers off Roanoke Island, 'all our Cardes (i.e. maps), Bookes and writings, were by the Saylors cast ouer boord'. This is clearly an exaggeration. Harriot certainly saved some of his notes, possibly the major part of them, and White many, if by no means all, of his drawings, but the effect was to leave them only with a sample of a sample, together with what they could piece together from memory. It was this which led Harriot to stress that further inquiry would be necessary before a complete picture of the natural resources of the area could be published. Writing about the fauna of the area, he said 'after wee are better furnished and stored vpon further discouery, with their strange beastes, fishe, trees, plants and hearbes they shalbe also published'.[24] It is highly probable that while the primary purpose of the survey was to inform Ralegh and his associates of the major features of Virginia as a basis for colonial development there, from an

18. Theodor de Bry, *America*, part i, Frankfurt, 1590. See also Quinn, *Roanoke voyages*, I: 413–44.

19. Two specimens only of the mainland flora were separately drawn and described (Hulton and Quinn, I: 113–15; II: pl. 49, 50); though others appear in their natural setting without description, notably in II: pl. 42 (I: 102–4).

20. *A briefe and true report*, 1588, sig. B1–D4^v; Quinn, *Roanoke voyages*, I: 325–66; Hulton and Quinn, *American drawings, passim*.

21. *A briefe and true report*, Sig. B2, B3^{r-v}, D4–E1^v, F2^v–3^v; Quinn, *Roanoke voyages*, I: 327–8, 331–4, 363, 366–7, 382–5.

22. *Ibid.*, I: 54–5, 329 n., 339 n., 340 n., 347 n., 348 n., 353–4 n.

23. *Ibid.*, I: 293.

24. *A briefe and true report*, Sig. D3; Quinn, *Roanoke voyages*, I: 359.

early stage in the process of their survey, Harriot and White had in mind the preparation from their collections of a systematic illustrated survey, covering both natural resources and ethnography. With its illustrations and maps this would make a full picture of part of America available on a scale and with a thoroughness not hitherto attempted in print. (It will be remembered that Oviedo's full text did not appear until 1851 and that the records of the Francisco Hernandes survey of Mexico in the decade before the Roanoke voyages were never published directly from the drawings and texts at all.)[25]

In July 1586, when he landed at Plymouth, Harriot's active association with the New World ended so far as his participation in its exploration and direct study was concerned—indeed he is never known again to have left England for parts more distant than Ireland and may rarely for many years have stirred from London and its near surroundings. He had had enough of voyaging and of distant lands. But he was to sit down over the next few years after 1586 to extract all that he could out of his own knowledge and that of others so that as much as possible could be salvaged from the survey and from the other knowledge obtained by participants in the 1584 and later voyages, so that alongside the descriptive record a detailed dossier on which a narrative could be based could at last be assembled. His and Ralegh's reasoning was to the effect that the discovery and settlement of Virginia was an enterprise which would make the fame both of England and of its promoter Sir Walter Ralegh, so that any and every record must be kept of its progress as well as the descriptive and scientific data which had emerged, with whatever gaps and deficiencies, from the Harriot–White survey.

We can see Harriot in action later in 1586. Alongside the Reverend Richard Hakluyt, home from Paris and his embassy chaplaincy there for a time, he interrogated Nicholas Bourgoignon, a Frenchman liberated at San Agustín by Drake and brought eventually to England along with the Roanoke colonists. The surviving version of the interrogation is concerned largely with what the Spaniards had discovered about the interior of what is now South Carolina through their occupation for some years after 1566 of the fort and colony of Santa Elena on Port Royal Sound. This was published by Hakluyt in 1600.[26] But Hakluyt was able to publish as early as 1589 the Barlowe report to which reference has already been made, a narrative of the 1585 Virginia voyage and a report by Ralph Lane on the colony of 1585–6,[27] all of which appear, with a high degree of probability, to have derived from the archive which Harriot was assembling on the enterprises, and which he passed on to Hakluyt, with, no doubt, the active approval of Ralegh. (Hakluyt did not get a narrative of the 1586 venture and it is probable that he derived the narratives of the expeditions of 1587 and 1588, as he did that of the last in 1590, directly from John White.) For some months after his return we can imagine Harriot busily

25. See Hulton and Quinn, *American drawings*, I: 31–3.
26. *Principal navigations*, III (1600): 361–2; Quinn, *Roanoke voyages*, II: 763–6.
27. *Principall navigations*, (1589), pp. 728–47.

interviewing those who had been on each of the preceding enterprises, obtaining their unvarnished narratives and their opinions on the ventures, and storing them away towards the major chronicle which he was engaged in compiling as his material reached some degree of finality. In my opinion Harriot was able during the first eight months after his return from Virginia not only to collect but to write up in draft his material on the history of the enterprises of 1584 to 1586. When he said at the end of his *A briefe and true report of the new found land of Virginia,* published in 1588, 'I haue ready in a discourse by it self in maner of a Chronicle according to the course of times and when time shall bee thought conuenient shall be also published' he was writing I believe, not of February 1588 (new style) but of February 1587.[28]

We must, I think, place the writing of *A briefe and true report* not in 1587-8 but in 1586-7. The pamphlet speaks of Ralegh's work in sponsoring voyages of discovery, settlement and supply in 1584, 1585, 1586 'and now of late this last yeere of 1587'[29] and I would suggest that the last phrase is wholly an addition made near the time the finished work was sent for publication in 'February. 1588' (as the text concludes). It goes on to report that of the voyages already made, the 1584 expedition stayed only six weeks and that the main discoveries were made in the 1585-6 colony when the colonists stayed 'a whole yeare'. He says 'the others after were onlie for supply and transportation, nothing more being discouered then had been before'. It seems most unlikely that had he been writing the pamphlet in 1588 he would have expressed himself thus and ignored altogether the colony which had gone out with John White in May 1587 and from which John White had returned in search of additional supplies in November 1587.[30]

I would suggest that the tract was prepared originally to support the following up of the 1585-6 colony by a new venture in 1587 and that it was intended to be published about January or February 1587, but that for some reason this was not done. It may be remembered that on 7 January 1587, Ralegh handed over the settlement of the City of Ralegh in Virginia to a corporate body, headed by John White, to found the colony, some of whose members were to go and others to remain in England.[31] The city was to be established on the southern shores of Chesapeake Bay and the grant did not comprise more than a small section of the territory included within the terms of Ralegh's grant of 1584. We do not know to what extent Ralegh himself contributed to the financing of this corporate enterprise, or indeed whether he did so at all at this stage. But it must be realized that the promotion of this colony was from January onwards in the hands of the company and not of Ralegh himself. Clearly Harriot wrote his tract for 'the Aduenturers [that is investors in], Fauourers, and Welwillers of the enterprise for the inhabiting and planting in

28. Sig. F4^v; Quinn, *Roanoke voyages,* I: 387.
29. Sig. A3; Quinn, *Roanoke voyages,* I: 320.
30. *Ibid.,* I: 538.
31. *Ibid.,* II: 497-502.

Virginia.'[32] as he said in the opening paragraph in the published version. It was designed to counteract the unfavourable reports circulated by some members of the first colony who returned in 1586 and to present a conspectus of the natural resources of the country, so that intending settlers would gain some insight into local conditions there and receive some guidance while preparing to invest or settle in America. He also wished it to be regarded as an advertisement for the illustrated survey he and White planned to produce. For some reason it would appear that this tract did not commend itself to the promoters of the venture, and its publication in 1587 was not carried out. It may be that White and his associates thought the picture painted by Harriot was not sufficiently glowing, but it is more likely that it was ready rather too late to do any good. If it was completed late in February 1587 it would not be available until well into March and by that time, it is not unlikely, White hoped to be at sea with a body of at least 150 settlers bound for the foundation of the City of Ralegh: that they did not leave in the end until May was probably fortuitous.[33]

By the beginning of 1588 the situation had changed once more. White had come back in November 1587, urgently demanding assistance from Ralegh (and anyone else with whom he could make contact) for the colony.[34] Ralegh undertook to despatch a pinnace, but if it was prepared in the month or six weeks after 20 November it did not sail, probably because weather conditions made it impossible for its men to put to sea. Ralegh, however, decided to make a further great effort to revive the whole Virginia venture, as well as to relieve the City of Ralegh colonists, and to get a formidable squadron to sea as early as possible in 1588. The embargo on overseas voyages imposed by the privy council on 9 October 1587 meant that special permission would be needed for such an expedition, but it would seem that Ralegh, and Sir Richard Grenville who had undertaken to lead the expedition for him, had reason to believe that they would get an exemption for their squadron, as it could be argued that the establishment of a firmly-based American colony would be a valuable gambit in the war with Spain. The seven or eight vessels preparing at Bideford may have been held up by uncertainties about this during February 1588, but it was expected to get them to sea in late March or early April.[35] It was in these circumstances that Harriot's pamphlet, held over, it is believed, in 1587, was hurriedly put into print with no further changes than redating it to February 1588 and a few verbal alterations, and appeared towards the end of the month or at the beginning of March. Its purpose at this point would be somewhat different from that which had previously been intended. Its principal object would now be to establish the fact that Sir Walter Ralegh was still vitally concerned with the Virginia ventures. The title-page stressed that it was Ralegh

32. *A briefe and true report*, Sig. A1 (Title page), A3; Quinn, *Roanoke voyages*, I: 318; 320.
33. *Ibid.*, II: 498–500.
34. *Ibid.*, II: 505, 532–8, 553–4.
35. *Ibid.*, II: 554–5.

who had sent out the 1585 colony and that the author, Thomas Harriot, was 'seruant to the abouenamed Sir Walter', while the association was reinforced by printing on the back of the title-page Ralegh's armorial achievement.[36] Harriot's stress on the advantages of Virginia still carried weight but, it is suggested, it was Ralegh's revived interest or, we should probably say, continued interest which it might now seem most important to stress. The publication may indeed have been part of the campaign, now seen to be necessary, to convince members of the court and of the privy council that the Virginia enterprise was an important objective of state policy and worthy of exemption from the embargo. Yet the attempt to get a licence failed in the end: Grenville was forbidden on 31 March to engage in the voyage and on 9 April was told to bring his ships to join Drake at Plymouth: he was allowed only to detach two small pinnaces to carry White and some stores to Virginia, though they were later forced to put back to England, badly damaged by pirates, and so were unable to carry out their task.[37]

The countermanding of the 1588 expedition altered again the perspective inside which Harriot worked. It would seem probable that his tract attracted a good deal of favourable attention on its publication, because it subsequently proved so popular. It was important because it was the first broad assessment of the potential resources of North America as seen by an educated Englishman who had been there. Its constant use as a standard of reference for so many years indicates how substantial a gap it filled. At the same time it can scarcely have seemed to Harriot himself much more than a stop-gap. In 1586–7 it is highly probable that he was working out with John White some plan for the publication of at least a part of the graphic materials collected in Virginia, and it seems likely that before White set out in 1587 he had completed a number of finished drawings from his earlier sketches, possibly including the greater part of the fine set which survives in the British Museum, while Harriot was involved in putting his notes in order to provide a text—a learned Latin text no doubt—with which they could be engraved and published. Ralegh was in close touch at this time with another American reporter and artist in the person of Jacques Le Moyne, who was busy preparing for Ralegh a set of his drawings, first made in Florida in 1564–5, with appropriate texts added to them, for another illustrated monograph.[38] It is probable that these collections were proceeding for the time being as ones which would remain in manuscript until such time as it should seem desirable or possible to publish them. The interim report (*A briefe and true report*), intended originally for use in the particular circumstances of 1587, was to be as far as Harriot was to get, for the time being, with publication.

36. *A briefe and true report*, Sig. A1–2, F4ᵛ; Quinn, *Roanoke voyages*, I: 317–19, 387.

37. *Ibid.*, II: 555–6, 562–9.

38. Epistle by the translator, Richard Hakluyt, to Sir Walter Ralegh, René de Laudonnière, *A notable historie containing foure voyages made by certayne French captaynes vnto Florida*, London, 1587, Sig. [] 2ᵛ; Quinn, *Roanoke voyages*, II: 546–7.

Later in 1588, probably during the early summer, Richard Hakluyt came home for good from Paris, full of his desire to get his volume of English voyages into print as soon as possible.[39] It is clear that he wished to stress particularly the significance of North America as an objective of English interest. It was, then, as has already been indicated, that Harriot was able to give him a selection of the materials he had gathered for the voyages of 1584–6. All these were edited, or we might say tampered with, to some extent before they were finally published and it is likely that Harriot carried out for Ralegh such re-shaping as he considered desirable, and which was intended to show him up in the most favourable light, while still concealing certain information from the Spaniards and possibly other English rivals or critics. The 1587/1588 narratives which Hakluyt printed, we think, as he got them from White, are much franker and fuller.[40] To them Hakluyt was able to add as his book, *The principall navigations*, went to press, the agreement by which Hakluyt, with a number of London merchants undertook at the opening of 1589 to underwrite further Virginia voyages.[41] He also reprinted Harriot's tract.[42]

Hakluyt had been closely associated with the plans for building up illus-trated records of American voyages, as he showed in his remarks on Le Moyne published in 1587.[43] and it was most probably through him that Theodor de Bry, the Frankfurt publisher, had come into contact with Ralegh, Harriot, and Le Moyne when he was in England in 1587 to discuss the possibility of some such publication as Harriot had in mind. It does not seem that agreement was reached at this point. Le Moyne does not appear to have been attracted by whatever plan De Bry put forward. But the latter on a further visit in 1588 to England returned to his project: by this time Le Moyne was dead and his widow did not sustain his objections. Hakluyt too, was in England; Ralegh was reconciled that for some time the war would prevent the revival on any scale of the Virginia ventures; *The principall navigations* came out shortly afterwards and attracted much attention in England, and it appears to have impressed De Bry very favourably. An agreement for De Bry to publish both an illustrated Le Moyne volume and an illustrated White–Harriot volume was worked out, with Hakluyt's active assistance, and so the project for a multilingual, American voyage series was born.[44]

America, part i, as we know it, took shape in 1589. It represented an enor-mous boost for Harriot in that his *Briefe and true report* was to come out in Latin, French, and German as well as, for the third time, in English. (He long afterwards noted the multilingual appearance of this edition with pride.)[45] He

39. D. B. Quinn and R. A. Skelton, eds., Richard Hakluyt, *The principall navigations*, (1589), 2 vols. Hakluyt Society, 1965, I: xiv–xix.

40. *Principall navigations* (1589), pp. 764–73.

41. *Ibid.*, pp. 815–19.

42. *Ibid.*, pp. 748–64.

43. See note 38, *supra*.

44. Hulton and Quinn, *American drawings*, I: 25–7.

45. Quinn and Shirley, *op. cit.*, XXII, 26.

was also asked to supply notes for the illustrations which De Bry selected from amongst White's drawings for engraving. Though Harriot wrote the notes in Latin it is likely that he did them in a hurry and it is likely that De Bry changed them about somewhat as he made his final selection of drawings from which to engrave the plates once he got back to his Frankfurt workshop. (The crude versions of the captions in English were attributed by De Bry to Hakluyt, but some are so garbled it would seem that De Bry himself may have been responsible for them—the Latin versions, if altered, were in the careful hands of Charles de l'Ecluse who undertook the translation of the *Briefe and true report* into Latin.)[46] The note which appeared under White's drawing of the arrival of the Englishmen[47] is more appropriate to the 1584 than the 1585 entry, and it is possible that it should be taken as some slight evidence that Harriot was a member of this enterprise. What is quite clear is that in whatever version we read them these notes are rather elementary in character and it is hard to see in them much evidence of the intellectual detachment shown in the *Briefe and true report*, though they do include some useful points on Indian culture traits and help appreciably to make the illustrations intelligible which, after all, was their main function. Several possible reasons for their simplicity suggest themselves. One may well be that though Harriot was pleased to have his tract brought out in a multilingual edition, he regarded the whole project as very much an essay in vulgarization. Instead of a whole gallery of natural history specimens and a systematic body of material on the Indians, his rather elementary tract (as he would have considered it) and a few pretty pictures of Indian life were to replace the series of folio volumes which it appears he had in mind in 1587. The notes may be seen therefore as the popularized remnants of an unwritten, or at least incomplete, ethnographical treatise, filling out the brief but cogent section on the Indians in his published tract. It may be remembered that Harriot was, or became, a perfectionist, letting nothing of his, or scarcely anything, emerge in print during his lifetime. Another factor in the slight appearance of the notes, or perhaps it would be more accurate and less misleading to call them captions, is that Harriot's interest in Virginia may have been fading as he became more absorbed in mathematical problems. No clear sequence in his scientific activities is yet evident, but we know that his scientific interests were growing as his ethnographical ones were receding. Perhaps the captions then reflect his writing at a point when he had ceased to care very much about such matters as the peculiarities in the dress and social customs of the American Indians he had left behind in 1586, though it would be interesting to know whether he met and conversed with the Indian brought back by Grenville from his 1586 voyage, who was christened on 27 March 1588, and died in April of the following year.[48] A decline in his ethnographical interests is more probable than a

46. Preliminaries to T. de Bry, *America*, pt. i (1590), Latin.
47. *America*, pt. i, pl. 2; See Hulton and Quinn, I: 84–5; II: pl. 123(a); Quinn, *Roanoke voyages*, I: 413–15.
48. *Ibid.*, I: 495.

comparable decline in his interest in the Algonquian language he had learnt between 1584 and 1586; this was still a living thing for him as late as 1602 and perhaps later. His only other 'Virginia' writing at this period, or perhaps of this period, is a brief note for a paper, which he may never have written, contrasting the character of a trading corporation with the closely similar, but by no means identical, chartered colonization venture:[49] it would have been of great interest to have had this topic developed by his hand. We can say, however, that between 1584 and 1589 the affairs of North America were a major preoccupation, though it is unlikely that thereafter they formed more than an occasional interlude for him in the midst of a sea of scientific enterprises and speculations.

Up to 1590 we have a reasonable range of documentary material on which to base a study of Harriot's concern with the Americas. Thereafter, from 1590 to 1621, our information is very scrappy and incomplete. That Harriot retained and perhaps developed his interests in some respects is undoubted, but it is premature to attempt any detailed analysis. In regard to Ralegh's Guiana enterprises which preoccupied him from 1593 onwards it is clear that he depended on Harriot to an appreciable degree. Harriot worked out detailed instructions for the navigation of Ralegh's ships from England to the north coast of South America.[50] He was given responsibility, when Ralegh went to sea in 1595, for administering a complex scheme regarding the financing of the voyage which was called in question in the courts many years later.[51] He worked on the maps brought back by Ralegh and was engaged on preparing one for Sir Robert Cecil[52]—though whether he completed it we do not know. While Ralegh was on the Cadiz voyage in 1596 he had the task of trying to prevent leakage of information and maps on Guiana through members of Lawrence Keymis' expedition.[53] He was, moreover, highly praised for his intelligence and by implication for his intellectual contributions to the Guiana venture in a poem prefixed to Keymis' published account of the 1596 venture.[54] How these disparate facts add up is not wholly clear. We appear to see Harriot taking a greater share in such proceedings as a business and technical consultant and less as a personally-involved participant. Harriot the business manager—or at least adviser—takes the place of Harriot the field-worker and explorer.

He is increasingly concerned with maps and in the years before 1600 is found in close association with Richard Hakluyt in the collection and inter-

49. British Library, Additional MSS 6798, f. 523ʳ.

50. E. G. R. Taylor, 'Hariot's instructions,' *loc.cit.*, pp. 345–51.

51. J. W. Shirley, 'Sir Walter Ralegh's Guiana finances,' *Huntington Library Quarterly*, XIII (1949), pp. 55–69.

52. Historical Manuscripts Commission, *Cecil*, VI: 256–7; Edward Edwards, *Life of Sir Walter Ralegh*, 2 vols., London, 1868, II: 420–3.

53. Historical Manuscripts Commission, *Cecil*, VI: 256–7, 300, 321.

54. Lawrence Keymis, *A relation of the second voyage to Guiana* (1596); reprinted by Hakluyt, *Principal navigations*, III (1600): 672.

pretation of cartographic materials and, possibly, in map construction, but once more our evidence is partial, and it is difficult to draw from it specific conclusions, as for example, on what part he may have had in the compilation of data (or other more specific involvement) in the Wright–Molyneux world map of 1599.[55]

During the period 1593 to 1605, Harriot's links with Ralegh became less exclusive. He was in close contact with Henry Percy, earl of Northumberland, as early as 1591 and became his pensioner in 1598. By 1601 he had settled at Northumberland's house at Syon,[56] though his status as an associate of Ralegh's—rather than a dependent—is strongly emphasized in the Ralegh will of 1597.[57] He may have continued his residence in Durham House until 1602 or after.[58] Thus when, from 1600 onwards, Ralegh again involved himself actively in Virginia voyages, Harriot's expertise was called on. We have shown him to have been involved in drawing up lists of supplies and trade goods for Samuel Mace's trading and exploring voyage to the Carolina Outer Banks in 1602 and he even designed copper gorgets to be disposed of profitably to the Indians. He revived his interest in the Algonquian language he had learnt in 1584–6 and may have provided the explorers with a wordlist.[59] He went on later in 1602 to help Ralegh in tracking down sassafras brought from what is now Massachusetts by Bartholomew Gosnold and Bartholomew Gilbert in apparent defiance of Ralegh's chartered monopoly of trade with North America.[60] It is highly probable that this revived association with North America would have been maintained and developed had Ralegh not fallen and lost his charter, and almost his life, in 1603.

We cannot tell how far Northumberland shared Ralegh's and Harriot's concern with North America before 1603, but it is likely that he took at least a benevolent interest in their plans and may have been prepared to invest in them. We have no evidence, however, that between 1603 and 1605 Harriot enlisted Northumberland to carry out any of the American projects which Ralegh—in the Tower—was unable to continue.

After 1605 when Northumberland joined Ralegh in the Tower and when Harriot became their principal mutual link with the outside world, it might seem that Northumberland's interest in North America was somewhat more closely engaged. But Harriot for all his expertise on Virginia is not known to

55. A study of Hakluyt's maps by the late R. A. Skelton, including the one referred to, has been contributed to *The Hakluyt handbook*, ed. D. B. Quinn, Hakluyt Society, Second Series, 144–5, 1974.

56. J. W. Shirley, 'The scientific experiments of Sir Walter Ralegh, the Wizard Earl, and the three Magi in the Tower,' *Ambix*, IV (1949): 59.

57. A. M. C. Latham, 'Sir Walter Ralegh's will,' *Review of English Studies*, XXII (1971): 129–56.

58. That Harriot maintained both establishments is indicated by British Museum, Additional MSS 6786, f. 554ᵛ, where Harriot computes the distance from observations taken at Syon House to Durham House, and the reverse.

59. Quinn, 'Hariot and the Virginia voyages,' *loc. cit.*, 268–75.

60. *Ibid.*, pp. 275–9.

have been consulted in the long series of discussions from which the Virginia Company charter emerged in April 1606: he was, during the crucial months, peripherally suspected of involvement in the Gunpowder Plot, was arrested, and retired after his release to obscurity at Syon. At the same time it is probably significant of his continuing interest and influence that George Percy, Northumberland's brother, sailed with Christopher Newport in December 1606 and became an important member of the struggling Jamestown colony until his return in 1612. Like Harriot, George Percy was a pensioner of the Earl and during his absence his pension was largely paid out under Harriot's supervision to provide him with necessities and an occasional luxury in Virginia.[61] He may well have given Percy, before he left England, some instruction in Algonquian, and a word list, as there appear to be indications that Percy could converse, at least to the extent of a few words, with the Powhatan Indians of the James River—whose language was very close to that of the Indians of the Carolina Outer Banks in 1607.[62] We can reasonably assume also that he provided Percy with a copy of *A briefe and true report* which would instruct him in the natural history and ethnology of the region, perhaps in De Bry's edition with its engravings from the White drawings. It may be—though the indications are in no way specific—that it was Harriot who encouraged Percy to keep a journal, and it is probable that he read the version which it would appear Newport brought home in 1608. There are a few reasonably specific traces of Harriot's influence in the Northumberland household accounts which cover payments on behalf of George Percy or which arose from his presence in Virginia.[63] Thus, one of the entries in the accounts of 8 February 1608–3 February 1609 clearly exhibits Harriot's hand. In January 1609 Christopher Newport returned once more after 'crowning' Powhatan as 'king' or 'sub-king' of Virginia under James I. He had with him one of Pow-

---

61. J. W. Shirley, 'George Percy at Jamestown,' *Virginia Magazine of History and Biography*, LVII (1949), pp. 227–43.

62. George Percy, 'Discourse of the plantation of the southerne colonie in Virginia,' P. L. Barbour, *The Jamestown voyages, 1607–9*, 2 vols., Hakluyt Society, 1969, '. . . we knew little what they meant' (not nothing of what they meant), p. 136; 'one of the chiefest . . . with a bold vttering of his speech, demanded of vs our being there, willing vs to bee gone,' p. 138; 'two Sauages . . . came as Messengers from the Wirowance of Paspihae; telling vs that their Werowance was comming and would be merry with vs with a fat Deare', pp. 138–9; 'they told vs the rest were gone a hunting with the Werowance', p. 139; 'this Werowance made answere againe very wisely of a Sauage, Why should you bee offended with them as long as they hurt you not, nor take any thing away by force, they take but a little waste ground, which doth you nor any of vs any good', p. 141.

These references carry Percy beyond the interpretation of signs to the understanding of words. There had, however, been Indians, probably from this area, brought to London in 1603, who might have, alternatively to Harriot, perhaps, established a linguistic bridge. See D. B. Quinn, ' "Virginians" in the Thames in 1603,' *Terrae Incognitae*, II (1970): 7–14.

63. The Syon and Alnwick accounts of the Earl of Northumberland (Historical Manuscripts Commission, *Sixth Report*, pp. 221–9, 300–19; G. R. Batho, *The household papers of Henry Percy, ninth earl of Northumberland*, Camden Series, 1962; and the extracts in Shirley, *Ambix*, V: 57–9; Shirley, *Virginia Magazine*, LVII: 235–42) make up a mine of information. The items cited are in the last item, pp. 234–6, and in the Hist. MSS Comm., *Sixth Report*, p. 229.

hatan's sons (we do not know his name). This young man was duly brought to Syon. Here he would have found Harriot still able to understand (we think) some of his own language and speak it. Harriot advised that no expensive gift be made to him but that he would be satisfied with copper decorations only, so that there duly appeared in the accounts a payment of three shillings 'for 2 Rings and other peeces of copper giuene to the Virginia prince'. Similarly, we can identify as probably chosen by Harriot, amongst the goods sent to George Percy in July 1608, 'for blewe beades' six shillings and 'for Read copper' nineteen shillings and sixpence, objects Harriot had long ago found the Indians anxious to have. In return we have Percy sending over attractive, if not valuable, stones, some of which were in 1609 set into a ring, probably under Harriot's supervision. When Percy returned in 1612 the two men are likely to have reinforced each other's knowledge and understanding of the North American scene.

It may well have been through Harriot that Richard Hakluyt obtained a copy of Percy's 1607–8 journal which in due course was passed to Samuel Purchas who printed a selection from it in 1625.[64] Percy's later journal, 1608–12, formed the basis of his 'True Relation' which he completed about 1625, after Harriot's death.[65] We may see George Percy, though still rather dimly from the existing evidence, as a significant continuing link between Harriot and the early settlement of Virginia in which he had been so important a precursor.[66]

We know Harriot to have been consulted only once by the Virginia Company. This was in February 1609 when the revision of the Virginia Company charter was under discussion and some widening of the scope of English economic activity was being considered. It appears highly likely that he was cross-questioned about a wide range of North American topics as probably also was his old associate Richard Hakluyt. We know only, through Hakluyt,[67] that he gave evidence of what he believed to have been Indian practices in obtaining alluvial copper on the Roanoke River during his stay in North America over twenty years before. We have no other evidence of his involvement with Virginia, but as late as 1622 the Virginia Company purchased a copy of his 1588 tract, perhaps either to send out to Jamestown or to add to their own reference collection.[68]

Harriot's name as an American pioneer appeared prominently in John

64. *Pilgrimes*, IV (1625): 1685–90; D. B. Quinn, *Observations gathered out of 'A discourse'*, Charlottesville, 1967; Barbour, *Jamestown voyages*, I: 129–47.

65. 'A true relation,' *Tyler's Historical and Genealogical Magazine*, III (1922): 259–82. The manuscript is in the Elkins collection in Philadelphia Public Library.

66. P. L. Barbour, 'The Honorable George Percy, premier chronicler of the first Virginia voyage,' *Early American Literature*, VI (1971): 7–17.

67. Gentleman of Elvas, *Virginia richly valued*, 1609. Dedication by Richard Hakluyt, the translator, Sig. A3ʳ. See Quinn, *Roanoke voyages*, I: 388.

68. D. B. Quinn, 'A list of books purchased for the Virginia Company,' *The Virginia Magazine of History and Biography*, LXXVI (1969): 348–9, 359; see below, 384–5, 395.

Smith's *Map of Virginia* (1612) and in his *General historie* (1624), and also in William Strachey's 'Historie of travell in Virginia Britania' which circulated in manuscript from 1612 onwards.[69] Purchas likewise, in successive editions of his *Pilgrimage* (1613, 1614, 1617, 1625) and in his *Pilgrimes* (1625),[70] refers to him with respect. De Bry and his successors kept his name alive on the continent as an authority on America by the repeated reissue of the Latin edition of *America* part i. As early as 1597, as Harriot was to note about 1602,[71] Cornelis van Wytfliet took over some of the Harriot material in De Bry, making due acknowledgement to Harriot. A full tracing of his European reputation in this area still remains to be made.

Harriot as a young man in his twenties made a major contribution to European knowledge and understanding of eastern North America. He not only did significant pioneer work as an observer and student in the year he spent in what are now North Carolina and Virginia, but he became a popular authority on the natural history and ethnography of the region, so that his name and reputation in the literature of the subject endured. His active associations with North America after 1590 were slighter and indirect but up to perhaps 1613 at least they had some thread of continuity. As late as 1613, he was in correspondence with Sir Thomas Aylesbury about the implications of recent Northwest Passage voyages which had led to the penetration of Hudson Bay. And he continued to purchase books about the overseas world into which he had penetrated.[72] Yet, if Harriot's retreat from exploration, geography, and ethnography to the mathematical sciences was not complete, his later life saw his New World interests recede, and become largely a memory for him, an aspect only of his widely ranging intellectual activity, a facet only of his enduring fame.

69. John Smith, *Works*, ed. E. Arber, 2 vols. Edinburgh, 1910. I: 55, 189, 234, 310–11, 315, 317, 319, 325; II: 685, 703, 964; William Strachey, *The historie of travell into Virginia Britania*, ed. L. B. Wright and V. Freund, Hakluyt Society, 1953, pp. 21–2, 49, 142, 144–5. The Bodleian Library, MS Ashmole 1758, copy of Strachey contains the De Bry plates from *America*, pt. i, with the Harriot captions.

70. *Pilgrimes*, IV (1625): 1645–6.

71. Quinn and Shirley, *op. cit.*, pp. 12, 26.

72. He noted the purchase of a number of books on American affairs, e.g. Antonio de Herrera's *Historia general*, Madrid, 1601 'Herera Spanish, 2 vol.'—British Library, Additional MSS 6784, f. 39, in or a little after 1602.

16

THE ATTEMPTED COLONIZATION OF
FLORIDA BY THE FRENCH, 1562-1565

URING THE FIRST HALF OF THE SIXTEENTH CENTURY France had established herself as the chief challenger to the monopoly of the Americas claimed by the Iberian kingdom.[1] Concerned with Brazil from 1503 onwards, she had first traded with the Indians and then, between 1555 and 1559, attempted to establish a colony there in rivalry with the Portuguese. In the Caribbean, French privateers had been active since the 1520s, while Verrazzano had been the first, in the service of Francis I, to make an effective coastal voyage from south to north along the North American coastline. His voyage had been followed up by the expeditions of Cartier and Roberval into the interior of North America by way of the St Lawrence, between 1534 and 1543, though the attempt to establish colonies in modern Canada had failed. France rapidly, after about 1509, built up the largest annual fleets at the Newfoundland Banks, on the shores of Newfoundland, Cape Breton, southern Labrador, and the Gulf of St Lawrence and, after the ending of the Cartier-Roberval ventures, appears to have kept going the annual fur trading mart at Tadoussac. As early as 1546 a French vessel is found in Chesapeake Bay trading with the Indians. Like many of her kind she was primarily engaged in piracy, privateering (during the years when France was formally at war with Spain), and trade in the Spanish West Indies, and came to the shores of North America to get water, fuel, and rest for her men while doing a little trade on the side. Many other French vessels must have done likewise. The Spaniards had become so alarmed in the late 1550s at French activity in Florida, the name then covering much of eastern North America, that Tristán de Luna was sent in 1559 to forestall them by establishing a permanent Spanish settlement at the Cape of Santa Elena. When he failed to do so, Villafañe, in 1560-1, attempted to take over, but he also had to abandon his attempts.[2] The treaty of Cateau-Cambrésis in 1559 had brought to an end for a time the struggle of Habsburg with Valois in Europe, but no agreement was reached about American waters. The Spaniards failed to force the French to observe their monopoly claims and the French regarded themselves as

---

[1] On French acitivities in America in the sixteenth century see C. A. Julien, *Les voyages de découverte et les premiers établissements* (Paris, 1948); M. Trudel, *Histoire de la Nouvelle-France*, I, *1524-1603* (Montreal, Paris, 1963). The older general book, still valuable for events in Florida, 1562-74, is Woodbury Lowery, *The Spanish settlements within the present limits of the United States*, II, *Florida, 1562-74* (New York, 1911).

[2] H. I. Priestley, ed., *The Luna papers*, 2 vols (Deland, Florida, 1928), especially I, pp. xix, xxiii, lxi, 123, 185, 193, 195; II, pp. 25, 39, 49, 137, 147, 149.

free to trade and to settle where the Spaniards had not occupied the land. Such was the situation when the first attempt was made by the French in 1562 to establish a colony in southeastern North America.[3]

A more specific reason why certain Frenchmen should have gone out of their way to hamstring the Spaniards was the position of the French Protestants. They enjoyed, precariously, some measure of influence in France, but they were in a very dangerous situation. At any moment, as a militant minority, they might be forced out of the country, if not destroyed by force. The idea of a place of refuge, a bridgehead overseas which might be enlarged to cope with an enforced migration, not surprisingly in these circumstances, had attractions for them. The notion seems to have emerged during the unsuccessful attempt to settle in Brazil in the 1550s and shifted its direction and emphasis in the 1560s to southeastern North America. There was a contingent reason too: Spain was the spearhead of the militant Catholic Church, she was anxious to destroy Protestants and Protestantism wherever she might find them. The Huguenots regarded Spain as the ally of the Catholic forces in France which could, if the expectation of plunder was sufficiently high, perhaps be induced to support an overseas war against Spain. To attack Spain, to rob her colonies, to settle within the boundaries which she claimed, but had never occupied, seemed not only a patriotic but a religious duty. Southeastern North America too had attractions of its own. It was out of the tropical heats and fevers of Brazil; it was well to the south of the bitter winds of Canada. Verrazzano had praised its fertile shores and fine woods. No doubt many privateers, coming northwards along the shore from the West Indies, had seen something of its attractive climate and its apparently rich vegetation. It is highly probable that some of them had seen gold and silver in the hands of the Indians, whom they encountered. The hope of treasure, perhaps as great as that of Mexico and Peru, was one incentive to French enterprise in the area. With these attractions the French had adequate motives for colonization. Moreover, with unofficial war or piracy going on against Spain in the Caribbean, a permanent French post or posts, with a colony to back them, offered great advantages for continually enlarging attacks in the West Indies. The colony could provide bases for ships where they could be refreshed and re-equipped for new assaults. The inspiration of French overseas enterprise of an aggressive character in the 1550s and 1560s was Gaspard de Coligny, Admiral of France, and, until his murder in 1572, the mainspring of French activity on American shores. It was he who was primarily behind the reconnaissance of 1562, the colony of 1564, and the first supply of 1565, and was in a real sense the father of the French Florida colony. All the same these ventures were not government-sponsored ones and though they involved French royal investment they could be repudiated by the Crown if expedient.

[3] As sources there is little beyond Jean Ribault, *The whole & true discouerye of Terra Florida*, ed. J. T. Connor (Deland, Fla., 1927) and the first part of René de Laudonnière, *L'histoire notable de la Floride* (Paris, 1586), the best edition of which is S. Lussagnet (see p. 5 n. 14), pp. 27-80.

II

On February 8, 1562, two ships with 150 men left Le Havre for North America.[4] Jean Ribault, their commander was a veteran of the English and French marine, whose thoughts had first turned to America well over a decade before.[5] His second in command, René Goulaine de Laudonnière, had previously commanded a royal vessel for the King of France. Apart from the sailors, the men were mostly trained soldiers, their captains being Albert de la Pierria, an Italian who had taken part in the Brazilian adventure, and Nicolas Barré. Their leaders were Huguenots as were almost all the men. The expedition made a rapid and efficient voyage across the Atlantic and made its landfall at the cape of Anastasia Island, at 29° 52′ N. lat., which Ribault named Cap François on April 29. On May 1, at 30° 24′, he found the entrance to the St Johns River, which he named the Rivière de May. This attracted him greatly and he made his first exploration of Florida by entering its channel. He encountered and made friendly contact with the local Timucuan Indians and in particular with the important chief Satouriwa, whose relations with the French were to make up an important section in the history of the attempts at colonization. He also erected a stone pillar (the materials for which he carried with him) on the south side of the river as an indication of French sovereignty.[6] From there he moved fairly rapidly northwards, noting each entry and river and exploring the entrances by boat. He named the entries successively after the rivers of France: Seine (St Mary's River), Somme (Satilla River), Loire (St Simon Sound), Charente (Altamaha River), Garonne (Sapelo River); then he made up names of his own: Belle (Ogeechee River), Grande (Savannah River), Port Royal (Port Royal Sound), at 32° 13′ and Belle a veoir (St Helena Sound) at 32° 20′, his most northerly point before turning back to Port Royal. Thus he traversed a good part of the modern eastern coast of Florida, Georgia, and South Carolina, though remaining within the zone broadly known to the Spaniards as Florida.

Port Royal Sound offered a number of different channels into the country. Ribault liked the situation and believed that he could find a site which would be suitable for a French outpost. It is not improbable that the estuary was known to earlier French visitors and that the advantage it offered of distance from waters patrolled by Spanish vessels and of concealment from their reconnaissances were its major attractions. Again he signalled the accession of French authority by the erection on May 26 of a stone pillar bearing the arms of France. Ribault and his men closely examined the

---

[4] The course of the expedition can be accurately followed for the first time with the aid of W. P. Cumming's study of the Spanish copy of Nicolas Barré's map, not now otherwise extant, 'The Parreus map (1562) of French Florida', *Imago Mundi*, XVII (1963), pp. 27–40, hereafter referred to as 'Parreus map'.

[5] Henry VIII hired Ribault towards the end of his reign 'In respecte of a certaine voyage which by his hignes licence and apoynctement he went abowte'. He was given a pension of £75 running from September 1546 to September 1547, which was paid to him by order of July 25, 1547, in the next reign (warrant

of the privy council, Pierpont Morgan Library, New York, MS. R.V. Roy. E, Edw. VI). He seems to have been involved in an Anglo-French project regarding the Amazon in 1550-1, to have drawn a chart of the Arctic seas in 1551, and to have planned to sail with Sebastian Cabot over the Pole: see *Calendar of state papers, Spanish, 1550-52* (London, 1914), pp. 115, 217, 492-3; D. B. Quinn, *Sebastian Cabot and Bristol exploration* (Bristol, 1968), p. 23.

[6] See P. Hulton, *The Work of Jacques Le Moyne de Mergues,* 2 vols. (1977), II, pl. 100.

Pedro Menéndez de Avilés, *Retratos de los Españoles Illustres* (Madrid, 1791)

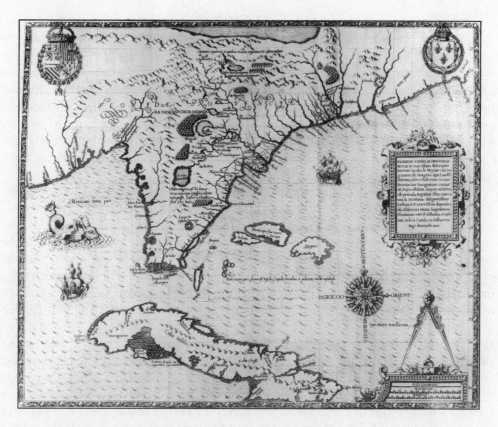

18 Engraving of map of Southeastern North America, after Jacques Le Moyne des Morgues, Theodor de Bry, *America*, part ii (Frankfurt, 1591)

complex of channels which entered the sound. One of the rivers was named by him the Chenonceaux; it was apparently Battery Creek. On it, near the site of the small modern town of Port Royal (not on the traditional site on Parris Island), he decided to establish his fort. This was rapidly accomplished and, leaving only thirty men to man it, Ribault set out to return to France. He made a fast passage, reaching Dieppe on June 22. His expedition was handled with great speed and efficiency. But it remained to be seen whether his outpost would do the job for which it was intended, namely to establish a French presence on American soil and to familiarize a small number of Frenchmen with the problems of living in North America.

Charlesfort, as the outpost was named, had a short uneasy history. Its commander, Albert de la Pierria—Captain Albert, as the French called him—showed considerable enterprise in making contact with a number of Indian groups, especially with the Oristan Indians (apparently the later Edisto of Edisto Island)[7] under their chief, Adusta, to the north, and explored the hinterland of the fort, mainly towards the south. But the supplies left to the men were inadequate and not enough food could be obtained from the Indians during the latter months of the year when the harvest had been spent. In maintaining discipline Albert was too harsh for the temper of his men and they reacted sharply against his authority, overthrowing him and setting the veteran, Nicolas Barré, at their head in his place. Under him they decided to abandon the fort, and having sufficient trained craftsmen among their numbers, they constructed a small sea-going vessel. The Indians collected large quantities of fibre for them from which they made ropes, and early in 1563 they got to sea. Unfortunately their provisions were inadequate for such a long voyage in a ship which was barely seaworthy and which is likely to have been a slow sailer. The end of the food produced a crisis and the eating of one of their number. Eventually they reached the approaches to the English Channel and were boarded by an English privateer. On her, by an extraordinary coincidence, was one of Ribault's men who had been with them in Florida. The survivors, some of them in a poor state, were brought to England and finally made their way to France. The precise date in 1563 is not known. Thus the attempt by Ribault to establish an advance post in America had failed. It was too weak to live of its own. Manned by soldiers, it had, in the absence of a successful search for precious metals, little reason for continuance, especially when Ribault failed to bring reinforcements and supplies within the time he had promised. The main legacy of the garrison was Barré's map of the coast, the first detailed survey to have survived.[8]

By the time Ribault reached France hostilities had broken out between the royal forces and the Huguenots. Ribault from July onwards was involved in the defence of Dieppe. The Huguenots made an agreement with Queen Elizabeth in 1562 to obtain English aid in return for the temporary occupation of Le Havre, which was undertaken

[7] J. R. Swanton, *The Indian tribes of North America* (Washington, 1952), p. 94.

[8] Cumming, 'Parreus map', pp. 37-8, discusses the controversial issue of the location of the Charlesfort site, citing the relevant literature. It cannot be considered fully settled unless traces of the French occupation are established by excavation, but the suggested location has at least a very high degree of probability.

by an English force in October. It would appear that Ribault encountered old English friends of his in Le Havre and conceived the idea of associating himself with an English contingent in order to relieve his Florida post and to carry on the exploration and settlement of southeastern North America. His report to Coligny[9] had strongly stressed the natural resources of Florida, the many inlets which led into the country and the characteristics, mainly favourable, of the Indian peoples he encountered. We do not know when he arrived in England; it was probably early in January 1563. He had a copy of his report with him and used it, after arranging for its translation into English, to circulate in manuscript in order to arouse interest in Florida.[10] It would seem that he obtained entry to the Court and it may have been the Queen herself who suggested to him that he should link his fortunes with that of a young courtier, Thomas Stukeley (or Stucley).[11] By March Stukeley had received his royal licence to depart, had armed, equipped, and manned (with 300 soldiers) five ships, the *Anne Stucley*, the *Thomas Stucley*, the *William Stucley*, the *Trenite Stucley*, and the *Fortune Stucley*, his passport on March 26, 1563, saying he was bound for 'the Contrey called Terra Florida for the farther discovering of those partes which as yet be unknown'.[12]

Ribault was by this time, no doubt, chafing at the delays (we do not know at what stage he learnt of the rescue of the Charlesfort survivors by the English ship). Moreover, the political tide was running against him. Disillusioned with their English allies, the French Huguenots turned against them in March 1563, and as a result of the concessions made to them in the Edict of Amboise, were soon allied with French government forces in besieging their former allies (whom they forced to surrender in August). From March onwards therefore Ribault was suspect by the English as a potential enemy, while he himself gradually lost any enthusiasm he had for English participation in the exploitation of Florida. Stukeley, who had Catholic leanings, had meantime been advised by the Spanish ambassador to keep away from Florida.[13] At the same time Ribault's report to Coligny was put out in a printed form early in June 1563 as *The whole and true discouerye of Terra Florida*,[14] to broaden the range of public interest and participation in the project, though too late. Ribault himself gave up the enterprise and, trying to make his way back to France in the same month, was arrested and put in the Tower. Stukeley left London with a great flourish early in July, picked up some of his ships at Plymouth and set sail, still ostensibly for Florida, but in reality to plunder

---

[9] No trace of his report in French has been found, but *The whole and true discouerye* as we have it is this report in English. It may well be that the original gave more detail on certain aspects of the expedition than was later circulated in print.

[10] Copies in a secretary hand are known in B.L., Sloane MS. 3644; in Phillipps MS. (imperfect) in the Paul Mellon collection at Yale; and at Exeter College, Oxford.

[11] The events of 1563 in England are detailed in John Izon, *Sir Thomas Stucley c. 1525-1578: traitor extraordinary* (London, 1956), pp. 32-49, but documentary sources are not indicated and it is consequently difficult to know how far it can be relied on.

[12] P.R.O., High Court of Admiralty, Exemplifications, H.C.A.

14/5, nos. 32, 36, 37, 38; H.C.A. 14/6, no. 4. These are cited by Izon, pp. 32-3, pl. III, but without references.

[13] It is from the Spanish ambassador in London, Quadra, that we learn most of the details of the Stukeley enterprise, see *Calendar of state papers, Spanish, 1558-67* (London, 1892), pp. 323, 333, 334-6.

[14] The publisher was Thomas Hacket, who had French affiliations. The title-page was dated May 30, 1563, so that publication must have taken place a very short time later. Another pamphlet, in verse, by Robert Seale, *A commendation of the aduenturus viage of Thomas Stutely* [1563], may have been published a little earlier as propaganda for the expedition.

shipping in the approaches to the English Channel and off the west coast of Europe.[15]
Ribault remained in detention as late as July 1564 but was subsequently released. His
failure in England and his imprisonment had meant that he had no share in organizing
the second and principal Florida venture which was ready in 1564.

III

The driving force here, as with the first expedition, was undoubtedly Coligny.[16] At
this point he was well established in the good graces of Catherine de Medici and
enjoyed for the time being the confidence of Charles IX. Armed with Ribault's report
and the impressions and reports which others such as Laudonnière brought back,
Coligny was able to get some unofficial support from the government and the goodwill
of the sovereign in recruiting participants at Court, the King himself making a contribution of perhaps as much as 100,000 francs.[17] René Goulaine de Laudonnière was
commissioned as lieutenant of New France by the King and on him rested, under
Coligny, the main burden of organizing the expedition.[18] Its maritime focus lay in
Huguenot Normandy, especially in the ports of Dieppe and Honfleur.[19] Honfleur
supplied the *Ysabeau*, Captain Jean Lucas, which was to be the flagship; Dieppe the
Petit Breton, Captain Michel Le Vasseur, whose brother Thomas and the painter
Le Moyne, all three Dieppois, were on board, and the *Faulcon*, Captain Pierre Marchant.
Other pinnaces accompanied them or were carried on shipboard. The total complement
was 300 men. The expedition made good progress.[20] Leaving Le Havre on April 22
and Teneriffe on May 5, they reached the West Indies fifteen days later. After refreshing
themselves at Dominica, they sailed through the passage between Anguilla and Anegada
and sighted the Florida coast north of Cape Canaveral, picking up Anastasia Island
(Ribault's Cap François) and making their way on June 22 into Matanzas Inlet, though
pushing on almost at once to the St Johns River. They there made contact with the
Indian chief Satouriwa, who received them with great enthusiasm, and whose son
Athore later brought them to the pillar set up by Ribault, which by this time had come

[15] Stukeley's treachery and his subsequent desertion to the
Catholic side left a bitter memory in England which lasted many
years (see Sir William Fitzwilliam to Sir William Cecil, May 24,
1571, State Papers, Ireland, Elizabeth, S.P. 63/32, 44, and Sir
Thomas Smith to Fitzwilliam, April 27, 1573, Bodleian Library,
Carte MS. 56, f. 57). As late as 1597 William Barlow, *The nauigators
supply*, sig. L2 v., remarked: 'It is euen a most irkesome and wofull
sight, to behold a company of courageous yong Gentlemen to be
led on blindfolded (as it were) in marine actions, by such as haue
no feare of God before their eyes; and many times by those, that
are very ignorant of almost any thing that good is (if any thing
might be accompted good, where the feare of God is not) but onely
can tell of their owne experience, howe they haue dissimboched
from *Terra Stolida*, making their voyage toward the Isle of
Pickery: gracing themselues (as they suppose) with swearing and
staring, and wishly lookes. A few such monsters hauing the chiefe
gouernement in Ships, and voyages, are a greate deale more
dangerous, then all the monsters in the Sea.'
[16] See *Narrative*, p. 119   ; Laudonnière, *L'histoire notable*

de la Floride (Paris, 1586), Hakluyt's translation being *A notable
historie containing foure voyages made by certayne French captaynes
vnto Florida* (London, 1587); *Coppie d'une lettre venant de la
Floride* (Paris, 1565): the edition used is that in H. Ternaux-
Compans, *Voyages . . . pour servir à l'histoire de la découverte de
l'Amérique*, XX (Paris, 1841), pp. 233-45; a translation with the
plan of the fort is in C. E. Bennett, *Laudonniere & Fort Caroline*
(Gainesville, Fla., 1964), pp. 65-70; Nicolas Le Challeux,
Discours de l'histoire de la Floride (1566), translated as *A true and
perfect description of the last voyage . . . attempted by Captaine
Iohn Rybaut* (London, 1566). There are good secondary accounts
in Lowery, *Spanish Settlements*, Trudel, *Histoire*, and Julien,
Voyages.
[17] Hulton, *Le Moyne*, I, 119.
[18] *H.N.*, p. 81; *Narrative*, p. 119.
[19] *H.N.*, p. 81.
[20] The details of the voyage and the selection of a site for the
fort are in Hulton, I, 119-20; *H.N.*, pp. 81-96.\

to be honoured by the Indians as a holy place. Laudonnière could understand a little of the Timucuan language and had with him one of Ribault's sons who had learnt rather more and so could carry on some sort of dialogue. In the next few days the hinterland was explored, Indian villages with their cornfields were inspected, and then, near the river's mouth, some agreement was reached with Satouriwa. He encouraged the French to stay in his territory; they in their turn promised to aid him against his enemies in the interior, from whom the metals, copper and some gold and silver, which he had, came (or so the French appeared to understand). How precise this agreement could have been is not clear; there was no doubt that it had mutual disadvantages. Satouriwa saddled himself with the French without realizing the economic burden they could prove to be to his people; the French committed themselves to one chief who might, after all, not be the most powerful or significant in the area or the best able to lead them to the mineral sources which they believed to exist in the interior. Both sides, but the French first, found it expedient to break their engagements.

After exploring the coast to the north of the St Johns, a site upstream of this river, six miles from the mouth on the south bank and on a bluff overlooking it, was chosen for the fort. Its chief advantage was the presence of deep water close to the shore, which would facilitate the anchoring of at least smallish vessels there—this is the reason too why the site has been eroded completely in modern times by an incutting current. The fort was laid out in triangular form[21] and was surrounded by a ditch. Satouriwa, coming to see what the Frenchmen were doing, responded favourably to their request for Indian labour and supplied it; this helped to get the fort built without delay. Inside the defences, which included gun platforms, there was living and storage accommodation and in the centre a courtyard eighteen yards square where a barracks was built, and a house for Laudonnière as commander. One of the larger buildings, Le Moyne tells us, did not withstand the first strong winds and had to be rebuilt to a rather more modest height. The fort was named 'La Caroline' in honour of the King. Laudonnière also put in hand the building of two substantial craft, larger than the ships' boats, with the aid of which the coast and river valleys might be effectively explored.

The position of the French was ambiguous. What precisely their occupation of Fort Caroline implied was not clear. It was a holding operation certainly, intended to secure some part of the territory Ribault had explored. It is clear that Laudonnière had built up substantial hopes of wealth in the minds of many of the volunteers who had joined him from amongst the court nobility. This was based apparently on the sight of copper and gold, together with some silver, and also stones believed to be precious, in the hands of the Indians of the territories explored by Ribault. It seems possible that the choice of the St Johns was made on account of the relatively large amounts of these commodities seen in the hands of the Indians there. Trade with the Indians for such things was envisaged, but also incursions into the interior where Ribault had

---

[21] Two plans exist, one in *Coppie* (see Bennett, *Laudonniere*, p. 69), the other in De Bry, pl. 102, which are difficult to reconcile. For descriptions see Hulton, I, 142; *H.N.*, pp. 97-9; *Coppie*, p. 241.

understood that metals were to be found. While medicinal plants, skins, feathers, and such might prove useful trade objects, there can scarcely have been any high hopes of making early significant profits from them. No preparations were made for agricultural activity. Leaving France late, reaching Florida when the corn was ripening, meant that no crops could be sown to see the colony through the winter. There is no mention even of herb and vegetable plots, the 'French gardens', which were to be so early a feature of other French ventures in America. On the other hand, Laudonnière had promised his volunteers adequate provisions for a year but had not brought this quantity or anything like it. Indeed wine was soon tightly rationed, and luxuries were also in short supply. Additional supplies from France were expected within a few months but did not come.

The result of these circumstances was to make the colonists almost wholly dependent on Indian supplies of corn, supplemented by their lesser food crops and by meat, mainly venison, a situation which placed an intolerable burden on the inhabitants since the Indian economy produced no surplus adequate to maintain several hundred additional men. In any event idleness was the fate of a large part of the colony. Had they all been professional soldiers, recruited solely for garrison duty, they might have settled down to a barracks routine, but the bulk of the men were adventurers not soldiers. What was there for them to do? What would keep them reasonably contented? The use of the fort for short-term raids on the Spanish islands was clearly feasible. Ribault had certainly thought of this as a long-term objective, but Laudonnière had been instructed to keep out of the Spaniards' way and so this possibility was, at least technically, not open to him. Parties of men were sent out to explore the coast as soon as the new shallops were available. They searched for minerals, did some trading, and were useful in extending the area within which corn could be purchased from the Indians. Others, as we shall see, were sent to make contact with chiefs in the interior who, from time to time, had the services of some French men as soldiers in their inter-tribal wars. Other specialists, like Le Moyne and the apothecaries of the party, were busy assembling data on medicinal plants, on the economic resources and customs of the Indians, making charts of coastal entries, and drawing pictures of Indian activities. Yet no single objective undertaken was sufficient to convey to the majority of the men at the fort any sense of purpose or much hope of riches. Laudonnière acted more like a diplomat whose task was to reach tolerable compromises than as an inspiring leader. He was too cautious to commit more than one or two parties of thirty men at a time to aid the Indians in their wars.

Reading between the lines of the accounts, it is clear there were considerable personal frictions amongst the colonists evident from the beginning and Laudonnière was not strong enough to keep them in check. Dissension among the higher ranks, and especially on the part of the young noblemen, was rife. Though almost all the members of the expedition were Protestants, it is evident that a division soon appeared between the courtly Huguenots and the devoted Calvinists from Normandy. To the latter the failure to bring a minister, for which Laudonnière was held, probably rightly, to be responsible, was demoralizing. These various discontents quickly gained common ground in the shortage of food supplies. Indian food and wild produce collected near the fort seemed quite insufficient: a basic diet of maize was certainly not suited either to the taste or to the digestion of Europeans. Discontent seems to have been most prevalent amongst the young who had come to Florida for action and for riches and were finding neither, getting indeed little save dull garrison duty. Their first major mischief was to set Laudonnière at odds with his loyal Sergeant, La Caille, forging documents which implied that the latter was plotting against his commander, forcing La Caille to take refuge with the Indians and then, with the leadership divided and suspicious, they plotted a mutiny in order to seize supplies, shipping, and munitions to mount a raid on the Spanish islands in the Caribbean. This offered the excitement both of adventure and plunder and appealed also to the more radical Huguenots who were violently anti-Spanish. From the point of view of the malcontents, this made sense. They were within easy reach of the Spanish Indies and they might as well attempt to use Fort Caroline as a privateering base. Otherwise they could see no point in remaining there, short of supplies and acting as a static garrison, to further the long-term plans, still unknown to them, which Coligny and the Ribaults (Jean and Jacques) were devising in France.

Laudonnière had got rid of his larger ships as quickly as he could. They could not be brought inside the bar and it was necessary to get them away before the hurricane season began. The *Ysabeau* sailed homeward while the fort was still building; and another ship, probably the *Faulcon*, left on July 28. It seems probable that the *Ysabeau* had left behind one or more pinnaces or large shallops (the two thirty-foot bark built for war and coastal work can also be thought of as shallops). The *Petit Breton*, the only ship capable of crossing the bar of the St Johns, had also been retained. On September 4, 1564, a ship, commanded by Captain Bourdet, put into the river. She was not directly connected with the expedition and was almost certainly returning from a privateering raid on the West Indies. Bourdet had planned a voyage to Florida in 1563; he had become interested in the area by meeting some survivors of the 1562 expedition.[22] He left some of his sailors and two carpenters behind at Fort Caroline when he sailed about September 10. He may have been able to report that Jean Ribault had joined his son Jacques in preparation for the relief expedition. It seems to have been his visit, and the activities of the men he left behind, which provoked the first outbreak, fifteen men seizing the *Petit Breton* and another small vessel (apparently one of the shallops) and making off to the West Indies.[23] This in turn set off a greater commotion. The extremists who wanted to emulate the successful efforts of the first group induced

[22] *H.N.*, pp. 119-20. Charles IX wrote to Jarnac on January 16, 1563, to get from Bourdet some men returned from Florida, Nicolas Symon and others he had on his ship, so that they could report to him. The King said he knew Bourdet intended to go himself to Florida. It is not improbable that on his 1564 expedition he was collecting information for the King (including some Le Moyne sketches?) and bringing an unofficial report of the situation at the fort. The latter is now at Fort Caroline National Memorial Site, Florida, and there is a translation in C. E. Bennett, *Settlement of Florida* (Gainesville, Fla., 1968), p. 129.

[23] *H.N.*, pp. 119-24.

the moderates, including La Caille, to represent to Laudonnière the need to send another vessel to the West Indies to get food somehow or other by trade or robbery. He faced them with a moderately firm refusal. He had been instructed not to interfere with Spanish subjects and he saw a reasonable chance of the Indians supplying enough food and other supplies to see them through the winter. He succeeded for a time in allaying the discontent, but on November 23, apparently, the extremists revolted. They put the leaders, including La Caille, in custody and imprisoned Laudonnière in a bark on the river. Over the next fifteen days they hastily equipped the shallops for warfare, taking many of the guns and munitions, and no doubt other stores as well, from the fort. Laudonnière was released when they set sail on December 8 with the consent of the majority who remained, whose precise number cannot be estimated from the surviving sources. The first party of insurgents reappeared on March 25, 1565, with the *Petit Breton* and a Spanish brigantine taken in the West Indies.[24] Laudonnière got control of their vessels by a trick and, having had four leaders executed, reincorporated the remainder into the garrison.

The relations of the colonists with Satouriwa were governed both by demands for corn and beans which Laudonnière made on him and also by external affairs. The chief returned victorious from his raid on Outina's territory, the latter being somewhat pre-occupied by his commitments against other hostile tribes to the south and elsewhere. Laudonnière demanded from him two of his prisoners so that he could interrogate them, and when Satouriwa refused Laudonnière took them by force. Moreover, it seems that food was taken by the same means, instead of by barter, and that some of the Frenchmen individually behaved savagely towards the Indians. In any event, as the year passed through autumn towards winter, corn surpluses were used up, and the Indians were left with little to barter. Satouriwa behaved with great restraint, showing his resentment but giving the French little excuse to take any very drastic action against him and gradually withdrawing his people from contact with them.

The shallops had been built for exploration work. An expedition up the St Johns took them, it was said, some thirty leagues into the country to a lake, Lake George, and to an attractive island in the river which they saw on their return voyage. This was the border of Satouriwa's influence or beyond and the Indians met may have been of the Oçita or Acuera encountered by Soto. (Laudonnière does not tell us that this expedition was to the south and it is implied that it was directly to the west or north.) Later, under Le Vasseur, the shallops were employed to range up and down the Atlantic coast searching for Indians with food to barter. The chief Adusta (of the Edisto Indians), on Port Royal Sound, sent them away with substantial food supplies and other cargoes were also obtained. But the relief was only temporary. The winter was indeed a hard one. Towards the end of 1564 it seems probable that the French had so depleted the local stored resources in maize, beans, and other commodities that the Indians were

---

[24] The *Petit Breton* is reported as having been taken by the mutineers on December 8, 1564, and to have been present in the harbour in June 1565, so that she must have been brought back in March. See *H.N.*, pp. 120, 143.

forced to begin their winter hunting season a little earlier than usual. By the beginning of January they had disappeared from the vicinity of the fort altogether and gone to hunt deer and other animals in the forests and to catch fish in the streams, leaving their villages virtually unoccupied save for a few old persons and children.[25]

These were the worst months for Laudonnière: there was very little in reserve to keep his men going and they were soon miserably hungry. We do not know how far they learnt self-help, to hunt and gather, to fish and dig for roots. By the time the Indians returned at the end of March the French were very much less arrogant. At this stage they pleaded with the Indians to give them meat or fish, but now the latter would only do so at substantial prices in commodities which they specified, arms in particular, and this trade further depleted the resources of the colonists. Finally, Laudonnière decided to see what he himself could do.[26] With fifty men he entered Outina's country and passed southwards upstream to Lake George. Here too he found the Indians unwilling to produce supplies of corn or beans. Finally he decided to put pressure on Outina and, entering his chief village in friendship, treacherously took him prisoner as a hostage. This took place apparently to the west of the St Johns, a considerable way down the peninsula. The Utina Indians refused to respond to any attempts to get them to buy their chief back for supplies of corn, as apparently they thought Laudonnière would kill him in any case, and also no doubt because their remaining corn was seed designed for the later maize sowings. Finally, in June, after Outina had been a prisoner for some time, emissaries from his villages promised to bring maize and when this was done he was set free, only for the party of Frenchmen which brought him home to be ambushed, suffer a number of injuries and lose much of its corn on the way back. By this time, however, the crops were coming in nearer at hand and the shallops were being used up and down the coast to barter corn from the Indians as in the previous autumn. We hear little of Satouriwa at this time; he seems to have continued to keep out of the way of the French as much as possible.

With the Utina tribe alienated the prospect of penetrating the interior was slight. Laudonnière was clearly unwilling, even had it been possible, to move his base to the north in order to outflank these tribes, for the strength of the colony had been seriously depleted. Many of the men were in poor physical condition, including Laudonnière himself, and it is likely that some at least were slowly recovering from scurvy. There were few resources with which to begin again. Ribault was late, having promised to arrive as early as possible in 1565, April at the latest, and it was now June and it therefore seemed sensible to begin preparations to abandon the settlement and return to France. This involved building sufficient craft to give them a chance to cross the Atlantic safely.

Laudonnière still had one ship in hand, the *Petit Breton*, of 80 tons, and the brigantine; his shipwrights had also laid down the keel of a galiot. There were still too many men to be accommodated on the ship so that the brigantine, little more than a boat, had to be completed or enlarged by having sides built on her. To begin with she was

[25] *H.N.*, pp. 141-4.   [26] *H.N.*, pp. 145-6; Hulton, I, 129.

put in hand and the houses inside the fort perimeter taken down, as well as the stout palisade round the fort, to provide timber for her construction. Such good progress was made that early in August all the vessels were apparently almost ready, the two smaller ones being described as pinnaces of 15 tons each.

On August 4 four ships were sighted, one a great ship. These caused great alarm until a pinnace arrived at the fort carrying John Hawkins, who was on his way back from his second West Indian voyage, well laden with plunder, though his men were suffering from lack of water.[27] It is probable that before leaving England in 1564 he had arranged to look in at Florida on his way home in order to see what sort of a country it was. The Spaniards later claimed that he had arranged with Ribault, before the latter returned to France, for a joint enterprise in January 1565 to erect a fortress on Los Martires, the islands guarding the Florida Channel, from which the *flota* could be attacked and Cuba later invaded. Laudonnière was somewhat suspicious of Hawkins to begin with and refused his offer to take the garrison back with him to France. Instead, Hawkins offered a ship for sale. The men wished Laudonnière to buy the ship for silver but he considered it unwise to let the English know he had enough to do so (they found out all the same), and so he agreed to hand over some cannon from the fort and to pledge himself to pay for the rest on his return. The Spaniards discovered later, they said, that Hawkins took with him the Spanish goods which were in the brigantine when she returned from the West Indies (indeed they thought there were two cargoes), and to retain some assurance that Hawkins would keep his engagements two Englishmen, who were afterwards killed by the Spaniards, were left with Laudonnière. Hawkins contributed flour for biscuit (a virtual necessity for an ocean voyage) and some dried beans, while he also gave shoes for the men and provided some delicacies for Laudonnière's table. He was not encouraged to stay, and indeed was anxious to get home as rapidly as possible, so he sailed off after three days.

With his basic wants supplied, it might be expected that Laudonnière would leave almost at once. Instead, he displayed a curious reluctance to sail, and hung around the fort for a further three weeks awaiting, he said, a favourable wind. But a steady easterly of this duration seems improbable and we do not hear that he made any serious attempt to get out of the river, in spite of the fact that he knew the peak of the hurricane season was at hand. This delay was to be fatal for almost all his men. On August 28 a further squadron was sighted: relief had come at last, four months late.

In the meantime much had happened on the European side of the Atlantic. In May and June 1564 an expedition under Fernando Manrique de Rojas, of which the French learnt nothing, had scoured the coast of Florida to see if Laudonnière's men were still in occupation.[28] Eventually they located Charlesfort where they took the precaution

[27] See Richard Hakluyt, *Principall navigations* (London, 1589), p. 539 (John Sparke's brief narrative of Hawkins's visit in 1565 supplies some useful sidelights on the fort and its occupants); Bennett, *Settlement*, p. 166; *H.N.*, pp. 159–63; Hulton, I, 131.

[28] Lucy L. Wenhold, 'Manrique de Rojas' report on French settlement in Florida, 1564', *Florida Historical Quarterly*, XXXVIII (1959), pp. 45–62, reprinted in Bennett, *Laudonniere*, pp. 107–24.

of razing what remained of the French fortifications and removing the pillar set up by Ribault to claim the territory for Charles IX. This in turn led Philip to take the decision to send a major force to Florida, one which would ensure a permanent occupation and would eliminate any Frenchmen who might be there and of course prevent any others from establishing themselves. His choice of Pedro Menéndez de Avilés was, from the Spanish point of view, an excellent one.[29] He had already, in 1561, made a reconnaissance of the Florida coastline and entered Chesapeake Bay, so that the problems of sailing along the coast were familiar to him, as were a number of the major inlets. He had much administrative experience and above all he was a hard and ruthless fighter on sea and land. He was also implacably hostile to Protestantism and Protestants. He had the additional advantage of being rich and willing to spend his extensive Asturian patrimony in the King's service. His preparations were going on vigorously in Asturian ports from early in 1565, and though Coligny eventually learnt he was making ready for sea, he believed his fleet was bound for Mexico.

Before he was ready Menéndez was supplied with three of Laudonnière's men, taken in the West Indies in the early autumn of 1564. They were rushed back to Spain to act as guides for the Spanish fleet to the St Johns River, with its little island (now Fort George Island) at its mouth and Fort Caroline ensconced a few leagues up the estuary. Menéndez was able to follow, from reports sent by Spanish agents in France, the preparations being made there, and thought he might be too late to forestall French reinforcements. But when he set out on June 29 he made excellent time, reached Puerto Rico and left again on August 15 to pick up reinforcements from Santo Domingo and Havana, and also to collect some of his own vessels which had been scattered by a storm, but then he changed his mind. He would omit the call at Havana and sail direct to Florida with such forces as he had, in case Ribault had arrived already. On his five ships he had 500 soldiers, 200 sailors and 100 supernumeraries, including the wives of some married soldiers. On August 25 he sighted the Florida peninsula.

In the meantime the French preparations had been going on in a surprisingly leisurely manner.[30] Soldiers were beginning to congregate at Dieppe from late January or early February 1565, but instead of leaving for Florida in time to get there by April, or soon after, the ships were ready only in May. Jean Ribault, who had returned to France in the latter part of 1564, was put in command; as Laudonnière's senior officer he was instructed to replace him as the King's representative and to have Laudonnière sent home. Ribault took up his command and planned to sail on May 10, but it was June 14 before he could get clear of the English Channel, though the Spaniards thought

---

[29] The fullest Spanish source is Gonzalo Solís de Merás, the Spanish text being in E. Ruidíaz y Caravia, *La Florida*, I (Madrid, 1893), translated by Jeannette T. Connor, *Pedro Menéndez de Avilés . . . Memorial by Gonzalo Solís de Merás* (Deland, Fla., 1923; reprinted Gainesville, Fla., 1964); Bartolomé Barrientos, 'Vida y hechos de Pedro Menendez de Auiles', in Genaro García, *Dos antiguas relaciones de la Florida* (Mexico, 1902) and translated as *Pedro de Menéndez de Avilés, founder of Florida*, by A. Kerrigan (Gainesville, Fla., 1965), is also useful, as is Francisco López de Mendoza, 'Memorial', translated in B. F. French, *Historical collections of Louisiana and Florida*, I (New York, 1875), pp. 191–234, reprinted in Bennett, *Laudonniere*, pp. 141–63. The letters of Pedro Menéndez de Avilés, in Ruidíaz, *La Florida*, II (1893), offer the most immediate evidence from the Spanish side and are basic sources. Letters of September 11 and October 15 translated by Jeannette T. Connor are in Bennett, *Settlement*, pp. 147–77.

[30] Julien, *Voyages*, pp. 237–9; Trudel, *Histoire*, I, pp. 205–6.

he had gone some time before. He reached the Florida coast on August 14. His direct voyage to Florida thus took two months, which was reasonably good sailing. With seven ships and some 800 men in all, he was very much the equal of Menéndez's five vessels, though the latter was being seconded by a much larger force. Ribault wasted valuable time in probing many harbours on the Florida coast and appeared at Fort Caroline only on August 28.

The reunion of the Fort Caroline garrison with the relieving expedition was accomplished with much goodwill,[31] even though some members of the former may have regretted that they had not got to sea before Ribault appeared and so obtained a release from Florida ties. But food and supplies were handed out to the garrison who had for so long gone short and the two forces settled down amicably together, perhaps spending a little too much time and energy in their celebrations. In the meantime Ribault had handed Laudonnière his commission and a letter from Coligny. The latter explained his supersession by the need for him to go back to France to report fully on the situation in Florida and also to answer various complaints, some clearly frivolous and others rather more serious, that he had behaved arbitrarily and taken too much on himself, and that he had been responsible for the maltreatment of Indians. But it was made clear to him that he was being recalled honourably on the completion of his mission and not in disgrace. In spite of his former relationship with Ribault he received this news with some resentment. Ribault behaved in a kindly way towards him and offered him, if he wished to stay, the post of second-in-command. But Laudonnière said he would go back. None the less he complained that from this time on he was treated and fed like a common soldier. Laudonnière by August 28 had already begun to demolish the fort; Ribault put in hand the rebuilding of the ramparts and the reinstallation of artillery, but not all the breaches had been repaired when the first Spanish ships were seen off the mouth of the St Johns and the first slight engagement between Spanish and French naval forces took place.

IV

Pedro Menéndez de Avilés sighted the four French ships which were anchored off the bar at three o'clock in the afternoon of September 4.[32] He later claimed that he intended to attack at once but was driven off by a thunderstorm. He returned at night, anchored close by, and started to taunt the French and to threaten them all with death. They cut their cables, he said, and sailed away. In fact the storm had come up again and the action of the French was largely at least dictated by the weather. He followed for some time and then came back to find the entrance to the river barred by three ships and defended by batteries. He therefore broke off the action and retreated south, pounded by the winds and losing the mainmast of his galleon. He had reconnoitred the inlet at the end

[31] See Bennett, *Settlement*, pp. 148-55.
[32] *H.N.*, pp. 172-3; Le Challeux (in Lussagnet), pp. 214-15;
Narrative, p. 132   ; Solís de Merás (Connor), pp. 80-9;

Barrientos (Kerrigan), pp. 38-43; Bennett, *Laudonniere*, pp. 151-2,
Settlement, pp. 148-50.

of Anastasia Island and the reach of sheltered water which lay inside the barrier islands. He now decided to make his base there and chose a site for a settlement on the island. With his smaller vessels he began hastily to unload his personnel, supernumeraries, soldiers, guns and munitions, and some supplies of food. He became anxious about the safety of the galleon which could not cross the bar and so resolved to send her back to Santo Domingo, out of harm's way, though she still held much of his food supply. In any event he wished to establish contact with the remainder of his force there. He says that two of the larger French vessels came up and had a chance of challenging his somewhat hampered fleet, but refused it. They were actually concerned mainly to report the location of the Spaniards to Ribault, though they could well have missed an opportunity for attack which would not recur. On September 8 Menéndez went ashore, formally took possession, and named his base San Agustín, because it was on this saint's day (August 28) that he had first found the inlet. He then proceeded to despatch the galleon to the West Indies.

In the meantime Ribault had decided to take the initiative by way of an all-out attempt to destroy the Spanish fleet.[33] All ships which he judged capable of fighting were prepared for battle and most of Laudonnière's men were invited to volunteer to go with him. The defences of the fort were further depleted, only four guns being left behind in it, while breaches in the walls still remained unrepaired. Laudonnière himself was ill and he was left to do the best he could with a motley collection of women, children, servants, some 150 men, many of them ill or recovering from wounds, and perhaps twenty to twenty-five effective soldiers in all. He did make some attempt to complete the restoration of the fort but failed to do so in time.

There were disagreements among the French as to whether Ribault's plan was the correct one. It was urged against him that the best thing would be to attack the Spaniards by a land march to the south. The danger to the fleet of hurricanes at this season was stressed. But Ribault refused to be deflected. His vessels, four large ships and a number of smaller ones (the Spaniards claimed there were as many as eight pinnaces), were ready by September 8, but he could not get clear of the river until the 10th. On that day the winds began to rise again, and, over the next few days, gradually reached hurricane intensity. By that time Menéndez had been warned; he too had put all his ships and supplies in the best position he could. When the French squadron put in towards the bar at Anastasia Island he was encamped there with his artillery and 150 men to cover the entry. The French ships were unable to cross the bar. Had they awaited the turn of the tide and pressed home an attack they would have had a fair chance of success. Instead we learn that they sailed southwards after the galleon and that this was the last to be seen of them as a coherent force. If this is so then Ribault was guilty of a major strategic error, since the galleon was not of immediate military significance. Shortly after this the hurricane gathered force and Ribault's fleet sailed on to its destruction on the beaches not far to the south of the Spanish base.

---

[33] *H.N.*, pp. 174–6; Le Challeux (in Lussagnet), p. 215 ; Hulton, I, 133.

Menéndez determined, as soon as the storm developed and ended temporarily the threat of a French attack on San Agustín, to make an excursion northwards against Fort Caroline.[34] In spite of the rain and wind he got 500 men together, his whole fighting force, and marched northwards. He carried on through sodden country until at dawn on September 20 he was approaching the fort. He had a French prisoner with him, one of those taken in the West Indies, and used him to find out where to attack. This he did at once.[35] Inside the fort the rain had drenched the sentinels and finally the master of the guard had withdrawn all of them to their quarters except for a single man at the gate. Him the Spaniards decoyed by a trick. They then broke through the postern while others brought twenty scaling ladders into play and still others found an un-repaired breach in the ramparts. The result was that there was virtually no resistance. Laudonnière ran out, armed, and tried to gather a group of his men round him in the courtyard, but the Spaniards were entering in such numbers that he realized it was hopeless and ran off to the woods through another breach, thus showing how impossible the fort was to defend. Le Moyne, awakened by the commotion, also saw that the position was hopeless and got away as fast as he could.[36] So did other individuals who gradually gathered into little groups and pushed their way down through the swamps towards the mouth of the river in the hope of being taken on board by one of the French ships which lay there.

Inside the fort all the men—and perhaps some of the women and children—were simply killed off as they were caught, 132 that night and ten more found wandering about during the day. The fort was completely plundered, only the meal, guns, and munitions being reserved by Menéndez from the spoil. During the next day or so some fifty women, girls, and boys under fifteen were assembled and left alive; how many had already been killed we do not know. Menéndez seriously considered having them killed off too, since, in his own words, 'very great is my anxiety at seeing them in the company of my people, because of their evil sect'.[37]

Not all the French were killed. The younger Ribault (Jacques) was in the river in command of two of the ships which his father had brought, and there were also the small vessels which had earlier been prepared for Laudonnière's abortive plan to sail back to France. Jacques Ribault made no attempt to bring his guns to bear on the Spaniards, but he did appreciate quite soon that he could share in a partial rescue expedition. Laudonnière, sick (hit on the head with a pike, the Spaniards said), swimming strongly at times over streams, supported half-dying at others by his com-panions, formed the nucleus for one group which included Jacques Le Moyne; eventually it was rescued from the swampy borderlands of the estuary. Nicolas Le Challeux was one of another group which was taken on board. There were agonizing

[34] Solís de Merás (Connor), pp. 91–3.
[35] *H.N.*, pp. 178–80; Le Challeux (in Lussagnet), pp. 216–21; Hulton, I, 134;   Solís de Merás (Connor), pp. 100–2; Barrientos (Kerrigan), pp. 46–55; Bennett, *Laudonniere*, pp. 156–60, *Settlement*, pp. 161–3, 173–4.
[36] *H.N.*, pp. 180–3; Le Challeux (in Lussagnet), pp. 217–25; Hulton, I, 134.
[37] Ruidiaz, *Florida*, II, p. 87.

decisions to be made. How long dare they wait to pick up survivors? Not long enough it appeared, for one group arrived soon after the ships had sailed and its members were picked off by the Spaniards. Should they go south and hope to join up with the main fleet which might well be straggling back northwards after the storm? Had they done so they might have formed a nucleus of help for the shipwrecked main body. But their weakness was too apparent to allow them to take any more risks. On September 25 two vessels set sail for France, the others having been scuttled. Pilots had not been allocated between the ships; Ribault's, piloted, got safely to La Rochelle; Laudonnière's, without proper navigation, the men suffering great hardship, ended up in the Bristol Channel, in Swansea Bay, from which slowly and painfully Laudonnière, Le Moyne, and a handful of others got back to France. They could report the Spanish victory, though not its full extent.

Meantime, in Florida, the last acts of the French tragedy were taking place.[38] After the capture of Fort Caroline was complete and it had been renamed San Mateo, Menéndez hurried south to San Agustín, finding it intact—it might well have been attacked by part of the French force which had gone after the galleon. He heard soon after that some Frenchmen had come ashore farther south. Reconnoitring with fifty men, he eventually located a large group of Frenchmen, three of whose ships had been sunk, on the other side of a water channel. Concealing his soldiers, he sent over messages and learnt in reply that there were some 140 men there under La Caille, Ribault's lieutenant, while they, in turn, believed there were some 200 more farther south where Jean Ribault's galleon had grounded, all that was left of the four major ships and many pinnaces which had been wrecked. The French asked for terms of surrender. Menéndez alleged he had told them he had come to 'wage a war of fire and blood against all who should come to people these lands and implant their wicked Lutheran sect'. La Caille came across the stream under safe conduct and offered to surrender 'provided I spared their lives', but met the reply which Menéndez claimed he had given, that they must 'place themselves at my mercy'. They did so; they came across the stream; they submitted to having their hands tied behind their backs and when all was ready they were butchered with knives like sheep. Sixteen, for various reasons, were spared. Fifty men had destroyed nearly three times their number without a shot. Had these resisted the outcome might have been less final.

Menéndez, after this massacre, settled down for a time to fortify his base, but kept up his vigilance to find out what had happened to the other survivors. Eventually he heard that a number had come north to the place where the first party had been killed. It seems that a small group under Le Vasseur had gone on a reconnaissance to the north, reached Fort Caroline and come back to report that it was in enemy hands; it was burned down later on October 10, perhaps by some of Le Vasseur's Indian friends. Menéndez went down to look for Ribault's men, this time with a hundred soldiers. He

[38] Solís de Merás (Connor), pp. 107–22; Barrientos (Kerrigan), pp. 58–67; Le Challeux (in Lussagnet), pp. 226–33; *Requeste au Roy* (in Lussagnet), pp. 234–9; Bennett, *Laudonniere*, pp. 161–3, *Settlement*, pp. 165–6, 174–5.

found about half the survivors from Ribault's ship, some seventy persons. At the first contact, Menéndez alleged, he told them that they 'must put themselves at my mercy, for me to do with their persons as I might wish'. Ribault himself came over under safe conduct and, Menéndez said, made various propositions to him for the safety of himself and his men, which he rejected. According to one or two Frenchmen who escaped, Ribault reported that Menéndez had undertaken by 'a signed oath' to spare their lives. When Ribault arrived with almost all his men they too had their hands tied and were knifed, except for five retained by Menéndez. Other parties, warned by a few who got away, did not put themselves in Spanish hands and scattered along the shore. The place where these episodes occurred has been known as Matanzas, the place of the massacres, ever since.

Menéndez has had his attackers and defenders ever since 1565. He had acted with impeccable skill and daring in carrying through the attack on Fort Caroline, and certainly his actions there, however drastic, could be justified by the military practice of the period, especially as he had to regard San Agustín as most vulnerable at the time, and it was essential for him then to avoid tying himself down with prisoners. His position as regards the other groups is less clear. To accept the unconditional surrender of unarmed men with whom there had been no fighting and then to kill them off in cold blood was, even by the standards of the time, a savage act. It differed from a surrender 'at mercy' after a siege. Even if, in the case of the first party, he might claim that he was still too insecure to take prisoners, this was not the case with Ribault's men. There was here only the desire to kill. Whether or not an agreement was broken, Menéndez was deliberately, in this case, showing his contempt for France and for French Protestantism in particular. It is indeed his view of the Protestants as subhuman monsters which is most revealing of the naked hatred of the Spaniards of the Counter Reformation. But it was national sensibilities that he most affronted when his actions became known in Europe and it was a Catholic, Dominique de Gourgues,[39] who in 1568 overran San Mateo, hanged all the Spanish garrison and affixed to the bodies the sardonic placards: 'I do this not as unto Spaniards, nor as unto mariners, but as unto traitors, robbers and murderers.' This episode survives in the broader fields of history as one, not soon forgotten by either nation, in the long Hapsburg–Valois struggle. Spain was determined to keep France, especially Protestant France, out of North America; France retained the will to re-establish herself, and the creation of French Canada in the end reflected in some degree a long-term reaction to the Florida killings.

Whatever doubts might be had about the methods employed by Menéndez, his decisiveness removed all danger of a short-term French recovery. He went about the business of rooting his settlement in the land with the greatest speed and efficiency. As for Laudonnière, ill, and with his forces and defences in the fort grievously depleted, there is little that he could have done to resist the Spaniards even if he had not been surprised. Ribault is more difficult to evaluate. His judgment on the need to fight at

[39] Gourgues (in Lussagnet), pp. 241-51; *H.N.*, pp. 187-200; Bennett, *Laudonniere*, pp. 166-70, *Settlement*, pp. 218-22.

sea was proved wrong by the course of events, but we can see that he was seeking for a decisive blow which could only have been obtained at sea since he did not wish to involve himself in a campaign of attrition. We can see that he would have been in a stronger position if he had mounted a dual attack on Menéndez, sending a force by sea to blockade the entries to his base and simultaneously another overland to attack his establishment. He can be criticized for failing to read the weather signs aright, but that was not perhaps easy. If he took his ships south from Anastasia Island in chase of the Spanish galleon he was undoubtedly guilty of a bad, probably even a fatal, misjudgment. Once he was trapped on shore, having lost most of his strength, he showed little initiative. Neither he nor La Caille seems to have appreciated that the only chance for them was to move away from the Spaniards and find a place where they could concentrate to resist them or to escape by water. Had they joined forces, salvaged what they could on improvised rafts and moved either into the interior or to the south they had a bare chance. They did not take it but behaved as if they were fighting in Europe and not beyond the boundaries of such civilization as they knew.

From the more limited aspect of the contribution made by the French between 1562 and 1565 to the exploration and understanding of North America, it is difficult to claim that they did as much as they might have done to illuminate the interior geography of southeastern North America. Yet though they supplied misleading evidence—a question for separate discussion in the following subsection—they provided a base on which all subsequent information could be erected. The solid core of reliable information they did contribute was substantial. They charted the coast in detail and their work undoubtedly helped later French vessels to work their way along it. Its outline, through the Le Moyne map, found its way into general maps of North America. Their main contribution to our knowledge is in the detailed and scholarly accounts which Le Moyne and Laudonnière alike made of the Muskhogean peoples of the coast and the interior of the southeast. Laudonnière wrote clearly and well about the Indians and Le Moyne preserved for us significant details of their way of life, mainly in graphic form, though some of it is difficult to interpret. Through this information we gain important insights into the relatively developed Indian cultures of the area, stemming from and linked with the striking centres of the Temple Mound II Culture, of which Etowah in central Georgia was still such a significant example. Through their writings and illustrations, moreover, a number of Indians of the area, Satouriwa especially, Outina, and others, come to life as personalities. For the French ethnography becomes, for a short time, history and this is an important factor in the growing understanding of Amerindian cultures and of culture contact. They carry on the tradition of detached yet not impersonal observation begun by Verrazzano and continued by Cartier, and later still by Champlain, on which so much of our limited knowledge of the Indians of the contact period depends. In this respect the achievements of the French expeditions to Florida are not isolated but are part of a sequence of great importance for North American history in its earliest literate phase.

From the aspect of attempted colonization the French efforts were not very effective or very intelligently conducted. Laudonnière's colony was primarily a garrison rather than a settlement. Only a few of its members took any part in extending knowledge of the interior even though the hope of finding precious metals there provided a great apparent incentive. Some Frenchmen did gain a great deal of knowledge of the country and of its peoples, but did not necessarily interpret correctly what they learnt. Their information was not exploited for the benefit of the settlement as a whole, but rather for individual gain. The French seem to have made little attempt to make themselves self-sufficient except by retaining and perhaps somewhat enlarging the small groups of livestock they had with them. They made wine from native grapes. They collected specimens of gold and silver from the Indians with such greed to begin with that the latter reacted sharply against disclosing what they had in later stages, and also acquired pearls but found them frequently blackened by being taken from oysters or mussels roasted for food; in addition they collected 'unicorns' horns' (the 'sword' of the sword-fish?). They investigated Indian dyes and may have obtained some samples of dyestuffs as also 'apothecary herbes, roots and gumme', especially sassafras and storax, it would seem. How far they accumulated furs and skins is not clear. Ribault brought substantial amounts of cloth and other goods for barter which the Spaniards eventually found in Fort Caroline. But all this was on too small a scale for viability. Laudonnière brought no women (or only one) and Ribault only a small number and some 'lackeys' (servants intended for menial tasks), but even with these recruits there were not enough people deeply involved in the project to give much hope for a successful settlement. The same focus remained until the end, so far as the interior was concerned, one which was coloured almost entirely by the expectation of supplies of gold and silver, a new Mexico.

The Spaniards were right in thinking, it appears, that the main purpose of the colony was to act as a base for aggression against the Spanish Indies. The armaments Ribault brought were not meant to be merely defensive. The Spanish story that Ribault intended to occupy Los Martires, a strong point on the Florida Keys, from which to pick off ships of the *flota* as it entered the Florida Channel is probably correct, though the notion that it was intended also as a jumping off point for an attack on Cuba was probably exaggerated. If this was so the possession of a fort along the coast higher up, on the St Johns, and perhaps one at Port Royal as well, would enable the process of cutting out ships from the slow-moving *flota* as it proceeded northward on the Gulf Stream to be continued over a long stretch of coast. Thus the Spaniards were right in thinking that the French threat to the continuity of their commerce with the Indies was a real one. In these circumstances, their insistence on mounting an effective counter-attack and in establishing a permanent garrison themselves in Florida is understandable. The extra animus and hate which religion gave was only an added incentive to a primarily political and strategic development. The major effect of the French Florida enterprise was thus to provoke Spain into establishing and maintaining the first permanent European garrison and colonial settlement on the eastern coast of North America.

V

As has been suggested above, the evidence supplied by the French narratives and Le Moyne's map is at variance in some essentials with the actual topography of the Florida peninsula. For this reason it is necessary, without prejudice to the cartographical discussions in Chapter IV,[40] to indicate some of the problems presented by this conflict of evidence.

The St Johns was in fact the worst river the French could have chosen if their object was to reach the mountains which Ribault had heard lay inland and which might be a source of precious metals. It rose far to the south in the Florida peninsula and flowed north. Lake George was a large expanse of water on its northern course and was probably as far south as the French penetrated. The river turns sharply eastwards near presentday Jacksonville and enters the sea about a dozen miles farther on. Its only relevant tributary was a small stream, the Trout River, rising on the narrow ridge which separated the St Johns from the swamp-ridden valley of the St Mary's and flowing eastwards. There was, on account of vast swamps, no practical route northwestward and no route westward, except along a narrow, discontinuous ridge from which it is possible to branch off northwestwards about halfway along its course.[41] To the piedmont, taken as beginning at the 600 foot contour, the distance from Fort Caroline, as the crow flies, is about 200 miles and by a practicable route which avoids the swamps at least 250 miles. The uplands of the Appalachian range, masked by the 1500 foot contour, are another 100 miles beyond that.

We are confronted with a situation in which the narratives frequently refer to activities taking place to the south or southwest of the fort, along the St Johns River, as if they were happening west of the fort, and to events which took place to the west, as if they occurred in the northwest. This bias is enhanced by the maps. John White's has the St Johns, his 'R. de May', running steadily from west to east,[42] as indeed the narratives would suggest; to the north it is bounded by a great lake and beyond it to the northwest there is shown a high mountain range, the 'Mountaigne Pallassi'. On the Le Moyne map Lake George is shown far to the southwest,[43] the course of the St Johns from it is shown as first northeast and then, in a long sweep of what might well be a hundred miles, southeast to the Atlantic. This last stretch corresponds to the mere twelve miles of the actual course described above. The river is joined, just after it bends to the southeast, by a major tributary coming from the northwest where it rises in high mountains, 'Montes Apalatci', which are shown as having precious metals in their streams. This tributary is non-existent, the terrain was and is entirely swamp and the actual mountains are at a vastly greater distance away than is shown. This map, therefore, and to some extent the White map also, conveys the idea that the French were operating westwards

---

[40] See Hulton, I, 45-54.
[41] The ridge now carries Routes U.S. 90 and Interstate 10 from Jacksonville westwards to Tallahassee, a distance of some 150 miles approximately, the only old practicable route to the Appalachians.   [42] Hulton and Quinn, pl. 58.
[43] See *pl.* 92 below.

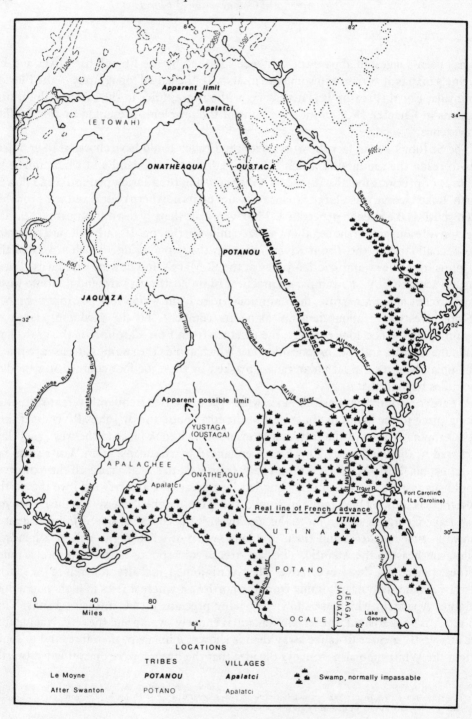

19 Franco-Indian locations, *c.* 1565.

and northwestwards from Fort Caroline rather than towards the south, southwest, and some little way to the west.

These confusions of topography are compounded in the locations of the Indian tribes.[44] A vital part of the activities of the French colonists lay in their relations with the Indians, in particular with the Saturiwa, their immediate neighbours. Satouriwa, their chief, was actively concerned in the inter-tribal politics of the area to the north of the St Johns and to the west and southwest. Consequently, the French, if they were to extend the range of their activities inland—and one of the major factors in the choice of the St Johns was the possibility it offered of penetrating into the interior—had either to ally with Satouriwa against his rivals or else bypass him and themselves make direct contacts with the chiefs in the interior. The Saturiwa Indians were located in the angle of land between the south bank of the St Johns and the sea, occupying the north bank of the estuary also, though the width of this angle on the two contemporary maps gave them a considerable variation of territorial range. It was in fact very narrow. To the west of the bend in the St Johns lay the Indians who were under the command of Outina, the Utina (or Timucua) Indians. The narratives say the Utina comprised some forty or more villages or bands. Modern discussions suggest that their tribal lands extended westwards from the St Johns River to the Suwannee River and perhaps to the west of it. There they were in contact with the Apalachee Indians, centred round the site of the modern city of Tallahassee, whose territory extended perhaps as far west as the Apalachicola River. Both these rivers appear approximately in the correct locations on the Le Moyne map, though the town of 'Apalatci' is sited in the high mountains far to the northwest, on the upper course of the mythical river which is shown joining the St Johns when in fact it was about 150 miles due west of Fort Caroline and far distant from any mountains. The Yustaga (Oustaca) and Onatheaqua tribes occupied land to the northwest of the Utina and were likely to have separated them from the Apalachee. The Potano tribe was located south and southwest of the Utina, but all these were placed on the map in the vicinity of modern Macon and Atlanta, some hundreds of miles away from their proper location. The main conflicts between the chiefs Outina and Satouriwa lay not west or northwest of the St Johns, but in the area where it runs northward from Lake George. There the Utina tribe was attempting to make good its hold on the east bank of the St Johns and the Saturiwa tribe was attempting to repel this intrusion and to push the Utina back westwards across the St Johns.

[44] The Indian tribal names have received in J. R. Swanton, *The Indian tribes of North America* (Washington, D.C., 1952; reprinted 1968), an accepted nomenclature (see also F. W. Hodge, *Handbook of American Indians*, 2 vols, 1907–10) which is used in the text, though the personal names of the chiefs during this 'French' period, from which in a number of cases these tribal names derive, have been kept in the forms used most frequently by Le Moyne and Laudonnière. Thus the tribal names, Saturiwa (Swanton, *Indian tribes*, pp. 138–9). Utina (or Timucua, pp. 147–52), Onatheaqua and Hostaqua (p. 135). Potano (pp. 137–8). The map in Swanton, *Indians of the southeastern United States* (Washington, D.C., 1946), p. 34, is also invaluable for locations, which have in general been borne out by archaeological and anthropological work (such as that in Gordon R. Willey, *Archeology of the Florida Gulf Coast* (Washington, D.C., 1949), especially pp. 517–33; John M. Goggin, *Space and time perspective in northern St Johns archeology* (New Haven, 1952); and William C. Sturtevant, 'Spanish-Indian relations in southeastern North America', *Ethnohistory*, IX (1962), pp. 41–94).

We may indeed go so far as to suggest that there was no range of mountains known to the Indians as 'Apalatci' and that the modern name was derived from the mistakes or misapprehensions made by the French and embodied on the Le Moyne map. It may have arisen because the Apalachee Indians, in contact with the Utina, and hence in some degree with the French, are likely to have known of the great range of mountains far to the north of their tribal locations. Because of this knowledge the French in turn transferred the tribal name to the mountains with which it had no relationship. There is no evidence that Indian travellers, from the Utina as well as the Apalachee tribe, had made the long journey to the piedmont and uplands and possibly to the high mountains, though it is not at all improbable that they had done so; it appears out of the question that any of the French settlers made this journey. From Fort Caroline to the high mountains would have taken a period of some eighty to ninety days for the return journey of about 900 miles, and such extensive travels would surely have been specified by either Laudonnière or Le Moyne in their narratives, even if it had been feasible to make them. Much less problematic were contacts between the Frenchmen, who had become familiar with journeying in the Indian country, and the Apalachee tribe within a range of less than 150 miles from Fort Caroline.

These considerations have to be taken into account before we can assess the information, or alleged information, on metal supplies conveyed by Le Moyne and Laudonnière. The gold and silver used by the Utina tribe were represented as native products obtained in the mountains of the northwest—with which, as we have indicated, the French had no direct contact whatsoever—instead of, as they were, products of wrecked Spanish vessels.[45] That the Indians, almost certainly the Apalachee Indians and possibly the Utina as well, obtained metal from the interior is also undoubted, but this was copper (the Indians having a single name for all metals), not gold or silver. Some Lake Superior copper may indeed have been traded as far as the Muskogean tribes in the southeast, but it now appears probable that their needs were supplied, either by occasional trading missions or else by transmission through intermediaries, from the localities still dominated by the Temple Mound Culture II,[46] from the Etowah area in particular, whose plentiful supply of copper seems to have come mainly from native deposits in the area where the piedmont shades into upland, some 300 to 350 miles from the centre of the Apalachee tribal area. That alluvial copper may well have been panned in such a way as is shown in Le Moyne's illustration (*pl.* 133), is by no means unlikely, but it purports to represent panning of gold not copper. (His map indicates alluvial silver in the mountains.) If our analysis is correct, no Frenchman can have seen this operation take place, the evidence being from second or third hand description by the Indians, whether of the Utina or other tribes. This, in turn, would

[45] Some Spaniards rescued from the Indians told Laudonnière that the gold and silver were of Spanish origin: see *H.N.*, pp. 137–8; Bennett, *Settlement*, p. 166. John Sparke discovered the same thing when he visited Fort Caroline with Hawkins: see Hakluyt, *Principall navigations* (London, 1589), p. 530.

[46] On the Temple Mound cultures in their later phases see G. R. Willey, *An introduction to American archaeology*, I (Englewood Cliffs, N.J., 1966), pp. 300–9.

account for the somewhat unrealistic elements in the engraving. From all this it is evident that the narratives, maps, and engravings, in so far as they affect the topography and natural resources of the area, cannot be taken at their face value and applied to the modern topography of the region. Consequently precision in interpreting exactly what happened and deciding what elements of truth there are in certain statements made by Le Moyne and Laudonnière cannot be obtained. It may well be that more careful examination of Indian sites and a more rigorous assessment of the topographical pattern as it existed in the sixteenth century may produce more accurate results, but at present only rough approximations appear possible.

When, therefore, Laudonnière was advised by those Frenchmen who had worked with the Indians in the interior to establish a chain of posts on the way to the mountains and to make contact with the chiefs of various tribes who would help to ease the way of the Frenchmen to the mines, which they assured him were within five days' journey from Fort Caroline, we are entirely in the realms of fantasy; locations of tribes, the possibilities of travelling in a particular direction, and the prospects of arriving at particular locations are all being distorted so greatly that they become not merely misapprehensions but conscious deceptions. Spanish prisoners released from the Indians could have told Laudonnière the truth. Whether or not Laudonnière was deceived, he did not stress, when he himself made forays up the course of the St Johns, that he was operating to the south and not to the west or northwest of the fort. For the construction of a misleading picture too, Le Moyne as well as Laudonnière must bear part of the responsibility.

In practice the growing desire of the French to exploit the supposed riches of the interior to the exclusion of the more vital problem of establishing the colony on a viable basis in its coastal situation, complicated the day-to-day relations between Laudonnière and Satouriwa, on whom to an appreciable extent the continuing welfare of the colony depended. There was a brief and effective period of co-operation from July 15, 1564, onwards, but when Ottigny and others, sent to explore the basin of the St Johns, came back with stories of gold and silver in Indian hands and brought with them sufficient specimens to establish the existence of precious metals, Laudonnière turned cool towards Satouriwa, refused him aid in repelling the pressure of the Utina tribe east-wards and in taking the offensive against them. This led to strained relations between them, Satouriwa regarding Laudonnière's hesitancy as a repudiation of his earlier agreement, which in turn absolved Satouriwa from his own engagements to look after the food supplies and comfort of the fort. Even though Laudonnière temporized rather than said 'No', and demanded a further two months before he would be ready to march at Satouriwa's side, the latter remained dissatisfied.

Ottigny and La Roche-Ferrière contributed a few arquebusiers to Outina's force which attacked the rival Potano tribe, helped him to win a skirmish, and opened the way for a series of small French raiding parties to fight alongside Outina's forces in the area to the west of the St Johns during the latter months of 1564. The pretext for this aid to Satouriwa's enemies, which the pioneers developed for Laudonnière's benefit when they returned to Fort Caroline, was that by assisting Outina to clear the smaller tribes, the Onatheaqua and Yustaga as well as the Potano, out of the way, the route which would bring the Frenchmen to the mountains in the northwest would thereby be cleared. As these tribal areas lay to the west, southwest, and south of Outina's own territory we must here clearly suspect deliberate deception on the part of La Roche-Ferrière and Laudonnière's other informants on their location. There is no indication whatever that Laudonnière treated these reports critically or interrogated Indians himself to find out whether they could be substantiated. Instead, he contributed successive contingents to the local Indian wars being waged by Outina without any advantage to the French plans, except the short-term one of keeping a certain number of the discontented settlers employed in military activities. It is ironical that had Laudonnière joined Satouriwa, as he had first agreed, in an assault on the Utina tribe, he would have had a reasonably good chance of taking from them substantial amounts of Spanish silver and gold which they had accumulated. Instead, for him, far-off mountains only were golden.

The crucial matter in the confusion surrounding the Le Moyne-Laudonnière evidence appears to be the existence and specification of 'Apalachen' or 'Palachen'. These two forms of the word are what Narvaez heard, according to Cabeza de Vaca, when he landed at Tampa Bay in 1528.[47] The local Indians (Oçita or Mococo) told him that the province of 'Apalachen' (or 'Palachen') was far away, apparently to the north, and had much gold. So far as one can discover this chance statement created the name for the whole Appalachian range. It appeared in the Zamora edition of the travels in 1542, in the Valladolid edition in 1555, and in Ramusio in 1556.[48] On the other hand, the real location of the tribe had been published in Portugal in 1557, and this was in the narrative by the Gentleman of Elvas of the Soto expedition.[49] He made it clear that the Apalachee tribe lived in Western Florida and that from their territory to the Cotifachique (in South Carolina) was some 450 leagues along the piedmont. He gave no encouragement to the view that the tribe lived anywhere except on level ground reasonably near the Gulf coast and was in no way associated with mountains. But this latter book was probably not yet known in France in 1564.[50] The Cabeza de Vaca mention had already, before 1564, affected a number of Spanish maps of North America. Typical of them, perhaps, was the Diego Gutiérrez printed map of 1562 where 'Apalachen' is a name already attached to mountains far into the interior.[51]

[47] Conveniently accessible in F. W. Hodge and T. H. Lewis, Spanish explorers in the southern United States, 1528-1543 (New York, 1907), pp. 21-2.

[48] La relación que dio Aluar Nuñez Cabeça de Vaca, translated into Italian in G. B. Ramusio, Navigationi et viaggi, III (Venice, 1556), ff. 310-30.

[49] Hodge and Lewis, Spanish explorers, pp. 160, 161, 188, 271-2.

[50] Fidalgo de Elvas, Relaçam verdadeira (Evora, 1557). There was no French edition. It was not known in England until after 1600. The parallel evidence from Rangel was recorded by Oviedo but was not published until the first full edition of his Historia, 4 vols (Madrid, 1851).

[51] This map was compiled before 1554 and was the most detailed and influential map of North America to be printed up to its date of publication; reproduced in W. P. Cumming, The southeast in early maps (Princeton, 1958), pl. 6; and see L. Bagrow, History of cartography, revised R. A. Skelton (London, 1964), p. 114, pl. LXIX.

In this map all the major rivers from this range found their way into the Gulf of Mexico. The tendency thereafter was for this name to retreat farther into the interior of North America. On the Zalteiri map of 1566,[52] for example, 'Apalachen' lies between two mountain ranges in juxtaposition with New France. The earliest map so far seen to bring it back towards Florida was the Mercator world map of 1569.[53] On this there is a great line of mountains, lying northwest to southeast, well behind the eastern coastline, which throws a long spur down towards the Atlantic: in the angle a wide river ('r. Sola') runs down to the sea at the northeastern end of the Florida peninsula. In this area also, situated northwestwards from Florida, is the location 'Apalchen'.

The use by Laudonnière of the dual forms 'Appalesse' and 'Palassi' (also 'Palacy' and 'Pallacy') would suggest that he already knew of the Cabeza de Vaca reference.[54] His knowledge of a map of the Gutiérrez type would allow him to reinforce the association of a rich, gold-bearing province, of which he had some vague reports, with the interior range of mountains depicted on North American maps. If it could be established that a map of the Mercator type was current in 1564, showing the name in a position northwest of the St Johns River, and associated with a river descending to the sea from that region, the transition to the story told by Laudonnière and Le Moyne, and recorded on the Le Moyne map, would be almost complete.

It has been suggested that the deception may have been deliberate. This may not inevitably have been so. Certainly Laudonnière could, in the absence of any effective map of the area made as the result of French experiences, have felt himself entitled to make the deductions he did. But what of Le Moyne and his map? Le Moyne undoubtedly had the names, including 'Apalatci' (and probably also the 'Pallassi' which appeared in White[55]) along with the names of 'Potanou', 'Oustaca', and the rest which he finally placed in what would now be central and western Georgia. But it is just possible that he had them on sketches made for him by others which he had forgotten how to fit into his general picture. If the site of the village of 'Apalatci' is rotated southwards about 60 or 70 degrees it falls roughly into place with the real village of Apalachee, seat of the Apalachee tribe, in the vicinity of modern Tallahassee, and then, Potanou, Oustaca, etc., if moved in the same way with it, fall, if not precisely, at least approximately into place where they are known to have been located. Thus the misleading picture could have been a combination of wrong analysis in good faith by Laudonnière and of the muddled association of sketches by Le Moyne, both contriving to operate in the same direction. It is possible, alternatively, that Le Moyne and Laudonnière both intended to deceive. The most difficult thing to understand, if Le Moyne did not, is how he could depict an enormous tributary joining the St Johns on the north bank, which he had himself traversed and should surely have remembered, even if he had

---

[52] Justin Winsor, *Narrative and critical history of America*, II (London, 1885), p. 451.

[53] Republished separately, *Imago Mundi*, Supplement no. 2 (1961). A legible section reproduced in Winsor, *Narrative and critical history*, IV (Boston, 1885), p. 373.

[54] *H.N.*, pp. 41, 137, 171.

[55] 'Montaigne Pallassi', Hulton and Quinn, p. 136, pl. 58.

depended on various field parties, which he did not accompany, for the sketches which he managed to confuse. Finally, we must not eliminate the distinct possibility that he made his final layout of his sketch material with the Mercator map of 1569 before him and that he could well have fitted his data into its broad pattern even at the cost of recording inaccurately the topographical information he had obtained in 1564-5.[56]

---

[56] Discussion between Dr Skelton and Professor Quinn on their respective emphases in these matters was still in progress at the time of the former's death. Dr Skelton stressed 'the probability that Le Moyne had to fit together separate map-sketches' and the likelihood of his having difficulty in 'adjusting them to the Spanish map framework' and 'the possibility that he tried to do so honestly'. He also stressed that 'one cannot expect uniform scale all over a map like this, especially at (or beyond) the periphery of knowledge'. He thought therefore that, besides the misapprehensions of the expedition leaders, 'the limitations of the cartographer and, particularly, of his compilation materials' should be emphasized. An attempt has been made above to balance these considerations, even though much must remain conjectural.

17

THE VOYAGE OF ÉTIENNE BELLENGER
TO THE MARITIMES IN 1583: A NEW DOCUMENT

BETWEEN THE RETURN OF THE CARTIER AND ROBERVAL EXPEDITIONS and the revival of the St. Lawrence penetration of North America by France under Champlain there is a long gap, only very partially filled by the revival in interest though not in action which the appointment of Troïlus de Mesgouez, marquis de la Roche, to act as royal governor in New France, 1577–8, seemed to mark, and the undoubted re-penetration of the river by small, fur-trading expeditions from 1581 onwards.[1] What has not been examined, and indeed has seemed incapable of examination for lack of materials, is French activity southwards from Cape Breton in the last quarter of the sixteenth century. The predominance of Breton fishing vessels using the Cape Breton area, evident in the earlier part of the century, had given way to the dominance of the Basques, mainly French but with Spaniards amongst them, later in the century. It is highly probable that before 1580 they ranged not only down the coast of Nova Scotia, but also along the New England shores where Englishmen were to find traces of them at the opening of the seventeenth century. But, being fishermen, with some though probably not major fur-trading interests, they left no trace, it appears, in the records of their home ports of precisely where they went. Indeed, what little knowledge we have of them in action comes, in the 'nineties, from English sources. This absence of information gives all the more value to what can be gleaned of a Norman voyage under the command of Etienne Bellenger in 1583 which explored the coasts southwards from Cape Breton, coasted the southern shore of Nova Scotia, and then turned along its north coast into the Bay of Fundy, following its limits around southern New Brunswick and, in open sea again, some way along the coast of Maine, before turning homewards for France.

For the Bellenger voyage there have hitherto been available only two paragraphs included in 1584 by Richard Hakluyt in "A particuler discourse concerning the greate necessitie and manifolde comodyties that are like to growe to this Realme of Englande by the Westerne discoveries lately attempted." This was first

[1]The best summary remains that of Charles de la Roncière, *Histoire de la marine française*, IV (3rd edition, Paris, 1923), 307–19.

published by Charles Deane in 1877 as "Discourse on Western Planting"[2] and the name, in the form of "Discourse of Western Planting," has stuck to it in the later and better edition by E. G. R. Taylor.[3] From 1877 on the voyage of "Stephen Bellanger," as Hakluyt called him, has made a modest appearance in works on the beginnings of French enterprise in North America.[4] Only Ganong,[5] on the basis of an inadequate reproduction of a French map of 1584, was able to make some additional deductions which pinned Bellenger down to the Bay of Fundy and seemed to make him its first explorer if not its discoverer.

It is now possible to say rather more about the voyage. In 1917 Phillippe Barrey published some materials from the records of the *Amirauté* of Le Havre which threw a little light on how Bellenger became involved in the venture;[6] while the maps of Jacques de Vaulx, when examined in detail (which Ganong had no opportunity to do), give some further information on his progress. But, with the identification of a manuscript in the British Museum (Additional MS 14027, ff. 289–90v.), which somehow escaped H. P. Biggar's eye, a narrative, brief but significant, gives a new perspective to the voyage. Moreover, this was written by and is in the handwriting of Richard Hakluyt, and elaborates appreciably what he is already known to have written. He thus increased our debt to him for preserving such few records as there are of French activity in American waters between 1541 and 1585. The document is among the papers of Dr. (later Sir) Julius Caesar, judge of the High Court of Admiralty, to whom Hakluyt may have sent it, though it could equally well have been passed on to him by Sir Francis Walsingham who was at that time very much concerned with American colonization. The manuscript, as printed below, offers some problems of interpretation, not all of which the present edition attempts to solve, but that it adds significantly to our knowledge of French enterprise at this period, and to the gradual uncovering of the shores of eastern Canada and the United States, cannot be doubted.

II

Little is so far known of Etienne Bellenger before his voyage of 1583. He was a Rouen merchant who lived in the Rue des Augustines next door to the sign of the Tuile d'or. He was concerned in the financing and victualling of overseas voyages. On May 10, 1582,[7] he was given an acquittance for the money (evidently

[2]In *The Documentary History of Maine*, I (Cambridge, Mass., 1877), 26, 84.

[3]In *The Original Writings and Correspondence of the Two Richard Hakluyts*, (Hakluyt Society, London, 1935), II, 227, 266.

[4]E.g., in N. E. Dionne, *La Nouvelle France de Cartier à Champlain* (Québec, 1891), pp. 120–1; H. Harrisse, *Découverte et évolution cartographique de Terre-Neuve et des pays circonvoisins* (Paris and London, 1900), 161; H. P. Biggar, *The Early Trading Companies of New France* (Toronto, 1901), 33; La Roncière, *Histoire de la marine française*, IV, 311; A. Anthiaume, *Cartes marines, constructions navales, voyages de découverte chez les Normands, 1500–1650* (Paris, 1916) II, 42, 92–3 (see G. Lanctot, *Histoire de Canada*, I (Montréal 1959), 114).

[5]W. F. Ganong, "Crucial Maps in the Early Cartography and Place-nomenclature of the Atlantic Coast of Canada, IX," Royal Society of Canada, *Transactions*, 3rd series, vol. XXXI, s. 2 (1937), 119–25.

[6]P. Barrey, "Le Havre transatlantique de 1571 à 1610," in Julien Hayem, ed., *Mémoires et documents pour servir à l'histoire du commerce et de l'industrie en France*, V (Paris, 1917), 86–7, 183.

[7]C. & P. Bréard, *Documents relatifs à la marine normande et à ses armements aux XVIᵉ et XVIIᵉ siècles* (Rouen, 1889), 267; Barrey, "Le Havre," 87n.

advanced to him earlier) which he, with Louis de la Chandre, merchant of Honfleur, had paid to members of the expedition which, under orders from Catherine de Médici, took Phillippe Strozzi to his fighting death in the Azores. Next month, on June 27,[8] he was given authority by Captain Bertrand Campion of the *Belle Etoile* to borrow 200 crowns for him at the current rate. No doubt other similar transactions will be traced when the departmental archives at Rouen are thoroughly combed for them. But they suggest that he was in a substantial way of business. More significant for the present purpose, he had already been twice across the Atlantic Ocean to Cape Breton. Since this information was obtained from him when he was discussing the quality of the fish taken off the Cape we may safely assume that he went on fishing voyages. We can also assume that he may well have done some fur trading along the coast, as the Bretons and Basques had been doing for so long. It is possible that he was then in command of a ship of his own, though, if so, it is strange that he has not yet come to light as a shipowner in the French records. More likely, he went as cape merchant of one of the ships he victualled in order to see how the fur and fishing trades were carried on. What he saw evidently made him anxious to investigate further, even, it seems, to take the risk of establishing a shore station, well to the south-west of Cape Breton, where the fur trade might be exploited more profitably.

The story of the 1583 voyage appears to begin on November 24, 1582, when the experienced Le Havre pilot, Michel Costé, acquired a third share in the bark *Chardon* of 50 tons, which belonged to Jacques de Chardon, sieur de Tressonville, gentlemen of the Chamber to the aged Cardinal-Archbishop of Rouen, cardinal de Bourbon. This transaction laid the foundations for a contract under which the Cardinal used Tressonville as cover for financing an expedition to North America. The agreement, signed on January 24, 1583,[9] contains almost all we know about the business side of the voyage. By it, Michel Costé, as captain of the *Chardon*, undertook to conduct Etienne Bellenger, with twenty men, to a destination which Bellenger was not to disclose to Costé until the ship was out of the English Channel. On arrival at this undisclosed destination Bellenger was to be put on shore, together with twenty men and such victuals as he would need, and Costé was to hurry back and report fully to Chardon. In the charter-party between Costé and Chardon the value of the merchandise carried was put at 400 crowns and the ostensible destination of the ship as "les côtes de Cap-Vert, Sierra Leone,

---

[8]Barrey, "Le Havre," 87*n*.

[9]"Le 24 Janvier 1583 Michel Costé qui, le 24 novembre précédent, avait pris au tiers la barque le *Chardon* de Jacques de Chardon, sieur de Tressonville, gentilhomme ordinaire de la Chambre du cardinal de Bourbon, demeurant à Jouy, près d'Evreux, s'engageait avec lui pour conduire Etienne Bellenger, accompagné de vingt hommes au lieu designé à ce dernier par Chardon, sans que Bellenger soit tenu de dire et declarer le lieu où il devait débarquer avant d'être hors des relâchements, c'est-à-dire en dehors de la Manche. A son arrivée, Bellenger pourroit prendre les victualles dont il aurait besoin, excepté celles qui seraient necessaires au navire pour revenir au Havre. En outre, les lettres qu'il remetrait à Costé devaient être portées à Chardon en la plus grande diligence, ce qui laisse penser que le navire devait l'attendre quelque temps, les réflexions faites en cours de traversée ne devant sans doute pas présenter grand intérêt pour son commanditaire. Cet engagement était conclu moyennant 133 écus un tiers et le chargement que Chardon avait promis." (*Ibid.*, pp. 86–7.)

"Le *Chardon*, de 50 tonneaux, capitaine Michel Costé.

"Marchandise et avaries 400 écus.

"Pour les côtes du Cap-Vert, Sierra Leone, le Brézil, Cannibales, îles et terre ferme du Pérou etc. Jacques de Chardon, écuyer, sieur de Tressonville, capitaine en la marine, bourgeois et victuailleur." (*Ibid.*, 183.)

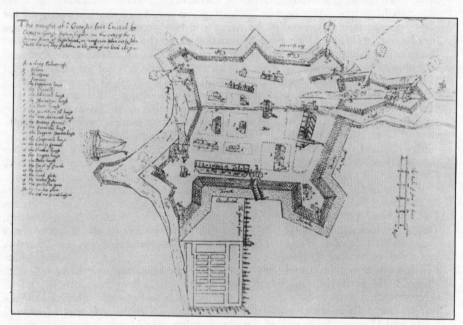

20 Fort St. George, Sagadahoc (Kennebec River), 1607-1608 *(Archivo General de Simancas, Estado Inglaterra 2586, f. 147)*

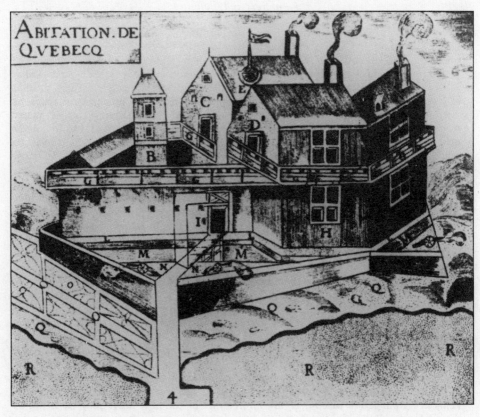

21 *Habitacion*, Québec, 1608, Samuel de Champlain, *Les voyages* (1613)

le Brézil, Cannibals, îles et terre ferme de Pérou etc." What makes sense of these obscure transactions is the information given both by the French cosmographer royal, André Thevet, and by the king's skinner, Valeron Perosse, to Richard Hakluyt in Paris early in January, 1584,[10] almost a year later, "that Duke Joyeuse [Anne de Joyeuse, duc de Joyeuse] Admiral of France, and the Cardinal of Burbon and their frendes, have had a meaning to send out certayen ships to inhabit some place for the north part of America, and to carry thither many friers and other religiouse persons." The plan was evidently one for a colony of settlement under powerful auspices, the ostensible object of which was to establish a base for missionary enterprise amongst the American Indians, though, no doubt, to do so on the basis of an effective trade in furs. But, Hakluyt adds—"I think they be not in haste to do yt."

It is difficult to comment on the implications of this major project without knowing much more of the background than we do at present, but it must be stressed that La Roche was still the king's lieutenant, on paper, for New France, and that he was again preparing an expedition to the St Lawrence. Was this to be a parallel or a rival venture? It would seem, though it would be unwise to be positive about it, that it was the latter. La Roche was associated with the Huguenots and linked with the Queen Mother; the Cardinal and the Duc de Joyeuse with the Catholic party. It might well seem that they wished to establish a foothold in the New World which would prevent the Huguenots, and the Bretons in particular, having a monopoly of New France. Hence too the missionary motive. Until more is known, however, it is essential to be cautious in drawing broad conclusions. Yet there are no major ambiguities, though a number of minor ones, in what actually happened on the voyage. The new Hakluyt narrative is in some respects an elaboration of what he included in "A particuler discourse" (or, more correctly, since the former was written first, the items in "A particuler discourse" are an abstract of the new narrative). It is not as detailed as we would like, but it dovetails so closely with the evidence to be derived from the de Vaulx maps that most of the difficulties of interpretation which it presents can be resolved.

III

We cannot say for certain when the voyage began. Hakluyt dated the setting out of the *Chardon* as January 19, 1583 (evidently New Style, i.e., January 29, 1582[−3], English style), but the date, January 24, of the Chardon-Costé contract strongly suggests a later start. Furthermore, it was not unknown for Breton fishermen to make a western crossing in January, though it was unusual. The northerly movement of the Azores high-pressure system which made this practicable was more frequent in February, while English fishermen were usually unwilling to set out before April or May. We may, provisionally, suggest mid-February as the approximate time of sailing from Le Havre. A few days later, if the pre-arranged plan was carried out, Bellenger would have declared his intentions to Costé and a preliminary decision would have been reached about how and when to land the former with his twenty men, leaving only ten men with Michel Costé to sail the ship home. In from twenty to thirty days, that is, if mid-February was the time of setting out, in early or mid-March the vessel reached Cape Breton. We do not know what, if anything, Costé knew of the

---

[10]Taylor, ed., *Hakluyts*, I, 207.

coast, though Bellenger was evidently knowledgeable from his earlier visits. The ship was prepared for her exploration of the shores to the southwest of the Cape which was an essential part of the purpose of the expedition, even if it was not so stated in the Chardon-Costé contract. The pinnace had been carried on deck and was now equipped for coastal discovery and charting. Under Costé's pilotage the vessel moved down the coast, penetrating harbours and rivers as she went and sending fairly frequent shore parties to make contact with the Indians and, where possible, to trade with them. Rocks, islands, and shallows were logged and indicated as coastal charting (no doubt varying in its detail with the weather and with local conditions) proceeded, and soundings were taken often, good depths of water being frequently noted inshore. Between 50 and 60 leagues southwest of Cape Breton Bellenger sketched the northeast shore of an island which, when it had been fully recorded, proved to be some 50 leagues long from north-east to southwest and was roughly triangular in shape. He identified it as the Ile de Saint Jehan (Isle of St. John) which had appeared in various locations on the maps of earlier days. Here it seems that the northeast shore must represent Halifax harbour, explored perhaps to Bedford Basin, though not further, to which Indian indications of portages to the Minas Basin would add proof of its continuity (which, indeed, the Minas Basin, when found, would tend to confirm).

At some point along the coast the Indians he met became less savage and treacherous. This may have taken place gradually as the Frenchmen began to leave the aboriginal sites frequented by other Europeans, or it may represent a tribal boundary. If it was the former it would not be surprising that contact with violent, drunken, fire-armed European fishermen and part-time fur traders should have rendered the Indians at least equally violent and, perhaps, more treacherous. But the Micmac did not, universally, have a bad reputation amongst the whites. By April they would probably be back in their villages after the winter hunting and would be ready to trade their furs. Evidently some of the villages were large: one of them, some 100 leagues from Cape Breton, and so, perhaps, forty to fifty leagues from Halifax harbour, that is not far from Cape Sable, comprised 80 houses, covered with bark, on the bank of a river up which Bellenger penetrated. If these were long houses, as they probably were, rather than summer shelters, this was an unusually large aggregation for an Algonkian tribe, amounting perhaps to 800 people or more. However, it is possible that it was an early encampment by tribesmen who had collected for the summer fishing near the sea, though this would have been more likely at the time of the *Chardon's* return up the coast than on her way down it.

We learn nothing of how the *Chardon* worked her way, with her pinnace, around the southern end of Nova Scotia towards the Bay of Fundy, but we are informed that the entrance to "a great Bay of that Iland" was very narrow, only the width of a culverin-shot. This indicates, clearly enough, that they eventually found themselves in St. Mary's Bay and were obliged, so as to proceed into the Bay of Fundy, to work through the narrow passage between Briar Island and Long Island (Grand Passage), or through that between Long Island and Digby Neck (Petit Passage), into the Bay of Fundy. From then on it was plain sailing for some 25 leagues, evidently northeast along the Nova Scotia coast, and eventually, probably after a look at the Minas Basin (though possibly without exploring it), a point was found which was thought to mark the termination of the Bay. This was probably between Ram Head and Cape d'Or, in which area an old marker was found by Champlain in 1607,[11] or it could have been as far round as Cape

---

[11]See Ganong, "Crucial maps, IX," 129.

Chignecto. There the Cardinal de Bourbon's arms were affixed to a tall tree and, perhaps also, a wooden cross was erected. It was probably at this point, though it may have been at a later one, that it was decided that Bellenger should not after all remain with his little party to start a trading post as a nucleus for a settlement. Yet the formal taking possession of the head of the Bay of Fundy indicates that it was believed to be a new discovery which should be solemnly secured for France through the Cardinal de Bourbon, and was also probably regarded as a possible site for future settlement under his auspices. It may, too, have been from this area that Bellenger obtained from the Indians the ore, thought to have silver and tin in it, which he brought home. The *Chardon* continued down the west shore of the Bay of Fundy, though we know this not from the narrative sources, but from the maps. The width of the Bay Bellenger put at 20 leagues. If this is to be taken literally, the "great river" which was entered with the pinnace about 20 leagues to the west "of that Iland," i.e., the Isle of St. John, would, most likely, have been Passamaquoddy Bay, but, had he passed along the Maine shore keeping Great Manan Island to port, as he is not unlikely to have done, it is, more probably, in spite of the inadequate distance indicated, the Penobscot. This is made the more so as the Rio de Gamas on the de Vaulx maps, almost certainly the Penobscot, is the only one shown which might have accommodated the pinnace easily for 7 leagues and have then suggested that it might be navigable for 60 or 80 miles more (or have been pointed out as penetrable for a long way by the Indians). We may assume that the *Chardon* spent between one and two months on the southwesterly exploration and would thus have reached the Penobscot, if that was the terminal river shown by de Vaulx, in late April or May. It must have been a mild spring since there is no mention of ice, snow, or cold weather. The decision to turn back may have been due to the identification of the "great River" with the Rio de Gamas of the traditional Spanish maps and the consequent reaching of a boundary on a coast which, it could be assumed, had previously been explored and its features named.

We are given no direct information on the return voyage except for one incident. Working back along the coast already discovered, that is the southern shore of Nova Scotia, within 80 to 60 leagues from Cape Breton, the pinnace was sent inshore to trade with the Indians. Through the cruelty and treachery of the natives, and the trustfulness of the French, so Hakluyt tells us, the boat was attacked, two of the men killed and the rest decoyed away in some manner so that the Indians could seize the pinnace.[12] If Bellenger had not already decided to abandon the intention of establishing a trading post, he did so then. To set up a post midway along the Nova Scotia coast might well have been one of a number of alternatives considered by him, but the Indian attack would tend to demoralize his men, and the loss of the pinnace, which it must have been intended to leave behind, would so immobilize the settlers that the fulfilment of the primary intention of the expedition was no longer possible. Thereafter, it is likely, he hurried on to Cape Breton where he could make contact with fishing vessels, if he wished to buy food or obtain news, and so set out back across the Atlantic. We do not know how long, this time, Costé took to bring the *Chardon* to her home port, but it was probably not more than 30 days. The total time taken for the voyage out and back is given either as four or four-and-a-half months. If the date of departure was about February 19 this would mean a return between the middle and end of June (or perhaps at the beginning of July), after an absence of some 117 to 132 days.

---

[12]The place was evidently named Terre des mauvais, see *infra*, p. 298, n. 45.

IV

Considering the relatively detailed character of the reconnaissance, covering as it did over 700 miles of coast in some 80 days and including 10 to 12 landings during this period, the amount of material information on the land and on the Indians is comparatively small. Hakluyt's narrative, welcome as it is, is only a summary of the knowledge gained from the voyage. It may, indeed, be only a short version of a longer account which he put together after he had met and talked with Bellenger. One difficulty with it is that we are not able to sort out the objects brought from Cape Breton and Nova Scotia from those acquired, say, in Maine, or within the Bay of Fundy. So far as flora or fauna are concerned this may not affect us very much, since the Maritimes have a certain geographical and climatic unity, but it is a little confusing where Indian traits are described not to have locations specified more fully so as to differentiate the sub-cultures of Micmac, Malecite, and Penobscot peoples. At the same time the narrative can be made to supply a good deal of valuable data, provided due caution is exercised, even before expert work has been done on it by Indian specialists.

The limits of latitude are stated as 42 to 44 degrees, where they are, in fact, 44 to 46 degrees approximately. The whole coastline seen is said to have been pleasant and warm, very much like the Bay of Biscay coast from Bayonne to Nantes, and varying only a little as the land lay towards the north or the south. The country was well wooded, with oaks, "cypresses" (red cedar), pine trees, hazels, and so on, admirable for shipbuilding. There were examples, more especially in the Minas Basin, it would seem, of flat beaches where salt could be panned and evaporated in the sun as at La Rochelle. Some mineral matter thought to contain silver and tin was brought back as giving promise of metals. The fishing along the shores was very good. Bellenger, from his three voyages to the Cape Breton coast, testified that the fish (cod) was better than that of Newfoundland, but here Hakluyt does not particularize where to do so would have been very valuable. Moreover, there were good harbours for the fishermen. But this was all the direct geographical information that Hakluyt recorded.

The more general evidence on Indian life has already been mentioned, the difference between the Indians relatively near to and distant from Cape Breton, and the large size of at least one of their settlements. Their physique was generally very good. They were naked (women presumably as well as men) except for a skin breechclout secured by a long belt, fringed at the ends, and decorated with red-dyed porcupine quills. From the belt hung a small bag containing the materials for fire-making. Their hair hung to the waist at back and front except for a cut across the brows. They used long bows, some 6 feet in length, with arrows half as long, tipped with indented bone points attached by a leather thong. They prepared finely dressed and ornamented skins, elk (?), deer, and seal. They also dried deer meat in long (12-inch) strips. This makes up a credible and useful, though strictly limited, picture.

The Indians were, everywhere, prepared to trade. Their willingness to do so might suggest that even in the Bay of Fundy European traders were already common. But this is not necessarily so, since the long-established seasonal contacts with the French and Basques at Cape Breton alone would have been sufficient to create fur production for sale through middlemen amongst the tribes living at a distance, within the catchment area. The main things that the Indians Bellenger met had to sell were skins and furs; large decorated skins, the staples of their own production, and the smaller, more valuable, furs called for mainly by European demand, beaver (already sought for hats), lynx (a rarity), and otter. The Indians were also willing to dispose of bows, porcupine quills, dyes (reds, yellows, grey, and blue), castoreum, and samples of pemmican. Whether they also supplied the metallic ore already mentioned is not stated. In return, they were willing to accept knives, looking-glasses, bells, and other trinkets, having not yet developed a taste for heavier weapons or for European spirits.

v

What happened on Bellenger's return? Some things we know, many others we do not. He sold his furs for good prices. His trade goods had cost him 40 livres (£4) and he sold what they had bought for 440 crowns (£88), disposing of 600 beaver pelts and having his lynx skins valued at 6 to 15 crowns. The profits were high though the scale of the transactions was small. He presented to the Cardinal twenty lynx skins and two Indian bows and arrows, with probably other samples of the products of the country. He sat down to compile from his journal and sketches a detailed map ("a fayre Carde") of the coasts explored which he also put into the Cardinal's hands. It is most likely that he added to it a detailed narrative of the voyage, though, if so, it has vanished without trace. What we do not know are what were the precise reactions of the Cardinal to the results of the reconnaissance. On the one hand, the primary purpose of the expedition, the establishment of a holding post on North American soil, had been frustrated, and the local Indians of part, at least, of the coast shown to be savage and treacherous. On the other, the reports contained, we can assume from what we know, much that was novel about Ile de Saint Jehan, our Bay of Fundy, and the Rio de Gamas (our Penobscot), and indicated that the fur trade, at least, was worth pursuing on economic grounds.

During 1582 Anne de Joyeuse became admiral of France and governor of Normandy and it was probably when he visited Normandy in 1583 that he became associated with the Cardinal de Bourbon's American projects.[13] Our next and only piece of information concerning them is that picked up by Richard Hakluyt at the beginning of January, 1584, and already noted, to the effect that Joyeuse and the Cardinal were in the field with a colonizing venture, but one which they were taking no very active steps to set forward. It may be worthwhile assuming that Bellenger was encouraged to go ahead with a further commercial enterprise to follow up his 1583 voyage, while the settlement plan was held in suspense for the time being. This would explain what is otherwise hard to understand, why Bellenger, who was bound to secrecy about his objectives at the beginning of the 1583 voyage, was willing and even anxious to talk about western prospects at the beginning of the following year.

It is mainly through what he said that we know anything whatever about the ventures in which he was engaged. The Reverend Richard Hakluyt had arrived in France at the end of September, 1583, as secretary and chaplain to the new English ambassador to France, Sir Edward Stafford. His primary purpose, in the short run at least, was to collect information about North America and about French projects for voyages to America, in the interests of his master, Sir Francis Walsingham, who was closely concerned at this time, as was Hakluyt himself, with English plans for trading to and settling New England, the Maritimes, and Newfoundland. His scholarly interests and his flair for collecting information rapidly made him an expert in economic espionage so that he extracted from merchants

---

[13]He was in Rouen March 25, Le Havre, April 14 (R. Herval, *Histoire de Rouen* (Paris, 1949), II, 95; A. E. Borély, *Histoire de la ville du Havre* (Le Havre, 1885), I, 165).

and academics alike invaluable information about French trade with Canada and, from Valeron Perosse and André Thevet, the king's skinner and cosmographer, respectively, the information about the Cardinal de Bourbon's recent venture and also, it would seem, the name of the man, who had undertaken it for him. Consequently, he hurried down to Rouen. There he made contact with the Rouen instrument-maker, André Mayer, whom he knew already, and who was a relative of Bellenger's, and, with an introduction from Mayer, introduced himself to Bellenger in the Rue des Augustines.

Bellenger, receiving the learned and curious young clergyman in this informal way, did not regard him in any way as an English intelligence agent. Consequently, he spoke freely about his voyage, probably allowing Hakluyt to take notes of what he said, showing him the draft of his chart, the fair copy of which he had passed on to the Cardinal, and also, apparently, some of the journals he had made in the course of the enterprise. He also exhibited specimens of the goods and curiosities he had retained for himself from those brought home on the *Chardon*, and gave Hakluyt a sample of the ore which was supposed to contain silver and tin. He told him that other things had been discovered on the voyage on which he did not wish to speak, so that it would seem that he regarded himself as being in possession of economic and geographical information which he had undertaken (to the Cardinal most likely) not to disclose. It is astonishing, however, that he talked so freely and with so little secrecy. Hakluyt even got him to address a small meeting of English merchants and sea captains in Rouen to whom he repeated a brief account of his voyage. Hakluyt had a specific purpose in view in the latter activity. Both Sir George Peckham and Christopher Carleill had at that time expeditions in preparation to explore and settle the territory to the southwest of Cape Breton. Bellenger's information on its character and products tended to encourage good hopes from these expeditions (though neither in the end reached North America) and to lead to the offer of subscriptions. It was the need to report the willingness of the English in Rouen to subscribe to English ventures, on the strength of what Bellenger had to say about his voyage, which led Hakluyt to send to England the document now first printed below.

Whatever the plans of the Cardinal de Bourbon and the Duc de Joyeuse, there is no reason to doubt that what Hakluyt said was true that, at the time he wrote the document now published, namely late January or early February, 1584, Etienne Bellenger was rapidly pushing forward preparations for a new fur-trading expedition. He was not, this year, going to use the *Chardon* (indeed Tressonville got into financial difficulties and had to dispose of her during 1584),[14] and this may demonstrate his detachment from the Cardinal's long-term projects. He had, instead, hired or acquired a small bark and pinnace which he was fitting out at Honfleur for a voyage on which he proposed to embark before March 1, 1584. There is every probability that he did so, but nothing has so far certainly come to light about his success, or, indeed, about himself. While he may have returned home safely, it is also possible that he was lost on the voyage and that this is the reason why the fur trade was not more vigorously plied on the coasts of the Maritimes by Norman merchants and mariners in succeeding years. A little more information may still lie buried in French archives.

The Cardinal and the Duke continued their overseas partnership, but their objectives proliferated. In 1584[15] Joyeuse prepared an expedition under Guillaume

---

[14]Barrey, "Le Havre," 86–7.

[15]*Ibid.*, 88, 189; E. Gosselin, *Documents ... pour servir à l'histoire de la marine normande* (Rouen, 1876), 167. See also La Roncière, *Histoire de la marine française*, IV, 312.

le Héricy, with Jacques de Vaulx as chief pilot, which was, ostensibly to coast and chart the whole of eastern America from Brazil to Labrador. The expedition was delayed until the following year and it remained at sea for some two years. It is known to have occupied itself, seriously, with Brazil, but whether it ever touched the shores which Bellenger had explored and on which the hopes of the Admiral and the Cardinal had earlier been centred is not yet known.

VI

The final group of sources for the Bellenger voyage, the maps of Jacques de Vaulx, make up a subject of great interest in themselves, but they cannot be discussed here in any great detail. They comprise two illuminated volumes and a map in the Bibliothèque nationale. Though they have been dealt with by Charles de la Roncière, Albert Anthiaume, and W. F. Ganong,[16] it is necessary to revise accepted views of their chronology if their relevance to the Bellenger voyage is to be understood. The volumes are each entitled "Les premières euvres de Iacques de Vaulx pillote en la Marine" and are two versions, differing only slightly from each other, of a general work on cosmography, which have numerous highly decorative illustrations and maps, including a number, larger and smaller, of America. It is clear from internal evidence that the less fine copy of "Les premières euvres," MS français 9175, was composed first,[17] even though at least one map was added at a later date and the dedication to M. de Riberpré made in 1584, i.e., in the year after its completion. The fine copy, MS français 150, was, on the other hand, commissioned by and completed for the Duc de Joyeuse during 1583. (What happened was apparently that de Vaulx soiled his primary copy and had to start again, but that he refurbished it for presentation to another client in the following year.) Of the many small variations between the two, those of significance for the Bellenger voyage concern only the maps showing northeast North America. Thus in MS français 9175, f.25, de Vaulx shows a stereotyped (Spanish-type) outline from Cape Breton westward to the Rio de Gamas, while in MS français 150, f.26, he shows a triangular "Isle St. Jehan" and makes other alterations which show that he has subsequently assimilated something from the Bellenger voyage. He went on to use similar "improved" material for a map of the Atlantic (*ibid.*, ff. 29–30) in the same volume, and then, it would seem, turned back to include a copy of this "improved" map in his earlier version (MS français 9175, ff. 29–30). This is, at least, a provisional reconstruction of the sequence of events. In all respects, however, considering the smallness of scale in the three cases cited, the Bellenger outline of the "island" and "great bay" (southern Nova Scotia and Bay of Fundy, respectively) are clearly indicated, and for the first time, though no names are added except that of "Isle St. Jehan." The closeness of the association of Joyeuse with de Vaulx on the one side and with the Cardinal de Bourbon on the other, and the known possession by the latter of Bellenger's chart, is the most likely explanation of the use by de Vaulx of the Bellenger data. De Vaulx went on, however, to make a more detailed chart of America, dated 1584, which also survives in the Bibliothèque nationale (Cartes, réserve géographie,

---

[16]C. de la Roncière, "Une carte française encore inconnue du nouveau monde (1584)," *Bibliothèque de l'Ecole des Chartes*, vol. LXXI (1910), 588–601; A. Anthiaume, *Cartes marines, constructions navales, voyages de découverte chez les Normands, 1500–1650*, I, 129–46; Ganong, "Crucial Maps, IX," 107–26.

[17]The freshness of the figure drawings in the one, their wooden, though competent, copying in the other is sufficiently evident. I was fortunate in having, in my study of them, the expert advice of Mr. P. H. Hulton, Department of Prints and Drawings, British Museum, whose opinion greatly reinforced my own view of the sequence.

C. 4052). This preserves a nomenclature from Cape Breton to the Rio de Gamas, including several names for features on the Bay of Fundy (which is called "Passaige de St Iehan"), which undoubtedly derives from Bellenger, though not all the names may have been given by him. Collectively, though several are difficult to read and may be differently interpreted by successive scholars, they make up, with the new coastline, an impressive cartographic record of the 1583 expedition.[18] They show that it made a substantial addition to the map of North America so that the new narrative, together with the de Vaulx maps, combine to provide an intelligible outline of an important, and neglected, achievement.

VII

As he was to show some knowledge of the new coastal profile of the Maritimes which the 1583 voyage produced on the de Vaulx maps, it is likely that Hakluyt recorded, though perhaps only from memory, a sketch of Etienne Bellenger's discoveries. The prominence of the "I: S. Joan" on the Molyneux globe of 1592, to which Hakluyt contributed, suggests the influence of the 1583 voyage, which appears to be more pronounced on the famous world map on the Wright-Mercator projection, made for the second edition of Hakluyt's *Principal Navigations* in 1599.[19] There the "I: S. Iohn" is elaborated to a size compatible with Bellenger's account of it, though it has also been elongated and moved northeastwards, so as to lie parallel with, not southwestwards of Cape Breton Island. A long inlet running southwestwards into the mainland, and named "B. menin" (*Menan* being the Micmac name for the Bay of Fundy),[20] is probably an attempt, though a distorted one, to show the great bay which Bellenger explored, though fresh information on nomenclature had come to Hakluyt in the meantime. A rough sketch which the mapmakers were to interpret loosely, rather than the detailed chart which de Vaulx had in 1584, would best fit the circumstances under which something on the Bellenger voyage, though nothing very precise, filtered through to the English maps of 1592 and 1599. Yet Hakluyt and his associate Edward Hayes were obtaining some new information on the Maritimes in the 'nineties. No English voyage to follow up Bellenger's discoveries is known, and Richard Fisher who coasted Nova Scotia in 1593 did so only because he had missed the entrance to the Gulf of St. Lawrence.[21] Hayes, however, in a treatise written between 1593 and 1595 refers to a French discovery of a mine in this region,[22] and gives more specific information of its location on the Bay of Menan in a published tract in 1602,[23] which might suggest that he was harking back to Bellenger's finds, though his information is probably too specific for him to be doing so. More likely, this represents information picked up from those Frenchmen who aroused the interest of the English briefly in the Gulf of St. Lawrence in the years 1591–7, during which they collected a good deal of other information on eastern Canada. Concern with this area fades away in England in 1602: it begins to revive in France in 1597 and to take effect in the voyages of Champlain and de Monts in 1603 and

---

[18]Anthiaume, *Cartes marines*, II, 527.

[19]Reprinted in R. Hakluyt, *The Principal Navigations*, I (Glasgow, 1904), 356. See W. F. Ganong, "A monograph of the cartography of the province of New Brunswick," Royal Society of Canada, *Transactions*, 2nd series, vol. II (1897–8), 346–7, and "Crucial Maps, IX," 121–2.

[20]*Ibid.*, 123.

[21]Hakluyt, *Principal Navigations*, VIII (1904), 157–61.

[22]Cambridge University Library, MS Dd.3.85, ff.2–2v.

[23]John Brereton, *A briefe and true Relation of the Discoverie of the North part of Virginia* (London, 1602), 16, 47.

1604. This new generation of French explorers, it seems, knew nothing of Bellenger or of de Vaulx and so had to repeat from scratch the exploration of the Maritimes.

THE RELATION OF MASTER STEPHEN BELLANGER[24]

The Relation[25] of m*aste*r Stephen Bellanger dwelling in Roan[26] in the street called Rue de Augustines at the syne of the golden tyle in frenche thuille deor[27] of his late voiadge of discoverie of two hundreth leagues of coast from Cape Brittone nere Newfound Land West southwest at the charges of the Cardinall of Borbon[28] this last yere 1583. With mention of some of the comodities fownde in those Cuntries and brought home into Fraunce by hym./

M*aste*r Stephen Bellanger nowe dwelling in Roan in the streete of the Augustines nexte howsse to the signe of the golden tyle in frenche thuille d'or; departed from Newhaven[29] the 19th of Ianuarii 1583[30] in a barck of Fiftie Tons and a little Pinnesse loose within board accompanied with M*aste*r Cottee an excellent Pilott of Newhaven[31] and thirtie men and boyes at the ch*ar*ges of the Cardinall of Burbon, and within lesse then a Moneth[32] arrived at Cape Bryton a little to the sowthwest of Newefownde Land./

From thence he toke his course following the Coast along to the southwest for the space of Two hundreth Leagues the draught and particular discription whereof he shewed me/

He discovered[33] all the Bayes, Harbors, Creekes, Rivers, Sand*es*, Rockes, Islandes, Flatt*es*, with the depthes of Water along as he went which were in some places. 15.30.40.44.50.60. fathoms which he had dilligentlie noted downe in writing within. 50. or threescore Leagues to the west and by south of Cape Briton he had drawne the Iland of St. Iohn which lieth east and west the space of Fiftie leagues, and lieth in forme of a Triangle/[34]

---

[24]The italics in the document are for expanded contractions.

[25]British Library, Additional Manuscript 14027, ff. 289–90v. It was listed in British Museum, *Catalogue of Additional Manuscripts* (London, 1843), p. 27, but it was not included in the manuscript list of contents with which the volume opens.

[26]The form in the French documents, *supra*, 286-8, is "Etienne (or Estienne) Bellenger de Rouen."

[27]Mistaken, as the text below says that he lived next door to the sign of the Tuile d'or in the Rue des Augustines. The precise house has not been ascertained or the existence of the sign corroborated, but the street is well known.

[28]Charles de Bourbon-Vendôme, cardinal de Bourbon, brother of Antoine, King of Navarre, was Archbishop of Rouen from 1550 to his death in 1590. R. Herval, *Histoire de Rouen*, II (1949), 70.

[29]Le Havre.

[30]The document in the Rouen archives shows (*supra*, 300) that the contract for his ship was signed only on January 24 so either Bellenger or Hakluyt is mistaken. A date of February 19 would be more likely. (He repeats January without a precise day in Taylor, ed., *Hakluyts*, II, 266.) He is using new-style dating for the day and year (the equivalent English dating would be January 29, 1582[–3]).

[31]Michel Costé, pilot of Rouen, see *supra*, 287.

[32]Hakluyt elsewhere says twenty days (Taylor, ed., *Hakluyts*, II, 266).

[33]"Discovered" means, for the inlets, that he entered them, probably charting, or at least sketching, each feature, as well as sounding.

[34]Bellenger gained the impression, from entering Halifax harbour perhaps, or hearing Indian tales of portages to the Minas Basin, that southern Nova Scotia was insular and triangular (it is more nearly a parallelogram). See W. D. and R. S. Wallis, *The Micmac Indians* (Minneapolis, 1955), 19.

In a great Bay of that Iland[35] which at one place of the enteraunce is so narrowe that a Colverin shott can reache from one side to the other,[36] and after you are passed that streight is xxv leagues vpp and 20 leagues broad he planted the Cardinall of Burbons Armes in a mightie highe tree[37] and gave names to many places/

To the west of that Iland about.20. leagues he fownde a great River into which he ran vpp with his smale Pynnasse seaven Leagues and thincketh it is navigable three or fowrescore leagues/[38]

He wente on shoare in Tenn or twelve places which he fownde verie pleasaunt And the coast lieth in 42 43 44 degrees of Latitude more or lesse,[39] and is as warme as Bayon, Bordeux, Rochell, and Nantes varieng a litle as it lieth more to the North or the south/

Salt   He thincketh verilie that verie good salte may be made there in great quantitie in divers places along the Coast seeing there wanteth no heate of the sonne nor lowe of flattes like those of Rochell fytt for the purpose/

Trees   He fownde the Countrev full of good trees to build Shipps withall and namely great plentie of oakes, Cypresses,[40] Pynes, hasels etc and divers good herbes as sorrell etc.

Trafficke   In many places he had traffique with the people which are of verie good disposition and stature of Bodie

They weare their hayre hanging downe long before and behynde as lowe as their Navells which they cutt short only overthwart their browes[41]

They go all naked saving their priuities which they cover with an Apron of some Beastes skynn, and tye it vnto them with a long buff[42] gerdle that comes three

---

[35]The great bay can only be the Bay of Fundy. Hakluyt says nothing of the gradual change of course of the *Chardon* as she rounded Cape Sable.

[36]This can only mean that Bellenger found himself in St. Mary's Bay and emerged into the Bay of Fundy by one of the narrow channels to the north or to the south of Long Island (if there have been no major changes in the coastline since 1583).

[37]Three or four leagues north of Cap de Poutrincourt—Cape Split (that is, between Cape d'Or and Ram Head) Champlain on July 11, 1607 found an old cross covered in moss almost wholly rotted away (S. de Champlain, *Voyages* (Paris, 1613), 152). Almost W. F. Ganong's last word in his last paper was to call attention to the cross, after arguing brilliantly that Bellenger might, in fact, have circumnavigated the Bay of Fundy in 1583 ("Crucial Maps, IX," 122–30 (see especially p. 129)).

[38]He is now speaking of the exit from the Bay of Fundy. Just as the evidence for his coasting of the north shore depends on the nomenclature of the de Vaulx chart, so does our interpretation of his narrative, implying that he had come out of the Bay by the Great Manan Channel and had worked along the Maine coast until he entered the Penobscot with his pinnace. The map evidence here associates the great river, which is the terminus of his voyage, with the Rio de Gamas, a traditional feature of the Spanish-style maps of the coast and most probably to be identified with the Penobscot. It must, however, be indicated that Hakluyt's evidence could possibly fit several other estuaries on the Maine coast.

[39]Actually between 44° and 46° (a mistake of two degrees in latitude reckoning is not unknown but it is rather higher than it should have been with an experienced pilot like Costé.)

[40]Red cedar here, not cypress.

[41]The long hair is a characteristic feature, but the cutting of the hair on the brow is not (cf., Wallis, *Micmac*, 83–5). It may be that Bellenger is describing the Indians he saw on the later stages of his outward journey who would be Malecite and Penobscot. (I have had the benefit of the advice of Mr. Wendell S. Hadlock on this and other Indian items.)

[42]Pliable leather here, not "buffalo." For the breechclout and girdle, see Wallis, *Micmac*, 78–9.

times about them beeing made fast behynde and at boath the endes it is cutt
into litle thynn thonges, which thonges they tye rownde about them with slender
quils of birdes fethers wherof some are as red as if they had byn dyed in
cuchanillo/[43]

Their girdells haue also before a litle Codd or Pursse of Buff wherein they putt
divers thinges but especiallie their tinder to keepe fire in, which is of a dry roote
and somewhat like a hard sponge and will quicklie take fyer and is hardlie put
out./ Their weapons whereof he brought hoame store to the Cardinall are Bowes
of two yardes long and arrowes of one yarde hedded with indented bones three
or fower ynches long, and are tyed into a nocke at the ende with a thong of
Lether/

In divers places they are gentle and tractable. But those about Cape Briton and
threescore or fowerscore leagues Westward are more cruell and subtill of norture
then the rest. And you are not to trust them but to stond vpon your gard/[44] For
among them he lost two of his men and his smale Pinesse which happned through
their owne follye in trusting the salvadges to farr/[45]

Commodities brought home   He had traffique with them in divers places and
for trifles, as knyves belles, glasses, and suche like smale marchaundize which cost
hym but Fortie liuers which amount but to fower Poundes Englishe he had by
waie of traffique comodities that he sould in Roan at his retourne. for Fower
hundreth and Fortie Crownes/[46]

Theis were some of the Comodities which he brought hoame from thence, &
showed them me at his howsse./

1   Buff hides reddie dressed vpon both sides bigger then an Oxe,[47]
2   Deere skynes dressed well on the inner side, with the hayre on the outside/
3   Seale[48] skynns exceding great dressed on the ynnerside/
4   Marterns enclyning vnto Sables[49]
5   Bevers skynes verie fayre as many as made 600 bever hattes
6   Otters skynnes verie faire and large
7   A kynde of liquide muske or sivet taken out of the Bevers stones/[50]
8   The fleshe of Deere dried in the sunne in peeces a foote Long/
9   Diuers excellent Cullors, as scarlet, vermillion, redd, tawny, yellowe, gray
    and watchett/[51]

---

[43]Most likely to be dyed porcupine quills.

[44]Does he mean that the Micmac were savage and treacherous and the Malecite and
Penobscot friendly? Or does he rather imply that the treacherous Micmac were those
in regular contact with Europeans, the others not being so? Hakluyt also twice mentions
elsewhere "a Towne of fourscore houses covered with the barkes of trees upon a ryvers
side about C leagues from ... Cape Breton" (Taylor, ed., *Hakluyts*, II, 227, 266).

[45]This must have taken place on the Nova Scotia coast on the return up the coast as
the pinnace was used to explore the great river before he turned northwest again. The
"Terre des mauvais" on the de Vaulx chart is probably associated with this episode,
but is placed on the mainland (probably by mistake) on the north side of the Bay
of Fundy.

[46]One livre is two shillings, one crown four, thus for £4 Bellenger had £88.

[47]Here elk rather than bison would seem to be intended.

[48]The hair seal.

[49]The fisher, *Mustela pennanti*, rather than the Canadian sable, *M. americana*?

[50]Castoreum ("a kynde of muske called Castor," Hakluyt, in Taylor, ed., *Hakluyts*,
II, 227).

[51]Hakluyt also speaks of "divers beastes skynnes as bevers, otters, marternes, lucernes,
seales, buffes, dere skynnes all ... painted on the innerside wth divers excellent colo[rs] as
redd, tawnye, yellowe, and vermillyon" (*ibid.*, II, 227). "Watchet" would be a blue
dye (cf. Wallis, *Micmac*, 87–9, and Nicolas Denys, *The Description and Natural History*

10 Fethers the quils wherof are redd as vermillion
11 Luserns, which the frenche call Loupceruiers[52] Whereof twentie he gave to
the Cardinall of Burbon for a present, and divers others to certaine of his
frendes which I sawe, and was enformed that they were worth some
6.8.10.12.15 crownes a skynne/
12 A kynde of mynerall matter which as some that haue seene thinck houldes
sylver and tynn, whereof he gave me a peece/[53]
Divers other comodities he fownde the secrites whereof he was loath to disclose
vnto me/
He affirmeth by his owne experience that fishe of that Coast on the which he hath
byn thrise,[54] is bigger and better then that of New found Land; and that the
havens are exceding good/
He was out vpon his voiadge but Foure Moneths and a half[55]
He hathe drawen a fayre Carde of all his discoverie which he presented latelie
to the Cardinall of Burbon./
His first draught he shewed me at his howsse and all the comodities aboue
mentioned and gave me parte of each of them for his kynnesmanns sake one
Andrewe Mayer the Compasse maker of Roan. which made me acquaynted with
hym/[56]
He hath also made brief relation of his voiadge in the presences of divers
Englishe men of Credit whome I brought into his Companie that they might here
the same   And namely of one Master Harvie of Lymehouse the owner of the Barck
called the Thomas & Iohn of Master Malym master of the barck called the
Christian of one Moyser an englishe merchannt of Roan and one Howe a sayler
& other honest men/
And this present yere 1584 he setteth fourth agayne for further Traffique in the
same voiadge with a barck and a smale Pinesse which are in preparing ayenst
the first of Marche at homefleur vpon the Coast of Normandy[57]
Vpon knowledge of this voiadge made by Master Stephen Bellanger divers
englishe merchauntes of Roan haue conferred togeather to contribute to the
furthering of the voiadge which is nowe to be sett forth in England[58] namely
theis/

---

of the Coasts of North America (Acadia), W. F. Ganong, ed. [London, 1908], 411,
413, the latter alone mentioning voilet and blue).

[52]Lynx.

[53]Cf., "a kinde of mynerall matter supposed to holde silver, whereof he gave me
some" (so Hakluyt, in Taylor, *Hakluyts*, II, 226).

[54]Bellenger's statement that he had been three times, in all, including 1583 it
would seem, to the Cape Breton coast indicates a degree of Norman activity in the
area not known from other sources.

[55]The total time is also given by Hakluyt as four months (*ibid.*, II, 266). If Bellenger
left in mid-February (not January 19) and reached Cape Breton in between 20 and
30 days, he could have spent from late March to the beginning of June in exploration
and sailed back by early July.

[56]The map is not known to be extant, but its main features are assimilated into de
Vaulx's chart. Hakluyt evidently made his own version from the rough version he had
seen with Bellenger (if indeed he did not get a copy of the finished map later). André
Mayer has not been identified further.

[57]Hakluyt is thus writing before March 1, 1584 (N.S.). Nothing is known of the
result of this voyage.

[58]The English expeditions in preparation at this time were those of Sir George Peckham (to follow up Sir Humphrey Gilbert's recent voyage, on which he was lost) to
southern New England, and Christopher Carleill's which seems to have been directed

Master Greene, Master Lacie, Master Grove, Master Martyn, Master Moyser, Master [   ][59] his chamber fellowe, Master Walbn, Master Smyth the owner of the Inne called the Diepe, Master Harvie of Lymehouse, Master Richardson of Hull, Master Malym, Master Bellpytt and Master Mychell both of Weymouth, Master Vyney, &c.[60]

[*Endorsed*] A discowrse of the newefound land. 1584.[61]

---

rather further north along the American shore (the Maritimes and possibly St. Lawrence). It is probable that these offers of assistance were for Carleill (who was more concerned with trade than settlement), but his venture ended no further away than Ireland in the summer of 1584—see D. B. Quinn, *The Voyages and Colonising Enterprises of Sir Humphrey Gilbert* (1940), I, 91–5.

[59]Blank in manuscript.

[60]The Englishmen fall into two groups, those who were members of the English colony settled in Rouen, and those who were seamen and traders who chanced to be in the port. In the first group we can place Thomas Moyser, a prominent merchant, Reynold Greene, and Robert Smyth (possibly also Robert Stacey if Hakluyt got his name confused and reported him as "Lacie") (cf., petitions of Sept. 13, 1582, and Feb. 11, 1583, in P.R.O., *Calendar of State Papers, Foreign, 1582*, 332, *Calendar of State Papers, Foreign, 1583 and Addenda*, 123), while Grove, Martyn, and Walyn may also have belonged to it. Of the rest, Thomas Harvey of Limehouse had his ship stayed at Le Havre in December, 1586 (British Museum, Lansdowne MS 148, f.145 (Dec. 23, 1586)). He could possibly have been the Thomas Harvey, grocer and citizen of London, who sailed with Sir Richard Grenville in April, 1585, as cape merchant in the first English colony on Roanoke island and returned from there in July 1588, but it is not very probable—see D. B. Quinn, ed., *The Roanoke Voyages, 1584–90*, (1955), I, 232–4. The others have not yet been traced.

[61]The body of the document is in Richard Hakluyt's hand throughout, the endorsement in a clerk's, presumably Caesar's. Mr. T. N. Marsh contributed a useful description and discussion of the document ("An Unpublished Hakluyt Manuscript?") to the *New England Quarterly*, XXV (June, 1962), 247–52, which appeared after the present paper had been completed. He also put a case for the manuscript being in Hakluyt's hand. The manuscript was mentioned as Richard Hakluyt's in Quinn, ed., *The Roanoke Voyages*, II, 779 (and cf. I, 77, n. 4), and was specified as being in Hakluyt's hand in D. B. Quinn et Jacques Rousseau, "Hakluyt et le mot 'esquimau,'" *R.H.A.F.*, XII (May, 1959), 600.

18

NEWFOUNDLAND IN THE CONSCIOUSNESS OF EUROPE
IN THE SIXTEENTH AND EARLY SEVENTEENTH CENTURIES

Newfoundland, — the fish of the Banks, the inshore cod fishery, the whale fishery on its northern flank — may in the end prove to have been for Europe during the sixteenth and early seventeenth centuries as valuable a discovery as the gold and silver of the Spanish empire. Whether or not the statisticians can ever add up the calories of nutriment provided to Europe by Newfoundland products between about 1500 and 1650 and balance them against the ounces of bullion extracted from Mexico and Peru so as to assess their respective effect on human life in western Europe I do not know; I am brave enough to guess that the balance might well go either way, and possibly in favour of Newfoundland produce.[1] And yet there is the strangest anomaly in the histories of the time. The conquest of the Spanish Indies is dramatic and colourful, was written about extensively at the time and ever since, while Newfoundland and its produce has remained, relatively, a backwater in world history, something to be taken for granted perhaps, but not assessed as being in any way of major significance for European development as a whole. Europe was aristocratic in this age; fishing and fishermen were decidedly not. Fishermen were poor and smelly; their ports were crammed with unattractive vessels; their produce was mainly employed in feeding ordinary people, who were of little account in the social scale, or in victualling ships and armies whose main tasks were far removed from the unattractive food their men ate;

---

1 Alison Quinn told me after I wrote this that I was not being original, since Thomas Morton, in his *New English Cannaan* (Amsterdam, 1637), pp. 86-7, boosting the fishing potential of New England, says: "The Coast aboundeth with such multitudes of Codd, that the inhabitants of New England doe dunge their grounds with Codd; and it is a commodity better than the golden mines of the Spanish Indies, for without dried codd the Spaniard, Portingal, and Italian, would not be able to vittel of a shipp for the Sea; and I am sure at the Canaries it is the principall commodity: which place lyeth neere New England very convenient, for the vending of this commodity, one hundred of these being at the price of 300. of New found land Codds, great store of traine oyle is mayd of the livers of the Codd, and is a commodity that without question will enrich the inhabitants of New England quicly; and is there a principall commodity." Without going into the vexed question of whether the average New England cod was better, bigger or more valuable than that of Newfoundland, we must grant Morton of Merrymount priority in his remarks.

   If I refer in subsequent notes rather frequently to publications in which I have had a hand, it is for convenience rather than vanity. Excellent reproductions of maps cited may, for example, be found elsewhere in print.

while the oil that illuminated their dwellings, lubricated their carriage wheels, formed a basis for much of their soap (where such was in use) was accepted as something to be grumbled about from time to time for its ineffectiveness or price but offering little attraction to human curiosity. Those who dealt in Newfoundland produce might even be rich, but they were usually socially insignificant. It was not until one and a quarter centuries after the discovery of Newfoundland that it was thought worth mention in an English parliament. What is true is that Newfoundland and its adjoining areas did attract the curiosity of chart and map makers in some numbers, even if they could not agree about the nature of the island even in outline for more than a century. We know very well indeed that it was again a century and a quarter before any considerable amount of material on Newfoundland was put into print, and we know too that, underneath the layer of significant state papers and letters on which so much narrative history has been based, there survive masses of materials on the business aspect of Newfoundland industry which are only now beginning to be uncovered. So the development of clear ideas about the discovery of Newfoundland and adjacent lands in the west was a slow and irregular process, beset with ignorance, lack of interest, and misunderstanding for a very long period indeed, and that Newfoundland surfaced in print in any detail only when proposals and attempts to colonize the island appeared in the first thirty years of the seventeenth century. As regards the fishery itself no one made any very systematic attempt to describe its nature and distribution at any time during the first one hundred and fifty years of its existence, though they did provide useful information on certain aspects of it.

Though we must rejoice that the site at L'Anse aux Meadows has given firm evidence of a Norse presence in Newfoundland at the opening of the eleventh century, it cannot establish, nor can the surviving sagas, that Newfoundland, as Vinland or whatever, was established in the European consciousness during the Middle Ages. For a few years the Vinland map looked as if it might provide such evidence, but its exposure as a fake meant that we had to start again with the fifteenth century and work forward to attempt to see at what point Newfoundland could be said to have become, for Europeans, a distinctive entity. This is not easy. The wide Atlantic as we know it was discovered slowly and tentatively and names firmly given only when many voyages had been made into it and across it, and even then for many years the precise appearance of Newfoundland on the maps remained as tentative as its very name. The first new islands in the Atlantic west of the Canaries shown on the marine charts, Antilia and Satanazes, appeared as early as 1424[2] and were located subsequently at various places far out to sea[3] —

---

2   James Ford Bell Library, University of Minnesota, Minneapolis; *New American World,* 5 vols., edited by D.B. Quinn, with the assistance of Alison M. Quinn and Susan Hillier (New York, 1979), I, pl. 5 (hence simply *NAW).*

3   e.g. the Andrea Benincasa chart of 1470, British Library (hence BL), Additional MS 31318; *NAW,* I, pl. 8.

in one map, the Paris map of between 1490 and 1493, Antilia has changed its name to the Island of the Seven Cities and appears in the Atlantic opposite Ireland.[4] This might fit in with the possible discovery of an island, conceivably Newfoundland, but described as Brasil and the Island of the Seven Cities, by Bristol men in 1481, though this is not certain. There is no news of what we know as Newfoundland until after the return of John Cabot from his voyage from Bristol in 1497. Much has been written on this subject. A favourite first landing (appearing to me circumstantially backed) is Cape Breton;[5] S.E. Morison's final choice was Cape Bauld,[6] and many other candidates in eastern Newfoundland have been fancied. The statement that his course lay between the latitudes of the mouth of the River Garonne and Dursey Head in County Kerry seems sound as a basis, but allowing for defects in latitude-reckoning, this does not take us much farther.[7] The Cosa map of 1500 gave us the first picture of a coastline — "Mar descubierta por ingleses"[8] as the basis of an unscaled sketch sent from England to Spain in 1498, which I have attempted to interpret in my own way, suggesting a course from Cape Breton to Cape Bauld.[9] At least something was on the maps from 1500 onwards. But what?

Until 1507, and in some minds not until much later, what we know as Newfoundland and the adjoining lands were regarded as part of Asia. The Martellus World Map of about 1490 had a "Horn of Asia"[10] sticking into the ocean in the farthest east, while Behaim's globe of 1492, the year Columbus sailed, had a similar 'Horn' but this time much farther south and adjacent to an enormous Cipango across a very narrow Atlantic.[11] That English voyages continued over the years 1501-1506 is now clear, and that cod, remarked on by Cabot, were brought to Bristol in 1502 and 1504 has been demonstrated.[12] Portuguese voyages to lands across the Atlantic in 1501 and subsequent years gave us maps which were to add confusingly to our knowledge of the western ocean. The land said to be that of the king of Portugal, recently discovered, as it appears on the Cantino map of 1502,[13] indicated what we might well call a proto-Newfoundland, an Atlantic island well out to sea and southwest of what

4 Paris, Bibliothèque Nationale, (hence BN), Section de Géographie; *NAW*, I, pl. 13, p. 480 (and D.B. Quinn, *England and the Discovery of America* (1974), pp. 69-71).

5 e.g. J.A. Williamson, *The Cabot Voyages and Bristol Discovery under Henry VII* (1962), 69, but very cautiously.

6 Samuel E. Morison, *The European Discovery of America: the Northern Voyages* (1971).

7 See John Day's letter in *NAW*, I, 98-99.

8 Madrid, Museo Naval; *NAW*, pl. 16.

9 D.B. Quinn, *North America from Earliest Discovery to First Settlements* (1977), pp. 117-118.

10 Beinecke Library, Yale University; *NAW*, I, pl. 14.

11 At Nürnberg; *NAW*, I, pl. 16.

12 Alwyn Ruddock, 'The Reputation of Sebastion Cabot' *Bulletin of the Institute of Historical Research*, XLVII (1974), 98.

13 Modena, Biblioteca Estense; *NAW*, I, pl. 19-20.

appears to be Greenland, but very far from the Spanish discoveries to the south and southwest. Maps of the years following, based on Portuguese voyages, known and unknown, add some reality to the lands discovered. The Oliveriana map of perhaps 1504 marks tentative coastlines in positions which could indicate the Maritimes, Newfoundland and Labrador.[14] The maps known as Kunstmann I and III (after 1504) give us something like an insular or at least peninsular Newfoundland, and supply moderately realistic latitudes with the later of the two giving an early recognition of variation by way of its oblique meridian.[15] There is no doubt that before 1507 English, Portuguese and French fishermen could find their way moderately easily across the Atlantic in the spring to the Banks and the inshore fishery and return again safely in the autumn (though there may have been more loss than we realise amongst these unnamed pioneers). But what did they call it? In 1497 Cabot gets credit only for finding "the new isle": but in 1502 we have the first mention of Newfoundland, but in the form of four separate words, "the newe found lande," in a grant of 1502 (in 1503 it is "the newe found Ilande" and in 1504 back to "the new Ilande" once more). It is not quite certain that some of these references, that of 1502 for example, may not be to the North American mainland rather than to the island, but there seems no doubt about the 1504 reference to the fish brought back from the islands called "Newfounde lleonnd,"[16] the "New" and the "Founde" being joined. This was to be a form which had a long continuance in England, frequent references well into the seventeenth century referring to "Newfound Land" with the first two words joined and the last separate. The Portuguese avoid reference to any name for the island or adjoining land for some years, but by 1506 "Terra Nova" clearly appears as the location for a fishery, and with this, in its Spanish form, "Tierra Neuva," the Spaniards were familiar by 1511 at latest. The earliest dated appearance under its name in French appears to be in 1510 when it is "Terre-Neufsve"[17] with two words adjoined by a hyphen, as they continued to be in many subsequent documents. We may conclude that by the end of the first decade of the sixteenth century the four western countries of Europe had a clear concept of an island or a group of islands to which they went to fish and to which the name "Newfound Land" or "New Land" in one or other form could be attached.

We cannot yet say that Newfoundland and the land adjacent to it had still been located clearly and firmly on the world map. The printed Contarini-Rosselli map of 1506[18] clearly places the new lands north of the Spanish

---

14   Biblioteca e Musei Oliveriani, Pesaro, *NAW*, I, pl. 23.

15   Bayerische Staatsbibliothek; *NAW*, I, pl. 24; H. Harrisse, *Découverte et évolution cartographique de Terre neuve* (1890), pl. v.

16   These can be traced in *NAW*, I, 109-110, 116-119.

17   *NAW*, I, 158.

18   Map Library, BL; *NAW*, I, pl. 26.

discoveries in the Caribbean (to the south of which a new continent is emerging), but as part of Asia, and as the still-surviving "Horn". It was Martin Waldseemüller who attempted in 1507 to break away from cosmographical precedent and instal two new continents beween Europe and Asia, though still hesitating about a name for the northern one in which Newfoundland would be located, but christening the southern one "America."[19] This was not accepted (or even firmly adopted in subsequent maps by Waldseemüller himself) and the Ruysch map of 1507-1508,[20] and later issues, continued to place the northerly discoveries, but with something that could be interpreted as a depiction of Newfoundland, lying off the "Horn of Asia" which was now making its ultimate appearance. Indeed, by 1519 Reinel (in the Miller Atlas)[21] was able to show what could be recognised as the Avalon Peninsula, though no western boundary for Newfoundland (and no firm name) was yet attached to it, but it was no longer part of Asia. It, too, was part of America, Waldseemüller's name having conquered both continents. "America" appeared clearly in England for North America at about the same time.

It remained for a name for Newfoundland to go on the map. Almost all our early cartography of this area comes from the Portuguese. In the Miller (Reinel) atlas the name "Terra Corte Regalis" appears, and this is endorsed in the map of Girolamo Verrazzano, the first non-Portuguese map of the area to contain a name, as "Corterealis," with a peninsular character for Newfoundland and with the land to the north labelled "Lavorador."[22] Verrazzano, in the French service in 1524 did not penetrate so far north. but we may take it that for the northern region he depended on Portuguese prototypes. The English map of Robert Thorne (published only in 1582 but compiled in 1527) compounded confusion by placing on the mainland north of a peninsula equivalent to Newfoundland the inscription "Nova terra laboratorum dicta."[23] The most systematic map of the eastern North America coastline thus far was the 1529 world map of Diogo Ribeiro[24] in which a peninsular Newfoundland was given the name of "Tiera Nova de Corte Real" while the mainland to the north (said to have been discovered by a Portuguese "Labrador" for the English) was given as "Tiera de Labrador."

The most influential group of maps on the early history of Newfoundland were those made at or near Dieppe from about 1538 onwards, but they were begun under strong Portuguese influence and one of the earlier maps, that in

19 Wolfegg Castle; *NAW*, I, pl. 29, 30, see pp. 481-482.

20 Ptolemy, *Geographia*, (Rome, 1507), *NAW*, I, pl. 27; see T. Layng, *Sixteenth Century Maps Relating to Canada* (1956), pp. 14-15.

21 Harrisse *Découverte*, pl. VII; for variants of Portuguese names see Williamson, *The Cabot Voyages*, p. 316.

22 Bibliotheca Apostolica Vaticana (hence BAV), Borgiano; *NAW*, I, pl. 44.

23 Richard Hakluyt, *Divers voyages* (1582); *NAW*, I, pl. 43.

24 BAV; *NAW*, I, pl. 47.

the Hague Atlas of *circa* 1538-1539, still has a peninsular Newfoundland.[25] Jean Rotz[26] in maps made in 1540 or before was the first to depict Cartier's Newfoundland. Cartier sailed up the east coast of Newfoundland, along the north coast and down the west coast in 1534 and completed the circumnavigation of the island in 1536, on official French voyages. Rotz is also the first to show Newfoundland as an archipelago, a tightly knit group of islands, having the general shape of Newfoundland but divided by a number of wide channels. This is followed by the so called 'Harley' map in the British Library,[27] the Desceliers world map of 1546 in Manchester[28] and that of 1550 in the British Library[29] on to the Desceliers atlas (which has not been precisely dated) in the Pierpont Morgan Library,[30] which all carry depictions of Cartier's second voyage, and show Newfoundland as a group of islands. The Desliens map of 1561 (not 1541), destroyed at Dresden in 1943[31] is followed by his map of 1566 in the Bibliothèque Nationale.[32] Both are in the same style but show the group of islands representing Newfoundland in varying degrees of compactness and with differing numbers of islands. The so-called Vallard map of 1547 (thought to have been made for, rather than by, someone of that name, and having some affinities to the Rotz maps) in the Huntington Library[33] records the Roberval expedition of 1543, but it follows the general tradition of the Dieppe School, established by Rotz, of showing Newfoundland as an archipelago. The so-called Sebastian Cabot map (preserved in Paris) made some of these features accessible, for the first time in 1544, to a wider public in a printed form.[34]

In the meantime, the Newfoundland fishery had become a major international attraction since its resources for a supply of fish protein appeared unlimited. The Dieppe cartographer artists began a tradition of indicating fishing banks extending from the eastern tip of Labrador (which in their maps is much extended to the east) in a sweep across the ocean well to the east of Newfoundland to below Cape Breton. The details of the fisheries on the Newfoundland Banks will always remain somewhat shrouded in the fogs of that area, but French and Portuguese and later Basques fished there in great

---

25   W.P. Cumming, R.A. Skelton, and D.B. Quinn, *The Discovery of North America* (1971), pl. 54.

26   BL, Royal MS. 20. E. IX, folios 23v-24r; *NAW*, I, pl. 53. The Rotz Atlas is being published in facsimile for the Roxburghe Club, edited by Helen Wallis.   Jan Rotz, *The Boke of Idrography*, edited by Helen Wallis, for the Roxburghe Club (1981).

27   BL, Additional MS 5413; *NAW*, I, pl. 54.

28   John Rylands University Library, Machester; *NAW*, I, pl. 55.

29   BL, Additional MS 26065.

30   This is described in Walters Gallery, *The World Encompassed*, Baltimore (1956).

31   Reproduction in BL, Map Library.

32   BN, Section de Géographie, for photographs of which I am indebted to Dr. Helen Wallis.

33   Huntington Library, San Marino; *NAW*, I, pl. 57.

34   BN, Section de Géographie; *NAW*, I, pl. 56, see p. 485.

numbers. I think we can say, however, that the Banks tended to be dominated by the Portuguese though the documentation is slight. At the other extreme in the north, as Selma Barkham has established, the Strait of Belle Isle from the early 1540s tended to be dominated by Basque whalers. In between, especially on the east coast, the many small harbours were shared by ships of many nations. The English in the 1530s and 1540s tended to concentrate north and south of Cape Spear, while the coasts north of St. John's appear to have been especially used by the French. The English gradually come to predominate in the small harbours from Ferryland southwards but shared them amicably with the Portuguese on whom they were dependent for salt. To the south and west of the Avalon Peninsula the French predominated and later accommodated more and more French and Spanish Basques (often not easy to differentiate) so that Placentia became very much of a meeting place (as well as shore-drying centre). On the east, St. John's fine harbour was never, so far as we know, monopolised by one nation though the French were most predominent there until well after the middle of the century. A Spanish force, under Basque leadership, drove them temporarily from the harbour in 1555. We first hear of an English ship sharing the harbour with both French and Portuguese in 1536 and it would appear that the sudden growth of English activity in the inshore fishery in the 1570s brought the centre of their fishery northwards to St. John's and that they tended to dominate the harbour, though without any exclusive right to drying spaces. The harbour became, as Placentia became in a lesser degree, a place of rendezvous, where ships destined for other grounds, or putting in laden from the Banks, could come to exchange food and stores of various sorts. The growth of the port admiral system remains obscure. In most harbours the captain of the first ship is claimed to have some arbitral or quasi-judicial powers over later arriving skippers, which was acceptable as a necessary way of lessening disputes. But at St. John's it seems that the English established by about 1580 the right to appoint the port admiral there and this paved the way for Sir Humphrey Gilbert's formal annexation of 1583, although most of the vessels in the harbour in early August 1583, were still Portuguese and French. St. John's remained an international rendezvous, though the Portuguese were gradually driven away as their absorption in the Spanish empire made them enemies to England, and though French supporters of Henri Quatre and the Guises fought in Newfoundland waters for nearly a decade after 1589 so that ships from Catholic League ports may not always have been welcome there. Even though English privateers tried to track down Basque vessels wherever they could find them, yet the old internationalism of the late sixteenth century was not wholly destroyed.[35]

The new and more conscious nationalism of the late sixteenth century emerged in a period when cartographers were at last beginning to set

35 D.B. Quinn, *North America*, (1977) pp. 347-368, 417-422, summarizes these developments, which are reasonably well known.

Newfoundland somewhat more correctly on to their maps. Mercator's great world map of 1569 still showed it as an archipelago,[36] as did John Dee's map presented to Queen Elizabeth in 1580[37] but Boazio, showing Drake's homeward track by way of Newfoundland in1586, reverted to an earlier form and showed it as a peninsula.[38] The French map of Pastoret in 1587,[39] when the French should have known much better, showed it as four islands, while Wytfliet in 1597[40] split it into still more sections.

André Thevet published a map of North America in 1581 (of which only the copy in the Lessing Rosenwald Collection, Division of Geography and Maps, Library of Congress survives) in which the strange notion appears that there were two major islands at the mouth of the River St. Lawrence, "Terre Neuve" and "L'Isle de S. Julien." Newfoundland is one major island with a number of smaller appendages (one representing the Avalon Peninsula) and "L'Isle de S. Julien" is southern Labrador. In his unfinished work, "Le Grand Insulaire," composed between 1581 and 1584, which is Bibliothèque Nationale, MS français 15452, folios 142b. and 148b., he describes these two "islands" and provides engraved maps of them, which he had specially cut, though they were never published. Here we have on the Newfoundland one a major insular form "Terres Neueues on Isles des Molues," showing mountains and forests for the first time. The south-western section is separated from the main body by a narrow channel, and well away to the southeast is the Avalon Peninsula, detached as "Partie de la Nouvelle France," while to the north of it his own, invented, island, "I. de Theuet" is shown. The strait to the north is called "Sein de S. Laurens," and its northern shore is the southern shore of his wholly imaginary depiction of southern Labrador as "La grand Isle de s. Julien." The separate map of this "island" is oriented more or less southwest-northeast with "Mer des Molues" to the south and "Bouche du grand fleuue de Canada" to the north, while there is a major inlet from the east. To the west is "Golfe Carre ou de S. Laurens." Thevet certainly gave a new complexion to the whole area, even if a great deal depended on his imagination. Nonetheless, his impression of Newfoundland is a striking one, even though it does not fit easily into any chronological or realistic sequence.

The earliest printed map I know of to show Newfoundland whole is that of Peter Plancius, now dated (circa) 1592, and reprinted by the British Library in 1975,[41] but a wider circulation was achieved by the fine world map

36 Museum Maritiem, Prins Hendrik, Rotterdam, NAW, IV, pl. 112.

37 BL, Cotton MS, Augustus I. i. 1; Quinn, The Voyages and Colonising Enterprises of Sir Humphrey Gilbert, II (1940), pocket at end (hence Quinn, Gilbert).

38 Beinecke Library (Paul Mellon Collection); NAW, III, pl. 97.

39 Harrisse, Découverte.

40 Cornelis Wytfliet, Descriptionis Ptolemaicae augmentum (1597), NAW, III, pl. 129.

41 BL, Map Library.

constructed by Edward Wright, added to the second volume of Hakluyt's *Principal navigations* in 1599,[42] even though it was on a small scale. Though Newfoundland appeared as a single unit on Lescarbot's map in 1609 it was very much distorted in shape. It fared better in the English map in the New York Public Library of about 1610,[43] and best of all in the remarkable map of late 1610, made in England but sent to Spain, which we know from its sender as the Velasco map.[44] Its shape was still some way from perfection but it appeared in recognisable detail. Champlain's famous map of 1612[45] is however very much the turning point: the island is not only recognisable (if still imperfect) but some precise locations for the fishing banks are given for the first time. His final map, that of 1632, did not substantially improve on the earlier version.[46]

We can thus see there were three main stages in the evolution of Newfoundland on the map: down to 1540 it is essentially part of the mainland, first of Asia and then of the New America. From about 1540 to 1600 it is an archipelago containing usually four major islands, sometimes many more, occasionally approximating in general outline to the island as a whole, more often not. From about 1592 it is most often a single island, recognisable, if far from perfect. It was to keep a somewhat mis-shapen appearance until well into the eighteenth century, but from 1600 it was at least a single entity. Even if many stages of this process are moderately well known to Newfoundlanders, though not all my examples may be familiar, as one statement of my theme, however, this cartographical history is essential, since it demonstrates how even professional cartographers saw the place which was known as Newfound Land, as Terre-Neuve, as Tierra Neuva, as Terra Nova but rarely as Newfoundland. This was, we should continue to remember, in the second half of the sixteenth century, as well known to thousands of fishermen in western Europe as the shores of the bays and rivers of their home countries in which they, themselves, grew up and learned their fishing. To them Newfoundland was almost regarded as an outpost of Europe itself.

Yet in another sense there is the paradox that to Europeans of the sixteenth and early seventeenth centuries Newfoundland was scarcely known at all. It was simply taken for granted. Everyone knew of its primary product, the cod, whether wet-salted or dried, but this was a brand-name; in England it was simply "Newland fish," or, derisively, "Poor John," for dried cod and "codfish" for the wet. There was little curiosity about the island itself. The Spanish officials of the Consejo de Indias who wrote so learnedly on so many

---

42   R. Hakluyt, *The principal navigations*, III (1599); *NAW*, III, Pl. 99; see Quinn, ed. *The Hakluyt Handbook*, I (1974), 69-73.

43   I.N.P. Stokes Collection, New York, Public Library. *NAW*, V, pl. 119.

44   Archivo General, Simancas, M.P.y.D.I.I, Estado 2588/25, *NAW*, V, pl. 140, III, pl. 108, 111.

45   Champlain, *Works*, portfolio, pl. LXXXI, (1612).

46   Ibid. pl. (1632).

parts of America scarcely ever bothered to ascertain where Newfoundland lay. Some of them thought of it as part of the mainland, or islands lying off the mainland a little north of Chesapeake Bay. Officially Spain regarded it as within the Portuguese sphere, as defined in the Treaty of Tordesillas, even though it was far to the west of that line. It was very different in northern Spain where the Basques built up their fortunes on both the cod and whale fisheries. Unofficially, it was known there as "La Provincia de Terra Nova," almost part of the Iberian peninsula itself, as again Selma Barkham has made clear. The French were, frankly, and not surprisingly, much more interested in Canada after 1534 than in Newfoundland itself. To the Portuguese, outside the northern fishing ports and the Azores, it had a very minor interest as compared with their Oriental or even their Brazilian possessions and little or nothing appears to have been written about it after the early Corte Real period.

The appearance of descriptions of Newfoundland in print was slow, far between and sketchy. The *Brief recit* in 1545 for Cartier's second voyage[47] gave some account of the south coast but was not very informative without the material in the narrative of the first voyage. This appeared, with a further version of the second, only in the Italian of Ramusio's third volume of the *Navigationi et viaggi* in 1556,[48] and at no time in the sixteenth century was it translated and published in French. It had better luck later on in England when John Florio's translation, sponsored by Richard Hakluyt the younger, appeared in London *(A shorte and briefe narration of the two nauigations and discoueries to the northweast partes called Newe Fraunce)* in 1580 and was reprinted in the third volume of Richard Hakluyt's *The principal navigations* in 1600.[49] The first French printed book which contained anything specific about Newfoundland was Jean Alfonce's *routier, Les voyages auantureux* (Poitiers, 1559).[50] It is now known to have circulated in manuscript in the 1530s and 1540s. This does speak of Newfoundland as if it were a single island. In Ganong's translation (Crucial maps, pp. 364-5)[51] "La Terre-neufe has the best ports and harbours of the entire sea, and great rivers, abundant fisheries. It is all covered with trees, pines and others such. The coast runs north and south to Cape de Ras.... Beyond Cap de Ras the coast turns to the west as far as the gouffe de S. Jehan. Before you approach this gulf is another which makes Terre-neufve an island." This was a small working book for seamen and its manuscript versions were more widely known in the ports than in Paris. The same is scarcely true for northern Spain and the French Basque country of the

47 Rouen, 1545.

48 Venice, 1556.

49 London, 1580; Hakluyt III (1600).

50 Copy in BN.

51 G.W. Ganong, *Crucial Maps in the Early Cartographer and Place-nomenclature of the Atlantic Coast of Canada* (1964), p. 364.

second *routier* to be published, that of Martin de Hoyarsabel, *Voyages auentureux du Captaine Martin de Hoyarsabel, habitant de Gubiburu* (Bordeaux, 1579).[52] It gave invaluable detail on the northern approaches to the Gulf of St. Lawrence. In England (apart from Hitchcock in 1580 who will appear later), there was nothing specific until 1589, though Sir George Peckham had referred briefly to Sir Humphrey Gilbert's attempt to annex Newfoundland to the English crown in 1583 in his pamphlet of that year, *A true reporte of the late discoueries*.[53] Richard Hakluyt's *Principall nauigations* (1589) provides in two documents the first conspectus of Newfoundland as it appeared to Englishmen. Anthony Parkhurst in the letter he sent to the elder Richard Hakluyt in 1578 conveyed briefly but cogently some impression of Newfoundland itself and of the activities of the European fishing fleets there. He had visited Newfoundland several times with fishing vessels he owned and he had taken the trouble to make some excursions into the exterior. He had convinced himself by sowing seeds and watching for their appearance and growth that European vegetables and grain could flourish. He was able to enumerate the kinds and quality of trees in some little detail. He gave a convincing account of the variety of fish and crustacea, besides cod, which were to be found in Newfoundland waters. He advocated Newfoundland as a place for English settlement, saying "you shall understand that New found land is in a temperate climate, and not so colde as foolish mariners doe say, who finde it colde sometimes when plenty of Isles of Ice lie neere the shore: but up in the land they shall finde it hotter than in England in many partes of the countrey toward the South." He had something to say about the numerous lakes and the birds to be found there, and also on the seabirds, animals to provide venison, caribou and furs. He even said something about the Basque whale fishery in the Strait of Belle Isle, and called attention to the quantity of iron ore (and he hoped richer minerals) which were in Newfoundland. His favourable view of the island was to be reprinted in volume III of the second edition of *The principal nauigations*, in 1600.[54]

The other descriptive piece on Newfoundland in this volume was contained in Edward Hayes' account of Sir Humphrey Gilbert's voyage of 1583.[55] Besides his graphic account of the annexation on August 5, 1583, he described what he had seen of the country (though on the basis of a limited view of part of the Avalon Peninsula alone). He was defensive about its climate and attempted to explain it: "The common opinion that is had of, in temperature and extreme cold that should be in this countrey, as of some part of it may be verified, namely the North, where I grant it is more cold then in countries of Europe, which are vnder the same eleuation; euen so it cannot

---

52 Copy in BN.

53 London, 1583; reprinted in *NAW*, III, 34-60.

54 Pp. 674-77, III, 132-134, *NAW*, IV, 7-10 (with his earlier letter, pp. 5-7).

55 III (1600), 688-90 *NAW*, IV, 23-42.

stand with reason that the South parts should be so intemperat as the brute
hath gone...the cold cannot be so intollerable vnder the latitude of 46, 47 & 48.
(especially within land) that it should be vnhabitable, as some doe suppose."
The months from June to September were warmer than in England and even in
November men have not found it colder, though, from November onwards, he
admitted that those who have come there "haue found the snowe exceeding
deepe" but it would be no colder than in Sweden or Russia at the worst where
people could live comfortably, and where "the rigor of colde is dispensed with
by the commoditie of Stoues, warme clothing, meates and drinkes: all which
neede not be wanting in the Newfound land, if we had intent there to inhabite."
He is able to give (partly from secondhand sources) similar information on
natural resources to that which Parkhurst had supplied, but with more
emphasis on the land animals and their value for food and furs. With
Parkhurst, Hayes emphasized the desirability of settling Newfoundland
before any foreign nation did so, and in private papers, unpublished at the
time, he provided elaborate plans for doing this.[56]

Newfoundland continues as an archipelago of four or more islands, with
relatively narrow channels between them, sometimes approximating in
general outline to the island and at other times not. For this we can, I think, see
several causes. First of all there is the model provided by the lost Cartier charts
which initiated it; secondly, there was the inherent conservatism of
cartographers, who when they found a plausible model for a particular area
tended to stick to it, unless they were presented with graphic and
incontrovertible evidence that they were wrong; thirdly, there was the
traditional reservation of sections of the coast mainly or exclusively to one of
the European nations engaged in the fishery which made them accept
traditional patterns of representation since there seemed no advantage in
altering them; fourthly, there was the fact, arising out of the foregoing, that
there was no incentive on the part of any European country to have a
comprehensive chart made, since the Cartier model worked adequately for
practical purposes. The final stage, beginning at the end of the century sees
Newfoundland emerging single and whole on the charts. We cannot pin down
precisely when or why this took place. My own view is that war conditions
ultimately led English and French fishing interests (or even possibly the
governments of these countries) to ascertain more accurately where their own
and their enemies' fishing vessels were to be found. The change came suddenly
and, I believe, through English enterprise. The Molyneux globe of 1592 had
relatively advanced information on North America, but it still showed the
break-up of Newfoundland into numerous islands, while the Edward Wright
map, completed in 1599, showed a single identifiable unit as Newfoundland.
Who was responsible for the charting which brought about the change, I do
not know. After French activity in the Gulf and River of St. Lawrence had

56   Printed for the first time *NA W*, III, 124-138.

accelerated from 1600 onwards it was inevitable that they, too, should have made and used reasonably accurate charts of Newfoundland as a whole. That this was done some years before the Lescarbot printed map of 1609 we can be certain, but once again we are not aware of when or precisely under what circumstances it took place. The first separate map of Newfoundland, showing it in some detail, was published by Captain John Mason at Edinburgh in 1621.

Many students of early Newfoundland will be familiar with the main outlines of the cartographical history I have discussed, but it demonstrates how little, after the early Portuguese initiatives, and in particular the naming of particular harbours which adhered to them, many until the present day, the actual fishing fleets felt the need for accurate charts. Experience, passed on from generation to generation, formed the main source of the knowledge of Newfoundland amongst the fishing community of western Europe. They took it for granted and did not need very much in the way of guides or charts. To thousands of seamen, over three or four generations, Newfoundland has become not a new land but almost part (or at least an outpost) of Europe itself.

At least it could be argued that Englishmen were reasonably fully informed (if in a somewhat partisan form) about Newfoundland by 1600, and that they were the first European people to have that information readily available to them. By 1600 Newfoundland was known and knowable and even plainly set out for them on Edward Wright's map. The same was not true of the other western European lands.

French interest and concern for North America was concentrated largely on Quebec and the beginnings of New France (even though Terre-Neuve was regarded as part of it) and, to a lesser extent, on Acadia. Newfoundland appears sparsely in the literature. Marc Lescarbot's *Histoire de la Nouvelle France* contains some account of Newfoundland. He commented on the mists in which Newfoundland was shrouded and tried to explain them,[57] and he went on to say a little about both the wet-fishing on the Banks and the dry-fishing carried on at a great number of ports "in Newfoundland and in Bacaillos," but he reserved most detail for a description of "the oil of the fish of Newfoundland," obtained from the whale and the walrus (pp.285-90). By his third edition in 1618 he had come to accord a much higher status to Newfoundland. In his dedication of that edition to Louis XIII, he said, "she hath long time supported by her fish the whole of Europe alike on sea and on land." He went on to compare the fishing at Newfoundland to mining the sea rather than the earth: "the sailors who go from all parts of Europe to fish off Newfoundland, and beyond,...find excellent mines in the depths of the waters, and in trading for skins and furs....Let this much be said in passing with regard to Newfoundland, which, though thinly inhabited and in a cold climate, is yet visited by a great number of people who yearly pay their homage from

---

57 M. Lescarbot, *Histoire de la Nouvelle France,* ed. H.P. Biggar and W.L. Grant, I (1911); *Nova Francia.* ed. H.P. Biggar (1928), 32-33.

further afield than is done to the greatest Kings of the earth."[58] This was a fine tribute indeed, but he made clear subsequently that to him "Terre-Neuve," "New-found-land," or "Bacaillos,"cod-fish land, comprised not only the island but all the lands adjoining it up to the mouth of the River St. Lawrence as well. As a result of his outward voyage in Acadia in 1606 he was able to provide a first-hand account of the climate of the Grand Banks and of the location of its subsidiary banks. He now elaborated what he had said of the Banks and inshore fishery and of the oil-bearing whale and walrus.[59] Over all, Lescarbot may be said to have paid for the first time adequate tribute to the Newfoundland fishery, without, however, giving any topographical description of the island itself. Champlain, on the other hand, gave little attention to Newfoundland in his writings. It was only in the 1632 edition of his *Voyages* that he paid even a cursory attention to its characteristics, but then gave[60] a useful brief account of its location and of the harbours most used by the French together with the information that the northwest and west coasts were scarcely known. "The land," he said, "is nearly all mountainous, covered with pine, spruce, cedar, birch, and with other trees of little value. A large number of streams come from the mountains and fall into the sea. The salmon-fishing is very good in most of these rivers, as well as that for other kinds of fish. The cold there is severe, and the snow, which falls to a great depth, lasts for nearly seven months. Moose (=caribou), rabbits, and grouse are plentiful. The island is not inhabited." This was scarcely an enthusiastic introduction to the island (and there were, of course, both Beothuk and English inhabitants), though he dealt at some length elsewhere[61] with whaling and with the Grand Bank and its subsidiaries.

It was during the first decade of the seventeenth century, at a period when her fishermen were flourishing at Newfoundland that the English turned to the possible colonization of the island. Publicity by word of mouth about the island began in 1609 and a settlement was started at Cupids in 1611, under royal charter granted in 1610. It is very strange that so far as we can tell no attempt was made to interest the English public in Newfoundland by printed material during the whole of the first two decades of the new century. This is a strange fact, since during most of this period Virginia had been vigorously promoted in print, and before it ended New England had also received an appreciable amount of printed publicity. So English opinion on Newfoundland, except for the appearance of an English version of Lescarbot's first edition, translated by Pierre Erondelle, as *Nova Francia,* in 1609, had to be formed by means of manuscript tracts, by letters, and by word of mouth. It

58   Lescarbot, *Histoire,* I, (1911) 7, 41, 304-307.

59   Ibid., III (1914), 234-245.

60   *Works,* ed. Biggar, V (1936), 57-61.

61   Ibid. II, 149-153, IV, 120-124, V, 300-307.

is therefore difficult to assess how much knowledge and understanding of the island developed during this period. For the first time, however, English men and women were going and coming not merely to fish during the summer months, but to live in Newfoundland throughout the year, and so they could on their return spread information, good and bad, favourable and unfavourable, about Newfoundland's soil and climate and resources. How far they did so we have so far no reliable guide, though the Middleton papers, in Nottingham University Library, offer numerous suggestions as Gillian Cell has brought out.

In 1620 so far as printed information, and propaganda masquerading as information, was concerned, the situation changed again. A flood of publications about Newfoundland appeared in the following decade. Mostly they were small, evanescent tracts, but they contained some solid works, and above all they represented a considerable variety of approach. They constituted, almost, if we are not too critical, a body of literature on Newfoundland which could not fail to circulate widely enough amongst the literate public to create some impressions of the island and its resources, whether those who read these tracts believed what they read or not. The key figure was of course Richard Whitbourne, whose *A discourse and discovery of New-found-land* was in 1620 a major contribution to the history, description and propaganda about the island, and was followed by *A discourse containing a loving invitation to adventurers, in the New-found-land* (1622) and a further edition, with additions, in the same year. There was then also, before the end of 1622, a further composite edition of both tracts, with more revisions and another in 1623. These five publications, repetitive though they were,[62] made up a substantial body of information and publicity. Moreover, they were extracted by Samuel Purchas for incorporation in his vast *Hakluytus posthumus, or Purchas his pilgrimes* in 1625, along with material dating between 1610 and 1612 on the establishment of the first English Colony at Cupids,[63] which ensured for early material on Newfoundland a permanence not given it by the pamphlets and a wider and more discriminating readership. John Mason's *A brief discourse of the New-foundland* (Edinburgh, 1620) was a succinct, knowledgeable account of the island with a good map, and with propaganda for settlement. Mason was the best informed of all the pamphleteers of these years. The smaller pamphlets at this time[64] have less substance. Edward Winne's *A letetr* [sic] *written by captaine Edward Winne to Sir George Calvert, from Feryland in Newfoundland, the 26. of August 1621* (1621)[65] is very brief indeed, but *T.C.'s A short discourse of the New-Found-*

---

62 The sequence is made clear in A.W. Pollard and G.R. Redgrave, *Short-title Catalogue of English Books, 1475-1640*, (2nd. edition), ed. W.A. Jackson and K.F. Panzer, II, (1976), nos. 25372-25375a (hence *STC.*)

63 IV (1625), 1882-1889, 1, 1875-82.

64 *STC*, 17616.

65 *STC*, 25854.

Land (Dublin, 1623)[66] is the first piece of printed material to be published in Ireland on any part of the Americas (as Mason's had been in Scotland), and so played some part in widening the scope of interest in, and concern for, Newfoundland. Very different was Richard Eburne's *A plaine path-way to plantations,* (1624)[67] which had little specific to say about Newfoundland as a place, but a great deal on the whys and wherefores of plantation in America and, more specifically, the colonization of the island. Sir William Vaughan in his three works, *Cambrensium Caroleia* (1625), *The golden fleece* (1626), and *The Newlanders cure* (1630)[68] coloured the literature with much rhetoric and, for the first time, celebrated Newfoundland in his first and, in part, his third with verse eulogia of the island. Robert Hayman's *Quodlibets, lately come over from New Britaniola* (1628),[69] had also sung the praises of Newfoundland, and much else, in verse which was the first, so far as we know, to have been printed from matter composed in Newfoundland itself. These publications launched Newfoundland in a flood of words no doubt, and must indeed have informed a considerable readership about it, but it was an evanescent one, which faded rapidly after 1630, if it had not done so already by that date. Newfoundland description and colonization propaganda for a long time had had its day, for reasons with which I am not here concerned. For a very long time Newfoundland appears only rarely in the literature of discovery and settlement as a place worthy of a writer's or publisher's attention, but the Lieutenant Edward Chappell who entitled his book, published in 1818, went much too far. He entitled it *Voyage of His Majesty's ship* Rosamund *to Newfoundland and the southern coast of Labrador of which countries no account has been published by an British traveller since the reign of Queen Elizabeth.*[70] So far as Spain and Portugal were concerned Newfoundland seemed scarcely worth writing about.

There is a third aspect too, besides maps and narratives. It is part of the parodox of Newfoundland's image that a vast number of people in Europe took its products (its wet and dry fish and its train oil) for granted, and so they did the territory which furnished the background for the industry which fed them, or in which they traded. Newfoundland fish and oil played a substantial part in Western European business at almost all levels, but fishing in the western Atlantic was only part of Europe's dependence on fish for protein which dominated the exploitation of the waters round her own coasts and as far afield as Iceland in one direction and the Cape Verde Islands at another. Much of the fishery business was local and small-scale and was considered to

66 *STC,* (1st ed., 1926) no. 4311, wrongly dated 1630; copy in Memorial University Library.

67 *STC,* (1st ed. 1926) 7469-7471.

68 *STC,* 24604-24605. 24609, 24619.

69 *STC,* (1st ed. 1926), 12974.

70 London, 1818.

be of little standing or prestige, simply a routine way of earning a living in a somewhat despised occupation. The bigger and more long distance fisheries were big business but they were everyday business. Consequently it was not thought necessary to write, or at least publish, about even such a remarkable new development of the sixteenth century as Newfoundland and its fishery. Thus, though there are endless business manuscripts of the fishery still in existence, there was very little put in print and those outside the business had very little idea of what went on at or near Newfoundland. There was consequently some doubt, even amongst businessmen, about how precisely to describe Newfoundland. A City of London committee of merchants in 1577, examining the question of marine insurance, decided that there should be no maximum time laid down for the settlement of insurance claims "from ye East and West Indies, and from the Coast of Labrador commonly called ye new found land."[71] Robert Hitchcock in *A politique platt, for the honour of the Prince* (1580) is the first Englishman to discuss the business aspect of the fishery in print. He was arguing for the building of an all-purpose English fishing vessel which could operate effectively against the Dutch in the North Sea and also in Newfoundland. He gives some detail how the "five hundredth sailes" of French ships were financed every year, and how, somewhat differently, a much smaller number of English Newfoundlanders were financed and set to sea. He also indicated that a 70 ton ship should bring home in August at least 20,000 wet fish and 10,000 dry fish, which would realise in France £500. (His figures are too low.) He wished the English to compete on more even terms. Forty years later, Richard Whitbourne, in his *Discourse,* gave comparable information and advice, but he thought a 100 ton ship could bring 200,000 dry fish and 100,000 wet fish.[73] John Smith, in *The generall historie of Virginia*[74] used some of Whitbourne's figures to calculate that a resident fishing population in New England could do very much better than this from the Gulf of Maine, with cod twice the size of those of Newfoundland. In *The description of New England* (1616)[75] he gave his own estimates of Newfoundland production: *"New found land,* doth yearely fraught neere 800 sayle of Ships with a sillie leane skinny Poore-John, and Corfish [wet fish], which at least yearly amount to 3 or 400000 pound...2000 pound will fit out a ship of 200. and 1 of 100 tuns. If the dry fish they both make, fraught that of 200. and goe for *Spaine,* sell it but ten shillings a quintal (but commonly it giueth fifteen or twentie, especially when it commeth first, which amounts to 3 or 4000 pound; but say tenne, which is the lowest), allowing the rest for waste it

---

71 *The Mariner's Mirror,* LXV (1979), 266.

72 *STC* (1st ed. 1926) 13531, sigs, Flr- Flv; *NAW,* IV, 105.

73 See G.T. Cell, *English Enterprise in Newfoundland* (1969), pp. 3-4.

74 London (1624), pp. 224-226.

75 London (1616), pp. 12-13, 22.

amounts at that rate, to 2000 pound; which is your two ships, and their equipage. Then the returne of the money, and the fraught of the ship for the vintage or any other voyage, is cleere gaine, with your ship of 100 tuns of Train and oyle, besides beuers and other commodities; and that you haue at home within six monethes, if God please but to send an ordinarie passage." But, he contended, a New England-based voyage would be more profitable still.

A final profit and loss account to be cited here is that of Lewis Roberts, whose large volume, *The merchants mapp of commerce* (1638), has something on "Estotilland [Zeno's mythical land of 1588] or New oudland." [76] He wrote of it as a place "where some have gone to plant, but the colde heth beene found to be too extreeme for the English constitution; but in the Summer season the Seas here are found to abound with Fish in such abundance, that a man may take in an houres space a hundred great Fishes, which being opened, salted and dried upon the rocks and beaches, are then transported to all parts of Europe; and known in England by the name of New-land fish...; five hundred sayle great and small doe from England yearly sayle to the coast, and to a place called the Banke, a sand of 15 in [to] 20 fadome deepe, thirtie leagues off this Coast, and these depart from our Coast at about the end of Februarie, and arriving there about the middle of Aprill, unrigge their shippes, set up boothes and cabanets on the shore in diverse creakes and harbours, and ther with fishing provisions and salt, begin their fishing in Shallops and Boats, continue it until September, and in this time does not onely catch as many fishe as will lade their shippes, but also as many as will lad vessels of greater burthens, that in the Summer come hither from England and other parts, to buy up the same, and purposely to transport it for Spaine, Italie, and other countries; and their fishing ended and the cold beginning, they leave their stations and booths and repassing abroad their shippes, lade their fish, and rigging their vessels, returne to theire native homes, where the fishermen winter, and then become husbandmen; so that their lives may be compared to the Otter, which [is] spent halfe on lande, and halfe in Sea. This fishing is found to be wonderfully beneficiall to our westerne parts of England, whose inhabitants, confiding upon the constancy of the yearly fishing upon this Coast, it is usuall with them to sell the said fish either by tale or by the hundredweight in England by contract, before they either depart their homes, or before the said fishe be caught, at profitable rates; and when their Summer is once spent, and that the cold approacheth and that the fish beginneth to leave the Coast, they returne contented to their Families; where oftentimes in Winter they merrily spend what in Summer they have painfully fisht for. Other notes of trading, worthy observation at there being in my younger dayes, I observed not. The Waights and Coins of England passing there currently amongst the English and the price of fish, once generally Cut at their fishing Stales, doth afterward in lieu of Coine, by way of Commutation, all that yeare passes current for all needfull Commodities, and is esteemed as a valuable Consideration amongst them from one man to another."

No comparable material has so far been found for other western countries but it may well exist in print. The statistics are given as their writers cite them without critical comment, but it must be stressed that Hitchcock, Whitbourne and Smith have each their own axes to grind, while Lewis Roberts is compiling a neutral-minded handbook to world commerce and exchange as he understood it. But most of those whose frequent food the cod was knew nothing of these writers and cared less; nor indeed did the many shipbuilders, victuallers, financiers, and fishermen whose livelihood Newfoundland was. The island remained in the background of the great business which the fishing had, before the middle of the seventeenth century, become.

What then can we conclude about the place of Newfoundland in the European consciousness during the first 150 years after Cabot's discovery? The only firm point of knowledge is that millions of people associated Newfoundland in some way or other with the dried or wet-salted codfish they ate. The knowledge was largely unspecified in that it did not imply any real knowledge of the Bank or the inshore fishery or of the island itself. Apart from Cartier, no major explorer of the period whose works were well known to an educated public at first, second or third hand said anything very distinctive about Newfoundland and Cartier's revelations were swallowed up in his major discoveries farther west. In England it was only after 1589, and then largely through Richard Hakluyt, that some information (reliable and otherwise) filtered through to an English public and to such continental Europeans who studied him, probably mainly the Dutch. Newfoundland was not taken up as an area of interest in, for example, any of the great popularizing series like that of Theodor de Bry. In France, before Marc Lescarbot in 1609 and subsequently, there was no material in print which would attract a wide readership. The "rash" of English, Scottish and Irish publications on Newfoundland between 1620 and 1630 were probably read by relatively few and made little impression, except possibly the writings of Richard Whitbourne which appeared in several editions and which were given wider currency by collectors and popularizers, Captain John Smith and the Reverend Samuel Purchas. We can legitimately doubt whether the French *routiers* of Jean Alfonce and Martin de Hoyarsabel were of much interest outside the seamen and their merchant backers in the west and north coasts of France and the north coast of Spain. We can also conclude that what specialist writers like Robert Hitchcock and Lewis Roberts said about the conduct of the fishery and its economics were little known outside a very narrow circle.

This leaves us with the maps. The majority of them remained in manuscript and were virtually unknown. Enough printed maps were in circulation during the period 1544-1599 which showed Newfoundland as an archipelago for a considerable number of people if they took the trouble to look (which we cannot comment on with any authority), to know where and what Newfoundland was supposed to be. The Edward Wright map in 1599, the Lescarbot map of 1609 and the Champlain map of the *Les Voyages* (1613) all informed a considerable number of readers that Newfoundland was a single island. Since both the Hakluyt collection in which the Wright map appeared and that of Lescarbot had texts attached which gave some fairly precise information to go with the maps, we can probably conclude that the educated public in England and France which read these works with some thoroughness was moderately well informed about Newfoundland if it cared to be so and was not focussed primarily on Virginia or on Canada. What is of some interest is that in the 1620s publications on Newfoundland should have appeared both in Scotland and Ireland as well as England, showing that it was hoped that the spread of information on Newfoundland there would attract settlers from those countries, though their effect was not very great. France and the Iberian nations might be involved at a commercial level very intimately with Newfoundland, but as John Mason, quoting a common saying, said it was held that "Fishing is a beastly trade and vnseeming a Gentleman." Not all the efforts of the colonial promoters were able entirely to overcome that prejudice, and so Newfoundland did not appear so predominently as it might well have done in the educated consciousness of Europe.

19

JAMES I AND THE BEGINNINGS OF EMPIRE IN AMERICA

In 1603, when James I came to the English throne, there was no permanent English foothold beyond the Atlantic: six years later a colony had been established in Virginia, and was in fair way towards becoming a permanent settlement. In the intervening period Anglo-Spanish relations were affected to some extent by this development as a minor element (though, as I shall try to show, not an insignificant one) in a complex web of diplomatic exchanges which it is fortunately not necessary for me to attempt to traverse as a whole. Diplomacy was only part of the matter. Virginia was involved in general questions regarding English trade with the Indies and English trade with Spain itself and the conditions under which it could be carried on. Virginia too was a matter of successive maritime expeditions and the fortunes of certain of them involved diplomatists and statesmen in both countries. The situation was a fairly tangled and rapidly changing one. I can attempt to give only a rather impressionist sketch of its development.

From 1603 to 1606 Englishmen were looking for places in eastern North America in which to settle (and were incidentally, it may be as well not to forget, searching for colonists left in what is now North Carolina in 1587 and believed by some to be still alive and flourishing). From 1607 to 1609 Englishmen were attempting to create firm colonial settlements in the places which they had selected, and were doing so under charters conferred by the crown and supervised by a royally appointed council. During the earlier years the Spaniards were constantly trying to prevent English expeditions being sent to find sites for settlements or at least to provide as much discouragement as they could to such as went. In the later years, once colonies were in

being, Spain turned rather towards inducing or coercing the English
king to give up the North American enterprises and admit that Spain
had a prior claim to the territories which the English had begun to
occupy. Whether James did right from the English point of view in
keeping the issue open to some extent in his dealings with Spain or
whether he would have done better to have ignored Spanish claims and
gestures altogether remains questionable. Perhaps we can judge it a
little better when such evidence as I have has been presented.

It might be useful to clear France out of the way before we come
on to Anglo-Spanish relations on this matter. Henry IV had made the
treaty of Vervins in 1598 with no mention of the Indies, but he maintained then and after that he was under no obligation to keep his
subjects out of territories in the New World not actually occupied by
the Spaniards, and he behaved as if New France, effectively defined as
North America north of about 45°, was his own to deal with without
any Spanish interference. Indeed from 1598 onwards there is a
continuous record of French intervention and attempted colonisation
in the St. Lawrence Valley and the Maritimes. In 1603 his patent to
Pierre du Gua, Sieur de Monts, lengthened his reach down to 40°,
approximately to modern New York. But after the exploring expeditions of Champlain, 1604–7, the Sieur de Monts lost his patent and
France retracted her claims to her former limit (approximately the
Penobscot River in modern Maine), leaving the English to occupy the
coastline to the south. From time to time between 1603 and 1609
Henry IV suggested to James I that they might mutually co-operate
to drive Spain from the Indies, but it is scarcely possible to guess how
seriously he contemplated a major offensive against the Spanish empire.
His policy of ignoring Spanish interests in the New World while serving
his own and those of France appears to have been successful, but then
he had no desire for any close links with Spain in Europe as had
James I.

Why should the position of England have been more complex than
that of France? In the first place Spain had never interested herself
seriously in North America north of 40°: she had acquiesced in the
early Portuguese assumption that Newfoundland, Labrador and the
Maritimes came within her sphere under the demarcation of 1949: her
geographers and statesmen rarely knew which was which. French
activities in this area were not of vital importance to her, even while
they were of continuing interest. English concern with North America
was concentrated mainly on territory much nearer the Spanish sphere
of influence. Spain had herself, at various times, conducted expeditions,
annexed territory, established missions or otherwise intervened intermittently, though without permanent results, as far north as 38° in
Chesapeake Bay. Her own Florida colony, even if confined by 1603 to
a garrison at San Agustín at approximately 30° N. and extending
northwards only through a series of missions and contracts with the
Indians, was considered to have its effective boundary somewhere about
32° N., that is in modern South Carolina. The English concentration
was on the coastline between approximately 34° and 37°, roughly

between Cape Fear and Cape Henry, though the Spaniards were not sure precisely where the attempted colonisation of 1584–7 had taken place. They had followed news of these Elizabethan settlements sponsored by Sir Walter Ralegh with interest and some trepidation and would probably have taken action against them if it had not been for war commitments elsewhere in 1587 and after. Indeed, as we shall see, some Spanish officials believed that an English settlement continued to exist after 1590 somewhere in this region. Any new English initiative in this area was therefore construed as a threat to Spanish Florida in providing potential bases from which ships might prey on the home-going Indies fleets. There was also the complication that to reach Ralegh's Virginia (the North Carolina and Virginia of today) the only safe route was thought to be the long one from England to the Canaries, the Caribbean and the Florida Strait, thus offering continued scope for hostile Spanish interception which she was not unwilling to provide. Direct passage from England to these parts of North America had not yet been developed. This tended to put English expeditions to some extent at the mercy of Spain though they could in fact often slip through the Spanish zone unscathed. The attitude James was to take about English trade with the Caribbean made openings for the exercise of Spanish pressures: James's line was that he was against piracy and would help suppress it, but he favoured free access by sea for trade except to ports where it was expressly forbidden and prevented by Spain. He could thus be bullied by treating all traders in the West Indies as pirates (indeed many were), but he was concerned also with reopening the potentially valuable English trade with Spain itself, as a source of raw materials and luxury foodstuffs and as a market for cloth (itself mainly destined for the Indies), so that pressure on traders in Spain might be used to induce him to give concessions elsewhere. James too, became obsessed with the desire to make a marriage alliance with Spain to enhance his own position as potential arbiter and peacemaker in Europe. Spain, for her part, could attempt to use these overtures to keep England from closer co-operation with France or the Dutch, and saw them as a possible lever to obtain concessions for English Catholics or even secure a Catholic succession to the English throne. These last, well-known, even hackneyed, motifs, tended to complicate the question of Spain's acceptance of or resistance to English acquisitions of territory in eastern North America.

It is hard to know how far James was himself involved in the sponsoring of expeditions to North America in the short time after his accession, and before the peace with Spain, from March 1603 to August 1604. The first book advocating English settlement in North Virginia (the later New England) on the strength of a reconnaissance in 1602, Brereton's *A briefe and true report*, had two printings just before Queen Elizabeth's death.[1] An expedition to the coast just south of Roanoke

1. John Brereton, *A briefe and true report of the discoverie of the north part of Virginia* (1602; two issues).

Island in 1602 had done some trading with Indians and was possibly the third since 1600 to visit this area. 1603 saw no less than four components of English expeditions to North America sail and return:[2] one at least brought Indians to show off their skills in a canoe in the Thames in September: the same ship may have brought some evidence indicating that the Lost Colonists of 1587 (left there by Ralegh's expedition and found to have moved out of sight when looked for in 1590) were still alive. We have no certain evidence that the king had any involvement in any of these voyages directly, but we do know that Robert Cecil had some concern with at least two of them. Nonetheless, the arrest of Sir Walter Ralegh in July 1603 led to the transfer of his charter rights on the North American coasts (technically extending to 600 miles north and south of Roanoke Island) to the king and he cannot have been unaware that future initiatives in this area lay with him. We have evidence that the negative terms of the Treaty of London (which we shall examine) left him quite clear in his mind that the road to the Americas still lay open to the English.

In the diplomatic shifts and turns of the years 1603–9 the question of the English right to establish settlements on the North American coast crops up more often than might be expected. After all the major issues were the opening of the road to the Portuguese Indies, a matter of basic prestige for England once the first East India Company venture had returned in 1603, and also the terms on which some arrangement could be made to bring about a peace (or, *faute de mieux*, a truce) between Spain and the United Provinces on terms which would safeguard Dutch overseas commerce. Beside these, the question of the Spanish pressure against English activities in the Western Atlantic seemed peripheral. Nonetheless, the question of rights, of access to and settlement in North America, emerged very often as one of the key issues. The reason was that it was crucial to the principle of the maintenance of the Spanish monopoly. Spain had undoubtedly stronger precedents on her side than England to have carried through early exploration and attempted settlement in the area claimed by the English as Virginia. Yet the claims she actually made were rarely based on such specific instances. They were based, surprisingly often, in terms of the old papal donation of 1493, but more generally on the assertion that the indivisibility of the American domain was a matter of Spanish royal prerogative which could not be impugned by, or even discussed in detail with, a foreign power. England's main claims were based on freedom of the seas for her ships and effective occupation as the basic indication of sovereignty, though occasionally precedent was called into play. James and his ministers were inclined to shelter their North American claims behind a more general claim to freedom to trade to and to have access to American waters and shores: Spain was more likely to bring up the special case which English penetration of the North American area and especially her attempts at settlement created

2. *Terrae Incognitae*, II, 1–8.

as being subversive of long established and undoubted Spanish rights. Much of the argument was verbal sparring only, but both sides tried to use it to obtain their larger ends, England towards easing open the Spanish monopoly while still keeping the marriage alliance option: Spain sticking to a traditional position, but varying her responses by diverting James by offers relating to the marriage alliance, the English Catholics, or the Dutch, or else varying her pressures on Englishmen captured in the western ocean in a kind of diplomatic blackmail.

2

The negotiation of the Treaty of London in 1604, both in its preliminary and final stages, saw a great deal of shadowboxing by all the parties concerned. It was clear from the beginning that England would not settle for anything less than the Vervins terms, that is the *status quo*, with each side reserving its position on the Indies—though the English hoped that the threat, if the treaty broke down, of an Anglo-Dutch drive into the East and West Indies, might gain them some concessions. Henry IV, through Rosny (the later Sully), had already tied James in July and August 1603 to a tentative agreement to join France and the Dutch in such an offensive which he did not particularly want to keep. The Spaniards for their part were slightly embarrassed by their belief that the English already had some settlements on the North American coast. A Spanish memorandum in March[3] reported that the English could claim that 'for almost forty years not only had they navigated to that region, but had footing and abode towards that part of the New World that is called Labrador,' perhaps a reference to Newfoundland, perhaps to Virginia, while the head of the Spanish delegation to London, the Constable of Castile, Juan de Velasco, admitted later that when he came to England (for the signing of the treaty in August) 'he considered that if he specifically tried to exclude the English from the Indies, and from Virginia, he foresaw the difficulty that they are in peaceful possession of the latter for more than thirty years'.[4]

In the negotiations both sides of course went through the motions of citing precedents.[5] Cotton's brief for Northampton[6] had brought up

3. Archivo General de Simancas, Estado Inglaterra 841, nos. 10–12; R. D. Hussey, 'America in European diplomacy, 1597–1604', *Revista de Historia de América*, no. 41 (Mexico, 1956), p. 22.

4. Barbour, *The Jamestown voyages, 1607–9*, I (1969), 121–2, p. 4.

5. The series of documents in Archivo General des Simancas, Estado Inglaterra 841 is very consistent in defining the Spanish attitude. The official instructions to the English commissioners, 22 May 1604 (P.R.O., S.P. 94/10, ff. 17–23; B.L., Cotton MS, Vespasian C.XIII, f. 61; F. G. Davenport, *European treaties bearing on the history of the United States* (4 vols., Washington, D.C., 1917–37), I, 247), stated that 'we are contented to prohibit all repaire of our subjects to any places where they are planted, but onely to seeke traffique by their own discoveries in other places'.

6. Sir Robert Cotton's brief is in Cotton MS, Vespasian C.XII, ff. 47–50. The East India Company's brief (ibid., ff. 23–4) concentrated on the limits of Portuguese and Spanish occupation east of the Cape of Good Hope.

the John Cabot patent of 5 March 1496 as evidence of early and continued concern by England with North America. In the debates[7] Northampton made a curious gaffe on the basis of this by claiming that 'for the first pointe of privilege we did produce patents granted by Henry VII yet on record to Columbus etc., for the discovery of the Indies 5 March in the 7th year of the reign [i.e. 1492]'. If he did produce such a document it is a pity it was not otherwise recorded, but of course the date 5 March makes it clear it was the Cabot patent of 1496 (the 11th year) which was in fact cited. Northampton was on rather better ground when he said 'that if first discovering might give occasion for any such prohibition, that the Queen's majesty might have restrained their fishing in the northern seas notwithstanding the Spaniards took liberty to use it'.[7] Rovida, for Spain, virtually ignored these statements. He also set aside arguments based on freedom of the sea 'because the Indies was a New World'. Cecil told Parry, the English ambassador in France, in June that England would settle for the Vervins formula[8] and this she did in Auugst, the phrase on commerce being that it should be 'agreeably and according to the use and observance of the ancient alliances and treaties before the war'.[9] Cecil told Parry after the signing of the Treaty of London that they had denied 'that any Prince could bar his majesty from plantation in uninhabited countries or from trade with those lords and kings of countries where the Spaniards had no actual possession'.[10] For Henry IV's benefit he expressed the hope that the article could be regarded as 'a pregnant affirmative for us rather than against us', though the day before, writing privately to Winwood, he was not so sure: the words 'according to usage ... doth rather make for them against us'.[11] James, according to the Venetian ambassador, had no doubts about the effects of the Treaty so far as trade with the Indies was concerned. When asked if the English were debarred from the Indies trade he said 'What for no? The meaning is quite clear'[12]—time indeed would have to tell, but in 1604 the English rights to the North American shore remained to be what they could make them.

Velasco had raised, of course, immediately after the signing of the Treaty, the question of a marriage alliance. Its ramifications from then onwards are part of the accepted history of the time, but it may not have been sufficiently stressed that in James's mind, from 1604 to 1609, the prospects of a marriage for Prince Henry and the Infanta were most commonly and strongly associated with plans for the

7. 'A jornall of the conference,' Bodleian Library, Rawlinson MS C.688, f. 48; Watson, *Philip III*, II (1808), 564.

8. P.R.O., S.P. 78/51, f. 192.

9. 'In quibus ante bellum fuit commercium juxta et secundum usum et observantium antiquorum foederum' (Davenport, *European treaties*, I, 253, 256).

10. 5 September 1604. S.P. 78/51, ff. 253-4.

11. Sir Ralph Winwood, *Memorials*, II, (1725), 28.

12. *C.S.P. Ven. 1603-7*, pp. 189-90; J. D. Mackie, 'James VI and the peace with Spain, 1604', *Scottish Historical Review*, XXIIII, (1926), 248.

assumption by the happy pair (if they were ever joined in matrimony) of sovereignty over a reconciled United Provinces, enjoying under the benevolent tutelege of the Spanish crown the rights, and more, assigned to the Belgian provinces under the Archdukes. This, in turn, had implications with regard to access to the Indies by England and the United Provinces of which James was well aware, though Spain always refused to be specific on whether she would make trade concessions to a reconciled Netherlands. We can see now that the chances of any such arrangement succeeding were minimal from the first, but James did not. Yet it was because he was so obsessed with this aspect of the negotiation that James was specially vulnerable to Spanish pressure about current English activities in American waters, and it is clear that both Philip III and Lerma were willing to exercise such pressures quite ruthlessly while at the same time remaining wholly cynical about the marriage negotiation.[13]

Though the treaty was ratified in 1605 there was considerable disillusionment in England about its practical results. The restored Spanish trade did not flourish: the balance of trade was unsatisfactory, monetary transactions on either side appear to have been difficult to complete. Spanish bureaucracy and judiciary alike proved tardy, obstructive and inefficient. The English agent at Bayonne, Richard Cocks, wrote in 1606 'it was generally thought that our peace with Spain would bring in mountains of gold, but now it proveth molehills of earth'.[14] In the Caribbean, in spite of continued appeals by James about the freedom of the seas, the Spaniards refused to make any distinction between armed and unarmed English ships and between those engaged in piracy and those engaged in peaceful trade (usually of course with the connivance of local Spanish officials), and as a result a merchant said in 1606 without exaggeration: 'If we yield and depend upon their friendly promises we lose our goods and are made slaves; if we make any resistance we are all thrown overboard.'[15] Summary execution or the galleys was the normal fate of Englishmen taken at sea especially in the Caribbean. Spaniards had, of course, legitimate complaints: English piracy continued in both European and American waters though James did try to deter pirates by repeated proclamations and by fairly frequent resort to death sentences. The Englishmen brought to Spain for trial were kept in prison for long periods and in the end usually, if they had not died or escaped, went to the galleys.

Since the Caribbean had been the main bone of contention in the sixteenth century why, we may ask, did it not remain so in the years

13. See S. R. Gardiner, *History of England*, I, 343; Winwood, *Memorials*, II, 147, 160-1, 24 October 1605, Cecil urges caution as an alliance was liable to involve James in war with the United Provinces (P.R.O., S.P. 9/150, p. 100); March 1606 the King decides this should not be further pursued (ibid., pp. 130-1).

14. Quinn, 'The voyage of *Triall* 1606-7', *American Neptune*, XXXI (1971), 100. See below, 378.

15. See below, 379.

after 1604? The answer is that the issues were more ambiguous. James at the same time forbade piracy and hanged pirates, while advocating and upholding the virtue of legitimate trade even in the Indies (apart from the scheduled ports). Spain regarded both trade and piracy as equally penal, but when the capture of an English ship in the Caribbean took place and the case was argued in England or Spain, the English line was always that the ships were engaged in trade, while the Spanish was that they were engaged solely in piracy, and so it was very hard to get a clear cut issue. In the case of Virginia the issues were more sharply defined. The English could claim that they had no evidence of Spanish occupation at any time; they could claim precedents of first discovery and earliest settlement; they could, from 1607, assert effective occupation, and, if these arguments failed, they could urge that ships bound for Virginia were free of the seas through which they passed since these were oceanic not territorial waters. Spain could challenge the English claims on each of these grounds, but one of her favourite methods was to bring the matter to issue if a ship going to or coming from North America could be captured and ship and crew used as bargaining counters. This provided a basis on which the arguments and counterarguments could be marshalled, with the men concerned being merely counters in a diplomatic tussle. These considerations explain what happened when a ship bound for North America was actually taken.

3

In February 1605 the Spaniards got their first chance to play their cat and mouse game with such an expedition. The ship *Castor and Pollux* and her pinnace the *Pollux and Castor* were captured by three Spanish war vessels in Saint Helena Sound, in modern South Carolina, and their mixed English and French crews either killed or captured.[16] This was just on the outer edge of the coast regularly under Spanish surveillance from San Agustín. Pedro de Ibarra, the governor of Florida, had heard there was now peace with France and England, so, instead of killing off h s prisoners in the usual way, he sent most of them inland to the care of Indian chiefs and there they remained, lost to view, until they were either absorbed, sacrificed or died. Out of the three he selected to take to San Agustín, and from materials found on the ship, he obtained an interesting, if tantalising story. In January 1604 Henry IV had granted a patent to Guillaume de la Mothe, messenger and translator in the household of the French ambassador in London, the Comte de Beaumont, and this gave him licence to make an American

16. The chief source is the depositions and enclosures in A.G.S., Estado Francia K.1607.10, ff. 1–17. Mary Ross, 'The French on the Savannah', *Georgia Historical Quarterly*, VIII (1924), 167–94, used the correspondence in Seville, Archivo General de Indias, 54.5.9 (now Santo Domingo 224), to construct a preliminary account of this episode. The location is wrong and the surviving letters give only an outline of what took place, but she made the story as intelligible as was possible before the depositions came to light.

voyage (ranging under the vague but generous French formula from the River Marañon—the Amazon—to Cape Breton). This was evidently arranged under licence from the Sieur de Monts who held a monopoly above latitude 40° N. The interesting thing is that the permits were for English ships, the *Castor and Pollux* and *Pollux and Castor*, and that they were issued during the time when Henry IV was trying to involve England in anti-Spanish activity in the Indies and before the treaty with Spain was completed. But it was some four months later (when a Spanish representative was already in London to take soundings for a peace conference) that the ships sailed: John Jerome, a Plymouth man, was captain of the ship, La Mothe's partner, Bertrand Rocque (from St. Malo) of the pinnance. The main backer of the voyage was Pierre Beauvoir, a merchant long established in London (he was from a Guernsey family which had strong connections in St. Malo), and the crew was mixed; the pilot was English and we do not know the proportions of French and English amongst the seamen. An unidentified and somewhat mysterious character was the man that Spaniards called 'Juan de Bona Semana', described as a physician and herbalist: he was, he said, from Burgundy, he was a Catholic, he knew Spanish. We wonder whether he was a spy in the French, English or even Dutch interest or just an innocent expert sent out to look for medicinal herbs. The programme laid down for the ships was to visit Trinidad to collect tobacco, which they did, and then make a quick voyage up the North American coast (which they began only after several piratical attacks on Spanish shipping in the Caribbean). The pinnace, a Spanish vessel swapped for their own in the Indies, made herself conspicuous on the way up the coast of Florida by sounding the inlets from San Agustín northwards and this led to the tracking down and capture of both the mother ship and the pinnace in February 1605. By their instructions the ships were to trade with the Indians and they were doing this when they were caught in Saint Helena Sound. They were disposing of a large and lethal collection of arms, axes, spears, butchers' knives and the rest (enough to arm several tribes to the teeth): they were collecting herbs and medicinal woods, sassafras and China root, in particular, and doing a little trade in skins with the Indians as they had been instructed. The rest of their programme remained, owing to the capture, potential only. They were supposed to go up the coast to about 36° N. to Croatoan where they were expected to find the English colonists lost since 1587. This was because in 1590 John White, when he had gone to look for the colonists, found signs saying they had moved down the coast from Roanoke Island to Croaton but was unable to follow them there. They were to make contact with them and report and also to collect quantities of silkgrass (leaves of the Yucca or down from the milkweed plant). They would then sail successively to the Penobscot and the Bay of Fundy, looking for mines, and so return to report on the resources of North America— a most ambitious programme. The Spaniards were alarmed, since this provided not only evidence of renewed French interest in the area immediately north of the Spanish zone but also indications of a new degree of co-operation with the English. This was sinister, as was the news about the presumably surviving English colony farther north. It is just possible also that the expedition had the task of sketching out, in a preliminary way, French and English zones of influence on the coast north of Spanish Florida, but this cannot be established on the present evidence.

The depositions got to Spain well before 1605 was out and news of the capture and 'disappearance' of the men leaked out or was allowed to leak out in the spring of 1606. When the marquis of San Germano arrived in England in April to congratulate James rather tardily on having survived the Gunpowder Plot and to make fresh murmurings about the marriage alliance,[17] he was confronted with a demand from some of the king's ministers to know what had happened to the *Castor and Pollux* and her men who had been, it was said, on a peaceful trading mission.[18] Pierre de Beauvoir, the man who had helped to set out the ship, was friendly with Sir Thomas Edmondes, the English ambassador at Brussels, and was able to stir up trouble. His case was that the ships were engaged on a voyage of exploration to Virginia, Norumbega (that is New England) and Acadia and were peacefully trading with the Indians when they were set upon, and their men killed or taken prisoner.[19] The Earl of Salisbury wrote to Sir Charles Cornwallis, who was now installed as ambassador in Spain, to take up the matter; and so did Edmondes from Brussels. From July to September 1606 Cornwallis tried to bring up the case; but he was out of favour ('my leaves are blasted' as he put it in July);[20] he wished to take a strong line about the ship but was put off; he groaned about Spanish pride; and the last we hear of the case he was saying 'I am yet doubtful in what sort to frame my suit; neither have I cause to conceive much hope of obtaining it, their jealousy of their Indies being such and so extreme as they resolve to make it capital to all such as shall fall into their hands there'. He never did get any satisfaction.[21] The Spaniards had been given a chance to show that they could and would deal ruthlessly and effectively with any English and French intervention in what they regarded to be their exclusive North American sphere. Indeed, the case was handled in such a manner as to show James what could happen if he sent or permitted colonists to go to Virginia.

It is true that an English captain operating in the vicinity of Cumaná in 1606 had the audacity to claim that he had a commission from the Earl of Nottingham, Lord High Admiral of England and one

---

17. See Edmondes to Salisbury, 23 March 1606, S.P. 77/8, f. 93.

18. See S.P. 94/12, ff. 202–11, placed July or August 1606, but perhaps earlier.

19. See Edmondes to Cornwallis, 12/22 June, Cotton MS, Vespasian C.IX, ff. 448–9; Winwood, *Memorials*, II, 234.

20. Cotton MS, Vespasian C.IX, ff. 453–4; Winwood, II, 235.

21. A.G.I., Santo Domingo 191 (transcript in B.L. , Additional MS 36319, f. 96, 14 August 1606). Information from Dr. K. R. Andrews.

of the commissioners sent to Spain in 1605 for the ratification of the Treaty of London, and the 'emperor' of Spain to go to search for new lands to the north of Florida.[22] But whether he expected Spanish officials in the West Indies to believe him is another matter.

The English discovery of Spanish action in the case of the *Castor and Pollux* concided with the grant to the Virginia Company of its first charter on 10 April 1606. This authorised settlement between 35° and 45° N., that is from just beyond the limit of effective Spanish control and into the zone already pre-empted by France for her own subjects. Moreover, it created a supervisory royal council to administer and make rules for colonies which was manned largely by a collection of government officials of the second rank as well as of prominent merchants, and it could be held to commit the king to a policy of continuous intervention in North America. There were immediate and repeated Spanish protests from the ambassador, Zúñiga, and there is no doubt that the freezing out of Cornwallis, in Spain, in July, had much to do with this, as had the tough, uncompromising Spanish line taken on the *Castor and Pollux* capture. The English were expected (and were probably told) to deduce that any Englishmen found on the North American coast would be wiped out by the Spaniards. Nevertheless, during 1606, the English attitude remained firm: no suggestions that the Virginia Company charter might be abrogated at the wish of Spain are known to have been made.[23]

Then in August a ship, the *Richard*, under Captain Henry Challons, left Plymouth to make the long voyage by way of the West Indies to reconnoitre a site for a company settlement in Mawooshen (modern Maine): in December a three-ship expedition under Christopher Newport, which was to establish Jamestown in Virginia in May 1607 followed. Newport encountered no obstacles in the Caribbean. The *Richard* made her way peacefully and safely through the Caribbean also but in November 1606 had the ill-luck to be picked up in the Florida Strait by a Spanish fleet which had been delayed at

22. See Huntington MS 1242, Henry E. Huntington Library.

23. The French ambassador La Broderie, who had replaced Beaumont, saw Salisbury on 7/17 June 1606. He raised the question of whether the Dutch were strong enough to engage themselves in the West Indies as well as maintaining their trade to the East unless they had French and English support. Broderie reported Salisbury as replying 'que pour eux ils avoisent une Flotte prête à partir en Virginie ... que si nous en voulons faire de même, nul non pouvoit nous en empêcher; & que peu a peu néanmoins y procèdent de cette sorte les affaires d'Espagne s'trouveroient assez incommodées, sans en venir a une autre plus manifeste démonstration.' (*Ambassades*, I (1750), 117–18.)

On 1 November 1608 Sir George Carew reported himself at a loss for a reply when Henry IV said: 'Oh sayeth he if you would join with us the only way for the piece of Christendom were to drive the Spaniard out of the Indies and range him within Spain.' (S.P.78/54, f. 196.)

Havana.[24] She was treated as a prize, her men were dispersed and no notice was taken of the plea that they were going to the English king's territory in Virginia. These men too might have disappeared if one of the Spanish ships, with some members of the English crew on board, had not put into Bordeaux under stress of weather, and there the prisoners managed to get the ship put under arrest early in 1607. These men got home and started diplomatic proceedings moving. Spain again was to make the most of this capture to put pressure on James, though in rather a different way, over Virginia.

The case of the *Richard* was to cause Cornwallis more trouble than any other single episode in his not untroubled career as ambassador, and it produced a considerable correspondence with Salisbury, Philip III and Lerma over the two years' debate to which it led. It did so at very varying temperatures and was a useful index of how the major diplomatic procedures of the period were moving. Dutch overtures for a truce were commended by Henry IV to James before the end of 1606, and early in 1607 he took them up with enthusiasm, raising again his hopes of seeing Prince Henry regent of a reconciled Netherlands or, at the least, envisaging himself as the grand mediator in the great quarrel between Spain and her estranged subjects. Against this background the existence of the Virginia Company, its colony-establishing activities, and such things as the existence of the royal council for Virginia, were an embarrassment, as the Spanish government was at pains to point out to Cornwallis from time to time. Cornwallis was allowed to plead for the *Richard*'s men for a time, as we shall see, only on humanitarian grounds. The astute Constable of Castile thought James's bluff ought finally to be called on Virginia by destroying the Jamestown settlement as soon as its existence was known in Spain, but his advice was not heeded. James on the other hand, and Salisbury also, took the line of giving the Spaniards the impression that they could not care less about what happened to the Virginia settlement, even though Salisbury was at the same time vitally concerned with seeing that it was supplied and reinforced. In this atmosphere the surprise eight-months' truce in March 1607 between the United Provinces and the Archdukes (tardily assented to by Spain) upset the longer-term calculations of Spain, England and France. These were renewed and revised later in the year. Spain made a dead set at James, trying to entice him into an alliance with Spain with the prize of the marriage alliance and possibilities of an arbitral position attractively set out; Henry IV trying, at the same time, to draw England into

24. The sources on the *Richard*'s capture in English are voluminous. There is a narrative of the voyage in S. Purchas, *Pilgrimes*, IV (1625), 1832–7 (supplemented by P.R.O., H.C.A. 14/38, 18; H.C.A. 13/38), Diplomatic correspondence is in H.M.C., *Cecil MSS*, XIX, XX (some items in full being in J. P. Baxter, *Sir Ferdinando Gorges* (3 vols., Boston, 1887–90)); Winwood, *Memorials*, II (1725) (supplemented by P.R.O., S.P. 9/312, ff. 817v–22v., S.P. 14/28, 35, S.P. 94/13, pt. ii, ff. 147 etc., S.P. 101/90, f. 241; B.L., Cotton MS, Vespasian C.X, and XI, Additional MS 39853, f. 144). No adequate search for material has so far been made in Spain.

an alliance with the Dutch in which peace could be dictated against Spain's resistance or else war resumed on very advantageous terms. James's attraction was towards Spain, Salisbury's towards a medial position between the two extremes which was that eventually adopted by James at the end of 1607.

In these circumstances extreme caution was the watchword of English diplomacy on North America during the early months of 1607. Sir John Popham, the lord chief justice, who was vitally associated with the Virginia Company, thought that the king himself must intervene to get the *Richard*'s men released ('I understand it will be in vain to seek for the delivery of such as be in captivity unless it be by order of the king himself', he wrote to Salisbury); but Salisbury in April (after the truce) was certainly unwilling to involve the king in anything of this sort. Instead he cautioned Cornwallis against permitting the circulation of any reports in Spain that he himself and Popham were involved in the *Richard*'s voyage in any way ('I must needs disavowe that it was any part of mine adventure and so I pray disperse that folly'). At the same time he set out a line for Cornwallis to follow: 'First that Virginia was first discovered by our nation and that Spain never since nor before was possessed of it. Secondly that these men had committeed no manner of offence to Spain unless it be an offence to come into their seas which by the law of nations ought to be free, *quoad navigationem*, but were only going towards a place which is yet disputable, whether it be allowable or not according to the treaty.'

A working paper of his (in the hand of Levinus Monck)[25] represents his thinking at this time, the basis of which is that the king should not be tied by rigid adherence to the Virginia claim to the prejudice of major issues. He thought that, for example, 'adventurers into the Indies' should be 'left unto the peril which they should incur thereby' and that 'although it is disputable whether Virginia be part of the Indies, even though it be situate upon the same continent as the West Indies, yet for avoiding of the occasion thereby to fall into the general question of the Indies and our trading thereunto, it might be advised that it were better to leave these prisoners to their fortune rather than by bringing it in question to stir up some greater inconveniences that might ensue of it'. Read into the wider context, he is advocating leaving the Virginia question in abeyance, avoiding the Spanish challenge over the *Richard*'s crew, and preferring to have the general question of access to the Indies merged in the wider context, that of the Dutch negotiation of which it was a vital part. The only case for argument was, as he had told Cornwallis, the free seas one which could be pleaded more or less independently of the territorial issue. Yet when Cornwallis tried this out on Lerma he was met with a tirade: Lerma said that 'to restrain access to those countries, he had an inclination rather to cruelty than to clemency'. There was no case for

25. Cecil MS 119/149 Hatfield House (printed in Baxter, *Gorges*, II, 132–3).

freedom of the seas: 'the case for traffic and navigation thither', he said, 'was far different from that of other parts of the world ... it was to them Regum Novum and therefore until their being better settled and fortified therein they were with great reason jealous and fearful to object either to hungry or curious eyes on so precious and desirable a jewel, and, lastly, that the dominion and possession was theirs and therefore lawful both by rule of nature and nation to appropriate it to themselves and exclude others, and so 'it was not fit for them to suffer any use of navigation thither.' (So much rhetoric about such a minor incident concerning a handful of seamen justified Salisbury's caution in the context of the time.)

The announcement by the Dutch in June that they would negotiate for a treaty only under the guarantee of France and England was the loophole for entry into the wider negotiation which James's diplomacy required. So Spain must be appeased for the time being. The *Richard*'s men must cease to be an embarrassment: Salisbury told Cornwallis that he must proceed by entreaty, 'not engaging his majesty'. There was considerable embarrassment, too, early in the summer, when the Spaniards brought up the case of another ship, the *Triall*.[26] She was a vessel that had gone out to make a voyage in 1606 to Virginia, not under the auspices of the Virginia Company but as a private venture, and after attempting to raise support for such a voyage in Ireland her expedition had degenerated into a piratical attack on Spanish shipping off the Spanish coast very early in 1607. The House of Commons too, irritated by merchant grievances in Spain and bad treatment of Englishmen taken at sea, openly attacked Spain in June, declaring that not only could merchants get no redress in Spain but were being killed and enslaved in the Indies. Salisbury, addressing a conference of lords and commons, promised to make representations; but he brought up the case of the *Triall* which had, he said, by pretending to go to Virginia as a cover for a piratical expedition, given the Spaniards just the kind of excuse which justified some of their actions.[27]

However, the return of Christopher Newport in July with the news of the foundation of Jamestown excited Salisbury and his circle (though their hopes of gold to be found there were soon dissipated) and incited the Spanish ambassador, Zúñiga, to renew protests at the licence given to the Virginia Company to intervene in what he insisted were Spain's territories. At a time when Spain was using especial blandishments to James to keep him out of the hands of the Dutch and French, Zúñiga had an interview with him on 27 September[28] and

---

26. Spanish verbal protests were probably made in May. A list of Spanish complaints dated 3 July also includes the *Triall* (*American Neptune*, XXXI (1971), 102).

27. Reported by Bacon to the Commons on 15 June (*American Neptune*, XXXI, 101)—'This very last voyage to Virginia, intended for trade and plantation where the Spaniard hath no people nor possession, is already become infamous for piracy.'

28. 28 September/8 October, A.G.S., Estado E2586,68 (Barbour, *Jamestown voyages*, I, 117–19).

brought up the question of Virginia. James put up a pretence of bland ignorance about Virginia and of the Spanish case concerning it. He never knew that Spain had any claim to Virginia since, as he said, 'it was a region very far from where the Spaniards had settled'. Zúñiga and he were at cross-purposes too on what the Treaty of London actually contained: James said it was not specified in it that the English and French could not go to new regions, and he was right: Zúñiga said it was stated they were not to go to the Indies, he was wrong. James was asked to stop his people going to Virginia: he stonewalled and said he never knew it belonged to Spain, but since he was assured that it did and that piracy might be practised against Spain from there he would look into it, and would tell his council to give the ambassador satisfaction. It was a very curious interview. Was James being cool and ironic? Or was he preparing the way for a sell-out of the Virginia colony if Spanish offers on other matters seemed to make it worthwhile? The answer is surely that he was keeping several options open.

Salisbury, again according to Zúñiga,[29] who may of course not be an entirely accurate reporter, told him much the same thing as the king and even went a little further. 'If the English were to go where they cannot go they are to be punished', he said, 'and that it now appears to him that they cannot go to Virginia, and therefore if something bad happens to them let it be their fault for it will not appear to him a thing against friendship and the terms of the treaty.' The indication of a sell-out is here more plain, but again there may be an ironical undercurrent or Zúñiga may be stretching things a little to fit in with his own recommendation, which, as we saw the Constable of Castile was to endorse, that Spain should attack Jamestown at once, 'hanging the settlers while so little is needed to make it possible'. But clearly Philip III regarded Zúñiga's intervention as a valuable one and sent his personal thanks to his ambassador for the services he had performed with the king on the subject of Virginia,[30] and also for 'converting the earl of Salisbury to my service'.

In Spain itself Cornwallis became moderately hopeful as he received from Lerma promises that cases pending against Englishmen would be speeded up and brought to a conclusion, though he had to add that nothing was in fact done about the *Richard*'s men. Spanish approaches to James also ended abruptly when James drew back in December from discussion of a general alliance with Spain which would in fact, it was seen, separate him wholly from France and the Dutch. On December 10 Cornwallis was told to say 'No', and did so. That brought to an end the period of Spanish wooing of England over Virginia.

29. 6/16 October, Estado E2586,69 (ibid., 120–1).
30. 6/16 October, Estado E2571,215 (Barbour, I, 122–3).

4

The atmosphere was wholly different in 1608. In this year James was taking Salisbury's advice and was carefully picking his way towards a realistic position in regard to the Dutch settlement: he refused the offensive alliance with the Dutch which Henry IV considered necessary to bring matters to a head, but he cautiously moved towards a defensive alliance which would give him some degree of arbitral status between the Dutch and Spain without wholly antagonising the latter.[31] On the question of Virginia there is no further word about drastic concessions, but no open defiance either, though Spanish intransigence over the *Richard*'s men was putting even James's back up. The second supply to Jamestown went off quietly in January, so that there was no interruption of support for the Virginia Company: Newport sailed indeed with all the insignia necessary to turn Powhatan, the Virginia chieftain, into an Indian sub-king under King James, so that withdrawal was not apparently now contemplated. At length, too, in February, Cornwallis heard that an adverse decision had been taken about the *Richard*'s men: all those over twenty years of age were to be sent to the galleys. Cornwallis expressed the opinion that they were being made scapegoats: 'by what hath passed may sufficiently appear unto your lordship,' he said to Salisbury, 'how much they take to heart his majesty's purpose of planting in Virginia.' The English consuls in Seville and Lisbon were even more specific, and one of them said 'It seems they mind to make them a precedent for others, for our settling in the new discoveries is very distasteful to them.' Cornwallis wrote a characteristically careful protest to Philip III[32] without any overt challenge on Virginia, but a strong reassertion of the doctrine of the freedom of the seas. The only result of this was a respite in enforcing the sentence until May, and a slanging match with Lerma,[33] in which the latter got furious when Cornwallis explained that the papal donation held no authority for the English. In May and June Cornwallis was sending warnings that ships might indeed be preparing to attack the Virginia settlement, though ostensibly the Spaniards were tactful enough to refuse to recognise that it was the English who had established a foothold in North America. They admitted however that 'some strangers' had 'strayed' into part of the Indies and would now have to be removed. But then tension died down again for a time and all the talk was of the interminable complexities of the Dutch negotiation. Finally, however, out of the blue, in November, Prada, the secretary of state, signed releases for the remaining eighteen men from the *Richard*[34] and they were all released from the galleys to which they had ultimately been sent,[35] after having been almost two years in custody altogether. The

---

31. F. G. Davenport, *European treaties*, 270.
32. Winwood, *Memorials*, II, 382–4.
33. Ibid, II, 386.
34. S.P. 94/15, ff. 156–7.
35. Winwood, *Memorials*, II, 400.

case had been allowed to fester: the Spaniards had tried to use the lives, or at least the liberty, of the men as blackmail: by doing so they had used up any goodwill they might have accumulated by a more generous gesture at an earlier stage. My impression is that James's ministers, and quite possibly the king himself, were ultimately so affected by the Spanish actions that they were persuaded to make Virginia a matter of prestige as well as a marginal colonial speculation. So it might seem that the survival of Virginia owed something to Spanish intransigence, though how much it is difficult to assess. In 1608 and thereafter it might seem that English attitudes to Spain over North America approximate more closely to those adopted by Henry IV ever since 1598.

Indeed, Cornwallis did not know all that was going on behind the scenes in Spain 1608–9.[36] Between August and October 1608 the Council of War, the *Junta de Guerra*, with the king's approval, was indeed trying to find ships to send to Virginia to destroy the colony, but could not easily locate suitable vessels. There seems to have been some division of interest in Spanish councils, since the sending of additional ships from Europe to the West Indies at that time might weaken Spain in her posture of defiance against the Dutch. But one positive order at least was given. The governor of Florida was told to send a vessel north to make a close inspection of the English settlements and to send reports to Spain as soon as possible. The reconnaissance was duly carried out in 1609 by Ferdinando de Éjica, who had captured the *Castor and Pollux* in 1605, but nothing came of it. He came into the Chesapeake, observed the English, was observed in turn and departed, to make still another long report on English activities.[37] Virginia remained in being, if not wholly freed of Spanish threats. Already, in 1608, the mild Cornwallis had been moved to write critically of the Indies, drawing attention to the weaknesses of the Spanish empire:[38] the Indies were being neglected, many reforms were needed, the populations there were by no means reliable; the vaunted Spanish empire might well crumble if the Dutch were free to attack it, while the Virginia enterprise was on its way to weaken it also. If this was mainly wishful thinking, there was something in it. Spain was weak in action and dilatory in discussion. Instead of destroying Jamestown soon after it was planted, time was wasted in haggling over the *Richard*'s men and in diplomatic shifts and turns. Spain had lost an opportunity of asserting decisively her monopoly position. Lack of readily available resources in the Indies as well as at home may have been as much responsible for this as lack of will.

Before the end of 1608 Spain made it clear she would not accept the independence of the United Provinces: the guarantors of the

---

36. Though Cornwallis did give some warnings in June (Winwood, *Memorials*, II, 409–10), and in October (p. 439).

37. A.G.I., Patronato 19, ramo 29, brought to my attention by Mr. P. L. Barbour.

38. Winwood, *Memorials*, II, 380.

negotiation, France and England, with the firm support of the Archdukes, endeavoured to salvage at least a long truce.[39] In the end, too,
that had to be patched up rather than be openly signed and sealed.
Spain would commit herself to nothing allowing the Dutch formal
rights of access to either of the Indies. The Archdukes got leave in the
end, as will be remembered, to issue a public statement that the Dutch
would not in fact be interfered with on their way to or from these
parts of the Indies not actually occupied by Spain, and this statement
was duly endorsed by the guarantors France and England.[40] France
and England indeed got something out of this rather unsatisfactory
solution since clearly they would not tolerate a less favoured status
than that of the Dutch, even though Spain had reserved her position so
firmly.[41] The nine year truce was duly signed in March, and at almost
the same time Zúñiga reported from London that Spain might well
have left her intervention in Virginia too long; the English were at last
putting their backs into the Virginia enterprise, Lord De La Warr was
going out as governor at the head of a large expedition. Action, he said,
was necessary at once if the English were to be eliminated. After this
expedition reached Virginia only a major struggle which would breach
the peace between the two countries would get them out. Once again
his warnings were ignored and no action was taken by Spain. Indeed it
was by 1609 obvious that the Virginia question had become a matter
of national prestige for England as well as of diplomatic bargaining. A
new charter for the Virginia Company on May 23 granted 'Virginia and
other parts and territories in America', two hundred miles north and
south of Jamestown, to a reorganised company whose membership now
comprised a broad swathe of court and mercantile enterprise. But at the
same time the royal council of 1606 was quietly eliminated: it had
never once been mentioned in the diplomatic exchanges but, potentially,
it was too direct a royal involvement for it to be retained. The English
commitment in the west was to grow rapidly (Newfoundland in 1610,
Bermuda in 1612), but it was to emerge piecemeal, with royal licences,
though not under royal direction, and with no impediment from Spain.

In 1609 we may consider that Spain was defeated, almost it might
be said without a battle. The integrity of her western Indies had been
breached by the Dutch truce, but also, and more positively, by the
English establishment of the Virginia settlement within what she could
credibly claim to be her sphere of influence. Diplomatic turns and shifts

39. The treaty of guarantee between England, France and United
Provinces was signed 7/17 March 1609. The truce of Antwerp followed on
March 29.

40. Davenport, *European treaties*, I, 271–2, prints the certificate. It was
ratified by France 16/26 July, and by England 10/20 July. Ibid., I, 270–4.

41. Note that in the instructions sent to the English commissioners on
2 March (Winwood, *Memorials*, II, 481–3) it was stated that the Dutch should
be content to trade to the parts not settled by the Spaniards, but the commissioners were instructed that 'you do not conclude by any words directly or
collaterally that his majesty's subjects are excluded from trading into any
places'.

had not saved Spain, but of course they did not save James either from further humiliations after he took up again his marriage alliance policy. At least we can say, however, that in this later diplomacy he was only lightly embarrassed by his successful if marginal breach of the Spanish monopoly in Virginia.

20

AN ANGLO-FRENCH 'VOYAGE OF DISCOVERY'
TO NORTH AMERICA IN 1604-1605, AND ITS SEQUEL

In May an expedition left Plymouth for the Caribbean and the eastern shores of North America. A later English complaint, in rather poor Spanish (¹) stated :

'Pedro de Beauois y otros Mercadeles sequexan que ponendo a la mar vn nauio lamado el Castor y Pollux con vn pattaxe aparexado con 35 hombres con diuersas suertes de marcadurias de grande valor por discourir la costa de Virginia Norembegh y Cadia en las partes de america el qual nauio y pataxe entrando en Chañel de Bahama y Nauigando la costa de florida para cumplir su vaxe pretendido fueron fuersados a entrar en vn rio lamado St Helena para aguar y refrescarse y estando alla serto tiempo tratando con los soluaxes no siendo parte de baxo del Gouernador despana no de ningun ministro del Rey.'

They were then set upon by three ships of the governor of Havana, Pedro de Valdés, the vessels taken, the crews killed or taken prisoner, to be ultimately sent as slaves to work on the fortifications of the Indies.

This brief and not wholly accurate reference covers a curious episode in the relations of France, England and Spain over part of southeastern North America in the opening years of the seventeenth century. We might think indeed that 'discovery' of the coast northwards from Florida was not strictly necessary after the many sixteenth century voyages had revealed the general outline of the shores of eastern North America. Nonetheless there were many questions left unanswered about the coastal territories north of Florida, not least, of course, the question of which, if any, European power should be able to establish its claim to exploit them.

(1) Public Record Office, London (hence P.R.O.), State Papers Foreign, Spain, S.P. 94/12, ff. 202-11.

Spain had, it is true, at one time or another explored and attempted to missionize or occupy most of the coastal lands between the tip of the Florida peninsula and the head of Chesapeake Bay. But one after another her connections had been given up — Santa Elena, when Drake's threat developed in 1586, many mission posts after the Indian rising of 1597, and so on, so that early in the seventeenth century Spain held only San Agustín, some mission posts near the mouth of the St Johns River and on Cumberland island and a vague sphere of influence over the Indians extending to Port Royal Sound or a little farther to the north.

Though the French had been driven from Florida in 1565 they had repeatedly come back to trade with the Indians along the coast immediately north of Port Royal Sound, though we cannot so far follow their associations with this area in any continuous pattern. After 1597 too there are signs that the French were renewing contacts with the Indians well to the south, namely those inside the missionized zone around the mouth of the St Johns River. There are indications that Englishmen were co-operating with them. In 1603 a vessel of which we know no details was on the Florida coast : it had two Englishmen on board and apparently at least one Frenchman who spoke Timucua and which made contacts in this area and then apparently went on to trade on the coast to the north of Port Royal Sound. So much was gathered by the Spaniards when investigating the *Castor and Pollux* in 1605. It is clear from later events that some Indians were pro-Spanish and some pro-French but whether this reflects any long-standing alignment is not at all clear. French and English were in the last years of the sixteenth century and the early ones of the seventeenth friendly rivals in the robbery of Spanish vessels in the Caribbean and in trade with Spaniards and natives there and out of this association had evidently sprung a measure of co-operation in trading to and investigating the shores of the North American mainland.

Henry IV, when he signed the treaty of Vervins in 1598, had given up no French claims in western waters and the French admiralty, under Villars, had gone on issuing broadly embracing commissions for French ships to make trading voyages to the Amazon ; 'Perou' (a cover name it seems for the Caribbean), New France, Acadia and so on. (²) These were effectively commissions for privateering activity as well as trade. In 1603 Rosny (the later duc de Sully) had visited England to attempt to get the

---

(2) Examples may be found in P. BARREY, *Le Havre transatlantique de 1571 à 1610*, in Julien HAYEM, ed., *Mémoires et documents pour servir à la histoire du commerce et de l'industrie en France*, V (Paris, 1917), pp. 86-183.

association of James I in an aggressive co-operative policy against the Spanish Indies. Though James signed agreements to do so he turned away from France to work towards peace and co-operation with Spain in 1604. One aspect of Henry's policy had been to consolidate his claims to the more northern part of the North American coast by granting to Pierre de Gua, Sieur de Monts, on 8 November 1603 ([3]) a monopoly of intercourse with the coast north of 40°. Henceforth Frenchmen operating in this area needed to have licences from de Monts and it appears that he had printed handbills containing a reprint of his second commission of December 18 circulated to publicize his monopoly, but it was not clear how far this extendad to cover those who had wide authority to sail to and trade as far as Cape Breton included on their admiralty commissions. One of the coastal traders, set out by Antoine Bonnet, a member of the household of the admiral himself (*La Levrette* of Havre de Grâce, captain Jean Rossignol), was seized by de Monts on her homeward voyage at Port-Mouton in April 1604, though four years later he had to pay compensation for her capture. ([4]) It would seem, however, that de Monts had approved the penetration of his reserved area by the *Castor and Pollux* and her pinnace the *Pollux and Castor* when, in due course, on 10 January 1604, a patent was issued in the king's name to Guillaume de la Mothe and Bertrand Rocque of Saint-Malo to take them to the western ocean. ([5]). The commission authorised them to make a voyage to the mainland and islands of America from the River Marañon (the Amazon) to Cape Breton in order to trade and to discover lands and places for the royal service. They were commended to the care of friends of France and were authorised to treat as enemies those who tried to impede them.

The commission concealed a good deal more than it revealed. The ships were English and were intended to be manned by a combined English and French crew. While Rocque and a number of the men were from Saint-Malo and represented a French investment, the ships were fitted out largely with London capital. La Mothe was, at this time, in London, a member of the

---

(3) See W. I. MORSE, *Pierre du Gua, sieur de Monts* (London, 1939), pp. 8, 49.

(4) S. DE CHAMPLAIN, *Works*, ed. H. P. Biggar (etc.). I (Toronto, 1922), 237, 276, P. LE BLANT and R. BAUDRY, edd., *Nouveaux documents sur Champlain* (Ottawa, 1967), pp. 169-72.

(5) The bulk of our information comes from the *dossier* on the affair in Archivo General de Simancas, Estado Francia, K. 1607, 10, ff. 1-17, and can be taken as authority for statements in this paper for which no other reference is given. The text is translated in D.B. Quinn, A.M. Quinn and S. Hillier, *New American World*, V (1979), 110-26.

household of the French ambassador, Christophe de Harlay, comte de Beaumont. We know little about him though, in 1606, after he had returned to France, he was described as a man in the confidence of the French king ([6]) and fit to represent French interests in a case which had arisen in England. Moreover, the main backer of the venture was a merchant, Pierre de Beauvoir, a member of a Guernsey family with connections in Saint-Malo, living in London where he had contacts in official circles. ([7]) This was, therefore, a venture built up on an earlier association between French and English privateers in the West Indies and, almost certainly, a direct successor to that of 1603 since several of the men, French and English, were common to the two expeditions. The January 1604 grant was not however brought into effect until May 1604 by which time England had begun to treat for peace with Spain, the signing of a peace treaty with whom in August made the position of her nationals in any conflict with Spain in the Indies rather ambiguous, since James I had declared himself both against piracy and against any interference with Englishmen trading in western waters.

Le Mothe did not propose to go himself and *Castor and Pollux* was confided to a Plymouth captain, John Jerome ([8]), who had with him an English pilot, who had probably been on the 1603 voyage : Rocque took command of the pinnace. On 16 May 1604, at Plymouth, La Mothe handed the captains their instructions. They were to go from England direct to Trinidad and to buy all the tobacco they could and also acquire there and in other islands both tobacco and maize. They were then to make their way to Santa Elena (on Port Royal Sound) in Florida and to sell such tobacco and maize as they could and also to trade for sassafras (*Sassafras officinale*, much

(6) It would seem that Guillaume de la Mothe was a relative of Pierre (or Peter) Beauvoir since J. Beaulieu was Beauvoir's cousin and he in turn refers to La Mothe as his cousin (Historical Manuscripts Commission (hence H.M.C.), *Downshire MSS*, II (1936), 5-7, 11). On 4 February 1606 Sir George Carew, English ambassador in Paris, wrote to Lord Salisbury of William de la Mothe, who was going to Paris and England to deal with certain cases relating to Frenchmen in the English courts, 'I find La Mothe himself, a man ready to do good offices to his Majesties ministers here,' (P.R.O., State Papers Foreign, France, S.P. 78/53, f. 13).

(7) A coherent biography of Pierre (or Peter) Beauvoir is not yet possible, though his activities can be partly reconstructed from H.M.C., *Cecil MSS*, XIV (1923), 31 ; *Acts of the Privy Council, 1598-9* (1905), pp. 425-7 ; H.M.C., *Downshire MSS*, II (1936), 16, 27, 33, 52, 72, 104, 107, 111, 113, 125, 164, 172, 282, 325, 408, 419, 437, 439, 440, 442, 459, 477 (a few of these references apparently being to a younger cousin of the same name).

(8) John Jerome, married to Elizabeth Jenkins at St Andrew's Church, Plymouth on 4 July 1603, is almost certainly he. *Register of St. Andrew's, Plymouth*, ed. M. C. S. Cruwys (Exeter, Devon and Cornwall Record Society, 1954), p. 254.

prized in medicine), China root (*Smilax pseudo-china*, a substitute for *Smilax china*, another favoured medicine), and — we gather from other sources — a bark known as 'Tus' (*corcho de los Tus*), which has not been identified, and the wood of aloes. When they had done so they were to explore northwards along the coast with both vessels, disposing of the remainder of their maize as they went, until they came to the place where the English settlers were living at Crotuan (at 36° 30' N. lat. one of the men said), with whom they were to make contact. They were to trade there for 'Oysan' or 'Bissanque' from which grass silk could be obtained. This was either the Milkweed, the down and fibre of which could be spun into fabric, or the Yucca, whose leaves provided fibre, or both of these plants. They were not told what dealings they were to have with the English settlers though they may have been carrying some supplies for them.

Proceeding northwards, they were to explore the river of Gama (the Penobscot) to see if there were any mines there and finally to visit Acadia where they were to locate a copper mine at 44° 15' N. lat. before returning to Plymouth. They were to report there at the house of Jacques Prevost or the Captain 'Jiraldo' : while if they put in at the Channel Islands they were to make contact with James Beauvoir or Master Belian at Guersnsey. During the course of their expedition along the North American coasts they were to keep a constant watch for the articles specified and also for the herb 'Aneda' (Amado, Adoaneda, Guinida, Humeday), Cartier's anti-scorbutic, *annedda*, a great beast called 'Orontes' (moose), and to report on the drugs, fruits, herbs roots, timber, dyes, flowers and minerals, they found, to bring back specimens and also to mark (presumably on a chart) the sites where they were found. This was an extremely ambitious programme, but it certainly involved exploration as well as trade. The proposed survey of the natural resources of the coastal lands was even more extensive than that performed by Thomas Harriot and John White in 1585-6. Jean de Bonnesemaine, [10] a physician and herbalist, was to be in charge : there would clearly be a chartmaker : we do not know if there was also to be an artist.

(9) For a James Beauvoir of Guernsey, who is probably the same person, see *Acts of the Privy Council, 1597-8*, pp. 26, 237, 243, 285-6 ; *A.P.C., 1599-1600*, p. 236 ; *Calendar of State Papers, Domestic, Addenda, 1580-1625*, pp. 269, 475.

(10) Juan de Bona Semana in Spanish. He does not appear in published records of physicians in England. He claimed to be a Catholic and a native of Burgundy, but it is possible that he was a Protestant Walloon in the English or French service. His claim not to be able to read English (and so disclaim knowledge of the contents of heretical books on board) is unlikely to be true. He could, conceivably, be an Englishmen named Goodwick (= good week = Bona Semana), but this a mere guess.

A primary English objective in North America at the opening of the sixteenth century was to find the Lost Colony, which had been left at Roanoke Island in 1587 and had disappeared when relief at last arrived in 1590 though with indications that it had gone to an island called Croatoan, some fifty miles to the south. From about 1600 onwards Sir Walter Ralegh was sending out expeditions to look for the colony and to trade with the Indians of the region to the south of Roanoke Island for sassafras and other medicinal plants. Samuel Mace in 1602 traded in this way in the vicinity of Cape Fear and brought back a cargo to England, but does not appear to have made contact with or to have heard news of the colonists. Bartholomew Gilbert was sent out by Ralegh in 1603, but was lost on the voyage, though there may have been a further vessel under Mace employed in the venture, since some Indians were brought to London in September and about this time a ship is known to have kidnapped some Indians from the Chesapeake Bay area. This could even have been the ship with the Anglo-French crew which was recorded as active on the Florida coast in this year though we have so far no evidence which supports the connection. But in July 1603 Ralegh was arrested, lost his American commission, and was sent prisoner, convicted of treason but reprieved from execution, to the Tower of London by the end of 1603. It is possible that he had had some previous contact with La Mothe or Beavoir and helped to set them on the track of the Lost Colonists, but there is no evidence for this so far. [11] However, the story of the Lost Colonists was well known at this time in England. [12]

It is clear that the organisers had some sort of clearance from de Monts since the ships were carrying with them a printed copy (*Vn bando escrivo de molde*) of his commission of 18 December 1603 and that they had, in their own commission from Henry IV, specific authority to work along the coast as far as Cape Breton. The 'mine' which they were told to search for in the Bay of Fundy was the copper deposit at Advocate Harbour reported by Prévert in 1602, of which Champlain had been told in 1603 and which he was indeed to explore himself in 1604. [13]

(11) The rather scrappy evidence of English activity in North American waters in these years is discussed in my *England and the discovery of America* (New York and London, 1974), chapters 15 and 16, while on the Lost Colony see chapter 17.

(12) Largely through the documents in Richard HAKLUYT, *Principal navigations*, III (1600), 285, 295.

(13) The copper mine at Advocate Harbour about which Jean Sarcel, Sieur de Prévert, had learnt in 1602, to be 'par les 44 degrez & quelque minutte,' had been publicized by CHAMPLAIN in *Des sauuages* (Paris, 1603), ff. 34-5. Champlain had gone to look for it in May 1604, with somewhat inconclusive results (cp. CHAMPLAIN, *Works*, I, 180-4 and 260-4).

Whether there was any broader objective we cannot be sure, but it is not out of the question that with the extensive de Monts project under way, covering the coast from the Gulf of St Lawrence to the southern limit of the later New England, and with several English groups jostling to take up some share in the coastline, the expedition may have been intended to sketch out in some rough and ready way a division of the coastline between the zone of Spanish occupation and 40° N. so that France and England should not directly compete against each other but would agree on their respective spheres of influence. At the time when Henry IV granted the commission to La Mothe and Rocque, the prospects of Anglo-French co-operation against the Spanish Indies, on the lines of the agreement of the summer of 1603, were good : by May 1604, with the arrival of a Spanish envoy in London to prepare the way for a formal treaty of peace, they were fading. But Robert Cecil in 1603 had cautiously favoured the French approaches and could well have had the desire to map out some programme of North American acquisition in collaboration with France should the Spanish treaty break down. Both he and the lord high admiral, the earl of Nottingham, had been in contact with Ralegh's attempts to revive North American voyaging in 1602. These, however, are speculations not based on any appreciable amount of evidence. But if the two English ships, with their mixed French and English crews, were to discover lands for the French king's service on the North American coast, as their commission instructed them, then it is highly probable that there was a mutual English interest in such discoveries also, whether or not James I was aware of such an association. (14)

We have a brief outline, without dates, of the progress of the expedition in its early stages. The vessels sailed to Trinidad and at the port there had no difficulty in acquiring a reasonable amount of tobacco (150 lb., obtained for implements, shirts. linen and wine), though we do not know how successful they were in purchasing maize. From there the vessels traversed the Caribbean, but at this point intent on plunder rather than trade. They worked westwards along the mainland coast to Punta Araya, not far from Cumaná, to take salt from the pans which were frequented by the Dutch. Off the coast they attacked two caravels from which they took a quantity of flour. Then, sailing northwards to Los Jardínes. the islands off the south

(14) A discussion of English relations with Spain over access to America, 1603-9, in which an attempt is made to place the 1605 episode in perspective, appears in my paper, 'James I and the beginnings of empire in America', in *Journal of British Commonwealth History*, II (January, 1974), 135-52; see above, 321-39.

coast of Cuba, they found a large Dutch ship aground and abandoned. On board they found a cargo of wine still largely intact, of which they removed forty pipes. They then sailed to a known prize-mart off Guanahibes in Hispaniola where French, English and Dutch privateers (or pirates) exchanged their spoils, and sold the wine for cash. They then turned back to Cuba, passing Jamaica, and met two small vessels lying in close to the shore. This was off Cabo de la Cruz. One vessel, a large fishing boat (*lancha*), was run aground by her crew and abandoned. By this time the pinnace, *Pollux and Castor*, was in bad shape and it was decided to abandon her and take over the fishing boat instead. Captain Jerome transferred into her along with his pilot so that she could be used for reconnaissance work once the tip of Florida had been rounded, and also, as she was a Spanish vessel, because she might well attract less attention from Spaniards and their Indian associates on shore. The other small vessel had yielded a few hides only. At length, apparently early in January 1605, the two ships entered the Florida Strait. Not long after, they were unlucky enough — as it turned out — to encounter a small ship coming from San Agustín which they robbed, but then allowed it to proceed to Havana. It was under 'the command of Gonzalo Juan, the factor of the San Agustín garrison. They stripped him of 2000 pesos in reals, a gold chain, 4 lb. of amber, and some 'appopala' wood (which has not been identified), and let him go on to Havana where he was able to inform Pedro de Valdés, the governor, of the presence of the foreign pirates, and was almost certainly responsible for the arrival of two of the three vessels which were to put an end to the expedition. ([15])

On their way up the Florida Strait a storm blew up and the two vessels were separated, but they had evidently arranged a provisional rendezvous and this did not unduly disturb them. The *Castor and Pollux* made her way along the coast fairly rapidly — though making a few contacts with the shore — until she was some eight Spanish leagues north of Santa Elena in the Bay of Shoals (Bahia de Bajos or Baxos), that is she was in the modern Saint Helena Sound, the entrance to which lies some sixteen miles to the north of that of Port Royal Sound. There her men settled down to trade with the local Coosa Indians with whom they were on good terms, to identify and dig up sassafras roots, and, no doubt, to begin, under Dr Bonnesemaines's guidance, their survey of the natural resources of the district. The smaller vessel meantime, once she had sighted land, was proceeding

(15) Ibarra in his statement on April 13 said that Pedro de Valdés had sent them because he had learnt there were enemy ships on the coast. This is also implied in the English complaint with which this paper opens.

much more slowly. Her captain and pilot were determined to use her to reconnoitre in detail the entries through the outer screen of islands along the coast so that they would know precisely where, and where not, the Spaniards were in occupation. Sailing along the outer shore of Anastasia Island, the vessel put into the inlet across which, on the mainland, San Agustín lay. This was on February 3. She began to sound the bar at the entry and then turned across the inlet towards the town itself. Captain Jerome may well have thought he would be identified as a Spanish fisherman, but his activities soon aroused suspicion amongst the garrison, which was always on the look-out for enemy vessels. When Pedro de Ibarra, the governor, was alerted, he watched the activities of the *Pollux and Castor* (for so she is likely to have been renamed), and, suspecting her to be in enemy hands, he was apprehensive in case she might be the forerunner of more serious foes. He had, moreover, not a single vessel in the harbour, the small ship plundered by Jerome in the channel being the regular advice boat on its way to Havana. Eventually, having carried his charting as far as he thought necessary, Jerome took his vessel back through the entry and made his way northwards along the coast. Ibarra at once selected eight men and put them under the command of Corporal Quadro, who could speak the Indian languages, with instructions to make their way on foot as fast as they could along the coast to alert the Indians to the presence of the vessel and to send word ahead so that information on its progress could be gathered. At Cape Tres Días the Indians were able to tell him that she had passed by and had put into the mouth of the St Johns River, where her men were trying to make friendly contacts with the Indians. There were eight men in her, they said, including one who could speak the Timucua language, and they were inquiring about the large ship with which they had lost contact. Continuing on his way a further eighteen leagues, Quadro was able to reach San Pedro, on the St Johns River, where the resident Spanish missionary, Father Francisco, and the local Indians were able to confirm and add to earlier reports on the small vessel which had now gone on to the north. The great ship was reported to have been seen very recently at Cumberland Island (known to the Spaniards as Guale), eight leagues farther on. Indian informants said that she had many guns and a crew of twenty-seven men, so that she must have made some contact with the Indians of this stretch of coast also. Later still, good news came in. The pinnace, which was trying to catch up with the great ship, had been attacked by the Indians on the shores of Cumberland Island. The local chief, who was in the pay of the Spaniards, had become suspicious as the vessel sounded and charted the bars and estuaries. He enticed her crew on shore and then subjected them and their vessel to a mass attack in the course of which two men were killed (unluckily for the expedition they were Captain Jerome and his pilot), while two more were captured. The other four had regained the vessel and eventually rejoined Captain Rocque in Saint Helena Sound with the tragic news of the death of the commander of the expedition and his pilot. Whatever Rocque's reaction to this news may have been, it did not lead him to expect any immediate danger from the Spaniards. He was well to the north of any force they could mount on land while he did not believe they had any shipping with which to pursue him effectively. So trade went on as if nothing untoward had occurred. By March 5 they had accumulated about 5415 pounds (217 arrobas) of sassafras root, a small barrel of China root, and 43 bundles of sarsaparilla (which was either one of the local smilaxes or *Smilax sarsaparilla* from the Caribbean). They had also 54 hairy skins and 40 jackets of cut leather, almost certainly taken in the West Indies. Much of their tobacco was gone, only 65 bundles being left. Clearly they had begun with some success to wean the Indians of this part of the coast from their native *Nicotiana rustica* in favour of the richer-flavoured Trinidad tobacco, *Nicotiana Tabacum*.

Whether they had brought maize to sell also we cannot tell. The plan to do so was an ingenious one. Ralph Lane had indicated that the Roanoke Island Indians during the spring of 1586 had gone short of all but their seed-corn and though storage was more general farther south, the carriage of maize on a spring trading visit may have been well judged. ([16]) Their trade goods were still in good supply for the completion of their trade at this spot and for further commerce at Croatoan, the Penobscot and the Bay of Fundy. They had 20 great copper kettles, which would provide enough neck gorgets to keep many a tribe happy, 39 iron frying pans, and 43 hatchets. The rest of their stock was made up of a varied array of weapons and tools, curved knives, butcher's knives, large knives, small knives, scissors, rasps, dagger-points, hammerheads, reaping hooks, harpoons, pikeheads and bills, as well as smaller objects. Clearly then, large-scale trade was envisaged, probably spread over many months. When the Spaniards saw this list of some 1400 objects, nearly all potentially lethal weapons in Indian hands, they must have been alarmed at the degree to which the natives peoples were being armed. But nemesis was about to descend.

(16) See D. B. QUINN, *The Roanoke Voyages, 1584-90*, I (Cambridge, 1955), 280-4 ; R. DE LAUDONNIÈRE, *L'histoire notable de la Floride* (Paris, 1586), ff. 6v-7 ; T. DE BRY, *America*, part II (Frankfurt am Main, 1591), plates 21-22 (captions by Jacques Le Moyne de Morgues).

The reports which came back from Quadro to Pedro de Ibarra increased his apprehensions about what the foreign vessels intended. He had, however, a piece of luck. The *patax, La Asunçión*, a vessel not much larger than a good-sized pinnace, put into San Agustín on February 8. The governor quickly mobilised twenty of his men and placed them and the vessel under the elderly but highly competent officer, Captain Francisco Fernández de Écija, and packed them off with arms and supplies to locate the enemy ships. They were at sea very quickly and on February 9 crossed the bar of the St Johns River to San Mateo where Father Quetana, head of the mission there, told them that the foreign pinnace, after sounding the entrance to the St Johns, had proceeded to the north, and had joined the great ship, the Indians said, in the vicinity of Santa Elena. The *Asunçión* then followed in her track until at the Indian village of Asseo on Cumberland Island Écija learnt that the pinnace had crossed the bar of Cofunufe nearby and had been attacked by the Indians under the *casique* of Guale, the captain and pilot being killed, two others taken and the four survivors, as we have seen, having made their way towards Santa Elena. Finally, the *Asunçión*, after inspecting the inlets near Santa Elena, located the ship and pinnace in the Bay of Shoals (Bahia de Baxos) some five leagues to the north, now, as we consider, Saint Helena Sound. There they learnt that the foreigners were busy collecting sassafras and China root. The *Acunçión* returned to the mouth of the St Johns from which she relayed to San Agustín the news about the location of the vessels. She reported the heavy armament of the *Castor and Pollux* to be nine guns, and asked for further instructions.

Meanwhile fortune had smiled again on Pedro Ibarra. Two well-armed vessels entered San Agustín, apparently sent as the result of the warning given to Pedro de Valdés at Havana. One was the frigate *San Josephe* and the other a smaller ship of the same type. This provided a naval force sufficient to ensure victory over the enemy, especially if he could be taken unawares. The two ships, under Lieutenant Arotre, were instructed to join Éjica at San Pedro and under his command to attack the enemy. The rendez-vous was made and the three vessels sailed to Port Royal Sound. There they learnt that the foreigners were still trading peacefully at the Bay of Shoals, to which the Spanish ships then made their way. Before disclosing his strength, Éjica sent forward a boat with a soldier and an interpreter who could speak French, to inform them of a Spanish presence and to call on them to yield themselves, since they were illegally intruding on King Philip's territory.

This demand, made on March 5, they evidently did not take seriously, rejecting it out of hand, not crediting that the Spaniards had sufficient forces available to do them any harm. Indeed they so far ignored the challenge that they went on trading, the pinnace going to the land with a number of the leading men on board. They were undeceived only when the three Spanish ships, one the *San Josephe*, a large and powerful vessel, came in sight, when the guns on the *Castor and Pollux* were hurriedly manned. Éjica decided that he had sufficient force to board at once rather than open the action with a long range gun duel. He himself positioned the *San Josephe* on one side to do so while Arotre was instructed to do the same with the smaller frigate, followed by the *Asunción*, on the other. There was a short and decisive struggle. The *Castor and Pollux* was unable to keep the Spanish ships from closing and a lucky shot set her on fire as they prepared to board. The Spaniards poured in under cover of the smoke and confusion and very rapidly dealt with such resistance as there was, killing five men in the attack and taking the rest prisoner, while the fire was extinguished with little damage being done. The pinnace had come out from shore to see what was happening and she too, and her men, were taken. In all, there were twenty-four prisoners, including Captain Rocque, Dr Bonnesemaine and the cape merchant Julien Baudoin (Bodian). Two of the *San Josephe's* men had been killed and a number of others injured.

After this striking victory on 5 March 1605, the most considerable the Spaniards had had in this region for a generation, the prizes were manned and brought southwards in triumph to San Agustín. The whole counter-operation had been very well planned and executed, though it was fortunate for the Spaniards that naval assistance arrived so opportunely. But the planned Anglo-French exploring venture was brought abruptly to an end and the many interesting consequences which could have flowed from its successful completion were frustrated.

Almost all we know of the expedition was compiled by Pedro de Ibarra and his officials during the two months which followed the Spanish victory. The ship and pinnace were inventoried and the varied mercantile cargo listed, though some objects were regarded as confidential and were reserved for transmission to Spain. Ibarra himself compiled a lengthy account of the episode, and had Captain Écija formally examined on April 12 to give him the opportunity of making the most of his part in the story of the capture. Interrogatories were compiled so as to obtain information systematically from the prisoners. The scrivener, Alonso Gracía de la Vera, was set busily to work recording the depositions (or *autos*). Ibarra had an efficient translator from the French in his service, but no one who could command sufficient English : on the other hand several of the prisoners had an adequate command of Castilian. One suspects that questions were asked of all those taken but that only partial and incomplete information was derived from the great majority of them. Finally, three of the captives were selected to make full depositions. The first, on April 13, was Bertrand Rocque ('Beltran Rogues'), acting captain of the *Castor and Pollux* after Captain Jerome had transferred to the unlucky Spanish *lancha*. Since he was, with La Mothe, the joint grantee, as well as second in command of the expedition, his information was especially valuable on the origins as well as the course of the voyage and also on the various documents captured with the ship. He had good Spanish. He was, he said, a native of Saint-Malo and a Catholic. The second was Dr Jean de Bonnesemaine (Juan de Bona Semana) whose lack of Spanish led to his being examined through the French-speaking interpreter, Pedro Chico de Haxo. He claimed to be a Frenchman, born in Burgundy (Borgona) and a Catholic, but he could well have been a Walloon in the French service, though no identification of him is so far possible. His evidence on the collecting activities of the expedition was interesting. Finally on April 14 there came Julien Baudoin ('Julian Bodian'), the cape merchant, whose Spanish was also adequate, who said he also was from Saint-Malo and was a Catholic. He too was able to add details on the activities of the ships in the course of the voyage and during the trading with the Indians in the Bay of Shoals. All three stressed that the Frenchmen taking part were Catholics and two of them tried to imply, though they did not assert it unequivocally, that the English or some of them were also, and only one (Bodian), classed them clearly as Protestants. In view of the Spanish tradition in Florida of massacring all Protestant captives on sight this emphasis is scarcely surprising.

The questions appear to have been well chosen. They were answered in most respects fully and with little hesitation, and the three depositions are, on all major issues, mutually consistent. There is room for some ambiguities of meaning, especially in the interrogation of Dr Bonnesemaine, but by and large they give us a full, though not necessarily exhaustive, account of the venture from its inception in January 1604 to March 1605.

The evidence of the prisoners and that provided by the inventory was supplemented by documentary materials taken from the ship. These were translated from French into Spanish and helped to provide some of the information on which the interrogatories were based. There was, primarily, the royal commission of 10 January 1604 which provided an outline of the ostensible objectives of the voyage and implicated the French king in its sponsorship, though it did not authorise any of the piratical activities undertaken in the Caribbean and in Florida waters. In questioning the prisoners particular attention was paid to the personality and activities of

M. de la Mothe, but beyong making it clear that he was in the French service in the ambassador's household in London, that he was employed as a translator, that he carried messages to and from Paris and was said to be in the confidence of Henry IV, nothing came to light on why he had involved himself in the venture. Further, almost nothing was elicited about the nature of the English involvement in the voyage, which remains very largely unexplained.

Closely linked with the commission was the set of instructions given to the captains by La Mothe when the ships left Plymouth on May 16. They emphasised the trading and exploratory character of the voyage and again gave no authority, implicit or explicit, for privateering or piratical activities. What they did contain was an ingenious and well-informed summary of outstanding questions on the resources of eastern North Africa which La Mothe desired to have answered, and which we have already noticed.

The question of how far these (and such supplementary information as was drawn from those who were questioned) were drawn from printed sources and how far from recent observation in North America is of some interest. Cartier's *annedda*, which they were to look for, had been known from Ramusio for more than half a century, had been in print in English since 1580 and been reprinted in 1600. ([17]) Prévert's mine had come from *Des sauuages* (1603), as we have seen : this also had *Orignac* (now *Orignal*) for the Moose (probably the basis for the *Orentes* of the documents) but only in a list, so that the description of it as a great beast presumably came from observation or from oral evidence. ([18]) Thomas Harriot's description of Sassafras and China Root had been available in his *Briefe and true report* in English since 1588 and in French and Latin since 1590. ([19]) Harriot had also described silkgrass, but as the fibre of the Yucca (*Y. filamentosa*) not the milkweed. The Milkweed (*Asclepias syriaca* or *A. incarnata*) had been drawn by John White (*circa* 1584-7), but his drawing was still unpublished and his note on it referred only to its medicinal qualities. John Gerard, in

(17) Jacques CARTIER, *A shorte and briefe narration of three nauigations to Newe Fraunce* (1580), pp. 67-8 (as *Ameda*) ; R. HAKLUYT, *Principal nauigations*, III (1600), 227, 234 (as *Ameda* or *Hanneda*), see H. P. BIGGAR, *The voyages of Jacques Cartier* (Ottawa, 1924), pp. 213, 254. The conifer concerned was identified by Jacques Rousseau ('L'anneda et l'arbre de vie,' *Memoires du Jardin Botanique de Montreal*, n° 31 (1954)) as White Spruce, *Picea Glauca*.

(18) Orignal, MOOSE *Alces americanus*, CHAMPLAIN, *Des sauuages*, f. 20v. ; *Works*, I, 146.

(19) Sassafras (1588), sig. B2-B2v (based on Monardes), China Root (1588), sig. C4-C4v ; reprinted in de BRY's *America*, pt. I (1590), in English, French, Latin and German, and also in HAKLUYT, *Principall nauigations* (1589) and *Principal nauigations*, III (1600). See QUINN, *Roanoke voyages*, I, 329, 348-9.

his *Herball* (1597), had published an engraved version of it in which he called attention both to its seed-pods, 'stuffed full of moste pure silke'; and also the fibre which produced silky strands : he called it *Wisanck*, so this was probably the source of the *Ossanc* or *Bissanque* of the documents. [20] On the question of the location of the Lost Colonists, the indication of the location to which they were bound, carved on a tree on Roanoke Island, which White saw in 1590, is spelt 'Croatoan', and on De Bry's printed version of White's map (*America*, part i (1590)), the island to which it refers, near modern Cape Hatteras, is also spelt 'Croatoan' which is very near the 'Crotuan' of the document. [21] Similarly the reference in the depositions to Virginia having been settled by Sir Walter Ralegh, could clearly have been derived from Hakluyt, since Ralegh is stressed in *Principal navigations* as the inspirer of all the voyages between 1584 and 1590. An intelligent use of printed sources could thus have lain behind the instructions given by La Mothe and the supplementary information imprinted on the minds of Captain Rocque, Dr Bonnesemaine and Julien Baudoin. Yet it is possible that some of Ralegh's friends and former associates, notably Thomas Harriot and, possibly even, John White, if he was still alive, [22] may have given some help to the organisers. There is little indication of the accumulation of new data on natural history or resources as a result of the Anglo-French voyage made to the same area in 1603. The brief list which we have of the products brought back by the Samuel Mace expedition in 1602 [23] includes 'Radix Chinae or the China Root', 'Benzoin' (perhaps *Lincera benzoin*) ; 'Cassia lignia' (possibly here *Liquidambar styraciflua*), and 'a rind of a tree more strong than any spice yet known', which could well be *Magnolia virginiana*, and might possibly link up with a product mentioned in the documents, the bark of a tree called *Tus*, for which no published analogue has been found so far, nor is it clear what the 'palo de Aloes' (Agave?) was or where it had been heard of.

(20) Milkweed, *Asclepias syriaca* or *A. incarnata*, is in GERARD, *Herball* (1597), p. 752 and for its association with John White, see : QUINN, *Roanoke voyages*, I, 444-6. HARRIOT, *A briefe and true report* (1588), sig. B1-B1v., has a silk grass which is clearly a Yucca (*Y. filamentosa*, most probably) : see QUINN, *Roanoke voyages*, I, 325-6.

(21) HAKLUYT, *Principal nauigations*, III (1600), 293 : see QUINN, *Roanoke voyages*, I, 462, II, 614.

(22) Though White may well have been alive in 1604 our last certain reference to his being in Ireland is either 1593 or 1594, probably the latter : see P. HULTON and D. B. QUINN, *The American drawings of John White*, I (London and Chapel Hill, 1964), 22-4.

(23) This would have been available to La Mothe in John BRERETON, *A briefe and true relation of the discouerie of the north part of Virginia* (London, 1602), p. 14 : see QUINN, *England and the discovery of America*, chapter 15.

There were two other documents which were also translated. The first was a printed broadsheet ('*vn baldo en letras de molde*') dated 18 December 1603, stating that by royal grant, dated November 8 previous, the Sieur de Monts had been granted authority over the lands between 40° and 46° N., and that no subjects should for ten years intrude on this area under threat of confiscation and fines. The places specified inside these limits were Cape Race, Cape Breton, the Bay of 'Conclor', Chaleur, the 'Ile Oredade', Gaspé, 'Gigique des Metanes', 'Quirino', Tadoussac, and the River of Canada (the St Lawrence). The Spaniards were clearly alarmed at the presumption of the French in warning off intruders from an expanse of the North American coast to which they regarded themselves as in some way entitled. The remaining document was something left behind from an earlier venture, being a grant of authority to the constable of Saint-Malo, the Sieur de Fougerai (Fezerai), dated 14 July 1600, to authorise the ship *Saint-Pol*, 400 tons, under Captain Billibagui, and François Angot, master, to make a voyage to the eastern Mediterranean.

It is highly probable that Pedro de Ibarra sent off word of his success as soon as he could dispense with the *San Josephe* and her consort to Pedro de Valdés at Havana, and it is possible also that he despatched some of his prisoners with them. He did not however wish to be embarrassed by having in his charge Englishmen and Frenchmen some of whom were heretics and who, together, could constitute a subversive influence. At the same time, since he had heard that technically Spain was now at peace with England as well as France, he did not feel justified in following the traditional practices of his predecessor, Pedro Menéndez de Avilés, and kill them out of hand. He retained Captain Rocque and Dr Bonnesemaine, in case their expert witness should be required in Spain at a later stage, but he distributed the remainder amongst friendly Indian tribes in the interior, from which it does not appear that any subsequently escaped. Whether they settled down with their captors or were duly sacrificed to provide them with sport or ceremony is not known.

By May 10 he was at last ready to write to the king, summarizing the events which had taken place, telling of what had been done since the ship had been captured, and assembling the *autos* and translated documents which he had had compiled. Lieutenant Juan Rodríguez was sent direct to Spain with them, and was to remain there so as to be available in case oral testimony was required of him, while Rocque and Bonnesemaine would be held in case their presence was required in Spain. He more or less repeated the contents of this despatch in a further letter to the king on May 15 which was probably sent as a duplicate by another route. ([24]) Except for the report and *autos* we have considered, these letters provide all the documentation so far found, except for a summary of events sent on November 15 following by Juan Menéndez Marqués, a veteran official of the Florida colony, to his friend Fray Miguel de Avengoza. ([25])

Ibarra was not satisfied that he had done all that he could to track down the contacts which the Anglo-French intruders had in mind. He knew something of the Roanoke voyages from his colleague Juan Menéndez Marqués but he was intrigued with the indication that survivors were still living at Crotuan, a place whose location he did not know. He therefore, in August 1605, equipped the *Asunçión* (now described as *fragata* not *patax*), putting Captain Francisco Fernández de Écija in charge of the sailors and soldiers who made up its complement of twenty-three men. These included several who were familiar with the various Indian languages to be found along the coast.

As the ship made her way northwards she picked up a Guale Indian, Filisse Corestiano (Felipe Cristiano?), who was able to reinforce the interpreters already available. Écija put in at the successive Indian settlements along the coast as he made his way to the north to make inquiries about vessels which might recently have passed that way and to see whether there was any news of activites of foreigners on the coast.

Santa Elena, on Santa Elena Bay, our Port Royal Sound, was, he estimated, at 32° N. latitude (the actual figure is 32° 13') and he reckoned to begin his search for the English settlement at the Bay of Shoals, the scene of his earlier victory, which he placed at 32° 10', that is about ten miles north of Port Royal Sound. The Indian *casique* at Santa Elena, 'Resscamasu' or 'Descamacu', told him he knew of no foreign ships in his tribal area or in that of the Cayagua immediately to the north. He went on to Oristan, which he placed at 32° 15', searching minutely the small river Rioxa, the bay of Pintia, the bar at Oristan, the bar at Ybracasen (places not yet easily identifiable). At Cayagua, indeed, he heard that there had

(24) The letters are in Archivo de Indias, Santo Domingo 224 (old numeration 54-4-9), n[os] 58-60, and were used by Mary Ross, in her pioneer article ' *The French in the Savannah, 1605*', *Georgia Historical quarterly*, VIII (1924), 167-94, to give some account of the 1605 affair, though as she considered the Baya de Baxos to be the Savannah River rather than St Helena Sound, her paper referred it to modern Georgia rather than South Carolina. Her views were accepted by P. QUATTLEBAUM, *The land called Chicora* (Gainesville, 1956), p. 82.

(25) Printed in C. M. LEWIS and A. J. LOOMIE, *The Spanish Jesuit mission in Virginia, 1570-2* (Chapel Hill, 1953), pp. 200-4. The source given, the legajo formerly numbered 54-4-9, does not now appear to contain this letter.

been some foreign vessels on the coast. Only a week before, early in August, a great ship had crossed the bar of Joye and a boat with five men on board had put in to shore. The Indians had set on them and killed two and retained the three others as prisoners. He hurried on northwards passing the river Xorton and then the River Jordan (Xordan) which he located at 33° 11' and on August 23 came in sight of Cape Román. He made contact with the *casique* of Joye who had taken the French boat and was told the French had come to trade for marten skins and to make inquiries about the interior. They were searching he said for the 'Cabo de Graçia' (which has not so far been located on contemporary maps). Écija was now in the area explored by Ayllón in the 1520's and near where his colony had perished in 1526, but it seemed that all knowledge of the district had vanished from Spanish memory. The chief told him that he believed part of the interior was occupied by white men but he could not say whether they were French or Spanish. When he was asked whether, if the river was followed, gold or silver would be found, he said that the Indians did indeed trade up-stream, exchanging fish for salt (perhaps brought across the Appalachians from Tennessee), and that there was rich copper and other things of value to be found far in the interior. There was a village (*pueblo*) there, near a high mountain, where the Indians had many beans and chestnuts. The current was strong and Écija could not easily enter the river : in any event the chief had nothing relevant to his mission to report.

Écija's search had been detailed and protracted, and it was now September 4, so that hurricanes along the coast might be expected at any time. He therefore decided to turn back, leaving the Lost Colonists, if they were indeed at Croatoan (which appears, at this time, unlikely), undisturbed. He reached San Agustín on September 21.

He was not entirely empty-handed. He had picked up two of the French prisoners taken at Joye, probably from the chief of the Cayagua tribe, and he had an Indian (Panço) from this area also and another from Santa Elena, a Christian convert named Alonso. At San Agustín the usual formal inquiries were held. The Indians were diffuse and unspecific in their references to the interior and the coast to the north of the places where they lived. There were vague tales of a rich and fertile interior. When they were asked specifically if they knew of any Europeans, 'people like us', they knew nothing of any such persons living to the north along the coast, indicating they had never heard of the Lost Colonists. They had, indeed, heard of a strange people in the interior, in the province of Tahamua, who were white like Spaniards, but there were many hostile Indians on the way, and none of the coastal peoples had ever been there. So much for Indian geographical information in this case.

One of the French prisoners gave some more tangible information on his immediate background. He was Guillaume de Nau (Guillermo de Nao), of Le Havre, who had sailed on a ship belonging to that port, commanded by Captain Basanil le Sueur (Baxanyl le Suer), who had a commission from M. de Villars, governor of Le Havre (and also admiral of France). They had brought axes, hatchets, knives and implements to sell to the Indians. They had traded in the Caribbean at Dominica, probably with the Caribs there, and had then come north along the Florida coast. So far their expedition had followed much the same sequence as had the *Castor and Pollux*. They put in at latitude 32° N. for water, but a storm had blown up suddenly, their ship had put to sea without them, and the Indians had attacked them, killed two and taken three as already related. He had no knowledge of any settlements, English or French, to the north on the coast where he had been captured. He had however met an Indian chief at Le Havre who was said to have been brought from latitude 40° N. on the coast, and he had seen things brought from that part of America and understood the French were making settlements nearby, though this was only a garbled account of what de Monts and Champlain had been doing rather farther north than 40° in 1604.

Honour was now satisfied. Ibarra could report, with the documents collected embodying Écija's report and the *autos* accompanying it, which showed that every effort had been made to find the English settlement at 'Crotuan' but without success : it appeared, if it existed at all, to offer no immediate threat to Spanish Florida. He thought that, the following season, in May 1606, a further expedition might be sent to the coast rather farther to the north, ([26]) but no such investigation appears to have been considered necessary.

The depositions so carefully garnered on the victory of the Bahía de Bajos were turned over for diplomatic use in Paris so that Henry IV could be reminded of his illegal actions in commissioning vessels to intrude into territory which was clearly that of Spain, but we do not know what reaction was made by the French court to any protests that were delivered : Spain was, in any event, late in 1605 being served only by a *chargé d'affaires* in Paris, her ambassador having been transferred to London and not yet

(26) The report and autos are in A.G.I., Patronato 1-1-1/19, ramo 29. They were located and kindly put at my disposal by Mr. P. L. Barbour.

replaced. But the affair leaked out in England in the spring of 1606. We do not know precisely how this had happened. Pierre Beauvoir had become a founder member of the Spanish Company at the time of the issue of its charter on 31 May 1605 [27] and it may have been through his mercantile contacts in Spain that he got to hear of it. It could possibly have been reported by either the English ambassador in France, Sir George Carew, if it had been brought to Henry IV's attention, or through Sir Charles Cornwallis, the new English ambassador in Spain, who had recently begun recruiting informants on the fringes of the Court. There is a distinct possibility that it was deliberately allowed by the duke of Lerma to reach English ears in order to impress on King James the salutary treatment by Spain of intruders on her American territory in North America.

When the marquis de San Germano reached England in April 1606 on a special diplomatic mission he was surprised to be confronted by a demand from several members of the Privy Council to explain the actions taken against Englismen peacefully trading on a part of the North American coast which was not in the actual possession of Spain : it is clear he knew nothing about the matter. But it seems that Robert Cecil (now earl of Salisbury) wrote to Sir Charles Cornwallis in Spain to investigate the case of the *Castor and Pollux*. Beauvoir too was soon active : he knew and wrote to Sir Thomas Edmondes, the English ambassador at Brussels about it ; Sir Thomas wrote to Cornwallis in June saying that the English Privy Council had already made representations in Spain but he had heard of no result. The case as passed to him by Beauvoir was very much in the terms of the complaint quoted at the opening of the paper : the *Castor and Pollux* was, 'bound for trade and merchandise to ye Coaste of Virginia & Norambergh' and was seized by Spanish ships in 'the river of Helena', in spite of the fact that her men 'went not to make theire trade in those partes where the king of Spaine possesseth any thinge, but in those partes which euer beene reputed Common & free for all Nacions to resorte vnto'. [28] Cornwallis, on receiving this letter, wrote a hasty note to Edmondes in reply, saying that

(27) Pauline Croft, ed., *The Spanish Company* (London Record Society Publications n° 9, 1973), p. 97. Abraham Beauvoir of Guernsey, most probably a relative, was admitted on 18 September 1605.

(28) Edmondes to Cornwallis, June 12/22, British Library, Cotton MS, Vespasian C.IX, ff. 448-9 (and for a somewhat corrupt version Sir Ralph Winwood, *Memorials*, ed. E. Sawyer, II (1725), 234). Edmondes mentions the confrontation of the marquis de San Germano by the Privy Council on this issue. For San German's reactions to his reception in England see Antonio Rodríguez Villa, *Correspondence de ... Dôna Isabel Clara Eugenia* (1906), p. 148.

he could do nothing about the matter as he was out of favour at court, possibly for already raising the case ('For my leaues are blasted, howsoeuer my Coate must for a tyme endure'). ([29]) He was still actively concerned in the matter in September when he wrote to Salisbury :

For the shippe called the Castor and Pollux and I am yett doubtfull in what sorte to frame my suite, neither haue I Cause to Conceaue muche hope of ob- teyninge it, theyr Iealousie of their Indyes being such and soe extreame as they resolue to make it Cappitall, to all such as shall haue or fall into theire handes there. ([30])

The Spaniards here had the whip hand. The English might claim to have the right to trade with and settle in parts of North America not actually oc- cupied by the Spaniards. They, in turn, could claim that not only had they had control of the Bay of Shoals in the past when they had a fort at Santa Elena, but they had the power to enforce their claim to exclusive occupation well beyond their continuing settlements. It was this authority that they wished to assert over the whole of the east coast of North America, and the episode was evidence that they meant to attempt to do so. On the other hand their complete ignorance, by this time, of the coast north of Cape Román, left the English in fact free to insert themselves there with little direct danger from Spain unless she wished to go to war with England. Thus the Virginia Company, whose charter was granted on 10 April 1606, was able, though not without further threats from Spain, to establish its colony safely in Jamestown in 1607.

The last word we hear of the case of the *Castor and Pollux* is in still another catalogue of English complaints against Spain for actions taken against English ships, dated between 1610 and 1613 : ([31])

A ship called the Castor and Pollax was taken by the Spaniards vpon the Coast of Florida which they confiscated and executed all the men in her, or kept them slaues for that we could neuer vnderstand what became of them since their takinge this ship with her merchandise worth - 15000[li] -0[s] -0[d].

It does not appear likely that any of her crew got back to England from their exile amongst the Indians or even that Captain Rocque or Dr Bonnesemaine were ever repatriated. It may be that the Archivo de Indias, when more

(29) Cornwallis to Edmondes, July 8/18, B.L., Cotton MS, Vespasian C. IX, ff. 453-4 (WINWOOD, *Memorials* II, 235).

(30) Cornwallis to Salisbury, September 6/16, B.L., Cotton MS, Vespasian C. IX, f. 528.

(31) Henry E. Huntington Library, San Marino, California, Huntington MS 1242.

thoroughly searched, may provide us with some further clues. Yet the Spanish sources, thinly helped out by information in England, give us more about this episode than about many comparable ones, and throw a bright though flickering light on relations between Englishmen, Frenchman and Spaniards only a very few years before the foundation of Jamestown and Québec when French and English alike began to plant permanent roots in the continent which Spain still hoped, after 1600, to reserve for herself.

It would be reasonable to expect some overlap between the organisers of the Anglo-French expedition of 1604-5 and those English groups who had carried on the detailed study of the natural history of south-eastern North America after the pioneer work of Jean and Jacques Ribault and René de Laudonnière (and indeed Cartier), and so to fit the voyage into the pattern of the growing accumulation of knowledge and practical experience which led at length to English settlement in Virginia. But with Ralegh in prison and probably unable to exercise any appreciable influence on external events at this time, and without clear evidence of links between Beauvoir or La Mothe with Richard Hakluyt, Thomas Harriot, Edward Hayes or Samuel Mace, all four of whom were active in 1602 and 1603 (if not certainly in 1604) in North American affairs, it seems unwise to make too confident claims for such an association, especially since so much of the briefing of which we are aware could have been drawn from sources already in print. At the same time, Beauvoir had connections in official circles, so that some official encouragement on the English side for the launching of the venture cannot be ruled out, even if, on present information, it cannot be established. And so too there may be some common inspiration amongst the unofficial enthusiasts for America which spanned the gap between the Roanoke voyages, the tentative experiments from 1602 onwards, the French interests inspired by Champlain's voyage in 1603 and those who eventually organised the Virginia Company on the English side and the settlement of the St. Lawrence valley on the French. The co-operation of English and French in the venture of 1604-5 strongly suggests that at this time their common interests were more significant than their differences.

21

THE VOYAGE OF *TRIALL*, 1606-1607:
AN ABORTIVE VIRGINIA VENTURE

AFTER George Waymouth came back from his voyage to Maine in 1605 he found Lord Arundell had given up his project for sending an aristocratic Catholic colony to North Virginia and had taken himself off to the Spanish Netherlands in command of an English regiment: a scheme for the recruitment for the American colony of several thousand English ex-soldiers from the Spanish armies had also been abandoned. Waymouth was left only with the backing of the Plymouth merchants for a fishing voyage in 1606. However, Sir John Zouche, the head of a collateral branch of the family of which Edward, Lord Zouche was the head (who may well himself have been an earlier backer of Waymouth's), came into the picture and undertook to lead a colonizing party to Maine in 1606 in close association with the Plymouth venture and under the command of Waymouth.[1] It was to mobilize support for this joint venture that James Rosier's well-known pamphlet,[2] which appeared towards the end of 1605 or possibly as late as January 1606, was designed. It gave an attractive, if somewhat exaggerated, picture of Maine as partly explored by Waymouth in 1605. It is probable that this pamphlet was the origin of the interest of a group of London fish merchants—members of the Fishmongers Company—in the North Virginia coast. Then too contacts—we do not know by whom—were made with Sir Ralph Bingley in Ireland. Bingley had commanded the royal guardship, *Tramontana,* on the south coast of Ireland[3] and was in 1606 closely associated with the lord deputy and other high officials. It seems that he may have been brought in partly be-

[1] 30 October 1605. Manchester Papers, P.R.O. Formerly in the Public Record Office, London; printed in Alexander Brown, *The Genesis of the United States* (2 vols. 1890), I, 32-35. See *The American Papers of Sir Nathaniel Rich, Property of his Grace the Tenth Duke of Manchester* (Parke-Bernet Galleries Sale, 5 May 1970), p. 80, now in the Alderman Library, Charlottesville, VA.

[2] John Brereton, *A briefe and true relation of the discoverie of the north part of Virginia* (London, 1602).

[3] See Public Record Office, High Court of Admiralty, H.C.A. 1/46, ff. 51^r-51^v (30 May 1603).

cause it was proposed to recruit some Irish Catholics for the venture in lieu of those English Catholics whom Lord Arundell was to have led to his proposed American seignory. If we are right in associating Zouche in some loose manner with the Fishmongers and Bingley we have here a grouping which was distinct from that which obtained the Virginia Company charter from the king in April 1606. That grouping represented a broad concentration of City and Court interests in London and merchant and landowner interests in the Southwest, especially in Devonshire. The main architects of it were Sir John Popham, Lord Salisbury, and Sir Thomas Smith, with Popham being the main influence in bringing the London and Southwestern interests into close association, though the device of associating two semi-autonomous syndicates, the one directed from London to South Virginia and the other from Plymouth to North Virginia, with a royal council separate from the Company to direct them both, was probably concocted by Salisbury and Sir Walter Cope. It is generally assumed that the charter of 10 April 1606 was an exclusive one, since it authorized the grantees to exclude competitors from the territories they occupied, but this was not so, since the London Fishmongers, the Irish venturers, Lord Zouche's men, and assorted English participants, in close association or otherwise, operated in 1606-1607 quite independently of the company and were able to obtain passports for the setting out of their expeditions from the Lord Admiral, the Earl of Nottingham. That they did not in effect constitute a threat to the monopoly of the chartered company was because they failed to get any ships to Virginia in 1606 or 1607 and their ventures faded away in controversy and litigation. A good deal is still unknown about their precise plans and backing. Because they played in fact no direct part in the exploitation of American lands, they are not of great significance in the story of the beginnings of English colonization, but what is known of their progress and failure helps to underline the careful, systematic and on the whole effective operations of the Virginia Company of London and even those of the less successful Virginia Company of Plymouth.

We might suppose that originally Waymouth had been intended as the leader of the northern ventures of 1606, but the Plymouth merchants, his original backers, cut loose and he may have felt too obligated to Zouche to follow them. Zouche, if we read the signs aright, substituted a London syndicate, composed of merchants interested in London in the fishing off the New England coasts as recently demonstrated by Waymouth, for the Plymouth grouping. Negotiations for the Virginia linkup of Plymouth with other London and Court interests may have gone so far by March 1606 that Waymouth did not feel ready to transfer to the rival London grouping. He therefore fades out of the American project altogether. It was presumably at this point that contacts were made with Bingley and plans were made to concentrate some ships in Ireland and, most probably, add some Irish Catholics to the venture, though here again there is a considerable element of conjecture involved. There had been a number of suggestions for bringing Irishmen, soldiers left over from the Nine Years' War, to America. These were renewed during 1606-1607.[4] The assumption rests on Bingley's association with the London venture, and the concentration of shipping originally intended for Virginia at Dublin, which make likely Irish participation in a colonizing plan.

On 10 March 1606 an agreement was reached for the hire of the ship *Triall* of London of 160 tons' burden to go to Virginia. The charter was for nine months, to end on 9 December 1606 and the rate £30 a month (making a total of £270). The ship was owned jointly by Lewes Owen, William Lancaster, William Angell and John Halsey, who were described as citizens and fishmongers of London.[5] The registers of the Fishmongers Company of London begin only in 1600 and only a small number of those actually members before 1600 can be named.[6] William Angell was certainly one of the latter and so was John Halsey, while the 'Lancaster' without a Christian name known to have been a member was probably William. A Lewes Owen who was probably a son of the Lewes Owen here named was admitted as an apprentice in 1615. William Lancaster was probably an uncle of the famous navigator who was the leading commander in the service of the East India Company. William Angell[7] was a member of a family extensively engaged in trading and shipowning both at London and Bristol and was especially involved in trade in fish. One of his ships had been captured by the Spaniards after King James had

---

[4] D. B. Quinn, *The Elizabethans and the Irish* (1965), pp. 119-20.

[5] Public Record Office, London, High Court of Admiralty, interrogatories on behalf of Lewis Owen [etc.], [September 1607], H.C.A. 24/72, 97; examination of Roger Bamford, 3 September 1607. H.C.A. 13/39. Between them, these documents contain the major part of our information on the case. The Bamford deposition was known to J. F. Jameson ('Notes from the English Admiralty Papers,' American Antiquarian Society, *Proceedings*, new series, xviii (1907), 275-76) but he did not appreciate its significance, thinking it to be linked with the Sagadahoc expedition, 1607. Dr. David Ransome included several documents in Virginia Record Survey Report 3,922 (copies in Research Department, Colonial Williamsburg and Swem Library, College of William and Mary).

[6] W. P. Haskett-Smith, *The Worshipful Company of Fishmongers of the City of London. Lists of Apprentices and Freemen* (London, privately printed, 1916), pp. 6, 8, 9, 23, 28, 32.

[7] On William Angell see Sir Ralph Winwood, *Memorials* (2 vols., London, 1729), II, 225; Public Record Office, State Papers, Foreign, Spain, S. P. 94/13, part ii, folio 89; H.C.A. 13/164 (personal answer of William Woder and Robert Angell); H.C.A. 24/73, part ii, folios 13-15 (charter party of *Margaret*, 1609); *Calendar of State Papers Colonial, East Indies, China, and Japan, 1513-1616* (London, 1860), 240. For a John Halsey, quite possibly the same man, see Alexander Brown, *The Genesis of the United States* (2 vols., Boston, 1890), II, 919.

come to the throne in 1603 (she was possibly engaged in trade or privateering in the West Indies). In 1607 a ship belonging to the family firm was at Newfoundland fishing and William Angell was on board her. In 1612 he appears as a member of the Northwest Passage Company. It is clear therefore that he had some substantial overseas interests. Less is known of the two others. It is highly probable that all four not only hired their ship for a Virginia voyage, but themselves invested in the venture also, though the full extent of their commitment has not been ascertained. The charterers were Arthur Kennithorpe, also a member of the Fishmongers Company, and Arthur and George Chambers. We know little about them or who they represented. Arthur Chambers, however, was to be master of the ship and he had had previous experience at sea,[8] though he had not won a good reputation. In 1604 he had been amongst a number of men tried in connection with a piratical attack on a French ship, had been convicted but had been pardoned. The employment of such a man as master, even though he was to be watched and supervised to some extent by Roger Bamford who as purser was to represent the owners and particularly his own employer, William Angell, was a fatal mistake. To Chambers more than to any other the failure of the expedition was due, even though it is necessary to point out that most of what we know of his actions arises in proceedings in the High Court of Admiralty against him after the expedition had failed, and is therefore by no means unbiased.

The ship was heavily armed; she was a fast vessel of a Dutch type (being described in one place as a flyboat). Her victualling was apparently for the nine months of the charter period. She is not known to have carried trade goods though she may have done so, but she had a substantial quantity of salt. There is no indication that there were colonists on board. Her captain may not have been chosen at the time the charter was made. It has been surmised that perhaps George Waymouth was originally intended to command her. The captain finally chosen for her was Sir Ralph Bingley.[9] He had served as a soldier in Ireland during the Nine Years' War before commanding *Tramontana* on the Irish coast. He had been rewarded with a grant of confiscated land and was made a member of the privy council in Ireland. The arrangement was, apparently, that Chambers would take *Triall* round to Dublin and that Bingley should join her as captain there. On 28 May following a passport was duly issued[10] by the

---

[8] Indictment of Thomas Price and others (including Arthur Chambers) for piracy against *Esperaunce* of La Rochelle, H.C.A. 1/5,40; petition for pardon for Arthur Chambers, H.C.A. 1/5,60.

[9] See note 3 and *Calendar of State Papers, Ireland, 1603; 1603-1606; 1606-1608, passim.*

[10] Draft passport for Bingley, as captain, and Chambers, as master, of *Triall*, 28 May 1606, H.C.A. 14/38,6.

Earl of Nottingham, Lord High Admiral, to Sir Ralph Bingley as captain and Arthur Chambers as master of *Triall* (though on the *recto* of the surviving draft—the *verso* is correct—the name is given as Sir Richard Bingley, apparently a confusion with the Richard Bingley, probably his brother, who had served as his lieutenant on *Tramontana* in 1604). We have in this document the objective of the voyage as being *pro navali expeditione ad partes Virginia pro novo commertio deligendo,* 'assigned for an expedition by sea for new trade with Virginia,' a sufficiently vague description. It does suggest very strongly a North Virginia rather than a South Virginia destination.

We know in very considerable detail the early course of *Triall*'s voyage.[11] It has not in itself any value for the early history of American colonization except as an example of what a bad commander could do to wreck an overseas venture. At the end of May 1606 *Triall* was fitted out in the Thames and was ready about 1 June to move down the river to Woolwich on the first stage of her journey to Weymouth, her first port of call. It is possible that this intermediate stop indicates that Weymouth fishing interests were also concerned in the venture, though there is no indication of this in the surviving town records. Chambers was not on the alert at the beginning of June when winds were favorable for getting out of the Thames. He took *Triall* down to Gravesend only, and then went ashore for three days. After he returned, winds had turned unfavorable and the first of a long series of delays took place. The weather in June was bad enough to win a place in the chronicles:[12] on 8 June there were heavy rains and tidal waves. Eventually *Triall* got out of the Thames and rounded the Kent coast into the English Channel. As so often happened there was further delay, waiting for favorable down-Channel winds, and the ship anchored in the Downs, in Dover roadstead. We learn from the purser that Chambers was soon ashore again, pilfering, it was alleged, two coils of new rope and a bolt of canvas, together worth £4 or £5, 'to maintaine his vaine & lavish expenses on shore.' Moreover, he gave at least one lavish party on board ship. Chambers

invitted many of the towne [Dover] on board to drincke & make merry, and the mariners takinge example by the Masters prodigality and seeing his slender government invited likewise many of their mates & acquaintances and made them drinck so liberally that there was draw[n] out above a hogshead of stronge beere at that time as the Stewarde affirmed & this examinate [Roger Bamford] beleveth yt was not lesse, for theere were upwardes of xxx guestes on borde besides the ships company who dranck so many healthes that many of them were drunk and in the

---

11 From the examination of Roger Bamford see note 5 above.
12 John Stow, *The Abridgement of the English Chronicle* (London, 1611), p. 462.

feasting & quaffing of healthes there was shott off by the Masters commaundemente elleven peeces of ordinance of this examinates certaine knowledge then beinge presente.

Nor did this end the festivities. On the next day, Monday, 'there came on borde thre maide servantes as yt seemed by theire habett, whom the said Master interteyned & at his goinge on shore with them he would have a piece [gun] geven him which was donn, & dischardging the peece, yt brake & tore downe the deck where yt stode . . . to the grate hurte of the shipp & dammadge of the owners.'

After five weeks *Triall* got to Weymouth, which would bring her there about the end of the first week of July. At Weymouth Chambers again went on shore. This time, Bamford said, he made off with the ship's lading in a wholesale fashion, taking away sixteen barrels of salt, belonging to the owners (which indicated they had victualled the ship and supplied it with the means of engaging in fishing and so were not the charterers only). This time, Bamford claimed that he tried to intervene on behalf of the owners. 'He reproved the said Arthur Chambers the Master for makinge such spoile of the owners goodes, and he answered that this examinate had nothinge to doe with the shipp nor ought to her belonging, and that he avouched with a grevous oathe For he sayd he and his frendes were bounde [i.e. had signed bonds] for the shippe and he would be sole commander in her both of men and goodes, and therefore [warned] this examinate not to interupte him in eany thinge he did, for yf he [did] he would unship hym.' Bamford took the position that he would submit to Chambers, but only in order to be available to look after the owners' interests in a passive manner—though we may wonder why he did not communicate with them from Weymouth and try to get *Triall* held up and taken out of Chambers' hands. Eventually *Triall* left Weymouth and worked her way into the Irish Sea, where she may have lain for a short time in Drogheda Bay before she cast anchor at Clontarf in Dublin Bay ('Glamtath in Dublin Water').

The scene shifts to Beaumaris, a small port in Anglesey, from which there was much shipping to Ireland. A small pinnace was lying there.[18] She was a London ship, bought from William Banning, possibly one of the London Baynings, for a tobacco voyage to the West Indies, by Rowland Buckley, a young gentleman aged twenty-three of Beaumaris. He had brought her round to buy ironware at Chester Fair 'to cary for the Indies.' Sir Ralph Bingley appeared at the port with a number of men and arranged that Buckley should carry them to Dublin for the sum of

18 Examination of Rowland Buckley, 7 April 1607, H.C.A. 1/46.

£18. We cannot tell whether Bingley had been belatedly in London receiving instructions from the London syndicate on their and his part in the proposed Virginia expedition or whether he had been to his own home in Flintshire where, amongst other things, he may have collected some recruits for his venture. On his way to Dublin Bingley proposed to Buckley that he, his pinnace and his five-man crew should join in his, Bingley's, venture.

Bingley told Buckley 'that he was bound for Virginia & had his shipping in Ireland appointed for that viadge & soe persuaded this examinate [Buckley] & his men that they consented to go with them.' When they arrived in Ireland, according to Buckley: 'there were thre ships in the bay of Tredath [Drogheda Bay], called the Dragon of London sometime the Bevis of Southampton belonging to Sir John Ferne knighte, the Triall of London belonginge to master Angell & others & the Greyhound of Bridgwater apperteyninge to Sir Henry Thyn which were appointed to goe for Virginia under the commaund of the saide Raffe Bingley as yt was given out.' This is the fullest indication of the range of English backing for the expedition that we have,[14] but it does not provide much indication of its nature and significance. Nor is it at any point made clear what backing there was for the venture in Ireland itself, and how far it represented an attempt to pave the way for a Catholic Irish colony in North Virginia. We have, however, a considerable range of interests concerned to act in some way independently of the Virginia Company, though it is not yet clear precisely how they were made up.

Buckley may not have been very accurate in his dating. He claims that he was hired 'at midsomer.' Technically this would be 22 June, but we might regard late June as being accurate enough. He states however that *Triall* was already in Irish waters when he arrived there himself. This is most unlikely. She cannot have left Weymouth before 8 July at earliest or have got to Ireland before the latter part of the second week of July. Discrepancies such as this make it necessary to be cautious about what happened next. It is clear, however, that Bingley's return precipitated a crisis. His associates may have agreed in principle that they would take part in a Virginia expedition in which *Triall* was to play a part. It may have been that the expected support in Ireland from a group of would-be

---

14 Sir John Ferne of St. Gabriel Fenchurch, London, was in 1609 in trouble for illegally exporting ordnance (H.M.C., *Cecil MSS.*, XXI, 88). Sir Henry Thynne was himself knighted only this summer, on 23 July 1606 (Shaw, *Knights*, II, 122), the honor conceivably having some connection with his Virginia involvement. He was the second son of the second marriage of Sir John Thynne the elder, of Longleat, Wiltshire (died 1580), and was later established at Kingwood in the same county (Beriah Botfield, *Stemmata Botevilliana* (London, 1858), pp. clxxviii-clxxix). The maritime interests of these men would repay investigation, Thynne being commissioned in 1612 to command an expedition to Persia (H.M.C., *Cecil MSS.*, XXI, 359).

Irish Catholic colonists did not eventuate. More probably it may seem that some of the English backers had gone into the venture from the first as a cover for the preparation of a piratical expedition against Spain, either in European waters or in the West Indies. The next we know, indeed, is that Bingley's associates largely deserted him. Buckley says that this happened 'within four days' of his coming to Ireland, but it is more probable that it took place about the middle of July. The story is confused and difficult to establish. According to Buckley it was Bingley who changed his mind about the purpose of the expedition: that he decided to go instead to north Russia and raid St. Nicholas (on the advice of a Captain Boorde), and that this precipitated the breakup of the squadron originally intended for Virginia, *Greyhound* returning to England (which meant that Sir Henry Thynne broke off his connections with the venture) and *Dragon* setting sail for the Straits. The latter destination, the Straits of Gibraltar, strongly indicates that *Dragon* was bound for a piratical cruise in the Mediterranean where a considerable number of ships were so engaged against the Venetians and other Italian city merchant fleets. But there is no real evidence that Bingley intended to divert *Triall* to some such venture and it is probable that the Virginia venture was not given over by him for some time further.

The precise sequence thereafter is not fully evident from our sources. Buckley says *Triall* was brought to Clontarf to be 'trimmed,' that is made ready for sea, by Bingley after having been for a time in Drogheda Bay, and implies that this was under duress of some sort. Similarly, he says that his own pinnace was forcibly brought under Bingley's orders to Clontarf and later to a creek at Bullick (Bullock Harbor, Dalkey, Co. Dublin) 'to be trimmed and kept there.' We have next an account by Roger Bamford[15] of a quarrel between Chambers and himself at Clontarf:

the said Arthur Chambers gave occasion of difference by reason he would be sole Captain and Commander of the shipp, and he came to this examinate and willed him to be silente and not to meddle with eany things he did, and sayd this examinate should not have eany thinge to do with eany thing in the shippe, and this examinate answered he would have as much to doe & command in his place beinge purser and with that belonged unto him as he should in his place, And yf he the said Master had don that which belonged unto him and as he oughte to have don, he mighte have had more to doe then this examinate where uppon the said Chambers would have sente one William Crowe to Sir Raph Bingley to sertify him that this examinate denied Sir Raphe his authority in the shippe, but the said Crowe refused to goe knowinge the messadge was ridiculous & false, yet sente he others, & affirmed him self to Sir Raph that if he had not byn carefull to prevent yt with his diligent

15 Examination of Roger Bamford, 3 September 1607 (see note 5 above); examination of Rowland Buckley, 7 April 1607 (see note 13 above).

watchfulness over this examinate, this examinate would have ron away with the ship before Sir Raphes arrivall in Ireland.

It is not possible, of course, to check anything in these allegations in detail, but Buckley, on the chronology of her voyage from London which Bamford gives, would make Bingley arrive in Ireland before *Triall* could have reached there.

We then run into some further chronological difficulties. Buckley alleges that when both vessels, *Triall* and his own pinnace were being 'trimmed'—'the purser of *Triall* being Master Angell his man made a petition to the Lord Deputy of Ireland [Sir Arthur Chichester] complayninge that the tyme was expired for the which Sir Raffe had hired the said shippe and that yt was not his masters intention the shipp should be imployed further & desired that the shipp mighte be stayed and Sir Raffe Bongley not to be suffered to proceed to sea therein.' He then alleged that Bingley responded by threatening Bamford and said 'he would hange him for yt,' and said that Bamford was then kept prisoner on *Triall* and not allowed to go ashore. Bamford himself makes no such allegation of any such happenings at this stage. While it is clear that the charter had not expired as it was only late August or early September when *Triall* finally left Dublin Buckley is, in fact, anticipating events which occurred later. Clearly Bamford got information on the breakup of the expedition to Angell and the other owners about the end of October or the beginning of November. The result was that on 3 November; the owners were able to get the Lord Admiral to issue a warrant for the arrest of *Triall* and the bringing of Sir Ralph Bingley and Arthur Chambers to London to answer charges made by the four owners of *Triall*. To bring suit in the High Court of Admiralty in this way was one thing, to get such orders executed was another. The writ of the Lord Admiral did not run in Ireland and he could get compliance with his orders only by the consent of the Lord Deputy, Sir Arthur Chichester, and this was not easily or quickly done.

Whatever the relations of Sir John Zouche's venture were with that of *Triall* the two seem to have proceeded without much contact for some time at least. Zouche's agreement with Waymouth on 30 October 1605 had specified that he would contribute two ships and two hundred men 'before the last daie of Aprill nexte cominge' to the intended joint expedition with the Plymouth men. This, however, we must regard as having become abortive on the bringing of the westerners into the Virginia Company in April. He had intended to go ahead on his own account and it was possible as early as April when, with two ships and a pinnace ready, he approached the Lord High Admiral, the Earl of Nottingham, for a passport.[16] He met with unexpected delays and a rebuff. This was not simply because the Virginia Company charter stood in the way of further Virginia enterprises prepared before it was issued, for, as we have seen, Bingley and Chambers had received a passport on 28 May for a similar ostensible purpose. Nottingham admitted later that the delay was due to 'some private reasons knowne to myselfe,' though we do not know precisely what they were. Later, some months later, he stated that he was subjected to considerable pressure to release Zouche on his voyage, saying 'I have been much laboured to geve Sir John Zouche leave to passe away with his shippes in his intended voyage for Virginea.' It is possible that this was in connection with a further plan to send English Catholics to Virginia. William Udall reported to Lord Salisbury on 16 June 1606[17] that there was a plan on foot to petition King James for a royal license to permit 'thre hundred Catholic Housholds at theyre owne cost & Charges, to depart this land to inhabit Virginia to hold such part as shalbe allotted to them, for his Majesty and his Successors.' He was able to follow this up on 28 June by reporting[18] that John Digby, then a young man holding a position in the royal household, had agreed to present the petition to the King. The diplomacy behind these activities is not intelligible, but we may venture a few assumptions. Both Salisbury and Nottingham represented the old guard of statesmen, left over from the Elizabethan regime. Their basic suspicions of Catholics and of international Catholicism went deep and they were unlikely to look with favor at what might appear as a concession to them at this time. The Gunpowder Plot of November 1605 had revived old antagonisms and suspicions. James, who had favored Catholics before the plot, turned savagely against them afterwards, but he blew hot and cold repeatedly in the years which followed. We can at least say that where the possible emigration of Catholics on favorable terms was possible, from an English aspect, before November 1605, thereafter it was tied up with many currents and crosscurrents of feeling and policy. It seems likely that pressure was being exerted on officials both for and against this project.

It is not unlikely that Nottingham was thus subject to such influences in regard to the passport. He was, however, also influenced against granting it by other factors. He considered that Zouche might very well become

16 James Franklin Jameson printed Nottingham's letter of 13 August, from which most of our information is derived, and also the bond and obligation (from High Court of Admiralty, Miscellanea, Bundle 1140) in *The Virginia Magazine of History and Biography*, XIX (1911), 195-96; drafts of the bond and obligation being also in H.C.A. 14/39, 239.

17 Cecil Manuscripts, Hatfield House, 192/96 (Historical Manuscripts Commission, *Cecil Manuscripts*, XVIII, 173).

18 Cecil Manuscripts 115/123 (H.M.C., *Cecil MSS.*, XVIII, 181-82).

embroiled with Spanish or other European ships at sea—as indeed Bingley and Chambers were, deliberately, to do. Consequently, he insisted that bonds should be entered into 'that Sir John Zouch shall not in the whole discourse of his voiage comitt any act either prejudical to the State of England or dishonorable to the peace and amitie which his Majestie hath now with forrain Princes.' This clearly put Sir John Zouche in a difficulty. Finally, though perhaps only after some further delay, he persuaded Edward, Lord Zouche, an elderly and respected peer, to act as his guarantor. He was the head of the main branch of the family, but only a very distant connection of Sir John's. The bond agreed was for £1000. That being arranged, Nottingham wrote to the Judge of the High Court of Admiralty, Sir Thomas Crompton, on 13 August 1606, authorizing him to issue a passport to Sir John Zouche. The bond and passport were completed and issued the following day, 14 August. The passport, recited in the obligation attached to the bond, stated that 'Sir John Zouche knight is licensed to passe uppon an intended voyadge for Virginea with two shippes and a Pinnace and their Captaynes, Masters and Companyes.' After so much, we cannot tell whether the ships ever put to sea. If they had been waiting since April for their release it is likely that their stores were badly depleted by mid-August and Zouche may not have had the ready cash to replace them. It would also be late in the year for a voyage direct to New England. At this time only a long haul by way of the West Indies would be possible; such a voyage in fact Henry Challons began in *Richard* on behalf of the Plymouth syndicate in the Virginia Company in the same month. If our assumption that Zouche may have been acting in association with Bingley and *Triall* is correct, it would seem likely that Zouche knew enough of the progress of that venture to realize that it was still held up in Ireland. Consequently, he may have made some attempt to join Bingley there and have been frustrated either by maritime mishaps or by the news that the venture there had begun to split up and was no longer viable as an American one. In that case, we may suggest that Zouche disbanded his ships in September or October. If they made an attempt at a direct crossing we have no news of it whatever. But on our present information the assumption that Zouche was tied up with Bingley and Chambers is wholly without direct evidence to support it.

Sometime later, probably early in November, *Triall* and Buckley's pinnace were at last ready for sea. Bingley ordered them to sail round to Kinsale on the south coast of Ireland from which, he still contended, he meant to set out for Virginia. It may have been this intention, with which he did not wish to comply, which led Chambers into some obscure plan to take over Buckley's pinnace and bring her to the West Indies, as Bamford alleged,[19] although this may have been based on gossip or have been an invention—since Buckley does not mention it.

Chambers continued to be dogged by either ill luck or his own incompetence as he failed to bring *Triall* to Kinsale without further accident. He sailed across the Irish Sea from Dublin and put in at Studwalles, 'being a wilde & open roade,' near Pwllheli ('Pothely') in North Wales. Chambers went ashore to visit friends who lived some way inland. In the morning the wind was fair for the ship's departure but Chambers had not returned and the men would not set sail without him (though we may think that Bamford tried to get them to do so). Eventually he came aboard with his friends,

one Master Mondre [Mundy?] & other gentlemen of the Cuntrey to see the shipp & to feast them, which was done all that afternoon untyll yt was nighte & to late as he sayd to sett saile being winter and the nightes longe, and beinge also to late for these gentlemen to goo home that nighte they at the request of the master stayed on borde all nighte, the winde continuinge still faire and blowinge hard at east north east and still increasing more and more in the night untill it grew to a greate tempest in so much that although the maine topp mast was striken and the shipp moved with two of her best ankers & cables. Yet grew the storme so grevois that had not the bows spritt and foremast gone by the boorde & close by the deck doubtlesse without the greate mercy of god the shipp had perished with this examinate and all the rest theron. And yet after the bowspritt & mast were gon by the borde one of the cables brake and yt so pleased god that presently after the winde began to abate, otherwise he verily thinketh they had perished.

Bamford had some gift for vivid description and it is a pity, perhaps, that he did not have the opportunity to display it in an American context. Clearly, now, *Triall* was in no shape to go to Virginia, if she were seriously intended for there. Jury masts were rigged and the ship limped to Waterford. It was there that Bamford records that Bingley arrived to see about the ship and where there was a confrontation. Bamford had petitioned Chichester saying that the nine months' charter was up (it was now the beginning of December) and that he suspected the ship 'would be caried away uppon unlawfull adventures,' namely on a piratical cruise. Bingley committed him prisoner to the ship and threatened to punish him.

But Bingley and Chambers were also at odds.[20] Bingley proposed to put in a certain Captain Farmer over Chambers' head. Chambers objected and declared that Bingley had promised to retain him in command (he does not seem to have intended to take over personally). Bingley is

19 Examination of Roger Bamford (see note 5 above).
20 Examination of Rowland Buckley (see note 13 above).

said to have replied to Chambers that 'his viadge had not bin so good to make him in love with him, & therefore if he would be gon he should, for he woulde neyther entrete him to stay or goe but for his leudness he should never goe Master whiles he had the shippe.' Chambers went off and stayed in Waterford for some time until his associates amongst the seamen had demonstrated to Bingley that they would not sail under another captain. Consequently, Bingley gave way and appointed Chambers captain. Under him *Triall* was put in order (according to Buckley, Bingley sold Buckley's pinnace, which was not his, in order to raise the money for repairs).

At Kinsale Bingley still maintained he was preparing an expedition to Virginia. According to Buckley he was consorting with known pirates, Captain Swedon, Captain Isaack (who was somewhat notorious), Captain Davis, Captain Thomas Coward, Captain Henry Duffield and Captain Thompson. One group had brought a French ship to Kinsale laden with Spanish wool and other goods and had fitted her out as a man-of-war for armed piracy. The southern Irish ports, Youghal, Cork, Kinsale and Baltimore in particular, had become a major pirate center. The prize mart had developed during the sea war between England and Spain from 1585 to 1604 when much prize-taking was legitimate but where the disposal of captured goods at an Irish port, where payment of customs to the Crown and levies to the Lord High Admiral might be evaded, was advantageous. With the gradual imposition of embargoes on privateering 1602-1604, the peace with Spain and attempts to end sea robbery, which was all now clearly piracy, the Irish ports, with the connivance of English officials and of Irish merchants alike, became one of the main base areas for continued piratical activity; the other was the Mediterranean where the pirates operated in association with Algerian and Moroccan sea rovers. Bingley may have become acquainted with a number of the English privateers during his period in command of *Tramontana*, but how deeply he had been involved with piracy hitherto is not known. His association may indeed have dated only from his arrival at Kinsale before the middle of September.

On 17 December 1606 Sir Ralph Bingley was at Kinsale with *Triall*, still ostensibly 'bounde for the laund of Virginia,' when he decided, it was said, to augment his stores by seizing a ship which was lading in Cork Harbor. He alleged, we are told,[21] she was a Dunkirker and, since Dunkirk was a pirate center, fair prize. Actually she was owned by an English

21 Richard Roche, Sovereign of Kinsale, to the Earl of Nottingham, 5 January 1607, H.C.A. 14/39,196.

merchant named Sweet though we do not know her name. Arthur Chambers was put in command of *Triall*'s longboat and with men drawn from *Triall* and from other pirate crews attempted to take her: however she had warning of the attack and ran under the guns of Haulbowline Fort where they did not dare attack. Instead, they made up the river Lee towards Cork and there encountered a small locally owned pinnace of seven or eight tons (one version says they went overland and surprised her in harbor). In any event she was captured, some of her men were beaten up, and wine, salt and other goods belonging to merchants named Thomas Farris and John Quyne of Cork and Richard Nagle of Kinsale were taken. (The vessel seems to have been taken to the Severn where after making some depredations there she was arrested at Cardiff.) Some of the spoil went to *Triall*.

Nonetheless when Bingley at length took *Triall* out on a cruise from Kinsale, he was at pains, in a later apology at least, to suggest that he had done so in an attempt to make the long-deferred voyage to Virginia. Roger Bamford[22] is very reticent about this aspect of *Triall*'s career. He says that eventually Bingley made Chambers captain of the vessel, 'and they wente to sea one viadge & returned to Baltimore' (and elsewhere refers to 'one viadge to the quost of Spaine'): he had probably gone himself on the voyage and wished to withhold his defense if anything criminal was later urged against those who took part.

Sir Ralph Bingley's defense, though not made until April 1608,[23] is worth giving at this point. He wrote to Lord Salisbury:

I know y[t] my doinges at sea have bein lykwyse made verie odious to your lordship good my lord geive me leave to set them downe unto you fullie, and trulie, for a more honorable Judge I cannot fynde,

First when through a most terrible storme I had beine tossed for vj weekes together uppon the coast of Spaine, all my lower Tyce [tier of barrels] of bere, and vj Tonne of water was leakt out, almost viij score men aboarde mee, & not above three buttes of drinke lefte in the whole ship, with a badd winde for England, In this distress I met with a smale barke y[t] had in her some title quantitie of Syder & water, which I tooke and gave the owners my bill for, of this if anie on complayne I knowe he had neither Comission nor Cawse to doe it. Another time I was forced for Savinge of my selfe & Companie when wee weare seekinge out a harbour after a great storme to save our lyves in, to them of this ship because the men desyred to be sett on shoare. I gave directions where they shold fynde me out, and receave back boeth ship & such goodes (which was onlie wheate) y[t] was in hir, which I after performed as the honorable Deputie [Chichester] can certefie your lordship which

---

[22] Examination of Roger Bamford (see note 5 above).

[23] Sir Ralph Bingley to the Earl of Salisbury, 5 April 1608. Public Record Office, State Papers, Ireland, James I, S.P. 63/223,64.

I doe here most earnestlie protest on my fayethe and credit was all & everie jott of harm that in all my voyadg I did at sea which if anie man can emplefie with a larger relacion (most honorable lord) I am well content to lose my lyffe.

When I intended first my voyadge to sea, my thoughtes did soare to high to stoope at those base & forbidden baytes y^t Pyrates oft are wont to byte at,   And at my beinge at Sea, when that men did see how my businies was bruisde, & my voyadge broken, woulde I then have changed my mynde, as my fortunes did change. . . .

At no point does Bingley state specifically that he was on a voyage to Virginia, but as he gives no other explanation at all for having put to sea and as he denies all intention or practice of piracy the implication is that he was still bound for Virginia at this time, and that what caused the final abandonment of the project was his misfortune in losing supplies and being subject to bad weather in its course. That he was still in European waters after six weeks at sea would indicate he was either very unlucky in the weather or else was looking for ships to seize. One hundred and sixty men would also be a large complement for a 160-ton ship on an Atlantic voyage.

Roger Bamford, however, in his evidence against Arthur Chambers,[24] is quite explicit that, before the charter of *Triall* expired in December, continuance of the Virginia voyage was already out of the question: 'he seyth the said Arthur Chambers both [before] the expiration of the nine monethes & after did well knowe that the viadge intended for Virginea could not be performed Fo[rasmuch] that there was not victualle & other provision for the viad[ge which] could not be provided.'

Sir Ralph Bingley had powerful backing from the Irish administration, both from the Lord Deputy, Sir Arthur Chichester, and from the Lord President of Munster, Sir Henry Brouncker. It may be that as a result of this he was dismissed from any charges of piracy during the criminal sessions of the High Court of Admiralty on 25 June and 7 July 1607, though the name of the person so dismissed is given as 'Richard Bingley' (but this we saw was what the clerk put as Sir Ralph Bingley's name on the passport to him in May 1606). The list of cases is not fully self-explanatory, so it cannot be claimed with certainty that no further proceedings for piracy were taken against him, though none have been found. Early in June Bingley had handed over a pinnace and a barque, one 'taken in the Bay of Biscay,' for the use of the Earl of Nottingham as Lord High Admiral. This, though reported by Chichester to Salisbury only on 16 July, may well have been the consideration that ensured that charges of piracy against Bingley were dropped on 7 August. Chichester wrote,

24 Examination of Rowland Buckley (see note 13 above).

urging that he should be released but this had probably already been done.[25] The case of *Triall* when it was eventually heard in September 1607, was a civil one. Though Bingley was named with Chambers in this as a defendant no attempt appears to have been made to get him to appear and the evidence we have in the case is mainly directed against Chambers. It thus appears that Bingley escaped any legal liability for turning the Virginia enterprise into a piratical one. At the same time he incurred political obloquy in Parliament.

After 1604 English merchants expected to be able to reopen the profitable trade with Spain which they had carried on before war began in 1585. They found instead that they were hampered by bureaucratic restrictions and by the hostility of many officials and of some merchants. They made many complaints that the revived Spanish trade was unprofitable. As Richard Cocks, a merchant engaged in this trade, wrote to Thomas Wilson,[26] an official in charge of a number of trade matters, on 26 September 1606, 'it was generally thought that our peace with Spaine would bringe in Mountains of goulde, but now it proveth molehills of earth.' Further, English ships found on the high seas were frequently attacked by Spanish naval vessels and merchantmen on the assumption that if they were English and at sea it was legitimate to take for granted that they were pirates, heretics and enemies. It is true that there were English pirates operating off the Spanish coast—as there were pirates of other nationalities—after the treaty of London, but many of the English vessels attacked were peacefully attempting to restore prewar commerce. There were too a number of English ships which still made their way to the Spanish Indies. There are indications that after 1604 they were mainly engaged in trade rather than piracy and that their trade in tobacco was largely with parts of the north coast of South America where there were no Spanish settlements. Official Spanish policy, which had been stated at the time of negotiations for the peace treaty in 1604, was that no English or other foreign ships had any right to appear at sea in any part of the Indies. Spanish commanders at sea were evidently urged to enforce this exclusion rigorously (which they did by seizure of ships and frequently the summary execution of the crews). Some were inclined to exert this

---

25 H.C.A. 1/5,150; H.C.A. 1/62,29; Chichester to Salisbury, 16 July and 6 August 1607 (*Calendar of State Papers, Ireland, 1606-1608*, pp. 224-25). Investigations were resumed in 1608, when merchants of Bayonne took proceedings for the recovery of *May* of Bayonne, allegedly taken by Bingley (H.C.A. 24/72, 95; H.C. 14/39, 149). On 13 April 1608, Chichester wrote to Salisbury that he could find no grounds for the adverse information against Bingley which Salisbury had been given; he claimed that he had told Bingley to write a full explanation to Salisbury. This was, presumably, the letter already cited (see note 21 above) which is much less than a full explanation. See *Calendar of State Papers, Ireland, 1606-1608*, p. 473.

26 Public Record Office, State Papers, Foreign, Spain, S.P. 94/13, part ii, folio 97.

policing duty on ships found any distance out at sea from the Spanish coast, whether or not there was evidence of intrusion in the Indies. Again many complaints were made to England. William Squier, a responsible English merchant in Lisbon, wrote to Lord Salisbury[27] on 29 March 1606: 'if we yield and depend upon their frendilie promises we loose our goodes, and are made slaves, if we make any resistance we are all throwen over-board, as they did in this voyage to a shippe of Master Edwardes of London, which they tooke at Margarita & threw all the men overboord, saving three which certain dayes after were put to death by the generalles order, so that none escapt but one boye, which a Capten begd to serve him.'

It is clear that many Spaniards and many Englishmen too were still carrying on a semiofficial war well after official peace had been made. Petitions to the House of Commons and the House of Lords by aggrieved merchants met a ready response, and in June 1607 a conference of both Houses of Parliament was held to consider the merchants' petitions for redress and, as some thought necessary, revenge. This was a considerable embarrassment to King James who was busy trying to create a political entente with the Spanish monarchy. At the same time, his ministers were unable to take too pliable a line with regard to Spain. Lord Salisbury stated the government point of view to the conference, which was duly reported on 15 June 1607[28] to the House of Commons by Sir Francis Bacon (in whose version we have the statement). Bacon had to point out that the Spaniards had been equally rigid with all non-Spaniards in regard to access to the Indies. King James had refused to accept the Spanish point of view. In the treaty of London the matter had been left in suspense, 'neither debarred nor permitted.' The consequence was that 'they that went thither must run their own peril.' It was quite possible for the king to have arrested men released if he conceded the point of principle, but he was not ready to do so. At this point he brought in the case of Sir Ralph Bingley which was an embarrassment to the crown as it gave the Spaniards an excuse for continuing their policy of repression of English shippers. Still reporting Lord Salisbury, Bacon said, 'the offences and scandals of some had made this point worse than it was; in regard that this very last voyage to Virginia, intended for trade and plantation where the Spaniard hath no people nor possession, is already become infamed for piracy: Witness Bingley, who first insinuating his purpose to be an actor in that worthy action of enlarging trades and plantations, is become a pirate, and hath been so pursued as his ship is taken in Ireland, though his person

---

[27] Cecil Manuscripts 115/148 (H.M.C., *Cecil MSS.*, XVIII, 77-78).

[28] James Spedding, *Letters and Life of Francis Bacon*, III (1868), 353-54; J. F. Stock, ed., *Proceedings and Debates of the British Parliaments Respecting North America*, I (1924), 8-18.

is not in hold.' The affair of *Triall* thus became public property, though we do not know how much detail was disclosed about the venture either in the conference of the two houses or in subsequent debates in the House of Commons.

The English ambassador in Spain, Sir Charles Cornwallis, was probably hampered in his representations on behalf of imprisoned or aggrieved English merchants by these proceedings. The Spanish ambassador, Pedro de Zúñiga, on 3 July,[29] added his mite by presenting a long list of Spanish grievances against English seamen. They included, with special emphasis, the depredations of 'Raph Binle,' whom it is not difficult to recognize as Sir Ralph Bingley. He is said to have brought a number of prizes into Irish ports and to have sold them there, and to be still operating under the protection of 'le Viceroy d'Irelande,' Sir Arthur Chichester. If, indeed, it was Sir Ralph Bingley and not Richard Bingley who was dismissed from the criminal cases in the High Court of Admiralty about this time, Zúñiga was not very wide of the mark.

Though *Triall* had been recovered before Bacon spoke in the House of Commons, Chambers seems to have got clear away. When the ship's owners commenced proceedings in their civil suit against him and Bingley in the Admiralty Court in September, their main purpose seems to have been to put the facts of the case, as they saw them, on record, in case either Bingley or Chambers should happen to come within the jurisdiction of the court. We do not know when, if ever, this took place. Bingley's letter of 5 April, 1608 to Lord Salisbury, already quoted, was a formal but rather cursory apology and denial of criminal offences. This, it appears, was all that was required of him. He was soon afterwards awarded a share in the rich spoils of the Ulster Plantation, reaping there as much or more than he would have done from a successful Virginia venture.

The chief interest of this episode for early American history is that it shows that independent Virginia ventures were being planned, even if not successfully executed, after the Virginia Company's charter had been granted. The inefficiency and double-dealing by which the voyage of *Triall* was distinguished underlines how fortunate the Virginia Company was in its chosen servants, notably in Christopher Newport, whose skill and reliability alone enabled the Jamestown colony to remain in existence, even though by a narrow margin.

The venture also underlines the overlap between projects for Virginia and for Ireland in the early seventeenth century: the exploitation of both areas by England was closely interlocked. There was a strong inclination

29 Cecil Manuscripts 115/148 (H.M.C., *Cecil MSS.*, XIX, 170-71).

to attempt to solve the problems of one area by trying to shift them to the other. The problem of the pirates on the south coast of Ireland grew steadily between 1607 and 1609, and appeared beyond the power of local English officials, even if they had the will, to resist and reduce. They concentrated on trying to get them to go elsewhere. Sir Richard Moryson, one such official and a brother of the celebrated travel writer Fynes Moryson, wrote to Lord Salisbury from Youghal on 22 August 1609:[30] 'Should his lordship please to allow of their employment in the intended plantation of Virginia, which he has not yet motioned to them, he thinks good use might be made of them for the present there, both in defending them now in the beginning, if they be disturbed in their first settling, and in relieving their wants from time to time.' We have not the full context for this suggestion, nor do we know that any attempt whatever was made to follow it up, but the thinking is clear enough. It is impossible to clear the pirates quickly from the Irish coast, therefore let us try to find a basis on which they can be induced to go elsewhere. Virginia remains under some threat from Spain; these pirates are mainly interested in carrying on the old sea war against the traditional enemy if it can be done profitably. Therefore, it would make sense to employ them as a maritime defense force for the Virginia colony and so protect it from Spanish attacks. At the same time the pirates could supply the colony with many of its wants, because by raiding the Spanish West Indies and by attacking Spanish ships at sea they would have much spoil to dispose of to the colonists. Virginia could therefore develop as a pirate base on the flanks of the Spanish empire. Such thinking was a reversion to the ideas of the 1580's when it was hoped to make the Roanoke colony viable by similar means. Had Moryson's proposition been adopted the course of Virginia history could have been considerably altered.

[30] Sir Richard Moryson to the Earl of Salisbury, 22 August 1609, Public Record Office, State Papers, Ireland, S.P. 63/227,20 (see *Calendar of State Papers, Ireland, 1608-1610*), p. 278); Alexander Brown, *The First Republic in America* (1891), p. 105, and *The Genesis of the United States*, I (1890), 325.

NOTE: J.C. Appleby printed the charter party (from H.C.A. 30/843) in *American Neptune*, XLVII (1987), 79-82, establishing Bingley's participation in the venture from the beginning.

22

A LIST OF BOOKS PURCHASED FOR THE VIRGINIA COMPANY

The late Philip Barbour found among the Ferrar papers in Magdalene College, Cambridge (Case 13, Miscellaneous 2, no. 1284) a list of books, apparently unpublished hitherto, which were purchased for the Virginia Company and which he suggested I might care to annotate. It is amongst the papers of Nicholas Ferrar the younger (1593-1637), who was deputy treasurer of the Virginia Company[1] between May 22, 1622, and July 1624; the account was put in, according to an endorsement, on March 30, 1623, and payment was made by Nicholas Ferrar on May 8 following. The books listed were bought for the Company "at seuerall times" by John Budge, bookseller of London, a member of the Company of Stationers and, from 1620, of the Virginia Company. We cannot say precisely what period before March 30, 1623, the list covers but from internal evidence it goes back to 1621 and possibly to 1620. The list covers the cost of the whole issue of one pamphlet, the numbers not specified, and the purchase of 116 copies of 14 other titles, the earliest published in 1588 and the latest towards the end of 1622.

In his article on "Books in the Virginia Colony before 1624,"[2] Mr. William S. Powell demonstrated that the Virginia Company was concerned that its officials and settlers at Jamestown should have books at their disposal both for recreation ("some good book alwayes in store, being in solitude the best and choicest company" as John Pory put it) and for instruction. Bibles, prayer books, and works of piety were sent by the Company and taken by intending settlers, as were practical handbooks for use in the everyday affairs of the colony. The Company published and sponsored extensively the publication of promotion literature and used print to serve the business operations on which it was engaged. Some of its promotion literature was

---

[1] On Budge see H. G. Aldis et al., A Dictionary of Printers and Booksellers (London, 1910); Alexander Brown, The Genesis of the United States (Boston, 1890), pp. 595, 904; Paul Guerrant Morrison, Index of Printers, Publishers and Booksellers in the Short Title Catalogue (Charlottesville, 1950), p. 15; S. M. Kingsbury, ed., Records of the Virginia Company (Washington, D. C., 1906-1935), 372; II (1906), 93, 327, III (1933), 62, 65-66.

[2] William and Mary Quarterly, 3rd ser. V (1948), 177-184. In the absence of the early Court Books, we lack much essential information on this subject but the later years of the Company are reasonably well documented (see Kingsbury, Records, I, 589; III, 178, 397-400, 447, 507, 576, 643; IV, 271).

used to encourage settlers and to direct their activities into potentially profitable channels. How far the Company felt it necessary to equip its officials in Virginia with a reference library is not at all clear, but it is possible that John Pory as secretary, when he wrote about his intention to read when he was not employed on the Company's business, may have been able to draw on some small reference collection in the colony and that this was built up during the years from 1619 to 1624. Similarly, the Company would have needed some books of reference at headquarters in London and it seems likely that these were added to during the energetic treasurership of Sir Edwin Sandys so as to build up some small library through which the Company's activities could be seen in perspective.

The present list of books throws some further light on the use of books by the Company, though the precise reasons for the purchase of some of the items is not clear. This is particularly so in the case of a group of nine volumes devoted to colonization and its history, mainly in North America, published between 1588 and 1616. It is most interesting to find the Company purchasing works whose interest was mainly historical—though they had some residual practical value also. They may have been part of a reference collection that was being made for the use of the Company's officers in London or in Jamestown. In the former case, as will be shown, their purchase may be associated with plans to publish an official history of the Company and its predecessors. John Pory and Captain George Thorpe both wrote to England that reference books were needed in the colony so that the making of this little historical collection may, alternatively, have been a response to such requests from Virginia. It is also possible that the books were being collected for another purpose in Virginia since books were being assembled from private donors, 1620-1621, for the use of the College which it had been decided to create at Henrico. It is impossible to discriminate firmly between these various possibilities though, as will be shown, the notion that they were connected with a plan to publish a history of the Company has its special attractions.

The earliest of the historical sources to be found in Budge's list is Thomas Hariot's *A briefe and true report of the new found land of Virginia*, which had been published as far back as 1588. That Budge was able to supply a copy for one shilling more than thirty years following its publication is surprising and interesting. Published primarily as a promotion tract and probably in a small edition, only six copies of this twenty-four leaf tract have survived down to modern times. Despite the smallness of the price—and, ironically, of its immense monetary value in the twentieth century—it is probable that this was a used copy charged at double its originally published price which is likely to have been sixpence only. This tract, the fruit of the Roanoke voyages, 1584-1587, was still a primary source of considerable value on the history of English exploration and attempted colonization of North America. How much practical value it still had as a guide to Ameri- can plants and fauna and to the American Indian is not clear, but it had been cited by John Smith and by William Strachey on these topics not many years before, so that it may have been regarded as still of some use, and not a historical source only. Its appearance is a tribute to its continuing repu- tation.

We should expect to find, in any collection of works on American coloniz- ing attempts, Richard Hakluyt's *Principal navigations*. Here Hakluyt is represented by the three volumes of the second edition, published 1598- 1600, and still in the 1620's very much a standard work. The cost, thirty- six shillings, that is twelve shillings a volume, would be, nearly enough, the price of a bound set at the time of publication, though it might, of course, have gone out of print and so it might represent a used copy. Hakluyt had given an exceptionally full coverage of the early English colonizing attempts by Sir Humphrey Gilbert and by his successors who penetrated the St. Lawrence in the 1590's, as well as almost all we have today of the docu- mentation of the Roanoke voyages, 1584-1590. The collection was essential reading as historical perspective for the role of the Virginia Company since its foundation in 1606, and it also retained a certain practical value as a work of reference more than twenty years after its publication.

Hakluyt's earlier collections on North America, the *Divers voyages* of 1582 and the first collection on the Roanoke voyages in *Principall naviga- tions* (1589), which we can now see as being of independent value, were evidently not considered relevant to the purposes of the Company, but another work, for which Hakluyt was responsible, appeared on the list. In 1609 Richard Hakluyt's translation of the Fidalgo de Elvas on the expe- dition of Hernardo de Soto, 1539-1543, had been published as *Virginia richly valued*. It was dedicated by Hakluyt to the Council of the Virginia Company, and he pointed to its contents as containing valuable lessons for the Company on the geography and resources of the interior of North America. It was evidently found to command a public and was reprinted in 1611 as *The worthy and famous history, of the . . . discovery . . . of . . . Terra Florida*, the altered title thus detaching its contents to some extent from Virginia as settled by the Company, with which, indeed, it had nothing directly to do. As the form in which it appears in Budge's list is

"Historie of Florida," it was probably the second edition which was purchased on this occasion, the cost being one shilling and sixpence, which could well have been the published price. The continuing regard for Hakluyt's work even though he had died in 1616 is of interest.

By taking the two Hakluyt works on the list together some violence has been done to chronology. The earliest work on the list after *The principal navigations,* is John Brereton's *A briefe and true relation of the discoverie of the north part of Virginia,* published in 1602. Besides containing an account of Bartholomew Gosnold's New England expedition in 1602, the tract had a considerable amount of additional information on the resources of the more northerly parts of North America, to which it is almost certain that Richard Hakluyt contributed, but it is not clear that he acted also as its general editor. This book would be mainly of historical interest though the data it contained could still have some practical uses.

Next in order of publication is an item which does not refer directly to Virginia. It is entitled in the list "Plantation of Vlster" and is very likely to be Thomas Blennerhasset's *A direction for the plantation in Ulster* (1610),[3] or else one of the official publications of 1608 and 1610 which set out the terms offered to planters in Ulster. Many members of the Virginia Company had investments in the plantations in Ireland—especially that in Ulster —as well as in Virginia, and they thought of the two ventures in very similar terms. The existence of an Ulster plantation tract in a series of books on English colonization is, therefore, by no means anomalous.

"Captaine Smithes book att larrge" is clearly John Smith's *A map of Virginia, with a description of the countrey* (1612), which was still the most comprehensive account of the earlier colonizing attempts as well as of the Virginia Company's own achievements in America, while it also contained the fullest description of American Indian society in Virginia yet to be printed. The Company is likely to have bought copies of this work repeatedly from the time of its appearance, its map in particular being an essential guide to colonizing parties. The acquisition of two copies at this time indicated that it was still of practical value, but its association in the list with earlier historical items would suggest that one of these was acquired for reference purposes of some sort. With this was bought no less than three copies of John Smith's *A description of New England* (1616). Clearly, at least two of these copies were intended for practical rather than reference use. The map it contained was invaluable to sea captains who might come

---

[3] Dr. Barbour pointed out to me that Thomas Blennerhasset was connected by marriage with two Virginia pioneers, Bartholomew Gosnold and Edward Maria Wingfield.

homewards by a northerly route, while the Company had a lively interest in the fishing off the New England coast. Indeed, the information on the country and its resources had a practical bearing on Virginia also since the Company was, through its plans for particular plantations, concerned as far north as the borders of a New England defined roughly for the first time when the Council for New England was created in 1620.

The first seven of the volumes so far described were undoubtedly of more historical than practical interest, while copies of the two works by John Smith considered with them can be said to have some historical content also. The nine, together, made up a very useful small collection on English colonizing enterprises in North America down to 1616. Of the four alternatives suggested as possible explanations for the collection of this material, the notion that they may have been connected with the plan to compile a history of the Company, with some reference to earlier events, seems at least worth canvassing in a little more detail. By 1621, after some fifteen years, the Company had a past worth looking back upon, a period of varied fortunes it is true, but one containing a record of persistence and of achievement in the face of many unanticipated difficulties. Now that the Company had distributed much of its land to the settlers and had begun the diversification of the Jamestown nucleus by means of the particular plantations, it would seem that the period of experiment was over and that a description of its character was worth putting on record. Nor was this opportunity for retrospection merely a matter of academic historical interest: there was a political motive in existence also, namely the need to justify to shareholders, present and potential, the regime under which Sir Edwin Sandys had pumped large amounts of new money into the Company's activities. By comparing recent experience with the smaller and less spectacular phases which had preceded it, experiment might be seen to emerge into the glorious achievement—before the 1622 Indian massacre—of the present. A history too could be used for promotion, amongst a wider circle still, of the Company's achievements, so that new subscribers and much-needed capital could be attracted. Sandys was, we know, very anxious to publicize the Company by further political propaganda and would respond favourably to a proposal to compile such a history. He was present at the meeting of the Virginia Company Court on April 12, 1621, when a motion for the compilation and publication of such a history by the Company was proposed.[4] The proposal was received with "a very great applause" and accepted as

---

[4] Kingsbury, *Records*, I, 444-452, the motion on "a faire & perspicuous history" being on pp. 451-452. I am much indebted to Mr. Barbour for his assistance on this question.

"fitt to be considered of and putt into practise in his due time," was given, in effect, approval in principle.

The proposal was made by "Mr Smith." Both "m^r Iohn Smith" and "m^r Smith" are recorded as being present at the meeting, so that "m^r Smith" remains unidentified specifically. He could have been either George Smith or Robert Smith both of whom were at that time active in the Company's affairs. As Captain John Smith eventually wrote a general history, it has been tempting to earlier scholars to identify him with the proposer, but it is now agreed that although Captain John Smith appeared on the list of subscribers in 1620, he has not been identified as attending meetings of the Court. Robert Smith[5] was, indeed, placed on a committee in the following November to revise the Company's laws and to prepare for the publication of new edition of them and so could be associated, not wholly inappropriately, with the motion. But the favourite candidate is John Smyth of Nibley, a man who fits best the compliment paid him on his motion, that he put forward "alwaies mocions of speciall consequence," and who was himself interested in authorship.

The grounds on which the proposal was made are interesting. The first objective was publicity. Now that the lotteries for the support of the Company were suspended, it was necessary that "the real and substantiall food" on which the Company subsisted, namely injections of new capital, should be obtained by promotion. The Virginia plantation, Smyth considered, would be advanced "in the popular opinion of the Common Subiectes" by the publication of "a faire & perspicuous history . . . of that Countrey, from her first discouery to this day." The reliance on history to provide continuing and broadening interest in the Company and capital for its enterprises is very clearly in the mind of the proposer and was acceptable to his colleagues on the Court. He considered that a history would put on record "the memory and fame" of many now dead, such as Sir Thomas Dale, Sir George Somers, Sir Walter Raleigh, Lord De la Warr and Sir Thomas Gates. Others yet living, some of them present at the Court, also deserved to have "their honorable and good deservinges commended to eternall thankefullnes," though he forbore to flatter them by mentioning their names. He considered that the plantation of Virginia deserved to be put on record for its own sake, and that no part of Spanish America under the Spanish government, in their annals and histories, "afforded better matter of relacion then Virginia hath donn," thus introducing a nationalist note. He thought that recent pamphlets published by the Company—those of 1620 noticed below

---

[5] Kingsbury, *Records*, I, 564.

were probably specially in his mind—had had an excellent effect on their readers so far as their interest in the Company was concerned, so that "a generall history (deduced to the life to this yeare)" would be still more effective "throughout the Kingdome with the generall and common Subiect." He added that it was desirable to compile such a history soon as many of those who had taken part in the Company's affairs might well die off or lose their clear recollection of what happened—so that he envisaged the collection of a body of oral evidence on the Company's history. He also expected to have assembled "those letters & intelligences which yet remaine in loose and neglected papers," and consequently anticipated the adding of private papers to the Company's formal records. The range of inquiry and the objectives sought are indeed most significant. We can only regret that they were not fully implemented.

Mr. P. L. Barbour, who has clarified so much in Captain John Smith's life, has not so far been able to link the Smyth of Nibley motion with the birth of John Smith's *Generall historie*. Certainly Smith's prospectus[6] strongly implies that he had got no financial help from anyone:

I haue endured gratis: and had I not discouered and liued in the most of these parts, I could not possibly haue collected the substantiall trueth from such an infinite number of variable Relations, that would make a volume of at least a thousand sheetes: and this is composed of lesse then eighty sheets besides the three Maps, which will stand me neere in an hundred pounds, which summe I cannot disburse: nor shall the Stationers haue the coppy for nothing.

But Smith went on to urge that the publication of his history would "stirre vp a double new life in the Aduenturers," which was what Smyth of Nibley had thought in 1621 a general history could do. Moreover Captain John Smith used Hariot, Hakluyt, Brereton, and the Fidalgo de Elvas in his summaries of earlier colonization prefaced to his *Generall historie*. He had reached 1590 at least during 1622, about the time the Virginia Company bought these books.[7] When, in his history, he was apologizing for the length and disproportion of his narrative,[8] he implied that the work was commissioned from him by the Company: "in the Companies name I was requested to doe it." Few things in John Smith's life are wholly unambiguous, but it may be that Smith was the beneficiary of John Smyth of Nibley's motion for a general history of Virginia in 1621 and it may even be that the volumes

---

[6] *Captain John Smith's Circular or Prospectus of his Generall Historie of Virginia, New-England, and the Summer Isles,* edited by Luther S. Livingston (Cambridge, privately printed, 1914), sig. A i[r].

[7] John Smith, *Works* (Birmingham, 1884), p. 331.

[8] Smith, *Works,* p. 622.

listed by Budge and discussed above were acquired by the Company for his use, even if they did not supply money as well. This chain of circumstantial evidence is far from complete and too much should not be made of it, but it has some interest as a possible explanation of the acquisition by the Virginia Company of certain items on the list.

Propaganda, as we have seen, was a substantial element in the proposal made to the Company for a general history: John Smyth of Nibley said[9] that it would "worke throughout the Kingdome with the generall and common Subiect, [as] may be gathered by the little Pamphlettes and declarations lately printed." These latter publications are represented on Budge's list by two entries of the "Book of Virginia." *A declaration of the state of the colonie and affaires in Virginia,* was brought out by the Company in June 1620 with four other items, two of them particularizing the supplies sent to the colony in 1619 and listing current subscribers to the Company. As a report on the Company's activity and as publicity for its further expansion, these tracts, now usually found in collected form, were widely circulated. There were in all two editions and five issues before the end of the year. Both copies specified in the list are there because they are specially bound presentation copies which Budge prepared. One was for King James, "gilt for ye Kinge with strings," and the price, 2s 6d, is not extravagant even though it may well represent the cost of the binding alone, the copy being supplied by the Company. This is not unlikely to have been a copy of the first edition. The second, presented to John Donne in November 1622, which appears on the list as "gilt for ye Deane of Paules," is more likely to have been one of the latest issues published towards the end of 1620, including the standing orders of the Company. The cost was 3s, and the occasion was almost certainly Donne's sermon to the Company, two years later, on November 13, 1622. This sermon, in its printed form, *A sermon upon the VIII. verse of the I. chapter of the Acts of the Apostles,* also appears on the list, six copies being purchased for distribution, at a cost of 6d each. Writing to Sir Thomas Roe[10] after the sermon, Donne said: "I preached, by invitation of the Virginian Company, to an honorable auditory, and they recompensed me with a new commandment, in their Service, to printe that." He expected the printed text to be available so that he could send it, with the letter dated December 1, to his correspondent.

---

[9] Kingsbury, *Records,* I, 452.

[10] John Donne, *Complete Poetry and Selected Prose,* ed., John Hayward (London, 1929), p. 478. Dr. Donne was admitted to the Company on May 22, 1622, and was made free and of the council in July of that year (Kingsbury, *Records,* II, 76, 89, III, 65).

On April 12, 1621, the same day that the motion for a Virginia history came up, Edward Bennett, citizen of London, was made a free member of the Company [11] for his services in appearing before committees of the House of Commons and "for a treatise which he made touchinge the inconvenience that the importacion of Tobacco out of Spaine had brought into this land." Budge's list reveals that Bennett's pamphlet, which is now represented only by two copies, one in Cambridge University Library and the other in the Public Record Office, London, was published by the Virginia Company. This was *A treatise divided into three parts, touching the inconveniences, that the importation of tobacco out of Spaine hath brought into this land,*[12] Budge's bill "For printinge of master Bennetes Booke" was only £2 10s in all. It would probably be retailed at 6d a copy, so that the cost could represent at this rate an edition of only 200 copies. This may have been large enough for a tract with a limited and largely free distribution, but as production costs were substantially less than 6d for six pages of print, the edition may, in fact, have been as much as 600.

Five items on Budge's list are concerned with the attempt to stimulate silk culture in Virginia and they cover 91 copies of two tracts which were employed mainly amongst the settlers in Virginia to teach the craft (already an old European introduction into Mexico) which Mr. Charles E. Hatch has already dealt with fully in this *Magazine*.[13] Jean Bonoeil, King James's gardener at Oatlands, was the source of information and instruction for both publications. His *Obseruations to be followed, for the making of fit roomes, to keep silk-wormes in* were almost ready by December 13, 1620, and the tract, dealing to a considerable extent with the culture of mulberry trees, is likely to have been published about the end of the calendar year. In it he observed that "other things concerning the ordering of silk-wormes, you shall know by another booke which is to be printed."[14] The larger treatise, dealing specifically with silkworm culture and containing illustrations, was ready by October 31, 1621,[15] and it was hoped to get it translated from the French, printed and despatched to Virginia with some rapidity. But this did not happen, and it was well into 1622 before it was ready. The Virginia Com-

---

[11] Kingsbury, *Records*, I, 447.

[12] This is a single-sheet, quarto, tract without separate title-page and with the author's name at the end. (Copies in Public Record Office (S. P. 14/135) and Cambridge University Library only.) (I am indebted to Miss Katharine F. Pantzer, The Houghton Library, Harvard University for her help on this and on the Jean Bonoeil items below.)

[13] "Mulberry Trees and Silkworms in Virginia," *Virginia Magazine of History and Biography*, LXV (1957), 1-61.

[14] *Obseruations* (1620), sig. C 3ᵛ.

[15] Kingsbury, *Records*, I, 543.

pany records report it as "lately published" on September 5, 1622,[16] when it was decided that a letter from the King to Lord Southampton, dated July 9, 1622, recommending that the Company should proceed rapidly with their silk projects, should "be printed and affixed to the Silkworme book of master Bonnelle the Frenchman." We have no separate copies of the silkworm tract of 1622 with a distinct titlepage, though it is possible that some were already on their way to Virginia before the decision to print the royal letter was taken.[17] Surviving copies are entitled *His majesties gracious letter to the Earle of South-Hampton . . . and to the councell and company of Virginia heere. . . . Together with instructions how to plant and dress vines . . . and other fruits. By John Bonoeil.* It does not seem possible to discriminate between the editions of 1620 and 1622 in Budge's list. It might appear that "Silkewormes large" would mean the larger edition of 1622 and that this is confirmed by the price, which was 1s a copy, but though two items would support this view, another has "Silkewormes large" at only 6d, so that probably here "large" implies a large-paper copy, perhaps for presentation to some of the Company's patrons. The principal item, of "78 Silkwormes att Seuerall times" at 6d each,[18] is likely in the main to represent copies sent to Virginia. The "Silkwormes" items well represent the use of print by the Company for the practical instruction of its colonists in Virginia.

Many of the Company's tracts must have found their way to Jamestown, but Budge's purchases discussed so far were not wholly for use inside the settlement. The remaining titles on his list were purchases specifically to meet colonial needs. A Bible "of Boss large," that is containing raised ornaments on the binding, represented the large church Bibles sent out from time to time as they were needed. The cost of a Bible in the Authorized Version, folio size and bound, was more like 40s than the 12s charged here.[19] The copy could, however, have been a less expensive quarto edition, either in the Geneva or Authorised Versions, or even a used copy of an older publication. The "Service booke large," costing 4s, was probably intended for the

---

[16] Kingsbury, *Records*, II, 101-102.

[17] Miss K. F. Pantzer writes "We have no evidence of an earlier issue of the *Treatise* without the King's *Letter* prefixed, but that is possible. The first two quires of the Harvard copy collate A1 missing; A2r title; A2v blank; A3r-4r *Letter*; A4v blank; (a) 1r-2r Southampton's letter, (a) 2v blank; unsigned leaf with recto blank and errata on the verso." The Treatise then follows, signed by Edward Bennett.

[18] It may be worth noting that the Boies Penrose copy of the *Obseruations* (1620) (photostat in the Folger Shakespeare Library), bears on its title-page in a contemporary hand the price "2d." (two pence) only, so that Budge's prices were high.

[19] Equivalent to 25s unbound (F. R. Johnson, "Notes on English Retail Book-prices," *The Library*, 5th series, V [1950-1951], 97). Other comments on prices of books in Budge's list are based on this paper, in which great caution in dogmatizing about prices is advocated.

use of the same church as the Bible and the "large" could have meant a large-paper copy, rather than a larger-sized book.[20] So many editions of the Bible and of the *Book of common prayer* were available that it is not practical to suggest which issues these may have been.

The remaining books listed are practical ones needed in the colony. William Wellwood's *An abridgement of all sea-lawes* (1613) was a sensible guide to carriage of goods by sea and of the rules—such as they were—of maritime intercourse. It would certainly have been of use to officials concerned with the receipt and despatch of ships at Jamestown. Philip Barrough's *The method of phisicke* (1610 and 1616) was an equally specific guide to diseases and their supposed remedies. Current since 1583, it was little altered from edition to edition, and is likely to have been more misleading than helpful to settlers who were trying to acclimatize themselves to American conditions and doing so unsuccessfully in the face of heavy mortality from diseases for whose effects textbooks such as this offered little remedy. There was, finally, a standard work on agriculture and horticulture, a French treatise by Charles Estienne and Jean Liebault, translated by Richard Surflet as *Maison rustique or The country farme*. It first appeared in 1600 and there were editions of 1606 and 1616, the latter claiming to have been revised and augmented by Gervase Markham. The book contained the earliest account in English of how tobacco could be cultivated and is likely to have influenced appreciably the attempts to introduce tobacco cultivation into England. This has its ironical sides since James I had tried for long to curb the spread of tobacco-addiction in England, while the Virginia Company, though greatly concerned to increase tobacco-consumption, was, equally strongly, attempting to get tobacco-growing in England stamped out so that, with the prohibition of Spanish tobacco which was also being worked for, the Company's Virginia tobacco would have the sole monopoly of the English market. Whether *Maison rustique* played any part in inducing better cultivation of tobacco in Virginia is not known.

As a sample of what must have been a number of similar accounts presented to the Company from time to time, Budge's list is of appreciable interest. It may record, as is suggested above, one stage in the building up of a small historical library: it throws some further light on the nature and extent of the use of print for promotion purposes by the Company, and it shows a little of how the Company responded to the practical needs of the

---

[20] Binding prices are indicated in the tables in *The Library*, 5th series, V, 96-112, but varied greatly with the size of the book and the quality of the binding. The prices cited above were somewhat above the average for a book of this size (1s 6d to 2s perhaps) but were not particularly high.

colonists in Virginia for books. It is also a small addition to the data collected by F. R. Johnson on book prices in this period and may, in expert hands, be made to yield some further light on this subject.

The list is published with the permission of the Master and Fellows of Magdalene College, Cambridge, through the courtesy of Mr. A. L. Maycock, then Keeper of the Old Library.

Deliuered and layd outt by mee Iohn Budge Stationer for the vse of the Virginia Company at seuerall times. These Books following vizd [21]

Imprimis: For printinge of master Bennetes Booke [22]	02 : 10 : 00
1 Silke wormes large [23]	00 : 01 : 00
1 Country farme [24]	00 : 09 : 00
2 Silkewormes large [25]	00 : 02 : 00
1 Bible of Boss large [26]	00 : 12 : 00
1 Service Booke large [27]	00 : 04 : 00
1 Hackluites Voyadges whole [28]	01 : 16 : 00
3 Method of Phisicke [29]	00 : 10 : 06

[21] *videlicet*, namely.

[22] Edward Bennett, *A treatise deuided into three parts, touching the inconueniences, that the importation of tobacco out of Spaine, hath brought into this land* (no printer or date). A. W. Pollard and G. R. Redgrave, *A Short-title Catalogue of Books Printed in England, 1476-1640* (London, 1926), no. 1881 [hereafter S. T. C.]. Copies in Cambridge University Library and Public Record Office, London, only. With acknowledgements to Miss K. M. Pantzer, Houghton Library, for her assistance.

[23] Possibly the brief *Obseruations to be followed, for the making of fit roomes, to keepe silk-wormes in* (1620) (S. T. C. 18761), but more likely *His maiesties gracious letter to the Earle of Southampton. . . . Also a treatise of the art of making silke. . . . By Iohn Bonoeil* (1622) (S. T. C. 14378). Title-pages reproduced vol. 65 (1957), 17, above. This is presumably a large-paper copy. (Sabin 99883, 99886.)

[24] Charles Stevens [Estienne] and John Liebault, *Maison rustique or The countrey farme*, trans. Richard Surflet (A. Hatfield for J. Norton and J. Bill, 1606) (S. T. C. 10548); (A. Islip for J. Bill, 1616) (S. T. C. 10549). A copy of the 1600 edition (S. T. C. 10547), bound, sold for 6s, unbound 4s 6d (*The Library*, 5th series, vol. 5, 102).

[25] As note 23 above.

[26] One folio Geneva Bible (S. T. C. 2244, 1616), two folio Authorised Version Bibles (S. T. C. 2245, 1616; 2247, 1617), and six quartos (S. T. C. 2253-2254, 1619; 2258, 1619(-1620); 2258a, 1620(-1621); 2262, 1622(-1623)), were published during the period 1616-1623 which represents, approximately, the range Budge may have covered. The copy could possibly have been a large paper copy of an octavo edition of which there were eight within these years.

[27] *The boke of common praier*. Unless this means a large paper edition of an octavo edition, of which there were five, 1616-1622, this was probably one of the folios, S. T. C. 16347, 1616; 16347a, 1616; 16349, 1617; 16353, 1619(-1620), or quartos S. T. C. 16351, 1619; 16354, 1620; 16357, 1621; 16359, 1622. A copy of S. T. C. 16353 sold for 3s unbound, so that a bound copy at 4s could be one of the folio editions (*The Library*, 5th series, vol. 5, 105).

[28] Richard Hakluyt, *The principal nauigations*, 3 vols. (G. Bishop and R. Newberie, deputies to C. Barker, 1598-1600). (S. T. C. 12626-12626a; Sabin 29595-29598).

[29] Philip Barrough, *The method of phisicke*, fourth edition. (R. Field, 1610); fifth edition (R. Field, 1617). (S. T. C. 1512-1513.) The 1583 edition (S. T. C. 1508) sold for 5s bound, 3s 8d unbound, and that of 1634 (S. T. C. 1515) for 3s 6d bound, 2s unbound (*The Library*, fifth series, vol. 5, 101).

1 Historie of Florida [30]   oo : o1 : o6

3 Smithes New England [31]   oo : o6 : oo

8 Silkewormes [32]   oo : o4 : oo

2 Silkewormes large [33]   oo : o1 : oo

1 Plantacion of Vlster [34]   oo : oo : o6

1 Sea Lawes [35]   oo : o1 : oo

1 Captaine Gosnols booke [36]   oo : oo : o6

78 Silkewormes att Seuerall times [37]   o1 : 19 : oo

o2 Captaine Smithes book att large [38]   oo : o2 : oo

o1 Heriotts booke of Virginia [39]   oo : o1 : oo

o1 Book of Virginia gilt for yᵉ Deane of Poles [40]   oo : o3 : oo

---

[30] Fidalgo de Elvas, *Virginia richly valued, by the description of the maine land of Florida*, translated by Richard Hakluyt (F. Kyngston for M. Lownes, 1609); reissued as *The worthye and famous history, of the trauailes, discouery, and conquest of that great continent of Terra Florida. . . . Accomplished . . . by . . . Don Ferdinando de Soto* (M. Lownes, 1611). (S. T. C. 22939-22940; Sabin 24896-24897.) The second issue is the more probable.

[31] John Smith, *A description of New England* (H. Lownes for R. Clerke, 1616). (S. T. C. 22788; Sabin 82820.)

[32] See notes 23 and 25 above. These may be either copies of the smaller version of 1620 or normal-sized copies of the larger edition of 1622. The price, 6d each, might suggest the former. They may have comprised one consignment sent to Virginia (see note 37 below).

[33] See notes 23, 25 and 32 above. These are half the price (6d for 1s) of the items in notes 23 and 25, so that they may represent large paper copies of the earlier, 1620, edition. Or perhaps "large" is a slip in this case.

[34] Most probably Thomas Blennerhasset, *A direction for the plantation in Vlster* (E. Allde for J. Budge, 1610). (S. T. C. 3130.) Budge in this case was the publisher. It could possibly be either *A collection of such orders and conditions as are to be obserued by the vndertakers . . . in Vlster* (Deputies of R. Barker, 1608), or *Conditions to be obserued by Brittish vndertakers . . . in Vlster* (R. Barker, 1610). (S. T. C. 24515-24516.)

[35] William Welwood, *An abridgement of all sea-lawes* (H. Lownes for T. Man, 1613). (S.T.C. 25237.) A copy sold for 6d unbound (*The Library*, fifth series, vol. 5, 112), so that this is probably a bound copy.

[36] John Brereton, *A briefe and true relation of the discouerie of the north part of Virginia* (G. Bishop, 1602), Two editions. (S. T. C. 3610-3611; Sabin 7730.)

[37] See notes 23, 25, 32, 33 above. These bulk consignments were intended for the colonists. Copies of the 1620 edition were sent to Virginia by the Company in February 1621 and probably reached Jamestown in June (Kingsbury, *Records*, I, 431-432; Hatch in vol. 65, 12, above). Privately sent copies were despatched in September 1620 (Kingsbury, III, 400). A more extensive distribution of the 1622 version was arranged by the Company, copies leaving England in September and reaching Jamestown in December 1622 (Kingsbury, III, 663-664; Hatch, 18). The price (6d a copy) might suggest the smaller 1620 edition but the place of the item on the list and the number of copies would fit the second edition better.

[38] John Smith, *A map of Virginia. With a description of the countrey* (Oxford, J. Barnes, 1612). (S. T. C. 22791; Sabin 82832.)

[39] Thomas Hariot, *A briefe and true report of the new found land of Virginia* ([T. Charlewood], 1588). (S. T. C. 12785; Sabin 30377.) This was presumably a secondhand copy and it is surprising that it should have been available at such a modest price (1s for its probable initial cost of 6d).

[40] *A declaration of the state of the colony and affaires in Virginia . . . 22 Iunii 1620* (T. Snodham, 1620). (S. T. C. 24835-24836; Sabin 99877-99881, distinguishing five issues between the two editions.) One of the later issues is most likely to have been bound especially for John Donne for presentation after his sermon to the Company on November 13, 1622, the probable occasion when this was given. This copy has not been traced.

06 Doctor Donns sermons of Virginia [41]   00 : 03 : 00
01 Book of Virginia: gilt for yᵉ Kinge with strings [42]   00 : 02 : 06

09 : 08 : 06   09 : 08 : 06

To yᵉ Right Honorable Henry Earle of Southampton
Treasurer of yᵉ Company for Virginia—

                                                    09li : 08 : 06
                                                    9li : 08 : 06

Wee pray your Lordship to pay vnto Iohn Budge Stationer for
Books deliuered and layde outt at seuerall times the Some of Nine
pounde viijs.6d. accordinge to the note beffore specified and this
shalbe your Lordships warrant

March the xxxth 1623

                    NICHOLAS FARRAR Deputy
                    RICHARD CASWELL
                    IOHN BLANDE
                    THO. WHITLEY
                    FRA: MEVERELL [43]

that the 8 of May 1623. of master Nicholas Farrar according to
this warrent the summ of nyne poundes viijs. 6d.
                    per me Io: BUDGE

---

[41] John Donne, *A sermon vpon the VIII. verse of the I. chapter of the Acts of the Apostles. Preached to the Honourable Company of the Virginia Plantation.* 13° *Nouemb.* 1622 ([A. Matthews] for T. Jones, 1622). (S. T. C. 7051; Sabin 20601.) It is probable that one or more of these copies were sent to Virginia, the others being for the Company's officers.

[42] *A declaration* (1620), as note 40 above. The occasion on which this specially bound volume, gilt, with ties of cloth, ribbon or leather, was presented to King James has not been identified, nor the copy traced, both copies in the British Library being in modern bindings.

[43] Richard Caswell, John Bland, Thomas Wheatley (or Whitley), and Francis Meverell were all experienced members of the Company's committees. Bland and Meverell were on the general committee from May 22, 1622, to the following November, and Caswell and Wheatley from November 27 onward (Kingsbury, *Records,* II, 30, 154). Bland and Wheatley signed the audit of Nicholas Ferrar's books on May 12, 1623, and Bland that of Southampton on the same day (Kingsbury, II, 417). It would appear that Budge's bill was passed by Ferrar and his co-signatories so that it could be included in the forthcoming audit.

23

WALES AND THE WEST

EARLY westward expansion from the British Isles has usually been thought of in terms of the actions of English monarchs, of citizens and sailors of Bristol and London and of the restless and enterprising gentry of, mainly, the English south-west. But there was no insurmountable impediment to the participation of ports like Galway or Milford, Waterford or Carmarthen, Cardiff or Wexford, to take examples of active, if small, merchant and fishing communities in Wales and Ireland, sending ships out to search for fishing grounds and islands in the wide Atlantic. Both areas were regularly sending fishing ventures into the deeper waters of the continental shelf before America was found. Galway, for example, was deeply involved in the Iceland trade, though we do not know if this was through the medium of Bristol vessels only or whether Irish vessels also took part in the fifteenth-century Iceland voyages. Nothing of this sort is so far known for Wales itself, but Bristol had an active Welsh community, which was concerned in some degree in the earliest English Atlantic enterprises and continued to concern itself with later ones. A Welsh community in London also was not backward in such activity as marked the early faltering years of official enterprise. However, the essential factor in the absence of independent Welsh expansion westward—except latterly in the Newfoundland fishery—was the comparative backwardness of the Welsh economy and the lack of disposable capital except among a small section of the gentry class. In general, it is Welshmen who had migrated to England or men of Welsh descent established there for a generation or more who are, with a few exceptions, to be found in the meagre records of early westward enterprise from England, Wales and Ireland. There was, too, the question of nomenclature. How are we to say that a particular Jones or Thomas or Davies, or such like, was indeed Welsh when such names spread over much of England and were especially frequent in the English border counties and in the south-west? The answer must lie in many cases in guesswork rather than proof, with, however, the occurrence of a Welsh forename as being one useful guide. Anglo-Welsh names offer their own problems.

In the first recorded voyage of exploration westward from Bristol, made in 1480 to 'the island of Brasylle in the western part of Ireland', the ship's master, described as 'the most knowledgeable seaman of the whole of England', was named by William Worcestre, in his draft chronicle, as '[blank] Thloyde'. We are entitled to conclude that this was a Welsh seaman called 'Lloyd', the 'Th' being an attempt to reproduce the Welsh double 'l'; but there was a Thomas Lloyd in Bristol at this time and the form of the name may therefore represent someone whose Welshness was not, at least, recent. The expedition did not find the supposed island, though another in 1481 perhaps did so, in the shape of a glimpse of Newfoundland, though this is not certain. Whether Lloyd was involved in this too is not recorded.[1] But under the part-Welsh monarch, Henry VII, many more Welsh men and women made their way to the capital and elsewhere in England. It was then that the successful voyage of John Cabot was made in 1497, the Newfoundland fishery begun in 1502, and much of the North American coast explored by 1509. Richard Ap Meryke (or Merrick) was customer of Bristol at the time and he was undoubtedly Welsh. On the strength of his association with the payment of John Cabot's pension between 1497 and 1499 and of his name, A. E. Hudd made the audacious assumption that the name America derived from him and not from Amerigo Vespucci,[2] even if the evidence to sustain this claim has not found acceptance, but for a time it was a potential feather in the Welsh cap. A John Thomas was certainly involved in the Bristol voyages of the early years of the century, but who is to say that he or his forebears came from Wales?

Though under Henry VIII westward voyaging (except for the development of the Newfoundland fishery, the growth of which is very obscure but which was actively pursued by the 1530s) was infrequent and intermittent, it may be that the Welsh trans-Atlantic fishery began then, since we have an example of a Kinsale ship being engaged in it in 1537 and there is no reason why Milford, for example, should have lagged behind. But hard evidence has still to be produced. Certainly men with Welsh names who were members of the Mercers' and Drapers' Companies of London—Philip Meredith and John Appowell in the Mercers and Master Vaughan, Thomas Howell, Robert Ap Raynolds and David Greffeth among the Drapers—proved willing to support a venture by Sebastian Cabot to sail through a Northwest Passage to trade with China, even if sufficient support for it was not obtained and it remained a project only.[3] In what little we know of the participants in North American voyages in 1527 and 1536 no Welsh-sounding name stands out. The only well-researched group of merchants for the mid-Tudor period are those who were involved in the Muscovy Company in 1550:[4] among them were Davie Appowell, a mercer, Philip Gunter, born at Dyffryn, Monmouthshire, a skinner, and Anthony Gamage of Coity, who accumulated extensive lands in Wales which, by the marriage of his grand-daughter Barbara Gamage to Robert Sidney, passed into the hands of that family. While both Gunter and Gamage were active in new branches of foreign trade, neither seems to have had any connection with American ventures, except very indirectly. The Muscovy Company indeed claimed to have a monopoly of venturing to the north-west as well as the north-east, and the London merchant Michael Lok had difficulty in getting recognition by the Company of the venture he sent out under Martin Frobisher in 1576. Mineral finds led to the formation of

[1] For the early Bristol enterprises, see D. B. Quinn, *North America from First Discovery to Early Settlements* (1977), pp. 112-35; *idem, England and the Discovery of America* (1974), pp. 5-24, 47, 144; D. B. Quinn, A. M. Quinn, S. E. Hillier (eds.), *New American World,* I (1979), 91-127.

[2] See A. E. Hudd, 'Richard Ameryk and the name America', in H. P. R. Finberg (ed.), *Gloucestershire Studies* (Leicester, 1957), pp. 123-9.

[3] Quinn *et al., New American World,* I, 174, 177-8.

[4] T. S. Willan, *The Muscovy Merchants of 1555* (Manchester, 1953), *passim.*

the Company of Cathay in 1577 and its activities brought to England in 1577 and 1578 much ore soon found to be worthless. William Williams, assay master at the Tower, is likely to have had Welsh associations. He astutely condemned the ore brought in 1576 as only 'marsquasite stone' but was over-ruled. He was involved in further assays of ore from America between 1577 and 1583 on which he returned mixed reports. There were a few subscribers with Welsh-sounding names such as Thomas Owine, and some of the humbler men may also have been Welsh: for example, Thomas Philips, who was to have been left as a miner-colonist on Baffin Island in 1578 (fortunately he did not have to stay), and in the ship *Aid* that year were sailors Robert Owen, Thomas Price, William and Harry Davies.[5] Whether this adds up to Welsh participation or not is debatable, but it illustrates the problem of assessing Welsh contributions to western enterprise.

From the middle of the sixteenth century, at least, the coasts of south Wales and southern Ireland were extensively used in the course of one of the most profitable 'trades' of the time, piracy. It might seem that whereas most of the shipping employed in stealing at sea was English, there was a Welsh element amongst its crews. Prize goods, taken from French, Spanish and Portuguese ships, as well as English, were brought to south Wales and Irish ports to be disposed of illegally. Sometimes the prize mart might be an Irish port like Kinsale, but the ultimate destination of the goods might perhaps be Cardiff, coming through the hands of Welsh middlemen. Valuable African goods from Portuguese ships were coming in this way before and after 1560. Some of the prize marts were in south Wales itself, perhaps the most blatant at Penarth. The first serious crack-down on this pernicious trade was made by a special commission in 1577, which seized ships, goods and men at Penarth and Cardiff, hanged some of the pirates and hoped the example would stamp out the trade. Instead, it temporarily diverted some of the shipping and men, and the backing which they evidently had from a number of Welsh gentlemen to an overseas venture designed both to penetrate and rob in the West Indies and also to reconnoitre a site for a colony on the shores of eastern North America. The inspirer of this was Sir Humphrey Gilbert, a Devonshire gentleman, fanatically hostile to Spain but also bitten with the desire to occupy the vast untenanted lands (so far as he knew) of North America.

In June 1578 Queen Elizabeth gave him a patent which was a blank cheque to seize and occupy land hitherto untouched by Spain in the west. Through the efforts of Henry Knollys, son of the queen's vice-chamberlain, and Simão Fernandes, the Portuguese pilot who had escaped hanging by selling his presumed knowledge of North America to Sir Francis Walsingham, Gilbert's backer, a number of former pirate vessels were enrolled. Among the ships which assembled at Plymouth (though we do not know whether or not she had had a career in piracy) was the *Red Lion*. Her captain was Miles Morgan of Tredegar, who had been high sheriff of Glamorgan a few years previously and who had mobilised a number of Welsh gentlemen to serve under his command. A vessel of 110 tons, well-gunned, carrying fifty-three sailors and soldiers, her master, John

[5] V. Stefansson (ed.), *The Three Voyages of Martin Frobisher* (2 vols., 1938), I, cxi, cxvi; II, 83-4, 112-13, 117-18, 217, 221.

Anthonie, had a good south Wales name, while his mate was Risa (Rees) Sparrowe (and the master's mate Black Robin, surely a stateless pirate!). The gentlemen – adventurers came from gentry families in Monmouthshire and Glamorgan: Edward Herbert, Edmond Mathew, Charles Brady (Bradney?), Risa Lewis, John Martin, Thomas Nycholas, John Amerideth, and Lewes Jones. [6] In making his will before leaving on the voyage, Miles Morgan (a son of John Morgan of Tredegar, and married to Catherine Morgan, daughter of Rowland Morgan of Machen) [7] stated that 'I . . . do intend and purpose by God's goodwill and sufferance to travel by sea in the company of Sir Humphrey Gilbert' and wished to 'order his affairs' before he did so. It may be noted that he left an annuity of 3*s*. 4*d*. to Rees Lewis, gent. (the Risa Lewis above), 'only if the said Rees Lewis do go with me to the seas this voyage in the company of Sir Humphrey Gilbert Knight'. This involvement of such a company in westward enterprises could have been a significant pointer to further participation if it had not had fatal consequences. Knollys and Gilbert quarrelled over their objectives and tactics, and Knollys took part of the squadron to sea to plunder off the coasts of Spain. Miles Morgan commanded one of the vessels which remained with Gilbert on his intended course, when they set out on 19 November 1578, for the Americas. But this squadron was soon scattered by storms and each vessel was left very much to its own devices. Gilbert himself with the flagship, *Ann Auger,* took refuge with some other ships in Irish ports. The crank old *Falcon* sailed south to the Canaries and evidently attempted to make westwards but was forced to turn back. The *Red Lion* evidently fell in with some of Knollys's ships and joined him in piratical attacks on friendly vessels, French ships, the *Marie* and the *Margerite,* on their way from Spain to Le Havre, robbing them of woollen and linen cloth belonging to Spanish merchants and said to be worth £2,700. Part of the spoil was put on board the *Red Lion* 'afore the aforesaid Master Morgan with the ship and goods were cast away'. The *Red Lion* sank and, evidently, her captain and crew with her. Gilbert, after he returned to England, heard of and mourned the 'loss of a tall ship' and (more to his grief) of a 'valiant gentleman, Miles Morgan'. [8] Though Gilbert was to sail again in 1583, annex Newfoundland, and be lost himself on the way back, the only Welsh subscriber we can trace in his venture was Sir William Morgan of Pencoed. [9] The loss of the ship and so many Welsh gentlemen-adventurers prejudiced the landed class in south Wales against direct participation in such ventures for many years.

The Newfoundland fishery, after it had been pioneered by Bristol ships at the opening of the sixteenth century, remains an obscure subject for over half a century. It seems that it expanded mainly in the hands of fishermen of Devonshire and drew in others from the Severn estuary; although when the first Welsh

---

[6] The book of pirates, 1577, PRO, SP 12/112; D. B. Quinn (ed.), *The Voyages and Colonising Enterprises of Sir Humphrey Gilbert* (2 vols., 1940), I, 198, 212; *New American World,* III, 191.

[7] G. B. Morgan (ed.), *Historical and Genealogical Memoirs of the Morgan family* (London, privately printed, 1891), pp. 112-18; G. T. Clark, *Limbus patrum Morganiae et Glamorganiae* (1886), p. 311.

[8] Thomas Churchyard, in the poem he composed before the expedition set sail (*A discourse . . . Whereunto is adjoined a commendation of Sir H. Gilbert's ventrous journey* [1578]), wrote 'Miles Morgan gaynes good fame'; Quinn, *Gilbert,* I, 202, 390; *New American World,* III, 204-9.

[9] Quinn, *Gilbert,* II, 332.

participation began we cannot say, by the 1560s it had started. Sir John Perrot was the leading figure in Pembrokeshire before he became involved in Ireland in 1570 and he was one of the first of the Anglo-Welsh gentry to be involved in the overseas fishery. His ship, the *Bark Perrotte* of Milford, 50 tons, David Wogan master, sailed from the Pembrokeshire coast to Newfoundland (though we do not know to what harbour) in 1566. She brought back the respectable lading of nineteen thousand cod (reckoned at 120 to the hundred) to Milford on 4 September. These were probably wet salted fish, some of which may have been shore dried before being exported. Consigned to Perrot himself and to Wogan, it was probably five thousand of these that were reconsigned to Bristol on 27 September, along with some friezes, in the *Turtaile* of Milford, Arnold Williams master, by John Synet (Synnot) of Haverfordwest. But this was not the first Welsh sponsored voyage to the fishery. On 31 March 1566 the *Michaell* of Laugharne brought a mixed cargo for Robert Toy of Carmarthen for Bristol, including six hundreds of 'Newfoundland fish' which are likely to have been the product of a 1565 voyage by a Laugharne- or Carmarthen-owned vessel. The *Turtaile*, rated at only 16 tons, was typical of the small coasting vessels in the Severn trade at this time, too small itself to have been at Newfoundland, but the fact that Perrot's ship was only rated at 50 tons shows how small were the vessels crossing the ocean at this time.[10]

Even earlier we find not only that there were Welsh-owned vessels at Newfoundland but also that they and their owners were closely tied in with the Devonshire fishery to the extent of employing a Plymouth master for a Tenby ship. On 13 April 1562, James Barret, gentleman, John Philkyn, John Pallmer and John Kibery, merchants of Tenby, owners of the *Jesus* of Tenby, whose master and 'governor' was John Garret of Plymouth, made an agreement with William Philpott of Tenby, James Barret of Tenby and William Lougher, apparently of Plymouth, victuallers. The *Jesus* was to sail from Tenby Quay 'to the Newfoundland with the first wind and weather', return with a full cargo and unload within twenty days, the catch to be divided in thirds between owners, victuallers and the ship's complement, a usual arrangement then and later. The ship duly set sail, made her lading, and was on her way back when she was caught in an Atlantic storm, driven northwards and was making her way, the long way round by the Orkney Islands, when pirates relieved her of her cargo but eventually allowed her to sail home intact.[11] The fact that when she sailed she was armed with artillery, shot and powder, bows and pikes (since piracy was so common) makes her easy looting a little suspicious. Was her lading sold off at the Orkneys or elsewhere or was it seized? We cannot tell, but owners and victuallers got nothing. What the document reveals is that Tenby was at this time engaged in a sophisticated manner in the fishery and may well have gone on trading in this way.

After Perrot returned from his first assignment in Ireland (1570-3), he appears to have built up a small fleet of vessels based on Milford. These may have been

---

[10] E. A. Lewis (ed.), *Welsh Port Books, 1550-1593* (1927), pp. 79, 85, 56.

[11] Quinn, *New American World*, IV, 99, with additional references in PRO, High Court of Admiralty, HCA 24/34, 90-3, 234-5, 272, 290; HCA 24/35, 208.

partly engaged in the fishery, but more likely in piracy. However, as relations with Spain worsened, open piracy gave way to 'reprisals': the seizing of Iberian ships and goods in retaliation for goods seized in Spain or, after 1580, when the kingdoms were joined, by Portugal. Perrot was evidently in close touch with a leading Southampton shipowner and merchant, Henry Oughtred (who had lost property, he claimed, at Spanish hands). Oughtred's *Susan Fortune,* 200 tons, Richard Clerke master, was joined with Perrot's *Popinjay,* 60 tons, Henry Taylor master, on a cruise to seize Iberian ships and their cargoes by way of reprisal at Newfoundland. At the harbour of Renews, in south-eastern Newfoundland, there were three Portuguese ships anchored, their crews out in boats, shore-fishing. Clerke decided to seize them, but the *Susan* was too large to enter the harbour. He, himself, with thirteen men 'besides the said Taylers whole companye' in the *Popinjay* sailed in to attack. There was no resistance and substantial quantities of fish and train oil (from the cod livers) were transferred to the *Popinjay* (some 120 thousand of fish and 3 or 4 tuns of train). Moreover, prize crews were placed on board and the ships were sailed to a nearby harbour, Fermeuse. There and at the Isle of Boys, a little farther north, two other Portuguese vessels were brought into the net. All five were stripped of everything of value, and much of the spoil was packed on one of them, so that the two raiders and their prize set out for Southampton on 31 August, leaving the Portuguese fishermen in a very perilous position. Relations between the English fishermen and the Portuguese at Newfoundland had hitherto been uniformly friendly. A number of English fishermen gave evidence in the High Court of Admiralty against Perrot and Oughtred when Portuguese representatives brought a case for damages against them, though the result of the case is not known. [12]

This aggression did not at once bring to an end the triangular trade between Newfoundland, the Iberian countries and the British Isles. By the 1580s the north Wales ports, in association with Chester, were engaged in the trade. In 1582 the *Victory* of Beaumaris (44 tons), fitted out at Chester, sailed from Beaumaris to Newfoundland, brought her lading of fish to Lisbon ('Lisburne in Spain') and was back in June 1583 with 350 barrels of salt (some perhaps designated for future fishing voyages), 400 pounds of Castile soap and 6 pecks of barley malt for a Manchester merchant, Henry Hardie, based at Beaumaris. [13] This is our sole glimpse so far of an interesting involvement of north Wales in a trans-Atlantic development of some significance. But the triangular trade with the Iberian countries was brought to an end by the Spanish seizure of English ships in Spanish ports in May 1585, though a few may have continued the triangular trade to Marseilles and Leghorn. Perhaps some Welsh vessels may some day turn out to have done so too.

The south Wales-Newfoundland fishery at Newfoundland continued, however, during the war years though, it might appear from surviving records, only on a small scale. We mostly hear of it at the redistributive end. Thus, on 4 November 1585 the *Margaret* of Carmarthen (18 tons) left Carmarthen for Bristol with a

[12] The story is outlined in Quinn, *North America* (1977), p. 363, and the documents printed in *New American World,* IV, 13-20.
[13] A. Eames, *Ships and Seamen of Anglesey* (Llangefni, 1973), pp. 27-8 (his note reference being faulty).

cargo including 4 hundreds of Newfoundland fish and 6 hogsheads of train oil, evidence of a returning fishing vessel in that year. The same voyage may have been responsible for the one tun of train brought on 14 February 1586 by the *Elizabeth* of Tenby for Walter Hooper of Bristol. A 1586 voyage, too, presumably lay behind the lading on 3 February 1587 on the *Mathewe* of Milford, John Fortune master, of two hundreds of Newfoundland fish for Bristol. [14] The arrival and lading of ships engaged directly in fishing off Newfoundland did not normally attract the attention of officials, since such fish entered without paying custom though sometimes customs officers mentioned the fact.

We have no further published records until 1600, when on 27 February the *Moises* of Cardiff (50 tons) landed at Cardiff 9 hogsheads of train oil, presumably going to Bristol or another port to unload her fish. Finally, just after the end of Queen Elizabeth's reign, the *Nicholas* of Milbrook (30 tons, but possibly really of 300 tons) landed no less than 500 tuns of train oil at Milford for Morgan Powell of Pembroke and Thomas Powell of Haverfordwest. [15] This was not normal cargo. Perhaps the *Nicholas* was a 'sack' ship, which went out to buy from fishermen at Newfoundland rather than to fish and render down oil, and had purchased oil in this quantity from English, or more likely French Basque, vessels (the quantity suggests whale oil from the strait of Belle Isle, rather than oil from the cod fishery).

No further records for the early-seventeenth century have yet been published, but it is clear that, in the later sixteenth century, ships of Welsh or Severn Channel ownership were engaged in most branches of the complex international trans-Atlantic trade in fish, train oil (possibly some of it whale or walrus oil), salt and other products. The extent of the capital and shipping available in ports like Tenby, Milford and Carmarthen for such enterprises is as yet unknown. The fishery, however, did much to widen Welsh horizons across the ocean.

The question of the emergence of the statement that Madoc ap Owain Gruffydd made a voyage across the Atlantic and that he established a Welsh colony in America has been treated in sufficient detail in the early part of *Madoc. The Making of a Myth* (1979), [16] to make it unnecessary to go into it in detail, but it forms an essential part of the Welsh contribution to western enterprise which must at least be noticed. Whether the myth of Madoc was constructed out of folk-memory, myth, lost medieval literature or wholesale invention must remain somewhat controversial. Its begetter appears to have been the antiquary Humphrey Lhoyd (Llwyd) who died in 1568, and who set it out in a preface prepared for his translation of a chronicle attributed to Caradoc of Llancarfan, of which John Dee, an enthusiast for ancient Britain, who was of Welsh descent if not birth, had a copy. It was not brought into the open, we think, before Dee in 1578 put it forward to Queen Elizabeth as a reason for challenging Spanish claims to the first discovery of America. The idea spread. Sir George Peckham, who as a

[14] Lewis, *Welsh Port Books,* pp. 111-12, 118, 140.
[15] Ibid., p. 234.
[16] G. A. Williams, *Madoc. The Making of a Myth* (1979), pp. 36-49, 55, 61-7. The classic piece of demolition remains T. Stephens, *Madoc* (1893), though the invention of the myth can now be surveyed within a wider context even if it remains one.

Catholic had little taste for impugning the papal division of 1493 between Spain and Portugal, seized on it after talks with Dee, and it appears as evidence for English rights to colonize North America in his tract, *A true reporte of the late discoveries . . . by Sir Humphrey Gilbert,* in 1583.[17] By this time, Dee had been joined by the Revd Richard Hakluyt, from a Herefordshire family with Welsh sympathies, and possibly as early as this by William Camden (though he is not known to have been a believer in the tale), and most actively by David Powel, whose edition of Llwyd's work, with his 'Madoc' preface, and further notes by Powel appeared as *The historie of Cambria* in 1584. This remained one of the primary printed sources on the Madoc myth down to the nineteenth century, though it was elaborated by Sir Thomas Herbert in *A relation of some yeares travaile* (1634). In 1584 it was brought before Queen Elizabeth in a more weighty form by Richard Hakluyt in the report on North American prospects, 'A particuler discourse concerninge the great necessitye and manifolde comodyties lately attempted' (now known less cumbrously as his *Discourse of Western planting*).[18] Here it was made, alongside the discoveries of John and Sebastian Cabot, part of the materials for an English challenge to the Iberian claim, at least so far as North America was concerned. Hakluyt continued to assert it, but it cannot be said to have done more than bring together a small group of imperialist (and pro-Welsh) intellectuals in London, rather than influencing Welsh activity in the west on which it had, at that time, no observed effect.

A side issue, which was to have a longer and stranger life, as Gwyn Williams has shown, was the myth of the Welsh-speaking Indians. In Newfoundland fishermen, some of them Welsh, encountered the strange flightless bird, the Great Auk, which was extensively killed for food. They gathered that the local Beothuk Indians called it 'Pengwyn', or something like it, which was translated as Welsh 'White Head' (in fact the oval white patch on the Great Auk covered more of its neck than its head).[19] So home came the tale that the Indians spoke Welsh, a slight base indeed. (The name 'penguin' was transferred to the birds of the southern continent in the seventeenth century.) Peckham publicised it, along with some Welsh-sounding 'Indian' words invented by the lying David Ingram, whose tales about his travels in North America in 1568-9 were for a time believed by Peckham and by Hakluyt, though by few others. Thus, Welsh visitors or settlers in America thereafter, who had probably never heard of Madoc, continued to repeat the more enduring myth about the Welsh-speaking Indians.

Gilbert's death in 1583 led to his patent being transferred to the more cautious and intelligent Walter Ralegh, his half-brother, under whose auspices five expeditions to North America were launched between 1584 and 1590, two of which led to the earliest English colonising experiments we know of in North America. No major Welsh participation in them can be traced, but that Welshmen were involved in both and Welsh women in the second is highly

---

[17] Reprinted in Quinn, *New American World,* III, 34-60.

[18] Reprinted in ibid., III, 74-123; a critical edition is in preparation by D. B. and A. M. Quinn.

[19] G. A. Williams is puzzled by the 'Pengwyn' story since penguins of the modern sort do not have white anywhere on their heads, but his knowledge of earlier natural history is at fault. For a century the Penguin was the Great Auk, and perhaps in northern waters for much longer.

probable though we have only the guess-work of names to go by. On the reconnaissance voyage of 1584 there is only the name of John Hewes as conceivably Welsh. In the colony which was left to explore the land and estimate its possibilities for permanent settlement (it spent from July 1585 to June 1586 mainly on Roanoke Island), there are more possibilities: among the gentlemen Captain (John) Vaughan, among the men (soldiers and labourers) Thomas and William Philippes, John Evans, Rowland Griffyn, David Williams and Hans and William Walters. But we know nothing of how they behaved, some well and some ill, in the year's course, until Sir Francis Drake took them all back to England in July 1586. The 1587 colony was to be a more serious affair, a community of families which would make a living for themselves in America, a first real colony of settlement. Certainly Gryffen Jones was Welsh. John Jones and Jane Jones (probably wife to one or the other) may have been, while there was also an Edward Powell—not a very convincing group, but a possible one, among the hundred-odd men, women and children that the governor, John White, left in August 1587 to speed supplies and never saw again, nor any other white man so far as we know. When White arrived back only in 1590 the Lost Colony had vanished, though some may have survived some fifty miles to the north for nearly twenty years. [20] Welsh association with these earliest colonising ventures remains tenuous in the extreme.

The privateering war against Spain and Portugal from 1585 to 1604 brought shipping from England to almost all parts of Spanish and Portuguese America, west coast as well as east. Amongst those manning the privateers there were, undoubtedly, a number of Welsh seamen. One ship from a south Wales port was the *Wheel of Fortune* of Carmarthen, Richard Nashe captain, which in 1589 took wines, calicoes, pepper and other goods from a French vessel laden with Spanish goods. [21] She may have been only one of a number of Welsh origin. 'Mr. Myddelton the merchant, of Tower Street', as the late A. H. Dodd called Thomas Myddleton, merchant, [22] and ultimately lord mayor of London and a knight, as well as many times a MP, based his many overseas activities on London and Weymouth, roping into them many of his relatives from Galch Hill and Llansannan, near Denbigh, and investing his great profits substantially in Welsh estates. He was active over the whole period of the war, and at a more peaceful level right through to his death in 1631. His 'Journal' in the National Library of Wales gives us much detail of his manifold enterprises. His brother Peter, his cousin William, and a nephew were all involved in expeditions which he financed in Atlantic waters. He emerges as one of the most enterprising and astute of the London merchants who invested in the cargoes of sugar, hides and bullion seized in the Caribbean or coming from Brazil. The list of them would fill a page. But he lost as well as gained. The voyage of Richard Hawkins to the

[20] Quinn, *New American World,* III, 281, 288, 321-2.

[21] K. R. Andrews, *Elizabethan Privateering* (1964), p. 261.

[22] A. H. Dodd, 'Mr. Myddleton the merchant of Tower Street', in S. T. Bindoff, J. Hurstfield, and C. H. Williams (eds.), *Elizabethan Government and Society* (1961), pp. 249-81; K. R. Andrews, *Elizabethan Privateering* (1964), pp. 113-18 (*passim*); 'A Jurnal of all owtlandishe accompts, 1583-1603', National Library of Wales, Chirk Castle MS. Fr. 12,540.

Pacific in 1592-3 was partly financed by him and he lost much when Hawkins was captured by the Spaniards; similarly, his investment in the last voyage of Drake and Hawkins to the West Indies in 1595-6 was a dead loss. He was quick to involve himself in peaceful trade with the West Indies as the privateering war ran down and his *Vineyard* made a successful trading voyage there as early as 1603. He was, too, an active participant in the Virginia Company when colonising restarted from 1609 (perhaps earlier) down to 1622. He demonstrated that if Welsh gentry and merchants were to engage in major commercial enterprises in peace or war their base had to be in London, not in Wales itself. But there were not many who could touch him for shrewdness and capacity for taking calculated risks which very often paid their way.

There was, after 1587, a long gap in English planning and attempts at colonisation in North America. The fishery alone went on in Newfoundland waters. The sea war was partly fought in the Caribbean by privateers and some larger expeditions, but the Spanish war made a hiatus in what might have been a continuous pattern of commerce and attempted colonisation. Before the war was quite over, indeed, ventures were made to what we know as New England. Bartholomew Gosnold planned a fur-trading post off the shores of southern Massachusetts, but his men would not chance staying. A Bristol venture in 1603, under Martin Pring, may have had some Welsh participants but we cannot be sure. His two small ships, *Speedwell* and *Discoverer*, were forced by contrary winds to put into Milford Haven; they stayed for a fortnight and may have made contact with some of the old Newfoundland fishermen of the port. There, before setting out, they heard on 10 April of the death of Queen Elizabeth, the end of an era. In 1605, again, Sir Thomas Arundell of Wardour, hoping to capitalize on the explorations of 1602-3 which had been valuable, sent George Waymouth to find a site for a mainly Catholic colony in the area recently reconnoitred. In 1605 the *Archangell* explored the islands off the Maine coast and the St. George River into the mainland. James Rosier, the later Jesuit priest, who was to collect materials on Abenaki Indian language and customs, was aided by a young man who was almost certainly Welsh, Owen Griffin. He was supposed to remain with the Indians and it was presumably thought he would make rapid progress with their language, if indeed they spoke Welsh or anything like it. As it was, none of the words he and Rosier collected had any similarity to Welsh. They were just another branch of the Algonquian languages spoken from modern North Carolina all the way to Cape Breton. [23]

A curious episode concerning persons from north Wales occurred in 1606-7. Rowland Bulkeley had at Beaumaris a 30-ton pinnace with which he contemplated a 'viadge in trade to the Indies for tobacco', since the illegal trade was developing in the West Indies. He went to Chester to buy commodities with which to trade and encountered there Sir Ralph Bingley, a Flintshire gentleman, who had collected a number of men for a voyage (he claimed) to Virginia. Bulkeley and his crew of five were given £13 to convey them to Dublin. On the journey Bingley persuaded Bulkeley to join him. He had a number of vessels lying off Drogheda, and it might seem that there was a plan to transport some settlers

[23] Quinn, *New American World*, III, 360, 372, 384-6.

from Ireland to North America just at the time the Virginia Company was organising its first voyages, but the whole thing may have been from the first a cover for a piratical venture. Previously, Bingley had induced a group of London fishmongers to appoint him captain of the ship *Triall,* which was to join him in Irish waters and take part in an expedition which its owners considered should bring them information on possible fishing bases on the Maine coast. It so happened that the master, Arthur Chambers, who was to bring the ship to Dublin, was a rascal and spent much of 1606 wasting his time and his masters' substance in visits to south-coast English ports. By the time the *Triall* reached Dublin, most of the other vessels had dispersed, giving up the voyage. But, according to Bulkeley, his pinnace was seized by Bingley and brought into Dublin Bay and eventually to Kinsale. There Bingley openly associated with pirate ships and from him Bulkeley made his escape, coming to Cardiff and eventually to London, to report that Bingley had in fact gone to sea but only to rob and seize Spanish ships in European waters. After Bingley's return, legal actions taken against him failed for want of evidence, his defence being that he ran out of supplies and could not get to Virginia. As both the lord deputy of Ireland, Sir Arthur Chichester, and the earl of Salisbury were prepared to overlook his crimes, he got away with them: the *Triall* was eventually recovered by her owners, but Bulkeley lost his pinnace and, perhaps, his taste for maritime adventure. His deposition in the High Court of Admiralty on 29 April 1607 constitutes a valuable sidelight on the confused situation after the end of the Spanish war, when Irish ports—and it seems Welsh as well (since Cardiff comes in marginally to the story)—were being used with the connivance of the local authorities to carry on a maritime war of plunder against all-comers. At this stage the cover of a voyage to Virginia could be used to disguise such operations. The London charterers of the *Triall* were genuine enough, but it is doubtful if Bingley ever was, or indeed if Rowland Bulkeley was as innocent as he made himself out to be. [24]

If Owen Griffin was employed in 1605 to collect information and a vocabulary from the Eastern Abenaki of the Maine coast, we might expect to find a Welsh element in the attempt by the Plymouth division of the Virginia Company (Bristol was involved as well) to establish a post on the Kennebec River in 1607, but it is not easy to do so with any certainty. What is clear is that two men, their surname both 'Davies' and 'Davis', were prominent in it, though research has not so far pinned them down to a Welsh origin. James was captain of Fort St. George on the Sagadahoc (Kennebec) River from August 1607 to the evacuation of the post late in 1608. He left a journal but this has been lost. Robert Davies is somewhat more prominent. He had evidently had experience both as a soldier and at sea. He was pilot of the *Mary and John* on the outward voyage in 1607 and, as master of the vessel (though his military rank was sergeant-major and he was a member of the

[24] D. B. Quinn, 'The voyage of Triall, 1606-1607: an abortive Virginia venture', *American Neptune* (above, pp. 363-81) ; *idem, New American World,* III, 396-402. Bulkeley's deposition is printed in full in D. B. and A. M. Quinn (eds.), *The English New England Voyages, 1602-1608* (1983). The first full study of Bingley is R. J. Hunter, 'Sir Ralph Bingley, *c.* 1570-1627', in P. Roebuck (ed.), *Plantation to Partition: Essays in Ulster History in Honour of J. L. McCracken* (Belfast, 1981), pp. 14-28, 253-6.

council), he explored the Maine coast to the south with Captain Raleigh Gilbert, the second-in-command of the expedition. He also accompanied him on boat searches upstream when the lower reaches of the Kennebec were explored. He commanded the *Gifte of God,* the larger vessel, back to England between October and December 1607, and the surviving journal, which is almost certainly his, is our main source of information on the activities of the settlers up to his departure. In England he reported on the rather poor prospects of the colony and later in 1608 was sent out in the *Gifte* to bring it aid. Instead, the settlers insisted on evacuating the fort, so that he conveyed them back to England late in 1608, a Virginia Company venture which set back the colonisation of New England for more than a decade. But we know no more about him. Perhaps he will appear when we learn more about the individuals, Welsh and non-Welsh, who took part in these early American ventures. [25]

When serious attempts at colonisation began we might expect to find traces of Welsh participation under the activities of the London division, which was charged with the settlement of the Chesapeake Bay area, and the Plymouth division, whose responsibility was modern Maine. Jamestown was established in May 1607. Settlers arrived between then and the end of 1608 in three separate groups. Among them we find names of men who were or could have been Welsh, mostly in humble positions: David Ap Hugh, artisan; Edward Morris, gentleman; David Ellis, carpenter; James Watkins, labourer,—William, labourer; and Hugh Winne, of whom we know nothing else. A young man, whose surname we do not know (he was called Thomas 'Savage'), was sent to live with the Indians and pick up their language and customs (which he did so well that he won his surname for his success); since it was still supposed the Indians might speak a kind of Welsh, his linguistic capacities might have been those of a Welsh boy, though Algonquian dialects soon revealed they had no Welsh elements that could be discerned. The only significant figure we can cite is Captain Peter Winne (Wynne), active among the first settlers and eventually appointed to the council of the colony but dying before he could take up office. Accompanying Captain Christopher Newport in the first expedition beyond the falls where modern Richmond stands, he penetrated the country of the Monacan or Siouan Indians and was one of the first to make contact with them. On returning to Jamestown, he wrote to his Yorkshire friend, Sir John Egerton, on 26 November 1607 that after going upstream on the James some 120 to 140 miles, 'afterwards I travailed between 50 or 60 myles by land, into a Country called Monacan, who owe no subjection to Powaton [high chief of the Indians lower down the river] . . . The people of Monacon speak a farr differing language from the subjectes of Powaton, theyr pronunciation being very like Welch so that the gentlemen in our Company desired me to be theyr Interpreter.' He had no success, yet it is clear that the myth was strong at Jamestown and that to a Welshman their language had some similarities *in sound* to Welsh. Unfortunately,

[25] Quinn, *New American World,* III, 429-37; D. B. and A. M. Quinn (eds.), *English New England Voyages, 1602-1608, passim.*

Winne died too soon to enlighten us further, and no echo of his efforts to speak and interpret Welsh to the Indians of the interior is on record. [26]

An amusing episode in 1614, however, illustrates how little the people of Pembrokeshire knew about what was going on across the Atlantic. The earliest Jesuit mission in north-eastern America, first started in 1611 at Port Royal, had only recently been re-established on Mount Desert Island when the Virginia Company of London sent Samuel Argall in 1613 to root it out as they did not want French Catholic competition along the Atlantic coast. He took some of the Jesuits and French civilians to Jamestown and brought two Jesuits back with him on a second raid in 1614 to show where the French civilian settlement at Port Royal was located (this he destroyed but did not catch its occupants who were away hunting). One of the vessels he had seized, with the two Jesuits on board, got separated from Argall and crossed the Atlantic eastward, putting into Milford Haven and remaining there for some time. In his *Relation de la Nouvelle-France* (1616), Father Pierre Biard S.J. recalled the visit. Though he labelled the captain of the ship, William Turner, a pirate and claimed he, along with his companion, Father Jacques Quentin, had been ill-treated at sea, he was anxious to impress himself on the local population as an educated man who was a victim of circumstances. He and Quentin were brought before the vice-admiral of Pembrokeshire at Milford, whom he names as Nicholas Adams, to explain their presence. When Adams heard the story he took them into his protection, had them lodged in the mayor's house and waited until he could hear from the authorities in London what should be done with them. In the meantime, the Jesuits in their habits had become a source of curiosity to the people of the locality. Even a member of the privy council, he tells us (who could he have been?), came to talk to them. The high point was when some local Anglican clergy were brought together to have a disputation with them, presumably with an interpreter present. Biard was amazed, he said, that so much of the traditional liturgy and ceremonial had been retained and that the hierarchy had remained unchanged (there was even an archdeacon present). We could do with a report from the Welsh side of their discussion but it was evidently more an informative talk than a theological wrangle. The people of Milford were able to hear at first hand something of what the French had been doing in Acadia (modern Nova Scotia and northern Maine) as well as learning some of the main points of difference between Anglican and Catholic. Finally, word came to send the Jesuits to London, where they were soon after repatriated. The basic irony of the situation was that, according to the laws in force at the time (strengthened in 1606 after the Guy Fawkes plot), any Jesuit landing in England or Wales was automatically liable to be tried as a traitor and to suffer as such. It was well for Biard and Quentin that knowledge of this law had not effectively penetrated to Pembrokeshire, and was not in fact being enforced by James I.

[26] P. L. Barbour (ed.), *The Jamestown Voyages, 1607-1609* (1969), I, xxv-xxviii, 245-6; Quinn, *New American World*, V, 285.

It is only recently that Biard's letter to the general of his Order, written in Latin shortly after the Milford episode, has been published.[27] The relief, and the irony, expressed in it may appear from the original:

> In Wallia capitaneus noster, cum ad urbem Pembrochium excendisset victus petendi causa, ob certa quaedam indicia, velut pirata captus est ac detentus. Ille enimvero, ut se liberaret, negat se piratam argumentumque innocentiae suae profert iesuitas duos, quos in navi haberet quosque si placeat accersere exipsis cognosci posse veritatem. O artificium divinae Providentiae! Erat tum hyens adulta et omnia in navi deerant. Ideoque, nisi provisum nobis fuisset, et frigore et malis peribamus. Quid multa! Extemplo accersuntur iesuitae et in urbem mirantibus omnibus deducuntur. Iubemur pro testimonio dicere. Nos enimvero quae vera erant proferimus: capitaneum scilicet nostrum officiarum esse regium non piratum, et quae in nos fecisset parendi necessitate magis quam voluntate fecisse. Ita capitaneus noster liberatus est, et non cum ipso in urbe, usque dum Londin[i]o responsum acciperetur, perhumaniter retenti sumus.

There is no evidence whatever that this episode, however illuminating to those who encountered Fathers Biard and Quentin, had any effect on Pembrokeshire's contribution to the western enterprise, which was confined no doubt, as before, to the Newfoundland fishery.

Much of the interest displayed by Welshmen in America in the early-seventeenth century was directed farther north. Sir Robert Mansel, again, was a leading figure in the North-West Passage Company, chartered in 1612 to develop Henry Hudson's discovery of the bay which took his name in 1611. Captain Thomas Button, an associate of Mansel's in naval affairs and another Glamorgan man, took two ships to explore the Bay in 1612 and managed to winter at the mouth of the Nelson River. His explorations revealed the outlines of the Bay but showed it to be a cul-de-sac. He did, however, import the names New North Wales and New South Wales to North American soil, though they did not remain there as long even as Button's Bay, which was his name for Hudson Bay. (The re-naming of Mount Desert Island in Maine as Mount Mansel, after Sir Robert who had thought of settling there in the 1620s, had no longer lease of life.)[28]

It was not until 1609 that nationwide support was sought and found for the Virginia Company of London and its Jamestown colony. Most of the money was drawn from the London merchant and craft companies (many of which had Welsh members) and also from individuals in the city, at court and from the nobility and gentry represented in parliament. How far systematic attempts were made to raise money in the outlying parts of England and Wales is by no means clear—probably none at this point. A wider range was drawn on in the next big subscription in 1612 and thereafter there was some countrywide participation in the annual lotteries which, until 1621, made up much of the effective income of the Company. It was not until it launched its new programme of expansion in

[27] Biard's *Relation* was published at Lyon in 1616; it is reprinted in I. Campeau (ed.), *La Première mission d'Acadie (1602-1616)* (Monumenta Novae Franciae, I, Quebec, 1967), pp. 595-7; the letter of 16/26 May 1614 to Father Claude Acquaviva, general of the Jesuit Order, is on p. 420.

[28] E. S. Dodge, *Northwest by Sea* (New York, 1961), pp. 129-34. There is a useful summary of Mansel's American involvement in A. Brown, *The Genesis of the United States*, II (1890), 573-4.

1618 that opportunities for speculation and employment in Virginia proliferated. Land was distributed to investors who would take it up themselves or induce others to take it off their hands, but most significantly private syndicates were empowered to receive large portions of land on which they could settle free farmers, craftsmen or, mostly, indentured labourers. In 1619 Sir Thomas Myddleton and Alderman Robert Johnson (the latter having been active in Virginia affairs from the start) combined to apply for a 'particular plantation' on which they might plant tobacco-growing colonists. Needless to say, neither Myddleton nor Johnson proposed to go himself, but under the care of Captain Peter Mathew (who appears as Mathewe and Mathewes but was almost certainly a member of the Glamorganshire gentry family of that name) a group of colonists was sent out. How many came from Wales we do not know, but at the very least some of the many dependents of the Myddletons would have gone, together with a selection from the London Welsh, and since south Wales was not prosperous at the time, we may suspect a number of labourers (who could indeed have been craftsmen or farmers in a better time) went too. The land assigned to them was well up the James River, three miles north of the second town in Virginia, Henrico. Its Indian name seems to have been Harrowhatock, and it is described as 'one of the best seats'. From November 1619 to March 1622 it appears to have had good fortune, though we know little or nothing about its internal development as yet. At Martin's Hundred, south of Jamestown, thanks to the excavations of Ivor Noël Hume in recent years, a comparable plantation is known to have established an extensive agricultural base and built a village, Wolstenholme, which bore every sign of developing prosperity. But then on 22 March 1622 came disaster for many of the colonists. The Powhatan Indians made a stand, too late indeed, as they saw their land being overrun by settlers now numbered in their thousands. Their rising killed more than 350 colonists but by luck, skill and good judgement (or a combination of all three) Captain Mathew kept his Anglo-Welsh plantation unscathed. Jamestown itself was spared and readied to begin a counter-attack: Captain Mathew's land was too near the frontier for safety and he and his men were called back. Though Mathew himself received a new grant and probably took most of the members of the plantation there, we do not know just where they went; perhaps some dispersed, since labour was short and indentures could not for a time be firmly enforced. Mathew himself was soon enrolling a force which he was to lead to destroy the Indian settlement of Tanx Powhatan, some way to the north of where the plantation had been. He went on to play a distinguished part as a member of the colony's council before and after the collapse of the Company and the setting up of the royal colony. More can no doubt be written about the Welsh in early Virginia but we at least know that they were present and active. [29]

Newfoundland was something different. There Welshmen had long fished and there they attempted to make their mark as organisers, proprietors and settlers, though with mixed success for some years and ultimately failure. A few Welshmen may have subscribed to the Newfoundland Company after it was

[29] S. M. Kingsbury (ed.), *Records of the Virginia Company of London*, III (Washington, 1933), 227, 246, 264, 570; V (1935), *passim.*

chartered in 1610, but none have been found among John Guy's settlers at Cupids Cove from 1611 onwards. It was not until the Company disposed of much of its right to lands in the peninsula to the south of St. John's Harbour from 1616 onwards that Wales took a stake in the country.

The man who is most closely associated with Newfoundland is William Vaughan, second son of Walter Vaughan of Golden Grove, Carmarthenshire, who after his marriage settled at Llangyndeyrn in 1605, and resided there until his death in 1641. But from 1616 to 1631 he focused much of his attention on Newfoundland. In his early moralising work, *The Golden Grove* in 1600, enlarged in 1608, he had noted the sufferings of poor farmers, oppressed by rising population and enclosures, and this was reflected in his works on Newfoundland, the first in Latin, *Cambrensium Caroleia* (1625), assuring the new king that almost all the ills of his kingdom would be solved by colonising Newfoundland; then *The Golden Fleece* (1626), under the poorly-concealed pseudonym of 'Orpheus Junior', assuring his public that by colonisation there 'we should performe miracles, and returne yearly into Great Britain a surer gain than Jason's Golden Fleece from Colochos' [sign, B3v.]; and descending to *The Newlanders cure* (1630), which dealt, prosaically for him, with the ills to which seamen and settlers were heir.

The extent to which practice accompanied (preceded or followed) theory has been debated. According to most Welsh historians, Vaughan visited Newfoundland in 1622 and 1628: later views suggest he never crossed the seas. He did indeed acquire a large tract of the southern part of the modern Avalon Peninsula from the Newfoundland Company in 1616, from Caplin Bay to Placentia Harbour, which was called Cambriola (the second territory to be named after Wales). From 1617 onwards he supplied John Mason, who was engaged in mapping the island (Vaughan printed his map in 1625 and 1626), with names like Glamorgan, Vaughans Cove, Golden Grove, Colchos, Pembrok, Cardigan and Brechonia for bays and capes already known by other names. But this was a smokescreen only. We now know that he sent his first settlers out to Aquafort (later transferred to Lord Falkland) in 1617. Nothing is known of how many there were or who led them, but they lived miserably in the huts the fishermen had built during the summer. In 1618 Vaughan appointed the experienced Captain Richard Whitbourne as governor for life of his colony and sent him out with fresh colonists. Whitbourne moved the first settlers and his new associates to Renews, a better fishing harbour. But he sent many of them home as unsuitable. One of their ships was despoiled by robbers. Finally, he left only six men to winter at Renews and came home to quarrel with Vaughan and to look for other means of colonising Newfoundland. In 1619 the survivors at Renews gave up—'the welch Fooles haue left of', said another colonist unkindly. The latest summary of his involvement is given by Professor Gillian T. Cell:[30]

---

[30] G. T. Cell (ed.), *Newfoundland Discovered: English Attempts at Colonisation, 1610-1630* (Hakluyt Soc., 1982), p. 25. The documentation on which she bases her conclusions will be found in this volume. However, D. W. Prowse, *A History of Newfoundland* (2nd ed., 1896), pp. 110-12, gave his authority to the placing of the Vaughan colony at Trepassy and said Vaughan lived there for some years. This was taken up subsequently by Welsh historians, notably A. H. Dodd, whose *Studies in Stuart Wales* (Cardiff, 1953), put him at Trepassy, considered that ill-health prevented him from making the crossing in 1622, but sent him there later. G. T. Cell, in her *English enterprise in Newfoundland, 1577-1660* (Toronto, 1969), pp. 83-92, put forward the view that the settlement at Trepassy never took effect, though Vaughan was planning it as late as 1630. In her *Newfoundland Discovered*, pp. 25-6, she gives a critical account of the significance of his writings, which for all their oddity make him significant as a pioneer propagandist for Welsh settlement in Newfoundland.

So William Vaughan's brief and unfortunate attempt at colonisation came to an end. There is no evidence that he ever sent out any more settlers to Renews or any other site. In his writings he refers only to the two groups of men and women whom he had despatched in 1617 and 1618, as well as to his hopes of reviving the venture and even of visiting the island in person. There is no good evidence that he ever achieved either of these goals, whether because of ill-health . . . or because of the financial difficulties to which Vaughan himself refers.

He continued to puff and blow about Newfoundland for some years, but his airy notions were at least based on the assumption that the real wealth of Newfoundland lay in its fish even if he built castles of air over this prosaic topic.

It may be true, however, that one or two of the men whom Vaughan was responsible for sending to Newfoundland, under other direction, became significant figures for a few years. At the instigation of his eldest brother, the earl of Carbery, Vaughan transferred in 1620 a small part of his grant to Sir George Calvert, who was interested in preparing the way for a Catholic settlement in Newfoundland, finally choosing Ferryland which had formed part of the original Vaughan territory. His chief agent was Captain Edward Winne who is not unlikely to have come over to Calvert from the Renews settlement when it dispersed. In 1620-1 Winne had created, with the assistance of men sent out by Calvert, a substantial building at Ferryland and had begun to grow crops by the time he wrote *A letetr* [*sic*] . . . *to Sir George Calvert, from Ferryland in Newfoundland, the 26. of August, 1621*, printed in London by B. Alsop with the date 1621. This was excellent work. Whitbourne, who had gone into the service of Lord Falkland's colony a little further north, published in a second edition of his *A discourse and discovery of New-found-land* in 1622, a further letter from Winne to Calvert reporting that a large house had been completed, timber cut for winter and various crops planted and now flourishing. Daniel Powell, almost certainly another Welshman, wrote on the same day to describe the country round Ferryland in flattering terms. Winne remained there until at least 1624 and laid foundations which impressed Calvert (now Lord Baltimore) that settlement was possible. So there was an indirect Welsh contribution to Newfoundland settlement after all. [31]

Over the whole field of Welsh activity in the early discovery, exploitation and settlement of the trans-Atlantic world we cannot say that Wales or Welshmen took an outstanding part, yet they touched on its successive manifestations at many points, even if largely peripherally. Welsh merchants, sailors and intellectuals in Bristol and London probably played a greater part than Welshmen in Wales. Yet this was not wholly true. Welsh fishermen from south Wales took part in fishing voyages to Newfoundland at least from the beginning of Queen Elizabeth's reign (and we still require to know much more of what they did before and after that reign). Welsh gentry in Monmouthshire and Glamorgan

[31] Vaughan, in *Cambrensium Caroleia*. For the Calvert colony, see Cell, *English Enterprise*, pp. 92-5, and full documentation in her *Newfoundland Discovered*, pp. 250-306. L. Codignola, *Simon Stock, Propaganda Fide e la colonia di Lord Baltimore a Terranova* (Venice, 1982), has interesting things to say about Vaughan and Calvert. For a general perspective on Newfoundland, see D. B. Quinn, 'Newfoundland in the consciousness of Europe in the sixteenth and early seventeenth centuries', in G. M. Story (ed.), *Early European Settlement and Exploitation in Atlantic Canada* (St. John's, Newfoundland, 1982), pp. 9-30; see above, pp. 301-20.

were attracted by the possibility of combining penetration of the Spanish zone in
the Americas with robbery. A few seem to have considered early settlement. But
Wales was relatively poor. It was not until the early-seventeenth century that an
appreciable number of Welsh gentry turned to the west. Perhaps this was because
it was now fashionable in England to do so; perhaps it was because they had more
mobile capital to expend on speculative ventures; possibly it was because the
economic situation at home in the early-seventeenth century was uncertain and
overseas investment and even settlement might prove more profitable than
investment nearer home. In all, the Welsh commitment down to about 1630 did
not amount to a great deal, but it was pervasive. We would like to know why it
was not more so. This is not likely to be possible until much more systematic
research on Welsh social and economic history of the period has been published.
Perhaps it may then be possible to present this topic as an integral part of the
history of Wales rather than as a series of largely isolated and only casually related
episodes. [32]

[32] Glanmor Williams, 'The Welsh in Tudor England', in *Religion, Language and Nationality in Wales*, pp. 171-99,
touches brilliantly on cognate topics. We still lack not only further research on Welsh people overseas in this
period, but also on the Welsh in Ireland.

24

NOTES BY A PIOUS COLONIAL INVESTOR, 1608-1610

WHAT we have too little of for the early stages of English investment and settlement overseas is the personal touch. For Virginia under the Company most of our literature is propagandist, and there is, especially, little record of the people who stayed at home but whose interests, material and intellectual, were involved in the New World. Sir Stephen Powle[1] has left us a little of this sort of information.

Powle spent the greater part of his adult life as a legal official. The summit of his achievement was to succeed his father as one of the Six Clerks of Chancery—a lucrative office—and to be knighted by King James at Theobalds in 1604. Like many of his kind, he collected copies of legal documents as formularies and precedents, and it is probable that his extensive commonplace book, which is now Tanner Manuscripts 168 and 169 in the Bodleian Library, Oxford, was intended originally as a legal reference book. But as it proceeded he got his clerk to copy into it many other materials: public documents which interested him, some of his Latin poems, letters to him and from him, tracts, and medical recipes. A few of these are in his own hand, and some have his marginal notes and corrections—in all, an interesting skeleton for a biography.

On the preliminary leaves of the commonplace book Powle wrote down a series of personal memoranda during the years 1608-10, interspersed with jottings of Latin verses and crossed-out notes of financial transactions rang-

---

[1] See Alexander Brown, *Genesis of the United States* (Boston, 1890), II, 971 and William Arthur Shaw, *The Knights of England* (London, 1906), II, 135. He is not in the *Dictionary of National Biography*.

ing over a longer period.[2] Three of the memoranda are concerned with the Virginia Company, one with a Guiana venture, and the rest with his personal affairs. The overseas items have been several times referred to, not always correctly,[3] but they have not apparently been published together and in their context. When read together, they reveal how good a diarist Powle would have been had he persevered in this genre. He puts down information about sailings to Virginia and Guiana which might be of value to him as reminders of his financial commitments; he also adds his prayers for the good success of the ventures. The combination of piety with successful business enterprise was not unusual in this period, but it is rarely so clearly illustrated.

Memorandum. 26° Ianuarij *1607* [-8][4]

I went ouer the *Thames* from the Parliament stayres to *Lambeth* bridge, attended on by *Iob Murcot, Iohn Wriothesly,* and *Richard Hoskin,* betwixt the houres of .8. and .9. in yᵉ morninge beinge at that tyme all frozen ouer,[5] in such sort that yt was an vsuall order of the way to walk

[2] The first leaf, now numbered fol. iii, was begun long before as follows:
Stephen Powle Clerus Coronae : 1597 : 9° Octobris
Thesaurus
The Cadence to all conferences
1. All is one
2. Lyke inough soe.
3. It is a goode leavinge
4. Woold I weare hee
5. The better for him
[3] See especially Charles M. Andrews and Frances G. Davenport, *Guide to the Manuscript Materials for the History of the United States to 1783, in the British Museum* . . . (Washington, D. C., 1908), pp. 375-376; Charles M. Andrews, *The Colonial Period of American History,* I (New Haven, 1934), 108-109; James Alexander Williamson, *English Colonies in Guiana and on the Amazon, 1604-1668* (Oxford, 1923), p. 152; and Leslie Hotson, *I, William Shakespeare* (New York, 1937), p. 221.
[4] The memoranda occupy foll. iii, verso—iv, verso.
[5] Cf. John Chamberlain to Dudley Carleton, Jan. 5, 1608, *The Letters of John Chamberlain,* ed. Norman Egbert McClure (Philadelphia, 1939), I, 251; *The great frost: cold doings in London* (London, 1608), listed in *A Short-title Catalogue of Books Printed in England . . . 1475-1640,* comp. A. W. Pollard and G. R. Redgrave (London, 1926), no. 11403.

theron from all the bridges vpon yᵉ *Thames,* the frost havinge continued from a Fortnight before Sᵗ *Thomas* day, till this present without any more then one dayes thawe within all that tyme. On which was shutinge, bowlinge, and bonefires and football playinge, as also little boothes for to vtter their ware in for shoes and drinks, besydes the resort of sondry kyndes of professions, as Pedlers Costermungers beggers, criples, I met when I was ¾ ouer an ancient gentleman my Clyent visited with a dead Palsey, and therefore carried in a chaire supported with .4. staues and borne vpon .8.mens shoulders and was presented in *Westminster* to Master Doctor Amy a Master of the Chauncery fer takinge of his Answere by oath in a suite dependinge betwixt the said Sir Iohn Poole and George Poole his sonne. Horses also with ther riders passed ouer at Lambeth ferry.

The 28ᵗʰ day of Ianuary .2. dayes after my man William Scott lead my horse and footcloth ouer Lambeth Ferry to Lambeth

Memorandum 9° Martis 1608 [-9]

Betweene the howers of 10. and 11. in the fornoone the day and yeere aboue written I deliuered to Sir Thomas Smith Treasorer of the viage to Virginia the summe of fifty powndes in mony towlde for which I receaued a noate with the armes of Englande testifyinge the receipt therof,[6] and am to be one of the Counsell of this expedition. My name also was inserted into the roule and booke kept by Master   [7]/ The successe of whitch vndertakinge I referre to god allmighty./

29 martij 1609. *Mia Consorte diceua che:*
Louers must wooe lyke Turtle doues: that is neuer wooe but once.
Embrace lyke Ivy: straightely, and dye when the thing embraced decayeth.
Kisse lyke Cockles: which is so to proportion ther affection, that the same be not fitted to any, but to one loue.

[6] Three copies of the original Bills of Adventure such as Powle received are among the Hastings Manuscripts in the Huntington Library (Huntington Library, *Bulletin,* no. 5 [1934], p. 57). Powle's name appeared in the Virginia Company Charter of May 23, 1609, and he was named a member of the Council for Virginia, while his "adventure" was entered in 1611 as £37 10s. (Brown, *Genesis,* I, 212, 232, 467). About 1618 Powle was down for £100 and in 1620 for £37 10s. (*Records of the Virginia Company of London,* ed. Susan Myra Kingsbury, III [Washington, D. C., 1933], 86, 331).

[7] Blank in MS. Probably the name is that of Sir Thomas Smyth's clerk whose name does not appear to be known.

Virginia

15. Maij. 1609 on monday in the morninge our .6. shippes lyinge at Blacke wall wayed Anker and fell downe to beginne ther viage toward Virginia. Sir Thomas Gates beinge the deputy Gouernoure vntill the Lord Delaware dooth comme theather which is supposed shalbe about 2 monthes hence. Capitayne Neweport captayne Sir George Sommers and 800. people of all sortes went in these 6. shippes besydes .2. moare that attend the fleete at Plymmouth and ther be inhabitantes allready at Virginia about 160: god blesse them and guide them to his glory and our goode: Amen

Guiana

13. Februarij 1609 [-10] being Twesday Sir Thomas Roe oure commander for the discouery of Guiana and Sir George Brooke (as I heard since) departed toward Dartmowth wheare oure 2 shippes and prouision for .2. pinnesses more bestowed in them lay at roade for his comminge : : parteners the Earle of Sowthampton 800ll. Sir Walter Rawley : 600ll. Sir Thomas Roe him sealfe with his parteners : 1100ll. : and my sealf : 20ll. : which viage god blesse : The 2 shippes departed from Dartmouth the .24. of Februarij 1609 [-10].

5 Martii 1609 [-10].

The Lord Delaware tooke his leaue of all the company on Monday at Sir Thomas Smithese in Fillpott lane treasorer of the Virginia Company : and on Satterday followinge .10. Martij departed towardes his howse in Hampsheere : from whaire he went to meete his shippes at Sowthampton readdy furnished with peopell res:[8] and plantes, seedes, and all other prouision of grayne as well to sowe, as to vittaile 1000 : men for one yeere. He had .3.shippes : one whear him sealfe was : of 200. tunn called the [*De la Warr*]:[9] a Flyboate of 400 tunne : and a pinace of 120. tunes : : his style was Lord Gouernour and captayne of Virginia . he tooke shippinge for that viage the [first] of [April][10] god blesse his worthy endeauours.

Die Veneris—9° Nouembris 1610.

Luna stella

The moone being .4. dayes oulde hora 4ᵃ. 5ᵃ. et 6ᵃ post meridien I sawe

[8] Latin *res* for "things," equipment to be taken on the voyage.
[9] Blank in MS. Brown, *Genesis*, I, 402.
[10] Blanks in MS. *Ibid.*

(in the sowthewest about the mark of the firmament of .3. of the clocke in the afternoone) a starr of the first magnitude neere the lower part of the moone with in lesse then one foote distant from the moone and so continwed in coorse and brightnesse proportionably to her greatnes with the moone many howers after.

25

ADVICE FOR INVESTORS IN VIRGINIA, BERMUDA, AND NEWFOUNDLAND, 1611

IN 1933 Memorial College, St. John's Newfoundland, acquired from the London booksellers Messrs. Francis Edwards a single-sheet news-letter, handwritten though not addressed, which is now in the Library of Memorial University, St. John's. It is dated June 29, 1611, and provides a useful conspectus of what news was considered worth sending from London to the country at that date. It has a particular interest in that it is largely concerned with the new plantations begun since 1606 which were attracting investors and settlers to Virginia, Newfoundland, Ulster, and Bermuda. There is, besides, both internal and external evidence that this Newsletter was deliberately slanted so as to attract financial support and settlers for the new colonies.

Newsletters as well as diaries[1] help us to extend the somewhat exiguous official documentation of the early years of colonial settlement. News material was found in considerable quantities in the letters of such men as John Chamberlain who, for a generation, towards the end of the sixteenth century and in the early part of the seventeenth century, gathered and disseminated information about current happenings in London and elsewhere in a professional manner if not for financial reward. Besides the gossipy letters which were exchanged between friends there were more professional newsletters exchanged between unofficial as well as official agents and their home government. European archives of the early modern period contain very many newsletters from such agents— we should call them intelligence reports—which supplement the formal dispatches of diplomatic envoys. Sometimes, as in the case of the Fugger correspondents, the agents were posted primarily to report on business conditions, though they included, incidentally, much that was of political or social interest. At the same time there were, in the sixteenth and early seventeenth centuries, more direct precursors of the newspaper press.[2] Many of the topical tracts published in the period filled the place

---

[1] Compare David B. Quinn, "Notes by a Pious Colonial Investor," *William and Mary Quarterly,* 3d Ser., XVI (1959), 551-555 ; above, 415-19.

[2] See Matthias A. Shaaber, *Some Forerunners of the Newspaper in England, 1476-*

of the later newspapers, but they were not periodical.[8] The nearest equivalent to the newspaper was the handwritten newsletter, supplied regularly to subscribers for a price. London was the center of most of the public affairs of King James's Kingdom of Great Britain, as he was attempting to persuade his subjects to call it, but it was separated by days and even weeks of travel from much of its hinterland. At the same time many members of the nobility and gentry had to spend some time there at Court or Parliament and consequently might wish to be kept informed of news and gossip during their residence at home in the country. If they did not have a friend who, like John Chamberlain, enjoyed sending weekly or more frequent letters of news and gossip they could employ a writer of newsletters to do so.

There is not a great deal known on who the writers of these newsletters were and how they worked. Nor are there, for King James's reign, whole files of their productions surviving. Presumably they had a clientele large enough in number to pay for their living expenses and yet not too large to impose too great a burden in hand-copying and dispatching letters Their clients had to be, to an appreciable extent, drawn from a homogeneous social group so that the same letter could satisfy all subscribers. How much was charged for a weekly newsletter we cannot say. Since postage was costly as well as insecure it cannot have been very much. The newsletter writer had to be in a position where he could obtain news. The scriveners, who wrote for other people, were in a good position to pick up, as well as disseminate, news. Legal clerks, minor secretaries, and messengers at Court could accumulate the right sort of information. They needed mercantile contacts too, as news from the provinces circulated mainly with goods coming by road or ship. It is quite probable also that they needed access to official channels of communication, the ability to get the letters carried with official correspondence by the messengers employed for this purpose. Written to meet a temporary need, circulated in a family circle and passed outside it also, the professionally written newsletter has survived in limited numbers only, where one or more happened to be inserted in files of correspondence or buried in a book. When one appears it must usually be treated in isolation and not merely as one of the series of which it once formed a part.

The Court normally formed the primary topic of interest. What the royal family was doing was important when the king ruled as well as

---

1622 (Philadelphia, 1929); F. W. Bateson, ed., *Cambridge Bibliography of English Literature* (Cambridge, Eng., 1941-57), I, 736-746; V, 330.

[8] See Douglas C. Collins, *A Handlist of News Pamphlets, 1590-1610* (London, 1943).

reigned. Parliament, if it chanced to be sitting, was also significant news. The comings and going of foreigners, public spectacles, the performance of stage plays were often noteworthy. During the Spanish War, down to 1604, the dispatch or return of expeditions was chronicled. Mercantile events were of interest only if they concerned a wide body of the nobility and gentry. Natural or man-made disasters, exceptional weather conditions, the birth of human or animal freaks made up the main incidents of provincial news circulated from London. As soon as substantial amounts of capital were being raised from country as well as City subscribers for companies concerned with overseas commerce or colonization, newsletter writers, amateur and professional, found them, too, worthy of chronicle and comment.

Though the year 1600, with the foundation of the East India Company, had marked a turning point in the organization of English overseas trade by mobilizing an unprecedented volume of capital from widely dispersed sources, it is 1606, with the launching of the dual Virginia Company having headquarters both at London and at Plymouth, which marks a further stage in acceleration. This was followed by a large number of additional ventures, the Ulster Plantation of 1609-10, the Newfoundland Company of 1610, the Bermuda Company of 1611-12 among them. These attracted a good deal of public attention and were accompanied by a considerable measure of publicity in the shape of pamphlets and broadsheets. It is clear that the launching of one venture helped to publicize the others and that by 1611 they were, individually and collectively, newsworthy. We do not have many typical letters for this year since the indefatigable John Chamberlain was abroad on the continent and there were no letters of his surviving dated from London between May 24, 1610, and November 6, 1611.[4] Consequently, the appearance of a newsletter covering an appreciable range of home and colonial news for June 1611 is very welcome.

The Newsletter of June 29, 1611, contains, on a single sheet of paper, seven items of news. Three items are of domestic interest—the swearing in of the new Archbishop of Canterbury, George Abbot, as a Privy Councillor; the arrival of Otto of Hesse, aged seventeen, a suitor for the Princess Elizabeth; and a brief reference to the collapse of a stand at the mayor-making at Norwich, which caused a number of casualties. These are all characteristic ingredients of the newsletter. Only that relating to Prince

[4] See Norman Egbert McClure, ed., *The Letters of John Chamberlain,* in The American Philosophical Society, *Memoirs,* XII, Pt. I (Philadelphia, 1939), I, 297-307; and the study of his career by Wallace Notestein in *Four Worthies: John Chamberlain, Ann Clifford, John Taylor, Oliver Heywood* (London, 1956), 29-119.

Otto's suit reveals any inside information, the writer referring to a conversation he had with the prince's principal gentleman. The remaining four items refer to the business of colonization on which Englishmen had so recently embarked. The meeting of the Virginia Company Court on June 25 is reported. Lord De La Warr is said to have apologized for his recent premature return from Virginia and to have promised to return there as soon as his health should have improved. This report was published shortly after. The Court also discussed the reports which had been coming in over the past year about the Bermudas. These indicated that the island was very fertile and the prospects of settlement seemed so good that the Company decided to send a colony there and received offers to go from many present at the meeting. This information is of some historical value since it does not appear to be precisely paralleled from other sources. The Company's action marks an essential step in the preparation of the Somer Islands, or Bermuda, Company which was launched under the Virginia Company's auspices in 1612. After Virginia and Bermuda, Newfoundland followed. The largest single item relates to the activities of Governor John Guy who had gone out to Newfoundland in 1610 with the first English colony and had recently reported to the Company on his successful wintering at Cupers Cove (now Cupids Cove) on Conception Bay. The writer had evidently obtained access to letters received by the treasurer John Slany and others and was able to report the survival of the colonists and their livestock, with Guy's undertaking to come over later in the year for a second party of colonists. The writer reports the success of the colonists in withstanding the severe winter climate and even undertaking some exploration during this season. He knows what furs and skins have been obtained and sent to England. He is even able to relate that enough stores are in hand for another year. The Newsletter is, therefore, of considerable interest for Newfoundland history, and this, in itself, would justify its publication. It concludes with a laconic statement that the Londoners were becoming weary of their Irish plantation. The Ulster Plantation, a much more extensive colonizing project than anything so far attempted in America, had involved the City of London in a very substantial investment in the part (Londonderry and Coleraine) assigned to the companies. From the beginning there was some hesitation on the part of certain companies about paying their contributions while the cost of building new towns in Ireland was proving an expensive business even before settlers had gone from England to inhabit them. Consequently, the reference to disaffection in the City about the Irish venture is probably correct though it is rather early in its appearance.

There is no doubt that the letter was written by a man who favored overseas colonization and who was attempting to make publicity in its favor; though interested in Irish as well as American colonies, he was, perhaps, biased against the former, even though at the time they were very much associated in men's minds with these being planted in Virginia, and Francis Bacon thought the Ulster Plantation to be of much more significance than that of Virginia.[5] The optimistic aspect of Lord De La Warr's report to the Virginia Company—that he expected to return soon to his governorship—is stressed. Bermuda is said to be so rich and pleasant that all men at the Virginia Company Court meeting were willing to go there. John Guy's achievements in Newfoundland are conveyed in flattering terms. His reports are so favorable that "all men" are anxious to invest in the second colony which Guy hopes to organize when he arrives from Newfoundland later in the year. The plantation is praised as "honest"—here equivalent to "worthy"—peaceful, hopeful, and likely to be profitable. On the other hand the City of London is said to be dissatisfied with the colony to which it had been committed in Londonderry and Coleraine as part of the Ulster Plantation, launched in 1609-10. The range thus covered is wide, the emphasis emphatic. Should we conclude that the writer was an enthusiast for colonies or that he had a more specific reason for seeking to promote them? It may help in answering this question if we look at the career of Edmund Howes, gentleman of London, editor of John Stow's chronicles between 1607 and 1632,[6] and himself a chronicler.

Edmund (or Edmond) Howes is an obscure figure. About 1602 he began to assist the aged John Stow with the continuation of his English chronicles, but the first edition of Stow's *Abridgement* (1607) for which he was responsible contained nothing about recent overseas voyages. The *Annales* of 1611, which he had continued, with some help from the City of London, to the summer of 1610, has, however, valuable summaries of the early achievements of both the East India and Virginia Companies, though little that can be regarded as overt promotion of their enterprises.

---

[5] See Historical Manuscripts Commission, *Downshire Manuscripts* (London, 1936), II, 258, 406; James Spedding, *The Letters and Life of Francis Bacon . . .* (London, 1868), IV, 123.

[6] John Stow, *The abridgement or summarie of the English chronicle . . . Continued . . . unto . . . 1607* (London [1607]), *The abridgement of the English chronicle . . . Continued . . . unto . . . 1610* (London, 1611), *The annales or generall chronicle of England . . . Continued . . . unto . . . 1614* (London, 1615), *The abridgement of the English chronicle . . . Continued . . . unto . . . 1618* (London, 1618), and *The annales, or, a generall chronicle of England . . . Continued . . . unto . . . 1631* (London, 1631 [-32]), all edited by Edmond Howes.

On July 26, 1612, Howes appears as a charter member of the Northwest Passage Company[7] which, under the governorship of Sir Thomas Smythe, who also headed the East Indian and Virginia Companies, sent out three unsuccessful expeditions, 1614-16, but he does not appear as a subscriber to the Virginia Company. Nonetheless, his edition of the *Annales* which appeared in 1615 contained a vigorous boost for overseas enterprises of many sorts, particularly the colonies in Virginia, Bermuda, Newfoundland, and Ireland. This might be taken simply as a token of his personal concern for such activities or as a reflection of an expanding public interest in them if it were not for a much later reference in the Court Minutes of the Virginia Company,[8] where, under May 20, 1622, the following entry appears: "Mr. Howe the Cronicler makinge a request for 12*li* of Tobacco, which he pretends was promised him yearely in consideracon of his paines and willingenes to doe the Companie service in his Booke relatinge the Passages concerninge Virginia, The Court was pleased to graunt his request for this yeare, givinge order that somuch should be deliuered him of the Companies Tobacco which he thankfully accepted of." Howes is shown offering for a fee to advertise the Company and to help create a favorable public image of it among the readers of the next edition of the *Annales,* which did not appear, in fact, until well after the dissolution of the Company. His reference to past services shows that he had done similar tasks earlier for the Company, but in the absence of minutes and accounts we cannot say when he began to do so. We could legitimately assume from the tone of his entries that it was before the publication of the 1615 edition of the *Annales* where, if he was taking money from the Virginia Company for boosting their product, he could also have been doing so for Sir Thomas Smythe's other overseas enterprises and also for the Newfoundland Company, since all the references have more than a trace of promotion literature about them. We must consequently look with some suspicion on the apology which Howes made in the last (1631-32) edition of the *Annales* when he said: "Plaine truth was the mark I aym'd at in the beginning, midst, and end, and in that simplicity of solid truth I end."[9] Whatever his truth might be it was neither so "plaine" nor so "solid" as he claimed.

If we look at Howes's survey of colonial affairs between 1606 and

---

[7] See Alexander Brown, *Genesis of the United States* . . . (Boston, 1890), II, 928; *Calendar of State Papers, Colonial, East Indies, China, and Japan, 1513-1616* (London, 1862), 231-233.

[8] Susan Myra Kingsbury, ed., *The Records of the Virginia Company of London* (Washington, D. C., 1906-35), II, 16.

[9] Stow, *The annales . . . Continued . . . unto . . . 1631*, Howes, ed., preface, 8v.

1614, added first to the *Annales* in 1615 and reprinted in 1631-32,[10] we may notice that his description of the activities of the Newfoundland Company has close parallels with that to be found in the 1611 Newsletter. He relates that Captain John Guy, under the charter of 1610, planted a colony of men and women in Newfoundland, and continues:[11] "hee also transported Hennes, Duckes, Pigeons, Conies, Goates, Kine and other liue creatures, all which did very well there: this Generall Gwy stayd there with the Collony both Winter and Summer, whose natures and conditions in generall agreed well with the soyle and clime. . . ." This compares very closely with the "quyck creatures . . . viz Ducks Geese henns Conneyes Goats Swyne and kyne" of the Newsletter, especially as there had been nothing else on these lines published on the 1610 settlement between 1611 and 1615. This would suggest, at least, that Howes was using some of the same sources as the writer of the Newsletter.

If, again, we look at the domestic events for 1611 presented in the 1631-32 edition of the *Annales,* we find that Howes considered eight events worthy of notice. One of them relates to the translation of George Abbot from the see of London to the metropolitan see of Canterbury, and continues: "And the twenty third of Iune next following, hee was sworne a Priuy Councellour of Estate, at Greenewitch."[12] This comparatively minor piece of information is included in the Newsletter. Again, Howes gives considerable detail on a more substantial episode, the mission of Otto, son of the Landgrave of Hesse, to pay suit to the Princess Elizabeth. He is said to have been attended by thirty persons, and his itinerary, though not his place of residence in London, is given. Howes tells us that "his chiefe Gentleman, and director of his affaires, was master Frauncis Seager, an Englishman, a sworne Counsellour vnto Prince Morris, the father of this young Prince, and one of his Captaines in Ordinary."[13] The Newsletter gives Otto's age but not his Christian name, says he was attended by twenty-six persons, but goes on to say that the writer had conversed with "his chief gentilman" who had told him something about the young prince's intentions.

The overlap in information between the Howes *Annales* and the newsletter is striking in regard to the details of Guy's Newfoundland venture of 1610-11 and the reference to Francis Seager. The optimistic view of Bermuda and Newfoundland colonization, remarked on above, is very like what a man who was in the pay of the Virginia Company and

[10] *Ibid.,* 1017-1022.
[11] *Ibid.,* 1019.
[12] *Ibid.,* 1000.
[13] *Ibid.,* 1001-1002.

probably other colonizing companies would write to promote their interests. The evidence is not sufficiently precise to enable us to say definitely that Edmund Howes wrote the 1611 Newsletter but it is adequate to allow us to suspect that he probably did so. No other newsletters have, so far as is known, been ascribed to him, but the writing of newsletters would seem a very appropriate occupation for one of whom Sir Sidney Lee, when writing a brief note on him in the *Dictionary of National Biography,* could find virtually nothing except his chronicling activities. The Newsletter itself is written in a not very distinctive secretary hand. Were more examples of Howes' handwriting known it would perhaps be possible to make a positive identification, though this is far from certain. What is of interest is that the hand is not that of a professional scrivener, but that of the author himself. The orthography is too irregular to be that of a professional and there are crossings out and a little rewording which show that the letter was being composed as it was written. This might suggest that the writer was making it for a single correspondent, but this is most unlikely in that it was not begun or terminated like a letter. It begins impersonally with a date and ends as impersonally at the end of the sheet. A wrapper, now missing, would have carried the address. We might take it to be the first copy of a newsletter which was later multiplied for the use of a small circle of correspondents. How many there were, how frequently the letters were sent out, and what the recipients paid the writer cannot be established, but they were paying for straight news. If, as seems very likely, the author was Edmund Howes, they were receiving from him, in part at least, information on colonial enterprises in America which was already chosen to illustrate their activities favorably and, in the case of the Virginia Company, had probably been paid for as advertising matter. The Newsletter is of considerable interest for the information it contains but even more, perhaps, for the light—feeble though it is—which it throws on the publicity methods of the early colonial promoters.

The newsletter is published below with the kind permission of Memorial University, St. John's Newfoundland.[14]

29 Iunij 1611
Last Sondeye[15] the Lord Archbyshopp was sworne A pryvye Counsellour at Greenewych

Last Sondeye heere Arryved the Landgrave of Hessons eldest Sonne of 17

[14] Contractions in the text have been silently expanded. The text has been established with the assistance of Miss Agnes O'Dea, University Library, Memorial University, St. John's, Newfoundland.

[15] June 29, as the Letter was dated, was a Saturday so that last Sunday would have

yeeres Age Atended with 26 persons and is lodged in a Duch Ghest house in Lombard streat[16][,] his chief gentilman And I had some Conference, Wherein he glanced At[17] an entention of A mach with the Lady Elizabeth marry he seyd that his Lords Comeing was to see this kingdom and to salute the kinge and prince etc.

The Laste weeke at Norwych vpon A Soleme show daye in chooseing their Maiour Through A greate Crowd which overthrew A scaffould there weare 32 persons slayne and many hurt som weare verye good Accompt[18]

Last Tewsdaye at A Virgynya Court the Lord La Warre in person made his Apollogye to the wholl assemblye[,] saying allso that so soone as he could recover health he would be as willing to returne to Virgynya as any man.[19]

The State and hope of the Bermodes was there fully dyscust And Concluded to send A Collony thither,[20] the place is so opulent fertile and pleasant that all men were willing to go thither

---

been June 23. This date is confirmed in Stow, *Annales . . . Continued by Howes* (1631), 1000, as the date of Archbishop Abbot's admission.

[16] The German *gasthaus* in Lombard Street has not been identified. Fynes Moryson, *An Itinerary . . .* (London, 1617), Pt. III, Bk. iii, 151, complained that German visitors to England tended to use German rather than English inns and to use non-English guides, so obtaining false impressions of the country.

[17] The expression 'glanced at' here suggests 'jested about' rather than 'referred to.' If so the meaning of the passage is that the gentleman, Francis Seager, cast doubts on the mission being intended for the courtship of Princess Elizabeth rather than as a sightseeing and courtesy visit. A treaty had recently been made between King James I and a number of the German Protestant Princes, including Maurice of Hesse. See Sir Ralph Winwood to Sir John Digby, Apr. 13, 1611, in Hist. MSS Comm., *Manuscripts of the Earls of Eglinton . . . and G. Wingfield Digby, Esq.* (London, 1885), 574-575, so that a courtesy visit by Prince Otto would have been appropriate enough.

[18] This happened on June 18. The account in Francis Blomefield, *An Essay Towards a Topographical History of the County of Norfolk,* 2d ed. (London, 1805-10), III, 364, differs: "On the 18th of June, (it being the gild-day) a sumptuous pageant was prepared at the new mayor's gate on Tombland, and certain fireworks, as had been usual, were fired off in the evening, some of which breaking, frighted the people (who were very numerous) to such a degree, that hurrying away in crowds for fear of hurt, there were no less than 33 persons trodden down and pressed to death, as the register of the parish of St. Simon and Jude declares."

[19] Lord De La Warr's explanation was published as *The relation of the right honourable the Lord De-la-Warre, lord gouernour and captaine generall of the colonie, planted in Virginia* (London, 1611), reprinted in Brown, *Genesis,* I, 477-483.

[20] The circumstances of the English discovery of Bermuda had been publicized by Silvester Jourdain in *A discovery of the Barmudas . . .* (London, 1610), the dedicatory epistle to which is dated Oct. 13, 1610. The report of the discussion on Bermuda at the Virginia Company Court of June 25, 1611, which this newsletter mentions, is not found elsewhere, and is therefore a valuable piece of information in the emergence of the "under company" (ultimately detached from the Virginia Com-

Master Guye of Brystow who the Last yeare very discreatly honestly and providentlye with a shipp And 30 honest persons well Accomodated with all necessaryes (as well of quyck creatures as other wayes Viz Ducks Geese henns Conneyes Goats Swyne and Kyne,) According to the Terme of his Letters pattents went to the Newfound Land,[21] where he very orderly hath seated hym self, buylded A Convenyent house, encreased all sorts of his Creatures, kyld many sorts of wyld beastes as Deere, Wolues Foxes & black foxes some of the Skynns and other things he hath sent ower for Testymony[22], and hath written vnto the rest of the Adventerers[23] his good estate, his farther Dyscovery of the Countrey even in the Winter Season, when his people haue healthfully endured the sharpest Could[,] and that he hath all things yet For one yeares Sustentacion,[24] The next Mychaellmas he Will com over in person[25] And prepare for further plantacion in that Contynent, whervnto all men are very forward to put in theyre moneyes[26][,] by reason this plantacion is very honest peacefull And hopefull, And very lykelye to be profytable

The Cytyzens of London are exceding wearye of theyre Ireyshe plantacion[27]

---

pany as a separate organization), supplementing Wesley Frank Craven, *An Introduction to the History of Bermuda* (Williamsburg, 1939), 27, and Henry Wilkinson, *The Adventurers of Bermuda,* 2d ed. (Oxford, 1958), 54.

[21] Gov. John Guy's letter from Cupers Cove, to the Treasurer of the Newfoundland Company, John Slany, dated May 16, 1611, and probably others sent to other members of the Company, formed the basis of the report. The letter to Slany was not printed until 1625. Samuel Purchas, *Purchas his Pilgrimes . . .* (London, 1625), IV, book x, 1879-1880.

[22] The dispatch of furs and skins is not mentioned in the letter to Slany.

[23] A small piece of the surface of the paper, affecting the ink, has been removed, the word "of" disappearing in the process.

[24] Guy told Slany he had sufficient stores for a further year.

[25] Guy was less specific in his letter to Slany, stating merely that he would return later in 1611.

[26] On the promotion and development of the colony, new material has been discussed by Gillian M. Cell in *English Enterprise in Newfoundland, 1577-1660* (1969), *Newfoundland Discovered* (Hakluyt Society, 1982), and in her article, "The Newfoundland Company: A Study of Subscribers to a Colonizing Venture," *Wm. and Mary Qtly.,* 3d Ser., XXII (1965), 611-625.

[27] The City of London had been enlisted in 1609-10 to play a large part in the Ulster Plantation by settling the country of Coleraine (now County Londonderry). A consortium of City companies (the Irish Society) had raised enough capital to put 527 men to work on building operations in Ireland by August 1611, but already a number of the contributing companies had begun to complain about the weight of the financial burden they had undertaken. See Theodore W. Moody, *The Londonderry Plantation, 1609-1641* (Belfast, 1939), 62-105. This appears to be the earliest critical comment on the dissentients' reaction to be circulated. As the Virginia Company was competing for City capital, the claim that all Londoners were dissatisfied must be treated with caution.

INDEX